# The Parents Answer Book

# The Parents Answer Book

### Everything You Need to Know
### About Your Child's Physical, Emotional,
### and Cognitive Development, Health, and Safety

*From Birth Through Age Five*

by the editors of Parents Magazine

St. Martin's Griffin  New York

**A Roundtable Press Book**

THE PARENTS ANSWER BOOK. Copyright © 1998 by Roundtable Press, Inc., and G+J USA Publishing. All rights reserved. Printed in the United States of America. No part of this book may be used or reproduced in any manner whatsoever without written permission except in the case of brief quotations embodied in critical articles or reviews. For information, address St. Martin's Press, 175 Fifth Avenue, New York, N.Y. 10010.
Revised in 2000.

10 9 8 7 6 5 4 3 2

**Library of Congress Cataloging-in-Publication Data**

The Parents answer book: everything you need to know about your
    child's physical, emotional, and cognitive development, health, and safety.
        p.   cm.
    Includes index.
    ISBN: 0-312-26372-4
    1. Child development.  2. Child rearing.  3. Children—Health and
hygiene.  I. Parents (New York, N.Y.: 1993)
    RJ131.P3   1998
    649'.1—dc21
98-23766
CIP

# Contents

Foreword by Sally Lee ..................... xv

## Newborn Basics

### *Getting ready* ........................... 2
Breast- or bottle-feeding ............ 2
Should you have your son
  circumcised? ............................. 4
Choosing a health provider ...... 5
Diapers—cloth or disposable? ... 7

### *What you'll need for your newborn* ...................... 7
The layette ................................. 8
Your baby's bed and bedding ...... 8
Feeding supplies ....................... 10
Diapering supplies and
  equipment ............................... 11
Health and grooming supplies ... 14
Travel and outing equipment ..... 14
Toys and other equipment ........ 17

### *Caring for your newborn* ....... 19
Holding and handling
  your infant .............................. 19
Feeding your infant .................. 21
Breast-feeding ......................... 21
Bottle-feeding ......................... 28
Caring for your newborn's
  navel ....................................... 32
Diapering ................................. 32
Newborn sleep patterns ........... 38
Bathing and grooming .............. 42
Dressing your baby .................. 47
Your baby's first outings ......... 50

### *Your newborn's health* ......... 53
The neonatal checkup ............... 53
Healthy at-home routines ........ 53
When to call the doctor ........... 56

### *Treating common health problems in newborns* ........ 58
Birthmarks ............................... 58

Colds ....................................... 59
Colic ........................................ 61
Constipation ............................ 62
Coughs ..................................... 64
Dehydration ............................. 64
Diarrhea ................................... 65
Ear infections .......................... 66
Eye conditions and vision
  concerns ................................. 66
Fever ....................................... 67
Hearing concerns ..................... 68
Hiccups .................................... 69
Infant jaundice
  (yellowing of the skin) ........... 69
Mouth cysts ............................. 71
Rashes and other skin
  conditions .............................. 71
Thrush ..................................... 73
Vomiting .................................. 74

## Part I  As They Grow

### Chapter 1:  The First 8 Weeks ... 76

### *Physical development* ........... 77
Physical changes ...................... 77
Your baby's senses ................... 79

### *The first days and weeks* ...... 80
Your baby's first well-baby
  checkup ................................... 82
Growth Charts for the
  First 12 Months ...................... 84

### *Emotional development* ........ 85
Your baby's feelings ................ 85
Adjusting to your new family
  member ................................... 86
Handling postpartum blues ...... 88
Comforting your fussy baby ..... 91

### *Cognitive development* ......... 93
How your baby learns ............... 94
Providing the right stimulation ... 94

**Special Section:**
**Your Premature Baby**......96

Care during the neonatal
period......96
Bringing your baby home......97
Your baby's development......98

**Chapter 2:  2 and 3 Months**......100
*Physical development*......101
Physical changes......101
Early speech development......104
Establishing a rhythm with
your baby......105
*Emotional development*......106
Your baby's feelings......106
The first steps toward separation 108
Your baby's personality......109
The daddy bond......110
*Cognitive development*......111
What your baby knows......111
Smart from the start......112
Games babies love......114

**Chapter 3:  4 and 5 Months**......115
*Physical development*......115
Physical changes......116
Introducing solids......118
Your baby's teeth......121
*Emotional development*......123
Your baby's feelings......123
Your baby's fears and frustrations 124
Your baby's self-awareness......125
The grandparent connection......126
*Cognitive development*......127
What your baby knows......127
Oral explorations......129

**Chapter 4:  6 and 7 Months**......131
*Physical development*......131
Physical changes......132
Your baby's unique development...134
*Emotional development*......136
Your baby's feelings......136
Self-comforting routines......137
*Cognitive development*......139
What your baby knows......139
How babies explore the world......142
Games babies love......143
Your baby's language
development......144

**Chapter 5:  8 and 9 months**......146
*Physical development*......147
Physical changes......147
Drinking from a cup......149
Crawling and walking......150
*Emotional development*......152
Your baby's feelings......152
Your baby's sense of self......154
*Cognitive development*......155
What your baby knows......155
Your baby's brain power......157

**Chapter 6:  10 to 12 Months**......160
*Physical development*......160
Physical changes......161
Developing bedtime routines......163
Encouraging your baby's
explorations......166
Your baby's coordination......166
*Emotional development*......167
Your baby's feelings......168
First friendships......170
Disciplining your baby......171
*Cognitive development*......172
What your baby knows......172
Games babies love......175
Communicating with your baby......176

**Chapter 7: 13 to 18 Months** ........177
*Physical development* .........178
Physical changes .........178
Good eating habits .........180
Great physical activities for toddlers .........183
Active games for toddlers .........184
*Emotional development* .........185
Your toddler's feelings .........185
Encouraging independence .........188
The family bed .........189
The fears of toddlers .........191
Your toddler's understanding of gender .........194
*Cognitive development* .........195
What your toddler knows .........195
Language development .........197
The meaning of mess .........199
Why toddlers love repetition .........200
Choosing toddler toys .........200

**Chapter 8: 19 to 24 Months** .........203
*Physical development* .........204
Physical changes .........204
Keeping up with your toddler .........205
Music and movement .........205
*Emotional development* .........206
Your toddler's feelings .........206
Letting dads be dads .........208
A toddler's sense of ownership .........209
The importance of security objects .........210
*Cognitive development* .........211
What your toddler knows .........211
Solo play .........212
The importance of make-believe .........214
Word games to enjoy with your toddler .........215
Games to encourage thinking skills .........216

What nursery rhymes teach your toddler .........216
From babbling to talking .........217

**Chapter 9: 2 Years** .........219
*Physical development* .........220
Physical changes .........220
Measuring your child's growth .........222
Physical play .........223
Teaching safety to your toddler .........225
Bedtime power struggles .........225
Your child's sexuality .........227
*Emotional development* .........230
Your child's feelings .........230
Routines that help your child feel secure .........232
Encouraging empathy .........236
What sharing means .........236
Your child's social style .........239
Fears and frustrations .........244
Handling nightmares and night terrors .........245
Regression .........247
*Cognitive development* .........249
What your child knows .........249
Your child's language development .........251
Reading to your child .........252
Boosting creativity .........254
Great games for 2-year-olds .........257
Helping your child learn math .........258
What pretending teaches .........259
**Special Section: Toilet Teaching and Toileting Routines** .........261
Signs of readiness .........261
Getting ready .........261
Beginning actual potty practice .........263
Working toward nighttime dryness .........267
Handling toileting difficulties .........268
When bedwetting continues .........269

**Chapter 10: 3 Years** ..................... 272

*Physical development* ..................... 273

Physical changes ..................... 273

Activities to promote
fine-motor skills ..................... 274

Helping your child dress
independently ..................... 275

*Emotional development* ..................... 276

Your child's feelings ..................... 276

Raising a can-do kid ..................... 277

Your child's fears ..................... 279

Your child's frustrations ..................... 281

Friendships ..................... 282

Make-believe violence ..................... 286

Teaching children about
differences ..................... 288

Gender and gender roles ..................... 290

*Cognitive development* ..................... 290

What your child knows ..................... 291

Understanding your child's
intelligence ..................... 292

Your child's imagination ..................... 294

Building your child's vocabulary ..296

Reading to your child ..................... 298

Dealing with television and videos 299

**Chapter 11: 4 years** ..................... 300

*Physical development* ..................... 301

Physical changes ..................... 301

Your child's handedness ..................... 302

*Emotional development* ..................... 304

Your child's feelings ..................... 304

Building your child's self-esteem ....306

Children's play styles ..................... 308

The sensitive child ..................... 310

Your child's anger ..................... 311

Handling stress-relieving habits ....312

Teaching manners to your
preschooler ..................... 314

Developing a conscience ..................... 317

*Cognitive development* ..................... 319

What your child knows ..................... 319

Your preschooler's
problem-solving skills ..................... 320

Preschool math and science ..................... 321

Your preschooler's artwork ..................... 323

Reading with your preschooler ..... 324

Language and learning ..................... 325

**Chapter 12: 5 Years** ..................... 327

*Physical development* ..................... 328

Physical changes ..................... 328

Saying good-bye to baby teeth ...... 329

5-year-olds and sports ..................... 331

Why children show off their skills 334

*Emotional development* ..................... 335

Your child's feelings ..................... 335

Introverts and extroverts ..................... 337

The perfectionist ..................... 338

Building self-confidence ..................... 339

Handling disappointment and
frustration ..................... 341

Relieving your child's stress ..................... 342

Fifth-year friendships ..................... 344

Your child's spiritual life ..................... 347

*Cognitive development* ..................... 351

What your child knows ..................... 351

Your child's learning style ..................... 354

Boosting your child's
pre-reading skills ..................... 356

What kindergartners know
about time ..................... 357

Your child's listening skills ..................... 358

What your child needs to know ..... 359

# Part 2  Through the Years

**Chapter 1:  You and Your Adopted Child** ............ 362
  Welcoming your child home .......... 362
  Special health considerations ....... 363
  Your child's emotional well-being  364
  Understanding your feelings .......... 365

**Chapter 2:  Childcare** ............ 368
*Finding the right care* ............ 368
  Group care ............ 369
  In-home care ............ 372
  When it's time for a change ...... 375
*Handling feelings* ............ 377
  When maternity leave ends ......... 377

**Chapter 3:  Discipline and Setting Limits** ............ 379
*Understanding discipline* ............ 379
  Your style as a parent ............ 379
  Understanding misbehavior ......... 381
*Encouraging positive behavior* ... 383
  Creating routines ............ 383
  Setting limits ............ 385
  Encouraging cooperation ......... 387
*Limiting unacceptable behaviors* ............ 388
  Responding to common childish behaviors ............ 388
  Handling unacceptable behaviors 393
  Discipline strategies ............ 400
  Handling your own anger ......... 401

**Chapter 4:  Early Education** ...... 404
*Nursery and preschool* ............ 404
  Is nursery school necessary? ...... 404
  What children learn in nursery school ............ 405
  The right age to begin ......... 407
  Different methods of teaching preschoolers ............ 410

Getting your child ready for nursery school ............ 414
*Kindergarten* ............ 417
  When to start kindergarten ......... 418
  Getting started at school ............ 421
  The kindergarten year ............ 422
  Handling school problems ......... 425
  School fears ............ 426
  School phobia ............ 427
  School bus safety ............ 429

**Chapter 5:  Multiples** ............ 430
  Getting in gear ............ 430
  Taking care of yourself ............ 431
  Helping develop individuality ...... 432
  The bonds between multiples ...... 434

**Chapter 6:  Raising Siblings** ...... 436
*Spacing your children* ............ 436
  One to two years apart ............ 437
  Two to five years apart ............ 438
  More than five years ............ 439
  What birth order means ............ 440
  Telling your first-born ............ 442
  Preparing your older child for changes ............ 442
  Introducing new siblings ......... 443
*What siblings gain* ............ 445
*Playing favorites* ............ 446
*Handling sibling wars* ............ 449
  Problem solving for children under age 3 ............ 449
  Problem solving for 3- to 5-year-olds ............ 450
  Preventing sibling wars ......... 451

**Chapter 7:  Single Parents and Stepfamilies** ............ 453
*Single parents* ............ 453
  Suddenly single ............ 454
  Single parents and dating ......... 458

*Divorced parents* .................... 459
  Helping children through divorce ... 459
  Custody and communication ........ 462
*Widowed parents* .................... 464
*Single parents by choice* ......... 464
  Helping your child understand
    your family .......................... 465
*Stepfamilies* .......................... 466
  Forming new relationships ........ 466
  Becoming a stepfamily ............. 468
  The new home ....................... 469
  The need to communicate ......... 470
  Blending lifestyles ................. 472
  Handling discipline issues in
    stepfamilies ........................ 474
  Stepsiblings ......................... 475
  From "yours and mine" to "ours" .. 475


# Part 3  Your Child's Health

**Chapter 1:  Healthy Habits** .......... 478
*Staying healthy* ....................... 478
  Good hygiene ......................... 478
  Bathing and grooming ............. 481
  Hair care ............................. 482
  Ears ................................... 484
  Nail care .............................. 485
  Daily care of teeth ................. 486
  Dressing and clothing routines .... 489
  Sleep needs .......................... 490
  Making exercise a part
    of the day .......................... 493
  Seasonal health concerns ......... 494

**Chapter 2:  Diet and Nutrition** ... 500
*Eating right* ........................... 500
  Handling dining dilemmas ......... 502
  Adding fun—and nutrition ......... 502
  Feeding your 1-year-old ........... 503
  Feeding your 2- or 3-year-old .... 503
  Feeding your preschooler ......... 505

The basic food groups .............. 506
Heart-smart eating for the
  whole family ....................... 509
Diet and weight ..................... 510
Food allergies and sensitivities ... 515
Foods to avoid or limit ............. 518

**Chapter 3:  Medical care** ........... 521
*Medical history* ...................... 521
  Charting your family's medical
    history .............................. 521
*Health-care professionals* ......... 525
  Working with your child's
    physician ........................... 525
  Your child's routine checkups .... 526
  What about alternative care? .... 528
  Handling emergency room visits .. 528
  When your child is hospitalized ... 530
*Professional dental care* .......... 533
  Choosing and working with
    a dentist ........................... 533
*Professional eye care* ............. 534
*Medications* ........................... 536
  Forms of children's medicines .... 537
  Giving liquid medications ......... 537
  Antibiotics .......................... 539
  Your family's medicine chest ..... 541
**Special Section: Immunizations** ... 543
  What to know about
    immunizations ..................... 543

**Chapter 4:  Symptoms and
         Treatments for
         Childhood Illnesses** ... 548
*When to call the doctor* ............ 548
*Conditions and illnesses* ........... 550
  Adenoiditis and tonsillitis ........ 550
  Allergies ............................. 553
    Allergies to animals ............. 555
    Allergies due to the indoor
      environment ..................... 556
    Allergies due to the outdoor
      environment ..................... 559

Anemia ....................................... 559
Apnea (sleep apnea) ................... 561
Appendicitis ............................. 562
Attention deficit disorder (ADD)
   and attention deficit
   hyperactivity disorder (ADHD) 563
Bowlegs and knock-knees ........... 568
Bronchiolitis ............................. 568
Bronchitis ................................. 569
Bruising .................................... 570
Canker sores ............................. 570
Cat-scratch disease ................... 571
Chicken pox (varicella) ............. 572
Colds, cold symptoms, and coughs 573
   Coughs ................................. 575
Constipation .............................. 577
Coxsackie virus (hand-foot-
   and-mouth disease) ............... 578
Croup ....................................... 579
Dehydration .............................. 579
Dermatitis/eczema .................... 581
Diarrhea ................................... 583
Diphtheria ................................. 584
Dislocations .............................. 585
Ear infections (otitis media) ..... 585
   Swimmer's ear ..................... 589
Encephalitis .............................. 589
Epiglottis .................................. 590
Eye concerns ............................ 591
   Amblyopia ............................ 592
   Astigmatism ......................... 592
   Blepharitis ........................... 593
   Blocked tear ducts ............... 593
   Color blindness .................... 594
   Conjunctivitis ("pink eye") ... 594
   Farsightedness (hyperopia) ... 595
   Nearsightedness (myopia) ..... 595
   Ptosis .................................. 596
   Strabismus ("wandering eyes"
     or crossed-eyes) ............... 597
   Stye ..................................... 597
Fainting .................................... 598
Febrile seizures ......................... 598

Fever ........................................ 598
Fifth disease ............................. 602
Flat feet ................................... 603
Food poisoning .......................... 603
Gassiness and flatulence ........... 606
German measles (rubella) ......... 606
Giardiasis ................................. 607
Growing pains ........................... 607
Headache .................................. 608
Head lice .................................. 609
Hearing concerns ...................... 610
Heart conditions ....................... 613
   Heart murmurs .................... 613
   Arrhythmia .......................... 614
Height and weight ..................... 615
Growth Charts for 1 to 6 Years ...... 617
Hematuria ................................. 618
Hepatitis A and B ..................... 618
Hernia (inguinal) ...................... 620
Herpes simplex ......................... 621
Hiccups .................................... 622
High cholesterol ....................... 623
Hives ....................................... 624
Hydrocele (infant hernia) ......... 624
Hypertension
   (high blood pressure) ............ 625
Impetigo ................................... 626
Infection ................................... 627
Influenza (flu) ........................... 627
Jaundice ................................... 628
Labial adhesions ....................... 628
Lead poisoning .......................... 629
Lyme disease ............................ 631
Malabsorption ........................... 632
Measles (rubella) ...................... 633
Meningitis ................................. 634
Mononucleosis ........................... 635
Motion sickness ........................ 635
Mumps ...................................... 636
Papular uticaria ........................ 637
Pertussis (whooping cough) ...... 637
Pigeon toes (intoeing) ............... 638
Pinworms .................................. 639

Pneumonia .................................. 639
Pyloric stenosis ........................ 640
Rabies (hydrophobia) ............... 640
Rashes ...................................... 642
Respiratory syncytial virus (RSV)... 642
Reye syndrome ......................... 643
Rheumatic fever ....................... 644
Rhinitis .................................... 644
Ringworm (tinea) ..................... 645
Rocky Mountain spotted fever ..... 646
Roseola ..................................... 647
Salmonella (animal-borne) ........ 647
Scabies ..................................... 648
Scarlet fever (scarlatina) ......... 648
Sinusitis ................................... 649
Snoring ..................................... 650
Sore throat ............................... 650
Stomach ache ........................... 651
Strep throat ............................. 653
Stress ....................................... 654
Swollen glands ......................... 654
Tetanus (lockjaw) ..................... 655
Tics .......................................... 655
Toe-walking .............................. 656
Tuberculosis (TB) ..................... 656
Undescended testicles .............. 657
Urinary tract infections ........... 658
Vaginal infections .................... 660
Vomiting ................................... 661
Warts ....................................... 662

***Caring for kids*** ......................... 663

**Special Section: First Aid** ....... 664
Handling medical emergencies ..... 664
Assessing and treating
    injuries ............................... 666
Allergies ................................... 666
Back injuries ............................ 667
Bites and stings ....................... 667
Bee stings and bug bites .......... 669
Bleeding (external) ................... 669
Bleeding (internal) ................... 670

Blisters .................................... 671
Bone and joint injuries—
    breaks and sprains .............. 671
Breathing difficulties ............... 674
Choking ............................... 676
Burns ....................................... 678
Convulsions and seizures ......... 682
Drowning (near drowning) ........ 683
Ear injuries .............................. 683
Electrical shock ....................... 684
Eye injuries .............................. 685
Fainting ................................... 686
Frostbite .................................. 686
Hand and finger injuries .......... 687
Head and neck injuries ............. 687
Heat exhaustion and heat cramps 689
Heat rash ................................. 689
Heat stroke and sunstroke ....... 690
Mouth injuries .......................... 690
Nose injuries ............................ 692
Poisoning ................................. 693
Poison oak, ivy, sumac, etc. ..... 694
Shock ....................................... 695
Splinters .................................. 696

**Chapter 5:  Your Special-Needs
            Child** ......................... 698
***Living with and loving your
special-needs child*** ............... 698
Your feelings ............................ 699
Your marriage ........................... 701
Your other children .................. 702
Helping your child cope ............ 704
***Accident-related disabilities*** ...... 706
Brain injury and spinal cord
    injury (SCI) ......................... 706
***Acquired/chronic illnesses*** ....... 707
Asthma ..................................... 707

Cancer .................................................. 712
   Acute lymphocytic
     (lymphoblastic) leukemia ..... 713
Diabetes (type 1) ............................. 714
Epilepsy ............................................ 717
HIV and AIDS ................................. 720
Juvenile rheumatoid arthritis
   (JRA) .............................................. 722
*Birth defects and injuries* ............ 726
   Malformations present at birth ..... 726
     Cleft lip and/or palate ................ 726
     Clubfoot ...................................... 728
     Congenital heart defects ............ 729
     Hirschsprung's disease .............. 731
     Spina bifida ................................. 731
   Metabolic defects ............................ 733
     Celiac disease ............................. 733
     Cystic fibrosis (CF) ..................... 734
     Muscular dystrophy (MD) ........... 736
     PKU (phenolketonuria) ............... 738
   Blood disorders .............................. 739
     Hemophilia .................................. 739
     von Willebrand's disease ........... 740
     Sickle cell disease ..................... 741
   Chromosomal abnormalities ........... 743
     Down syndrome ........................... 743
     Fragile X syndrome ..................... 745
   Perinatal damage ........................... 746
     Cerebral palsy (CP) .................... 746
*Emotional disorders and
mental illness* ................................ 748
   Depression ...................................... 748
   Obsessive-compulsive disorder
     (OCD) ............................................ 749
   Pervasive developmental delay
     (PDD)/autism ................................ 750
*Mental retardation* ......................... 752
*Sensory disorders* ......................... 755
   Hearing loss and impairment ......... 755
   Visual impairment .......................... 757

**Part 4 Safe and Sound**
**Chapter 1: Childproofing
       Your Home** ...................... 762
*Your child's room* .......................... 763
   Bedding ............................................ 763
   Toddler beds .................................... 764
   Adult-size beds ............................... 765
   Bunk beds ........................................ 765
   Playpens and play yards ................. 767
   Shelves, cabinets, dressers, etc. ..... 767
*Bathroom* ......................................... 769
   Water hazards ................................. 769
   Bathroom supplies .......................... 770
*Around the house* ........................... 772
   Doors, floors, windows, and
     stairways ...................................... 772
   Furnishings ..................................... 776
*Kitchen* ............................................. 777
   General safety in the kitchen .......... 779
   Stove ................................................ 779
   Refrigerators and freezers .............. 780
   Dishwasher ...................................... 781
   Garbage disposal ............................ 781
   Small kitchen appliances ................ 782
   Dining area ...................................... 782
   High chairs ...................................... 783
*Laundry room* .................................. 785
   Washer and dryer ........................... 785
   Iron .................................................. 785
*Indoor play spaces* ........................ 786
   Choosing safe toys ......................... 787
   Toy storage equipment ................... 788
*Electrical systems* .......................... 789
   General precautions regarding
     electricity ..................................... 789
   Household appliances ...................... 791
   Heating, cooling, and air-filtration
     systems ......................................... 792
   Furnace and air-duct safety ............ 794
   Fireplace safety .............................. 795

*Indoor pollutants* ............................ 796
  Asbestos ...................................... 796
  Carbon monoxide (CO) ................ 798
  Formaldehyde ............................. 799
  Household chemicals .................. 799
  Lead ........................................... 800
  Radon ........................................ 802
  Treated and pressurized wood ..... 803
  Water supply ............................. 804
  Tobacco smoke ........................... 805
  Other contaminants ................... 805
*Remodeling safety* ......................... 806
*Outdoor areas* ............................... 807
  Barbecue areas .......................... 808
  Balconies and decks .................. 809
  Hot tubs ..................................... 810
  Driveways and garages .............. 811
  Yards and gardens ..................... 813
  Outdoor play equipment ............ 815
*Away from home* ........................... 817
**Special Section:**
**Outdoor Water Safety** ................. 819
  General water safety guidelines ... 819
  Swimming lessons ...................... 821
  Pool and pool-area safety ........... 821
  Boating and dock safety ............. 823

**Chapter 2:  Safe Routines** ........... 824
*At-home activities* ......................... 824
  Knowing your home ................... 825
  Cooking and food-handling
    routines ................................. 825
  Household cleaning .................... 831
  Safe bath time routines .............. 832

*Pets and other animals* ................. 834
*Travel and outings* ........................ 835
  Stroller and pram safety ............ 836
  Pedestrian routines ................... 837
  Car travel .................................. 838
  Public place safety .................... 842
  Plane travel ............................... 843
  Shopping routines ...................... 844
  Bike, trike, and roller
    skate safety ............................ 846

**Chapter 3: Community Concerns** 850
*Environmental pollution* ............... 850
  Air pollution .............................. 851
  Water contamination .................. 853
*Public spaces and places* ............. 854
  Structural hazards in the
    community .............................. 854
  Playground safety ...................... 855
**Special Section:**
**Home Fire Safety** ........................ 858
  Fire prevention ......................... 858
  Fire escape planning .................. 859
  Fire extinguishers ..................... 861

**Index** .......................................... 862
**Acknowledgments** ....................... 880

# Foreword

When my daughter, Gracie, was born in 1997, my husband, Rob, and I had hundreds of questions—daily. Why won't she eat? Is she too warm? Cold? Why won't she stop crying? Like all new parents, we wanted to give our baby the best possible care and were terrified of making a wrong decision. Our pediatrician was wonderful and told us to call her anytime, but we were afraid to take advantage of her offer. It seemed silly to call a busy doctor because we couldn't figure out how warm the baby's bath water should be or how to keep her swaddled. And so, over time, we built a network of family, friends, and other new moms who gave us their wise advice on a whole variety of subjects. We also bought a library of books on medical and developmental issues to get the leading experts' opinions on a host of much more complicated topics.

Back then, we wished for one good book that could combine the expertise of a pediatrician with the warmth of a friend; the up-to-date research of an expert in child psychology with the down-to-earth advice of a wise grandmother; the reliability of a child-safety expert with the reassuring perspective of another mom. I know that other parents felt the same way, and that is why *The Parents Answer Book* is such a brilliant idea. This comprehensive guide to your kids' first five years has nearly 900 pages of practical advice from a source that has built its reputation on 74 years of child-rearing expertise.

Of course, this book can't pretend to solve some of the deeper mysteries of childhood, such as why, when your kids crawl into bed in the middle of the night, do they insist on sleeping horizontally, not vertically? And how come a 2 1/2-year-old can figure out how to use a VCR but can't eat a bowl of applesauce without spilling half of it? For some parenting questions, there are no answers. For all the others, there's *The Parents Answer Book*.

Sally Lee
Editor-in-Chief

# *Also by the editors of* Parents

Parents *Magazine's* It Worked for Me!

The Parents Book of Lists

The Parents Party Book

Parents  Play and Learn

As They Grow
    Your One-Year-Old
    Your Two-Year-Old

I Can Do It
    Physical Milestones for the First Twelve Months
    Physical Milestones for One-Year-Olds
    Physical Milestones for Two-Year-Olds
    Physical Milestones for Three- and Four-Year-Olds

# Newborn Basics

**T**aking care of your newborn's physical needs satisfies his emotional and intellectual growth, too. In this preview, you'll be provided with information about getting ready for your baby's arrival, handling your infant's daily care routines, and being attentive to any health concerns you have about your baby.

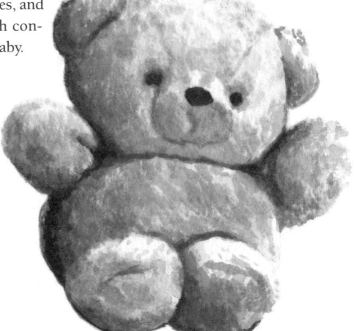

# Getting ready

Even before you meet the child you've been anticipating for so long, there are some issues of baby care and some decisions that you'll need to attend to now. *Will you breast- or bottle-feed your baby? Should you circumcise your son? How can you find the pediatrician that's right for your family?* It's important to arm yourself with the facts you need to make informed choices. Also, never underestimate your intuition: Do what feels right for you.

## Breast- or bottle-feeding?

Breast-feeding has gone through many cycles of fashion—from being almost the only choice, to being nearly outmoded, and back again to being the choice of most mothers. By the mid-1990s, between 70 and 80 percent of moms were breast-feeding, up from 40 percent in the 1970s, according to the La Leche League.

**The benefits of breast-feeding** One thing about breast-feeding has never changed: It remains the most healthful way for babies to be fed. Studies show both short- and long-term benefits for breast-fed children, including:

• **A lower incidence of SIDS (sudden infant death syndrome).** While the relationship between breast-feeding and SIDS is not entirely known, breast feeding does seem to reduce the risk.

• **Fewer first-year ear infections.**

• **Increased immunity.** Babies who are breast-fed during their first year seem to be less susceptible to infections later on.

• **Elevated intelligence.** A number of studies suggest that a breast-fed baby's IQ can be as much as 10 points higher than his non-breast-fed counterpart.

• **Reduced risk of obesity.** Research conducted in the late 1990s in Germany showed that bottle-fed babies are twice as likely to be overweight by age five as are breast-fed children. The longer a child is breast-fed, the less likely he is to become overweight.

• **Reduced likelihood of developing asthma and other allergies.** Breast-feeding may prevent children born with a family history of allergies from inheriting allergies.

In addition to being the nutritionally best choice for your baby, breast-feeding can work for you, too. Nursing your baby eliminates worries about preparing formula and cleaning up, and it offers many pleasant hours between mother and baby. It also confers long-term health benefits on moms as well as being the most economical choice.

### Concerns you may have about breast-feeding

• **Will I find breast-feeding too uncomfortable?** Some aspects of breast-feeding will be uncomfortable at first. Keep in mind that nearly *all* new moms, whether or not they breast-feed, experience some breast pain after birth. Nursing is the best way to ease the pain. Certain discomforts that come from nursing can be eased by practice and by taking care of your breasts.

• **What if I have to return to work shortly after the birth?** While breast-feeding for the first year is optimal, even a shorter period of breast-feeding is better than none at all. If you need to return to work after just six weeks or so, consider pumping breast milk to feed to your baby for the next few months.

• **How can I include my mate in our baby's feedings?** Since breast-feeding is eased by a relaxed environment, your mate can work toward easing any other stresses. He can, of course, join you, offering a back rub or glass of water to you as you nurse. He can burp the baby. He can take over the baby's care while you rest after a feeding. At night, he can bring the baby to you for nursing. Or he can feed expressed breast milk when you're unavailable or simply in need of rest.

*For more information on easing breast pain, see **page 27**.*

*For more information on easing breast pain, see **page 27**.*

**PARENTS RESOURCE**

For more information on breast-feeding, log on to www.breastfeeding.com or www.compleatmother.com

**Choosing bottle-feeding** Infant formula today is highly advanced, and comes very close to mimicking the nutrition of breast milk. Formula that contains fatty acids normally found in mother's milk (docosahexaenoic acid and arachidonic acid) have been shown to significantly boost mental development in babies to the same levels as breast-fed infants. In spite of the good reasons to breast-feed, there may be reasons to make bottle-feeding your choice. Bottle-feeding gives you considerably more freedom, and, of course, lets dad (and others) share equally in the all-important function of feeding the baby. Bottle-feeding is also the natural choice for adoptive parents.

Certain health conditions of a newborn or new mom may, in rare circumstances, preclude breast-feeding. Be aware, however, that bottle-feeding is far more costly and requires more preparation and cleanup than does breast-feeding. If bottle-feeding, you can and should have the same intimacy with your baby, cradling him in your arms during each feeding as you would if breast-feeding.

## Should you have your son circumcised?

Approximately 60 percent of all infant boys in the United States are circumcised; that is, they have had the foreskin, or prepuce, a fold of skin cloaking the end of the penis, surgically removed. The procedure is done for both religious and health reasons. Often, sons are circumcised simply because their fathers are circumcised.

Circumcisions performed for health and/or family tradition are usually done in the hospital by a physician within 48 hours after birth. Those done for religious reasons, according to both Jewish and Muslim custom, are performed in a ceremony on the eighth day after the birth. Some circumcisions are done later in the baby's first year, for a variety of reasons. Generally, babies must be five or six pounds before being circumcised. Therefore, the procedure isn't done on preterm or very small babies since the surgical instruments are simply too big to snip away the foreskin. Health problems, such as eczema and bleeding disorders, may also preclude early circumcision. Adopted babies, born in countries where circumcision isn't routinely done, may be circumcised later.

**What to know about the procedure** In most cases, the circumcision is done using a special surgical tool. In some hospital circumcisions, doctors perform circumcision using a technique in which a plastic ring is left on the penis, cutting off circulation to the foreskin.

Traditionally, circumcision was done without anesthesia because it was felt that a baby's experience of pain is fleeting and no greater than what he might feel during other newborn medical procedures, such as a heel prick to draw blood. New research, however, suggests the impact of pain from circumcision may not be so temporary. In a small study of 4- to 6-month old boys, circumcised infants cried longer and were judged to be in more pain after receiving a vaccination than uncircumcised babies. The researchers suggest that memories of pain from circumcision may have long-lasting effects on an infant's pain response and/or perception. Also, the pain of circumcision can disrupt a newborn's sleep and eating and make him more irritable for at least a day.

*For information about anesthesia, see **page 532**.*

Increasingly, doctors are using short-acting anesthetics to dull a baby's pain. Anesthetic options include a nerve-blocking injection at the base of the penis, less-deep injections just under the skin close to or on the incision site, and a topical cream that numbs the skin before it's cut. Also, a dose of acetaminophen one hour before the operation and every four to six hours afterward on the day of the procedure can help ease the pain. During the procedure, a sugar-coated pacifier may help comfort and distract the baby.

When boys are circumcised later in the first year, doctors usually give them general anesthesia to keep them from squirming.

**Making the decision** Increasingly, parents for whom circumcision is not a religious issue are deciding against the procedure. One of the main reasons is the potential for pain. The American Academy of Pediatrics does not recommend circumcision as a routine procedure, except to satisfy religious and/or cultural needs, and strongly recommends that boys who are circumcised be given pain medication.

# Choosing a health-care provider

Choosing your newborn's doctor is a major step, one you'll want to make before your baby is born.

**What to look for** Your child's health-care professional should be a pediatrician or a family practitioner who has received considerable training in the care of children. Make sure the doctor you choose is board-certified in pediatrics or family medicine.

The physician should also be licensed by the state in which she practices, and the license should be posted prominently in her office for your review. Also make sure the doctor is affiliated with a hospital near your home to avoid lengthy trips in case an emergency should arise.

**Finding a doctor** To find the right physician, ask your obstetrician/gynecologist or nurse-midwife for a referral. Friends, especially other parents in your neighborhood, are also good sources for referrals. If you've just moved to a new community, call the public

**PARENTS RESOURCE**

To find out if the doctor you're considering is certified, call the **American Board of Medical Specialties** at (800) 776-2378 or visit their website at www.certifieddoctor.org.

## Hospital Credentials

Just as you checked your doctor's credentials, check the hospital's to see that it is approved by the Joint Commission on Accreditation of Health-Care Organizations. If you choose an osteopath who is affiliated with an osteopathic hospital only, check that this facility is accredited by the American Osteopathic Association.

affairs department at the nearest teaching (university-affiliated) hospital or a respected local hospital or medical center for a recommendation. If the public affairs department isn't able to recommend someone, ask to speak with a pediatric floor nurse. Someone in that position is likely to be aware of the best doctors in town.

You'll want not only medical expertise, but a feeling of partnership with this professional whom you trust to address your baby's needs as well as your own need for information, help, and reassurance. You'll want him to be someone you feel comfortable calling with even minor concerns.

Some parents interview pediatricians to get a feel for their style. During such an interview, ask the doctor how accessible she is, whether she's available to take calls during the day and evening, how quickly she gets back to parents, how reliable her answering service is, and whether she has weekend and evening office hours—a must for parents who work outside the home. Pay attention to how well the doctor focuses on your needs, how well you feel your questions have been answered, and whether or not you feel rushed or your concerns are brushed aside.

Ask if your baby will see the doctor, a nurse-practitioner, or other service provider during routine visits. You'll want regular contact with a single party with whom you and your child can develop a relationship. If the doctor herself sees patients only for emergencies, you may want to look around since you will both be far more comfortable in an emergency situation with your baby's regular physician.

Find out if the physician and you share attitudes on such key child-rearing issues as breast-feeding, weaning, and nutrition. Keep looking if you feel that you and a particular doctor aren't a good match.

Convenience is also an important factor in choosing your child's physician. You don't want to have half an hour's drive between your home and the doctor's office, especially when your baby is ill. You may also want to consider having a doctor in a group practice rather than someone who has a solo practice. Then, if the doctor is on vacation or ill, your child can see one of her partners, with whom you are more likely to be somewhat familiar.

## Diapers — cloth or disposable?

Since you'll need to have a supply available, it's good to review the pros and cons of each kind of diaper before your baby is home. Disposable diapers have a number of advantages over cloth, though cloth remains a good choice for some.

**Advantages and disadvantages** Disposables keep your baby's bottom drier, which is especially helpful in preventing rashes. Disposables are easier to handle on outings. Important to tired parents, disposables require relatively little work and no additional equipment, such as diaper pails and diaper covers. Some parents opt for using cloth diapers at home and disposables while traveling.

The most economical choice, washing cloth diapers at home, requires an enormous commitment of time and resources. Using a diaper service to launder cloth diapers costs about the same as using disposables. Cloth diapers that are cleaned by a service and disposables have an equivalent, though different, impact on the environment, with disposables filling landfills and serviced cloth using cleaning chemicals, fuel, and water.

# What you'll need for your newborn

The array of cute and seemingly necessary items you've encountered in baby stores might lead you to believe that you'll need to spend thousands of dollars and fill every nook and cranny of your home with baby gear. You won't. Overabundance isn't necessary or even desirable, especially at first. There are some things you will need right from the start, however.

Talk to friends and other parents to find out what they found most useful and what items they found least useful during the early months. Also ask where in your area you can expect the best value and the best service.

## Stocking the Nursery

**Before your baby's homecoming, you'll need:**

Layette of clothing essentials

Bedding

Feeding supplies and equipment

Diapering supplies and equipment

Bathing supplies and equipment

Health-care supplies

Traveling and outing supplies and equipment

Equipment to soothe and entertain your baby

# The layette

In addition to diapers and seasonally appropriate clothing such as snowsuits and sweaters, these are the basic items that you'll need right away:

8 to 10 undershirts
3 "onesies"—snap-crotch T-shirts or bodysuits
4 to 6 sleeping gowns or kimonos
2 or 3 blanket sleepers (for winters and cold climates)
4 to 6 coveralls with feet
1 to 2 sunhats or cooler-weather hats, depending on the season
3 pairs of socks or booties
3 washable bibs
1 special dress-up outfit
2–3 receiving blankets

# Your baby's bed and bedding

*For information about childproofing your baby's room, see* **pages 763–67**.

Your infant's bed should be a soothing, pleasant environment, free from hazards. Be especially careful when choosing a crib, particularly a hand-me-down, to be sure that it meets current standards for safety, and do not use a hand-me-down that doesn't meet these safety criteria, which are detailed below.

**Cradles and bassinets** During the first few months, until your baby can sit up or crawl, you can opt for a cradle or a bassinet instead of a full-size crib. Cradles and bassinets are particularly useful because they take up less space during the early months when you may want to have your baby share your bedroom; they can be more easily moved from room to room, and the gentle rock of a cradle can be soothing to your newborn. Choose a cradle or bassinet that is sturdy and not easily tipped over; be sure that any collapsible legs can be firmly locked in the open position and that the mattress fits very snugly against the sides of the bed.

### Safety Seal

The Juvenile Products Manufacturers Association (JPMA) certifies that baby furniture and cribs meet the association's stringent standards, so look for their sticker before making any purchases.

**Cribs** A crib can serve as your child's bed from his first day home until age two or older, so you'll want to make sure that the crib you choose is safe. When purchasing a new crib, look for one with a certification seal showing that it meets national safety standards.

The U.S. Consumer Product Safety Commission guidelines stipulate that a safe crib has:

- **No missing, loose, broken, or improperly installed screws, brackets,** or other hardware on the crib or in the mattress support.
- **No more than 2⅜ inches between crib slats** so a baby's body cannot fit through the slats. Never use a crib with missing, broken, or loose slats.
- **A firm, snug-fitting mattress** so a baby cannot get trapped between the mattress and the side of the crib. If you can fit more than two fingers between the edge of the mattress and crib side, the mattress is too small for the crib and must be replaced.
- **No corner posts extending over $\frac{1}{16}$ of an inch above the end panels** unless they are over 16 inches high for a canopy so your child cannot catch his clothing on the post and strangle.
- **No cutout areas on the headboard or foot board** so your baby's head cannot get trapped.
- **A mattress support that does not easily pull apart from the corner posts** so a baby cannot get trapped between mattress and crib. (Mattress support hangers should be secured by a closed hook.)
- **No cracked or peeling paint.** Also be sure that any paint is lead free.
- **No splinters or rough edges.**

*See **page 767** for more information on choosing playpens.*

**Bedding** You'll need tight-fitting sheets and a waterproof mattress cover. Bumper pads are unnecessary. Quilts and pillows are fine for decorations, but shouldn't be used while your baby is in her crib or bassinet. For warmth, let your baby sleep in blanket sleepers. Other safety guidelines to keep in mind when choosing your baby's bedding:

• **Bumper pads,** if used, should fit around the entire crib, tie or snap into place, and have at least six straps (one at each corner and one on each of the middle of the long sides). To prevent your baby from chewing on the straps or becoming entangled in them, trim off excess length after tying so that no loose string or ribbon dangles into the crib, or choose bumpers fastened by Velcro. Use the bumpers until your baby can pull himself up to a standing position, then remove them so that he will not use them as steps to try to climb out of the crib.

• **Do not use pillows** for young infants in the crib. If you place pillows there for decoration, remove them from the crib whenever your baby is using it.

• **Remove and discard all plastic wrapping materials,** after unpacking a new crib. Tie the wrapping in a knot before throwing away.

• **Use only heavyweight, rubberlike covers beneath the sheets.** Never use thin plastic dry-cleaning or trash bags, or the plastic wrapping that came on the new mattress as waterproof mattress covers. These may cling to a child's face and cause suffocation.

## Portable Cribs or Playpens

If you're likely to be away from home overnight with your newborn, consider purchasing a portable crib or play yard now rather than relying on borrowed or makeshift equipment that may not meet safety standards. Mesh-sided models that can be easily assembled and dismantled and that can be stored in small areas, including car trunks, are well-suited for traveling.

## Feeding supplies

There's no need to purchase a high chair or any special solid-food servers right away. Both breast-feeding and bottle-feeding parents will need some feeding supplies, however. In addition to those listed opposite, also purchase some washable bibs and spit-up cloths, such as clean diapers, to handle burping.

**Nursing supplies** Nursing moms need:

• **A nursing bra** If possible, shop for a nursing bra before your baby is born—at around the seventh month of pregnancy—to ensure the best fit.

- **Nursing pads** These are useful for catching leaks, especially during the first few days after birth.
- **A breast pump and bottles if you're planning to express milk** Pumps come in a number of models, both electric and manual. Mothers tend to have strong preferences about pumps; before you purchase or rent one, ask around for opinions on the matter to see what pump would best serve you. Pumps come with complete instructions. Opt for opaque plastic over clear plastic or glass bottles for storing breast milk.

**Bottle-feeding supplies** Newborns generally start on four-ounce bottles, though you can just as easily fill a standard eight-ounce bottle half way for each feeding in the early weeks. Glass and dishwasher-safe plastic bottles are equally good for formula-fed babies since either can be sterilized. Some plastic bottles have plastic liners that you insert into the outer holder. On the plus side, these disposable liners make it easier at cleanup and they reduce the amount of air the baby sucks because they collapse as he drinks.

Unless you are using bottles with liners at all times, you will need a bottle brush to remove lingering traces of formula from the bottles before sterilizingthem Especially for late-night feedings, you'll also find that an electric bottle cooler and warmer is a good investment.

## Diapering supplies and equipment

Right from the start, you'll need a changing table and supply of diapers and bottom-care products.

**Disposable diapers** If you've decided to use disposables, purchase only a few packages of the newborn size. Your baby may quickly outgrow them; if she is large at birth, she may be out of the newborn size in a matter of days. Look at the different varieties available. Some brands provide different designs for night and day; others have reusable tabs, which are handy for checking to see if your baby needs a change. Some have elasticized waists and/or legs. Others are designed especially for boys or girls. You may want to try out a few brands and a variety of styles, experimenting to see which ones you like best before stocking up on any one type.

Optional equipment includes products that wrap and bundle

soiled diapers and store them odorlessly until the unit is full. Even if you're committed to using disposables, you might also want to have some cloth diapers and pins or diaper covers on hand in case you ever run out of disposables. The diapers themselves also serve as terrific burping pads, and the covers can be used to dress up an ordinary disposable.

**Cloth diapers and cloth diaper accessories** If you've chosen cloth diapers as your regular diapering material, purchase about six dozen in size large, which can be folded to fit and which won't be outgrown. A combination of flat and prefolded will give you versatility. Cloth diaper users may also want to use diaper liners, which can cut down on the laundry load by absorbing small amounts of urine while keeping the outer diaper itself dry for reuse after changing. Have about six pair of diaper pins or four to six diaper covers or diaper wraps with Velcro tabs on hand, too. (Avoid plastic pants, which can trap moisture and lead to diaper rash.) A covered diaper pail is an essential.

**Additional diapering supplies** In addition to diapers, you'll need:
• **Ointments** for preventing and/or treating diaper rash. Talk to your pediatrician for brand recommendations. Buy only the small sizes of whatever brand you're trying until you've settled on a product that you know works for your baby.
• **Sterile cotton balls** for wiping your baby's bottom.
• **A portable diaper pad** for changing your baby on outings.
• **A changing table.**

**Changing table** A changing table in the nursery should be a safe and sturdy spot to change and dress your baby. Over 1,300 infants a year are injured in changing-table-related accidents, mostly falls, according to the Consumer Product Safety Commission. Following are tips on choosing a suitable table:
• **Select a sturdy, stable changing table with a built-in strap.** If the table does not have a strap, purchase one separately and install it. Use the strap to restrain your baby whenever she's on the table.
• **Look for changing tables with at least a two-inch lip around all four edges** to help keep your baby from rolling off.

- **Choose a style that lets you have supplies and baby clothing in easy reach** to you but not your baby.

**Bathing supplies** During your baby's first few weeks, until his umbilical cord stump falls off, you can bathe him with sponge baths instead of submerging him. For sponge baths, you'll need:

- **An unbreakable bowl** in which to hold tepid water.
- **Cotton balls, swabs, and two soft washcloths** for cleaning and rinsing your baby.
- **Cleansing products** Use soaps and shampoos that are specifically made for babies since these are gentle and produce fewer tears if the soap gets into your baby's eyes. There's usually no need for lotions and baby oils.
- **A soft, absorbent towel** in which to wrap your baby while you hold him in your arms. Hooded towels are particularly useful for drying your baby's head and keeping him warm immediately after his bath.

*safety strap*

*2-inch lip*

*sturdy base*

*Safe changing table*

**Tubs and tub or sink liners** Once your baby is taking tub baths, usually by the third week or so, you'll also need a tub or a sink or tub liner. Tubs are available in both hard plastic and inflatable models that can be placed on any steady surface, including within the family's bathtub or a large kitchen sink. Freestanding models are also available, though these are cumbersome and not useful after the first few months.

Tub or sink liners are molded sponges that can be placed inside a baby tub or sink for the baby to lie on or, when the baby is older, for him to sit on in the adult tub.

**Bath safety items** To ensure that you can bathe your infant safely, you'll need:
• **Nonskid bath rug** Whether you're bathing your baby in a baby bath or in the bathroom or kitchen, be sure that the surface on which you're standing or kneeling is covered with a safety mat to absorb spills and to keep the floor from becoming too slippery.
• **Bath thermometer** These plastic submersible devices, available in most baby-supply stores and drugstores, are more accurate than the "elbow test" for measuring the bath temperature.

## Health and grooming supplies

Have the following on hand to take care of any minor health problems and for grooming your baby:
• **Bulb syringe** for removing mucus from your baby's congested nose
• **Rectal thermometer,** either mercury or digital
• **Petroleum jelly** for coating a rectal thermometer before use
• **Cool-mist humidifier** to help clear nasal congestion
• **Rounded-tipped scissor or baby nail clipper** for finger- and toenail clipping
• **A comb and/or hairbrush.** Opt for a style designed specifically for infants with soft brush bristles and rounded comb teeth. Adult and big-kid designs can scratch your newborn's scalp.

**PARENTS ALERT**

### *Keep Your Nails Short*

Long fingernails, particularly the glue-on kind, harbor bacteria that can be harmful to your baby. Hand washing alone does not eliminate the bacteria, so the best course is to keep your nails trimmed and to avoid artificial nails.

# Travel and outing equipment

To transport your newborn, you'll need a car seat, a stroller or pram, and a carrier.

**Car seats**  Car seats are not only essential safety equipment, they're required by law for young children. For your newborn, choose a car seat that's especially designed for infants or one that is convertible for infant use. For the larger convertible models, invest in a padded insert that keeps your newborn secure and comfortable.

A new car seat is generally a good investment. If you're using an older model, call the manufacturer to be sure that the particular model has not been recalled and to request a copy of the installation instructions. Do not buy or use a car seat that has been or may have been involved in an accident.

Car seats for babies under 6 months of age or 20 pounds should be installed in the rear-facing positions, buckled into the middle of the back seat. Since the introduction of passenger-side air bags and, in some models, side-air bags, sitting children in the front seat or in the back next to the doors has become a serious hazard for babies and children. Never place a child in the front seat, and, if you must place more than one child in the back seat of a car that has side-impact bags, have those bags disabled.

It is also essential to install the car seat properly. (A 1999 survey found that nearly 85% of car seats were improperly installed.) Follow both the car seat manufacturer's guidelines and the car manufacturer's recommendations. After installing, pull on the seat vigorously to ensure that it cannot be moved more than an inch or so in any direction.

**Carriers**  One good way to keep your newborn feeling secure during walks is a front carrier. A front carrier keeps your baby warm and cozy, and gives her the calming addition of being able to hear mom or dad's heartbeat. Backpacks aren't right for newborns, so if you have one, save it for when your baby is able to hold her head up and keep her back straight entirely on her own, usually at about 6 months.

Front carriers come in a variety of models, from the simplest to quite elaborate, in sling-designs, which rest on your hips, and in sack designs that straddle your chest. Before purchasing a carrier, experiment with a few and see which ones feel most comfortable to wear and which you find easiest to manipulate. (Consider trying them on while carrying a baby-size doll.) Front carriers are best for limited use, since overuse can put a strain on your back.

**Prams and strollers** Another good way of getting your newborn around is a pram-type carriage or a sturdy stroller that can be positioned to allow your infant to lay flat on his back. A pram or stroller is essential if you'll be doing a lot of walking with your baby.

Try out a number of carriages to see which one best suits your needs. Consider:

• **Handles.** These should be at a comfortable height for you and your spouse and whomever else will be walking your child regularly. If there's a big variance in height among those who will be using the stroller, look for a design with adjustable handles or invest in handle extensions for the taller parent or other caretaker. See if you feel more comfortable pushing a single straight bar handle or two umbrella-style handles.

• **Wheels.** The wheels should be easily maneuverable across a variety of surfaces. In general, rubber wheels offer a better ride and are easier to push than plastic wheels.

• **General construction.** The fabric should be washable, though not necessarily vinyl, which can get sticky and uncomfortable in warm weather. Cotton canvas is a good choice. If you'll be doing a lot of city walking, note that a design with springs in the chassis will provide more comfort for your baby.

• **Safety.** Check the construction and ease of using the seat belts that are built into all strollers. If you're planning to use a pram, make sure that it has a safety strap. Check that the brakes work well and easily. The stroller or pram should have a roof to block out the sun. Consider adding a removable stroller umbrella to increase sun protection.

• **Versatility.** A pram that converts to a stroller is an economical choice, as is a stroller that has a fully reclining position. Some stroller designs have movable handles and adjustable wheels that allow you to switch back and forth from front to back facing. If you've chosen a folding model, be sure that you can fold and open it without too much trouble using one arm.

- **Storage capacity.** If you'll be using the stroller while running errands, be sure that the model you choose has the storage capacity you'll need, preferably in undercarriage baskets. Storage bags and baskets that hang from the handles are not the best choice because, when they're filled, the weight can cause the stroller to topple.

**Carry-alongs** No matter how you're traveling, you'll need a multi-compartment diaper bag to store the essentials. Look for one that's washable, contains an insulated compartment for keeping bottles warm or cool, and a removable changing pad. Opt for wide, padded shoulder straps, which will be more comfortable than unpadded straps or than a handheld model. Consider buying a diaper bag in a color and design that your mate will feel comfortable carrying instead of the popular pastel, baby-print designs.

**PARENTS ALERT**

### No Sit-Up or Jogging Strollers for Infants Under Six Months of Age

Umbrella strollers— lightweight, fold-up designs— that do no have a full reclining position are *not* good choices for infants since they are not designed to support your baby's head and neck. Jogging strollers, though they allow your infant to recline, jostle the head and neck and can result in injury.

## Toys and other equipment

While newborns don't need lots of play equipment, some items will be useful early on to soothe and interest your baby. These include a self-winding infant swing, a bouncing seat, and a mobile and other visually appealing toys.

**Infant swings** A baby swing can provide entertainment for your baby in a confined environment. Your baby will be ready to recline in a swing safely at about six weeks of age. To choose and use a swing safely, follow these guidelines:

- **Make sure the swing is stable** and has skid-resistant tips on the legs. Braces between the legs and a wide base add stability.
- **Make sure the swing has a seat belt and crotch restraint** and use them every time your child is enjoying his swing.
- **The motor should be quiet.** A battery-operated model or one with a soft-winding crank won't startle a baby. Also, speed control lets you choose a gentle motion for a newborn and a faster pace for an older baby.

### No Bouncing Babies

Never bounce or shake your baby. Because a baby's head is so large in proportion to his body, any shaking can cause serious injury, including cerebral hemorrhaging, which, in turn, can lead to blindness and/or mental retardation or even death.

- **Look for an adjustable seat,** so you can recline it for a newborn, and raise it as her neck gets stronger.
  - **Look for padding** for extra comfort and washable fabric.
  - **Don't set the swing near a stove or hot appliance** or any other place where your child could be harmed.
  - **Follow manufacturer's weight and age restrictions,** which generally recommend that you stop using the swing when your baby reaches 25 pounds or 9 months.
  - **Limit use once your baby can crawl** and stop using the swing once your baby can pump her legs or grab the swing's legs.
  - **Always keep an eye on your baby** while she's in the swing. Also supervise an older child who may try to push the baby or climb inside the swing.

**Portable seats**  A lightweight, portable seat is a good investment, allowing you to keep your baby nearby as you go from room to room. Seats are available in stationery models; car seats can substitute for this kind of seat, although they are a bit heavy for everyday use. Molded plastic seats with handles make it possible to carry your baby when he's sleeping. Another kind many parents prefer, however, is a bouncing seat, which inclines at about a 45-degree angle and which responds to your baby's kicks with a gentle rocking motion that many babies enjoy.

**Toys**  Your infant will enjoy a few interesting distractions, such as a crib mobile, a baby gym, and perhaps a soft toy or rattle. Get these in strongly contrasting colors—black-and-white is best—which your newborn can most easily see. Many infants also like to see their reflections in safety mirrors and to listen to musical and chiming toys. When examining toys for your baby consider the following:

- **Will you have toys over your infant's bed?** So-called crib gyms and other brightly colored toys that stretch across a crib must be installed securely at both ends—never let cords or strings dangle into cribs. (You'll need to remove crib gyms, mobiles, and other hanging objects when your baby is 5 months old or is able to push up on his hands and knees, whichever comes sooner.)

- **Are toys, including rattles, too large to swallow?** They should be at least 1⅝ inches across. (Check all parts, including both ends of rattles.)
- **Are there small parts on toys that could fall off and pose a choking hazard?** Check to make sure all eyes or noses on dolls or stuffed animals are firmly attached. Check to make sure the squeaker in squeak toys can't be removed.
- **Are there any ribbons or strings on toys?** Remove before giving them to your child.
- **Are toy edges smooth?**
- **Are materials nontoxic, nonbreakable, and nonbrittle?**
- **Is the toy in good repair?**
- **Is the material washable?**

# Caring for your newborn

Handling the day-to-day care of your infant is both exciting and exhausting. There are some tricks to be learned to make the hard parts easier and the fun parts even more delightful. Here are the things you need to know about feeding, diapering, bathing, helping your newborn sleep, and other important information about handling his daily routines.

## Holding and handling your infant

Your newborn probably looks as fragile as fine china, but, in truth, she's quite sturdy. But even though she's relatively solid, she does need careful handling.

**How to support your baby** There are two factors to keep in mind every time you approach your newborn. The first is her obvious inability to support her head on her own. The other is less apparent, but just as important. Your baby, like all newborns, has an innate fear of falling. Through proper handling, you can see to it that she both is safe and feels safe.

*Provide good support when lifting your baby.*

When you start to pick up your baby, slowly move close to her to abbreviate the amount of time she must move through the air. Gently place one hand under her neck and head and the other beneath her buttocks and torso. Your hands should virtually surround her so that she has no sense of flying as you bring her to you. Give her time to adjust to the feeling of your hands protecting her before you lift her from her mattress or blanket. Similarly, when you hold your baby, cradle her with your arms or hands in such a way that she is comfortably snug. Be sure her head is placed on your shoulder or arm so that it cannot flop and keep your hand supporting her neck and head at all times. She may show a preference for being held on the shoulder or for lying in your arms. Most likely, though, she will enjoy both positions and happily change from one to the other as long as she is carefully supported.

*Approach your baby slowly when picking her up.*

As you prepare to put your baby down, move close to the surface first. Gently place her head on the mattress or other surface, remove your hand, and then slide your other hand out from under her back. Move slowly and carefully, giving her time to adjust, and you'll be letting your baby know in yet another way that she is secure and cared for in her new world.

### Protecting your baby's "soft-spot"— the fontanel

*"What is a baby's 'soft spot?'"*

*For information on premature fusing of the fontanel, see **page 103**.*

Soft spots, or fontanels, are the gaps between the bony plates of your baby's skull. They allow your infant's head to contract and fit through the birth canal. Later on, these soft spots allow room for the tremendous brain growth that occurs during the first two or three years of life. The skull plates gradually fuse to form a single protective bone mass.

In spite of the seeming delicacy of your baby's fontanel, you don't really need to be overly concerned about it. In addition to the skull, the brain is protected by a tough canvaslike membrane. This allows normal activities—holding, changing, shampooing—to take place without any danger to your baby. Obviously, though, you must be sure your baby is protected from dangers such as sharp objects or harsh blows.

Because of its pliant construction, you'll be able to notice some activity taking place under the fontanel. For instance, you'll no doubt see your baby's pulse on occasion. This is normal and should not alarm you. However, if the fontanel ever becomes tense or shows bulging, or if it seems to sink in, call the baby's physician. These kinds of changes in the shape of the fontanel could be signs of illness or dehydration.

**Can too much holding spoil a baby?**
*"Can I spoil my newborn by holding him too much?"*
It's impossible to spoil infants. At this age, if they are to form secure attachments, babies need to know that their needs are being met. So, by all means, respond to your baby's cries, and give him plenty of hugs and other attention. One reminder, though: babies are born with their own distinctive temperaments and while some infants seem to melt into their parent's arms for hours of bliss, others prefer being held for more limited amounts of time. You'll quickly discover your baby's own preferences for cuddling.

## Feeding your infant

Feeding is the most social of occasions and nourishes your newborn in many ways as you share lots of eye contact and conversation along with breast milk or formula.

## Breast-feeding

Even though breast-feeding is natural, knowing how to nurse does not necessarily come naturally. Breast-feeding is a learned experience for both you and your baby. Because the initial attempts to breast-feed may prove difficult and frustrating, it's important to review your good reasons for choosing breast-feeding, to practice, and to ask for help from others if you're experiencing any difficulties. Don't worry if you can't nurse easily in the first few attempts. During the first day, your baby may not be hungry and won't be

*There are a number of safe, comfortable ways to hold your baby (above and opposite). Always be sure to support the baby securely.*

harmed at all if he doesn't eat. If you're persistent, both you and your baby will figure out what you need to do.

To get started on breast-feeding, get into a comfortable position. Ignore distractions and concentrate on the softness of your baby's face against your breasts. If your baby doesn't immediately suckle— and not all do—get her attention for a feeding by gently stroking her cheek with your finger or your nipple. This triggers the rooting reflex and causes your baby to turn toward your breast for mealtime.

Learning to latch-on correctly is the next skill you and your baby must master. The key to successful latching-on is making sure that your baby's mouth encircles the entire nipple area, called the *areola*, not just the nipple itself. If her mouth encircles the nipple only, both you and your baby will be uncomfortable. Improper latching-on can cause your nipples to become sore and even crack, and your baby will not be feeding efficiently. Some babies take eagerly to the breast and have no trouble latching-on; others find it more difficult and need their mother's gentle prodding to help them. You can help your baby latch-on properly by placing your nipple in the center of her mouth, with the aureole entirely within her lips, making sure that your breast does not cover her nose and interfere with breathing. Don't be afraid to adjust your position to maintain your comfort during mealtime. The more relaxed you feel, the better for both of you.

*For information on burping your baby see **pages 30–31**.*

Allow your baby five minutes on each breast when you first begin nursing. Over the course of a few days, and depending on your baby's appetite, build to ten minutes per breast, and then to fifteen minutes. To break the baby's suction when you're ready to switch breasts, simply place your finger into her mouth, between the nipple and her mouth. Burp your baby before switching to the other breast.

When it's time to go to your other breast, gently reposition your baby, again helping her to latch-on properly. Start nursing on the opposite breast at each feeding, a habit that will keep milk being produced evenly by both breasts throughout your nursing experience.

For a few days after delivery, your breasts will produce colostrum, a nutrition-rich yellowish fluid, sometimes called "first milk." When the milk itself comes in, you may go through an uncomfortable period of about 72 hours because the milk overfills, or engorges, your breasts. This experience causes some new moms to think that breast-feeding is not for them. The engorgement, however, is normal among both breast-feeding and nonbreast-feeding mothers since all new mothers produce milk. Continuing to breast-feed and breast-feeding more frequently, in fact, is the best thing you can do to ease the pain. Express a small amount of milk from your breasts first if the baby has trouble latching-on because your breasts are swollen. Also try placing warm cloths over your breasts between feedings and taking warm showers to relieve engorgement problems.

*See **page 27** for more information on relieving breast tenderness.*

If you or your baby finds nursing difficult in the early days, seek advice. Ask your health-care provider or your friends who have nursed for suggestions.

### Infant vitamins while nursing

*"I'm nursing. Should I give my newborn vitamin supplements?"*

No. Nature designed the perfect food for young infants in breast milk. At about six months of age, your baby's need for iron will be greater than your breast milk can supply, but the cereals and other solid food your baby should be getting by then will fill this need.

### Nursing schedule

One of the areas in which babies show their distinct, inborn personalities is in nursing styles. Some approach the breast eagerly; others are laid back. Some babies want to nurse frequently; others fill themselves completely with fewer sessions. You'll quickly come to understand your baby's own style. In general, breast-fed babies eat more often than formula-fed babies because breast milk is less filling than formula.

Whatever her style, your baby should determine her own schedule. She will let you know if she's becoming hungry primarily through fussing, but also by nuzzling your breast and making sucking noises. From your baby's second day and for a week or so, she will need to nurse frequently—every hour is not uncommon—since her stomach can't hold enough to keep her satisfied for long periods of time. Since nursing can take anywhere from 10 to 30 minutes per session, you may feel as if you're rarely doing anything but nursing at the beginning, and that may, indeed, be what your baby needs. Of course, that will change as she becomes bigger and can eat more at each nursing session. Until about three months, however, nursing will take up a great deal of your baby's waking hours.

**PARENTS RESOURCE**

The **La Leche League** has local nursing-support hotlines with knowledgeable staffers and volunteers who can address your problems immediately. Call (800) LA LECHE or visit www.lalecheleague.org to find a support group in your area.

## What NOT to Eat While Nursing

If you have a family history of food allergies, it is best to avoid peanuts or peanut butter and shellfish while nursing. Also avoid alcohol, which can have the same effect on your baby as it does on you.

Even though nursing is such a focus of your baby's life, don't automatically assume each time your baby is fussing that she is hungry. If it seems unlikely she is hungry, such as right after a long feeding, look for other possible sources of her discomfort before offering her the breast again.

Your baby will no doubt go through a number of growth spurts, starting at about three weeks of age. You'll recognize a spurt because she will suddenly nurse much more than usual for several days.

**Judging breast milk intake** Your baby may get little substance in her first attempts at breast-feeding. This isn't a problem since she doesn't need much to satisfy her needs in the first few days. Once she is ready to consume more, you'll soon recognize the regular sucking motions in her face, and her gulping at your breast that tell you she is feeding well. Your milk supply is determined by how much the baby sucks. If she starts to need more milk, her increased sucking will prompt your body to produce more milk, so that by the next day, the amount of milk you have and your baby's feeding needs will be in sync.

Since you can't measure precisely how much your baby is consuming when you breast-feed, you'll need to look for other signs that she is getting enough nutrition. She should be wetting her diapers from five to eight times a day during her first few days and from six to eight diapers a day afterward. She should be gaining weight at a rate that satisfies her doctor. Most likely, your baby *is* getting all she needs. However, if you are concerned that she is not, consult your pediatrician.

**If you're not producing enough milk** Sometimes, women do have problems producing enough milk. If so, there are several considerations: Are you eating a healthful, nutritious diet with enough calories? Producing milk takes some 500 extra calories a day so you'll have to consume that much more than normal. Look, too, at your fluid intake. You are probably thirstier than usual because milk production requires liquids, so be sure that you are drinking plenty of water, milk, and juices to satisfy your body's needs. It's helpful to have a drink at your side as you nurse. You may need to cut back your activities for a time if your milk production is slowing down to assure your body the energy it needs for nursing.

**Feeding positions while nursing** There are several positions for nursing; some will just feel better to you and your baby than others, so experiment to see what works best. The classic position involves sitting up, with your baby positioned in a slightly inclined position. If you're smaller breasted, you'll probably be most comfortable with your baby cradled in your arms and your arms resting on a pillow. If you're larger breasted, you may feel more comfortable with your baby positioned on a pillow in your lap.

Some women with especially large breasts or with small babies prefer the "football hold" for nursing. To achieve this position, rest your baby along the inside of your arm with her head in the palm of your hand so that she is facing away from your other breast with her feet pointed toward your elbow. (See illustration.) When you are resting, or at night, you may find it more comfortable to lie on your side with your baby next to you, facing your breast.

Whatever position you are using, be sure your baby's entire body is facing you, rather than having her turn her head toward your breast. If your breast is blocking the baby's nose, press your breast down with your free hand to give your infant clear breathing space.

*Women with large breasts may find the football hold most comfortable for nursing.*

**Pumping breast milk** At some point, and probably often, you will need to express your breast milk in order to relieve an overly full breast, leave a bottle when you must be out, or keep up milk production when you can't nurse according to your usual schedule. Always wash your hands before you begin to express milk in any fashion.

Many women find hand-expressing simple and efficient for small amounts of milk or to relieve overly filled breasts. To express milk by hand, hold a clean container under your breast and place one hand around your breast with the thumb on top. Gently squeeze in a rhythmic fashion, pulling the thumb toward the areola. It's easiest to master this technique when your breasts are full.

You can also express milk with a pump, either manual or electric. A pump is generally more efficient than hand-expressing if you need to express bottles of milk. Follow the manufacturer's suggestions for using the pump. Wash and sterilize your pump immediately after each use or as soon as possible.

**Storing breast milk**  Breast milk must be placed in the refrigerator as soon as possible after pumping, preferably in the bottle from which the baby will drink. Use dishwasher-safe plastic bottles for storing breast milk. Breast milk stays fresh in the refrigerator for up to 48 hours. If you wish to freeze it, chill the milk first, put a date on the container, and place it in the back of the freezer, where it will stay coldest. Don't use the freezer door compartment because the milk will not stay adequately frozen. It will remain good for the baby to drink for several weeks in a single-door refrigerator, for three months in a double-door one, and for six months in a deep-freeze unit. Don't fill any container completely to leave some room for expansion of the milk as it freezes.

**Warming and serving bottled breast milk**  Frozen milk will thaw quickly if you run it under warm (about 110°F) water or place it in a bowl of warm water. Shake the milk after it's warmed, and test it on your wrist before giving it to your infant. The milk should be at room temperature for serving to your baby.

When feeding breast milk from a bottle, be sure to allow your child to stop eating when he appears satisfied rather than prodding him to finish the entire bottle after he's full. Do not offer your baby the leftover breast milk for a later feeding, either, since it is a breeding ground for bacteria once the baby has sucked from it. Discard leftovers after each feeding.

**Mixing breast- and bottle-feeding**
*"Is it okay to mix breast- and bottle-feeding?"*

Mixing breast and bottle may be necessary for a number of reasons, such as a mother's need to return to work. If at all possible, however, breast-feeding should be the exclusive choice until both you and your baby are fully comfortable with the nursing routine.

Introducing a bottle poses certain risks to the breast-feeding process: The bottle's nipple is easier for your baby to suck than your breast, so sucking from a bottle can make your baby lazy about sucking from the breast. Also, if the bottle you offer is filled with formula, you will reduce the amount of milk your breasts produce. Bottle-feeding pumped breast milk will keep your supply in sync with your baby's needs, however.

**TIME FOR YOU**

# *Soothing Tender Breasts*

Breast-feeding, natural though it is, can create breast discomfort. Engorgement and sore nipples are early problems, while mastitis and blocked ducts can happen at any time. Here's what to do.

| Condition | What Causes It | The Cure |
| --- | --- | --- |
| **Blocked duct** | Why a milk duct becomes blocked isn't clear, but the result is a red, tender lump around the nipple area. Usually only one duct is affected. | Avoid tight bras or clothes that put pressure on your breasts. Let your baby suckle on the affected breast; if you don't, milk may continue to back up and lead to an infection. If the blockage is painful or doesn't clear in three days, call your physician. You may need antibiotics if a bacterial infection has set in; if an abscess has developed, the duct may have to be drained. |
| **Engorgement** | An accumulation of milk in the breasts results in swelling that can make nursing painful. This is particularly common and dramatic the first time the milk comes in, a few days after delivery, and usually lasts about 72 hours, though it can recur later on. | Reduce the milk in your breasts by nursing or pumping. Warm soaks help remove excess milk. A supportive nursing bra can offer relief. Placing cold cabbage leaves on your breasts, oddly enough, may also help. If you are not planning to nurse, an ice pack can minimize pain. |
| **Mastitis** | An inflammation or infection. Triggers include a decrease in nursing, engorgement, stress, bacteria introduced by the baby's saliva through a crack in the skin, and tight bras. Symptoms are swelling, reddening, breast pain, and, often, fever and fatigue. | A warm soak or compress, moist heat, or, in severe cases, an oral antibiotic. Your doctor will know which medications are safe for nursing infants. Nurse through the pain; you'll feel worse if you don't. |
| **Sore nipples** | Usually because the baby does not latch-on properly. | Breast milk itself. Rubbing a bit of milk over the nipples is as lubricating as commercial nipple creams, possibly even more so. Air-drying your breasts after nursing also helps, as well as exposing your nipples to sunlight when feasible. If you continue to have problems with the baby's latching-on, a lactation specialist can coach you. |

# Bottle-feeding

Bottle-feeding is a straightforward affair as far as your baby is concerned. Your baby will probably not have trouble taking to it; the nipples are easier to suck from than the breast.

If your baby does appear to be having trouble, check that the nipple has the right-size hole for the formula to pass through easily. If your child seems to be frustrated and overstraining to get the formula, the hole is probably too small. On the other hand, if your baby frequently gulps and sputters, the hole may be too large. In that case, replace the nipple with one with a smaller hole for now. You can check the nipple by simply inverting the bottle and shaking to see the speed and ease of the flow.

**Bottle-feeding schedule** Feeding on demand is as appropriate for bottle-fed babies as it is for nursing infants. Start with a four-ounce bottle. For the first few days, he probably won't be terribly hungry as he recovers from delivery and adjusts to his new surroundings, and may not finish an entire four ounces. Soon, however, his appetite will pick up. He may not feed as often as a breast-feeding newborn because formula is more filling. Always allow your baby to decide when enough is enough. It's tempting with bottles—since you can see exactly how much or little formula is left—to cajole your baby into finishing it all, but this habit could result in an overweight baby. Over-feeding an infant who's not hungry can also confuse and upset him. Discard leftover formula.

*You and your baby should both be comfortable at feeding time.*

**Keeping bottles clean** Until your baby is 3 months old, you'll need to sterilize her bottles and feeding equipment, using either a bottle sterilizer, the dishwasher, or the stove top. Follow the manufacturer's suggestions for using a bottle sterilizer; when using the dishwasher, place plastic items on the top shelf and use a dish-washer-safe container to hold small items such as nipples and rings to keep them from falling into the motor. For stove-top sterilizing, place items on a rack in a large pot, submerge them in water, and cover.

Allow to boil for five minutes. Remember to sterilize the containers you store any feeding equipment in as well. After sterilizing, place cooled bottles, nipples, rings, and other supplies in the refrigerator, to keep them bacteria free.

**Choosing and storing formula** There are two different types of formula: cow's milk based and soy based, designed for allergy-prone babies. Most babies start with cows' milk-based formula and switch only if problems erupt. However, if your family has a history of allergies, your child's pediatrician may recommend soy-based formula from the beginning. Do not give your baby ordinary cow's milk in his first year because it doesn't have the nutrients that babies need.

You can purchase formula in three different forms: ready-to-feed, liquid concentrate, and powder. It is extremely important that you follow all label instructions for mixing and storage exactly. Ignoring them in any way, such as diluting too much or too little, can harm your baby. Refrigerate filled bottles until it is time to use them; for traveling, put the bottles in a thermal bag. Once you have opened a can of prepared formula or put formula into bottles, use it within 48 hours. The formula should be at room temperature for a feeding. New formulas are under development that contain fatty acids that mimic those found in mother's milk. Check with your pediatrician and/or the store where you purchase formula to see if brands with supplemental fatty acids are available.

**Feeding positions when bottle-feeding** Cradling your baby in your arms for bottle-feeding is easy and natural. Just remember to switch arms regularly both to relieve your own discomfort, and so the baby will learn to feel at home facing either direction. Angle the bottle in such a way, throughout the feeding, so that the formula always fills the neck of the bottle. This will prevent your baby from swallowing too much air. Don't prop a bottle for your baby. Not only is it a lonely dining experience for your infant, but the baby can choke from too much milk coming before he is ready. Allowing a baby to lie on his back while feeding has also been associated with inner-ear infections.

**PARENTS ALERT**

## *No Bedtime Bottles*

It's important not to allow babies to form a habit of falling asleep with a bottle during the newborn period since this habit will be very difficult to break. And, as your baby's teeth begin to come in, at about 4 months, bedtime bottles will make cavities far more likely since liquids will pool around their teeth as they sleep.

**PARENTS ALERT**

## Beware of Overheated Bottles

Bottled breast milk or formula should be served at room temperature. Cooled or frozen liquids should be warmed by running lukewarm water over the bottle or by using a commercial bottle warmer. Never boil a bottle in water, which can overheat the food. Also never heat a bottle in a microwave. Since a microwave heats from the inner core out, it is possible for some of the liquid to be scalding and you wouldn't know until the baby drinks it. Shaking the bottle does *not* greatly reduce the danger from one of these hot spots. Do not pour hot formula into a plastic liner, since these can burst if they are overheated.

### Feeding water to a baby
*"Should I give my baby water along with nursing him?"*

Water isn't necessary until your baby starts eating solid foods since both breast milk and formula provide needed fluids. In hot weather, however, or if your baby isn't feeling well, a few ounces of water can be helpful. Restrict the amount of water you give a baby under six months of age to no more than four to six ounces per day since his kidneys aren't mature enough to flush out the excess water. The water needn't be sterile, but you should be sure that your water supply is safe.

**Burping your baby** Babies must be burped. Their gastrointestinal systems aren't yet ready to do this work themselves, so you must nudge them along. A lack of regular burping can lead to painful gas. Some babies are gassier than others, and they need to be burped often and with vigor. Others need just a few pats. Breast-fed infants, because they take in less air while feeding, generally burp less than bottle-fed babies. Even if your baby doesn't seem to have much air in his stomach, you should routinely burp him, between breasts if nursing, or after every two or three ounces of formula, if bottle-feeding. Burp him again at the end of the feeding, although he might be ready to sleep. Simply pat him gently on his back as you hold him against your shoulder or in some other comfortable position. Always keep a cloth diaper or other fabric under the baby's mouth to catch the milk that often comes up with the burp!

**Burping positions** There are several positions for burping. You and your baby may develop a preference for one or another, or you may want to use all of them at different times. It's easiest to hold a baby who can't support his head—generally the first two months—on your shoulder. With his head steadied by your shoulder, use one arm to hold him under his bottom and lower back. Use your free hand to pat him gently on his upper back. You can also try a sitting-up position on your lap: Support your baby's chest and head with one hand. Keeping him slightly tilted forward on your lap, pat his back with your other hand. A third position is sometimes helpful to relieve gas, but you should avoid it if your baby spits up a lot since additional pressure on his tummy can trigger more spit-up: Place the baby across your thighs on his stomach, with his head higher than his chest. Gently pat his back or rub it in a circular motion.

**Nighttime feedings** Newborns and young babies don't know it's the middle of the night and that the rest of the household needs to sleep. They only know they are hungry, and it's time to eat. Until your baby's stomach is large enough for him to hold more milk— usually at about 12 pounds—and so sleep comfortably full through the night, you can be assured he will wake up for food. Gradually, the time he sleeps between feedings will grow longer and longer.

The nighttime feeding should be an efficient affair, with a minimum of communication or fuss. Unless your baby is a sound sleeper, change his diaper before feeding to avoid handling him and possibly rewaking him after feeding. Keep the room dimly lit while you feed, burp him, and return him to bed. These quiet routines will help your child develop the nighttime sleeping patterns that will best mesh with the rest of the family.

*Younger infants are easier to burp over your shoulder. Always place a towel or clean diaper on your shoulder. The sitting-up position can also be used.*

**Keeping baby awake during feedings**
*"My 2-week-old falls asleep one minute into her feedings and then wakes up hungry a half-an-hour later. How can I keep her awake long enough to eat?"*

Loosen her swaddling when you put her to your breast, and take off a layer or two of clothing so that she isn't overly warm. Tickle her cheek to rouse her, and the second she stirs, put the nipple into her mouth. Rock her, put her on your shoulder, jiggle the bottle or breast. In other words, experiment and do whatever works to stimulate her enough to remain awake during her feeding.

# Caring for your newborn's navel

During the seven to ten days or so that it takes for your newborn's navel stump to heal, you'll need to take special care while diapering, changing clothes, and sponge bathing.

**Avoid chafing** Many brands of newborn-size disposable diapers are designed with a cutout in the umbilical cord area that prevents the diaper from chafing against this delicate area. Some parents find, however, that simply folding the diaper—whether disposable or cloth—below the navel during this time prevents any problems. Some parents opt to cover the umbilical-cord area with a sterile gauze pad held in place with *paper* first-aid tape, which is available at all drug stores. Use only this kind of tape, which has a very mild adhesive, rather than any sticky type that could hurt your baby's delicate skin.

**Helping the wound heal** At each diapering, use a cotton swab to dab on a bit of rubbing alcohol to dry the wound. If the diaper or gauze pad covering the wound has stuck to it, do not forcefully pull it away. Loosen it with a cotton ball dipped into tepid water. When dampened, any covering can easily be removed.

If there's any sign of infection—oozing puss or increasing redness in the area—call your baby's doctor.

# Diapering

Changing your baby's diaper will quickly become the routine you know best—and with good reason. In the first year alone, you're likely to change your baby's diaper about 3,000 times! In spite of the work involved, diapering your baby provides you both with an opportunity to cuddle and play and get to know one another better.

**Comfort and safety routines** Always change your baby on a flat, sturdy surface, preferably a changing table, where she cannot roll and fall. Always use the safety straps on your changing table to secure her; if your table doesn't have safety straps, keep one hand on your baby at all times during changing because you can't be sure that she won't move in an unpredictable way, even at a very early age. Never leave a baby unattended on a changing surface, even when properly strapped. Before you begin, have all of your supplies on hand within your easy reach but out of reach of your infant.

**Diapering your newborn** To diaper your baby, place him on his back and unfasten his soiled diaper. Holding his ankles securely, lift your baby with one hand, leaving your other hand free to remove the soiled diaper and to clean his bottom. (It generally works best to hold your baby's ankles with your less-dominant hand and to do the rest with the hand you favor.) If the diaper is soiled, clean as much of his bottom as you can with the unsoiled portions of the dirty diaper. Wash your newborn's bottom and genital area with a sterile cotton ball or washcloth dipped in tepid water. Baby wipes that have little or no alcohol are fine to use on the baby after the first month or two, when the skin is less delicate, but should not be used on newborns.

*Place the diaper under your baby.*

In the early weeks, you'll probably be changing diapers before and after a feeding. As your baby soils less frequently, though, changing *after* a feeding is usually wisest since babies often have a bowel movement while they are feeding. If your baby doesn't generally have a BM after a feeding, diaper before middle-of-the-night feedings to avoid rousing him. If he does generally poop after a feeding, diaper him afterward to help prevent diaper rash. You'll learn your baby's normal schedule over time and can adjust your diapering routine as needed.

*Fold the diaper over.*

*Secure both sides.*

*For more
information on
constipation in
infants, see
**page 62**; for
diarrhea, see
**page 65**.*

**Knowing what's normal** New parents can be concerned when they first see the contents of their babies diapers, so it helps to know what to expect. Greenish or yellow-colored bowel movements are perfectly normal in infants, especially in the newborn stage. By the time a baby reaches 3 months of age, her poop usually takes on its typical light- to medium-brown color. Infants who are constipated may produce "rabbit pellets," small, hard feces. Diarrhea in newborns looks like water. Black, tar-like BM's, however, can indicate problems, including life-threatening internal bleeding, and must be addressed by the doctor.

Newborns' urine is pale yellow. Dark brown or pink-tinged urine calls for a doctor's attention.

**Diapering with disposables** When diapering with disposables, avoid getting any lotion, talc, or ointment on the closure tapes. This will prevent them from sticking.

Take care to discard soiled disposable diapers properly. Flush loose fecal matter down the toilet, then carefully wrap the diaper, securing it together with its own tapes, and place it in a leftover supermarket plastic bag before disposal. Keep soiled diapers together in a separate covered plastic trash bag and discard this frequently. Or, if finances allow, consider purchasing a device to wrap and store soiled disposables until trash day. Carry plastic bags on outings for sanitary disposal.

**Diapering with cloth** For a boy baby, fold the diaper to add extra bulk in the front of the diaper where the urine needs absorbing; for a girl, fold to bulk up the back. If you're using prefolded diapers, you can achieve the extra absorbency where you need it with diaper liners. With either prefolded or regular diapers, disposable liners can cut down on your laundry load and the need for more frequent complete clothing changes.

If you're using diaper pins, choose ones that have plastic protective heads. To store the pins, stick them in a bar of pure soap near the changing table, which makes them easy to find and easier to slide into the diaper. Shield your baby's tummy from a

**PARENTS ALERT**

## Use Talcs Carefully

Do not shake powder or talc onto your baby's bottom because your baby can inhale the product. Instead, put some carefully into the palm of your hand before applying it. Another talc problem: using talc on girl babies has been associated with cervical cancer in later life. Cornstarch-based powders, including cornstarch from the kitchen, are the better choice if a dry diaper-rash remedy, rather than an ointment, is needed.

possible prick by keeping one hand between the diaper and the baby as you pin with the other hand. Dispose of the pins as soon as the points become dull and difficult to use. Velcro-tabbed diaper covers can replace the need for pins and can provide a more secure fit as well as limiting leaks.

**Cleaning cloth diapers** For cleaning cloth diapers, empty all fecal matter into the toilet immediately upon changing the diaper; put soiled and wet diapers into a diaper pail partially filled with water. You can get a jump on removing stains by making this a mixture of one-half cup borax per gallon of water. Wash the diapers with a mild soap or detergent. Rinse several times to be sure all the detergent has been completely removed. If your baby has particularly sensitive skin, you may need to rinse even more. Do not use fabric softener on cloth diapers because this reduces their absorbency. Clean the pail regularly. On outings, carry plastic bags with you to store soiled diapers until you're home.

**PARENTS ALERT**

### Diapering After Live Polio Vaccines

If your child has received the Sabin polio vaccine, which contains the live polio virus, be sure to take special precautions to prevent spreading the virus to others. Child-care workers and others who may not have been vaccinated themselves are at risk of contracting the disease from contact with your child's feces within 48 hours after inoculation. Likewise, people with compromised immunity should *not* handle your child's diapers for two days after the inoculation.

**Diapering newly circumcised boys** Your son's penis will be red and raw for a few days after circumcision, but it's important that you clean it while diapering. Avoid wipes; the ingredients can irritate tender skin. Instead, use warm water applied with a real cotton ball, not a synthetic "cosmetic puff," which can irritate skin. Place a piece of gauze presoaked in petroleum jelly (available at pharmacies) over the penis tip to repel irritating urine.

Always check for signs that your baby's penis is healing as it should. A yellow secretion during the first week is a normal sign of healing, but if yellow-crusted sores develop or redness persists beyond one week, an infection may be present and you should call your doctor. After the circumcision heals, usually in about a week, no additional care is required beyond routine bathing. If your son was circumcised by a technique in which a plastic ring is left on the penis, call your doctor if the ring has not fallen off within 10 days.

**Diapering uncircumcised boys** At birth, the foreskin is attached to the head of the penis. It eventually separates, and the foreskin can be pulled back for cleaning. Do not attempt to retract the foreskin before it separates. Separation happens in half of all boys by the end of the first year. For some boys, however, it may take up to three years. Ask your child's doctor when you can safely retract the foreskin for cleaning. Until then, simply bathe the penis with soap and water, rinsing thoroughly. After separation, you may pull the foreskin back gently while bathing to clean the tip of the penis underneath, a practice your son will learn to do by himself.

**Diapering girls** To avoid the risk of vaginal infections, always wipe your daughter's bottom from front to back, making sure that fecal matter does not enter her vagina, which could cause an infection. Also be sure not to put talc or powder on her vaginal area, which is associated with cervical cancer later in life.

**Babies' awareness of wet diapers**
*"Can babies tell when they are wet?"*

For the most part, babies don't notice when they are wet. They do object to wetness and will cry when they feel a chill on their bottoms. Babies with exceptionally sensitive skin can also be bothered because the moisture triggers soreness. The awareness of wetness as a source of discomfort doesn't generally come until toddlerhood, which is just one of the reasons younger babies cannot be toilet trained.

**Diaper rash** Diaper rash is exceedingly common. There are a number of causes, but most diaper rash is due to the fact that babies live in diapers, and even the most conscientious parent can't keep a baby dry at all times. Some babies have naturally more susceptible skin, which makes them more likely to develop rashes. Sometimes, babies are particularly sensitive to a certain diapering product, including the diaper itself.

**Preventing diaper rash** To prevent or greatly limit diaper rash:
• **Change diapers often,** and as soon as possible when your child has had a bowel movement.

- **Switch diapering products** if irritation is due to sensitivity to a product. Discontinue using baby wipes when your baby has a rash, opting instead for a cotton ball or washcloth dipped in tepid water.
- **Make sure your baby's diapers aren't on too tight.** Put diapers on loosely, even if that may lead to some leakage.
- **Avoid overcleaning** your baby's bottom with either too much rubbing, too harsh a soap, or too much soaping generally.

**Soothing diaper rash caused by irritation**  In spite of your best efforts, it's likely your baby will get a rash at some point, especially once solid foods are introduced When rashes do occur, there are a number of things you can do to speed healing and to make your baby more comfortable:

- Give your child's bottom some "air time," in which she can go without a diaper for an hour or two, a few times a day. Don't apply ointment until you're ready to diaper her.
- Soak her bottom in a tub of clean tepid water. Don't use soap, which can further irritate her tender skin. When soaking isn't possible, use sterile cotton balls and warm water to clean her bottom. Avoid using baby wipes.
- If touching seems to hurt, use a spray bottle with a gentle mist of clean warm water to wash away feces.
- When diapering, apply a liberal coating of ointment to protect her from the urine in her diaper
- Cut away the elasticized leg opening of disposable diapers to allow air to circulate.
- Avoid nonbreathable fabrics in clothing when your child is suffering from a diaper rash. Wash all clothing in fragrance-free soap and use fragrance-free diapers
- If your child's skin is very inflamed, his doctor may prescribe a cortisone cream to relieve redness and discomfort.

     With care, most rashes go away in a few days' time. If your baby's hasn't cleared or if it's causing secondary symptoms, such as a fever or loss of appetite, call her doctor. Rashes sometimes require antibiotics and medicated ointments; the doctor will have to diagnose the nature of the rash and prescribe accordingly.

---

**"IT WORKED FOR ME"**

### *Changing Brands of Diapers*

When my 3-month-old developed diaper rash that just wouldn't clear up I thought I'd have to switch from disposable diapers to cloth ones. Then a friend suggested that I try a different brand of disposables—and that worked. My baby's diaper rash was gone within a few days.

### Diarrhea and diaper rash
*"Whenever my baby has diarrhea, he gets a rash on his bottom. How can I clear it up?"*

First, use a very mild baby soap and water to clean the diaper area; rinse well with tepid water and pat dry. Then apply a mixture of one to two teaspoons of an antacid suspension, such as Mylanta or Maalox, with an equal amount of water to the affected areas. Using a cotton swab, paint the mixture onto the irritated area and let it sit for five minutes. Rinse with warm water and pat dry. Apply a protective coating of petroleum jelly. Repeat at each diaper change until the condition is remedied.

• **Soothing yeast diaper rash.** This type of rash, which is triggered by candida—the same organism responsible for vaginal yeast infections and thrush—looks considerably worse than irritant diaper rash, with its red dots surrounding a big splotchy red area. A yeast rash can also invade the creases around your baby's hips, while an irritant rash usually won't affect the creases. Your baby may develop a yeasty rash during or after antibiotic treatment, or he may simply be prone to yeast, which thrive in warm, damp areas. Avoid using cornstarch baby powder on a yeast rash because the yeast organism will thrive by "eating" the cornstarch. Instead, keep your baby's skin dry; also leave his diaper off for one to two hours a day. Wash your hands scrupulously after diaper changes to avoid picking up the yeast on your fingers and introducing the yeast to other parts of his body. Your child's doctor can prescribe an antifungal lotion that will curb the growth of the yeast.
• **Soothing seborrheic diaper rash.** A red rash that affects the baby's bottom and hip creases, seborrhea doesn't cause the baby any discomfort. You can treat this form of diaper rash by cleansing your baby's bottom, genital area, and hip creases with a cloth or cotton balls soaked in water after each changing. Pat dry. Your child's doctor may also prescribe a cortisone cream.

## Newborn sleep patterns

Your newborn baby will spend the better part of her day asleep. At first, the word "schedule" won't really come into play. Your newborn doesn't yet have any sense of night or day and sleeps whenever her body tells her to, typically for a total of about 16 hours in a 24-hour period. Her sleeping time will likely be divided into about five 3- or 4-hour stretches. Don't worry about establishing a schedule during the newborn period. Your baby's stomach simply isn't big enough for her to take in enough food to see her through longer stretches between feedings. As your baby grows, she will naturally start to sleep longer at night, and be awake more during the day.

In the next few months, your newborn will ease into a two-nap-a-day routine on most days. She will be more alert during her waking hours as she becomes increasingly interested in what is going on around her. She will most likely start to skip at least one of her nighttime feedings by the time she is 8 weeks old, and be sleeping through the night by about 12 to 16 weeks.

Once they are sleeping through the night, some babies are early birds while others gravitate toward a later bedtime and wake-up time. There isn't too much you can do to change your baby's natural body rhythms.

**Sleeping through the night**  You can expect your baby to be sleeping through the night, at least an abbreviated form of night, by her third or fourth month. You may need to work on encouraging her, however. Limit afternoon naps, which could interfere with her being tired at night. Keep her at the breast a few extra minutes if you can, or gently encourage her to finish a complete bedtime bottle so that her stomach will stay full longer after her last evening meal. A dark room quite naturally encourages sleep, but a nightlight will make your job safer when you need to come into your

## TIMELINE *Infant Sleep*

**Newborn:** During the first two weeks of life and for some time after that, your baby's tummy will dictate her sleep routine. Breast-fed babies will need to eat every two to three hours; formula-fed babies every three to four. Infants are able to sleep for longer periods between feedings when they reach about 12 pounds.

**1 to 2 months:** As infants get older, they naturally become more alert during the day and more sleepy at night. However, most babies at this age still need at least two 1- to 3-hour naps each day. All babies nap for different lengths of time, but if your baby sleeps longer than three or four hours during daytime naps, wake her up so that she will be sleepy at bedtime.

**6 weeks:** Your baby will probably start to skip one predawn feeding and nurse longer right before bedtime to stock up for the night. Keep in mind, though, that it's normal for babies this age to fuss or wake up several times during the night.

**3 months.** By three months, babies are ready to have a more formal bedtime. Now is the time to get your baby used to falling asleep after feeding, not during it. At first, this may be difficult, if not impossible, but getting him used to being placed in his crib while he's at least partially awake will make the bedtime routine easier as he gets older.

**4 months:** At this age (or 12 to 13 pounds) most babies no longer need to wake up for middle-of-the-night meals. This means they now can—and do—sleep through the night.

## Getting the Sleep You Need

New parenthood is an exhausting experience. But the following will help you increase the amount you sleep and the quality of your sleep:

**Consider the baby's location and your sleep.** Some parents sleep better knowing their baby is in the room with them, easily in reach. Others find the whimpers and sighs a baby makes in sleep disturbing to their own sleep. Do whatever feels right for you.

**Take a nap every day.** Sleep research shows that even 10 to 20 minutes of daytime sleep has a powerful effect on adults, increasing their energy and vitality.

**Avoid caffeine, alcohol, and chocolate, especially after dinner.** All of these can interfere with sound sleep.

**Get some exercise every day, but not shortly before bedtime.** Regular exercise is one of the most effective ways to get a good sleep. Even better is getting exercise out of doors. Take the baby and go!

baby's room, and some babies are comforted by having the low light.

Create a bedtime ritual as your baby becomes ready for it. Give her a soothing bath, read her a quiet story, play soft music, rock her, and stroke her. However, put her into bed while she is still awake so that she doesn't depend on being in your arms in order to sleep. Don't let her take a bottle to bed with her; not only is it better for her to learn to sleep on her own, but milk or juice left in her mouth can pool around her teeth and eventually cause cavities. For your sake, it's best to avoid having her sleep with a pacifier as well. When the pacifier slips out of her mouth, she's likely to cry until you come in and find it for her.

By the end of the first year, your baby will probably sleep about 12 hours a night. Expect brief periods when she wakes during the night. Let her cry a few minutes before you go in; sometimes babies aren't really awake when they lightly fuss, and they go back into a deeper sleep naturally. In the event your baby cries for five minutes or is particularly upset, go in to check if the diaper is soiled or extremely wet, if she is in some other way uncomfortable, or if she isn't well. Once you're satisfied that everything is fine, just whisper a few quiet words of comfort, telling her it's time to go back to sleep, and leave. You may have to do this several times before she finally nods off again. As upsetting as it may be for you to avoid picking your baby up, in the long run this practice helps her by teaching her how to put herself back into sleep.

**Naps for infants**  After a few weeks of age, your newborn starts to move toward two long daily naps, one in the morning, and one after lunch. Babies sometimes take excessively long naps, of up to even five hours. This can wreak havoc on your child's nighttime sleep. If she isn't in need of extra sleep because of illness, wake her after a three-hour nap. You'll notice the morning nap getting shorter over time, but it won't disappear for most babies until nearly a year of age. The afternoon nap continues to be a long, full nap well into the toddler years.

### Sharing a bed with your newborn

*"Is it dangerous to nap with my 2-month-old in bed with me?"*

This is a safe practice as long as you follow certain precautions. You should remove pillows and comforters, and not be under the influence of alcohol, medications, or other drugs. To reduce the risk of SIDS, you should not sleep with your baby if you smoke; even the residue on your nightwear increases the risk. Don't let your baby sleep with you on a water bed, feather bed, or sheepskin, any of which could cause suffocation. Be sure your baby sleeps on his back, and don't overbundle him, especially since he will have your body heat as well as his own. Make sure he's in the center of the bed, away from the edges. There have been reports of babies being suffocated by parents, although this is extremely rare, and usually involves the parents' use of alcohol or drugs. You may be more comfortable putting the baby's bassinet next to you.

### Different babies' sleep needs

*"My sister's newborn sleeps about 16 hours a day, but my newborn sleeps only about 9 or 10 hours. Which is more normal? Does how they sleep now tell what kind of sleepers they'll be as they get older?*

Sixteen hours a day is typical of a newborn. You should review your practices to see if there is any way you can encourage your baby to sleep more. Are you putting the baby into the bassinet or crib for sleep on a regular basis so that she learns to associate a particular place with sleep? Having something of a predictable schedule will help establish sound sleeping habits, too. Are you picking her up at the first cry? If so, you could be unintentionally waking her. Give her a moment to soothe herself back to a full sleep before picking her up. Is the household quiet enough that she isn't being disturbed? The house doesn't have to be completely quiet since babies need to learn

**PARENTS ALERT**

### *Sleep Position for Baby*

To reduce the risk of SIDS (Sudden Infant Death Syndrome), always place your child to bed on a firm surface on her back. Do not put her to bed on soft cushiony surfaces. Do not place her tummy-side down.

## Working with Your Baby's Schedule

Almost every night, my 3-month old was falling asleep by 7 p.m. and then waking up, ready to eat again, at 1 a.m., just after we had gone to sleep. I tried to keep him up later in the evening, but it didn't work. Instead, I decided to attack the problem from the other end. I began waking him between 11 and 11:30 p.m., which was our normal bedtime. He was cooperative about breast-feeding in spite of his sleepiness. It wasn't a huge feeding, but it was apparently enough extra food in his stomach to keep him content and asleep until almost 5 a.m. That was the bonus I needed to get a sustained sleep.

to sleep through a normal level of household noise, but too much of a racket could keep her awake. Are you swaddling her? Swaddling could help calm her enough for sleep.

Try changing your routine to see if these changes can encourage longer sleep. While it's true that some babies are more wakeful than others, at this early stage, very little is predictive. In a few months or years, your baby may be a sound sleeper.

## Bathing and grooming

Some babies love their baths, squealing with delight as soon as they hear the water running. Others would prefer to skip the entire process. Your baby's temperament certainly influences how she'll respond to your efforts to keep her well groomed. Adapting your routines to make the process safe and fun, however, can make even the most reluctant bather a happy one.

**Comfort and safety routines** Bathing your baby is a routine both of you will come to enjoy. At first, however, you and the baby may find it unsettling. For the baby, being undressed and exposed to open air may cause some discomfort; for you, not yet having the confidence and know-how to hold and clean a slippery infant may limit your enjoyment.

Fortunately, you'll have plenty of time to learn. Because newborns should not be immersed in water—in order to protect their umbilical cord stump—you'll need only to sponge bathe your newborn. Unless the weather is warm and your baby is sweaty or she's spit up or has had a particularly messy bowel movement, you won't even need to use soap except on her hands, bottom, and genitals. Before you begin, be sure the room is warm and free from drafts. Gather all the items for the bath, and place these necessities, along with a clean diaper and your baby's clothes, within easy reach of the surface you plan to use.

**Giving your newborn a sponge bath** Here are simple and easy-to-master techniques for sponge bathing:

- **Fill the sink or a small bowl with tepid water.**
- **Undress the baby and wrap him in a towel.** Some babies are alarmed by being totally naked. If this is the case for your infant, keep him partially dressed as you wash one area at a time.
- **Dip a cotton ball in the water** and wipe your baby's eyes, from the nose bridge outward. Use a fresh ball for each eye. Wash his face and outer parts of his ears with a damp cloth; you don't need to use soap for his face.

- **After washing your baby's face, wash his scalp and neck, and working down the front of his body, lightly soap** (if you wish) the baby with a washcloth or your hand. Rinse the soap with the second clean cloth, and dry your baby as you go. Do not wash the umbilical stump.
- **Place your baby on his stomach** with his head turned to one side and repeat this soaping, rinsing, and drying procedure, to wash his back.

- **Wash his bottom and genitals last.** Use soap, and clean carefully in the folds and creases of your baby's skin. If your son has not been circumcised, do not attempt to retract the foreskin.
- **Pat your baby completely dry; diaper and dress.**

### The right bath temperature

*"How warm should the water be for my baby's bath? What's the best way to check it?"*

The water should be body temperature, or between 90° and 100° F. Check the water temperature with your elbow or, preferably, a bath thermometer, which you can purchase at most drug or baby stores.

**Immersion baths for young babies** Once the cord stump has fallen off, usually within ten days to two weeks, you may immerse your baby for a full bath. It isn't necessary to rush into this, however, if you are not yet comfortable with the idea. Sponge baths are sufficient for keeping your baby clean for at least a few more weeks.

Infants should not be placed in an adult-size bathtub until they are ready to sit up on their own—usually at about six months of age. Prior to that, most parents find a separate, portable baby bath to be most convenient. Using the kitchen sink is also an option, provided safety precautions are taken.

Decide what location is most comfortable for you while bathing your baby—the kitchen sink or a baby tub placed on a sturdy surface or placed inside the regular bathtub. Your attention will be on holding and supporting your infant, so it is important to choose a place that gives you maximum physical comfort. For most parents, leaning over the adult bathtub isn't the best choice until the baby can sit up on his own.

*Gently lower your baby into the tub. Be sure to hold onto your baby at all times during the bath.*

Gather everything you need, and put these supplies where you can reach them easily. Fill your baby's bath basin with warm water. Just a few inches of water will do the job. Check the temperature of the water before placing your baby in it. You can make the tub softer for the baby and less slippery for you by placing a towel or specially molded baby sponge liner on the bottom of the baby tub.

Cradle your baby in one arm with his head resting on that arm and your hand grasping his thigh. Slowly lower him into the water. Wash him just as you did when sponge bathing, starting with cleaning his eyes with cotton balls. To wash his back, carefully turn him, supporting his neck, head, and trunk. Remember to give his neck and head support as you lift him into the towel at the end of his bath.

### Bathing with your baby

*"Is it okay for me to take my two-week-old into the bath with me?"*

Under certain conditions, it could be fine to bathe with your newborn once her umbilical cord is fully healed. To keep her safe, follow these precautions: Make sure the bath temperature is right for her—about 90°F to 100°F—which will be on the chilly side for you. Have a nonskid mat in the tub. Be sure there's another adult nearby who can assist you if you need help, especially getting in and out of the tub. To reduce slipperiness, drape a towel between yourself and your baby. When getting out, wrap your baby in a dry towel immediately to prevent chills. Make sure, too, that you step onto a nonskid mat to limit the chance of falls on a wet floor.

### Bath frequency

*"How often does a newborn need a bath? Is it okay to skip a day?"*

You may skip more than a day. It is most important that you carefully clean your baby's bottom and genital area each time you diaper. By doing this, there is no problem in limiting his baths to once or twice a week since he doesn't really get dirty anyplace else. The exceptions might be if it's extremely warm and your baby would be made more comfortable by more frequent bathing, or if he has spit up or had a messy BM and needs a more complete cleaning.

**Caring for your baby's skin**  The best care, of course, is lots of loving caresses and routine bathing. Routine care of your baby's skin does not include applying lotion or oil. Parents often like to use one or the other because of the gentle scent, but nature has provided your baby's skin with its own protective qualities. If your baby has unusually dry skin—or if you really want that baby smell—it is okay to use a little baby lotion, but not oil, after each bath. Oil can clog your baby's pores.

**Washing your baby's hair**  Unless your baby is particularly sweaty or has somehow gotten her hair dirty, you don't need to wash her hair more than once or twice a week, especially if she seems to dislike the process. To wash your newborn's hair:

- **Dampen or wet his head** gently with a cloth or your hands.
- **Apply a small dab of baby shampoo**—a dollop about the size of a dime. (Newborns and very young infants will also do fine with regular body soap

---

### Warm Comfort

For added pleasure, warm up your baby's towel in the dryer or by placing it over a radiator before the bath. Just be sure it isn't too warm.

---

**PARENTS ALERT**

### Washing Your Baby's Ears Safely

Wash the outer portion of your baby's ears with a soft washcloth. Do not use cotton swabs to remove wax from the inner portion of his ears. The wax is there to protect the delicate skin that lines the ear passages.

provided that you're very careful not to let suds get in the eyes.) Gently work up a lather.

- **Rinse.** You can rinse a young infant's scalp by holding her over the sink or tub, her body along one arm with the back of her head resting in your hand. Rinse her head by gently wiping with the washcloth until all suds have disappeared. Between wipes, rinse and squeeze the cloth along her head and hairline so that as little water as possible runs into her face. As babies get older and they have more hair, use a cup filled with bath-temperature water instead of a washcloth. Don't hold your baby's head under the faucet to rinse. The running water may be frightening and the water temperature could suddenly change, either burning or overly chilling your child.
- **Pat dry.**

**Grooming your baby's hair** To groom your baby's hair, use a soft-bristled brush or rounded-tooth comb on it each day. If your baby has enough fine textured hair to work with, you can create a few curls if you wish by combing wet hair around your finger.

**Baby head bands**
*"Are those cute little head bands safe for babies?"*
Hair ornaments are not a good idea for babies. They could slip down onto the baby's neck where they could strangle her, or fall off and present a choking hazard if they are ingested. Tight-fitting headbands can be excruciatingly uncomfortable, too. It's fine to place a comfortable hairband or ribbon in your baby's hair for a picture as long as you remove it immediately after the shot is taken.

**Keeping your baby's gums clean** During infancy, make oral hygiene a regular part of the bath routine. Gently wash surface bacteria from your baby's gums with a clean bit of gauze or washcloth wrapped around your finger.

**Nail care for infants** Few things make parents more nervous than clipping their newborn's nails. There is really no reason to worry—baby nails are thin, making them easy to cut quickly. It's important to keep up with the trimming since newborns, in particular, like to keep their hands near their faces and can easily scratch themselves. Since baby's fingernails grow quickly, trim them whenever they look like they're about to grow beyond his fingertips.

Right after the bath, when the baby is relaxed and his nails are especially soft, is an excellent time to accomplish this job. You'll have more control if your spouse or another adult holds and entertains your baby while you snip, at least until you've had some practice.

To clip fingernails:
- Use rounded scissors or baby nail clippers.
- Hold each finger securely as you clip.
- Use your thumb to depress your child's finger pad so it isn't so close to the nail when you trim.
- Cut fingernails so that they are rounded.
- Use an emery board to smooth rough edges.
- If you accidentally snip into the fingertip and draw blood, gently apply pressure to the area using a clean, damp cloth or piece of gauze. Then smooth on a bit of antibiotic ointment.

For toenail clipping:
- Use rounded scissors or baby nail clippers.
- Grasp your baby's foot, holding the pads of fat down as you clip.
- Clip toenails straight across.
- Use an emery board to smooth rough edges.

## Dressing your baby

Learning to dress your baby is an art. New babies don't like the sensation of too much bare skin, and they certainly don't enjoy the tugging and pulling that are so often part of dressing them. You can get around both problems through the infant clothing you select, and by knowing some time-honored tricks for dressing your baby quickly.

Dressing time is more than a practical

**"IT WORKED FOR ME"**
### Help Staying Dry

I used to get soaked every time I gave my baby a bath. I was so afraid he'd slip out of my arms that I clutched him close to me as soon as I lifted him out of the tub. Now I tie a bath towel loosely around my neck before bathing my baby. It works like an apron to shield me from splashing water, and it's also a handy wrap for my baby when I lift him out of the water.

**"IT WORKED FOR ME"**
### Nighttime Nail Clipping Technique

My baby is constantly moving, which made nail clipping really difficult. In desperation, I waited until he was asleep to cut his nails. It was so easy, I haven't bothered to try any other way!

routine. It is also a great opportunity for playful pauses in the day with your baby. Talk to your child throughout the procedure, telling him what you are doing. This is reassuring as well as fun for him. It also distracts him from his annoyance at being dressed. And unless his clothes have become really soiled, don't change them any more than absolutely necessary to keep stress levels — and laundry piles — low.

**Easy ways to dress your newborn**  Use the same care when you're dressing your baby as you do during diapering. Before you begin, have all your supplies on hand and always keep one hand on your baby as you ease him into his clothing.

No baby likes having his face covered for more than a second so you'll want to get over-the-head items on and off quickly. Because a baby's head is more oval than round, the garment will slip on faster if you place it at the back of your baby's head first, and then ease it over his head and face. To remove this type of clothing, first stretch it out away from your baby's face and remove it front to back.

For one-piece outfits, start at the feet and legs. When putting on a two-piece outfit, start with the top and do the bottoms last. For two-piece items, most parents prefer bottoms that have easy-to-open snaps in the legs, though you may find it easier to remove bottoms entirely while diapering rather than resnapping a half-dozen or more snaps each time.

When you put a jacket or other piece of clothing with long sleeves on your baby, you can make it simpler by reaching through the sleeve from the wrist opening and pulling his hands through the garment rather than trying to push your child's arms through the sleeves.

**Adding to your baby's wardrobe**  When it's time to add to your baby's layette:

• **Look for clothes that are easy to put on and take off.** If you choose over-the-head items such as stretchy shirts and sweaters, look for ones that have large head openings or snaps at the neck. Since your baby will be lying prone for most of his dressing routine, opt for front rather than back closures.

• **Choose nonbinding styles.** Make sure that the clothing doesn't bind around the legs, arms, and neck, and that there are no loops of thread or strings that could catch on objects or wind around little fingers or toes.

- **Choose comfortable, breathable fabrics.** For daily indoor wear, choose soft, stretchy fabrics with oversewn seams that won't scratch your baby's tender skin. Many synthetics don't breath, and wearing outfits made of them can make your baby unpleasantly warm. If neck or other labels are stiff, remove them. (Save care labels if the garment requires any unusual laundering.) Limit fussy, dress-up clothing, since these tend to be uncomfortable and make dressing more difficult.

- **Avoid ornamentation.** Look for anything that a baby could swallow, chew off, strangle on, get tangled up in, or get cut by. Snaps are the best closures, but make sure they are securely anchored to the clothing, or else they, too, can pose a choking hazard.

- **Pay special attention to sleepwear.** At bedtime, dress your baby in long-sleeved footed pajamas unless it is very warm and you're not using air conditioning. If you turn down the thermostat at night or turn on the air conditioner, zip on a blanket sleeper with feet.

- **Go for a comfortable fit.** Clothing that's too large can snag on prams and other items, can more easily catch fire near an open flame, and can also be just plain uncomfortable to your baby. Too-small clothing is not a good choice either; it confines a baby's movements and is difficult to put on. Once your baby starts to outgrow an outfit, pack it away or pass it on to a friend.

- **Skip the shoes.** Baby shoes are unnecessary for nonwalkers. Footed garments are more practical, especially in cooler weather or chilly rooms. Socks and booties are helpful, although they tend to come off easily. If your child pulls off his socks regularly and his feet get chilly, use cotton tights instead of socks.

**Caring for your baby's clothing** Following the manufacturer's suggestions for laundering garments is the best route to take. (If you need to remove the garment labels because they're too stiff or otherwise uncomfortable for your baby, tape them onto a piece of paper and write the name or description of the item next to the label so you'll have a laundering guide at wash time.) In general, it's best

**PARENTS ALERT**

## Clothing Hazards

Avoid dressing your child in any garment that has ribbons or strings that could in any way encircle your baby's neck. Regularly check that buttons and other trims are securely fastened since these can present a choking hazard. *Always* remove any hood strings and pompoms from your infant's coats, sweaters, and sweatshirts. These items are extremely unsafe.

## Clear Storage for Baby's Clothing

With so many small pieces of clothing, I found I was having to rummage too much through my baby's drawers to find exactly what I wanted. The solution for me was an inexpensive tall, plastic dresser with many see-through drawers. I keep everything separate. T-shirts, jammies, stretchies, bibs, and dressier clothes each have their own drawer. Now I can track what I need quickly.

to use nonperfumed detergents and soaps. Note that flame-retardant sleepwear must be washed in soap, not detergent, to maintain its retardancy. To remove spit-up stains, presoak the garment. Add a touch of bleach to the presoak solution if the garment can withstand bleaching, and then wash as usual. Hold off on using prewash stain removers during the first few months, since these products are harsher and may irritate your child's skin.

### Prewashing infants' clothes

*"Is it okay to let my baby wear newly purchased clothing right away, or should I wash the items first?"*

It's best to wash the items that are stiff or that have dark colors. Washing heavily dyed fabrics will remove excess dyes that could irritate your child's skin. Otherwise, it's not necessary to wash clothing before wearing.

## Your baby's first outings

Pediatricians differ about the right time to take a newborn outside. Some are conservative, advising you to keep your newborn in the house for two to four weeks after birth. Others feel going out even in the first week is perfectly all right as long as your baby is sufficiently shielded from the weather. All pediatricians, however, agree that newborns should be kept away from groups of people to protect them from airborne germs. Consult with your child's pediatrician and count on your own judgment to decide what's right for you and your baby.

**Dressing your baby for cool and cold weather** When deciding what clothing to put on your baby in normally chilly or damp weather, consider what you wear for your own comfort. Babies respond to cold and dampness in much the same way adults do, and what you choose for your own comfort level should be your guide. For newborns, who can't regulate their own temperatures yet, however, add one more layer than you would choose for yourself.

Layers, in fact, are always a good choice since you can easily add or remove some of the baby's clothing when you're concerned that the baby may be getting too hot or too chilly. The air between the layers creates terrific insulation. Start with a one-piece undergarment made of soft loosely woven material. Avoid direct skin contact with wool, since it may irritate your baby's skin.

For the second layer, good choices include wool or synthetic polyester fleece, which is light-weight and breathable. For the outer layer, choose a water- and wind-resistant fabric to protect against wind, sleet, and snow.

On her feet, your baby needs only a pair of socks. If it's particularly cold out, add insulated booties. (Boots are too heavy for young babies.) It's very important that her head and ears be covered since body heat is lost mostly through her head. A snowsuit hood will also protect her neck. Slip on one pair of mittens, and shield her face with a light blanket if you go outdoors on a very cold day.

Don't overbundle your baby, which could lead to over-heating. Signs of overheating include sweating, damp hair, heat rash, rapid breathing, restlessness and, sometimes, fever. If your baby has any of these symptoms, reduce the amount of clothing on her until she is comfortable again.

For cold-day outings, you may want to put your baby in a front carrier. That way, your own body heat will keep the baby much warmer, and her face won't be as exposed to wind. If your baby's cheeks get very red or she starts fussing, bring her indoors.

If you must take the baby out in very cold weather, be sure her skin surface is covered, includ-ing her hands. To protect her face from frostbite, place a scarf loosely around her face, making sure, however, that you're not in any way restricting her breathing or creating a strangulation hazard. A plas-tic shield on the stroller or carriage will protect her on windy and rainy days.

## Being Prepared

Keep your diaper bag handy and fully stocked with the es-sentials. Put in several diapers, wipes, a well-insulated bottle or two if your baby uses them, and an extra blanket and set of clothing. Remember to add items to your bag as your baby starts to use them, from snacks and first books to a favorite toy. Keeping your bag stocked, except for last-minute additions of perish-ables, will save you lots of time and aggravation as you head out the door.

## Never Leave Your Baby in a Car

Never leave your infant in a closed, hot car for even a few minutes. Heat builds up quickly and the inside temperature could soar to over 100°F even when the outside temperature hovers in the eighties. Within minutes, your child could suffer heat stroke, which could be fatal.

### Winter skin protection

*"Should I put something like petroleum jelly on my baby's cheeks on cold, windy days? Could this kind of product increase the chance of winter sunburn?"*

A thin layer of petroleum jelly can help your baby avoid chapping due to wind. However, your newborn should not be out for any prolonged period on very windy days. On sunny winter days, be sure to use sunscreen or keep him in the shade to protect him from sunburn.

**Dressing for summer** In the warm weather, your biggest concern will be preventing overheating and sunburn. Sunhats are great, but they might bother your baby. Direct sunlight will certainly harm your baby's tender skin so be sure to use sunscreen and to keep him under the awning of his stroller or otherwise in the shade during your outings. Carry a sweater or blanket with you if you plan to be going indoors into air conditioning, which could make your infant quite chilly. To prevent overheating and dehydration, make sure your baby is drinking enough. Don't overdress him; diapers and an undershirt may be enough on really hot days. Bathing suits on babies are cute to see, but they leave too much skin exposed for safety. If you do choose to put your baby in a bathing suit, choose one that will make diaper changing easier—two-piece suits with a tummy-covering top, or a one-piece style with crotch snaps.

**Summer sun protection for infants** Sunscreen with an SPF (sun protection factor) of at least 15 that's specially designed for infants is a must if your baby is likely to be exposed to direct sunlight. The best protection again sunburn, however, is shielding your baby under an umbrella or other shade source and having him wear a sunhat that protects both his face and his neck, and long sleeved shirts and long pants to protect his extremities.

# *Your newborn's health*

Right now, you may sometimes wish that her health-care provider could move in with you. Happily, even though infants look fragile and are given to odd twitches and sounds, they are almost always both sturdy and resilient.

Nevertheless, their immune systems remain immature for several months. This immaturity, plus certain physical conditions, some of which are unique to newborns, mean that you must exercise vigilance and be prepared to follow up with prompt calls for medical expertise whenever your baby shows any symptoms of illness.

## The neonatal checkup

Your child's first medical exam will take place shortly after birth. During this exam, your baby's overall health will be evaluated, his measurements taken, and he will be checked for certain illnesses that affect newborns.

### Apgar scores
*"What does an Apgar score really mean?"*

The Apgar test, given to babies immediately after birth and again five minutes later, is used to determine the overall health of your newborn. The score is a way of alerting the medical staff about what attention is needed, from the usual post-delivery routine to urgent action. Ten is the highest score; most babies easily fall into the seven to ten range that indicates a healthy baby. Most babies who score a four or less, which calls for immediate attention, go on to develop normally in all ways, since this early score may indicate entirely correctable problems.

## Healthy at-home routines

During your baby's early months, adjusting household routines can ensure better health for your child for her entire life.

**Shielding your newborn from germs**  Naturally you want to show off your new baby, but it's wise to limit the amount of contact she has with others during the first few weeks since any illness can be more worrisome in a young baby than for an older child. Certainly you can stop by the office or your neighbor's house with the baby, but don't expose her to too many people or to anyone—

including family members—with a contagious illness. Have anyone who holds your newborn first wash his or her hands, preferably with an antibacterial soap. While this may seem like an extreme measure of caution, pediatricians now routinely advise it as an important protection for the baby. Avoid going places where there are large numbers of people, such as the mall or on public transportation, where passersby could cough or sneeze on your baby.

**Limiting ear infections** Newborns' inner ear canals are shorter and straighter than older children's. Thus, swallowed liquids are less likely to drain properly, which can lead to ear infections. To limit the occurrence of ear infections in your baby:
- **Do not put her to sleep with a bottle.**
- **Do not smoke** or allow anyone else to smoke in her presence, since second-hand smoke can inflame the inner ear and make drainage more difficult.
- **Feed her in a slightly upright position rather than a prone position**.

**Reducing the risk of developing asthma** Taking the following steps, especially during your baby's first 6 months of life, can reduce her risk of developing asthma:
- **Keep your baby away from second-hand smoke.**
- **Protect her against respiratory syncytial virus (RSV),** especially if she was premature, by limiting her exposure to others, particularly to other children in a child-care setting.
- **Avoid exposing your child to anyone with respiratory illnesses.**
- **Choose a small day-care facility over a big one** if she'll be in a child-care center, since fewer children means less exposure to germs.
- **Exclusively breast-feed your baby** for at least the first four months of her life to increase her resistance.
- **Keep her room, and other areas she is frequently in, as dust- and mold-free as possible.** Bare floors are preferable to carpeting, which can trap both dust and molds. Be sure to damp mop or vacuum often.
- **Keep pets out of your child's room** Move your pets outdoors or to a distant part of the house. Then vacuum and damp mop thoroughly; dander remains in dust for up to six months. If you keep pets indoors, bathe them weekly.

### Reducing the risk of developing food allergies

*"Food and seasonal allergies run in my family. Is there any way I can prevent my 3-month-old son from becoming allergic?"*

Whenever possible, babies born to highly allergic parents should breast-feed immediately after birth because the colostrum, which comes in before the mother's milk, offers a level of protection. Nursing mothers who are highly prone to food allergies should avoid cow's milk, eggs, peanuts, fish, shellfish, soy milk, chocolate, nuts, and strawberries. Those with an allergy to wheat should also avoid wheat products. Some research has indicated that highly allergic mothers should refrain from breast-feeding for more than four months. To determine if your allergies warrant early cessation of breast-feeding, talk to an allergist. It is also recommended that babies of allergic mothers who are bottle-fed be given a hypoallergenic formula, such as Nurtramigen or Alimentum.

Delay introducing solids until your baby is about 6 months old, and start with rice cereal, the food least apt to cause food allergies. From there, move on to vegetables and then to non-citrus fruits. Babies who are eating solid foods should refrain from eating any foods made with cow's milk and/or egg whites, such as ice cream or cookies. Introduce foods one at a time, waiting three days between each new food. Withdraw any that cause a reaction such as a rash, runny nose, gassiness, or wheezing. Do not reintroduce those foods for several months, until the food sensitivity is likely to have passed.

### Minimizing the risk of SIDS (Sudden Infant Death Syndrome)

Identified in 1969, this disorder causes affected babies to stop breathing. Some risk factors and possible causes have now been pinpointed, but others remain unknown. SIDS is most apt to occur in infants from 2 to 4 months old, although in rare cases, it can occur in babies up to 1 year old. It is more common in boys than girls and more apt to affect babies in cold weather.

Medical researchers have found that following these steps can significantly reduce the risk of SIDS:

• **Put your baby to sleep on his back.** Countries in which babies are now routinely placed this way to sleep have reduced the incidence of SIDS by half. For a long time, parents and pediatricians

**PARENTS ALERT**

### Hold the Honey

Honey should never be given to children under 12 months of age. Some honey contains spores of *Clostridium botulinum*, an organism that is harmless to adults but can cause botulism in babies. This illness can lead to pneumonia and dehydration. Baked good containing honey do not present a problem.

both assumed that an infant sleeping on his stomach was less likely to choke, but, with the exception of babies suffering from certain medical conditions such as an esophageal reflux, this is not so. Sleeping on their backs prevents babies from re-breathing their own air, which researchers now feel is related to SIDS.

- **Avoid cigarette smoke in the baby's environment.** Babies who are exposed to smoke before or after birth are three times more likely to die of SIDS.
- **Avoid overheating.** Babies should be dressed in the same amount of clothing as you are and their rooms should have the same level of heat as yours. Overheating babies, especially when they have a cold or other infection, has been linked to an increased risk of SIDS.
- **Use only a firm mattress in the crib.** The mattress should fit snugly in the crib to keep the baby from becoming wedged between it and the crib rails. Cover the mattress with a waterproof sheet designed for crib use (not a lightweight plastic such as a dry-cleaning bag) and a snug-fitting crib sheet. Don't put anything soft, quilted, or cushiony on or under the sheet. Keep pillows, plush animals, and bulky blankets out of the crib. For needed warmth, dress your baby in footed sleepwear. Be sure crib bumpers are securely fastened, well fitted, and firm rather than pillowy. It is never safe to let a baby sleep—even for brief periods—on sheepskins, bean bag chairs, foam pads, pillows, comforters, cushiony sofas, or water beds.
- **Breast-feed, if possible.** While there is not as much conclusive evidence about the relationship between breast-feeding and SIDS as there is with other risk factors, the rates of SIDS among nursing infants are lower.

## When to call the doctor

Never hesitate to call your infant's pediatrician when you're concerned about any aspect of her health or development. Because a newborn's immune system is not highly developed and because certain conditions become apparent shortly after birth, it's essential to call the doctor or take your child to the emergency room immediately if your baby shows any of the following symptoms during his first three months:

- **Appearance changes.** Your newborn just doesn't "look right" to you.
- **Behavioral changes.** Behavioral changes include lethargy; excessive sleepiness or wakefulness; excessive, continuous, or high-pitched crying; and/or the appearance of pain, indicated when,

if you touch him in a certain spot, he recoils or if he appears to be holding himself still to avoid discomfort.

- **Blue coloration or paleness.** This symptom could indicate that your child is experiencing a breathing or circulatory problem or allergy and should be treated as a medical emergency.
- **Bowel habit or urine output changes.** A change in the frequency, consistency, or color of your child's feces or urine could indicate diarrhea, dehydration, constipation or blocked intestines, jaundice, injury, or other serious condition.
- **Breathing difficulty.** Breathing difficulty is signaled by any gaps in breathing, rapid breathing, shallow breathing, wheezy or raspy breathing, paleness, or blue coloration. Breathing difficulty could indicate asthma or other allergies, apnea, a cold or other virus, pneumonia, an injury, or other medical emergency.
- **Bruising or any injury,** even if no bruising is apparent.
- **Convulsion or seizure.** This could indicate a fever, a seizure disorder, or other condition.
- **Fever.** A temperature of 100.1°F or higher.
- **Fontanel changes.** Any bulging or depression of the "soft spot" on your baby's head. This could indicate dehydration or other serious condition.
- **Skin conditions.** Minor rashes from diaper rash or other common skin conditions may not need a doctor's attention. However, wounds that ooze, don't heal, or get worse; or a rash that looks like pinpoint bleeding under the skin do require a doctor's care.
- **Vomiting.** Spitting up is normal. Projectile vomiting, however, while relatively common, must be addressed by the doctor to rule out pyloric stenosis, a rare but serious condition.
- **Yellowing of the whites of the eyes and/or the skin,** which could indicate jaundice.


Nonemergency conditions that need your doctor's prompt attention include:
- **Indications of hearing or vision problems.** If your child doesn't respond to audio and visual stimuli or if his eyes show any clouding or other abnormality.
- **In boys, tenderness and/or swelling in the scrotal area.** This may indicate a hernia or undescended testicles.
- **In girls, a closing of the labial tissues.** This could indicate labial adhesions.

# Treating common health problems in newborns

In the course of your baby's first few months, she will, no doubt, suffer a few bouts with germs and display symptoms ranging from sniffles to diarrhea. Though there is no reason to panic over every sneeze, it's essential that your infant's symptoms be discussed with her pediatrician. Even minor symptoms in newborns can signal major distress.

Following is an alphabetical list of common illnesses and symptoms, including possible causes and treatments.

*See Part 3,* **page 477** *for additional information on children's health.*

## Birthmarks

Birthmarks are common. And while some are apparent at birth, others do not show up until a few weeks after birth. Most are harmless and can be removed, if necessary, when your baby is older.

**Stork bites**  Many babies are born with marks on the nape of the neck or on the upper lip and eyelids. These salmon-colored patches, which are sometimes called "stork-bites" or "angel kisses," tend to disappear during the child's first two years of life.

**Mongolian spots**  Many babies have bluish marks, called Mongolian spots, on their faces or bodies. Asian, African American, Native American, and Hispanic children, as well as those of Mediterranean descent, are more prone to these blue spots, which fade by mid- to late childhood.

**Strawberry marks**  During your child's first two months, she may develop strawberry marks, also known as strawberry hermangiomas. Raised red bumps that look like ripe strawberries, they usually occur on the scalp or tummy. Strawberry marks are birthmarks caused by a vascular malformation and appear most often on girls and on preemies. Unlike port wine stains (another of this type of vascular condition, discussed below), which do not go away on their own, strawberry marks almost always fade over time. Before they fade, however, they first grow very rapidly in the first year of life, changing from barely visible to quite apparent. The mark's size generally plateaus when a baby is about a year old, and then it starts to fade. In most cases, the marks disappear entirely by the time the child is 6 to 10 years of age. In extremely rare cases, the mark may be in a place that interferes with functioning, for instance, over the eyes, nose, or mouth, or it may become infected. In these cases, laser treatment is available.

**Port wine stains** Port wine stains are purple-red birthmarks that can appear anywhere on a baby's body. They are made up of a mass of dilated capillaries, little blood vessels, that have collected near the skin's surface. (In adults, they often appear on the cheeks, nose, and chin and are known as broken capillaries). Although port wine stains may fade slightly, they do not disappear without treatment. Currently, laser treatments are used to remove port wine birthmarks.

**Moles** Between 2 weeks and 2 months of age, your baby may develop brown spots—or moles—that look like small, flat freckles. These are usually permanent. Because some moles become malignant during adulthood, they should be watched carefully throughout your child's life.

# Colds

Sneezing, running noses, congestion, and coughs may appear as a result of a cold virus or in response to other conditions, such as allergies. Having cold symptoms does not necessarily indicate the presence of the cold virus.

## Cold symptoms

- **Nasal congestion.** Mucus forms in your baby's nostrils, interfering with nose breathing.
- **Noisy breathing.** A baby with a cold may have a minor rattling sound in his throat and chest that is not, in itself, a cause for concern.
- **A slight fever.**
- **Irritability.** Some fussiness is normal in a baby with a cold. Because a cold in a baby could lead to a more serious illness and because cold symptoms could indicate another condition, you'll need to keep a close eye on her recovery. If your baby's symptoms get worse or last more than three days, or if she develops any of the following symptoms, call the doctor:

- **Difficulty breathing,** including wheezing, breathing rapidly or shallowly, or turning blue.
- **Persistent nasal mucus that is dark-green or yellow** and lasts more than 24 hours.
- **A fever of 100.1°F or higher.**
- **A decrease in appetite or excessive irritability.**

**Treating cold symptoms**  If your child is sleeping fairly well and behaving normally, you probably won't need to do much more than wait for the cold to run its course, while treating the symptoms to make her more comfortable. To be assured that the cold symptoms aren't worsening or indicating another illness, take her temperature twice a day to be sure it isn't higher than is safe for a newborn.

To help ease your baby's mild symptoms, try the following:
- **Run a cool-mist humidifier in his room,** especially at night, to help him breathe more easily. Clean the humidifier daily to keep mold and other organisms from accumulating, following the manufacturer's recommendations.
- **Unstuff your baby's nose with saline nasal drops** if stuffiness is seriously interfering with his eating and sleeping. Use just a couple of drops in each nostril before feedings and sleep. Saline drops are nonmedicated and available at drugstores. Do *not* use an over-the-counter decongestant or medicated drops in babies under 6 months.
- **Use a bulb nasal syringe,** available at drugstores, to suction nasal secretions if the baby's mucus is especially thick. Suction secretions just after using saline nasal drops, since the drops thin the secretions, making them easier to remove. Be aware that most babies dislike this process.
- **Give your baby plenty of fluids;** studies suggest that fluids help thin nasal secretions, so encourage extra breast milk or formula consumption.
- **Elevate his head during sleeping.** Place a pillow or several towels under the head of your baby's mattress to raise his head slightly and aid in draining mucus from his nasal cavity. Do not use pillows directly under your baby's head since they can cause smothering.

*Squeeze the bulb before inserting, then insert the syringe about ⅛-inch into the nostril. Slowly release the bulb to suction the secretion.*

**Bathing a baby with a cold**
*"Is it safe to bathe a baby who has a cold?"*

Yes. In fact, the humidity in the bathroom may help the baby breathe more easily. Just make sure the water and room temperatures are warm enough to keep the baby comfortable and prevent chills.

## Colic

Colic is a gastrointestinal disorder marked by extreme gassiness, irritability, and bouts of crying, oftentimes in the evening hours. No one knows for sure what causes colic, a condition that usually peaks at around 6 weeks of age but can last for three to six months. Some experts feel a colicky child is unusually sensitive to stimulation from lights, sounds, movement, or clothing. Others think the baby is gassy due to something in his diet. For breast-fed babies, that may be something in their mother's milk. Formula-fed infants may be sensitive to the milk protein in commercial formula.

**Recognizing colic**  The symptoms of colic include:
- **Apparent abdominal pain**
- **Extreme gassiness**
- **A distended belly**
- **Irritability**
- **Inconsolable crying that occurs daily,** typically starting at around 5 p.m., and that lasts a few hours, or crying that occurs sporadically all day and all night long.

*Try the colic carry to soothe a colicky baby.*

**Treating colic**  If your infant has symptoms of colic, have her evaluated by her physician to rule out other more serious conditions. If colic is confirmed:
- **Walk him.** Put your baby in a front-pack carrier and walk him in the house or around the block. In cultures in which babies are frequently carried, incidence of colic is lower.
- **Take him for a car ride,** securely fastened in his car seat, or for a walk around the house or neighborhood in his stroller.

- **Rock him.** Find a position that's comfortable for you both, and rock in a steady rhythm.
- **Massage him.** Lay him tummy-down across your knees and gently rub his back to help release pent-up gas.
- **Try swaddling.** You can also combine swaddling with gentle rocking.
- **Play white noise.** Make a tape of a vacuum cleaner or, the shower running, or invest in a noise machine that makes waterfall and rain sounds. Or, play soothing classical or nature-sounds music.
- **Try vibrations.** With your baby securely fastened in his infant carrier, place him on top of a running clothes dryer. The movement under him will lull him to sleep. Just be sure to keep a firm and constant hold on the carrier.
- **Try the "colic carry."** Position your baby so that his stomach rests on your forearm. His head should be turned to one side and supported with the palm of your hand or the crook of your arm.
- **Cut back on stimulation.** Lower the lights, turn off the TV, and speak softly to him.
- **Provide warmth.** If your baby seems to have abdominal pain, place a warm, wet washcloth on his tummy.
- **Exercise his legs.** With your baby on his back, gently "pedal" his legs in a bicycle motion to help him pass gas.
- **Adjust your baby's diet.** If nursing, and you have tried all other methods of soothing your baby, try changing your own diet by eliminating dairy products, caffeine, onions, cabbage, and garlic. If your baby is formula-fed, ask your child's pediatrician to recommend a different formula. The doctor may suggest one that doesn't contain cow's milk, such as a soy formula, an iron-free or reduced-iron formula, since iron can cause gas and cramping, or, if your baby isn't able to digest milk protein, a switch to a predigested formula.

## Constipation

Constipation is most often a symptom of gastrointestinal distress. Heredity may play a part in some children's constipation. For bottle-fed infants, a common cause is formula; soy formulas are particularly binding. Less common causes include lead poisoning, hypothyroidism, and Hirschsprung's disease.

Not all babies who fail to move their bowels frequently suffer from constipation. Bowel patterns vary in newborns and babies. Some babies move their bowels after every meal; others have a BM twice a day; and some move their bowels only every other day or so. Breast-fed newborns may have as many as 10 or 12 soiled diapers a day, before tapering off to just three or four a day for a few months, and then to fewer as they approach toddlerhood. It is also possible, however, for breast-fed babies to go for days without pooping.

If your newborn is not moving his bowels daily, call his doctor. Though this pattern may be normal for him, it's important that his pediatrician rule out bowel obstruction or other conditions.

### Recognizing constipation in infants

- **Fewer bowel movements than normal for your child.** If your child has been soiling two diapers a day and suddenly goes two days without a bowel movement, he may be constipated.
- **Stools are hard and difficult to move.** In infants, feces look like rabbit pellets.
- **Signs of discomfort.** Your baby grunts, grimaces, or cries before forcing out a stool.
- **Blood appears in or on the outside of the stool,** due to tiny fissures that form in the rectum because of straining.
- **Apparent tummy pain is relieved after having a large movement.**
- **Your child soils his diapers between movements** with a brownish liquid. This could mean that fecal matter is being forced around a hardened stool.

### Treating constipation in infants
If your baby has no other symptoms—no fever, no breathing difficulty, no vomiting, and no pain, treat the constipation as follows:

- **Resume breast-feeding, if possible.** If your baby has recently switched from breast milk to formula, resume breast-feeding if possible.
- **Bathe her bottom.** To soothe irritated anal tissue caused by anal fissures, seat your baby in an inch or two of warm water for 10 to 15 minutes several times a day. Also, apply diaper ointment to the affected area.

---

**"IT WORKED FOR ME"**

## Using a Rectal Thermometer to Loosen Stool

When I was concerned about my newborn's constipation, I decided to take his temperature. As soon as I inserted the thermometer, he had a large bowel movement. His pediatrician later said that this reaction is quite common and he recommends it before suggesting any medications to his young patients.

- **Offer water.** If your baby takes water, offer one extra serving per day—about 2 ounces for babies under 6 months of age.
- **Assist in getting her into position.** When your baby tries to move her bowels, help her by gently lifting and holding her knees up toward her chest. This will straighten the rectum and allow the stool to pass through more easily.

# Coughs

If your child is under 2 months and develops a cough, call his doctor. For children over 2 months, an occasional cough is no cause for alarm. Treat it as you do other cold symptoms. However, call the doctor if:

- **Your child has difficulty breathing.**
- **A cough lasts longer than a week.**
- **Coughing appears to be painful or is intense or persistent.**
- **Your child also vomits or turns blue while coughing.**
- **A cough comes on suddenly and is accompanied by fever.**
- **Your child develops a chronic cough after choking on food or a small object.** Children who have inhaled liquids or small objects may have long-lasting coughs that can't be linked to any cause.

# Dehydration

Dehydration can be caused by anything that triggers excessive fluid loss, such as diarrhea or vomiting or by a low fluid intake. Dehydration is a serious condition for newborns.

**Recognizing dehydration in infants** Call your pediatrician if your child shows any of the following dehydration symptoms:

- **Reduced urine output.** Your baby wets fewer than four diapers a day.
- **Dryness.** Your baby's mouth and skin seem dry and his lips are cracked.
- **No tears when crying.**
- **A sunken fontanel.** Your baby's fontanel (soft spot) is more sunken than usual.
- **A rapid heartbeat.** The child's heart beats at a faster rate than usual.
- **Listlessness.** Your baby doesn't make good eye contact or he has a "dazed" look.

- **Pale skin and fingertips.** His nails aren't as pink and his skin looks pale.
- **Sunken eyes.**
- **Irritability.**
- **Weight loss.**

**Treating dehydration in infants**  Always discuss symptoms of dehydration with your child's doctor. If the dehydration is not advanced, the doctor may recommend giving your baby an oral electrolyte replacement solution, such as Pedialyte, which will prevent severe dehydration. Severe dehydration may require hospitalization.

If your doctor recommends giving your child rehydration therapy at home, be persistent about getting the liquids into your child. Use a medicine dropper or bottle to feed rehydration fluids, carefully following your doctor's recommended dosage. Because bacteria grow rapidly in rehydration liquids, use opened bottles or powdered-mix preparations within 24 hours and discard leftovers. Thoroughly wash the medicine dropper between uses.

**Determining wetness**
*"I know my baby is supposed to wet about six to eight diapers a day, but because he's wearing super absorbent ones, I really can't tell if they're wet or not. Is there any way to be sure?"*

Yes. If your baby wears the extra-absorbent diapers, place a soft facial tissue in the diaper to determine if he is urinating. Check for urine every hour or so.

# Diarrhea

Systemic viral or bacterial infections are a primary cause of diarrhea, and diarrhea is sometimes a tip-off that your baby has an ear infection, urinary tract infection, a cold, or even pneumonia. Certain drugs, including antibiotics and antiseizure medications, can cause loose stools. Lactose intolerance—a sensitivity to the lactose (sugar) in milk-based formula—can trigger diarrhea in some kids.

**Recognizing diarrhea in infants**  In infants, diarrhea looks like water, whereas normal "baby poop" looks like thick pea soup. Call your physician if your child:

- **Shows any signs of dehydration.** Call the doctor if your baby may be dehydrated.
- **Has diarrhea for more than 24 hours,** alert her doctor.

**Treating diarrhea in infants** For a child with diarrhea that occurs every hour or so, but who has no signs of dehydration, continue breast- or bottle-feeding, and give rehydration fluids within four to six hours after diarrhea starts, as prescribed by her doctor.

## Ear infections

Infants are particularly vulnerable to ear infections because the inner-ear tubes are short, which prevents proper drainage of fluids.

**Symptoms of ear infections in infants**
- **Pulling at or tugging of ear.**
- **High-pitched crying.**
- **Signs of hearing loss.**

**Treating ear infections in infants** Your child should be seen by her physician, who may recommend a wait-and-see approach or may prescribe antibiotics. Increasingly, due to the development of antibiotic-resistant bacteria, physicians are recommending the "wait-and-see" approach. After your infant reaches 12 months of age, he can receive his vaccination against pneumococcal bacteria, which has the added benefit of limiting the occurrence of ear infections.

## Eye conditions and vision concerns

Certain eye conditions, such as a blocked tear duct, are relatively common to newborns. Congenital conditions, such as cataracts and glaucoma, are rare, but can affect newborns as well as older children. Occasionally, a visual impairment is diagnosed before the child leaves the hospital. Because premature babies are more susceptible to vision problems, the medical staff regularly checks preemies for clues of a vision deficit. But more often, it's the parent who notices that something isn't quite right.

**Checking your baby's eyes** If your family has a history of eye disorders, these should be discussed with your pediatrician in the hospital or at your baby's first checkup. If she shows any of the following symptoms, she should see her doctor as soon as possible:
- A tendency to startled or frightened every time you pick her up.

- Failure to focus her eyes on you or on a colorful toy a foot or so away from her, after 8 weeks of age.

- Failure to follow you with her eyes as you move across the room by the age of 8 weeks.
- Lack of reaching out for things, such as mobiles and toys or her feet, by 12 weeks.
- A tendency in an infant over 3 months to be quiet and not move around much; the baby seems more intent on listening.
- Clouding of the eyes, which may indicate cataracts.
- Discharge, crustiness, or other symptom may indicate infection.
- Wandering eyes, drooping eyelids, or other unusual appearance.
- Excessive tearing or mucus in one or both eyes, which may indicate a blocked tear duct.

# Fever

Fever is a symptom of bacterial or viral infections, allergic or toxic reactions, heat stroke, or dehydration. In newborns, a rectal reading of 100°F or lower is considered normal. A rectal temperature reading of 100.1°F or higher indicates fever.

While you can often sense the presence of fever, either by your baby's appearance or by touch, it is important to take his temperature to determine the exact reading. For an infant, use a rectal thermometer, either mercury-based or digital, for the most accurate reading. Armpit readings taken with a mercury thermometer or readings from a forehead-strip thermometer do not give an accurate core-body-temperature reading. Neither do digital ear thermometers because an infant's ear canal is too small for proper insertion.

**Taking your baby's temperature** If you are the parent of a newborn, do a "temperature-taking trial run" during your baby's first week at home. That way, when you suspect your baby has a fever, you'll know exactly how to take his temperature.

- If your baby has been bundled up, let him cool down in his diapers and an undershirt for 20 minutes before taking his temperature.
- Shake the mercury column of a glass bulb rectal thermometer down to below 96°F, or reset your digital thermometer.
- Smooth a small amount of petroleum jelly on the bulb end.
- Spread a diaper or other protective cloth across your lap; inserting a rectal thermometer may trigger a bowel movement.
- Place your baby tummy-down on your lap.

• Press the palm of one hand against your baby's lower back, just above her buttocks to keep her from rolling or squirming.

• Hold the thermometer between your thumb and forefinger or second and third fingers of your other hand, and slide it about one inch into your baby's rectum. Use your free fingers to hold your baby's bottom. If she raises up, your hand (and the thermometer) should move up with her to prevent further penetration.

• Leave the thermometer in for two minutes. Keep in mind that temperature-taking doesn't hurt—it just feels a little strange to your baby. Sing or talk soothingly to her during the procedure.

• After reading the thermometer, wash it with cool water and soap, then wipe with rubbing alcohol to disinfect it before storing.

**Treating your baby's fever**  Call your doctor for any fever over 100.1°F in a baby under 3 months and 100.4°F in a child between 3 and 6 months of age. Do not give your infant a cool bath or administer any fever-reducing medication to lower his fever without consulting your doctor. Never give your infant an alcohol rub, because inhaled fumes could cause intoxication.

## Hearing concerns

*For more information on encephalitis, see page 589.*

*For more information about detecting hearing loss in older babies and children, see pages 611–13.*

Newborns at high risk for hearing impairment or deafness include those admitted to a hospital neonatal intensive care unit because of any type of abnormality, infection, or difficulty during delivery; those with craniofacial malformations, including cleft palate; babies who are born prematurely and weigh less than 3 pounds, 4 ounces at birth; children with a family history of hearing loss; and those whose mothers had intrauterine infections, such as rubella.

Children with certain congenital abnormalities, such as Down syndrome, are also at increased risk for hearing impairment, either at birth or later in childhood. Other factors that put children at high risk of hearing loss include: bacterial meningitis; significant head trauma; infections; excessive noise exposure; and exposure to certain types of antibiotics

**Checking your infant's hearing**  High-risk newborns should be tested soon after birth. Older infants should be evaluated if they show symptoms of impaired hearing, such as:

- **Not reacting to loud noises.** Your baby isn't awakened by loud voices or loud noises.
- **Not responding to your voice.** He isn't soothed by your voice. He doesn't turn his head toward you or smile when you speak to him. He appears not to recognize your voice.

## Hiccups

Hiccups are triggered by a sudden spasm of the diaphragm. Many infants tend to hiccup after meals during their first few months. They are not harmful.

### Treating hiccups in babies
- **See if your baby needs to burp.**
- **Offer warm water.** Giving him an ounce or two of warm water in a bottle may help stop his hiccups.

## Infant jaundice (yellowing of the skin)

Newborn jaundice—also called physiologic or benign jaundice—is a common condition that affects about two-thirds of all newborns. Jaundice is a symptom of illness in only a small percentage of infants. No one can predict whether a newborn will develop jaundice, but babies who are born prematurely are more prone to newborn jaundice. Breast-fed infants are more likely to develop jaundice than those who are fed formula, although researchers aren't sure why. Sometimes stopping breast-feeding for 24 to 48 hours clears jaundice.

**Causes of infant jaundice** Jaundice is caused by an excess of a yellow waste product of red blood cells called bilirubin. It affects more than 15 percent of newborns whose livers are too immature to process the excess waste. A contributing factor in the development of newborn jaundice is the presence of too many red blood cells at birth. In approximately 3 percent of cases, jaundice indicates underlying liver disease or may be caused by an incompatibility between the mother's and the baby's blood types.

**Symptoms of infant jaundice** Newborn jaundice usually begins to show about 48 hours after the child's birth, peaks at three or four days, and lasts for approximately seven days. During your baby's hospital stay, the medical staff will regularly check her for signs of jaundice. But if you take your baby home before the third day after her birth, you'll need to examine her each day for symptoms:

- **A yellowing of the skin and the whites of the eyes.**
- **Behavioral changes,** including listlessness, unusual sleepiness, prolonged irritability or crying, hypersensitivity, sleeplessness, or sudden change in feeding or elimination.

**How to check for jaundice** With your finger gently press the tip of your baby's nose or his forehead. This will "squeeze" some of the blood out of the skin. If the skin looks white, the baby doesn't have jaundice. (This is true of black and Asian babies as well as Caucasian babies.) If a yellow tinge shows, the baby is developing jaundice and you should contact his doctor.

The yellow cast will progress from the nose and face to the upper chest and arms, move to the trunk, and then to the legs. If your baby is otherwise healthy and the yellow tint is light to moderate, there is no cause for alarm. But if the color deepens, looks very yellow, or extends to the soles or palms, his doctor will want to check his bilirubin level.

When checking for jaundice, hold your baby under direct sunlight or a white fluorescent light. Don't examine him under incandescent light—it has a yellow tint that can reflect on the baby's skin. For the same reason, be sure you and your baby are not wearing any yellow or orange clothing, and avoid rooms with yellow furniture or walls.

**Diagnosing and treating benign jaundice** Doctors diagnose jaundice through a simple blood test that measures bilirubin levels. A doctor's decision whether or not to treat jaundice depends on several factors, including how high the bilirubin level is climbing, the baby's age, and her general health. Some experts believe that in healthy, full-term infants, slightly elevated bilirubin levels are fairly harmless and don't warrant therapy. However, babies whose bilirubin counts are especially high or whose counts do not come down on their own in a few days need treatment to prevent brain damage. Treatment consists of placing the baby under special fluorescent lamps that convert the excess bilirubin into a water-soluble form that can be excreted in bile and urine. The treatment lasts for two to three days. Some hospitals are able to arrange for parents to rent home phototherapy equipment—long fluorescent lights that hang over the crib so the baby can be treated at home. Some offer a fiber-optic "blanket"—a sheet of plastic that has fiber-optic tubing running through it so that the entire blanket becomes a light source. Though doctors once routinely advised parents to expose infants with newborn jaundice to sunlight, pediatric dermatologists now caution that newborn skin is much too tender—and too prone to sunburn—to be exposed to direct sunlight.

Researchers at Rockefeller University in New York City have developed a drug—tin-mesoporphyrin (SnMP)—that can be given to newborns to lower their bilirubin levels significantly, lessening the need for phototherapy. However, the drug has not yet been approved by the U.S. Food and Drug Administration for use in infants.

**Diagnosing and treating abnormal jaundice** Approximately 3 percent of jaundice cases are illness-related and require special attention. Call your doctor immediately if:

• **Symptoms develop soon after or long after birth.** While benign newborn jaundice usually develops 48 hours after birth and lasts for approximately seven days, abnormal jaundice usually occurs within the first 36 hours after birth—or several weeks after birth.

• **The palms of his hands and soles of his feet turn yellow or the whites of his eyes become tinged with yellow.**

• **The baby acts sick, listless, has a poor appetite, and/or cries weakly.**

• **The baby's urine is very dark.**

# Mouth cysts

Mouth cysts—pearly white, fluid-filled cysts along the edge of babies' gums—look like miniature teeth erupting, but they are rounder than teeth and aren't as hard. Cysts can also develop on the roof of an infant's mouth. Mouth cysts are harmless and painless and disappear on their own without treatment.

# Rashes and other skin conditions

The perfection of your baby's skin may be temporarily marred by one of these common skin conditions:

**Acne and milia** These skin breakouts are often seen on babies under a month or so in age. Acne appears as pink pimples on the cheeks, forehead, or chin; milia are whiteheads on the nose. These will go away on their own and should *not* be squeezed or touched.

**Atopic dermatitis** Atopic dermatitis, a form of eczema, commonly occurs in infants who have a family or personal history of allergies or eczema. If your child has atopic dermatitis, the condition will most likely occur in phases. Between the ages of 2 and 6 months, he may develop small, itchy, red bumps on his cheeks, forehead, or scalp. The rash may then spread to his arms and trunk. In 50 percent of cases, atopic dermatitis clears up by the time the child is age 2 or 3 years old.

**Cradle cap and seborrheic dermatitis** Cradle cap is a red, scaly rash that may appear on your infant's scalp during his first few months of life. It is especially common between the ages of 2 to 4 months. No one knows for sure what causes it. Some experts think it's due to hormonal changes that mothers experience during pregnancy, which stimulate the baby's oil glands to produce excess oil, resulting in the rash. Others believe cradle cap is an overgrowth of a yeast normally on the skin. Cradle cap frequently extends to the creases behind a baby's neck, to his armpits, and behind his ears. When the rash appears on the baby's face and in the diaper area, doctors refer to the condition as seborrheic dermatitis, which is a form of eczema. This condition usually clears up by 4 weeks of age.

Cradle cap and seborrheic dermatitis are rarely itchy or uncomfortable and are not harmful to your baby. Cradle cap that's confined to the scalp can be treated with daily shampooing with a mild shampoo and gentle brushing to remove the flakes.

If cradle cap is severe, or persists for more than a week, call your child's physician, who may prescribe a medicated shampoo to help curb flaking and redness. Also call if the rash spreads to your

---

**PEDIATRICK**

### Cradle Cap "Cure"

If your baby's cradle cap is unsightly or the scales are unusually thick, apply slightly warmed mineral oil to her scalp. Leave it on for three to four hours. Then, using a children's antidandruff shampoo, wash her scalp, massaging it with your fingers to loosen scales. Comb your baby's hair with a rounded-tooth, fine-tooth comb to remove the scales from her hair.

baby's face, neck, and armpits, or diaper area. In this case, the doctor will probably recommend treating the affected areas with a cortisone cream or lotion.

**Eczema** Itchy red patches of skin on the cheeks, forehead, chest, arms, legs, and behind the knees or elbows are common in babies with a family history of allergies. To relieve symptoms, dress your baby in breathable cotton and other soft fabrics; ask your baby's physician about what kind of medicated lotion, if any, you should use.

**Heat rash, or prickly heat** These skin conditions are marked by red bumps on parts of the body that can overheat more easily than others. These include the neck, diaper area, behind the ears, the armpits, and behind the knees. Loose, lightweight clothing, lukewarm baths, and a light application of cornstarch can help keep heat rash under control.

**Peeling** Most babies have a natural peeling of the skin—which looks like the result of a minor sunburn—in the first few weeks. It requires no treatment.

# Thrush

Thrush is a mild fungal infection of the mouth caused by *Candida albicans*—the same organism that causes vaginal yeast infections. Thrush may make nursing painful for your child, but it's a relatively harmless condition and not a cause for concern unless your child has other symptoms, such as fever, and is excessively irritable.

Babies—especially newborns—often develop thrush when something disturbs the microbial environment in their mouths, allowing candida to proliferate. Antibiotics and illnesses are frequent triggers. Also, the sugar in breast milk and formula provides an ideal breeding ground for candida.

### Symptoms of thrush
- **White patches** on the insides of his cheeks, the roof of his mouth, and on his tongue that may appear to be dried milk, but don't wash off.
- **Inflammation** of the underlying skin and slight bleeding might be present.

**Treating thrush** Call your doctor if you suspect your baby has thrush. If your child is taking antibiotics, her doctor may change the dosage—if the thrush is seriously interfering with her ability to nurse or eat. The doctor may also prescribe a topical antifungal agent if the infection is severe.

Because your baby can transmit candida to your nipples during breast-feeding—and may be reinfected when she nurses—your obstetrician will probably prescribe a medicated cream you can apply to your nipples; the cream won't hurt your baby. You may also want to give your baby a little water after feedings to help wash the milk out of his mouth. If bottle-feeding or if your baby uses a pacifier, prevent reinfection by sterilizing his bottle nipples and pacifiers after each use, then drying them thoroughly.

## Vomiting

Vomiting is a symptom of many different illnesses. Unlike spitting up, true vomiting can be caused by many medical problems but is most commonly the result of gastrointestinal bacterial or viral infections, allergies, or gastroesophageal reflux. Other triggers include bacterial infections, food poisoning, and ailments such as ear and urinary tract infections, colds, flu, pneumonia, meningitis, and appendicitis. Although rare, infants may experience projectile vomiting, extremely forceful vomiting that literally projects across the room and is not related to feeding. Any instances of projectile vomiting should be discussed with your child's physician. A serious condition in newborns, pyloric stenosis, can lead to projectile vomiting and requires immediate medical attention.

Call the doctor for any instances of vomiting in an infant under 6 months of age. During a bout of vomiting or spitting up, keep your baby on his side to prevent him from inhaling the material.

### Distinguishing Between Vomiting and Spitting Up

Vomiting should not be confused with spitting up, a normal aftermath of feeding in many babies when a small amount of milk comes up with a burp or shortly thereafter. Vomiting is more substantial: it may not come directly after or consist of your baby's most recent meal.

# Part 1

# As They Grow

# CHAPTER 1

# The First 8 Weeks

The first days and weeks of your baby's life are filled with new experiences—for your baby and for you. It's a time of discovery, questioning, and learning. For you, there is the business of mastering the basics—diapering, feeding, dressing, and bathing—that easily fills your days and often your nights. Added to that is the awesome experience of getting to know your baby. Your baby is learning, too, figuring out what life outside the womb is all about, as she gets to know the people who hover around her, who care for her needs, and who are introducing her to the larger world. Your baby is also learning about herself. Her newborn unfocused squint will quickly become a careful gaze as she studies her hands, her toes, and you.

In your first eight weeks with your baby, you will go from fumbling to finesse. At the outset, you'll no doubt feel overwhelmed. But experience, some experimentation, wise advice from friends and family, and the reading you do will give you courage and confidence. It won't be long before you really will know what you're doing.

# Physical development

In the nine months before birth, your baby grew at a rate never to be matched again. The last few weeks of this astonishing metamorphosis were filled with preparation as he busily "practiced" for life outside the womb. He had a sleep schedule of sorts. He responded to stimuli of sound and light from outside his cozy uterine home, and he spent a good deal of time exercising motor movements—kicking and squirming—as you remember well. After making the traumatic journey from the warm womb to the outside world, your healthy baby comes to you well-equipped to get on with life.

## Physical changes

Your newborn's appearance will change quite dramatically over the next few weeks. Yours may have been born with an excessive amount of hair, including fine hair, called lanugo, on their backs and shoulders. Lanugo develops toward the end of pregnancy, and most babies shed this hair before they are born. But babies born before their due date are more likely to have body hair, which will disappear within a couple of weeks. Many newborns are born with a full head of hair—only to lose it during the first few weeks or months after birth.

The "belly button," or navel, marks that part of your baby to which his umbilical cord was attached, allowing nutrients from your body to reach him. At birth, the navel is clamped. The stump will take about seven to ten days to heal.

Newborn boys usually have startlingly large scrotums, caused by fluid around the testes that will gradually be absorbed into their bodies. Girls may have enlarged labia along with a drop or two of vaginal blood. Both boys and girls generally have a nub of breast tissue under their nipples and may even have a show of breast milk, all the result of their mothers' pregnancy hormones spilling into their bodies. Babies often have facial blemishes. In the course of the next few weeks and months, any peculiarities of this sort in your newborn are likely to fade away.

Right now, you can content yourself with deciding who in the family this remarkable creature most resembles. If you're like most parents, you'll decide he looks just like you. Over the next few weeks, as your baby's facial expressions take on a range from

## Baby's First Smile

That all-important expression, the first direct communication, erupts early in your baby's life. Fleeting smile-like expressions cross newborns' faces as they sleep. This is not, as once thought, the result of gas or even a momentary sweet dream. It is a reflex triggered by the central nervous system. You can expect to see your baby's first real smile, the one that says "Hi," by the time she is around four weeks old.

grimaces to wide smiles, you'll see someone else—the unique child he is.

**What your newborn can do**   Some physical changes are eventful enough to be considered milestones of sorts. While a newborn can only lift his head a few inches for a moment or so, by the time two months have passed, he'll be able to raise his shoulders as well and hold his head high from a prone position.

Feeding comes naturally to newborns. Because your baby knows how to suck, he can participate, even enthusiastically, in his feedings. He is also born with a set of reflexes—automatic physical reactions to specific stimuli. One you'll see often is called "rooting," which describes how babies turn their heads in search of a nipple and begin to move their mouths in anticipation of mealtime. Other reflexes include a stepping action that makes babies appear to be trying to walk when they are held upright over a surface, and a similar crawling-like motion when placed on their stomachs. When startled, your baby will display the "Moro" reflex, flinging out his arms, and then, just as suddenly, pulling them back toward his chest. This action may be frightening for you to witness because it looks as if your baby is upset, but it's a neurological, not a psychological, event. The reflex that may delight you most is the grasping one, which enables your baby to grab onto your finger when you place it in his palm. In time all of these reflexes will disappear, and more sophisticated and useful actions will follow.

Reaching for something that catches her eye, be it a shiny toy or your hand, is another milestone that excites parents. This thrilling event usually occurs when your baby is four or five months, but the process starts now. At birth, your baby's reflex gives her a strong grasp, but she has little muscle control. By the time she reaches two months, although she will have lost the grasping reflex, you'll start to see her swiping at objects that interest her. Not yet able to achieve a controlled, purposeful reach, your baby does have better vision, steadier hands, and a more focused gaze, all of which get her closer to the mark.

**What you can do** For an hour or so after delivery, your newborn is generally wide-eyed and alert. And it's no wonder! Now bright lights and excited voices suddenly replace the dark quiet he enjoyed before. At this moment, he is almost as curious about the people surrounding him as they are about him. This alertness creates an excellent opportunity for you to hold your baby, admire his tiny features, and put him to your breast as you examine one another in a whole new way.

In the first weeks of life, you can help your baby feel physically safe by holding him close and getting into the habit of placing your hand behind his neck and head whenever you handle him. Take this time to get to know your baby as you learn to read his signals. Also be sure to take time for yourself and your spouse, so that you'll have the energy you need to enjoy these fleeting weeks of your newborn's life.

## Your baby's senses

Babies are born with their senses surprisingly developed, although none are yet fully in operation. If their senses were highly tuned, babies would be overwhelmed by the sudden onslaught of so many new sights and sounds. Following is what you may need to know about the normal range of your baby's senses.

**Hearing** At birth, your baby is slightly hard of hearing because his inner ears have not yet completely matured. Newborns can hear exaggerated changes in pitch and tones and seem to prefer higher-pitched voices to lower ones—making their mother's voice especially appealing; his mother's voice is also the first one the child will recognize. Your newborn's natural preference for higher tones helps explain why many people instinctively speak to him in high-pitched "baby talk." Newborns also are able to distinguish one male voice from another, but the preference for their father's voice won't come until several weeks after birth.

*See **page 611** for information about evaluating your baby's hearing.*

**Vision** Parents have long wondered just how much their baby can see in the early weeks of life. While healthy newborns can see, your smiling face is pretty much of a blur. Newborns are very nearsighted, unable to focus clearly on anything beyond about 8 to 15 inches. Not coincidentally, this is the usual distance between a nursing baby and his mother's face. A baby's vision steadily progresses

*See **page 535** for information about evaluating your baby's vision.*

from the newborn's vision of about 20/400 (which means he's able to see at a distance of 20 feet what an older person with perfect vision can see at 400 feet) to 20/70 in just a few months. By six months, your baby has fully formed vision.

Your newborn's color sense is not fully developed either. Until he is about four months old, he is unable to fully distinguish among colors, which is why he responds more strongly to contrasting tones, such as black and white. When your baby studies faces, he's particularly interested in contrasts, such as the color and whites of the person's eyes.

**Smell and taste**　Both smell and taste senses are in place at birth. Newborns grimace when pungent odors, such as odors from vinegar, are introduced to them. On the other hand, pleasant smells such as vanilla will elicit their interest.

Your newborn will show a strong preference for sweet tastes. This is important to her survival because it makes naturally sweet breast milk immediately appealing. The only taste sensation newborns seem unable to detect well is salt. That ability begins to emerge at about four to five months of age, and it isn't fully formed until your child is about five years old.

**Touch**　The development of touch is particularly significant because it is the one sense that must be stimulated to assure your infant's survival. Your baby's need to be touched is intense. Without holding and stroking, babies show a physical and emotional failure to thrive; some even die from this lack of skin-to-skin contact. Besides human touch, infants have certain textural preferences, including, as you would expect, soft-textured blankets and clothing. However, it takes years for children to develop a more sophisticated sense of touch.

# The first days and weeks

In the next few weeks, you'll hear again and again, "get as much sleep as you can." This is not idle advice. As keyed up as you probably are and as overwhelmed as you no doubt feel, everything will be easier if you are better rested. It's nearly impossible to be well rested when you're responsible for meeting your newborn's needs, but grabbing a nap as she naps; going to bed as she nods off; letting someone else comfort, change, and feed her when possible will serve you both well.

Anxious though you probably are to master this situation and get things under control, your first priority should be to relax—as much as you can—and enjoy your baby. You've waited a long time for this, and you have the right to revel in the pleasure of new parenthood.

### Infant massage
*"Are massages good for babies? How should I do one?"*

While babies don't need massaging, a massage can be enjoyable for both you and your baby when properly done. Don't be overly gentle since that approach is more apt to tickle than soothe your baby. On the other hand, if you are rubbing too hard, your baby will make it clear that he doesn't like that style either. Aim for a touch that is firm without being forceful. Use a little vegetable oil on your hands instead of mineral oil, since your baby will likely be putting his hands into his mouth and could ingest whatever oil you use.

A good baby massage proceeds as follows: Be sure the room is comfortably warm. Lay your naked or almost-naked baby on his back. Then "walk" your hands across your baby's stomach, a motion that is soothing and good for relieving gas. On his face, make small circles on and around his jawbone with your fingertips. To massage his legs, wrap one hand around your baby's thigh, the other around his ankle, and gently squeeze and slide one hand to the other and repeat in the opposite direction. Then place your thumb on the bottom of your baby's foot and push forward, following an invisible line from his heel to each toe. For your baby's arms, grasp one arm with both hands, one hand above the other, near your baby's shoulder, and gently twist back and forth in opposite directions moving toward his wrist. (Your baby's arms should be straight for this, but if he isn't ready to uncurl them, don't force him.)

To massage his back, place him on his tummy, turning his head to one side. Place one of your hands on his buttocks. With the other hand, make a sweeping motion down from the top of his back to your hand. Repeat this motion to cover his entire back. Finally, for your baby's chest, gently turn him onto his back. Place both of your hands at the center of his chest and, in a heart-shaped motion, move each hand out to the side, down his rib cage, and then up the center to your starting position. If, at any point during his massage, your baby displays any displeasure, stop.

# Your baby's first well-baby checkup

*For information on your newborn's health, see **pages 53–74**.*

The first time you take your baby in for her well-baby checkup is a momentous occasion. For many babies, this is their first real outing, so you might have anxiety about both the visit and getting there.

Because this experience will be new to you, it's a good idea to write down any questions you have before the visit and to bring the list with you. Don't worry about appearing to be unsure of yourself. The pediatrician is your resource for learning about your baby's health and development and is ready and able to help you do the best for your baby. These tips will help make your first doctor's visit go smoothly:

• **Dress your baby in easy-on and easy-off clothing.** There's no need to make your baby uncomfortable with too much fussing about dressing and undressing. Bring an extra set of clothes in case of accidents.

• **Keep a receiving blanket handy.**  Not only can the doctor's office be chilly, but you'll want to cover up your naked baby to prevent chills during the exam.

• **Review your list of questions, and put it in the diaper carrier.** It's easy to forget to refer to your list if you don't keep it in a place where you're sure to find it.

• **Consider packing a camera** if you'd like to record this big day.

## Growth charts

*"What do the percentile scores on growth charts mean? Do they predict my baby's future growth?"*

*For more information about predicting your child's future height, see **page 222**.*

At each well-baby visit, your baby's physician measures your child's height, weight, and head circumference, and plots these measurements on a graph that shows how your baby's size compares to other babies her age. The median percentile ranking is 50, meaning that 50 percent of all babies of the same age are larger, and 50 percent are smaller than the number shown for each measurement. Babies in the 80th percentile, then, are bigger than 80 percent of other babies their age; babies who are in the 20th percentile are smaller than 80 percent of other babies their age. There is no correct percentile. Some babies score in the 20th percentile and are perfectly healthy. Likewise, a baby in the 90th percentile may be equally healthy. The important thing that the pediatrician is looking for is consistent growth and a balance between height and weight. If your baby is in the 40th percentile for height, he should be in a similar range for weight. If his weight fell far below or above the 40th percentile, that would be cause for concern.

Growth spurts and slow-downs are normal throughout the growing years, but most children stay within the same percentiles throughout their lives. However, switching from one percentile range to another in the first two years of life is more common and reflects his genetic makeup. By age 3, the percentile ranking is a valid predictor of future size.

### Eye color

*"My husband and I have brown eyes. How did our daughter get her blue eyes?"*

Even with brown-eyed parents, almost all Caucasian babies are born with blue or gray-blue eyes, and they remain a variation of blue for six months or longer. After that, your baby's eyes may turn brown since brown is the dominant gene. However, if both you and your husband carry a recessive blue gene, it is possible that your baby will inherit two genes for blue eyes. In that case, your baby's eyes will remain blue.

## Infant Health Checklist

These are the things your child's physician will check at his newborn, well-baby visit:

- Height
- Weight
- Head circumference
- Ears and eyes for clarity and signs of infection
- Glands for any swelling indicating an abnormality
- Heart rate and ease of breathing
- Temperature
- Reflexes
- Your baby's urine output and bowel habits
- Any symptoms the doctor observes and/or you report

# Growth Charts For the First 12 Months

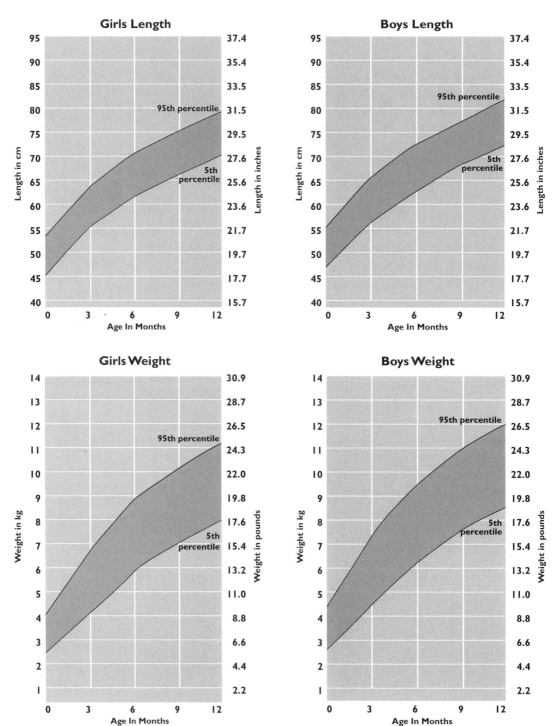

# *Emotional development*

A newborn is a funny little creature, all squints and twitches, cries and hunger. It's sometimes hard to realize—at the outset, at least—that every baby is also born with emotional needs as compelling as her physical ones, and a temperament that is uniquely her own.

## Your baby's feelings

Your newborn's principle emotional need is to be assured—and reassured—that her world is a secure place where her needs will be met.

**How your newborn develops secure relationships** Some babies seem to meld themselves into their parents' arms and lives with little awkwardness or struggle. Others seem almost impossible to please, crying frequently, and having long periods of wakefulness. It's part of the individual temperament babies bring with them. Learning to respond to your child's particular emotional makeup is part of the experience of getting to know your baby.

Whatever your baby's particular temperament, it's most important for him to have his needs promptly met. Being fed when hungry, cleaned and changed when wet or soiled, and cuddled and loved frequently when awake are the experiences that allow him to learn that the world is safe, and that he can depend on others—specifically, on you. The people in your baby's family are the faces he sees throughout the day, smiling and tending to his needs. These are the faces he learns to trust.

**What you can do** Your responsiveness to your baby's needs ensures that she develops an inner sense of security. In the long run, feeling completely cared for will make your baby calmer and easier to handle. This doesn't mean, however, that you must drop everything the instant your baby cries; a few minutes of fussing doesn't hurt as long as you appear in a relatively short time, prepared to make your baby comfortable again. Hold her closely, and when you handle her, do so in a protective fashion. This will prevent her instinctive fear of falling from interfering with her sense of security.

*Also see*
**pages 442–45**
*for information*
*about helping*
*siblings adjust.*

# Adjusting to your new family member

Whether this is your first baby or your fourth, the presence of a new child changes the dynamics of your family's life. Every new baby needs a place of his own—both physical and emotional—and everyone else involved must move a little to open up that space. If this is your first child, you are in the brand new role of parent. No doubt, there are moments when you feel overwhelmed with the responsibility that comes hand in hand with parenthood. You may wonder if you'll miss being the free spirit you were before. And there will probably be times when you miss those carefree days. You may even forget, for a moment here and there, that you have this new 24-hour-a-day job. A flash or two of resentment about the burden of caring for a helpless infant is hardly surprising, given the magnitude of the demands. Offsetting the awesome new responsibility you have, though, is the immense joy this new person brings you.

If married, you and your spouse are also undergoing enormous changes in your relationship. Now, you're not just friends, lovers, and roommates, but you're partners in parenting. Over time, you'll work out the "who-does-what" routine, and find that you may each have a different approach to child rearing and garner a different reaction from your child. It's important to remember from the start that, while you need to work out something of a united front on major issues on subjects such as discipline, you needn't be identical in the ways you relate to your baby. In fact, the different styles you bring to play and other interactions serve your baby well. If you're a single parent, you may feel overwhelmed by the demands. Don't feel that you must do everything for your baby yourself to assure yourself and others that you're up to the job. Invite others in to share in the work and the joy.

Now that you are a parent, the relationship with your own parents will necessarily undergo a change. For the first time, perhaps, you will have insight into what they went through as younger people bringing you into the world.

## This may sound crazy, but...

*"Everyone said that I would fall in love with my baby instantly, but it hasn't happened. What's wrong with me?"*

Nothing at all. Your reaction is completely normal and shared by many other new parents. In fact, in one study, an amazing 40 percent of new parents reported that immediately after delivery they felt mostly indifference! This isn't surprising when you consider how exhausting giving birth is. Furthermore, although you may have carried this child for nine months, meeting face to face is, in essence, meeting a stranger. Love develops over time and through shared experiences. One day, whether in a week, a month, or even longer, you'll look at your baby and realize, that, yes, it's love that you're feeling.

The first few months with your new baby is a wonderful opportunity to rebond with your parents in ways that are fresh and more equal. You can gain from their experience and wisdom about children, and you can empathize and share feelings with them as never before. You will probably also find that you begin to view your parents as people in their own right, not just as Mom and Dad.

**The truth about bonding** Bonding between mothers and their newborns has been one of the most discussed—and most misunderstood—aspects of new parenthood. Research showed that mothers who held their infants in the first few hours following birth were more responsive and affectionate toward their children in the early days of their children's lives. Some researchers wrongly concluded that a lack of skin-to-skin contact between mothers and their newborns in the first hours after birth resulted in a weakened maternal-infant bonding. Additional studies have shown, however, that bonding is a longer-term process through which you build an *enduring* emotional investment in your child, regardless of how soon you first hold him. Rather than being an instantaneous event, bonding evolves as parents care for their children over many hours, days, weeks, and months. While you can't force it, there are ways to facilitate bonding. They are:

- **Make feedings a time for intimacy.** Whether at your breast or from a bottle, feeding time with your new baby is an opportunity to cuddle, comfort, and communicate. When possible, invite the new father to sit with you in a close family circle.
- **Carry the baby in a sling or front carrier.** This arrangement allows you to stay physically close to your baby for many hours and it will help you learn to read his signals more quickly.
- **Talk to your baby.** It doesn't matter that he doesn't understand the words, your baby responds to the loving tone and familiar cadence of your voice.
- **Try reading to your baby.** It doesn't matter if he understands the material; it's simply a wonderful routine and an opportunity to share time together.

**"IT WORKED FOR ME"**

### Finding One-on-One Time with Your Baby

I had to go back to work just a few weeks after my baby's birth. Because my husband works at home, he became the chief child-care parent. I felt I wasn't getting any special time to know my baby so my husband and I came up with a plan. Each night when I come home, I spend an hour or so with the baby—just the two of us. I feel much better now that my son and I have this private time.

- **Don't be surprised by ups and downs.** It's only natural that some days you'll feel closer to your baby than others. Don't assume you've lost any intimacy on those days when you feel less connected.

**Your pet and your new baby**  Family pets often feel as displaced as first-born siblings when the new baby comes home. You can make it an easier transition, and a successful one, by taking a few precautions:

- **Interact with your pet immediately.** When you bring your baby home, spend a few minutes with your pet as soon as you enter your home. Introduce your baby after you've had a chance to interact with your pet. Give your dog commands to follow to keep it from showing too much excitement, such as "sit," and "stay." Also keep your dog on a leash during introductions. Cats, however, should be allowed to wander around the baby, to indulge their natural curiosity, but with strict supervision.
- **Include your pet in family activities.**
- **Reinforce the pet's good behavior with verbal praise.**
- **Spend ten or fifteen minutes a day exclusively with your pet.** Should that be out of the question for the time being, ask an animal-loving friend to stop by regularly to be your pet's pal.
- **Don't make assumptions about your pet's misbehavior.** Don't assume any aberrant behavior on the part of your pet is caused by feelings of resentment or rivalry. Urinating in the house, becoming droopy, and other changes could be symptoms of a serious illness. Check anything unusual with the vet.
- **Pay attention to warning signs.** If your pet growls, hisses, shows its teeth, or if its hair stands up when it is around the baby, you may have to find it a new home. Call your vet without delay to discuss aggressive behavior.
- **Remain vigilant.** Even if your pet seems delighted with or uninterested in your new baby, do not leave your baby and pet together in a room without you or another responsible adult present until your baby is old enough to call out for help, if necessary.

## Handling postpartum blues

About 80 percent of new mothers become weepy, anxious, and moody after giving birth. For some, these moods last just a few hours or days. For others, feeling low may persist for weeks or even months. Commonly known as "postpartum blues," these feelings can rob you of the joy of new motherhood. If you are suffering from feelings of helplessness or depression following your baby's birth, first recognize that these feelings are not your fault.

The hormones instrumental for developing your baby in utero drop dramatically shortly after birth, leaving you emotionally spent. Exhaustion—from delivery and from caring for a newborn—exacerbates the problem. You may experience the blues as nothing more than a blip on your emotional screen, a moment here and there of melancholy. Or, for you, the experience may be more intense, causing long crying jags and interfering with your ability to eat and sleep. For most women, these hormone-induced blues depart within a few weeks as your body returns to normal.

For some women, the blues may not be the result of fluctuating hormones, but may be caused by the enormous changes and responsibilities that accompany parenthood. Here are ways to help you combat the blues:

- **Face the day.** Shower and get dressed each morning. Wear whatever makes you feel and look your best.
- **Find other new mothers.** If you do not have any friends sharing your new-mother experience in your immediate circle, seek out some new friends. Check with the local Y or community center for new mother support groups. When you're at the mall or in the grocery store, strike up a conversation on the spot with any other new moms you see. Don't be shy. The chances are that she's in as much need for companionship as you are.
- **Listen to the voices of experience.** Not only new mothers, but experienced parents, can give advice and allay your fears. They may be more likely to have the energy to spare for helping you with some practical matters, such as giving you a break when you need one.
- **Stay connected.** Even though your childless friends, coworkers, and others less connected to your new-mom experience may have a limited attention span for baby discussions, it's important to remain in touch with them. Eventually you'll be invigorated by conversations that center on things other than babies for a change!

"IT WORKED FOR ME"

## Easing Postpartum Blues

When I was bogged down by the baby blues, I wanted to prevent them from getting worse. So when my friends called and asked what they could do, I told them! I needed help putting my house in order and getting some clean clothes in the drawers. My friends really pitched in for me, and having clean, tidy surroundings lifted my spirits right away. My friends also nudged me to get out of the house every day, even to run to the store. The fresh air and change of scenery were wonderful for me at that point, and, with their encouragement, I came back to the house feeling refreshed and happier.

**TIME FOR YOU**

## *Sharing the Caring with Your Spouse*

Since women give birth and many breast-feed their new babies, it's easy to understand why fathers sometimes feel left out. But there are many tasks and pleasures of baby care that Dad can enjoy. Dad's involvement brings him closer to his child and offers you the opportunity to have regular breaks.

To solidify his involvement, Dad can:

**Take on most of the responsibility for specific tasks.** There are a number of tasks Dad can make his own—diapering, burping, or putting the baby to bed among them—and doing so will assure him of his important role in the baby-care routine. Having specific responsibilities also helps get past the feeling that it's up to Mom to orchestrate all of the baby's care.

**Take the baby for regular outings.** The adventure of taking the baby out alone will strengthen Dad's sense of being this baby's parent, and it is shared fun that even an infant soon begins to enjoy. Public adventures also give Dad some positive reinforcement from the outside world as friends and strangers stop to greet the twosome.

**Spend time alone in the home.** It is equally helpful for Dad and the baby to spend time alone at home. Knowing he can handle the situation without you there as a safety net is terrific for his confidence.

**Become involved with the other important members of the baby-care team.** Dad can take turns taking your baby for his regularly scheduled visits to the pediatrician. He can also share responsibility in arranging for childcare, as well as regularly discussing issues with sitters and others who share the care.

**Spend time reading to the baby.** The baby will especially enjoy Dad's voice.

• **Keep fit.** A strong, healthy body will help you feel strong and in control. Watch your diet, get rest when you can, and exercise every day, even if only for a few minutes.

• **Take care of your marriage.** Set aside time for you and your spouse to focus on just the two of you. Being close to each other can give you both strength.

• **Get professional help.** In rare cases, postpartum blues can develop into full-blown depression. If feelings of anxiety and hopelessness overwhelm you, it's imperative that you seek help without delay. Medication and therapeutic treatment can restore your sense of equilibrium. Left untreated, depression puts you and your baby at serious risk. Discuss your feelings with your spouse. Contact your physician. Do not let anyone dismiss your feelings by telling you "it's all in your head." Seek out a sympathetic professional who can prescribe necessary medications and/or refer you to a support group or other therapeutic environments. You can find help by calling your local mental health agency, hospital, or university for a referral.

# Comforting your fussy baby

A baby's wail is upsetting to everyone. But it can become truly frustrating for you when you are unable to soothe your fussy infant. Gentle talk and light stroking tend to soothe most babies, but sometimes they need more.

*See **page 61** for more information about colic.*

   Here are several time-honored strategies for comforting your baby. If one doesn't work, try another, and remember—what may not calm your infant one day may be just the right approach the next.

- **Motion.** Rhythmic motion has a calming effect on most babies, perhaps because it mimics the movements that were part of their prenatal experience. If rocking, swaying, or walking with your baby in your arms doesn't do the trick, take her for a car or stroller ride. After about six weeks of age, your baby can go in an infant swing, something most babies adore.

- **Sucking.** Healthy babies are born with a strong sucking reflex, and many babies need to suck for more purposes than eating. Placing your finger in your newborn's mouth will frequently produce instant calm. Put your pinkie (washed and with the nail trimmed) in her mouth so that her tongue can curl around it. This technique soothes and encourages proper sucking from the breast. Many infants are soothed by pacifiers, though you should hold off on using them until breast-feeding

## When Your Newborn Cries

### Do...

report a sudden change in your baby's crying—frequency or type of crying—to his pediatrician.

take a time-out when you feel overwhelmed by your baby's crying. As long as nothing is wrong, some crying will not hurt a baby. Don't let your baby cry for more than five minutes, however.

be sure your infant is comfortably swaddled.

console him with gentle movement. Rhythmic motion such as rocking, swaying with the baby in your arms, walking, or taking him for a drive calms most crying.

give him something to suck, such as your clean finger or a pacifier.

### Don't...

respond to every cry with offers of food. Crying often has nothing to do with hunger.

regularly let your baby "cry it out." Studies show that the more attention parents pay to their baby's crying in the first three months of life, the less the baby cries by the end of the first year. If, however, you're feeling overwhelmed, it's better to ignore the cries for a moment while you handle your own feelings. If possible, have someone else attend to the baby, so you can get away for a break.

assume you are doing something wrong if your baby cries excessively. Some babies are born crankier than others and cry more than the average two hours a day that most newborns do.

## Choosing and Using Pacifiers

# Do...

choose a pacifier that most nearly resembles your breast nipple or the bottle nipple your baby is using. It should be made of one piece of nontoxic, flexible material, with a handle that's easy for your baby to grasp once she is old enough.

get a pacifier with a nondetachable shield or mouth guard that prevents the pacifier from fitting inside a child's mouth. It should also have ventilation holes so that any saliva that collects around it does not chap your baby's lips or cheeks.

consider taking your baby off the pacifier at 3 or 4 months of age, when his sucking needs begin to decrease and breaking the habit will be relatively easy. Break the habit gradually, and give him extra cuddling until he is used to the change.

consider choosing a pacifier made of silicon rather than latex. Latex rubber is more likely to trigger an allergic reaction in sensitive babies.

# Don't...

introduce a pacifier to a nursing baby in the first two weeks, before she has become adept at sucking from the breast. It may confuse her and delay nursing success. If the hospital has given your baby a pacifier, don't worry. Simply offer your breast to satisfy your baby's sucking needs at home, and do so until nursing is well established.

encourage your baby to sleep with a pacifier so that he doesn't wake each time it falls out of his mouth.

automatically put the pacifier in your baby's mouth without thinking through what other need he may be trying to express first.

offer your baby a pacifier that is worn or has holes or tears in the nipple. Tug on it to test it and replace it when it shows any sign of wear.

**NEVER** attach a pacifier to a string or ribbon around your baby's neck or attach one with a ribbon or string to his clothing, the stroller, or his crib; a string or ribbon could be a strangulation hazard.

is well established if you're breast-feeding. Don't let your bottle-feeding baby suck on an empty bottle since this will cause him to suck air into his tummy, which will cause gas.

• **Holding.** Close body contact is a real source of comfort for infants. Hold your baby snugly against your shoulder, or, if you suspect gas, place your newborn on her tummy, straddling your arm. Support her neck and chin with the palm of your hand. This is called the football hold, and it's one many babies and parents find especially comfortable while swaying and rocking together.

### Swaddling

*"Is swaddling my newborn a good idea?"*

Definitely. A newborn is making the transition from the womb to the world, and for the first three or four weeks after birth, being snugly wrapped in a receiving blanket soothes her. The swaddling also simulates the feeling of being cradled in her parent's arms, and helps calm her startle reflex. This "Moro reflex" —when the baby flings her arms out suddenly in response to a loud noise or jarring motion— can awaken and, thus, upset her. Being swaddled, with her arms tucked into the blanket, moderates the intensity of the reflex and can result in undisturbed sleep.

Be careful not to wrap your baby too tightly or allow her to become overheated. Also, after swaddling her, remember to place her on her back or side for sleep as a precaution against SIDS. By three or four weeks of age, or earlier for some infants, your baby will prefer stretching out to being swaddled.

# *Cognitive development*

In these first two months, your baby is developing from a newborn with almost no attention span, who responds to virtually every sound, to an infant who is alert most of his waking hours, and who associates activities to the voices he hears. He may learn, for instance, that the sounds of your approaching mean great things—perhaps feedings—are about to occur. At one month, your baby is aware of objects only fleetingly, for not more than a few seconds. By the second month, however, merely anticipating an object, notably the breast or bottle, excites him. These are quiet changes in your baby's behavior, but they demonstrate large leaps in his cognitive development.

*How to swaddle a newborn:*
- *Place the baby in the center of a receiving blanket with his arms folded in.*
- *Take one upper corner and pull it across the baby's body, tucking it under his back on the opposite side*
- *Fold the bottom of the blanket up over the baby's body then wrap the last corner around him, tucking it under his back.*

# How your baby learns

Your baby learns through his senses. His eyes are beginning to focus better, especially peripherally. This increases his ability to learn from seeing, and he starts to gaze more carefully. He particularly likes to examine other people's faces and his own hands. At around 2 months of age, your baby will start to explore objects such as his hands or his rattle by mouthing them. His mouth has many nerve endings, which makes it an ideal tool for learning. Sucking on things also soothes him. Your baby's listening ability is constantly improving; gradually he is learning to detect the differences in human voices and other sounds, and to respond accordingly, for instance, kicking his heels in delight when he hears you enter the room. Sometime during the second month, he will not only recognize his parents' voices in a crowded room, but he will also know the direction from which their voices are coming.

**What you can do**   Spend lots of time with your baby in activities that aren't directly devoted to his basic care. Beyond feeding and diapering him, talk to him. Give him the opportunity to observe his world. Take him on a tour of the house and the outdoors. Let him observe your regular routines. Because human faces are becoming ever more interesting to him, allow him time to gaze into your face as often as possible, and not just at feeding or diapering time. Seek out quiet moments throughout the day for the two of you to have close interaction, perhaps counting his toes or stroking his head. He is learning from this time, and enjoying your comforting presence. When he is awake and alert, let him join the activities of the rest of the family, propped in his infant seat or on your lap, where he can get a good view. And don't forget to sing to him—it's fun for you both, and represents another learning experience for your baby.

# Providing the right stimulation

Your baby's temperament will largely determine the degree of stimulation he wants. Your baby may show a preference for being in the middle of things whenever he's awake. Or he may want only small doses of excitement at certain times of the day. Don't assume, however, that an easy-going, laid-back baby doesn't need your attention or that a highly excitable baby requires constant attention.

Every baby needs to interact with his environment and especially with you. Your newborn's escalating alertness allows more time for active play as the weeks go on. Experiment to see what he likes today. In a week or so, try a few different things to see what new things interest him. Show him rattles and demonstrate how they can make noises. Play with textured objects such as his stuffed animals, guiding his hand to touch them. Gently tickle and kiss his tummy and feet. Hold a rattle or small toy in front of him and allow him to track it with his eyes. Pace your games according to his reactions. Keep going as long as you and he remain interested. Stop when he seems to have had enough.

It's important for you to respect your baby's feelings of irritability or fatigue by not trying to distract him with play when he needs to relax. When he is hungry, tired, or uncomfortable, meet those needs first before attempting to engage him in any other activity.

**Learning to read your newborn's signals** One of the few straightforward ways infants have of letting you know how they feel is crying. However, they also have a range of more subtle signals to display their interest in people and their need for quiet or for stimulation. By paying attention to his gestures, you can bridge the communication gap with your baby long before he can speak.

Your baby shows pleasure in your company by meeting your gaze, smiling, and following you with his eyes as you come and go. He will reach toward you. He becomes more alert when you speak to him, and may return your words with throaty sounds of his own. Likewise, he'll carefully watch and make noises in response to other things that interest him, such as toys or his own reflection in a mirror.

New babies can let you know that they've had enough attention and need to shut down for a moment by yawning, passing gas, or sneezing. When he needs some quiet time, your baby may cry and/or turn his face away from you. He may also turn away when he's decided that he's had enough to eat, even though you may feel he hasn't eaten enough. It's important not to take these gestures as any kind of rejection, but to recognize them as signs that your baby is doing his best to communicate.

# Your Premature Baby

Each year, some 300,000 low-birth-weight babies are born in the United States. This category, which describes any baby under 5.8 pounds, includes many babies born weighing much less, some as little as 2 pounds. Not too many years ago, babies who were just a few weeks premature could be at grave risk. Today, the vast majority of preemies not only survive, but go on to thrive.

## Care during the neonatal period

Depending on your baby's gestational age at birth and his condition, he will probably spend at least some time in the neonatal intensive care unit. Here, specially trained nurses supervise the care of babies 24 hours a day. For a time, you may be disturbed by the unit with its equipment, monitors, and buzzers—to say nothing of your newborn's translucent skin, and tiny, floppy body—but it is here that your baby's chance for survival is vastly improved, perhaps even made possible.

Your preemie's nourishment, and how it is delivered, is determined by his size and gestational age. The smallest babies are tube-fed a special blend of nutrients, based on what they would have been receiving through the umbilical cord at this point had their gestation proceeded. Larger preemies benefit from breast milk; this is because their mother's milk exactly matches the baby's needs at his gestational age.

Even if your baby starts on a tube-fed fluid, you would be wise to get your milk production into full swing in preparation for later feeding. You will have to express milk often, first as a supply for tube-feeding to your baby when he is ready; later, even when he is able to nurse directly, he will need nourishment every few hours because of his small stomach. Expressed milk will make it possible for him to have constant access.

When you do put your baby to your breast, expect him to take a great deal of time learning how to nurse. Preemies, without the size and strong sucking reflex full-termers have, need more time to become proficient.

**Working with your child's hospital caregivers**  After the distress of delivering your baby early, you may now have to deal with becoming an onlooker in your newborn's care. It is the medical team expertise that is responsible for your baby's well-being, and there isn't too much you can do in practical terms during the first critical days or weeks. You may feel helpless as you watch the nurses and doctors administer care to your baby, but there *are* ways for you to become, a member of the team. Get to know the health professionals by name, and make it clear to them that you are willing to do whatever you can to contribute to your child's care.

Once the crisis in your baby's health has passed, you will be able to spend a good deal of time in the intensive-care nursery. The staff will show you how to scrub and how you can handle your baby with your arms placed through his isolette or by holding him. Gentle massaging can be extremely beneficial for some preemies, and it is a wonderful way for you to bond with your child as well. Don't overlook the importance of quiet conversation with your baby. Your voice will be soothing to him, and talking with him will help you feel more connected.

The hours you are not in the hospital, waiting for your baby to come home, need not be taken up entirely with anxiety. Make a point of preparing for your baby's arrival home. Because of his prematurity, you probably didn't have a chance to make the baby preparations you would have as your due date came near. Go all out now getting the diapers, cotton balls, clothes, and equipment you need for your baby so that all will be ready when the big homecoming finally happens.

## Bringing your baby home
On the homecoming day, you may also have to bring home a plethora of needed equipment and medications in addition to your baby. The hospital staff will train you in how to use or administer all

of these life-saving devices and medications. Expect the early weeks or months to be stressful, but the knowledge that this is your baby's road to health and strength will make it easier.

You should be aware of the burnout problem for many parents of preemies. If you are called on to supervise monitors and medications, there is constant pressure on you. Having some form of backup for the care of your baby can work wonders for your health and sanity during this period. Ask close family members and others who can assist you to learn CPR as well as the routines your baby needs. Alert the local ambulance company that you have a preemie in your home; supply the company with a map with the route to your home highlighted for the EMS crew, just to be on the safe side, and keep emergency numbers posted by all phones. Keep a list and schedule of medications on your refrigerator door or other central location for easy access. Have everyone involved in your child's care who administers medication mark this master list accordingly. This way you have instant, up-to-date information about your baby's regimen. If your baby needs to have regular blood checks, consider learning how to do the needle sticks yourself. That will free you to drop the blood off at the hospital or lab for testing, rather than having to take the baby in on a regular basis. Of course, if the procedure would make you anxious, it's best to continue to bring your child to the doctor.

## Your baby's development

Once your baby's survival is assured, the next question you may have is likely to be the "catch-up" issue. Will your baby ever be as developed, mentally and physically, as other children the same age? The answer to this lies in looking at the calendar in a new way. You simply have to base your expectation of milestones on the due date of your baby, not on the date the baby prematurely arrived. Just as babies develop at a certain pace and in a predictable way in utero, they continue that pace and pattern even if they happen to be born early. This means your baby will match development with other infants who were born about the time he should have made his entrance into the world. For example, if he was two months early, take that into account when you anticipate his developmental progress, expecting him to reach the average development of a 4-month-old when he's 6 months old. This is called the "adjusted age." You may even prefer to use his adjusted age when you answer people's query about how old your baby is so that their expectations of him coincide with his development.

You can expect to think in terms of adjusted age until your baby is about 2½ years old, at which time development evens out. The long-term prognosis for preemies today is excellent. The vast majority have no long-term problems stemming from their prematurity; the problems that do evidence themselves in some children are generally minor and do not hinder them.

For information on health conditions that may affect preemies, refer to the following:

Eye Conditions, see **pages 66** and **591**; especially retinopathy of prematurity, see **page 758**
Hearing problems—see **page 68**
Cerebral palsy—see **page 746**
Infant jaundice—see **page 69**
Apnea—see **page 561**
Respiratory conditions— see **page 642**

## Resources for Parents of Premature Infants

**The Preemie Store and More!/TLC Clothing** offers a catalog of preemie clothing and accessories.
(800) O-SO-TINY
(714) 434-3740
www.preemie.com

**The International Childbirth Education Association Bookcenter** carries a wide range of literature on all topics related to prematurity.
(800) 624-4934
(952) 854-8660
www.icea.org/book.htm

**The American Academy of Pediatrics** offers referrals to preemie specialists in your area.
(847) 434-4000
www.aap.org

# 2 and 3 Months

With the newness of the first weeks behind you, you are now able to enjoy your baby more than ever. You and your infant have become comfortable together, and you are starting to enjoy a certain amount of predictability in your day. You're better able to discern your baby's needs—and your own. Your schedule is perhaps less hectic, with fewer guests dropping by to see the newest family member. Now is the time that your baby is smiling broadly at you, giving you an emotional reward that you'll remember.

For many new parents, this is the time when the reality of baby-care sets in. You may find a growing calmness as you settle into your routine of nurturing your child. Or you may find that suddenly, with the diminished attention of brand-new parenthood, you're feeling more alone than ever. It's important to remember that throughout your child's life—particularly during the first year—you'll feel ups and downs about your role as parent. Continuing to be responsive to your infant will serve you both, as will your continuing nurturing of yourself.

# Physical development

No longer an awkward newborn, your baby is growing in size and in strength. The reflexes that determined much of her earliest physical responses are being replaced by smoother, more purposeful motions.

## Physical changes

Slow and steady is the expression that best describes a baby's growth in these early months. Babies typically gain about 1½ to 2 pounds and grow from 1 to 1½ inches between 2 and 3 months of age. Your baby's head continues to appear outsized compared to the rest of her body; this situation will change over the first year as her body's rate of growth catches up with her head. Don't worry if your baby is round and chubby now. Soon she will start to move her limbs, and then eventually her entire body, and she will thin out as her motor development progresses. The fontanels on your baby's head will continue to be open during these months; look for the back one to close by the end of her third or during her fourth month. The bones of the front fontanel at the top of your baby's head will align at about 18 months; the bones won't fuse for years.

**What your baby can do**  An important development is now taking place. Your baby is getting strong enough to lift her head, and to support it without your help.  When on her tummy, she can lift herself on her arms. She no longer holds her hands tightly in little fists, but keeps them relaxed, grasping only when an object is placed in her hand. She also enjoys bringing her hands to her mouth to explore them further. Indeed, your baby's hands are rapidly becoming objects of great interest to her as she spends time staring at them, aided by her more fully developing vision. She enjoys looking at other objects as well, including her crib mobile, and will start swiping at this and other items placed within her reach. During this period, your baby may develop the ability to roll herself from her side to her back.

### Changes in Appearance

Your baby's skin now comes much closer to matching the picture-perfect baby skin you probably expected. The pimples and rashes that so many infants are born with should have faded, to be replaced by a beautiful, even-colored complexion. If she was born with hair, she may have lost much of it by now—or will very shortly.

**What you can do**  Because your baby is rapidly becoming more in control of her body movements, be sure she has plenty of opportunities to practice being in motion. Place her on a blanket on the floor, alternating between her back and her stomach. In this way, she will have different challenges and she'll get practice that will help her develop her neck muscles. Although your baby's stronger neck gives her more control and a better view of the world around her, her ability to fully support her head may not be complete for some time. So you should continue to protect her by watching carefully to see when you should offer her support, especially when you are picking her up or laying her down.

Your baby will probably enjoy a play gym now and for the next few months. These toys usually contain dangling objects in bright colors that simply move or make sounds when kicked or swiped at. Some models attach to the sides of the crib and hang above the mattress within reach of your baby's arms or legs. Others are designed as freestanding units to be enjoyed by your baby when she's on her back on the floor. When your baby's random kicks or hand motions connect to one of the gym attachments and cause it to move, she's encouraged to try again. This more purposeful kicking or batting gives her both an experience of having an impact on her environment and a demonstration of cause and effect.

### Watch for Rolling!

Your infant's new ability to roll over, though not very consistent yet, is your signal to exercise extreme caution when she is on higher surfaces, such as the bed or changing table. Always use the restraining strap to secure her on the changing table, or your firmly placed hand when she's on a bed, even if it seems unlikely that your baby could roll off.

### Ready for solid food?

*"My 3-month old seems to be hungry even after a long feeding session. Should I introduce solids to her diet?"*

Most 3-month-olds are not ready for solids, though a few may be. If by 3 months of age your bottle-fed baby is taking more than 40 ounces a day, and still seems hungry, or if your breast-fed baby has doubled her birth weight—or, conversely, has started to lose weight—it may be time to start her on solids, though the decision should be made after consulting with her pediatrician. The 3-month-old who seems satisfied after breast or bottle feeding may wait until closer to 6 months before his first solid meal.

*For more on introducing solid foods, see **page 503**.*

**Baby's belly button**

*"Why does my baby have an 'outie'?"*

Many infants have so-called outies when the navel protrudes above instead of sinking into the abdomen. The reason is that babies don't have the same fat covering on their abdomen that toddlers develop and retain for the rest of their lives. This fat layer surrounds the navel, giving it the more familiar holelike look. So, as your baby grows, her navel will seem to protrude less.

**Fused fontanels**

*"My 3-month-old daughter's 'soft spot' has closed. An X ray showed that her brain looks normal, and her doctor tells us not to worry. What caused this to happen, and what should I do next?*

Doctors check a baby's head circumference at each visit to determine that the brain is growing properly. If there's any slowdown of growth or if the fontanel appears to be prematurely closed, the doctor may order X rays to rule out any problems.

The triangle-shaped gap at the top of the head appears to close for most babies at around 18 months, when the bony plates of the skull come close together without actually fusing. (Fusion of these plates doesn't actually occur until young adulthood.) Occasionally, however, the plates come together as early as 3 months of age. In most cases, this early "closing" is not cause for alarm. As long as X rays indicate that all is well, you can relax.

There are two conditions that the doctor ruled out after reviewing your child's X rays: Microcephaly and craniosynostosis. Microcephaly, a condition marked by an abnormally small head, can result when a congenital infection or structural abnormality stops brain growth. It is usually associated with developmental delays and neurological problems. Sometimes, however, microcephaly is inherited as a normal trait and the child develops normally.

Craniosynostosis is a true permanent fusion of the skull plates. Surgery is needed to separate the plates again so that the brain can grown normally. The operation is usually successful, requiring only a three- to five-day hospital stay and bandages for about one week.

## TIMELINE | *Infant Hearing and Speech*

**Newborn:** In the first six weeks of life, your infant is startled and awakened by loud, sudden noises, such as a door slamming. She is able to recognize her mother's voice and particularly female tones. She is also becoming familiar with her Dad's voice

**By 3 months:** Your baby recognizes your voice; he looks toward you when you speak and may quiet down if he has been crying when you speak to him.

**Between 3 and 6 months:** Your baby will turn his head when he hears a new, unfamiliar sound. He will also respond to changes in your voice. He may be upset by an angry tone and soothed by a lilting one.

**Between 6 to 10 months:** Your baby responds to his name, can locate sounds on either side of him, and can understand some of what he hears. He enjoys sound-making objects such as rattles. He imitates sounds and starts to babble. He responds to a firm "no" by looking at you.

**By 1 year:** Your child begins to associate words with the objects they represent. He responds to simple requests, such as "Come here," with the help of your gestures and smiles along with your words. He mimics adult speech patterns and uses at least two words in addition to "mama" and "dada."

**Reversing a reversed schedule**

*"My 3-month-old son sleeps all day and is awake all night. How can I help him turn his schedule around?"*

Confusing night and day is common among babies at this age. You can help your baby—and yourself—by keeping him active during the day, and allowing less daytime sleep. Delay his bed hour until late in the evening. Give him a good feeding, and put him to bed. When he wakes during the night, take care of his needs as quickly as you can, without any socialization or even turning on the lights. Rouse him in the morning and keep the room he's in during the day brightly lit. At night, turn off the lights in his room. Eventually, he will adopt the traditional sleep pattern.

## Early speech development

Crooning a lullaby is the time-honored way to soothe a baby. Psychologists have found that music benefits babies in many ways from the earliest months of life, when connections in the brain are rapidly forming. By exposing your baby to music, you can enhance his ability to process information and stimulate language development by encouraging him to hone his listening skills and repeat the sounds he hears.

Babies have an uncanny ability to identify and imitate pitches. Amazingly, studies have found that if you sing a note to a 3-month-old, he's likely to sing the same tone back in almost perfect pitch. The awareness of different pitches helps an infant learn to recognize the beginnings and ends of sentences, because adults—particularly when they speak to babies—tend to speak in a slightly lower pitch at the end of a sentence, and a higher pitch at the beginning of a sentence or when they ask a question.

**Loud sounds and hearing loss**

*"My baby's sitter listens to music at a high volume. Could this cause hearing loss in my baby?"*

Loud music certainly could harm your baby's ears. Sound over the range of about 85 decibels or so—the noise level of city rush-hour traffic—can cause hearing damage, and loud music easily exceeds this noise level. Insist that your baby sitter give up loud music in your home.

Babies with profound hearing loss will babble as much as other babies, but they will not develop speech. Nor, of course, will they respond to sounds in their environment. Mild hearing loss is more difficult to detect; however, if a baby seems surprised to see something that sound should have alerted him to or his speech patterns do not seem to be progressing normally, a consultation with the baby's health professional is called for. This person will make a preliminary diagnosis and, if it's necessary, refer him to a specialist.

*For more on hearing, see* **pages 610–13**.

## Establishing a rhythm with your baby

As your baby settles into his surroundings, he will become somewhat more consistent, not only in his sleep/wake and feeding/eliminating cycles, but also about his likes and dislikes. It's still too soon to expect that your baby will follow the regular family schedule, but he is moving in that direction. The better you can anticipate how he will likely respond to his routines and to changes in his routine, the more prepared you can be to make the best use of his schedule—and to carve out your own schedule.

It would be a mistake to overstate a baby's consistency, however, since he will often fluctuate or change just as you think you know what to expect. The key is to remain flexible when developing your daily schedule with your baby and not to ignore your own scheduling needs completely. Don't be overly concerned, for instance, if your plans require that you be out

### *The Right Timing*

Your baby is probably awake for about 8 out of 24 hours now, creating time for more interactions between himself and others. Babies tend to be most wakeful in late afternoon, making this a good time for him to socialize with you and others. Your baby may be more of a lark, however, making mid-morning his preferred time for play. Planning activities around his present sleep/alertness cycles will serve you both. Notice, too, his response to routines so that you can make the most of his body rhythms. If the bath is calming for your baby, evening is the obvious best choice. If, on the other hand, the bath tends to excite your child, a morning or mid-day bath time may be better. He'll let you know if he needs to eat just after waking, or if he prefers a later mealtime, allowing you to plan accordingly.

during your baby's nap time. Take him along on your errands or arrange for other care. While your baby does benefit from consistency and needs to be fed whenever he's hungry, a too-rigid schedule is unnecessary. As long as you meet his basic needs of hunger, comfort, and love, he'll be fine.

The 2- to 3-month period can be satisfying for parents. Discovering what works best and when clearly demonstrates that you are getting to know your child. Learning to "go with the flow" lets you establish routines that meet your needs as well.

# Emotional development

By the time your baby is 2 months old, his energies turn outward. Although he had a primitive sense of self at birth—he could recognize his own cries—he is now beginning quite literally to explore who he is, as he ponders his hands and toes in seemingly endless fascination. He is becoming quite social and enjoys his interactions with others, particularly you. Not only does he respond to those around him with radiant smiles, he now gurgles and coos as well. You are the center of his universe, however, and it is for you he saves his broadest smiles, and his most cheerful coos.

## Your baby's feelings

Feelings are your baby's first language. Long before he can express himself with words, he communicates through his emotions—crying when he's upset or when he needs your attention, smiling when he's content, wriggling excitedly when he is happy. Although you may need to give thought to what feeling your baby is expressing at any given moment, for the most part, his feelings are simple and straightforward—pleasure and contentment, discomfort and unhappiness, alertness or fatigue.

**How your baby develops secure relationships** Virtually everything your baby is learning about the outside world, she learns from those who provide her daily care. A baby this age will smile at a full-face picture of any cheerful face, but she will respond with an even broader smile to the familiar face of a family member or caregiver. Meeting her emotional needs is as important as taking care of her physical ones. She has a singular strong preference for you as you take care of her daily needs. She also gets emotional support from others in her orbit who consistently shower her with affection and soothe her discomforts.

She will trust and feel safe in the arms of those who handle her gently and will even begin to show excitement at the slightly different handling that others provide. If her father is not the primary caregiver, she may kick her legs excitedly when he approaches, knowing that his loving care is a bit of an adventure outside the norm. But in times of distress, she may want the most familiar arms to hold her. Giving her opportunities to enjoy the comfort of a small circle of consistently loving caregivers helps her view the world as a safe and welcoming place. Responding to her needs in a reasonable period of time teaches her that she herself is important.

**What you can do** You are now starting to see the earliest steps of your baby's interactions with others. The first steps may be so subtle that you could easily miss them—perhaps her eyes peeking over the top of her crib bumper when you enter the room, or her hands quietly waving in response to your song. These subtle actions create thrilling moments because they show that your baby is reacting, not to being fed or changed, but to *you*.

In the next few months, you'll learn more and more about how to interpret your baby's interests and moods. Overriding all is your continuing responsiveness to her. When she gurgles and coos, stop and listen to her part of the conversation. When she looks at you, pause to make full eye contact. Engage her often this way, but heed her signals that say she has had enough. Sometimes, even a 2- or 3-month-old wants to be left alone. When your baby turns her head away, when she breaks eye contact, or stiffens her body, she's signaling that it's time for a break.

## TIMELINE

## Infant Social Development

**At 6 weeks:** An infant's smile is short-lived and often not directed at anyone.

**By 2 to 3 months:** Her smile lasts longer and is directed at people. She frequently returns smiles—mostly from family members—and smiles at her toys.

**By 4 months:** She also laughs, especially when tickled gently or when playing bouncing games. She may fret and cry around strangers, such as a new baby-sitter.

**At around 5 or 6 months:** A baby might raise her hand or graze an adult's arm to get attention or to hear a song again.

**At 7 months:** A baby uses specific gestures to express her wishes—such as lifting her arms when she wants to be picked up.

**By 8 months:** She will hug familiar people, and starts to enjoy interactive games such as peek-a-boo.

# The first steps toward separation

Birth is the first separation that a mother and child must endure. During early infancy, many mothers find it distressing to be away from their babies for even a minute while others are comfortable and even anxious to have a moment to themselves. For most new moms, the pendulum swings both ways as they both crave their newborns' company and need a break from it. Eventually, all moms find the need to be apart from their child; the child, too, eventually needs to separate. The process is rarely easy for anyone concerned.

If you're waiting for a sign from your child that she won't mind if you take some time off from parenting, you can stop waiting. It won't happen. Most likely, you will have to take the first step, whether because you have to return to work or because you simply need time away in order to regroup and come back emotionally calm and recharged.

Don't feel guilty about your need to instigate the separation. Without time for yourself, you're bound to break down, and that certainly won't serve your child well. Some new mothers become anxious because they assume that no one, not even the baby's dad, can give their child the right care. If that's your attitude, realize that it's important to your child as well as to yourself and your spouse that your baby learn that she has other caregivers she can trust. Many parents get into the habit of staying home with their baby because the baby cries if they leave. Even working parents who leave their babies in childcare during the week may forego leaving them for a few hours on the weekend. But the truth is, even now, your baby needs to practice separating and you deny her that learning experience if you never leave her side.

If your child is used to your more or less constant presence, make an effort to create regular opportunities for separation—even when you have no need to go out of the house alone. Infants are quick to pick up on routines and will eventually learn to accept your absences if you give them the chance.

## Easing Your Fears

If you are anxious about leaving your baby, talk to your spouse, a family member, your child's pediatrician, or a friend to help assuage your own fears. Getting your emotions out in the open can help you put them in perspective. Your child will take her cues from you about separation and the sooner you can put your own mind at ease, the better it will be for her.

*For information on separation when your child is in childcare, see **page 377**.*

# Your baby's personality

Much of your baby's personality comes into the world with him. While his environment and experiences will shape him, at core, he will always have the personality he was born with. In his second and third month, you'll see clues to that personality. Some babies are highly charged and excitable. Others are more mellow and are happy to observe the goings-on in a quieter fashion. Your baby may show a quick response to your words and actions. Or he may take a more wait-and-see approach to you and others.

It's important to be sensitive to your baby's personality, because to a great extent, working with his inborn nature will help you nurture him more successfully. The following chart shows the difference between a naturally responsive baby and a more reserved one.

## Understanding Your Baby's Inborn Personality

**In this imagined scene, you are counting your 3-month-old's toes.** You'll need to play this game over several days to gain more insight into your baby's personality—a quieter response one day might mean he's sleepy, not necessarily innately low-key. Over the next few weeks and months, you'll see more evidence of his inborn characteristics and his emerging personality.

| If... | Then you should... |
|---|---|
| he widens his eyes, waves his arms, and smiles, | maintain a consistent level of play, then slow down the pace before ending the game. *While they are easy to engage, responsive babies are also easily overstimulated.* |
| he stares placidly and remains still, | keep the game going, even trying a slightly more vigorous play. *While reserved babies are harder to engage socially, their placid demeanor is not a sign that they don't want to play.* |

## This may sound crazy, but...

*"I can't make love with our baby in the room. This is a real problem because we live in a one-bedroom apartment. Am I being overly concerned?"*

Spontaneous lovemaking is a common challenge for new parents who are regularly interrupted by their baby's cries. Because of your space constraints, you and your spouse need to become a bit more creative to assure that you're at ease.

If your baby is in a portable crib or bassinet, simply move it with your sleeping child inside, to another room, while you make love. Or move your lovemaking to another room. Enjoy making love at different times of day, when your baby is sleeping in the living room in a playpen or some other comfortable, safe place. Until you're able to get a two-bedroom home, if that's in your plans, create a room divider with secured shelving or by rearranging the furniture so that your bed and your baby's crib are not side by side. If you're not planning on moving to larger quarters for a while, consider transforming your living room into your bedroom with a sleep sofa. In any case, realize that in the not-too-distant future, your child will need some room of her own.

For now, you needn't worry about whether your baby is aware of what's going on, though by the time she's 6 months or so, she will be aware of activity, while still not understanding it.

Many new mothers are reluctant to resume sexual relations after giving birth. Your energy level and interest are focused on your baby's needs for your time and attention. You may feel overwhelmed and fear another pregnancy, even if you are careful about using birth control. You may be satisfying your need for intimacy with your love for your newborn. Talk to your ob/gyn or a trusted therapist about your feelings. Give your husband the opportunity to make you feel more comfortable. Give yourself time to adjust. Eventually, your life—including your sex life—will more closely resemble your pre-baby days.

# The daddy bond

Mothers and fathers do not parent in the same way. Their different styles serve their child well. From a very early age, children seem to understand that interacting with Dad means adventure, and is different from interacting with Mom.

Early involvement between a father and his baby forms the cornerstone of the "daddy bond." Fathers approach their babies and older children differently than do mothers. Dads stimulate different muscle groups and engage different parts of their baby's brain. A father's involvement, therefore, has developmental implications. One study showed that when fathers regularly talked, played, soothed, fed, and changed their babies during the first month of life, their children scored significantly higher on developmental tests of motor skills, pattern identification, word recognition, and problem solving at age 1. By interacting with their infants, fathers also provide an additional source of stimulation, which encourages babies to distinguish different sounds, faces, and touches at an early age. It also helps make infants more receptive to change, less fearful of new experiences, and better able—having established close ties with more than one person—to form trusting relationships with others.

# Cognitive development

Although the progress your baby is making in these early months lacks the drama of first words and steps, it will delight you nevertheless. As your baby peers intently at you, he will suddenly break into gurgles, displaying his pleasure with you and himself. He is beginning to find the world a most interesting place, even though his vision isn't yet fully focused and his ability to understand what's being said is extremely limited. When he is dry, fed, and warm, he busies himself by watching—and learning from what he sees.

## What your baby knows

One thing your baby knows clearly is you. He has recognized your voice, distinguishing it from all others, since he was just a few weeks old. Now he knows your face, your smell, and your style of cuddling. He also knows that other children are not adults, and he is starting to become particularly interested in them, an interest that will grow strongly in the months to come. You may find your baby is starting to practice his sounds, repeating the same ones again and again, often as he lies in his crib in the morning.

**How your baby learns** Just as you provide for his physical safety and his emotional stability, you are first, and most important, his teacher. He is learning by observation and listening. When you make noises to him, he'll surprise you by echoing your pitch and tone. He is in the early stages of using his mouth to explore, too. For a number of months to come, anything and everything will go into his mouth as he tries to learn more about these strange, interesting objects. His ability to predict is forming. He knows, for instance, that your appearance promises certain rewards.

**What you can do** With your help, your baby will become more aware of his body and his physical environment. Gently clap his hands together, bend his arms and legs, and tickle him when you are changing his diapers. Let him experience the various things his body can do. As you dress him, tell him what you are doing, naming his body parts as you handle them. Sing to him, inserting his name into the song whenever you can. Throughout the day together, hold

## Keeping Up Friendships with Friends Who Don't Have Children

Nurturing your friendships with your childless friends allows you to nurture the part of yourself that is not a parent. To keep your friendship thriving, while developing new friendships with other moms and dads:

**Make time for get-togethers in baby-free territory.** Meet coworkers for lunch. Make evening dates with others while leaving your child with a sitter. Take turns with your spouse to keep up friendships and hobbies that each enjoyed before the baby.

**Limit baby talk.** It can be difficult not to start every conversation with an anecdote about your baby's latest accomplishment. But joining in with others about non-baby issues will help keep you in touch with their lives, too.

**Invite friends over for more than baby play.** While your baby naps, enjoy lunch with a friend. When dinner guests visit, enjoy adult time. Consider hiring a sitter to help out so that you can devote your energy to the grown-ups.

**Make good use of the phone, e-mail, and regular mail.** Take whatever opportunities you can to keep in touch with those who matter to you and with whom you can't get together as much as you'd like.

conversations with your baby. Pause for his response—of course you won't get one yet, but you're teaching him about the art of conversation. Identify other objects that you handle in his presence by name, and talk some about what they are and do. For instance, you can describe the roundness of a ball, and the squareness of a block, and the softness of a stuffed toy. Have your baby touch the objects as you discuss them. He will soon understand concepts as well as cause and effect, and you are getting him off to a good start with a desire to communicate.

Be sure to give your baby plenty of opportunities to view the world from a variety of angles. Put him in his infant seat, have him sit in your lap facing out, let him enjoy his baby swing, all while there is activity around him for him to watch.

## Smart from the start

During the first 12 months of life, your baby's brain grows rapidly. This isn't due to an increase in the number of brain cells, but mostly because of connections that grow between different parts of her brain. The more connections she makes, the greater the growth.

Brain connections expand to form a network every time your baby has a thought—and this happens whenever any of her senses are stimulated. From the moment of birth, connections develop based on the sounds, sights, touches, feelings, smells, and tastes she experiences.

Cognitive development involves many different parts of the brain coming together to work in unison. Her senses interact with her thought processes; these, in turn, interact with her muscles. Muscles, thoughts, and senses work together continuously, strengthening each other. For example, through her sense of sight your baby sees her favorite toy. The thought process of memory gets her excited about it. Using her muscles, she reaches for it. By coordinating the use of her eyes and hands, she can grasp for and hold it. And by holding and playing with the toy, she learns. At 2 to 3 months, only part of the process is possible, of course. But by the end of the first year, a healthy baby has the cognitive and physical power to achieve the task easily.

Beyond the concrete experiences of touching and handling objects, this year your baby begins to grasp concepts, such as roundness, coldness, roughness, "animalness," and the uniqueness and similarities of various things. Within just a few months, she will know that her stuffed bear and her stuffed kangaroo or her bowl and her cup belong to a similar category of things. She will even find it funny to find things out of context, and will laugh if you playfully place a mitten on her foot.

### Talking to your baby

*"While I know it's a good idea to talk to my 2-month-old son, I feel silly. Does it really make any difference?"*

The importance of talking to your baby cannot be overstated. In fact, the conversations you're having now with him are as important as those you'll have 10 or 15 years from now. Research shows that the verbal interactions a baby has in his first year make an enormous difference in his cognitive and social development. Babies who are rarely exposed to conversation are significantly less astute as preschoolers and beyond. On the other hand, babies who enjoy lots of talk from their parents make earlier and more sustained intellectual and social development throughout their lives.

Try not to feel awkward about conversing with your infant. Read to him. Tell him what you're doing as you go about your routines. Stop to "listen" to his end of the conversation. When he shows interest in your speech, reward him with a touch and a smile. Sing to him. He'll soon sing along, even without any words. Not too long from now, he'll reward you by returning a few words of his own.

## Games babies love

Your baby loves interacting with you and others now. Any game that promotes this will please her. For starters:

• **Sing to her.** You will never have a better audience for your songs than your baby, especially if you personalize them with her name and the names of other important people in her life.

• **Dance.** Gentle rocking in your arms to the beat of your own song or other music will please her and help develop her sense of rhythm.

• **Look in the mirror.** Hold her close enough that she can clearly see herself—about 8 to 12 inches away. You can point to her reflection, say her name, name her facial features, and make faces of your own. Ask your child, "Where's my baby?" Then point to her reflection in the mirror and say, "There's my baby!" Be as silly as you like—your baby will love every moment of your antics.

• **Use sign language.** Wave, blow a kiss, and use other gestures that your child will soon understand and mimic.

• **Play peek-a-boo.** Although your baby won't respond until 8 months of age or so, this simple hide-and-seek game gives you and your baby a chance to practice playing the repetitive, predictable games she'll come to enjoy.

# CHAPTER 3

# 4 and 5 Months

At four and five months, your baby's development is steady but quiet. Her body is gaining strength and filling out; her vocalizing is becoming more precise, almost studied, and she is becoming alert and responsive for greater periods in her day. This subtle progress is setting the stage for the explosion of development to come.

## Physical development

Your baby is no longer making random movements, instinctive responses to internal or external stimuli. Now she moves in a purposeful way, sometimes for the sheer joy of moving; other times to practice her budding coordination in an attempt to swipe at something or to bring a toy or other intriguing object closer to herself. Her newfound strength is evident in many positions: On her tummy, she holds her head up and turns it from side to side at will. When you place her in a corner of the couch, propped with pillows behind her, she sits with little or no floppiness.

Fascinated as you may be by her growing physical abilities, she is even more intrigued by them and spends a good deal of her waking hours performing each new skill, again and again. Refining one skill opens the way for her to develop another physical feat, more complex—and more exciting—than the one that came before.

# Physical changes

Your baby now is surprisingly removed from what she was as a squinty newborn, captive to the reflexes she was born with. Her features are well-formed, her coloring is even, and her expression is often curious and alert. Although her body is not yet well proportioned, with her head still oversized and her lower body small relative to her torso and upper body, her skin is smooth and lovely. A Caucasian baby's eye color may be changing, going from the blue/gray she was born with to the brown, blue, green, gray, or hazel her eyes will become. Expect a fair amount of drooling to begin. First teeth erupt most typically in babies at 5 or 6 months of age.

Yet another change you'll notice your baby making is in her vocalizing. The coos and gurgles that so delighted you last month are slowly turning into purposeful sounds, and your baby no doubt spends much of her time awake practicing them. Don't be surprised if your baby lets loose with a screech now and then. As alarming as her occasional scream might sound, it's just another practice session to her.

**What your baby can do**   In many ways, this is the easiest time you will have with your baby, in part because of what she *can't* do. While she now has a relatively predictable routine, she isn't yet mobile, and this allows you to be somewhat more relaxed. Of course, she is on her way to that mobility, and you'll see her progress through these weeks. For instance, when you place your baby on her stomach early in her fourth month, she will be annoyed to find herself in such an awkward position, virtually unable to move. By the end of her fifth month, however, she will enjoy raising her head while on her stomach, and extending her arms and legs, to put herself into a "flying" position. Or she'll raise her upper body on her arms, the better to gaze around. At this stage, she'll also raise her bottom from the on-her-tummy position, a precursor to crawling. While on her back, she will grab her feet, often bringing them to her mouth, and stretch her arms out to reach for objects that interest her.

When propped in a sitting position, your baby may strain to pull to a full sitting position on her own; indeed, some babies successfully accomplish this marvelous task during this period. If you hold her up in a standing position, she extends her legs with her feet flat on the floor, and may stamp them. She will probably roll over from her stomach to her back—so be prepared to protect her from any potential fall.

With her vision finally near perfect, she has limitless possibilities for enjoying the view. Her excellent visual capabilities coupled with her newly strong neck—which allows her to turn her head at will—make her eager to take in all the sights around her.

No longer is your baby a sleepy-head most of the day. Now her sleep patterns are more clearly defined, and for the longer stretches of being awake she is alert and playful. She probably won't demand to be fed the minute she wakes up, and may play happily in her crib before hunger overwhelms her. While she will continue to get most of her nutrition from breast milk or formula, her health-care professional may well suggest you start your baby on solid foods sometime between her fourth to sixth month.

**PARENTS ALERT**

## Baby-proofing

Now's the time to remove play gyms that hang over your baby's crib, lower the mattress in the crib, and further remove any items within reach of the changing table and bath, since your baby's new mobility and unpredictable ability to reach and grab for objects puts him at risk.

**What you can do**  You can help your baby develop her back and neck strength by allowing her to spend some waking time on her tummy to practice and strengthen her new movements. Make these exercises more intriguing for her by placing an interesting toy in front of her which will encourage her to raise her head so that she can see it better. She may need you to make her more comfortable; you can gently extend her arms outward so that they are not curled awkwardly under her.

When you prop your baby in a sitting position, she will strain to lean forward herself, balancing herself by placing her hands forward. Again, you can encourage her early efforts to sit unaided—when she is strong enough—by placing objects of interest in front of her for her to reach. Offer rattles, plastic keys, and the like to her so that she can practice her reach and grasp; you'll notice that she will drop one toy to hold another rather than attempt to hold one in each hand.

Let your baby spend regular time in her crib with access to her bare feet. She will enjoy exploring her body, from fingering her toes to placing them in her mouth. She will continue to study her hands, gazing at them and turning them for long periods of time.

# Introducing solids

At one time, starting babies on solid food in the first few months was considered a sign of superiority. No more. Not only do babies get all the nutrition they need in the first four to six months from breast milk or formula alone, too early an introduction to solids is both not the best choice nutritionally and is potentially dangerous. Until they are about four months old, infants have an extrusion reflex, which causes their tongues to automatically push out any nonliquid substance that touches the front of their tongues. Solids placed further back in their mouths can cause choking.

*Symptoms of a food allergy include diarrhea, vomiting, constipation, fussiness, or rashes. For more on food allergies, see **pages 515–18**.*

**A guide to introducing solids**  Do not feed your baby solid food in his bottle, such as mixing cereal with formula because this reduces his ability to learn to swallow solids correctly.

Start your baby with iron-fortified infant cereal mixed with breast milk or formula; rice is generally preferred as the first of the first because it has virtually no allergens. Do not mix foods while you are in the introductory process. If your baby does have a food sensitivity or allergy, you can identify the trigger food by following this one-new-food-at-a-time procedure. Wait three to five days between introducing each new food.

The next group of foods to introduce should be vegetables, then fruits, but no tomatoes, oranges, or grapefruit, which can be too acidic for your baby. All food should be thoroughly pureed or prepared baby food in jars. Meat can be introduced last. The time to introduce finger foods, while convenient for you and entertaining for your child, depends on your baby's fine motor control and ability to gum or chew the food properly. For most babies, this development comes at about six or seven months, whether or not they have teeth. You can start your baby with small pieces of dry cereal, such as Cheerios and let him try to feed himself. Hold off on such things as sliced fruits and chunks of bread until your baby's ability to chew is well established.

When first introducing solids, be aware that your baby may not much like this new experience. To give him the best chance of trying, hold him in your lap snuggly with one of his arms pressed against you to help keep him from grabbing the spoon. If he doesn't take the food right away, don't force the issue. Simply try again in a day or so. When he moves forward toward the spoon, however, he's indicating he wants more.

**Choosing commercial baby food** When you purchase processed baby food, get into the habit of reading the nutrition label. Keep in mind that the first ingredient listed is the main ingredient, even if another ingredient is shown on the front of the package. For example, if a product is sold as "banana dessert" and the first ingredient shown on the list is sugar or water, then the product is made primarily of sugar or water. If the first product listed is bananas, that's your best choice. Steer clear of foods that have sugar or salt added; these ingredients are made to appeal to your palate and offer nothing for your baby.

**Storing, heating, and serving solid foods** Store jars of baby food in a cool, dry place, and serve them at room temperature. Babies do not have a preference for warmed foods; most parents warm foods simply because they like their own dinners heated. If you need to warm up food that has been refrigerated, do so in an electric feeding dish or by placing the open jar in hot water. Do not use the microwave, which can cause super-hot spots. Your baby's food should be served on a spoon and from a separate dish, not from the jar to avoid waste. Spoon out just enough and use a clean spoon if you wish to refill your baby's serving dish. Never feed directly from the jar and then refrigerate the leftovers, since the baby's saliva introduces bacteria into the food. Be sure that you have tightly covered any leftover foods before refrigeration.

**PARENTS ALERT**

### Baby Food Storage

Refrigerate baby food after opening jars. Discard meat or poultry products if you haven't finished them within one day, and vegetable products within two days.

**Eliminating 2 a.m. feedings**

*"My 5-month-old still doesn't sleep through the night. Should I add cereal to his nightime bottle so he won't be hungry at 2 a.m.?"*

No. Babies should learn to eat solid foods through the swallowing reflex, not the sucking one, which is what putting cereal in his bottle would produce. Instead, you have to consider why your baby is continuing to wake during the night. It may be that he isn't getting a large enough feeding before he goes to bed, or that he is in the habit of waking—and being fed—during the night.

Be sure you give him a substantial feeding shortly before he goes to sleep in the evening. This way you have the comfort of knowing it is unlikely that hunger is awakening him in the wee

## Helping Baby Sleep

Letting a baby cry for an extended period is extremely difficult for many parents. But it is important for your baby to learn to comfort himself and handle returning to sleep on his own. Babies, like adults, wake several times during the night naturally; unless you help your baby learn to go back to sleep himself, he may retain this habit for many months to come or even longer.

hours. You will need to break him of the habit of being held and fed during the night, which is probably behind his nocturnal risings. Check his diaper, and, if necessary, change him quietly in the crib rather than rousing him further by chatting or moving him to his changing table. Then you can either let him cry until he puts himself back to sleep, or you can go into his room, offer him quiet comfort, and leave. Simply say a few calming things to him, rub his back for a minute, and walk away. If he continues to fuss—and you are too troubled by it to ignore his cries—go in again, and repeat your earlier actions. Eventually, he will understand that you are not going to pick him up, and he will start to put himself back to sleep without disturbing you.

**Weaning from breast to bottle**  Weaning is an emotional as well as a physical event and represents a major milestone on the road to your baby's independence.  There's no reason to rush the process if you prefer to continue breast-feeding.  While it is best to continue nursing through the first year, you may choose now to introduce the bottle to your baby, filling it with either breast milk or formula.

Babies who have been fed only by the breast often find it tough going to drink from a bottle. You can make it easier by offering him a nipple bottle that most closely resembles the breast's nipple. Someone other than mom should offer the bottle until your baby is used to it. In fact, if possible, mom should stay out of the room entirely during the first few bottle feedings since seeing her will only frustrate and upset the baby who can't have the familiar breast.

To help ease the transition, consider filling his early bottles with expressed breast milk, so that the familiar taste will encourage him to keep trying. Also experiment with offering water or formula. And now that your baby is over three months of age, you can introduce diluted apple juice. Check with your pediatrician first, however. Some doctors do not want babies ingesting calories from juice yet, particularly if the baby had a low birth weight and still has some catching up to do.

Watch to see which choices are most pleasing to your baby, and which he is more apt to accept.  Assume the first few attempts won't be successful. Keep offering, and your baby will get used to this new way of feeding in a few days or weeks.

## Your baby's teeth

Your baby was born with primary "tooth buds" that will account for all her baby and permanent teeth. The baby buds are much bigger than those of permanent teeth and almost fully developed by 6 months, when the first one generally erupts. The permanent-tooth buds are tiny at birth and grow much more slowly.

Your child's baby teeth will probably begin to erupt by the fifth month, but keep in mind that each child is individual, and teeth tend to come in at different times in different babies.

### Symptoms of teething

• **Drooling.** When your baby is teething, he may drool more than usual. Drooling can lead to a rash on his chin or around his mouth since his saliva may irritate and dry out tender skin.

• **Minor coughing.** Babies who are teething sometimes develop a mild cough, usually because they are gagging on their drool. If your baby doesn't appear to have additional symptoms of a cold or other illness, you needn't worry about this minor cough.

• **Slight temperature.** Your baby's temperature may also rise a bit—to about 100.4°F—but teething doesn't cause an actual "fever," which is a symptom of true illness. If your baby develops a true fever—a temperature of more than 100.4°F, then she's probably suffering from a cold or another ailment.

**Handling teething pain** Teething may trigger a variety of symptoms, many of them mimicking a cold. No one knows for sure if "teething congestion" is caused by teething or if teething makes a baby more susceptible to the cold virus. Doctors do agree that coldlike symptoms in a baby should not be automatically attributed to teething, however.

**PARENTS ALERT**

### No Alcohol on Baby's Gums

Your own mom may have rubbed brandy or another alcoholic beverage on your tender gums when you were teething, but we now know that alcohol, even a small amount, can be poisonous to infants. Caution grandparents and babysitters to avoid rubbing alcohol on your little one's gums.

**"IT WORKED FOR ME"**

### Chilled Teethers

I was giving my baby chilled washcloths to chew on. Both the coolness and the texture seemed to soothe him, but they were somewhat ungainly to handle. Then I hit on an ingenious idea: I filled a clean cotton sock with ice chips, and tied a knot on the end. It was easy to handle, and my baby loved it.

## TIMELINE

### *Infant Teething*

An infant's primary, or baby, teeth begin developing in the womb. They are partially formed at birth, and some permanent teeth have already begun to develop in the gums above the primary teeth.

**At around 5 to 6 months:** Babies start to teethe. Gums may be red and swollen as the first tooth—usually a bottom front tooth, or lower incisor—emerges. (Tender gums occur throughout childhood as new teeth come in.) Each tooth takes several weeks to emerge fully after breaking through the gum. Because teeth appear in pairs, a baby's second tooth—the mate to the lower incisor—will appear often within days of the first.

**At about 8 months:** The two upper front teeth—or upper incisors—emerge.

**By 12 months:** The four lateral incisors appear and the first molars begin to emerge.

If your baby is, in fact, suffering from teething pain:

- **Clean up drool.** To cut down on skin irritation, periodically wipe his mouth and chin with a clean, damp washcloth. Ask your doctor to recommend a gentle moisture cream or lotion to combat dryness.
- **Offer pain relievers.** Ask your doctor to recommend a topical OTC teething preparation and/or a pain reliever such as acetaminophen to help soothe the pain.
- **Offer cold treats.** Once your baby is on solid food, you can also offer cold treats, including chilled pureed fruit, or frozen yogurt, which will curb pain somewhat.
- **Offer teethers.** Commercially made teethers, such as cold rings, can greatly reduce teething discomfort. Be careful not to offer any items that could choke or gag your baby, such as frozen bagels or cold spoons, however.

### Biting while nursing

*"Now that my baby is getting teeth, he sometimes bites me when he's nursing. I don't want to stop nursing him, but I need to know how to stop the biting. What works?"*

Anytime your baby bites your nipple, remove him immediately from your breast. Sternly say "no," to him as you do so. Do not shake or jar him, which could physically harm him as well as frighten him. If he attempts to hold on to your nipple with his mouth, put your finger between his lips and your nipple, which will immediately break the suction. You may have to do this several times, but he will learn that biting is an unacceptable behavior.

# Emotional development

At 4 to 5 months of age, your baby's personality and basic nature is coming to the fore. He interacts with the world around him now, and he expects the world to react in return. He is particularly sensitive to the way you interact with him; in fact, your behavior is an important determinant of his own. A highly social being now, your baby is looking to you for his cues on how to respond to the people and events around him.

## Your baby's feelings

Now a happily social creature, your baby is delighted by his family. Although he may be slightly wary of people he doesn't see regularly, he is nevertheless generally adaptable and responsive, even to strangers. These are the months in which he is making his primary attachments—to father as well as mother—and he is becoming extremely aware of who these important people are to him. His social needs are paramount, and he is perfectly happy to play for long stretches at a time so long as he has you nearby. He watches people, especially family members, with great intensity. He responds to the interest given him. Beyond observing, he wants interaction. The more he can get, as long as he is not sleepy or overstimulated, the better. Cutting him off from the social action when he is enjoying it will make him unhappy, even morose.

**How your baby develops secure relationships**  Social interaction is a primary ingredient of your baby's developing a sense of security in this period. Your baby's budding awareness that members of his family are special people in his life is producing a real bond to them. The continuity of his family members' presence reassures your baby that you are there for him, and through his interaction with you and other family members, he is learning that he is special, loved, and accepted.

**What you can do**  Accommodating her needs for socializing is nearly as important as responding to your baby's cries for nourishment, and should be taken just as seriously. Return her playfulness in kind, while continuing to give her ample amounts of cuddling, stroking, and love. She will want to explore your face and body now as you hold her. She will pat your cheeks, tug at your hair, and twirl a lock with her fingers. Allow her plenty of time for this especially tender way of getting to know you.

Boredom is a new factor creeping into your baby's life. With the many wonderful things he is discovering, he greatly enjoys exploring, and it's important that you give him the opportunities he needs to observe. When he is in the mood to watch and learn, lying someplace where there is little to see, or on his tummy where the view is limited, will not be to his liking for long. Expect him to protest in short order.

## Your baby's fears and frustrations

At this stage in your baby's life, you may begin to see situations that make him fearful or timid. Even this young, a few babies start to become alarmed by strangers; some babies may protest their bath or being left alone in a room. Your baby will be more secure if you accept that he may have fears and work around them rather than trying to force him to get past them—an impossibility in any case.

Gently help him through his fears. For instance, if he is put off by being naked, talk to him as you change his clothes, explaining each step you are taking, and try to keep at least a light blanket around him so that he feels covered. Likewise, if the bath frightens him, opt for sponge baths for a while. As long as he has your protective presence and actions, his fears are unlikely to overwhelm him.

In these months, your baby is apt to express frustration. The very fact that she is rapidly becoming more aware of her world increases her eagerness to take part in it. Something as simple as not being able to reach a toy can make her screech in frustration.

Depending on the nature of her frustration, don't be overly quick to resolve the situation. Naturally, if she is frustrated by being caught in the folds of her blanket, do what you must to make her comfortable again. But if you see her frustration is building as she struggles to move toward a toy or pacifier, give her a moment to accomplish the job on her own. Interfere only if you see that her goal is impossible or that the frustration is overwhelming her. Working toward a reachable goal, however, is good training for her as she prepares to meet the many physical challenges that lie ahead and to surmount the frustration that will often accompany the learning process.

**Handling intense emotion**

*"My son's pediatrician says he's an 'intense' baby because every-thing seems to upset him—getting dressed, going to sleep—any changes at all. What can I do to help my son relax?"*

Basic temperament, whether easy-going or intense, is largely inborn, and can be apparent even in infancy. Given that your baby is upset by daily routines, it isn't likely that he will turn into a child who can easily go with the flow. However, you can make changes in your baby's environment to help him adjust with little or no stress as you and he move through the day.

Time is a key element for you. When at all possible, allow plenty of it for your baby to make transitions—yours is not the kind of baby who deals well with surprise. Move slowly from one activity to the next. Handle him especially gently, and talk to him more or less continuously in a quiet voice, telling him what you are doing and what is coming next. You should also keep the general atmosphere calm. Play quiet music in the background, rather than nerve-jangling tunes or television sounds. Keep the lighting low. Minimize the hustle and bustle of the household as much as is reasonable, without going overboard. After all, your intense child will have to adjust, too. With a regular and calming routine, however, over time he will become more relaxed.

## Your baby's self-awareness

The fourth and fifth months are happy ones. Your baby seems to bubble with cheerfulness and is responsive to just about everyone he meets. He smiles and coos at all who take the time to smile and coo at him—which is to say nearly every person he comes across.

He is also on the path to self-awareness, learning who he is and how he fits into his environment. He is gaining awareness of himself through observing his own body, especially his feet and hands. His increased mobility and facility for controlling his body movements will give him many more chances to gather sensory information and to realize that he can manipulate his surroundings. These accomplishments create feelings of mastery that will greatly contribute to his sense of self.

**The role of separation** You play a significant role in your baby's development of self-awareness. His sense of being a separate person begins with separation, and it is parents who must first separate from the baby rather than the other way around. The first time you leave your baby alone in his crib, a process begins that evolves into greater separations later on. Separation is fraught with moments of anguish throughout life, but it must take place for a baby—and eventually a grown person—to discover his own identity. Creating a stable environment, dependable routines, and loving responses encourage your child to test the parameters of life, from learning to sit up to going away to college, and through these tests and risks he will develop his own sense of self.

## The grandparent connection

Having a grandchild is one of the great joys of life, and the child who has grandparents to dote on him is blessed indeed. For your child, grandparents are a powerful connection to the extended family as well as to the family's roots. The strength of that bond depends, of course, on you.

To help your child and your parents and/or in-laws develop a strong relationship, you must act as a bridge. When your child-raising philosophy differs from the previous generations', work toward an open-minded exchange of ideas. Share your thoughts and listen to theirs. It can be difficult to make the transition from child to parent with your own parents, and it doesn't have to be accomplished immediately. It helps to realize from the beginning that you and your child's grandparents all have your child's best interests at heart. Rather than simply defending your way of doing things, share current literature about babies—books such as this one, and relevant magazine articles—to acquaint the grandparents with current child-rearing knowledge so that they may better understand your own educated decisions. Be firm where you must be. For instance, a generation past believed that babies must lie on their tummies while sleeping. Since current research proves that this involves serious risks, you're right to insist that they abide by your wishes when they're watching your child.

In other, less serious matters, you may feel comfortable allowing the grandparents to do things their way. Make it a point to keep grandparents connected to the day-to-day developments of your child's life. If they live nearby, they might enjoy having time set apart with their grandchild just for them. Keep faraway grandparents in touch with videos, e-mail, photos, and letters. In your home, display their pictures—including recent ones—prominently so that your child becomes accustomed to their faces.

# Cognitive development

Your baby's more acute vision is a critical tool for her in her developing cognitive abilities. All her purposeful gazing now reflects the fact that she's seeing clear images, whether it is your face a few feet away, or birds that catch her interest as they sit on branches outside her window. Her newly acquired vocal skills lead her to mimic the sounds and cadences of her home language.

## What your baby knows

The reservoir of knowledge your baby can draw on is substantially greater now; her awareness of her special people—parents, siblings, and a regular baby-sitter—is obvious by the joyous smiles and happy kicks she reserves for this select group. She is also conscious of her immediate environment: her crib, her toys, and other baby areas such as her changing table and car seat. Your baby's understanding of cause and effect is emerging in some areas. For instance, you'll see this new understanding in her intentional kicks at objects now that she knows her actions produce predictable results. Her strengthened interest in the world around her, combined with her new physical abilities, make babyproofing her environment essential.

Your baby is also learning to anticipate. You might see this in a show of excitement surrounding your actions. She may vocalize excitedly or kick in pleasure as you are readying her bath, perhaps, or she may show signs of early cooperation while you dress or change her.

Your baby's interest in human faces continues to be strong. You may catch her babbling in "conversation" with drawings or pictures of people, including, even, such unlikely candidates as cartoon characters on her crib sheets.

**How your baby learns** Practice, practice, practice—it's an adage babies apparently come into the world with. You will be seeing ample evidence of your baby's determination, starting in these weeks, as she works to master her blossoming skills. Her vocalizing is mostly focused on vowel sounds that she repeats over and over, much like a singer warming up. You may notice consonants starting to nudge in as well; the letters *p*, *b*, and *m* are usually the first to make an appearance. She learns these sounds from the conversation around her. In fact, startling new research shows that babies have learned the unique, distinct sounds of their own language by the time they turn 6 months of age.

Games are part of your baby's learning tools now. When you hear her cough, you may worry at first that she is getting sick. It's far more likely to be the onset of a game you will both enjoy, and one that is teaching her more about conversational patterns: she coughs, and pauses, waiting for you to cough in return. Yet another sound she'll enjoy making with you is razzing—blowing through her lips, often with saliva bubbles, to make a vibrating sound.

Your baby is now starting to enjoy small changes in her environment. Simply shifting some crib toys to her play yard, or putting up new pictures around her changing table will please her. If you appear fresh from the shower with a towel wrapped around your hair, she will notice Mommy's new blue hair, as you'll see from the puzzled look that crosses her face. For some babies, the incongruity of seeing your changed appearance will cause broad smiles—the first sign of your child's emerging sense of humor. Other children (including those who will also have a strong sense of humor) may be frightened by your appearance. In either case, a reaction points to your child's new ability to discern the difference between the familiar and the new.

**What you can do** During these months, your baby will take a much stronger, more involved, role in her interactions with you. A game of peek-a-boo, which before elicited her watchful, quiet interest, will now garner giggles and much arm and leg waving. The game is also beginning to have new meaning to your baby because she is starting to suspect that people and objects don't cease to exist when she can't see them. In just a few more months, she'll play along.

Because she learns so much through observation, give her frequent changes of view. Place her infant seat in different parts of the room so she can enjoy differing perspectives. Take her out often, and give her plenty of time to observe colorful picture books while in your lap. This is an excellent time to show her pictures of objects that are familiar in her environment. For example, if you have a cat, find a board book featuring a similar-looking cat to read with your baby. Pictures of other babies will interest her, as will more mundane things such as household objects and toys.

It's important to keep conversations going with your baby throughout the day. Repeat the sounds she makes with you—the coughs, razzes, coos, and vowels—and do this in conversational pacing. Her silence after she makes different sounds is her tacit acknowledgment that it's your turn. Be sure to use many words with her as well. Identify objects around the house, and, when you go out, describe what you are doing. Talk to her about anything and everything. You'll know when she's had enough—she'll turn her head away, or her expression will indicate she is tuning out and wants a rest.

## Oral explorations

By the end of his fifth month, expect to see your baby start to put a variety of objects into his mouth. Previously, it may have been just his thumb, fingers, or his fist that he mouthed. Soon it will be virtually everything he can get his hands on.

Interestingly, the onset of a baby's mouthing objects coincides with much of the teething process, and you may well assume that your baby is attempting to relieve gum discomfort. No doubt he is doing that to some extent. However, there is much more going on. The nerves and muscles of a baby's mouth are highly developed even at birth, and his mouth is a very useful tool to learn about objects around him. More acute to his sense of touch than his hands, his mouth lets him know if an item he comes across is hard, soft, fuzzy, or smooth.

As time goes on, your baby's persistent mouthing of objects may become quite unnerving, especially after he has learned to crawl, when every tiny thing he finds on your floor goes right to his mouth—and an occasional bug is no exception. You can't stop your baby's mouthing, nor should you try since it gives him valuable learning experiences. But, of course, you'll need to be careful about what items he has access to. Ingesting some dirt isn't usually anything to be alarmed about, but you must be sure to have completed your childproofing before your baby becomes mobile.

Be sure to give your baby plenty of colorful, safe toys he will enjoy putting in his mouth, and don't allow him anything that is small enough to cause a choking hazard. This includes loose buttons on toys and clothing that he could pull off. Occasional washing of the toys and objects your baby regularly puts in his mouth is sufficient to keep them sanitary since it is his own germs on these objects. Naturally, when a toy falls on the floor, you should wash it with soap and water. Also wash after other babies have used the toys as well to protect your child from their germs.

By the time your baby is about a year old, he will lose his interest in mouthing everything that comes his way and will have shifted his attention to learning through his hands and eyes, using his mouth to eat and, increasingly, to communicate.

# CHAPTER 4

# 6 and 7 Months

Prepare yourself: Life with your baby is about to change rapidly. The hours of lying in his crib, quietly studying his hands, or sitting in your arms, gazing lovingly at your face are over. It's all systems go from now on as your baby moves into a monumental phase of development.

## Physical development

Babies develop their fine and gross motor skills in tandem, but in these months, the gross motor skills will be the focus of excitement. Yes, you will see your baby manipulating small objects much more effectively, but that accomplishment will most likely pale when compared with the other physical feats you'll witness.

You have started a long period in which you'll need to safeguard your baby a good part of his day. He is becoming both more active and more mobile, and there are a dismaying number of ways he can hurt himself—and your favorite breakable items. Childproofing, of course, is mandatory. But nothing replaces vigilance on the part of you, and the others who care for your baby.

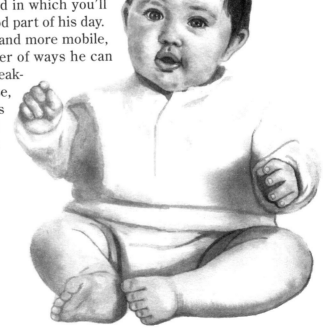

*"My 6-month-old daughter is balder today than the day she was born. When will she grow hair? I have very thin hair, and I'm worried she'll be like me."*

Some babies are born with an astonishing amount of hair, referred to as "birth hair," which generally falls out over the first few months. It is not unusual for these babies, as well as others born virtually without hair, to spend many more months with only fuzz on their scalps, hardly enough to be considered *hair*.

If you have thin hair, it wouldn't be surprising if your child inherits the same kind, but you needn't draw any conclusions too early. Eventually a full head of hair will grow in. But be patient—more than one baby celebrates her first birthday without enough hair to tie a bow in for the photos.

# Physical changes

One of the most striking changes a baby makes at this age is in his muscular development. Any scrawniness he may have had in his arms or legs is replaced by sturdy muscles and, generally, a fair amount of baby fat. His face is beginning to take on more form, and his body proportions are changing with the lower body becoming bigger and stronger.

A once-bald head may now be showing a bit of hair, probably far from luxurious, but enough to be reassuring. Overall, your baby is beginning to look less like an infant, and more like a person with his own distinctive appearance.

**What your baby can do**  The changes you can see in your baby's body are visible evidence of his greatly increased strength. He is now combining these strong muscles with his much improved coordination—and this combination is leading him to mastery of important baby feats.

The list of baby accomplishments is substantial. In these months, your baby will probably be sitting up fully, rolling over, arching his back to look around, and maybe clapping his hands and banging his toys on any surface as well. In his early sitting up, he holds a tenuous posture—balancing himself in triangular fashion with his hands on the floor in front of him. Shortly, though, he will sit firmly planted, arms waving, for up to 30 minutes at a time. He may even be able to keep objects in his hands as he sits, sure evidence of sitting-up prowess. He will now pass an object he is holding from one to the other hand and may even try holding an object in each hand simultaneously.

If your baby is now accustomed to eating solid foods, he will want to help out in the feeding process. Developing the ability to pick up tiny objects is a notable event during these months. Your baby will enjoy practicing this finger-grasping with small morsels of food. But he will also take great pleasure in attempting to get all manner of food—the messier the better—into his mouth... hair...ears...and anywhere else it lands or he slaps it.

*Squirming* is a word that will come to mind frequently in this period as you observe your baby try to change whatever position he is in to something else. The first mobility he is apt to demonstrate is squirming on his belly, and slithering in this position for some distance across the floor. Or he might discover that he can get across rooms quickly by bouncing on his bottom. Whichever kind of early moving he does, at some point after that, your baby will attempt to raise his body on all fours, the first signal of real crawling. When he is strong enough to start moving in this position, don't be surprised if his movement is in a backward direction rather than forward, a circumstance that will bother him not at all, and shouldn't upset you either. It's simply that his current strength makes a backward motion easier to attain.

Don't be surprised if he also pulls himself to a standing position for brief periods of time toward the end of this period.

**What you can do** The speed with which your baby is developing his physical skills now is awesome, and the more opportunity for practice you give him, the happier he will be. You can encourage his forward motion—whether on his tummy, bottom, or on all fours—by putting interesting toys far enough in front of him that he has to move to get them. To pull himself up to a standing position, he needs strong support. If you haven't already done so, it is essential that you lower his crib mattress to prevent mishaps. Likewise, scan the room for surfaces he might use to pull himself up, and be sure there are none that can tip or be pulled down, or items on the surfaces that can hurt him or break.

Although any self-feeding attempts are no doubt going to require substantial cleaning up, it's important for you to allow your child to feed herself at least some of the time. Offer different types of finger foods, and give her sufficient time to get some of the food into her mouth himself.

Your baby is extremely interested in your body now as well as his own. He will poke at you, pat your arms, breast, and face, in part from love, in part as a way of achieving a better grasp of what a body is. This activity is valuable exploration for him, and can be a pleasant pause in the day for you.

### Baby Views

Your baby is likely strong enough now to perch on an adult's shoulders as long as he is firmly gripped and to sit comfortably in a back carrier. He will no doubt find the wide-open view such a carrier affords him a great pleasure.

It is now that your baby may begin to find his genitals of interest. Should you discover that he is touching his as you change his diapers or bathe him, don't worry about it, or discourage the action. Touching this way gives your baby a sensation of pleasure that he will quite naturally want to repeat. It's completely normal.

# Your baby's unique development

Just as babies have widely differing temperaments and personalities, they also have individual paths of physical development. A baby who is particularly active, the kind who was born, it seems, with arms and legs flailing, is going to be extremely interested in developing her gross motor skills. Crawling, first steps, and walking give her that much more opportunity to exercise her on-the-move nature. It's hardly a surprise, then, that this kind of baby tends to reach these milestones on the early side of the usual ages. Less active babies are more apt to develop physical skills in a more drawn-out sequence. And if a baby is born prematurely, she's not as likely to reach certain milestones at birth age, but rather will reach them at her developmental age. The two will not likely be in sync for a year or more after birth. The manner and timing of her developmental milestones is far less important than steady development. Gaps of a few weeks or months between two different babies in attaining these skills has no bearing on their future abilities, since the normal range is quite wide.

Your baby's emotional temperament will also influence her physical development. If yours is one who particularly loves to socialize, she'll be more motivated to learn to sit because sitting gives her a better view of the people around her, and a better position from which to engage others in cooing and babbling. A more self-contained baby, on the other hand, is more content to enjoy the world from a lying-down position, at least for now.

Whatever your baby's nature, she will develop as she is ready, and in the progression that is right for her. Instead of worrying whether your baby is on target with the developmental tables, chart her personal progress as a way of better understanding her unique development.

## Limit Standing

While you and your baby will both marvel at her new ability to stand up, it's important that you don't overdo your encouragement. Until your baby is adept at sitting unaided and crawling, her skeleton isn't ready for long stretches of being upright and supporting her weight on her feet.

## Making comparisons

*"My neighbor's son sat up unassisted at 5 months, but at 6 months, my son is just learning to roll over by himself. Is my son's development lagging or is her son advanced?"*

All developmental charts give the approximate ages of when parents can expect their child to reach various milestones. When used correctly, these charts serve as broad guidelines. They are not meant to be standards that each and every child should meet at precise ages, so it's important not to take them too literally. To do so will only cause you unnecessary anxiety about your baby.

**Weighty issues of baby fat**    Parents are often amazed at the way their infant, whether breast or bottle-fed, can become roly-poly.

If you are concerned about your baby's weight at six months, ask her health provider to plot your baby's height and weight on a growth-curve chart, which shows how the growth of your child compares with that of other children the same age. As long as your child falls into an appropriate percentile for her weight and height, there is nothing to be concerned about. However, if your baby's weight consistently moves upward faster than her height, her pediatrician may want to screen her for any related medical condition. Once a medical problem is ruled out, as it usually is, the doctor will examine if overfeeding is the problem and help you adjust your baby's diet to be sure she is on a healthy track. The goal will not be for your baby to lose weight, but for her to grow into her weight.

**First haircut**    For many parents, this event is a rite of passage. Some babies are ready for their first cut by 6 or 7 months of age or even earlier, especially if the hair is growing in front of the child's eyes. If your child's hair is particularly wispy, a haircut will help it grow in thicker. If you choose to cut your baby's hair yourself, use blunt-end scissors, available at most cosmetic and drug stores. The cut will work best if your baby's hair is wet. The high chair usually makes a good home-barber chair. Give your baby a bath right afterward to remove any prickly hairs which can cause discomfort. If you have a professional cut your baby's hair, select a stylist who has experience working with babies. Don't forget your camera!

*See **page 84** for first-year height and weight charts.*

# *Emotional development*

Coinciding with your baby's physical development is a greater self-awareness on your baby's part. Babies this age know who they are. Overall, expect to see your baby's emotional life much more intensely displayed than in the past. With so much going on, the accompanying feelings can be a dizzying change of moods.

## Your baby's feelings

Your baby pulls herself to a standing position and you clap in obvious pleasure. She then rewards you with a smile that says, "I'm proud of myself!" Being proud is one of several new emotions your baby expresses at this stage of her emotional development. During this time, she may also become shy around people she doesn't know, burying her face in your shoulder if a stranger makes overtures. Her strong affection for you is something she makes ever more obvious—grinning when you come into the room, and fussing when you leave. If there are siblings in the house, the baby delights in their antics, and now she takes a more active role in their play. She loves to clown, and she has a hearty appreciation of a good audience.

For the many emotional reactions your baby has that make you smile, you'll experience the less joyful ones as well. Before accomplishing each new developmental milestone, your baby may be tense and irritable for a time. Should you try to cajole her into a better mood, you may find she doesn't focus on your efforts, however much your attempts might please her on another day. Being out of sorts while focusing on new developmental skills is normal. Your baby may also become clingier than usual during this period. Now that she can more easily look around, she is startled by the realization that her world is a bigger place than she had known, and she needs the extra comfort and reassurance that clinging to you provides.

**How your baby develops secure relationships**  To some degree, your role with baby has changed. Added to the many roles you already have is that of safety net. Both literally and figuratively, your presence provides the security that your baby's budding prowess demands. As she starts to squirm away from you, you may see her turn back to be sure you are still there. She may like to hide for a moment under a blanket, but only if she knows you are there to find her.

Because your baby is decidedly aware of the people close to her, she wants them to be with her on a regular basis. As social as she may be with the people she sees casually, she really relates to those who are close to her now. She is beginning to sense that those outside her immediate circle are "others," and her feelings of safety come from constant interactions with those at the center of her existence, the ones she knows she can depend upon.

**What you can do**  Although it is easy to become distracted by your baby's physical changes, it is important to remain particularly sensitive to her moods. She needs to know you are there for her, even as she is pushing her boundaries further each day. Sometimes she'll require just a quick smile in response to her furtive glances your way, enough to say that you're watching over her. If you leave her in the crib in her room, she may cry out in protest. Call to her from the other room with reassuring words that you are nearby and will return shortly.

Show your pleasure in both her progress and her antics. Be attentive to her emotional needs, letting her know again and again that her trust in you is well founded. Respect her moods—her sour ones as well as her happy ones. If the need to be contrary overtakes her, she has no choice but to go with that feeling and to act accordingly. Be aware that at this age, your child has no concept of doing anything purposefully naughty or irritating. Consequently, punishment in any form is inappropriate, even cruel, for a baby this age.

## Self-comforting routines

As exciting as the second six months of life are in development, they also introduce your baby more fully to the concept of separation. Probably she sleeps now in her own room, rather than in a bassinet near you; certainly she spends considerably less time in your arms and out of the front carrier and into her stroller. An important aspect of the greater separation your baby has is finding ways to comfort herself in your absence.

Sucking on pacifiers or thumbs offers a great deal of self-comfort for some babies. When your baby rouses during the night, she may put her thumb into her mouth—or cry out for her pacifier—and sucking one or the other will offer just enough comfort for her to return to sleep. Some babies resort to other, more alarming routines as part of their self-comfort. When she is strong enough to hoist herself onto her hands and knees, your baby may start to bang her head against the crib rails, and rock back and forth as she puts herself to sleep. As troublesome as head-banging and rocking are when you first encounter them, these behaviors are normal and do not reflect any underlying emotional disturbance. If head-banging becomes routine or particularly intense, discuss the situation with your child's pediatrician, who will likely reassure you that your baby isn't hurting herself with the action. Head-banging, rocking, and other physical routines as a means of self-comforting can go on for anything from a few weeks to a year or even longer. This behavior almost always goes away on its own, and you should restrain yourself from making any comments about it to your child.

### Thumb sucking

For information about pacifiers, see **page 234**. For information about helping children overcome habits, see **pages 312–13**.

*"My daughter, age 7 months, rarely stops sucking her thumb. I didn't mind when she was a newborn, but now I'm worried that she'll ruin her teeth. Is constant thumb sucking normal?"*

Thumb sucking is a completely normal behavior in babies; in fact, prenatal ultrasound pictures sometimes reveal a fetus with her thumb planted in her mouth. After birth, infants are apt to find their thumbs to fulfill the need to suck, but as they get past the first three or four months, they value thumb sucking for the comfort it brings them. There's no good purpose served by interfering with this form of self-comfort. Some children lose interest in sucking their thumbs around their first birthday; others continue it well into the toddler years.

Even though you may not like the way it looks, sucking her thumb is not a problem for an infant or toddler. Her permanent teeth will not come in until she is 5 or 6 years old at the earliest, and they can't be damaged before then. If thumb sucking goes on so long that it puts your child's teeth alignment at risk, her dentist can prescribe a special mouth device that will help her break the habit.

For more on security objects, see **page 210**.

**Security objects** At about six months of age, your baby may become attached to a so-called security object, such as a favorite toy or a blanket, an attachment that may persist for months or even years. Clutching her blanket or toy makes your child feel safer, and she can obtain this feeling on her own rather than from you, a considerable achievement for a baby. The comfort she gains from her security objects is especially valuable when she endures the stress of change—starting to crawl, meeting a new sitter, or entering child-care, for example.

Your baby's attachment to her security object is likely to be intense, so it's a good idea to have a duplicate because losing it will cause great distress. Also, get in the habit of washing it regularly, both to prevent it from becoming too unsanitary and to keep it from developing a particular odor, which will become part of its appeal. Once your child associates the odor with the object, it will be difficult for her to find comfort in it clean or with a replacement. As long as the object serves your child, allow her to take it with her when you go on family vacations, when she has a doctor's appointment, or any other time that could be stressful.

At some point in the toddler and preschool years—after age two and before age five—even the most devoted child generally gives up a once-beloved object. Until then, go along with your child's determination to have her security item, and enjoy the fact that through this, she has learned a great deal about self-comfort.

# Cognitive development

Expect to get into a repetitive mode with your baby during this period. He will practice new-found cognitive skills by replaying certain maneuvers again and again, and he will want you to repeat favorite games.

During his sixth and seventh months, your baby's attention span gains considerably. He is visually alert much of his waking hours, and he can maintain general alertness for several hours at a time, giving him greater opportunity to learn. Although your baby's language development is continuing in these months, the amount of vocalizing he does might actually decrease. He will laugh, he will grunt, but his primary focus will be on his physical development.

## What your baby knows

Last month, if your baby's favorite toy was hidden under his blanket, he would have assumed that it no longer existed, but now he is catching on to a new reality: Objects, even those he cannot see at the moment, continue to exist. This is called object permanence, and it represents a major cognitive leap for your baby. Of course, understanding object permanence also means your baby knows that you and others who matter to him exist, even when you're not there.

Memory goes hand in hand with object permanence, and you will start seeing considerable development in your baby's ability to recall people, objects, and events. He can anticipate some things—that at the end of the song you sing to him you throw your hands upward, that the jack jumps from the box—and you'll see the excitement build on his face as he anticipates the expected action. He knows, too, that hearing the key in the front door lock each evening means that a parent is coming home.

He is building his grasp of cause and effect; in fact, he is becoming quite sophisticated in his understanding that actions lead to other actions. A few months back, having his foot accidentally hit an attachment on his crib gym served to trigger an awareness that perhaps he could do that again; now he will delight in slamming his hand onto the water's surface in his bath for the purpose of watching it splash around him, or he will knock a bowl of cereal off his high chair tray for the excitement it causes.

He clearly understands a few words. When you ask him if he wants his bottle, he may wave his arms in a happy answer. If you wonder aloud where the dog is, your baby might look around the room. He will respond to his own name and to other important names, looking at Mommy when he hears the word *mommy*, and at Daddy, when he hears his name.

**How your baby learns**   Your baby continues to rely on his mouth to help him learn about objects he comes across. And now he is also learning a great deal through hand exploration. After his first months of having little or no control of his hands, your baby at 6 and 7 months of age is moving toward full, purposeful use of his hands and fingers. He may now be able to pass items back and forth, hold a toy in each hand at the same time instead of dropping one toy to pick up another. He can also position his hands as he wishes. He will pick up an object that interests him and stare at it for a while as he holds it upright. Then he may turn it around, turn it upside down, and hold it at various angles. Placing it at arm's length gives your baby yet another view of this intriguing object. He will pass it from hand to hand, shake it to see what sound it might make, and otherwise study it.

Your baby is also listening carefully now. As you recite a favorite rhyme, you'll have his rapt attention while he listens to the cadences of your words and phrases. His listening skills are matched by his visual attentiveness; he may now start to imitate some of your actions such as clapping his hands when you clap. He is still happy to observe his own reflection, and he is gaining awareness that this isn't just *any* baby he is looking at, it's him!

## Language Learning

The age of 5 or 6 months is a good time to start teaching your child words to describe his own body parts. While you dress him, point to and name his eyes and your own; his nose, and yours; his mouth and yours, and so on. Soon when you ask him where his eyes are, he'll point directly to them.

Experimentation begins in earnest in these months. Your baby is becoming extremely interested in finding out what things do; he'll bang one toy, poke at another, and shake still others to see which ones roll away, make a noise, or otherwise respond to him. A rudimentary awareness of relative size may start now, and he will experiment, trying to stack toys or nest them within one another.

**What you can do**  Daily interactions provide many opportunities to focus on and reinforce the concepts your baby is learning now. Because he is learning the implications of cause and effect beyond his own actions, talk to him about them. Point out, for example, how the key unlocks the door, how pouring out the water empties the glass, and the myriad other cause/effect situations in your day. Play frequent games of "Where is it?" Tuck his rattle under the crib blanket and ask him where it went; you'll see him progress from being somewhat unsure to being absolutely gleeful as he whips it out from its hiding place. When you hear the outside door opening, comment on it, and ask in a dramatic voice, "Who could it be?" When it's Dad or Grandma or another person familiar to him, say the name even though your child obviously recognizes the person. In this scenario and ones like it, you are reassuring your baby that his understanding of the world is valid.

Play different kinds of music for your baby now and watch his reactions. He'll let you know by fussing or turning away if rock and roll, for instance, is not to his taste. Similarly, your young country-music fan will respond with happy kicks and hand clapping if you're playing a bit of bluegrass on the CD. Whatever your taste, look for music that has a strong beat as your baby is becoming increasingly aware of and interested in rhythm. He'll continue to enjoy hearing you sing and may even mimic a few simple sounds from songs he knows well, perhaps responding to your rendition of "Baa, Baa Black Sheep" with a few *baa*'s of his own. Create or re-create songs to go with your routines: "I'm going to wash that soap right out of your hair," or "Now's the time to take your bath." And one of the great moments that will bring pleasure to both baby and you is having a dance together. Twirl and turn, take a few dips, and listen to his squeals of joy.

Continue to read your baby books that feature many aspects of his world. A picture book with pictures of babies, toys, familiar animals and vehicles, and other similar kinds of things will please him. Identify each object as you go along, and, when appropriate, make sounds that match.

## How babies explore the world

Your baby's ability to use his hands purposefully leads to other cognitive developments. At some point between your baby's sixth and ninth month, you'll catch the delight on his face when he suddenly discovers that the block he has in one hand fits into the cup in his other hand. And he'll laugh aloud when he sees that if he turns the cup over, the inserted block comes out again. Through this exercise your baby is beginning to understand the spatial concepts of *in* and *out* and *bigger* and *smaller*. And he's getting another lesson in object permanence as he observes the block disappearing inside the cup and reappearing when he empties the cup. He'll also use his hands to experiment with stacking objects, too, placing one block on top of the other.

The ability to grasp becomes ever finer. Earlier, your baby used his whole hand, much like a scoop, to hold something. Then he used his thumb and fingers together in a kind of clasping action. And finally, at about 8 months, he'll start to use just his thumb and forefinger, a highly skilled maneuver known as the "pincer grasp." By the time your baby is a year old, he will have refined this grasp well enough to be able to pick up even the tiniest of crumbs with precision.

Increasingly, your baby uses his hands in addition to (and, eventually, instead of) his mouth to discover more about texture and feel. He touches the soft blocks and notes that they are nice and nubby. He pats your breast and face and sees that they are smooth. This pleasurable learning technique is one of the reasons why *Pat the*

*Bunny*, a book that features different textures for baby to touch on each page, is such a popular book with babies.

## Games babies love

**Peek-a-boo** You can turn peek-a-boo into a more sophisticated game now, hiding objects instead of your face. Cover a toy and let your child uncover it. When she begins crawling, hide a toy while she is watching you, then let her find it. Next, hide two or three toys, and allow longer periods of time to elapse before encouraging your baby to find them.

**Pat-a-cake** Similarly, pat-a-cake will change now as well. Her enjoyment of the game will continue, but she will start to take a more active role in it. She will either clap her hands in the most developed level of the game, or she may clasp your hands and bring them together when she knows it is time for you to clap.

**Body games** More games of "This little piggy went to market," and "Where are baby's eyes, nose, etc." continue to please your baby at this stage, and they are especially on target now as baby is learning about her body.

**Singing games** In the months to come, take advantage of your baby's growing ability to anticipate the action by singing songs such as "The itsy-bitsy spider…" which feature repetitive and predictable hand movements. Help her perform the hand gestures herself along with you, though don't expect her to do these movements on her own for another year or so.

### Infant humor

*"Is it possible for a 6-month-old to have a sense of humor? My daughter laughs at many of her older brother's antics."*

Not only is it possible for babies this young to enjoy humor, many of them delight in it, even instigating the fun. A baby can get a big kick out of acting the clown, chortling as she upends a dish of yogurt, giggling as she pats the family dog, or when she sees something incongruous or amusingly unexpected, such as a favorite stuffed bear dressed in a frilly doll's hat.

Babies take special notice and interest in other children as well, clearly sensing that they are kindred creatures. It's no accident that your daughter's older brother pleases her so. In fact, a sibling can often elicit the baby's full-scale laughter by simply making a silly face.

# Your baby's language development

Though it may still be a few months before your baby is speaking, he's already learned a lot about language and is getting physically ready to talk. When you speak to him, he's absorbing the rhythms of his native tongue. When he sucks and eats, he's developing the muscles in his mouth. How you communicate with your baby greatly affects how his language skills develop. The more involved you and others who care for him are with talking to him, listening to him, and having basic "conversations," the more developed the language centers of his brain will become. To improve the circuits of his brain's language wiring:

- **Talk to him about what you're doing.** In addition to the conversations you engage in when you're feeding or diapering your baby, tell him about your actions as you run errands and are busy in the kitchen. The words may not mean much, but your child will know that you're talking to him.
- **Respond to his sounds.** Mimic your baby's coos. When he babbles, let him know that you're listening by talking back to him.
- **Sing and play with words.** Let your child experience your fondness for language by hearing you sing to him or play with sounds, such as repeating silly syllables to him.

### Your baby's understanding of spoken language

*"Does a 7-month old actually understand what people are saying, or is he responding only to the tone of voice?"*

A baby of 7 months is beginning to understand the meaning of specific words that he hears the most often, such as his name and the name of objects that are meaningful to him, like *bottle* or *teddy bear*. By the time he is a year old, a baby on average understands about 20 words. He learns these words in a variety of ways, including matching the tone of voice to particular content. That's why the word *no* spoken firmly earns early understanding. He also learns words by association. When you say a word—*mama*, for instance—and then point to yourself, your baby learns to connect the word to the meaning. He also learns words from your response to his babbles; if you excitedly repeat his babbles of *da-da-da* after him, and point to a beaming Daddy at the same time, your baby will come to realize that he's made a special sound.

Because all of these systems for learning to communicate—voice tones, association, babbling—work together, it's important that they make consistent sense to your baby. For instance, if you say, "No, don't touch," in a mild instead of firm voice, your baby will have more difficulty learning the meaning of the words. Likewise, if you say, "I love you," in a harsh voice, your baby will absorb more meaning from your tone than from your words. If you misname objects or use vague terms, such as calling many items *things* instead of using specific terms such as *teddy bear* or *rattle*, your baby will be limited in his vocabulary development. But when you use more precise words, respond to his babbling, and let your tone match your words, you're giving your child the tools he needs both cognitively and emotionally to encourage his listening and speaking skills.

### TIME FOR YOU
## *Little Luxuries*

You have enormous responsibility for others. Sometimes, in the flurry of getting everything done, you may feel there's nothing left just for you. That's exactly the moment when you should make a plan for your own pleasure. It's particularly satisfying then to take some time—and sometimes a bit of money—to give yourself a real treat. You've earned the privilege.

Following is a list of small indulgences that can pay off with big rewards.

**Get a spa treatment.** Treat yourself to a half day at a salon or day spa. You can select from a list of services those that will make you feel like a new person, such as a massage, facial, manicure, and/or pedicure. Some services may be arranged in your own home.

**Hire a professional organizer.** Even one session can help you put your surroundings in order, and help you feel you're back in control.

**Enjoy some cultural events.** Get yourself a series of concert, ballet, or theater tickets. For the more active type, sign up for tap-dancing or modern jazz classes.

**Eliminate one household chore.** Hire a cook to create a supply of in-a-minute dinners for your freezer. Cooking schools in your area will put you in touch with eager students, or you might offer to pay a friend with great cooking skills. Send the wash out instead of doing it yourself. Or schedule special or regular housekeeping services.

**Get a hair-care treatment.** Few things make new moms feel fresher than having hair cut and styled.

**Send yourself fresh flowers.** Better yet, arrange with the florist to send you flowers once a week for the next month.

**Buy some luxurious, lacy underwear.** It feels great against your skin, and adds some sexy self-awareness to your day.

# 8 and 9 Months

A t this point, your household has probably become a much noisier and busier place. Your baby's presence is felt—and heard—everywhere as he scoots or crawls around, getting into cabinets, dropping toys and food, and banging one object against another. He is having a wonderful time, making new discoveries daily. Naturally, you must make sure your home is safe for your baby's explorations, but you can maximize the fun for him by giving him plenty of secured spaces in which to move around.

The eighth month will likely be a continuation of the fast-paced months that went before. With your baby so busy learning, it's hard for him to quiet enough even to sleep. In his ninth month, however, you can expect to have a more peaceful few weeks. It is, in some respects, the calm before the storm that comes with his development of full mobility. Right now, he is content to be absorbing the many things he has learned in such a short period of time.

# *Physical development*

Mobility is the name of the game these months. Your baby will be ecstatic that he can get around on his own steam, and he will want to spend much of his time doing just that. The disproportionate amount of strength he had in his arms when he began to crawl, which in many babies results in crawling backward at first, is beginning to ebb. His legs are catching up now with repeated efforts to stand up, or even walk.

Your baby's physical abilities change almost daily, and you'll have to work hard to stay ahead of him.

## Physical changes

Not only have your baby's facial features become more clearly defined, the expressions that cross her face are now more pronounced and indicative of her internal state of mind. At times, her expression appears pensive, to be replaced, perhaps, by a curious look, and then one of unmistakable glee. She is still growing quickly. Her longer, stronger body is apparent as she maneuvers herself around, either crawling or even beginning to take some uncertain steps.

By about nine months of age, your baby will have enough control over each finger that he can use his index finger to point and poke. Pointing is an indispensable gesture for the child who is too young to express himself in words. It is also an important social skill. When your baby points at something, he is actually "talking" to you, and when you respond by giving him the requested object, he knows that you are listening.

**What your baby can do**  In these months, expect to have little peace. As you walk across the kitchen to prepare dinner, your new crawler will probably be right behind you. While she may have started creeping on her bottom or tummy, sometime toward the end of this period she will most likely get around on all fours. And she is astonishingly quick about it. Wherever you go, she will be at your heels.

You may see your baby start to climb in these months. From learning the move to stand—putting her hands on a surface and pulling her body up—your baby soon figures out that scaling a bookshelf or other high object is possible, too.

Sitting up, of course, is now old hat. But your baby will master an associated skill. From a lying-down position, she will roll over and push herself to sitting in an easy, smooth maneuver. She is also probably extremely facile at flipping herself over. This means you must be ever vigilant when she is on a surface, especially the changing table which she knows well and is no doubt bored by.

In your baby's many explorations, she will come across drawers stuffed with clothing, shelves filled with books, and wastebaskets full of trash. To her these offer entertainment value more wondrous than that of the most enticing, colorful toys. She will spend many happy hours pulling contents from the drawers and scattering them around her, yanking books from their shelves to the floor, and going through the trash. For your own sake, try to teach her that part of the game is putting things back. She won't be able to do this yet, but it will give you hope for future months. Of course, you must also make sure that there is nothing that can harm her in this activity.

## Baby Reading

At this age, your baby has a good time going through magazines. While the pictures interest her, she particularly likes to rip apart the paper. She enjoys the lovely sound along with her newfound ability to so clearly change an object by touching it.

**What you can do**   More and more, your baby needs continuous opportunities to explore her environment. She is strengthening her body this way, and perfecting her physical skills. Although it requires careful supervision on your part, giving your baby considerable freedom is extremely important. Don't put her playpen or safety yard away, but reserve its use for those times when you must have your baby in a secure place.

You can also make your baby's explorations ever more interesting for her. Try scattering pillows around the room for her to climb over or around; put toys in corners for her to discover, and roll balls filled with bells or other noisemakers for her to chase.

In general, you should allow your baby to do as much for herself as she can. Her self-feeding efforts no doubt continue to be messy, but it is through the pasta that lands on the floor, or the yogurt that gets smeared in her hair that she is developing not only the ability to feed herself, but also greater eye-hand coordination and finger dexterity. She may now be extending her arms or legs to help you dress her or grabbing the washcloth to assist in the bath; praise her for her efforts and encourage her to do more.

Rather than worry about a messy home, give your baby magazines of her own to rip, and access to drawers that have contents you can accept having strewn around. Keep your pots and pans in a cabinet your baby can easily get to, and watch the fun she'll have pulling them out, banging them together and beating on them. This alone can keep your baby entertained the entire time you need to prepare a meal or clean up afterward. Do be careful, however, to secure the doors to avoid pinched fingers.

Now, just before she learns to walk, is when your baby will take special pleasure from having you lift her by her hands. Take one of her hands in each of yours and pull her to a standing position. She'll want you to do this again and again, so only start the game when you have time to be relaxed about it. Be sure to be gentle in your movements, and avoid swinging her from her arms or pulling her up too quickly, movements that could result in injury. Your job is to provide support, while not overtaking her movements.

## Drinking from a cup

Most babies are ready to hold and drink from a cup by the time they are 8 or 9 months of age, so now might be a good time to introduce this new way of eating. Expect the first attempts to be messy ones and prepare accordingly. Get a cup with a weighted bottom, a spouted lid, and, of course, one that is unbreakable.

Hold your baby on your lap, or seat her in the high chair or infant seat. Then demonstrate for her how to sip from the cup. Don't put in more than an ounce or two of liquid

**TIMELINE** *Walking*

A **newborn's** legs are folded as they were in the womb, and look bowed. They straighten out in time.

When **2-week-olds** are held upright on a firm surface, they move in a march-like fashion, with each foot jumping up as it touches the surface.

By **2 months**, infants can bear their weight briefly when they are held in a standing position.

By **8 months**, many babies are crawling and by **9 months**, they start to climb onto things.

Between **9 and 16 months**, most babies start walking; they first pull themselves up to a standing position and cruise around by holding on to furniture. Eventually they walk unaided. Typically they hold their arms out and spread their legs for balance, and point their knees out and toes in or out.

By **18 months**, toddlers have graduated to a heel-to-toe gait and climb stairs one foot at a time while holding on to an adult's hand.

Most **2-year-olds** can walk backward and can also run with ease.

By **3 years**, preschoolers are able to jump with both feet off the floor at once, stand on one foot for several seconds, and walk up and down stairs on their own.

## Your Baby's First Shoes

### Do...

allow your baby to go without shoes in the protected environment of your home. Bare feet (socks might be too slick) actually help a baby learn to walk.

look for flexible shoes made of material that is porous enough to breathe.

start with smoother-soled styles that won't grip the floor and cause your new walker to trip.

### Don't...

buy the hightop shoes that were assumed to be the best choice for babies in years past. These are too confining around the baby's ankle.

put a baby in odd-shaped shoes such as cute little cowboy boots.

buy shoes with growing room. Although the toe box should be ample enough for the baby's foot to easily move, it shouldn't be so big it encumbers walking.

until she has the hang of it. She may well treat the cup as a plaything at first; this is a good way for her to become used to the cup. Water is usually the best beverage to start with. Have the cup accompany meal times. On hungry mornings, however, offer the familiar breast or bottle. Once your baby is accepting the mealtime cups, you can begin giving her cups more often in place of the breast or bottle except before bedtime, when she will want the comfort of her old routine for a while longer.

## Crawling and walking

For most babies this age, crawling will be the preferred means of travel, and their crawling positions will vary widely—from pulling themselves along on their bottoms to the smooth four-legged gait of a jungle cat. A few will make attempts at walking.

As she pulls herself to standing, your baby's posture may look as if it needs some work, but she's just trying to assure her balance. In order to have the full support she requires in early standing and walking, she automatically protrudes her belly, sways her back, and sticks out her bottom. She also stands on legs spread wide apart for additional support. This is normal, and a posture she will modify as she becomes a seasoned walker. Don't be alarmed, either, by her seemingly flat feet. There is a fat pad on all babies' feet that makes it look as if there isn't an arch, but there is and it will appear in time.

## Sit-down crawling

*"My 8-month-old daughter loves to get around from a sitting position, using her arms to propel her. When will she begin crawling on all fours?"*

Some babies become extremely good at getting themselves around in the fashion your daughter has learned. Given that they have developed a way of moving that works perfectly well for their purposes, they may be reluctant to learn a different one. Most babies do, however, eventually move on to crawling on all fours, as is more typical. Don't be surprised, though, if your daughter never crawls on her hands and knees, but goes directly to walking instead. It's unlikely, but possible, and should it occur, it's also nothing to worry about.

## Fear of walking

*"Whenever my 9-month-old son pulls himself up to a standing position, he begins to cry hysterically. Why?"*

There are several reasons babies respond with apparent panic when they first stand. It may be that your baby suddenly realizes—as he first views the world from a standing position he has achieved for himself—that he is rapidly becoming a more independent creature. However attracted he is to that goal, it also alarms him when an achievement in that direction is still new.

His tears may reflect a less philosophical issue, however. Babies figure out how to pull themselves up before they understand how to get themselves back down again. You can put an end to his tears by standing behind him, flexing his knees, and showing him how to get himself back into a sitting position. You may need to help him for several days or a week before he masters sitting down himself. Until then, expect tears of frustration each time he stands.

**PARENTS ALERT**

## *Dangers of Baby Walkers*

Babies enjoy bouncing and moving around, but babies in motion can spell trouble if you're not careful. Baby walkers are very dangerous. Every year, thousands of babies are treated in emergency rooms for baby walker-related injuries. Most are hurt when they fall down stairs. It's much safer to choose one of the many devices that will allow your baby to swivel or bounce, while remaining stationary. Take note, however, that overuse of the stationary bouncers—more than 20 minutes or so every day—can cause bone growth problems that can result in poor posture. Your best bet is to allow your child to learn to walk on his own with your close supervision.

# *Emotional development*

In these months, your baby will become a more emotional creature than you have seen before. This is a crucial period when many babies become fully overcome by a phase called stranger anxiety. Although researchers once thought all babies go through this stage—which generally lasts for as long as seven or eight months—they now recognize that, for unclear reasons, some babies do not experience this vulnerable stage. So you should consider your baby's withdrawal from people he doesn't know well completely normal now; if he shows no such reaction, well, that's normal, too.

You're apt to see other, new feelings erupt in this period, too. Fear and fussiness may play bigger parts in your baby's day than they did before as will a greater sensitivity to the activity in his surroundings. He may show a particularly strong attachment to one parent over the other—most often his mother. While this seeming rejection is understandably difficult for the other parent, it's nothing to be upset about. This, too, will pass, and the so-called rejected parent may become the new favorite when it does.

## Your baby's feelings

This is the age when your baby is absolutely clear who are the primary people in his life, and it is usually a small circle at that—his parents, his siblings, and his full-time baby-sitter if he has one. Anyone else, including the neighbors who could elicit a broad smile just last week, are now cause for suspicion. Your baby is probably feeling vulnerable in a way he hasn't experienced before; not only does he realize that most people are unknowns, his physical accomplishments are hurling him toward separateness that is completely new.

The result of your baby's feelings of vulnerability is that he is becoming extremely clingy. This is not the personality of a shrinking violet emerging, it is merely a part of your baby's emotional development. He may burst into tears now when you turn on the vacuum cleaner, or do something else that produces an unexpected noise, as if he feels the world isn't such a safe place after all. And, yes, he'll turn to you, hiding his face in your shoulder, determined never to let go of your arm. At this stage, your baby is equally demonstrative about his complete and total devotion to you. His love only grows more and more—and that look of total bliss is something to take to your heart and keep in your memory.

**How your baby develops secure relationships**  If your baby is one in whom stranger anxiety appears, you should view it as part of the process through which your baby is indeed forming more secure relationships. By identifying "other," he is turning toward "mine," and visibly forging an ever-tighter bond. Even if your baby continues to woo friends and strangers alike with his most winsome smiles, don't be fooled into thinking he is less aware of his family. Even though he manifests it more quietly, he, too, is creating a tight family bond.

It may not be enough for your baby right now to be across the room from you. You might find your lap is assuredly the spot from which he feels safest viewing the world. Your baby's desire to pull the security of his family, in particular his mother, around him will continue for at least several more months. He is building the emotional foundation that will give him the strength he needs to move forward in forming his own sense of self.

**What you can do**  This is a time for great patience with your baby. You may be tempted to scold him for his sudden reluctance to interact with people, and his new desire to cling to you. What he needs now, however, is your comfort. Consistently reassure him that everything is fine and that you are there for him. This, not scolding, is what will help him grow strong and independent.

You can also help your baby become more comfortable with his increasing awareness of so much that is new around him. If he reacts to the sudden noise of the vacuum cleaner, stop, and show him what you are doing. Let him see you are in control of the noise that frightened him so. Don't put it back on, however, if the sound continues to frighten him. This fear will pass soon enough and, in the meantime, save the activity for when he's not in earshot. Likewise, take your time making adjustments with him. Instead of rushing to go out shopping together, let him ease into the experience and explain as you go along what you are, and will be, doing.

In spite of his shyness or outright fear around strangers, your baby will still benefit from exposure to other people. Just be sure to introduce him gently to those he doesn't know or shows new shyness toward. Keep him in your arms, and allow him to pursue getting friendly with the other person at his own pace—and expect it to be a slow one. Give him lots of praise for his efforts; this is a difficult time for him and he deserves your kind words throughout it.

## Getting Rid of Guilt

It's not uncommon for parents to want to be perfect and loving at all times, to want to have all the right answers, and to be totally in tune with their child. Naturally, that is an impossible goal, but the very fact of having it somewhere in the back of your head creates guilt that you can't live up to such demands. Because this kind of guilt is unproductive, it's important to find ways to let it go.

To successfully free yourself from unwarranted guilt, and the cycle of vague depression it can create, you must first identify what is causing the feeling. More than likely, it's just that sense that you aren't reaching your overly high standards. Once you have pinned down what exactly is triggering your own guilt, you can go about getting rid of it in an appropriate way.

Here are suggestions that will help you banish the guilt from your life:

**Take ten minutes** to indulge your guilty conscience. Think about the things you don't do perfectly, and, when the time is up, focus on other, constructive thoughts.

**Ask yourself** if your current transgression, the one you are feeling so terrible about, will matter in a week.

**Remind yourself** that what you are feeling guilty about probably didn't bother your parents when you were young.

**Ask yourself** if the cause of your guilt is within your control. If the answer is no, your guilty feelings are self-defeating, and it's time to let them go.

# Your baby's sense of self

Even though your baby doesn't understand most or any of the words you direct at her, praise is as important in her first year of life as it will be in subsequent years. With the many accomplishments your baby is making this year, you will have frequent reason to lavish her with compliments. Your rapt attention, the happy expression on your face, and the tone of your voice as you tell her how wonderful she is all register clearly on her budding self-esteem.

While it's true that all healthy babies develop and progress in a more-or-less predictable pattern, every step forward your baby makes is hers alone. She already can feel proud of herself and her accomplishments, and your heartfelt words and smiles will add to that pride. The "I can do it" spirit she develops now will serve her throughout her life.

### Your baby's favored people

*"Do children under the age of 1 have people preferences? My 9-month-old gets very excited whenever my brother comes to visit. He doesn't have this reaction to anyone else."*

Between the ages of 6 and 12 months, babies develop strong people preferences. Generally, though, it is to one or the other parent, not someone in the extended family. Should your brother be unable to visit your baby for any length of time, prepare him for the possibility that he may tumble from grace. Most babies at 9 months are highly attuned to the people they see almost daily, and if your brother is no longer one of them, he will probably lose favor in your baby's eyes.

# Cognitive development

These months, your baby is learning and practicing new concepts, primarily those relating to spatial relationships. You'll see her turning a toy—or her head—to gain new perspectives on an item. She'll push objects off her high chair or any other surface she comes across to watch them fall and splat to the ground. Afterward, she'll peer at the now-grounded item, studying what it looks like down there. She may still show interest in her hands, but now it will be to look at them from many different angles.

Her attention span is increasing although she will probably start to show boredom if you repeat a game too many times for her taste. On the other hand, she may be quite annoyed if you decide to cut off any game she wants to continue.

Her vocalizing is more complex as she prepares to begin making sounds in real speech. She babbles in two-syllable sounds such as *ba-ba* or *da-da*, and may well employ a word or two for the object or person it represents.

## What your baby knows

With her eyes and hands working together and her rapidly growing cognitive skills, your baby is now able to do many more interesting things. She is catching on that her finger, for instance, will fit into a peg hole, and that if she spins certain toys, they will produce interesting sights or sounds. This is therefore the period of time in which she will start to become fascinated with an activity board in her crib or playpen. At this age, your baby is also figuring out how objects work together; a shape sorter, which requires her to match shaped objects to the correct hole, begins to intrigue her as does a ring stacker. At first she'll try to shove the rings on and the blocks in willy-nilly fashion, attempting to make up with force what won't work for size. Soon, though, she will grasp the concept that these toys work best when she combines looking, planning, and acting in a certain sequence and she will master the object of the game.

Object permanence—knowing that an object still exists even when she can't see it—is clear to your baby now. She'll get a kick out of making something disappear under a blanket and retrieving it again. Placing items into a container—and then shaking them back out onto the floor—will also be a favorite at this time.

It is also unmistakable that your baby understands a few key words now. *No* is often one of the first words babies clearly get; however, don't think that just because your baby knows what the word means she will follow the instruction. Additionally, this is the time you will begin to see early signs of her mimicking your hand motions. Some 9-month olds are beginning social body language, such as waving bye-bye.

**How your baby learns**    Your interactions with your baby and the experimentation she's conducting with her environment are the two primary ways in which your baby is learning now. Your interplay with her can't be stressed too much, not just because of the strong emotional base it gives your baby, but because of the impact it has on her cognitive growth as well. She watches you and other family members, seeing what each person does in given situations. As she moves through the day with you, your baby observes you open doors and cabinets, take out items you need, turn on faucets, feed the cat, prepare her lunch—all of these routines are going into her memory bank. She continues to listen to your sounds, and to engage you in conversation as she hones her understanding of how language works.

Similarly, she experiments on an ongoing basis. Her fascination with cause and effect hasn't lessened, but it has broadened far beyond the earliest stages when she realized her kicks could produce motion from something else. She will tug on toys to produce sound or movement, or pull on blankets and tablecloths to get an even bigger effect. Everything that comes before her is apt to trigger her interest and her desire to conduct a closer inspection; the bowl of yogurt at lunch makes a dandy hat—and even better if it makes Mom and Dad laugh; spoons are for pounding and poking, bottles are for feeding and throwing. Give her access to as many safe items as you can, while storing away those that can harm her.

**What you can do**    This is an exciting time for your baby, and toys take on a special place in her world, truly becoming educational objects. This has nothing to do with flashcards and other early, misguided attempts to increase a baby's intelligence. The toys you can provide for her now that will excite her and help her learn are simple: shape sorters, activity centers that have large buttons and bells, stacking toys, and nesting toys.

There is also a host of objects in your home that your baby will learn from and love. Pots and pans, measuring spoons and cups, the telephone, plastic bowls—virtually anything that is safe, especially if your baby can produce noise with it, is fair game for her learning play. Keep this in mind as you go through your cabinets; put some of these objects aside in a box for her to go through, especially when you need time to accomplish a household chore.

You will increase your baby's enjoyment and her learning by getting down on the floor with her on a regular basis, and demonstrating some of the wonderful things the items in her life can do. Because mimicry is starting to play such a central role in her learning, she will eventually follow your lead—but only when she is ready. However thoughtfully she may watch you, some things she won't be able to do until the time is physically and cognitively right. Enjoy showing her how things work, but allow her to master them at her own pace.

## Your baby's brain power

Researchers have established the extreme importance that the brain's development in the first year has for future cognitive development. Child development experts now recognize that it is in this year that the neurological foundations for rational thinking, problem solving, and general reasoning are put in place. This is because the physical neural connections are formed early in life. What is even more striking is that your baby's experiences determine how well the neural connections are made and so how well the brain eventually works. Therefore, the more brain-shaping experiences your child enjoys in his first year, the better his brain grows.

### Keep Talking

Hearing the spoken language is one of the most important experiences for brain development. In fact, there are those experts who feel the number of words an infant hears every day is the major predictor of later success, both scholastically and socially. This isn't to imply that you should get tapes and videos for your baby—quite the opposite. These words must come from another human being for them to serve any purpose in developing brain power.

You can help your baby maximize her brain power, but not by stimulating her with one activity after another. The simplest and most effective way for you to help your baby develop cognitively is to keep up the conversation. Chatter with her about what she is doing, what you are doing, how the weather is, even what the cat is doing. That and the emotional closeness and security you are giving her in your loving relationship, not games, toys, and activities specifically designed to stimulate intelligence, are what will give your baby a head start in life.

**Baby math**  The concept of one-to-one correspondence—knowing, for instance, that one shoe goes with one foot—involves fairly abstract mathematical thinking, but children seem to develop an understanding of it completely naturally. By the time babies are 6 months old, most have the beginnings of mathematical comprehension. In one study, babies between 6 and 8 months sat between two large screens. Projected on the right screen was a slide of three objects; on the left, the slide showed two objects. Immediately after seeing the slides, the babies heard a tape of either two or three drumbeats.

When the babies heard three beats, they tended to look at the slide of three objects; when they heard two beats, they looked toward the screen that had shown two objects. This is fairly strong evidence, say the researchers, that the babies have a rudimentary understanding of one-to-one correspondence

You can help your baby make this leap in baby math by pointing out when you dress her, one mitten for one hand, one shoe for one foot, and so on. Look for other games that incorporate this concept that she will enjoy as well, such as sharing a snack—one cookie for you and one for me.

### Learning a second language
*"What is the best time and the best way to introduce a second language?"*

There is considerable disagreement among the experts about the optimum time to start a baby in a second language. Of course, there are obvious advantages to speaking to a newborn in both languages if one or both parents are fluent in the other tongue; this way the baby learns automatically as she grows. The disadvantage of this, and what causes concern among some experts, is that being constantly exposed to two languages slows speech development in both. Even so, this is a temporary situation—the child quickly catches up by around age three. However, you can avoid that lag by waiting until your child is between two and three years old to introduce the second language.

Don't postpone introducing another language too long, however. Studies show that the window of opportunity for learning language naturally and fluently closes by school age. After that, the particular neurological pathways used to understand language are fully formed. Though a person can learn another language later on, it will not be as a native speaker.

Whenever you decide to begin your child's second language development, the only real way for her to learn it is by being continuously exposed to the language through a person who speaks it fluently. You can reinforce the language with books, records, or videos in that language, but it is the daily conversations in the home that will make any language a viable part of your child's hearing comprehension and speech.

............................................................

# CHAPTER 6

# 10 to 12 Months

B y the time you celebrate your child's first birthday, you will be in awe at what has transpired in 12 short months as your helpless newborn becomes a self-propelled rover. By the time this year ends, she will have developed the physical, emotional, and cognitive prowess that removes her from the ranks of babyhood, making her a full-fledged toddler!

## *Physical development*

In many ways, these months are a real coming together of the physical abilities your baby has been developing. From turning over to standing up, your baby has been on a crash course of motor-skills education. An infant's neuromuscular development starts quite literally at the top and moves down; first he learns to control his head and neck, then his torso, and finally his lower body as he prepares to approach—or even reach—the crowning achievement of walking by his first birthday.

At the same time that he is making such breathtaking, but obvious, strides, your baby is quietly working toward mastery of the many other skills he has learned as well. He will probably be quieter these months as he devotes so much attention to perfecting his skills, such as using his eyes and hands in coordination, and his persistence in practicing them will continue to amaze you.

Don't be surprised if your baby's eating pattern changes these months. He may decide he likes only specific foods, and no others. Or he may decide he prefers eating one large meal and several small ones instead of six small meals a day. Your best bet is to go along with his preferences, even though they may change regularly.

# Physical changes

When you take your baby for his first-year well-baby checkup, you can expect that he will have tripled his birth weight. He will also be about 50 percent taller, and his brain will now be three quarters the size of an adult's brain, three times the size it was at birth.

The rapid weight gain that defined so much of your baby's first year will have dropped off by now, and with good reason. He no longer needs the number of calories he did earlier to progress through the fast-paced physical and motor development that characterized the first year of life. He is also moving much more now, which, in addition to his decreased appetite, has no doubt thinned him out. Interestingly, the fact that he has become vertical instead of continuously horizontal means he has lost a small, nearly imperceptible, amount of height, a result of his spine becoming more compact from being upright. When your baby stands and walks, don't be alarmed by the noticeable bowing of his legs and his toes turned either too much in or out. This stance is normal and will correct in time. His arms will be long relative to the rest of his body; this seeming oddity makes cruising and walking easier for him to accomplish, and his proportions will even out in a few years' time.

Your baby may still have a nearly bald head or may sport a headful of curls. The physical differences in body types among babies will now be strikingly apparent. Your best friend's baby might weigh substantially more—or less—than yours and have a noticeably differing kind of bone structure. Virtually all babies this age, however, are alert, full of smiles, and appealing to everyone they meet.

**What your baby can do** A new world opened up for your baby when he learned to crawl. He discovered he no longer had to depend on someone's arms or the stroller to get around—he could do it himself! His mobility gave him the means to explore in new ways, to get to interesting areas of the house, and to come across strange and fascinating objects to study.

Imagine, then, how thrilling it is for baby when he stands up and realizes he can move forward on his feet, just as the others in his home do. He starts, of course, by pulling himself up gripping the coffee table or another handy surface. Now you'll see him cruise around the furniture, from the coffee table to the big chair, the sofa to the end table. Sometimes he'll let go—and often surprise even himself that he is standing on his own.

Although there is a wide window of time in which healthy babies begin to walk unaided, a great proportion of them do reach this milestone by the end of the first year; most of the others are well on their way to this accomplishment. The first steps will be halting, and may even startle your baby so much he cries or sits down and refuses to move forward again for days or even weeks. But once the walking desire is in place, your baby moves from haltingly attempting to cross the floor, with his arms outstretched for balance, to making the journey in steady and speedy fashion, in a matter of days.

Any stairs your baby comes across offer up a challenge to him now as well, although he'll take them crawling, not walking. He'll be content to climb up steps—but he'll be stymied about how to get down. To keep him from making the trip head first, teach him immediately how to back down the steps.

Your baby won't restrict his climbing efforts to those things that may appear to you easier to scale, such as shelves. He may well go for not only low stools and tables, but also the washing machine, the kitchen table, anything that has a surface and a means of reaching it.

Fine motor skills are coming along in these months as well. Your baby may grab a crayon or pencil and make some stabbing attempts to create with it, just as he sees others do. Not long ago, he could take a toy in each hand; now he can happily empty practically the entire toy pile into his arms, one toy after another. He can also maneuver his own clothing—something you'll appreciate as he helps you dress him. Don't be surprised, too, when you discover that he has stripped himself bare in his crib. Instead, just share his delight in his accomplishment, even if it means that you ended up with soaking wet crib sheets.

**What you can do**   This is a period which calls for you to be ever alert. The issue of safety can't be overstated as your baby is discovering the entire house, from the toilet to the basement stairs. Your observations are also important to help your baby in his development of motor skills. For instance, you can demonstrate for him how to reach his arm from one piece of furniture to another just slightly farther away, thereby increasing his range of successful cruising. You can show him how to make a mark on paper with a crayon, rather than just jabbing at it. He will want to push chairs and his stroller around now, as he practices his walking technique. Make sure he has chairs that can be pushed, and areas that are open enough for him to make some distance without crashing into furniture or walls.

Some babies who have lagged in their motor development start to catch up in these months. No one knows for sure why some babies are less interested in the physical milestones than others are, but many of them will make up for it now. You should encourage your baby if he is only now tackling crawling, pulling himself up, and cruising. Help him if he seems confused about just how to go about this, and stay nearby to offer encouragement when he needs it. Give him lots of praise for each move forward he makes.

With all the excitement and intensity that your baby's focus on new skills creates, he will probably have some trouble sleeping for the time being. He may resist sleep in the evening; he may sleep for short spurts in the morning, and then have trouble getting a reasonably early afternoon nap, thereby confusing his evening schedule. He may wake up even several times during the night. You can do a lot to help him get past this stressful sleeping pattern. In the evening, take some extra time with your baby. Stroke him gently as he nurses or drinks his bedtime bottle; rock with him and croon him his favorite lullabies. Delay putting him into the crib until you feel him relax, which, although it will take additional time from your evening, should help him sleep better during the night. To counter nap-time confusion, keep him awake as long as possible in the morning, and give him an early lunch if necessary. That way, even if he slips into sleep before the ideal naptime, at least it's postponed until afternoon.

## Developing bedtime routines

Pleasant bedtime routines ease the transition from being awake to being asleep by helping children feel more secure and comfortable about what they can expect at the end of every day. To create a bedtime routine that works for your toddler and that will serve him and you for years to come, put together a predictable sequence of events that you can consistently follow in the same order every night. The actual routine will evolve and change as your child grows, but the basics remain the same. At this age, the bedtime routine might involve the process of putting on PJs, brushing your child's teeth, and reading him a good-night story. Or, your routine may involve a bath and a song, and a story, and another song, and a glass of water, and

## Plan Routines Wisely

Whatever bedtime routines you choose, make sure they are ones that you'll have the time and energy to repeat every night and that sitters can duplicate. If you change the routine in length, or sequence, or activities, it's no longer a routine, and you'll lose the comforting effect of repetition. Once you've established a routine, sleep won't come easily if you try to skip a step or if your sitter doesn't know it in detail. Routines are all about consistency and repetition. Knowing what comes next gives your child a sense of control and power.

another story. It's up to you to decide if you want to make it quick and easy or if you want to allow 20 to 30 minutes for special and exclusive time with your child for reading, snuggling, and being together.

Bedtime routines work best if you reserve the hour before bedtime for quiet play. This will lower your child's activity level and prepare his nervous system for relaxation. Roughhousing, running, playing tickling games, and even watching action-packed TV shows or vidoes make peaceful transition to sleep especially difficult. The following illustrates beneficial routines. Yours can be anything that works for you and your child:

• **Set a specific time and stick to it.** Your child's body clock will adjust much more quickly to the routine if the routine follows a natural and consistent pattern.

• **Give a warning.** Just before bedtime, give your child advance notice that the day is winding down. Your child may be too young to judge time yet, so saying something like "five more minutes" is not likely to be understood. Instead teach your child by association. Begin the first part of your routine—running the bath water, putting the toys away, or however your particular routine begins to signal the start of the wind down. Some parents signal impending bedtime with the ringing of a kitchen timer or stove-top buzzer or even an alarm clock. By your setting the timer for five minutes, the child learns that the sound means bedtime. This allows an impersonal third party to announce bedtime and reduces the desire to complain, since even a toddler knows that you can't argue with a machine.

• **Offer a snack.** A light snack that includes both protein and carbohydrates—for example, a small piece of cheese and one half slice of whole-wheat bread—will induce sleep and help her stay asleep through the night. The carbohydrates make her sleepy, and the protein will help keep her blood sugar level on a even keel until breakfast. Be sure to brush her teeth after she eats.

• **Give your child a warm bath.** By raising your baby's body temperature slightly, you'll make him more prone to sleepiness. Also, playing with his bath toys allows him to relax.

- **Get dressed for bed.** Choose comfortable, non-binding pajamas, that are neither too warm nor too light.
- **Read a favorite story to your child.** This is a particularly comforting routine for your toddler, particularly if it's a favorite story that's associated with bedtime, such as *Goodnight, Moon.* (As your child grows, he'll want more stories and more variety.)
- **Play soft music while you read.** It's okay to let the music play as the child drifts off.
- **Make sure your child has a friend to sleep with.** A favorite doll or teddy bear provides comfort.
- **Limit or eliminate bottles.** If your child needs a bottle to fall asleep, make sure it contains only water. Milk, formula, or juice can pool around her teeth causing cavities, even in infants.
- **Keep last "goodnights" brief.** Say "goodnight" when it's time for you to leave the room and try not to come back if your child calls for you. This sounds harsh, but if you keep coming into the room, you will have taught your child that "If I call to Mommy, she'll come back." Kids learn how to "condition" parents very quickly! *Any* hesitation on our part may be picked up by your child as an indication that maybe you really aren't serious about this bedtime business and if she yells loudly enough you'll come back and play some more.

### Snoozing in the stroller

*"When I take my 1-year-old out in his stroller, he falls asleep. Is napping in a stroller as restful as in a crib? Should I move him?"*

The gentle motion of the wheels tends to lull kids to sleep, which is why parents of colicky or fussy babies often use carriage rides as a way to calm their over-wrought infants. The overall quality of your child's sleep probably isn't much different in a stroller than in a crib. Also, if he's a light sleeper, moving him to his bed could unnecessarily rouse him. If he's a sound sleeper and you're close to home, you can try. Ten minutes into a nap, many babies are sleeping deeply and can be moved easily. But if the child is 40 minutes into an hour-long nap, even a heavy sleeper may wake up if you try to move him, since he's near the end of a sleep cycle.

If you allow your child to continue to sleep in his stroller, make sure the stroller is in its locked position and he is securely strapped in. Keep close watch on him so you know when he wakes up.

## Encouraging your baby's explorations

Helping your baby explore while keeping his safety in mind can result in mixed feelings for parents. As you see your formerly immobile baby take on the household, your pride mixes with terror.

To keep the pride high while reducing your fears, your first item of business is to create a number of secure areas in your home. Review your childproofing to double check that the environment is safe for your little explorer. In the safety zones—the family room, his nursery, your bedroom, for instance—let him go and move around as he wishes. Naturally you or another adult will have to be in the room with him, but he should feel free to move about and to investigate most items he comes across.

He'll enjoy his explorations even more if the items he finds are particularly interesting. Supply him with a basket that holds children's books with textured pages, such as *Pat the Bunny* or board books with hard pages for him to turn by himself, a ball or two to roll, some cardboard or plastic tubes, and other odd-shaped items. (Be sure that none is small enough or chewable enough to pose a choking hazard.) His bath will probably be a source of real pleasure to him now, especially if he has toys that encourage him to discover the many varied things that he can do with water.

While you can nudge him into making more or further explorations, don't try to rush him. He'll take on the world at the pace he is comfortable with, and not before. Even so, you can point out to him where something is that you know he wants. When you're outdoors, show him the leaves and flowers, and let him touch the grass. With both his fine and gross motor skills well developed, he is equipped to having a meaningful interaction with his environment.

## Your baby's coordination

When you observe the wide variation of physical coordination among adults, from world-class athletes to those who can't hit a tennis ball, it's no surprise that babies, too, vary in their physical coordination. Some babies are monkeylike in their ability to climb and move their bodies through space, apparently without fear or caution. Others have trouble even pulling themselves up for what may seem the longest time, as if their bottoms appear glued to the floor.

Should your baby fall at either end of the coordination spectrum, you'll need to pay special attention. Very agile babies call for extreme watchfulness; they move so well and so quickly, in what seems like mere seconds, that they can get themselves into a dangerous position quickly. Less coordinated babies, on the other hand, may require you to work with them, demonstrating and encouraging their physical development to help them reach the level of competence they need.

Most babies, of course, fall in between these two extremes. It may appear that your baby is lacking coordination at times, when he is struggling to develop his new abilities. Just as when he first sat on his own, he toppled over, he will experience some clumsiness as he takes his first steps. He will balance himself with his arms extended out or slightly up. This toddler gait serves to help keep him upright as he staggers for a short distance, before wobbling back down or stumbling.

The physical tasks your baby is mastering in this one year of life will not be equaled at any other time. In short order, your baby will walk smoothly—an old pro—stopping to pick up tiny items here and there with a perfectly executed stoop.

**Diapering your older baby** The more mobile baby requires a bit more creativity when it comes to diapering. If your child dislikes diapering and puts up a fuss, it may be time to move from the high perch of a changing table to a blanket-covered floor to prevent mishaps. Experiment to see what location works best. Some parents find that their babies like to be diapered standing up. See if this works for you.

# Emotional development

Your baby is continuing to become a more complex emotional being with an expanding range of moods. While this is in some ways a demanding period for you—meeting your baby's emotional needs can be strenuous—it is also more interesting than ever as you see shades of feelings come and go in your baby's emerging personality.

# Your baby's feelings

Exuberance and timidity mix in the emotional package that is your 10- to 12-month-old. She will respond with unbridled enthusiasm to playtime with Daddy; she is more than pleased with herself when her efforts, at clowning or helping you as you wash her, win laughter and applause; but in the middle of a new activity (or even a routine) she may suddenly feel frightened and grab at you for reassurance.

Her sensitivity to your moods, and those of the others close to her, is evident now. If you show disapproval, she will acknowledge it; she may frown or look away or, even, occasionally stop what she is doing that you don't like. Your baby is making such rapid progress in so many ways, she may need to retreat now and then to an earlier phase. In spite of having made a few first steps, she may now resolutely keep herself in a stationary position, stubbornly refusing to continue on her independent path while she summons her courage again.

A sense of personal identity is continuing to grow—and to show itself—in your baby. She cries for specific reasons, not, as she once did, to release tension or as a generalized way of communicating. Now she lets loose to protest something, such as being removed from a game she is enjoying. She may also cry in response to strange and unknown people, and often to express frustration when something is not to her liking. She will favor certain stuffed animals and toys, and she has a sense of priority about what is hers.

At this time, she will begin to cross the line into behaving in ways she knows you don't like. Some babies delight in tossing objects from their high chairs and listening for you to say *no* yet again. The look on your child's face makes it clear she knows she is being naughty, and she loves every minute of it.

Early signs of compassion may emerge now as well. Your baby will show her tender feelings by gently patting her favorite animals—real and otherwise—and she'll give looks of concern when she sees another baby crying.

**How your baby develops secure relationships**　You may feel in these months that there is a baby permanently attached to you. While moving around the kitchen, preparing dinner, your child may never be more than a half-inch away from you unless she's restrained in some way. Rest assured that you won't spend the rest of your life with your baby in such close proximity, but for a number of months, she will need the reassurance of your constant presence. She is so aware that there is a world bigger than her immediate environment, and that there are other people beyond those close to her. This awareness prods her to refuel her feelings of safety and security by firmly attaching herself to you.

If you are physically away from your baby much of the day due to outside work, your baby will take great reassurance from her constant caregiver. You, however, remain the most important emotional connection she has, and that connection is reinforced in the many hours you do spend together. Indeed, babies who feel closely connected to their mothers are the very ones who are most willing to try out more independent actions. Such words from you as "I'm here," and "It's okay," give your baby great strength.

You will see your baby's clinginess increase even more when she doesn't feel well or is under an unusual stress, such as having a new caregiver or moving to a new home or even visiting an unfamiliar place. At these times, she will probably want only you, and it will be difficult to convince her that anyone else will do.

Your baby is watching you for cues more closely than ever now. She builds her sense of trust and security with others in large measure from how you behave with these others. As she observes you being friendly and relaxed with a visiting relative or the grocery-store clerk, she begins to think that maybe these folks are okay and that she can feel comfortable with them too. Such a change in attitude takes time, but it does happen.

**What you can do**  To a large extent, you should keep doing what you have been all along. Even though you may find yourself getting irritated by your baby's refusal to be away from you and go happily to others, don't scold her or make her feel upset about her behavior. Instead, when you must turn her over to another, speak to her gently, explaining what is about to happen. Reassure her that she is safe, and that this person will take good care of her. Much of what you do now should be with the long-term goal of helping your baby feel safe and secure, even when it takes special sensitivity and extra time from your schedule.

Your baby will bask in any praise you give her. Cheer her efforts, and instill in her the pride of accomplishment. Your reaction to her is on its way to being increasingly important; she will look for it and you should be quick to give her positive feedback. Of course, when it is behavior you don't want her to repeat, you should tell her firmly, but gently, what you do want. Scolding isn't necessary or helpful; firmness is.

You can strengthen your baby's emerging sense of identity by using her name, and chatting with her about her body, and her favorite possessions. Keep up the games about her body, what you're doing, and what she can observe; have conversations about the toys and animals she is starting to love.

When your baby has minor accidents, all part of her learning, be sympathetic, of course. But don't overdo your response. A simple, straightforward, "Oh, dear, I see you fell," accompanied by a hug and a kiss—as well as a check to be sure everything actually is all right—is sufficient to let her know you are aware and caring. Too prolonged or too intense a response from you will lead her to feel insecure and frightened about what might happen if she ventures on.

## First friendships

Experts once believed that children didn't develop true friendships until around age 5, but research has now proven that even babies can be buddies. From birth on, infants who regularly spend time together can develop bonds. Children don't need to be in daily contact to become socially well adjusted; the occasional playdate can be a rewarding experience if you know what to expect. Following are the key stages in the development of early friendships:

**At 3 months,** infants love to watch each other. When a baby becomes fascinated by smiling at himself in the mirror, he's old enough to enjoy being with another infant. They won't play, but they will observe and try to touch each other. You must be watchful, of course, because infants can't always tell the difference between people and objects and might swipe at one another.

**Between about 4 and 10 months,** babies try to copy their pals. Increasing strength and mobility let your older baby do more than just look. He can crawl over to another child or extend an invitation by picking up a toy and showing it to the other baby. Often, a baby will sit beside a playmate and do exactly what she's doing; mimicking is a baby's way of communicating that she likes a friend and wants to be just like her.

**Toddlers'** new and familiar playmates. One-year-olds in child-care centers often spend all day with a special friend, and some even cry when their parent or the other child's parent comes to take them home. On playdates, it's ideal to have more than one model of various toys available to prevent conflicts. Although it may be hard for strong-willed toddlers to share, they are also starting to develop a sense of empathy. So don't be surprised if your child tries to console a tearful friend by offering a prized possession—even his bottle.

## Disciplining your baby

Late infancy is not too soon to discipline your child, though, of course, you cannot punish a baby. Discipline at this age involves helping your child understand limitations—both his own and yours.

At about 10 months of age, your baby begins to understand that she can do things that make you frown—and she may delight in achieving your attention this way. This isn't any kind of manipulation or power play on your baby's part. Instead it reflects her growing awareness that she can have an impact on her environment, a healthy realization. Even so, you will need to set boundaries for her now if she persists in behavior you want her to stop. A common type of behavior for a baby this age is to turn on the TV or radio, and, if allowed, she might do it over and over. If this happens, don't overreact by becoming angry or scolding. Simply say *no*, and take your baby away from the source of the behavior. Follow up by distracting her with a new activity. When she heads for the TV buttons again, respond in the same way. By being consistent and not overly reactive, you accomplish two things: You let her know that a behavior is not allowed, and you reinforce your position as teacher and helper without becoming her adversary.

A few babies, as they approach their first birthday, also attempt a temper tantrum of sorts. They will lie on the floor and scream when they are frustrated about something. Although you'll probably be alarmed by such a reaction, it's best to ignore the behavior, and, after the storm passes, hold your baby and calm her with quiet talk. By acting unimpressed, you'll discourage any further tantrums for at least a number of months more.

# Cognitive development

If it hasn't already started, imitation will definitely appear and increase in these months as your baby learns how the world works. What he sees you do with your hands, he wants to do, too; this can work to your advantage in helping your baby with such skills as eating with a spoon. Imitation is a sophisticated social skill because, for example, when your baby waves good-bye, his gesture not only serves as a form of communication, but also elicits a response from the other person, often a smile and a wave back, which lets your child know that his attempts at communicating are successful.

Your child's verbal abilities—both speech and comprehension—will move forward now, but you'll probably be most impressed with how much your baby understands. He will shake his head *no* a great deal; don't assume, though, that he means a negative answer. It is easier to shake the head in that direction than the up and down for a positive response. He is practicing his newfound movement, not necessarily being negative.

He continues to be fascinated by seeing things in different ways and angles. You may be surprised the day he starts blinking—and keeps blinking, day after day. This isn't to indicate a vision problem or a nervous tick; your baby has discovered that blinking changes what he is looking at. It's interesting enough to keep doing it.

This is the time when a distinct hand preference begins to emerge in many babies. It is most likely the right hand, in keeping with the statistics, but if your child shows a preference for the left, don't discourage him. He will be able to make a few scribbles with a fat crayon, and it will most likely be with the same hand each time.

## What your baby knows

Now your baby is adding to the already impressive amount of knowledge he has built. His memory retention is greater almost every day. If you placed a toy somewhere out of sight yesterday, your baby will go looking for it there today. He has the usual daily routines easily memorized; he knows mealtime indicators, when you are preparing a bath, and the procedure for dressing him. In fact, he may well grab the spoon away from you before you start serving up lunch and attempt to feed you with it.

Communications of all kinds are rapidly rising. Your baby may see the picture of a kitten and respond with a meow if there is a family cat or if he is otherwise familiar with the sound that a cat makes. He understands when you shake your head no or say the word; indeed, he understands many words now—a hearing vocabulary of several hundred words is usual by the time a baby is a year old. Ask your child to hand you the wooden spoon he is holding, and he'll probably do so gladly. He recognizes what many sounds imply now as well. If he hears the squeak of his brother's toy robot from another room, he may go looking for his sibling. Likewise, the sound of the key opening the door will send him scurrying to welcome you or his other parent home if he's used to such a daily arrival.

Hand gestures are also on the rise and an important new way your baby has figured out to communicate with you. He knows to point squarely at what interests him for you to give it to him. Should he be ready for you to pick him up, he will reach his arms up to signal his wish. Yet another small gesture that tells you what he is thinking is when he extends his hand, palm up, and opens and closes his fist. Translation: "I want more."

His babbling will be melodic now as he moves faster and faster toward being able to talk. This seems to be a type of sentence he is putting together, but only he is privy to the meaning. He probably has at least several words he can say that others can understand, even as many as eight or ten.

Sure in his knowledge that he belongs to the family, your baby will exercise his rights as a family member. He knows what toys are his, and will protest if he doesn't want another person to take one.

**How your baby learns**   You, and the others around your baby, continue to be his most important teachers. Constant observation of your actions and responses is his principle learning tool; because he will have made mimicry a big part of his daily behavior, you are apt to become aware of how very watchful your baby is. He will grab a washcloth in the bath and attempt to wash your face as you do his. Your baby will imitate distinctive vocal expressions you have, whether a particular intonation, or even a swear word muttered at times. He will wave his hand as you do, and cock his head just the way you do when puzzled or amused.

His ability to absorb concepts is marching ahead, and it is exciting to watch him figure things out—the cup that fits into a larger cup, the way the rings fit on a stacking cone, that if he presses the doorbell, it results in a buzz. Anything he can hold he will study from many different angles—up, down, sideways, and from the back—to understand it better. He will shake it to find what kind of noise the object may make, and toss it down to see what happens when it hits the floor.

The games you play with your baby now both teach and reinforce his learning. He loves these activities because they're with you, but also because he is learning as you play together. He is listening to the words you speak as well; many of your descriptions may still elude him, but a surprising number of them are taking hold. With his memory improving each day, he is able to store information and to build on it. He will now stay with a toy or activity for up to 15 minutes at a time, and the increased attention span naturally helps him absorb that much more information.

**What you can do**  In your role of beloved teacher, you can be even more specific now with your baby. Instead of simply pointing to the picture of a dog and making a doglike noise, you should add words describing the dog—its size, color, how big its ears are, and so on. Do this in many of your conversations with your baby; point out how you are sorting socks by colors, how the big books go on the low shelves, why the large cookies won't fit in the small jar.

Encourage your baby to do as much for himself as possible. Allow him to flip the light switch on and off, to press the elevator buttons (with your help, of course!), and turn on the sink faucets. Again, explain to him what each thing is for and what will happen as a result of his actions.

Your games with your baby can become more complicated as you see his awareness gaining. Now when you play hide-and-seek, you can tuck yourself behind a chair completely, only calling to him if he is totally at a loss about where you are. Sit on the floor and roll the ball to him, and cheer him on when he realizes that he can roll it back to you. Use lots of counting games throughout the day, and add imitation to your playtime. Make silly expressions and watch him do them for you; clap in rhythms; open and close your fists; rub your head or tummy, and pull your ear. If you create a simple sequence of these, he will soon be able to anticipate what comes next and beat you to it.

Books will be more interesting than ever to your baby now. Because he understands more of the words, the bright colors and pictures he has enjoyed all along have greater meaning to him. Ask him to point to certain things on each page, a challenge that will delight him. Older babies are also enthralled by all sorts of tunes.

Experiment with a wide variety of music to see what your child likes. When he hears the familiar beat of a melody he knows and loves, he'll smile, wave his arms and legs, and move in eager anticipation.

Keep adding to the box of household items with which your baby can play. His love of water play, which will go on for some years, starts around this time. Give him plastic cups for the bath and watch how he'll pour water in and out and back and forth. Back in the kitchen, with wooden spoons and metal pots, he'll have a nice percussion instrument to pound on. If you add a baby brush or comb to his collection, he will probably attempt to groom his own hair.

At this point, you should be used to having an ongoing conversation with your baby all day long. This is when his awareness that things and people have names is starting to form, and you can help him a great deal by attaching those proper names. Although you may be reluctant to give up favored sounds for your baby's bottle, blanket, and the like, be sure to use the proper words for them as well. This is an appropriate acknowledgment that your little baby is soon to become a talking toddler.

## Games babies love

Your newly minted baby delights in just about any activity that puts you two together and allows him to control some of the action. You'll see in his game playing that he is using play to practice what he wants to learn. Some of his favorites include:

**Drop it** The next time your baby tosses dinner to the floor, remember that for him, it's a lesson in physics. Once your baby realizes that he can release an object at will, he will want to play the "drop it" game again and again. But he is not doing this to drive you crazy. When he drops his cup and listens for the sound it makes when it lands, your baby is learning about cause and effect. He is also discovering that different objects have different properties: The cup stays the same when it hits the floor, but the milk spreads out. And when you pick up that cup, your baby is learning that his actions influence yours, and he enjoys communicating with you.

**One more time** You go up a step to get from point A to point B. Your new toddler goes up a step to go up a step. Practicing a new skill again and again assures your child that he's really mastered it.

**What if?**  Continuing to experiment, but now with a higher level of understanding of what might work, your child will enjoy activities that involve unstructured play equipment, such as cardboard boxes, blocks, and other items that he can manipulate.

# Communicating with your baby

While most babies know a few words such as *mama* and *dada*, communicating more complex ideas is not easy for kids who don't yet have large vocabularies. A type of communication called "baby signs," however, allows nontalkers to say what's on their minds by using a form of sign language.

There's nothing very complex about the process. You and your child probably already have a useful "vocabulary" of gestures— waving hands to say *good-bye* for instance. Using baby signs, you can expand that repertoire, creating gestures that you both understand.

**Using "baby signs"**  Start with a few gestures that are easy to remember. You can rotate your hand in a gesture that signals opening the door while saying, "Let's go out." Use the sign each time you talk about going out.

As your child becomes familiar with the notion of signing, add ideas that matter to him. If he likes juice, create a simple gesture such as bringing your cupped hand up to your mouth. Repeat this gesture when you say, "Would you like some juice?" and "Here's your juice." Use the gestures often. Always say the word or phrase as you use the sign. It won't; be long before your child catches on and mimics you. Be alert to his own gesturing, too. Once he knows that movements can stand for ideas, he will find the gesture that works for him. For instance, he might move his fingers in imitation of playing the piano to communicate that he wants to play his piano. Or he might flap his arms in the air to tell you about a bird he sees. Just as you would praise an attempt at verbal speech, let your child know you are delighted with his attempts to communicate by signing.

Don't worry that signing will take the place of verbal communication or that signing will slow down your child's attempts to use words. On the contrary, these nonverbal "conversations" only serve to prod your child on toward further communication.

# CHAPTER 7

# 13 to 18 Months

**W**elcome to the world of the toddler! No other age is described by a word derived from a verb, but mobility certainly marks this stage of development. Between 13 and 18 months, the rapid physical growth that occurred in the first year now slows down as your child's ability to get around accelerates. Walking, throwing, and crawling up and down stairs take up much of her time and attention—and yours!

As your toddler moves away from you physically, she also begins to separate emotionally. During these months, your child will become increasingly aware that she is a person with her own will and wishes, anxious to explore the world.

This exploration leads to giant intellectual gains. Although your toddler isn't ready to carry on lengthy verbal conversations just yet, she is listening and learning constantly. Her hearing vocabulary grows rapidly during this period and so she understands much more of what you say. This is an exciting metamorphosis— the growth of a baby into a child.

# *Physical development*

Watch out—your baby is (or is about to be)—up on two feet and ready to go. As he grows taller and more slender, his movements will become more coordinated and agile. He needs plenty of room and lots of opportunities to experiment with his newfound physical abilities.

## Physical changes

Your baby's first-year growth spurt is slowing down now and won't reach such a fast pace again until early adolescence. Slow and steady growth will mark this second year. At 13 months, the average child weighs about 21 pounds and is 30 inches tall; by 18 months, this child will weigh about 24 pounds and will be about 32 inches tall. At the beginning of this year, your child still looks like a baby with his head and abdomen being proportionately larger than the rest of his body. His arms and legs are still relatively short and soft, rather than muscular, and his face still has its round fullness. As he nears 18 months, you'll see him begin to mature, developing more slender and muscular childlike features.

**What your child can do**  At this age, each day marks a milestone in physical growth as babies learn to toddle, walk, run, and climb.

**Gross motor skills**  Your baby can walk unassisted. Notice that she bends her trunk slightly forward, thrusts her arms out in front, and waddles with her legs wide apart. After a month or two of practicing these first steps, she will progress from this wide-based, stiff-legged gait to a more rhythmic step with knee-bending and a heel-toe step with her feet closer together.

Your baby can now throw things and will practice this new skill over and over again. The throwing motion is still immature and is more like a pushing action than an over-arm pitch.

Stacking blocks takes on a new fascination for your child because she can now stack two blocks herself with agility. Given the blocks, the opportunity, and the encouragement, she will keep trying for more.

Your baby can now crawl up and down stairs, an activity she'll want to try wherever there are stairs, so make sure that safety gates are secured at the top and bottom of all staircases. By about 18 months, she will learn to walk upstairs with you holding her hand. As her climbing skills develop, she may learn to climb out of the crib, high chair, and stroller.

**Fine motor skills** As your toddler's fine motor coordination improves, she will be better able to grasp small objects with her thumb and forefinger and no longer grab everything in a fist as she did a few months ago. This new skill enables her to manipulate small objects. She will take great pleasure in covering and uncovering containers and putting pegs into holes.

She can also remove small objects from a cup and put three or more objects into a container. She prefers to play with several small objects rather than with only one. She will pick them up one by one, drop them, and pick them up again. Be sure, of course, that the objects with which she plays are too large to put into her mouth, unless they are edible, such as bits of cereal or cubes of fruit.

When given a crayon, your child will scribble. Though she can lift the crayon in her pincer grasp to examine it, she will hold it in her fist when she first attempts to make marks with it, scrawling back-and-forth lines and an occasional wiper-blade semicircle. A bit later on, at about age 2, you'll see her begin to hold the crayon between her thumb and forefinger and control her waving arm. It won't be until about age 2½ or 3 that she'll begin to concentrate and think about making certain shapes and patterns, however.

**What you can do** Each success in physical ability is marked first by a trial-and-error process. To become physically competent, your child needs daily opportunities to explore, try, fail, and try again, so don't immediately step in to ease the way. Give your child lots of room and time to try new things, to move from place to place, and to risk "failure." Remember, she is unaware of any timetable to which others expect her to adhere, so she does not judge herself as failing when she needs to try again.

Toys such as blocks and sorters let her practice the skills of finger dexterity. Give her soft balls and racquets to practice eye-hand coordination and a push-pull toy that supports her efforts to stand on her own. Let her kick, roll, and toss a ball to boost body confidence.

Young toddlers also need a helping hand that shows them how to do things. Put your hand over your baby's hand and show her how to push the buttons on a new toy. Hold clay in your baby's

For information about your child's nutritional needs, see **pages 500–18**.

## Mealtime Routines

If you can't find any consistency in the time your child needs to eat, try creating a routine around the act of eating itself. Whether he eats three or ten meals a day, serve each meal at the table. Don't let your child get into the habit of eating while wandering around the house or when watching TV. Have him sit in the same chair or booster seat each time and give him the same bowl, cup, and utensils. This kind of ritual gives meals and snacks an important place in each day.

hands to show her how to mold it and change its shape. This kind of hands-on help combined with your own example will encourage your child to give new physical feats a try, and always, to try again.

# Good eating habits

While food is central to survival, most toddlers are not terribly concerned about eating. Yes, they want to satisfy their hunger. But satisfying you, eating on your schedule, tasting "icky" things, and eating beyond the point at which they are full make no sense to your child.

It's important from the start that your child learn what food is—the fuel that drives the engine. It's equally important that she not learn that food is a means of control and that eating is something she does to please you. To help your toddler develop good eating attitudes:

- **Serve small portions.**
- **Ask her to try foods,** but don't insist that she eat everything you place in front of her.
- **Make mealtime pleasant.**
- **Help your child recognize hunger.** When she asks for a treat, ask, "Are you hungry?" Help her see the connection between hunger and food, rather than letting her think that food satisfies other needs, such as reducing boredom.
- **Have your child eat sitting down.** Eating on the run is dangerous. It also diminishes the pleasure that should accompany eating.

**Scheduling your toddler's meals and snacks** Your child's physical growth is beginning to slow down now which causes a corresponding decrease in appetite—justifying the toddler label of "picky eater." It is a mistake, however, to insist on a three-meal-a-day routine without between-meal-snacking in the hopes of improving a toddler's appetite. Young children's stomachs have a limited capacity for food; toddlers need to eat frequent snacks in order to consume an adequate amount of food each day. The trick is to set up an eating routine that satisfies the child's need for small meals without turning your kitchen into a 24-hour open buffet.

Although some flexibility is necessary, a consistent eating routine helps toddlers regulate their appetites and also gives them a sense of security and emotional reassurance. When setting up this routine, watch your child for signs of hunger and create a meal and snack schedule around his needs. Is he always looking for food in the mornings? Does he refuse food if his play time is interrupted? Can he wait for dinner to be served, or does be become whiny while you're cooking? Don't fret if your child refuses food at the family's dinner time. If you can consistently offer food at the times of day when you know your child is hungry and willing to sit down to eat, you may be able to avoid many of the food battles that are characteristic of toddlers.

Your child's eating routine can better encourage good eating habits and provide for his nutritional needs if you remember these few pointers:

• **Don't expect your child to sit down like an adult and enjoy a complete meal.** Toddlers can't sit still for very long nor can they eat large quantities at one sitting, so rarely will they need to be at the table for more than 10 or 15 minutes. If you make your child stay longer than necessary, you'll find that he'll amuse himself by playing with the food.

• **Don't try to force your toddler to eat.** Mealtime becomes battle time when toddlers discover that refusing nutritious food gets their parents' attention. If you beg, bargain, and barter over food, you'll establish a routine of refusal rather than a routine of eating.

• **Don't judge your child's intake by what he eats at each meal.** Young children will rarely eat a lot or a variety of foods at one sitting. Instead, consider his intake over a 24-hour period.

Most often you'll find that your child is much more interested in running and playing than in sitting and eating. Scheduling a routine of frequent breaks for nutritious mini-meals is the best way to accommodate your child's on-the-run lifestyle.

### How much juice?

*"My 14-month-old prefers juice to any other drink or food. Is this healthy? How can I get her to eat a more balanced diet?"*

Kids like the sweet taste of juice, and a half cup a day isn't harmful to most kids. Certain juices, especially orange juice, are good sources of vitamin C, but juice is also loaded with sugar, and excessive juice intake may lead to obesity or shorter stature in children, as well as diarrhea, abdominal pain, and, in extreme cases, malnutrition.

A 1997 study of 223 children, published in the journal *Pediatrics,* found that children who drink 12 or more ounces of juice a day are more likely to be either short for their age or overweight. The researchers speculate that the kids who were short for their age had filled up on juice instead of eating more nutritious foods like milk, vegetables, and whole fruit. The researchers also theorize that those children who were obese ate a normal amount of food, but increased their caloric intake by drinking lots of juice.

To help your child eat a more nutritionally balanced diet, start by offering her whole fruits, along with a glass of water. The water will quench her thirst, while the fruit will satisfy her sweet tooth. Make milk more tempting by adding chocolate or strawberry flavoring, and give it to her in place of juice. Also try substituting noncaloric, fruit-flavored seltzer for fruit juice.

### A dislike of crunchy foods
*"At 12 months, my son still refuses to eat any crunchy foods. He eats baby foods from a jar, but won't eat other solids. How do I encourage his interest in a greater variety of food?"*

Many babies eat only pureed or mashed foods during their second six months of life. Mushy foods are easy to swallow and have a soft texture that's pleasing to infants. It's likely that your son finds crunchy foods intimidating. He may not like the way they feel on his teeth or gums since hard pieces of vegetables can irritate tender gums. Gradually introduce your child to crunchy foods by mixing them with soft ones. For example, sprinkle a little crisp rice cereal on top of yogurt, or spread cream cheese or mashed bananas onto a cracker. Offer him small portions and let him experiment.

### No green foods
*"My 1-year-old is a very picky eater. She likes anything white, yellow, or orange, but won't eat anything green. Is she getting the vitamins she needs without eating green vegetables?"*

If your daughter is eating a variety of nongreen vegetables, as well as whole fruits, she is probably getting her quota of vitamins. But you should continue to encourage her to eat green vegetables by placing just a few string beans or some mashed zucchini on her plate, along with the rest of her food. Also try mixing green veggies with other foods she does like. For example, if she loves cooked carrots and corn, add a few string beans to the mix. Top green vegetables with something appealing, like spaghetti sauce. Or grate zucchini or broccoli into a muffin mix.

# Great physical activities for toddlers

Your 13- to 18-month-old needs lots of active play—running, jumping, climbing—to develop her physical, emotional, and mental dexterity. Physical games let her practice muscle coordination, focus her abundant energy in positive ways, and help relieve the stress of trying to learn so many new things each day. With her suddenly increased activity level and ability to get into things that were once out of reach, your supervision of her activities needs to be focused and constant. But rather than anxiously hovering and interrupting your toddler's physical explorations, work toward creating a safe environment where your child can play freely and joyfully. Make time for plenty of outdoor play. Consider enrolling in a "Mom-and-Me" or other play group where your child can have access to a variety of safe and challenging play equipment. And for hours of fun at home, try these activities with your newly mobile child:

**Climbing**  Climbing games are a good way to satisfy your toddler's desire to scale new heights as he practices his coordination and balancing skills. Through repetition, he'll internalize safety precautions, learning, for instance, that holding onto a banister or your hand gives him the security to keep from toppling over. To encourage climbing, start with a staircase at home, which is especially fun because it's usually blocked off from his easy access. During playtime, let your toddler climb up and then teach him how to turn around at the top and come down backward on his tummy. Later, try another approach and let him come down in a sitting position, step-by-step.

**Gymnastics**  Tumbling on a soft surface gives toddlers a real sense of mastery over their environment as they jump, fall, and roll without fear of getting hurt. Take an old mattress or the one off your own bed and put in on the floor, away from any sharp-cornered furniture, and let the games begin!

**Throwing and catching**  Most toddlers are too young to toss or catch a ball, but they're not too young to enjoy the challenge. They'll have more success and less frustration if you provide easy-to-catch balls they can get a grip on—those made of soft cloth with a clutchable surface or bean bags that change shape to fit snugly into little hands.

*For information on creating safe play areas, see **pages 786–88**.*

### Handling a fearless toddler

*"My 17-month-old daughter has absolutely no fears. If I turn my back for a second, she climbs or runs into trouble. How can I get her to slow down?"*

Your daughter is old enough to follow clear and logical rules if you enforce them consistently. Make sure she knows where she can and cannot play. Periodically remind her of these boundaries, especially before you turn your back. Give her plenty of opportunity for running and climbing in appropriate settings and with your supervision. At other times, you can encourage calm and quiet play by praising her whenever she plays quietly indoors. Don't tiptoe past a quiet moment fearing you'll break the spell; stop and tell her how proud you are that she's able to play so. This will encourage her to do it more often. Also be sure to praise her active moments when she's following the safety rules you've established, since you don't want to encourage only quiet play, which, for her, would be unnatural. If nothing you try slows her down when you need her to be, you'll have to take solace in the knowledge that this whirl of excess energy usually slows down on its own somewhat by the time she's ready for school. In the meantime you'll need to be vigilant and patient.

## Active games for toddlers

In addition to unstructured physical activities, these more formal games will delight your newly mobile child:

**Ring-around-the-rosey**  This old-time favorite is not only hilariously funny at the end when everyone falls down, it is good for helping your child learn team work and coordinated balance.

**Lap rides**  Whether climbing onto your knee or your lap, your child will love the flip-flop feeling of being jostled around. He feels the thrill of being daring and adventurous as long as you're always in control and don't let him fall or jostle his head or neck.

**Hide-and-seek**  With his increased mobility, as well as his maturing mind, your young toddler loves to scurry out of sight knowing you'll be right behind to find him. Like a little ostrich, he believes that if he can't see you, you can't see him.

**Simon Says**  Given your child's natural inclination to copy your every move, this game is great fun as well as being a vocabulary booster. Make your moves simple: lift your arms up, squat down, make a funny face, kick one leg. Forget the rules about moving only when "Simon says" and in this toddler version, no one is ever "out."

### Toddler nap times

*"How many hours a day should a toddler nap?"*

There's no hard-and-fast rule. By 12 months, most toddlers usually take a morning nap and an afternoon nap, each an hour or two in length. At some point during the second year, the majority of kids start to stay awake during the morning and take only a one- or two-hour nap in the afternoon. But the daytime sleep needs vary from child to child and an individual toddler's sleep patterns may change from month to month. The best authority on how much sleep a toddler needs is the child herself. If she's moody and irritable, appears sleepy or overactive, you can bet she needs more sleep.

# *Emotional development*

How exciting and yet how frightening for your child to learn that he is his own person with his own feelings, thoughts, needs, and interests. His emotional development during this period will focus on this realization and the joys and fears of experimenting with independence.

## Your toddler's feelings

Your 1-year-old is becoming increasingly aware of "self" as a separate person, with power, and limitations. He is struggling to be independent and to control other people. As he goes about this task of defining self and establishing exactly what that means he will experience many abrupt emotional changes—swinging from wails of laughter one minute to screams of anger the next.

During this period, your child will become demonstratively affectionate. You will be the honored recipient of many kisses and hugs as your child explores the good feelings that come from physical contact.

Your baby continues to respond to praise. He enjoys applause and will repeat any performance that elicits response. It is your smiles,

## Finding Time for Yourself

You make time, somehow, for all the important things you must do each day involving your child, your spouse, your home, and your work. The easiest thing to let slip is finding time for yourself. But time alone, pursuing your own interests, is personally renewing. Time spent enjoying adult company enhances those relationships. So any time you can carve out for meeting your own needs serves your family and others who depend on you. Here are some ways to ensure some personal time.

**Schedule dates regularly.** Mark your calendar with regular appointment times to do those things you want to do—from having an every-other-Saturday night dinner out with your spouse to attending a class at the gym. Treat this schedule as seriously as any business appointment.

**Develop daily soothing rituals.** These needn't take long, but they should be regular and satisfying—anything from waking up 15 minutes earlier than the rest of the family so you can enjoy your morning paper and a cup of coffee in peace to taking a brisk daily walk after dinner, while your spouse watches your child.

**Engage others in your interests.** Rather than postponing your involvement in activities that matter to you, involve your family, either by bringing them along or by helping you find the time. If, for instance, you enjoy visiting art museums, take your baby in a backpack, or have another family member watch him while you go.

**Create a childcare co-op.** Take turns with another parent watching the children, while the other gets time to relax on her own.

applause, and praise that encourage him to practice his new skills until he reaches mastery.

You will also see the onset of negativism as he becomes willful, stubborn, and hardheaded. He will demand a great deal of personal attention and will throw things when he is angry. Narcissism is at its peak now and brings with it many new feelings including jealousy, self-confidence, anxiety, pride, and frustration.

Along with these new emotions comes the ability to express them in more subtle or indirect ways. Your child will go through phases in which he will be clingy in the morning and very independent in the afternoon. He may develop a fear of anything new. He may have difficulty sleeping. And he may have periods of regression in which he acts like a younger baby.

**How your 13- to 18-month-old develops secure relationships** During the past year, you have laid the foundation for a secure relationship with your child by teaching him that he can trust you—to feed him when he's hungry, change him when he's wet, hug him when he cries. This need to trust you continues to drive his relationship with you during this second year. He needs you to demonstrate your love with kisses and praise. He needs you to show your confidence in his faltering attempts to master physical skills. He needs you to notice his many accomplishments and show him the way to the next level. These kinds of concrete demonstrations tell your child that you understand his needs for emotional support.

At the same time that your child is seeing himself as a separate person, he is recognizing that adults too are separate beings with feelings of their own. He is learning to read your emotions and body language and will use these cues to decide what kind of relationship he can have with you and others each day. He's learning which of his behaviors win approval and affection and which ones make people angry. He's able to understand when you feel tense or tired, and sensing these feelings in you will make him tense, too. He will watch you closely to pick up signals about strangers and decide from your posture and expressions whether he should feel friendly or threatened. Without saying a word, you are constantly teaching your child how to relate to others.

It is not always easy to be emotionally supportive of a 1-year-old. In this narcissistic stage, your child's interpersonal relationships are almost completely dominated by the desire to take, not give. He takes your love, your help, your care, and hasn't any concept of returning the favor. But behind this apparent selfish attitude a secure parent-child relationship is forming.

**What you can do**  You can meet your child's emotional needs by taking time for lots of holding and touching. Your child notices how you show affection to him, your spouse, his siblings, and others, and he will learn to express his emotions by imitating you.

As you attend to your toddler's emotional needs with your constant love and affection, you can also help him gain self-reliance by providing him with opportunities to practice self-comforting. Don't immediately rush to the rescue every time he cries out in frustration or simply from fatigue. And don't get into the rocking-baby-to-sleep habit that teaches him to need you in order to fall asleep. When you're sure your baby is clean, fed, and in good health, let him try to fall asleep on his own. If he awakens during the night, give him a moment

## Step-by-Step Learning

During active times of the day, you can give your child a boost in self-confidence and self-esteem if you look for opportunities for him to feel a sense of mastery. This is easily accomplished if you break difficult tasks that your child is determined to do into small, manageable pieces. If he wants to feed himself, give him easy-to-handle finger foods. If he wants to build a tower of blocks, give him three large blocks rather than ten small blocks.

to calm himself back to sleep instead of responding immediately to the first sound. Falling asleep on his own or falling back to sleep usually takes only a few minutes. Give him the freedom to discharge tension and fatigue with a brief, self-calming cry. You can also help by giving him a comfort object like a blanket or stuffed animal when he's tired.

Strong emotional health depends on a toddler's ability to be self-calming, self-confident, and self-controlled when expressing emotions. With your help your child will begin to learn these things this year.

## Encouraging independence

This second year of life is a grand adventure for your child. Your once-dependent infant becomes the toddler who goes off to explore her world and begins the process of becoming a separate person with her own identity. Through the course of each and every day, there are many things you can do to encourage this growing need for independence.

• **Let her go.** More than anything else, walking sets the stage for separation. The capacity to see a wider world and the ability to run away from you gives your toddler a great sense of power. So let her walk in safe areas without hovering over her every move. Give her freedom to move away from you.

• **Let her explore.** Your toddler wants to find out things for herself now. She wants to know how cabinets open. She wants to take off her own coat. She wants to figure out how to get the spoon into her mouth. Don't do everything for your child all the time. Your intentions are good ones—you want to make life easier and happier for your child. But as your child reaches for independence, she has to learn all the many things she can do for herself.

• **Be patient.** It's so much faster and easier to pick up your child and plop her on the couch. But when you do that, you do the walking and climbing for her and increase her dependence on you. Slow down and let your child walk, climb, explore, try, fail, and try again. This is how she becomes her own person.

• **Practice separating.** Your toddler wants to separate from you, but only for a minute or two. She will still cry when you leave her with a sitter or even a beloved grandparent. If you try to avoid these tears by never leaving home without your child, you'll deprive her of the opportunity to practice coping with the sense of loss brought on by separation.

*For ideas on easing separation anxiety, see **page 108**.*

- **Be in charge.** While becoming independent, your child is also realizing that she is a relatively small, separate individual who must learn to cope on her own and who will not get what she wants simply because she wants it. She does not want to take a bath, but you insist. She does not want to leave the park, but you take her and leave anyway. Each time she does not get what she wants, she realizes that her desires and yours are not the same and that you and she are separate people—a very important discovery on the road to independence.
- **Be ready with praise and admiration.** Your little explorer never strays too far from your side. In fact, she is constantly concerned with your whereabouts, wants to share with you all her new skills and accomplishments, and demands your involvement in all her activities. This may not seem like the roots of independence, but it is—it's a plea for positive reinforcement that gives your child the courage to continue exploring. Your loving admiration is nourishing her development. Your pride in her achievements is reflected back to her, letting her take pride in herself; your pleasure in her confirms her self-worth. It is these things that feed independence.

*For more on discipline, see **pages 379–403**.*

### Handling a toddler's strong opinions

*"I never thought a 1-year-old could be so opinionated about his clothing! What can I do to respect my son's wishes while keeping him warm enough to go out?"*

Your 1-year-old probably doesn't really care what he wears when he goes out, but he knows he certainly doesn't want to wear whatever *you* say he has to wear. The battle here is not about fashion; it's about autonomy. You can keep your son warm without arguments if you let him choose which sweater he wants to wear, which pair of gloves, which hat, and so on. Don't overwhelm him with too many choices—limit his options to two, but let him feel that his selection of the red hat over the blue hat puts him in charge of his clothing.

# The family bed

Now that your child is a toddler, you may be making the decision for the first time or rethinking the decision you've made earlier. For parents whose child has been sharing their bed, you may be concerned that your child's growing awareness and increased nighttime mobility means it's time to move him to a bed of his own. Or, if your child has been in his own crib, he may now be able to climb

**This may sound crazy, but...**

*"I miss the complete dependency of an infant. Now that my 1-year-old is growing up, I just want a return to the time when he was content to be in my arms. Am I normal?"*

Yes, you are normal. It's hard for many parents to give up the time of infancy when children are completely dependent on them. But, like all parents, you can't hold your baby back. As he grows and moves away from the protection of your arms, you will move with him into the next stage and soon find yourself regretting that it too must pass. This process of hesitantly moving into stages and regretfully moving out of them will continue for the rest of your parenting days. The key to feeling content in your parent/child relationship is to learn to enjoy the moment and to accept the inevitable changes that come as children grow.

out—a clear signal that it's time to consider moving him out of the crib. When he crawls into your bed, it may simply be easier to let him stay there.

In many cultures, generational bed sharing is a common practice. Those who support this practice point out that children gain a great deal of security by having Mom and Dad right there if they should happen to wake up at night. Those opposed to the practice point out that children who share their parents' bed develop limited self-reliance. And there's the issue of parental privacy.

While it's true that children do enjoy the nighttime closeness that bed sharing brings, it's also true that regular bed sharing can actually make a child more anxious in the long run. Learning how to sleep in his own room and in his own bed increases your child's sense of autonomy and, ultimately, his sense of safety. Continuing to sleep with his parents, however, can rob him of his ability to soothe himself and to trust in his own ability to accomplish sleep.

The choice you make for your family is a very personal one. Should you choose to invite (or simply allow) your child into your bed, keep these things in mind:

• **Your sex life will be curtailed.** There's no room for spontaneity in bed when your child is under the covers with you.

• **It is a hard habit to break.** Many kids remain in their parents' bed well into their preteen years. For some kids, the move to their own bed will be traumatic at whatever age it occurs; for some, moving into their own beds when they're preschoolers or gradeschoolers comes naturally and without much fuss. It's just about impossible, however, to predict which child will follow which pattern.

• **Sleep may be interrupted.** The more elbows and knees that occupy a space, the more likely a few midnight collisions. If yours is a shared bed, opt for a queen- or king-size, if possible.

- **Parents need to agree.** If one parent resents the child being in the same bed, that's a good reason not to begin or continue the practice. Your child is better served by having his parents getting along than he is by sharing nighttime with you and your spouse.
- **Consider a compromise.** If you'd enjoy having your child in your bed some of the time, but not all of the time, find a time that works best for all involved, such as letting him come into your bed when he awakens in the morning before you're ready to get up.

## The fears of toddlers

One-year-olds vary in their vulnerability to fears. Some cope better than others; some are very sensitive to these emotions. It is impossible to predict exactly how your child will handle frightening and confusing events. Things that your child enjoyed yesterday may terrify her today. Situations that prompted screams in the morning may pass unnoticed by dinner. This is the world of a toddler.

Generally, three things spark the fears and the frustrations that accompany the fears of toddlers: (1) anything that thwarts their drive for independence, (2) anything that thwarts their need for dependence, (3) anything strange or unknown. On the one hand, your toddler seeks autonomy and fights against any effort to restrain or help her. She'll scream when you try to put her in the high chair at a time she thinks is inconvenient; she'll become infuriated if you try to show her how her new toy works. This "I-do-it" mentality can be extremely frustrating for her because so often what she wants to do far exceeds her abilities. On the other hand, she wants your support and protection even more. She'll shy away from strangers, cling to your leg, and holler when separated from you. This need for your presence and protection feeds her fear of separation, making her anxious and afraid.

The intensity of these feelings are new for your child. She has not developed defenses against anxiety and doesn't know how to cope with the range of emotions she feels. Unfortunately, parents' reactions may make things worse: When a baby gets hysterically angry, the parent may get angry, too. When a baby gets clingy, the parent may push her away in an attempt to make her brave. When the baby throws a tantrum out of frustration, it's all too easy for the parent to get frustrated, too.

These negative reactions only serve to slow down the growing-up process. Yet overreacting with understanding may backfire, too. Too much help and protection will clash with your child's need for independence. Too little will spark his fear of abandonment. As his feelings get out of control, he becomes frightened by their intensity and the original frustration transforms into fear.

So what can you do? Most fears and frustrations are best handled with patience, understanding, and just a bit of know-how. When your child collapses in frustration or cries out in fear, try these strategies:

• **Make allowances for inexperience.** Remember that children have an innate fear of the unknown and the unmanageable. They do not have background experience to rely on and so they approach new situations, people, and things with trepidation. Too little experience causes them to make broad and often erroneous associations:

## *Helping Your Toddler Make Decisions*

**The ability to make decisions is a learned skill that your 1-year-old can begin working on right now—if you give him the chance. To help:**

### Do...

offer reasonable choices, encouraging your child to select an option you can accept. For example, ask, "Would you like apple juice or milk?" or "Do you want the big truck or the little truck?" Limit the options, since too many choices can make a child feel overwhelmed or angry. Allow nonverbal children to make their choices known by pointing.

respect your child's decision and praise it as a good choice.

### Don't...

ask open-ended questions. If you ask, "What would you like for lunch?" you may get an answer you can't live with. Instead, ask, "Would you like a cheese or a bologna sandwich?" Likewise, refrain from asking questions you don't really want your child to answer, such as, "Don't you think it's time to clean up now?" If it's time to clean up, simply state the fact.

ask a child who is tired or hungry to decide anything. At these times, your child needs you to be wholly in charge.

push decision-making on a child who isn't ready for it. If your child can't handle choices now, try again in a couple of months.

If one dog barks too loud, aren't all dogs scary? If the boy in the story got lost, won't I? If my mother is afraid of spiders, shouldn't I be, too? These are not silly fears; they are very real and serious to your child.

- **Respect her fears.** Resist the temptation to make your child face her fears. Confronting fear will never help a child overcome it. Expecting a child to be "tough" only makes her more anxious. Instead, acknowledge the fear by saying something like, "I know that loud sirens can be scary." Praise your child for any effort, no matter how small, to overcome a fear. If she decides to deal with thunder by putting her fingers in her ears, praise her for being so clever.

- **Offer matter-of-fact reassurances.** Don't overdo your sympathetic response. Too much coddling may convince your child that there really is something to be afraid of. Matter-of-factly acknowledge the fear, praise efforts to deal with it, and assure your child that you will keep her from harm.

- **Don't introduce fear where none exists.** As a large dog approaches, don't be a catalyst for your child's fears by saying, "Don't be afraid." Maybe fear hadn't entered her mind. And don't threaten fearful punishments like, "If you don't behave in the store, I'm going to leave without you."

- **Create opportunities to explore fear-inducing objects and events in safety.** If your child fixates her fear on a particular circumstance or object, try to desensitize her response. If she's afraid of the vacuum, let her get acquainted with it while it's unplugged. Let her stand across the room with your spouse while you turn it on. Show her the off switch so she knows that you're in control. If she's afraid of dogs, let her watch a movie or read her a book about a child and a loving dog. Let her watch children with their dogs from a distance. Introduce her to a very small dog from a few feet away. Slowly let her decide when she feels comfortable about facing the object of her fear.

- **Expose your child to a wide range of experiences.** Most fears are rooted in the strange, the unexpected, and the unmanageable. Few children are afraid of steps and doors because they have seen them every day of their lives. Likewise, few kids fear people dressed as bus drivers because they are familiar, but someone wearing a clown costume might be terrifying. Fear of loud noises is

## Fears or Phobias

If your child's fears or phobias interfere with normal, daily living, talk to your pediatrician about the problem. If your child won't leave the house for fear of seeing a dog, or if she refuses to eat a certain food, this may signal something more serious than simple fear.

natural to young children, but few are fearful of the telephone because they hear the sound frequently. But many children are afraid of loud sirens, fireworks, and lightning. These are rare events and usually appear unexpectedly. The fears they arouse usually die out naturally as the child experiences the events more often. You can hasten this understanding by preparing your child for new experiences in advance when possible. Talk about things like lightning and alarms. Tell stories and read books that include new and untried experiences. The more your child knows, the less there is to be frightened about.

## Your toddler's understanding of gender

During this period of your child's life, he or she is just beginning to understand any notion of gender. In fact, it's not until your child is between 18 and 30 months that he or she even can correctly answer the question, "Are you a boy or a girl?" With this dawning of gender identity, your child picks up cues that mold his or her views of what is appropriate behavior for boys and girls. What becomes typical boy or girl play—from dressing up as a princess or a superhero to pushing a truck or a doll carriage—is evidence of your child's growing ability to observe, to categorize observations, and to mimic behaviors. The ways in which you respond to your son or daughter's behavior also signal what's expected of a boy or a girl. Videotaped studies have shown that parents more often encourage their boys to run free, but shadow their little girls anxiously. As a result, boys learn to take physical risks, while girls learn to become physically cautious. Similarly, girls are not as often encouraged to participate in activities that would help them develop physical strength and confidence, and are instead steered into quiet and safe activities. Meanwhile, boys are discouraged from nurturing activities such as playing with dolls.

Few children grow up unaffected by their culture's notions of appropriate gender behaviors. Forming a strong sense of being male or female is, in fact, essential to your child's emotional well-being. But there's a difference between identifying him- or herself as a boy or girl and learning to limit his or her potential based on stereotypical notions of masculinity or femininity. It's essential that all children be given the opportunity to explore the full range of their personalities, which always include both traditionally male and traditionally female traits.

The most important influence, of course, is you. Whatever you believe about boys and girls is very likely to be accepted at face value by your child. If the gender roles in your home show a clear division of labor and distinct male and female behaviors, your child will adopt those codes of conduct. If, on the other hand, both you and your spouse share in household tasks without strict male and female assignments and each displays a traditionally male and female range of behaviors, your child will be less likely to adopt a stereotypical role for him- or herself. If you allow your child to express certain emotions and pursue certain activities while limiting others based on gender, you risk distorting his or her emotional life. But if you accept a wide range of behaviors and feelings in both your son and daughter—allowing your little girl to play roughly and get messy and your little boy to express fear, for example—your child will incorporate a broader range of activities and emotions into his or her life.

At this point in your child's life, most of your teaching about gender roles is done through example. Later, you will be able to talk to your child about gender and will be able to help him view stereotypical gender roles with a more critical eye.

# Cognitive development

Your toddler is a learning machine, using everything at her disposal to understand the world. With so much to learn, she may shift her attention from one skill to another, speeding ahead in one area and regressing in another. For a while, she may concentrate on language development and let her walking skills regress a bit. Later she may become fascinated by toys that have unique shapes and colors and will stop talking for a while. This lopsided development will mark her learning well into the future.

## What your toddler knows

One-year-olds have an improved sense of objects, their permanence, and their use. They know that things and people exist behind closed doors. They will move one object aside to get at another. They try to take things apart to see what's inside. They may use one toy as a tool to reach another. They can recognize that an object is upside-down and turn it rightside-up.

The ability to imitate others develops at this age. This is a useful skill that helps your baby as he learns to talk, feed himself, and even laugh. One-year-olds are able to match words to concepts, for example to identify simple objects in a book. If you ask, "Where's the ball in this picture?" your child can now point to the ball. She can also form a mental picture of something she cannot see. For example, she can imagine her shoes and then go look for them if you ask her to.

The concept of cause and effect is further understood during this period as your toddler continues to learn that certain actions bring about predictable responses from you: If she drops a toy, you pick it up. If she reaches upward, you pick her up.

**How your 13- to 18-month-old learns** Your child is learning through a combination of methods, from the sensual to the higher level techniques of problem-solving. Each learning experience, as always, is built on other learning, and now, with so much accumulated knowledge as a base, his ability to learn is explosive. Primarily, your toddler learns by:

• **Using his senses.** When he feels wind blow through the window, when he compares the texture of a ball made of tin foil to one made of sponge, when he smells a flower, listens to a song, or sees the bark on a tree, your toddler is categorizing his experiences in ways that help him make sense of the world around him.

• **Experimenting.** Your toddler might drop a spoon on the floor over and over again, not to aggravate you, but to memorize the cause and effect of things. She will also vary an action slightly to see if the change affects the outcome. "What will happen if I drop the spoon and the fork together? What if I toss the spoon onto a cushion instead of the floor? Will it make a different sound?" All of these experiments prove that the world follows certain physical rules and enables her to make reasonable predictions. This knowledge gives her the safety to venture out, with the firm knowledge, for instance, that the floor is solid and will support her attempts to walk across it.

• **Manipulating objects.** Your toddler learns a great deal by "accident" as she handles objects and learns how one object interacts with another. For example, she may try to push a toy through the bars of her crib and find that, in the position she is holding the toy, it doesn't fit through. Eventually, by chance, she may rotate the toy and succeed at sliding it through the bars this time. The next time she tries the same action, she will remember to turn the toy so it fits through easily. She will push a wooden puzzle piece all around the puzzle frame until it finally falls into place. She learns the correct position by accident, and is able to retain this bit of information to use next time. This accidental learning, a form of experimentation, is the beginning of problem-solving.

**What you can do** By himself, your toddler can't change the scenery and expand his opportunities for stimulation. But you can encourage his intellectual growth by varying the sensations he experiences.

- **Introduce new playthings** to his collection of familiar toys. The rattle that was thrilling at seven months of age offers little new in the way of learning potential now. Include toys that challenge thinking skills, such as shape sorters and ring towers, which stimulate concentration and eye-hand coordination. Vary the shapes, colors, and textures of items within his reach.
- **Offer news twists to familiar playthings.** In addition to your child's traditional books, add some that have pop-up illustrations or textured pages. Add a bucket to your child's game with a ball. Put a new outfit on a stuffed bear.
- **Change the view.** Move your child's high chair to a new spot. Rearrange the bedroom furniture. Hang new curtains and pictures on the wall.

## Language development

This is the age of the parrot. Your one-year-old will listen and listen and suddenly cry out a sound in his attempt to imitate you. He is most interested in putting labels on the tangible, visible things around him. He first learns the names of things in his daily routine and environment, like "baby," "bottle," "bye-bye," "Mama," and "Dada." He learns these names by listening to you. As you walk through your daily routine, be aware that your baby is listening. Take time to point to objects and name them. As you pick up the spoon to feed him, say, "spoon." As you put on his hat, say, "hat." Say it simply and clearly. Don't confuse the lesson with full sentences like, "This is called a spoon." Just point and label. He

*For more information on toddler toys, see **page 787**.*

## TIMELINE
## Toddler and Preschooler Hearing and Speech

**Between 1 and 2:** Your toddler can point to pictures in a book when asked to, and can understand basic questions and commands without needing visual cues. He enjoys stories, songs, and rhymes. By his secont year, he starts to use two-word combinations, such as "want juice." His vocabulary consists of between 50 and 100 words.

**Between 2 and 3:** Your child's vocabulary expands to about 300 to 1,000 words. He starts using three- and four-word sentences and can follow two-part requests ("Get the ball, and put it on the couch"). He can locate sounds coming from outside his range of vision and replies when you call him from another room. He is attentive to a familiar voice on the phone.

**By age 4:** Your child knows between 1,200 and 2,000 words. He can answer "who," "what," "where," and "why" questions and can respond to basic questions asked by a familiar person on the telephone. At least 80 percent of his speech is understandable to a person outside the family. He begins to understand that words have opposites.

**By age 5:** Your child can understand most of what is said at home and in school. He can pay attention to a story, answer questions about it, and carry on a conversation. About 90 percent of his speech can be understood by a non-family member.

probably won't say the word at first. This is the time when your child does more listening and learning than talking.

Although it may appear that your baby is not doing much talking, don't underestimate the speed at which your child is learning language. Keep in mind that there are two kinds of language: words he can say and words he can understand. The 13- to 19-month-old may say very little, but understands so much.

When your baby does begin to speak, he'll first try the initial sounds of words and rely on you to fill in the rest. He may say "ba" for ball and baby and bottle and bad. But don't worry about how you'll know what he means. Your child will use the right tones and inflections and follow through with body language that leaves no doubt what he means. He will pull at your arm and point to the refrigerator as he says, "ba" meaning bottle. He will say "ba" as he holds out his ball. He will say "ba" as he points to the cat with a furrowed forehead and puckered lips to tell you the cat has been "bad." He will often practice his favorite word "no" by making an "n" sound and ferociously shaking his head. The use of simple sounds (like *b, c, d, n, m* and *g*) along with body movement and facial expressions is the way your baby shows you he is learning to talk.

Your baby quickly perceives that there is more to language than just words. You can hear him practicing inflection, timing, pitch, and volume as he jabbers in his own toddler jargon. Once in a while you'll even hear a recognizable word in his monologues. Encourage this exploration of language, and don't worry about trying to get your baby to speak "correctly." Talking to himself in words only he understands is an important step toward meaningful dialogue. When your child talks to you in his own language, talk back. Let him know that you understand he's trying to communicate. "Answer" him and then pause, leaving time for him to respond.

## The meaning of mess

Where you see chaos, your child sees skill-building fun. As frustrating as it may be for you, making a mess is part of growing up for your child—he can't help it; he can't stop himself, and there's no way you can (or should) completely outlaw it.

There's a good reason your child will flip a bowl of spaghetti noodles onto the floor: he's curious. One-year-olds are insatiably curious about the different ways that they can cause change. They want to know, "What happens when I pull all the books off the shelf or knock over the garbage in the kitchen? How will things look different?"

When your child overturns objects, he is also satisfying a need to exercise control over his environment. Toddlers are on a constant quest for power. This behavior, though exasperating at times, is a 1-year-old's way of discovering that he has his own will. He can make you react; he can immediately draw your attention to himself. This is an amazing discovery for a 1-year-old.

The compulsion to make a mess is also a young child's way of learning by using his senses. One-year-olds have to touch, smell, feel, and taste to explore their world with their whole bodies. You may look at a cup of pudding and know what it will taste like; your toddler needs to squish it through his fingers and smell it before he can decide if he wants to eat it. Getting covered in goo is not the issue—learning is.

Knowing your child's motivation will help you adjust your expectations of cleanliness, but it doesn't mean you have to lose all control. Even now, you can set limits on where and when potentially messy adventures can take place. If your child loves to empty drawers, clear out one bottom drawer and fill it with safe items he can play with; put drawer locks on the others. If he loves to squish his fingers through his mashed carrots, feed him this dish at home and just before he is about to take a bath. If you're in a restaurant, or whenever you don't want a mess, limit the menu to neater fare.

In general, it's best if you're prepared for and accepting of messes. Dress your child in old clothes, put down drop cloths, put him and his messy playthings in a small empty kiddie pool right in your kitchen. You can contain the mess to preserve some sanity, but don't try to stop it.

# Why toddlers love repetition

Your child's favorite word during this year will be "More!" Toddlers take special delight in doing the same thing over and over again because it's their own scientific way of investigating the world and mastering new skills.

While your child's insistence on doing things over and over again can seem tedious to you, she is actually introducing subtle changes into each repetition. For example, your child might bang a wooden block on the table and pay attention to how the sound changes when she bangs harder. Then she may use a plastic hammer and pick up other clues about the characteristics of the two materials.

While adults crave variety, a toddler needs repeated confirmation that things stay the same. So much is new and overwhelming for a one-year-old, but repeating an activity helps her learn what to expect. That's why repetitive songs such as "Old McDonald Had a Farm" are such a big hit at this age; there's a predictable pattern that empowers little ones with the knowledge of what's going to happen next. This is why your child may want you to read the same story over and over night after night. Knowing what comes next is the fun part. Being able to predict what characters are going to do is a skill one-year-olds don't possess in most other circumstances.

Repeated experience also seems to inoculate toddlers against forgetting. Even for adults, learning any new skill, from playing the piano to playing tennis, takes repeated practice. To your toddler, so much of what she does is a new skill, and repetition is her way of remembering how to perform it the next time.

Understanding your toddler's need for repetition may make it easier for you to grin-and-bear through one more reading of her favorite book. But don't hesitate to put limits on some activities also. If your child wants you to read the bedtime story for the tenth time, it's okay to put an end to the marathon and promise another reading in the morning.

# Choosing toddler toys

*For more information on toy safety, see **pages 786–88**.*

When choosing toys for toddlers, be sure to check the manufacturer's suggested age level, since toys meant for older children can present a hazard to younger kids who are apt to put small objects in their mouths. Age-appropriate toys for toddlers include:

- **Items to manipulate,** such as large wooden or cardboard blocks in a variety of shapes and sizes, and stacking cubes and rings.

- **Toys that encourage observation and categorizing,** such as shape sorters, simple puzzles, and nesting toys.
- **Toys that encourage empathy and cuddling,** such as stuffed animals and dolls.
- **Toys that encourage imaginative play,** such as toy food and toy cars.
- **Imitative toys.** Playthings such as pretend vacuum cleaners and tools can be introduced now as your child begins to enjoy mimicking adult behaviors.
- **Household items,** such a set of plastic measuring cups, pots and pans, and other safe objects also offer hours of play possibilities.
- **Water.** A basin of water is to your toddler what a 10-acre water park is to a teenager—the setting for hours of fun. Water offers opportunities to learn that some things float, some things sink, and some things dissolve. Provide some containers of different sizes, including perhaps a sieve and a turkey baster (great for squirting). You can demonstrate how the various containers work or you can just let your child make his own discoveries.
- **Sand.** Sand has a unique feel—not quite solid, not quite liquid. Dry sand is good for pouring and straining through a sieve. Wet sand is good for building and clumping. If you don't have access to a sandbox, a couple of pounds of cornmeal or rice in a basin is just as much fun. Add a few plastic cups for filling, emptying, and pouring.

*For information on water-play safety, see **pages 819–23**.*

*For information on sandbox safety, see **page 815**.*

**Gender and toys** When toddlers play, they are practicing life. They imitate family members and mentally place everyone into a category that helps them figure out how life works. Their early goal is to mimic adult—not male or female—behaviors. Toddlers will primarily copy the behaviors of their primary caretakers. If they witness housekeeping, they'll play at doing the wash and setting the table; if they see lots of home office work, they'll play at a toy computer. They will treat their dolls and stuffed animals as substitute selves, cuddling them as they are cuddled and sometimes scolding them, when they've been scolded.

Their view of gender differences may begin to emerge through this imitative play. Thus, the toys that are available for them can either limit or expand their sense of what it means to be a male or a female. When girls play with stereotypically boy toys or boys play with

## Gender-neutral play

You can use your children's play-time to encourage them to believe they can do anything they want to do, regardless of their gender:

• Offer gender-neutral items such as blocks, simple musical instruments, puzzles, and drawing materials, such as chalk.

• Offer traditional boy and girl toys, such as kitchenware and play tool sets and dolls and action toys, to both girls and boys.

• Encourage all kids to use toys that promote motor development, such as beginner trikes, balls, and wagons.

• Encourage a range of play, from active running to quiet reading, from messy artwork to block building, from cooking to fixing broken toys together.

stereotypically girl toys, it doesn't mean that they are unclear about their sexual identity. It simply means that they view a variety of activities as appropriate for males and females, a viewpoint that will serve them well as they grow. Children who are encouraged and allowed to play with whatever interests them develop a less rigid sense of appropriate boy and girl activities. They are freer to explore all aspects of themselves—the sensitive and timid parts and the rough and advenurous parts. When children are made to feel that certain toys are inappropriate, however, they must choose between pleasing others and following their own hearts, and this creates a conflict where none need be. When, on the other hand, children know that their gender doesn't limit their choices, they have a solid foundation of freedom on which to build their own unique talents and strengths.

# CHAPTER 8

# 19 to 24 Months

Full speed ahead! Your toddler is now running and can't stay still for long. She has no time to eat a full meal and no patience for sitting strapped into her car seat or stroller.

Emotionally, the 19- to 24-month-old is still struggling with the push-pull of independence. One minute she'll reject your kiss, the next she'll cry for your attention. An overload of these mixed feelings will frequently lead to meltdowns.

Rapidly increasing cognitive abilities give your toddler a greater awareness of her world and how it works. Now she can figure out concepts in her head without needing to hold or see what she's thinking about. She can also do some planning, considering a problem before rushing in with a solution. Her increasing vocabulary lets her talk about the world she is so actively exploring and gives you more opportunities to better understand her thoughts and needs. This advance in mental abilities makes the 19- to 24-month-old a bundle of fun and a very interactive member of the family.

# *Physical development*

The 19- to 24-month-old is full of energy and now has the physical ability to let it loose. He loves to run, jump, hop, and roll. His little fingers now cooperate with his mind and can turn, pull, and push even the smallest stereo knob or other gadget. This is a period of muscular growth and fine tuning.

## Physical changes

Your child is losing his baby fat and looking much more like an active toddler than an infant. His arms and legs will lengthen gradually, bringing his body into better proportion. His feet will now point forward as he walks, rather than out to the side. His facial features will lose their round appearance and become more defined.

**What your 19- to 24-month-old can do**  Your toddler is taking a great deal of pleasure in his newfound abililties.

　　**Gross motor skills**  Your toddler now advances from toddling and walking to full-speed running. Although he will not always watch where he's going at these top speeds, he actually gets around more safely because he can look down at his feet and maneuver around things that are in his way. He's switching from a flat-footed walk to the more grown-up heel-to-toe gait. By 24 months, your toddler may walk up stairs without holding the railing or your hand for support, and can walk down stairs while holding on. He will still go one step at a time, leading with the same foot, instead of alternating feet on each step.

　　As his motor skills develop, you'll see your baby enjoying his ability to jump, turn circles, stomp feet, and balance on one foot. This makes dancing and twirling to music especially fun. Acrobatics are another terrific way for your child to experiment with all the wonderful things his body can do. He'll be especially skilled at rolling and tumbling.

　　**Fine motor skills**  Your child can now turn the pages in a book one at a time once you've shown him how and will have great success with thick or cardboard pages. Lids hold a special fascination for your child; he'll open and close a shoe box, twist on and off the top to an empty jelly jar, and snap the plastic lid on an old container open and closed. He loves knobs and buttons. Your TV, stereo, and other electronics become his favorite toys; he has the dexterity to make them work and the mental ability to enjoy the cause-and-effect outcome. If you haven't already done so, put any put away dangerous yet alluring items.

**What you can do** You can encourage your child to develop motor skills by joining in his play. Playing tag in a safe and wide-open area helps your child perfect his developing skill at running. Play ball and watch his eye-hand coordination improve. Now is a good time to enroll your child in a toddler gym class where he'll find a safe place to run and jump to his heart's content.

You can also help your child develop physically by having patience. When you're reading to him, let him turn the pages, even though that will slow down the process. When going up and down stairs, take time to let him try it himself. When dressing your child, let him try to put on his socks or his pants; he needs time to practice these skills at his own pace.

## Keeping up with your toddler

Although a toddler's store of energy may far exceed yours, you'll find it easiest to keep up with this bundle of perpetual motion if you work with her, not against her. Don't confine her for too long. Strapping her into her high chair, plopping her in the playpen, or keeping her in her crib or room for long periods of time can lead to explosive tantrums as well as possibly dangerous struggles to find a way out.

Try to limit the amount of time you ask your child to stay in one place. If you take a rambunctious 2-year-old to church or a play, expect her to interrupt the speaker. Plan to work in needed breaks. Give your child daily opportunities to release excess energy. Take her outside as often as possible to a place where she can safely run and jump. After these excursions, you'll find her much more content at home, maybe enough to sit still and watch a video while you make supper (but don't count on it).

## Music and movement

Your toddler's energy level makes dancing and twirling to music especially fun. Movement is a natural and vital means of expression for young children; music brings joy and acceptance to this natural tendency.

Dancing is an excellent exercise for integrating movement and a degree of control for your 19- to 24-month-old. This is a time when motor abilities flourish, but large muscles are better developed than small ones. In general, muscle development is uneven and incomplete, and the large muscle groups cry for action. Dance helps children refine the development of such gross motor movements. Try some traditional dance games with your toddler, such as:

- **Ring-around-the-rosy.**
- **A variation of musical chairs,** in which no chairs are removed, but in which every player claims a seat when the music stops.
- **A marching game,** in which children parade around the room, perhaps with toy musical instruments, to the beat of a marching tune.

Body movement is also a form of communication for children with limited vocabularies. Creative rhythmic movement can be the child's way of interpreting thoughts and feelings; the body is the instrument and movement is the medium of expression.

Large movements of the arms, legs, trunk, and head also help your child become aware of his body in many ways, as a whole or in parts. Through body movement, he enjoys the exhilaration of galloping through space, of leaping higher and higher, and finding out how different body parts can move.

Through music and movement, children discover spatial relationships—tallness, smallness, highness, lowness, bigness, littleness, nearness, farness, roundness, squareness, and so on. They love to move through space—to jump, swing, bend—for the sheer fun of it!

# Emotional development

This 19-to-24-month period can be a very difficult emotional period for both child and parent. Your child's push toward independence and autonomy is at odds with her ever-present need to depend on you. This push-pull creates the core conflict of the second half of the second year.

## Your toddler's feelings

This age is marked by extreme egocentrism. Your child wants what she wants and she wants it now. In her mind, other people exist solely to answer her demands. She has become less affectionate and more adventurous. She doesn't always want to cuddle, and when she's had enough, she arches her back to slide off your lap. At times, she doesn't even want you touching her chair. She has just learned that she is a person separate from you and spends much of her time testing these boundaries.

The drive for independence is all-consuming right now and is very often frustrating for your child (and you!). Finding out that she is separate from you also means that she must to cope with the fact that she cannot get what she wants simply because she wants it. She now realizes that her desires and yours are not the same. And what a blow it is to her to learn that you are in control!

This is also an age when separation anxiety can be strong. The strong desire for independence and autonomy often evolves into excess clinginess or a tantrum. The tantrum itself adds to her confused emotional state. Your child feels anxious whenever her feelings begin to get out of control. The anger, which was intended to frighten you, scares her even more.

*For more on separation anxiety, see **pages 108** and **377**.*

*For advice on handling tantrums, see **page 398**.*

**How your 19- to 24-month-old develops secure relationships** Your toddler is pulling away from you right now, but at the same time she still wants you nearby to offer support and love when she needs it. You will teach your child to trust the tenacity of your relationship if you let her pull away when she needs to and come back when she's ready. If she refuses your kisses as she runs away, don't withhold your affection when she returns. If she insists on putting on her own socks and then turns back to you for help, simply offer your assistance. Most of this need-reject syndrome is caused by a struggle inside herself—not a struggle against you. You can secure the bonds of your relationship by giving your child the freedom to move away and to come back.

**What you can do** There are several ways you can help your child deal with her feelings at this age:

• **Create a safe, supportive environment** in which your child can try most of the things she wants to do on her own and can turn to you for help when she wants it without fear of being made to feel incompetent. For example, if your child wants to button her own sweater, instead of saying, "That's too hard for you; let me do it," let her try. Even if she mismatches the buttons to the holes, congratulate her on her achievement. If she finds that the task is too difficult, tell her that you're there to help if she wants you to.

• **Label feelings.** Giving your child the name of the feeling she's experiencing helps her gain more control and boosts her vocabulary. When your child is sad, for instance, say, "I know you're feeling sad right now."

• **Encourage acceptance and control of feelings.** Help your child accept all of her feelings as very natural. Then let her know that although you understand what she's feeling, you also know that all feelings can be controlled. Explain that anger, for example, does not have to be expressed by hitting.

• **Don't try to "make it all better."** Feelings are very real and shouldn't be erased before they're experienced. Let your child spend some time feeling sad, or angry, or sulky if she needs to.

• **Don't tell your child what to feel and what not to feel.** If you say, "You're not mad at your little brother," when indeed your child is feeling that emotion at the moment, you're telling her that her feelings aren't real, which is very confusing. Instead focus on her behavior. Say, "Yes, I know you're very angry, but you mustn't hit."

## Letting dads be dads

If you're a mom, don't be afraid to admit it: There are times you hesitate to leave the house because you worry your husband can't care for your child as well as you can. Sometimes, he plays rough. Sometimes, he doesn't pay close attention. Sometimes, he's insensitive. Sometimes, he disciplines harshly. Or he doesn't discipline enough. Experts report that all these things are true, which is precisely the reason that you should give your husband time alone with the kids.

Moms tend to offer their children closeness, comfort, and a sense of togetherness. Dads tend to give freedom and encouragement to explore the limits. Children need both of these parental perspectives. Take play, for example: Mom jumps in at the child's level of play. She provides the child with the opportunity to be in charge, to direct the game. Dads, on the other hand, play in a way that resembles an apprenticeship. Instead of bringing himself

### Letting Go

When dads are left alone with their children, they don't act like the child's mother—they act like a dad—and that's good. So take some time for yourself, kiss your husband and kids good-bye, shut the door, and stop worrying that things won't be the same without you. They won't be, and that's a good thing for all concerned.

to the child's level, most fathers automatically take the role of teacher. Dad encourages the child to learn new skills, to compete, and to push against the limits of her knowledge and abilities. Neither is the better approach. With Mom, children learn to feel important and better able to manipulate the world. With Dad, children gain a sense of belonging to a team, as well as a feeling of competence.

## A toddler's sense of ownership

As your child now begins to gain a sense of self that is separate from you, she also begins to understand that some things belong to her and nobody else. "Mine" becomes her favorite word, and her possessions become an extension of herself. She will hug her toys, hold them close, and carry them around everywhere she goes. These items remind her that she is a separate individual who can have things that are hers alone.

At around 21 months of age, your child will begin to understand that some things belong to other people, too. She will hand you your shoe and say, "Mommy." She may begin to put things in their "right" place. Your comb, address book, and pen go in a pile on one side of the room; her sock, doll, and book go in a pile on the other side of the room. She may get very upset if "your" things mix in with "her" things.

Your child may play with this division-of-property idea by gathering into her arms as many of "her" possessions as she can handle (and then a few more). She won't let anyone touch her things, and will scream if anyone tries to share or borrow what is hers. This attitude may appear selfish or greedy to you, but at this age, your child is not developmentally able to understand the concept of sharing. To her, something that is taken is gone forever.

Her dawning awareness that other people own some things that are not hers does not apply outside her home. If you visit a playmate or a toy store, everything is up for grabs. From her perspective, in the outside world, possession and ownership mean the same thing. If your child grabs a toy and won't let go, it is not stealing or taking; it is seeing something she wants, grabbing onto it, and assuming that once it's in her hands, she owns it.

After the age of 2, your child will be ready to investigate the idea of sharing. But right now, she needs the security of knowing what's hers is hers and nobody will take it away.

*For more on sharing, see **pages 236–39**.*

# The importance of security objects

Many toddlers attach themselves to their blankets, pacifiers, stuffed animals, or dolls for the comfort these objects offer. These worn and tattered items are generally called "security objects" or "transitional objects" because they give children something to depend upon as they make the transition from total dependency to independence. Toddlers want to venture out on their own, but because they're unsure of exactly what's out there, some need something to cling to for support as they give independence a try. These objects, also aptly called "lovies," are the tools that can help them become more independent and able to cope with stress on their own.

Although you try mightily to give your toddler all the assurances he needs during this developmental stage, there *are* times when you can't be there—when your child awakens in the middle of the night, at day care, or when a baby-sitter is there in your place, for example. Transitional objects, often something that was present when you held or fed him at an earlier stage in his life, act as your stand-in when you're out of sight.

Some parents worry that the need for a comforting object is a sign of an insecure personality. Research, however, shows that this is just not so. In a study of 108 children between the ages of 20 months and 4 years, children who were "attached" to their blankets were found to be no more fearful about separation, dogs, storms, and a variety of social events than children who didn't use these comforting objects.

Some children cling to their "lovies" with greater urgency and for longer periods than others. But by age five, most kids have put aside their transitional objects willingly and without fanfare, although some may continue to seek their comforting objects at nighttime or in times of stress or illness, even into their teens.

---

**"IT WORKED FOR ME"**

## *Double Up On Prized Possessions*

My daughter is very attached to a particular stuffed animal, which is getting frayed and worn. Since she never wants to let go of it, cleaning it became a challenge. Then it occured to me that if she ever lost it or if it completely fell apart, she'd be very upset. So I bought a second one just like the first. And she's comfortable alternating between the two. Keeping them clean has become easier and I'm a little less concerned about losing one.

# Cognitive development

This age is most notably marked by giant leaps in cognitive development. Through active exploration, your child is constantly learning the hows and whys of his world.

## What your toddler knows

Your child will begin to solve simple problems in her head. She will no longer simply solve puzzles, for example, by rubbing the piece over the hole until it fits; she can now look at the shape of the puzzle piece and the shape of the hole and turn the piece so it fits. When her pull toy gets stuck on the leg of a chair, she will no longer just tug and tug to free it; she will stop, look, think, and then lift the toy out of its trap. You can almost see her thinking as she invents solutions before acting to solve the problem.

Your toddler now also begins to anticipate consequences of her own behavior. She's learning, for example, that if she hugs you, you will smile, and if she has a tantrum, you will show your displeasure. She has a rudimentary understanding of physics: If she steps in a puddle, her feet will get wet. She can even consider possible outcomes: If she runs, she might fall.

Her curiosity shifts from objects to events and people. She spends more and more time looking out windows. She watches social interactions very thoughtfully, almost as if trying to memorize how it's done.

Your child's language development continues to progress. She has reached a cognitive milestone that allows her to use language: She can create an image of something in her mind that isn't really there and she gives these images names. She will know about 20 words at 19 months and about 100 or so words at 24 months. As she approaches her second birthday, she will begin to speak two-word "sentences" like: "Me go."

Time sense is expanding. Your child is still most aware of "now," but she also begins to see the order of sequence. When she sees you take out the juice, she will come to the table. When you put on your coat, she will go to the door.

Drawings begin to take some form. Scribbles now tend to imitate a shape.

**How your 19- to 24-month-old learns** Your toddler is no longer passive, dependent, and reactive; she is a thinking person who knows she exists as a separate individual.

She learns through active trial and error, which is why she will consider merely watching TV a waste of her time. It's too passive. Toys that make noise but are not contingent on her actions are also passive forms of entertainment that do not promote mastery of skills. Your child learns by doing and enjoys it. Toys that require interaction are all learning tools now. Blocks, trucks, dress-up dolls, musical instruments, puzzles, books, and toys that sound when the child hits them or pushes buttons are all opportunities for learning.

**What you can do** Give your child room to learn without your help. Certainly, your toddler still wants to be near you; she will play in the room where you are and she will bring her toys to your side. To help her learn:

• **Be a play partner, not the leader.** Your toddler's play involves exploring and experimenting and you interfere with this process when you direct the play by explaining how things work, how to hold objects properly, or how to do it "right." At this stage in your child's cognitive development, you teach her best when you don't teach at all.

• **Be the observer and the listener.** Ask your child to show you things, and then talk with her about what she shows you. If she brings you a rock, lead her to feel its shape and describe its hardness, texture, and color. Discuss where rocks are usually found and what they are used for. Don't make every contact with your child a lecture-lesson, however. Just talk about the world and follow her lead about what is interesting today.

• **Provide exposure to the world.** Now that your child is fascinated by people and events, try to make time for walks in the stroller to come face to face with others.

## Solo play

Now, while your child is experimenting with ways of expressing her independence, is a per-

---

**"IT WORKED FOR ME"**

### *Encouraging Solo Play*

My 18-month-old son is always right under my feet and doesn't play by himself well at all. To encourage him to amuse himself, I've made up a basket of special toys that I let him play with only when I need a few minutes to myself, such as when I'm cooking or getting dressed. The "special" quality of this basket holds his interest as long as he can still see me and hear me, which frees me to get things done.

fect age to encourage solitary play activities. Being able to play independently is the foundation on which she will build self-reliance. Solitary play helps your child practice focusing her attention and it strengthens her sense of identity apart from you. It also lets your child develop her own inner resources and creativity so she can confidently discover her world without needing you to navigate her every move.

Of course, there are also benefits that you'll enjoy when your child can play alone. Solo play gives you just enough time to finish a chore, go to the bathroom, or simply to answer the phone.

Whether a toddler can entertain herself naturally (without a few lessons) depends on several things: her personality, her birth order, and your style as a parent.

- **Personality.** Some children are naturally more introspective; and can sit quietly for quite a while to observe or play.
- **Birth order.** First borns may be less inclined to play alone if you or another adult regularly acts as social director and playmate. Because second-born and later-born children do not receive as much individual attention as first-borns, they often become more self-reliant and are better able to play by themselves (or with each other).
- **Parent style.** Some parents can step back from their children's play. They do not direct, explain, and stay involved every moment. Their children are better able to play by themselves than children whose parents always tell them what to do.

**Encouraging solo play** Most toddlers can learn to play alone for 10 to 15 minutes or more at a stretch. If your child doesn't naturally enjoy solo play, you can teach her how it's done. First, redirect the focus of play onto your child: let her choose the toy she wants to play with. Let her show you how to play. Back off as much as possible. The next step is to increase your periods of separation during play time. When your child seems absorbed in a toy, excuse yourself, walk away a few feet and come right back. Do this for several days, increasing the distance each time, so that your child gradually learns that when you leave, you will return. As you walk past

> ### *Good Play-Alone Toys*
>
> Toys that don't require winding up or other involvement from you are best. Some possibilities:
>
> - Blocks
> - Books with easy-to-turn pages
> - Unstructured materials, such as boxes or pots and pans
> - Coloring and drawing materials
> - Puppets, dress-up clothes, dolls, and action figures

your child, praise her, pat her back, stroke her hair. Give her positive attention for playing alone. Over two or three months, you can build up your time apart to ten minutes or more.

Always remember that "alone" doesn't mean being abandoned with a TV and a pile of toys while you go off to another part of the house. Even a toddler who can play alone happily for a while needs to check in with you repeatedly. For this reason, as well as for safety purposes, it's essential that you stay nearby without hovering. Teaching independence is an interactive process, and having you close by gives your child the security she needs while learning.

## The importance of make-believe

The ability to make believe is one of the greatest pathways to learning about the real world. Fantasy is not only fun in itself, but it stimulates your child's imagination, spurs his language development, and enhances his problem-solving abilities. Studies show that a child with a highly developed fantasy life tends to be better at concentrating on tasks, has more self-control, and is able to come up with creative, rather than predictable, responses to problems. These are all positive characteristics that you can promote in your child by encouraging opportunities for imaginative play.

Between the ages of 19 and 24 months, you'll see pretend play take up more and more of your child's time. Some of that pretend play will involve mimicking you and other adults, such as playing "mommy" or "daddy" with his dolls and stuffed animals. You'll also see evidence of his growing understanding of the world as he imagines an unseen participant in his make-believe game. For instance, though he may not yet be able to verbalize his fantasies, he may make up a story about a giant from whom he and his stuffed bears must defend themselves. He is now also able to hold onto an idea for a longer period of time so he can plan his play. For example, when he is having a picnic with his teddy bears, he can stop his game for a moment to gather the necessary toy plates and napkins he needs to continue.

Your toddler's ability to imagine also lets him have more play opportunities. He will freely substitute one thing for another if he doesn't have the exact object he wants on hand. He may hold a banana to his ear and pretend it's a telephone. Or his slipper becomes a toy car. This advanced thinking skill also gives him lots of material to develop his emerging sense of humor.

Imaginative play can also help your child deal with upsetting or unfamiliar circumstances. Before meeting a new baby-sitter, for example, a toddler may act out the baby-sitting situation with his dolls and animals. A child who is angry may let her action figures battle it out, which helps her feel more in control of the upsetting situation.

There are many ways to encourage imaginative play:

- **Provide plenty of real-world experiences to draw on** by getting out and going places. A dump truck or plastic farm animal sparks a higher level of imaginative play once your child has seen a construction site or visited a farm.
- **Have the materials on hand**—toys as well as household objects—to foster creative play.
- **Have the right attitude.** Encourage explorations without fear of mess, and enjoy playfulness with no particular goal in mind.
- **Don't force your child to play pretend,** but when he does, ask questions and make comments that show your interest and help your child verbalize his imaginative thoughts.
- **Don't ever "correct" your child's imagination.** If he colors a picture of an elephant purple and black, there's no need to remind him that elephants are really gray.
- **Play along.** If your child holds a toy teacup to his mouth, don't rush in to offer him something to drink from his real cup. Ask if you can have a sip, too. Just be sure to let your child lead the course of the story.

## Word games to enjoy with your toddler

Learning language can be even more fun for your child when you make it a game.

**Substitute words** When your child knows words such as "milk" and "cookie," for example, give her a cup of milk and say, "Here's your cookie." Let her giggle at your mistake and then correct yourself, saying, "Oh, this isn't a cookie. This is milk."

**Play telephone** This a fun way to practice two-way conversations. Call your child up on one toy phone, and let her answer on another. Or use extensions of your real phones, as long as you're able to remain in sight of one another. Then have a conversation.

**Name pictures** Using one of her books or your magazines, look at pictures together and name them.

**Rhymes and songs.** Nursery rhymes and songs help your child delight in the sounds and the rhythm of language.

## Games to encourage thinking skills

Games that reinforce your child's ability to make predictions, such as lining up toys cars on a ramp to watch them reach the bottom, can enthrall a child this age. Once that game is established, try varying the outcome a bit by placing a book on the ramp and seeing how the cars either stop or go around it. Encourage your child's sense of humor by playing with variations of some predictable routines. Play hide-and-seek games.

### TV time for tots
*"How much television should a 2-year-old watch?"*

TV viewing in itself is neither good nor bad. Certainly there are shows written for children to arouse their curiosity and reinforce your family's values. These can play a beneficial role in shaping your child's vision of life and you should encourage him to watch them. On the other hand, there are many mindless programs that stifle imaginative thought and present frightening ideas and images.

Your first step in shaping your child's viewing habits is to monitor the programs he watches and select only those that are a positive influence. Monitoring what he watches includes turning off the set when adult shows, such as soap operas, talk shows, and even the news are on if your child is in the room. Or instead of TV, offer quality children's videos. Then limit viewing to less than an hour or two per day to assure that most of his playtime is spent in more active, creative, and interactive pursuits.

Given more interesting options, toddlers themselves will choose hands-on play over passive viewing and will develop a TV habit only if they are given little else to do.

## What nursery rhymes teach your toddler

There's a reason that nursery rhymes appeal to generation after generation. Part of their appeal, of course, is tradition. But there's more. Nursery rhymes offer the perfect blend of rhythm and movement, predictability, and fun that has always appealed to toddlers. You've probably noticed that even infants enjoy the sing-song rhythm of "The Wheels on the Bus Go 'Round and 'Round," "Ring-around-the-rosey," "This little piggy…" and so on. Because they are one of the earliest forms of communication that a child learns, nursery rhymes have benefits for many aspects of a child's growth, from language development to social skills.

Now, as a toddler, your child is ready to throw herself into the action with hand gestures and body movements that she can repeat each time she hears the rhyme. At the first sound of patty-cake, she will clap her hands and laugh. Being physically involved helps your child pay attention. Pointing to body parts, playing with fingers and toes, and holding hands with others while turning in a circle helps them learn more because their bodies are brought into the sensory experience.

Nursery rhymes also add a comforting element to a child's day. The predictability of the rhyme means a lot in her world where so much is unstable. Hearing the rhymes' lines and rhythms helps your child develop a sensitivity to the flow of language and helps build her vocabulary. The repetition in the rhymes gives your child confidence that what she's saying is appropriate and will be responded to. She also learns how to listen and memorize. When the rhymes are read out of colorfully illustrated books, your child learns that there is some relation between what you are saying and what she sees in the picture, enhancing her love of books.

## From babbling to talking

Language skills blossom when your child feels he is being listened to and related to with respect. Your own body language conveys this message, so when you talk to your toddler, get down to his level, make eye contact, and stay close. This is a simple way to start building verbal competence. To further help your child develop his language skills:

• **Show your delight at your child's use of new words** and he'll work hard to please you with more.

**"IT WORKED FOR ME"**

### Making the Most of Storytime

Storytime at our local library was not fun with my 20-month-old. He couldn't sit still while the librarian was reading, and his running around distracted the other children. Now we "play" storytime at home. We line up all his stuffed animals and use books selected by my son from the library. I play the part of the librarian and he and his "friends" play the part of the children. Like the librarian, I remind him sternly that he and his friends must sit still. I keep the stories very short and each day he gets to practice listening and sitting. Because of these practice sessions, I think soon we'll be ready to join the other kids at the storytime program.

- **Clearly pronounce the name** of an object your child points to.
- **Encourage but don't insist that your child name objects** he points to. For instance, when he points to a book he wants you to read to him, say, "Do you want the book? Would you like to say, 'book?'"
- **Talk to your child in simple sentences** that refer to concrete objects and events.
- **Stress important words** in the sentence and exaggerate the intonation.
- **Pause between sentences** so your child has a chance to grasp your meaning.
- **Speak to your child in standard grammar.** This is the model he will copy.
- **Don't correct your child's sentence structure** or pronunciation while he's talking; his first need is to communicate. If he mispronounces a word, simply restate it correctly.
- **Provide a language-rich environment** that celebrates words. Read to your toddler, involve him in lots of conversation, ask questions, and play with words.

# CHAPTER 9

. . . . . . . . . . . . . . . . . . . . . . . . . . . . . . . . . . . . . . . . . . . . . . . . . . . . . . . . . . . . . . . .

# 2 Years

Every day is an adventure with a 2-year-old. His energy is bottomless; his curiosity is insatiable; and his heart is full of love. Sure, he can be stubborn, unpredictable, and wild, but the spontaneous exuberance of the 2-year-old makes him a joy to be around.

Life is easier for him now that he can walk, run, and climb better, and can use language to express his needs. This is also the age when children realize that other people have feelings too. They feel sad when you're sad; they show empathy for a playmate's hurt, and they'll go out of their way to make an older sibling laugh. With a steady supply of praise and encouragement, your 2-year-old can learn to handle the frustrations that come with a life so full of things to do and with so many restrictions on what he is allowed to do and what he is capable of doing.

Your 2-year-old has become a creative problem solver whose imaginary play will give you insights into his evolving thinking processes. He is honing his ability to plan, predict, consider cause and effect, and understand consequences. His increasing verbal capcity allows him to string sentences together, and question the way the world works with his favorite query—"why?"

Your most consuming task with your 2-year-old is finding the line between allowing your child the freedom he needs to discover how the world works and keeping him from getting into too much trouble. This is often an exhausting, but fun, part of raising a 2-year-old.

# *Physical development*

Your 2-year-old is eager to refine her motor skills so she prefers to gallop, roll, or jump rather than simply to walk. As her coordination improves, she is better able to control her movements and make her body do exactly what she wants it to.

## Physical changes

Your toddler continues the transformation from baby to child. You'll see his posture mature as his protruding abdomen slims down and his curved back becomes more erect. He'll develop a longer, leaner appearance. The growth of his head will drastically slow down because by age 2 your child has attained about 90 percent of his adult head size. Height and weight gain will slow for a while, too, so his appetite may diminish. He'll also continue teething, now getting additional molars.

**What your 2-year-old can do**  By the time your child is 2, early challenges such as walking and grasping objects have become routine. Your 2-year-old is now ready to learn new, more complex skills, as well as continue to refine existing ones.

**Gross motor skills**  Your toddler's unsure gait changes into a relatively smooth, confident stride at age 2 as her large muscles mature. She is able to round sharp corners and walk backward without her legs slipping out from under her. Now, as she walks, she shifts her weight from heel to toe, just like an adult. Falling is less frequent as she develops the ability to coordinate movement between her left and right sides. She is now ready to scoot up the ladder to the top of the slide, right hand with left foot and then left hand with right foot. Some 2-year olds have learned how to hop or even gallop—a sure sign of improved coordination and balance. With these developments comes the ability to engage in other activities while walking.

**Fine motor skills**  Skills involved in such activities as grasping and pointing are also showing marked progress. Two-year-olds no longer clutch objects in their fists, but hold them in the well between their fingers and thumbs. Your 2-year-old is now able to tackle such skills as dressing himself and holding a crayon or large piece of chalk with some dexterity and control. Feeding himself with a spoon and fork is less of a hit-or-miss activity. He's also able to begin to brush his teeth and take part in some other aspects of grooming, and he may also become adept at such tasks as unscrewing lids from jars and opening sealed containers—so be careful about what you leave in his grasp.

**Helping your child grow** Although you cannot rush your child's physical development, there *are* ways you can help him develop his emerging capabilities:

• **Provide lots of opportunities for physical play,** such as running, jumping, rolling, and climbing. Getting outdoors where there is plenty of space and a variety of play equipment is important to your 2-year-old's physical well-being. Indoors, ensure that there is a safe area in which your child can practice his skills. Instead of slowing him down with safety rules, childproof his play area, both indoors and out.

• **Get involved in your child's play.** Most 2-year-olds don't like to play by themselves for any length of time, and your participation in his activities will encourage him to take appropriate risks, to venture out, and to discover what he is physically capable of doing. For instance, hold his hand as he practices walking on a balance beam; cheer him on as he attempts to overcome any hesitancy about reaching the next rung on the ladder to a toddler-sized slide. Just be careful not to direct his play. If he's happily engaged in zooming his toy cars on the sandbox fence, allow him to continue without rushing him from this satisfying activity to another that you choose.

• **Encourage skill building by playing imitation games.** For example, have your child copy you as you practice such physical feats as touching your nose with your finger or jumping up and down or clapping in rhythm.

• **Make skill-building toys and household objects available.** In addition to developmentally appropriate toys, make safe household objects such as plastic containers available for physical exploration.

• **Don't get upset by minor mishaps.** Your 2-year-old is likely to suffer a few scrapes, bumps, and bruises as he explores his world and hones his abilities. He's also likely to spill more than a few glasses of milk and to get some finger paint where it wasn't meant to be. Hovering too closely, jumping in to kiss each and every boo-boo, or punishing the natural messiness of a 2-year-old can make him fearful and less likely to try out new skills.

# Measuring your child's growth

When it's time to measure your child, make it a special event, which will make your child feel proud of growing up. First, designate a place where you always measure and record height, such as a doorway. Decorated height charts that provide a record up to five feet tall also can be attached to the back of a door or a wall. In this way, your child will be able to check herself to see how much she has grown.

To measure height, have your child stand with his back straight and against a wall. Bare feet should be flat and his head straight. Place a ruler, a book, or other flat object on his head to line up with the wall. Then make your mark. You might also want to note the age and year next to each mark. Before choosing a door frame as your measuring spot, realize that you'll want to avoid erasing or painting over the marks in the years to come. You and your child will have fun looking back on how much he has changed.

To measure weight, always use the same scale. You may want to compare the measurements you take with those taken in the doctor's office, to make sure your scale is accurate. To keep your records consistent, try to weigh your child at about the same time of day and without shoes.

## Different Growth Rates

Don't be alarmed if your child is shorter or taller than other children her age. At around age 2, kids the same age begin to vary significantly in height and weight. For hereditary reasons, some perfectly healthy children don't grow as quickly as others during the second and third years. But by age 3 or 4, their growth rate speeds up, though they may not be as tall as their friends until they reach adolescence, when a major growth spurt occurs.

*For growth charts for 1 to 6 years see **page 617**.*

### Predicting adult height

*"Is there any way to tell how tall our 2-year-old will be when he's an adult?"*

Predicting your child's adult height is a tall order. That's because there's no way to tell who in your family tree your child will take after. Still, you can satisfy your curiosity with one of two easy-to-follow formulas. Just remember that these methods are unscientific, and your child may end up being shorter or taller than you guesstimate. The formulas work best in families of average height.

*Formula 1:* Add your height (in inches) to your spouse's. Divide the sum by 2. To predict a boy's height, add 2 to that number. To estimate a girl's future height, subtract 2.

*Formula 2:* Measure your child's height at age 2, on or close to his birthday, and double it.

**Your two-year-old's teeth**  During this year, your child's baby teeth will complete their eruptions, giving him a full set of 20 baby, or milk, teeth. This continued teething may cause some nighttime drooling, but is not as likely to cause any real pain as did his infant teething.

Here's what your 2- to 3-year-old's jaw looks like:

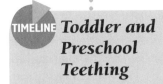

**TIMELINE** *Toddler and Preschool Teething*

**By 21 months,** all four first molars are in place.

**Between 15 and 21 months,** the canines, or pointed teeth, come in.

**Between 2½ and 3 years of age,** four second molars emerge next to the first molars.

*Upper Jaw*

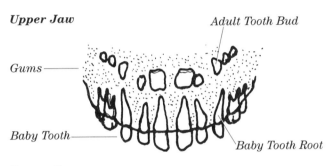

*Gums*

*Adult Tooth Bud*

*Baby Tooth*

*Baby Tooth Root*

*Lower Jaw*

*Gum line*

*Baby Tooth*

*Baby Tooth Root*

*Adult Tooth Bud*

*For information about daily care of your child's teeth, see **page 486**. For information about professional dental care, see **page 533**.*

## Physical play

Besides the necessary routines of sleeping and eating, playtime defines most of your toddler's day. At this age, your child needs lots of physical exercise, which will strengthen not only his muscles but will aid in his intellectual and emotional development as well.

These activities will satisfy his need for constant movement:

**Cycling**  Your child's ability to use both sides of his body to climb also means he can pedal a tricycle. Cycling is a terrific activity for toddlers because they can master it without working too hard and becoming overly frustrated. The trike models that sit close to the ground are best for beginning cyclers.

**Ball playing**  A 2-year-old loves to hit balls with just about anything. Give her a plastic bat, a tennis racquet, a toy golf club, a croquet mallet, a table-tennis paddle, a badminton racquet—anything! This swinging and hitting helps her practice her developing coordination. While you have the balls out, help your child practice throwing, catching, and bouncing. Large, soft balls are best for little fingers. Ball play requires your child to use eye-hand coordination; it makes her keep her eye on the ball; it encourages her to race after the ball, bend over, and pick it up without falling down. It also helps her practice the coordination required to aim at an object and throw the ball toward that spot. She will not likely be successful yet in her aim, but that does not trouble her.

**Climbing**  Toddlers are natural climbers. Give your child a safe toddler slide with a ladder to practice this skill which improves the development of large-muscle coordination. Also give him plenty of practice going up and down stairs.

**Balancing**  Your 2-year-old will love the challenge of walking across a narrow space such as a balance beam or a city sidewalk curb. Just be there to hold his hand. Also encourage him to try to stand on one foot, and then the other.

**Running**  Once your child learns to run, there's no stopping him—until he hits the wall. Create or find large areas for your child to run freely. Indoors, push the furniture aside to create an open space. Go outdoors to your yard or local park where your toddler can perfect this skill without injury. Race with him to a nearby tree. Take turns winning. Pretend to time his run. Create relays where he has to run across the room to pick up an object, such as a small stuffed animal, turn around, and run it back to you. Helping your child improve his coordination and muscular power protects him so that when he does run in the house, he can do it without hurting himself.

*For more on water play and teaching swimming, see* **pages 819–23.**

**Water play**  In well-supervised, shallow water, your 2-year-old can have hours of fun. Jumping up and down in waist-deep water is great aerobic exercise and it also teaches children to take their feet off the bottom without fear of going under. Teach your child how to play "motor boat" by standing in waist-deep water, bending over and blowing bubbles in the water as you run forward; this is good exercise and also teaches the basic breathing mechanism used in swimming the crawl stroke. Throw your child a beach ball as he stands in shallow water; he'll develop eye-hand coordination as he tries to catch it and the inevitable splash in the face will teach him that getting his face wet can be fun.

**Small-object manipulation** Your 2-year-old can now use his hands with improved dexterity. He enjoys stringing beads on a shoelace, unscrewing the lids of jars, and cutting dough with cookie-cutters. For quiet-time physical fun, try activities that let your child wiggle his fingers in water, sand, or clay. This helps him develop the finger dexterity he needs to write, cut with scissors, and dress himself.

# Teaching safety to your toddler

No doubt your home has been safety-proofed since your baby began to crawl. You've moved the cleaning products from under the sink; you've put safety latches on everything that opens; you've put gates across your stairs. But now that your toddler is better able to understand the word *no*, you might think it's time to ease up on the safety barriers. Think again. Although this is a good time to talk to your child about dangerous actions or situations like running into the street, it is *not* a good time to let down your guard and let him play unsupervised. He will listen to you when you talk about safety; he will agree with what you ask of him; he will intend to stay away from the curb, but then before you can blink, he'll be out in the middle of the road.

You can almost predict these disasters because 2-year-olds are impulsive. They act before they think. No amount of talking or explaining will change that. So although you may have warned your child a thousand times that it's dangerous to climb up on the bookshelf, and he may have promised never to go near it, you shouldn't be surprised when you look up and find him teetering on the highest point. No matter how cooperative your toddler may seem, never be lulled into thinking you can trust him not to let his curiosity lure him into trouble.

# Bedtime power struggles

A child's bedtime should be a welcome respite from a busy day, but all too often, parents find themselves locked in a battle with a child who's balking at going to bed. Bedtime battles often surface at around age 2 for a number of reasons.

• **Fear of separation.** A toddler may be afraid to go to bed if he has a problem with nighttime separation from his parents. Practice

*For more on
security objects,
see **pages 138**
and **210**.*

in making this separation will help. In the meantime, be sure your child gets lots of hugging and other reassurances during his waking hours and encourage his attachment with a security object to help him handle separation from you.

- **Fear of the dark.** If your child fears sleeping in a dark room, use a nightlight or keep his room door ajar with hallway light filtering in until he's sound asleep.

- **An upset schedule.** If his bedtime isn't regular—if he goes to bed at 7 p.m. one night and 9 p.m. the next—he probably won't be sleepy when you're ready to put him down for the night. When he gets off schedule, you may need to work gradually, over two or three days, to get back to his normal bedtime.

- **Curiosity.** Some kids simply don't want to miss out on anything going on in their fascinating environment—so they resist sleep. While you don't want to stifle your child's curiosity, you do need to be firm that certain hours of the evening and night are grown-up times. Also don't make an unnecessary show of anything interesting you're planning for after his bedtime.

- **Inappropriate associations.** Some children resist a going-to-bed routine because they've already learned to associate sleep with other activities. If your child has learned to fall asleep on the sofa while you watch TV, or in your arms while you rock in the rocking chair, or in your bed, this is his established bedtime routine. Unfortunately, these bedtime habits are tough to break and cause many sleep problems down the line. If your child resists the new bedtime routine that makes sleep a scheduled and natural part of each day, be prepared for some difficult nights ahead as you seek to undo bad habits.

---

**"IT WORKED FOR ME"**

### A "Goodnight" Ritual

When my 2½-year-old, Ben, decided that he didn't want to go to bed at his regular time, we tried pushing his bedtime back by one-half hour—but that didn't help. He didn't seem to want to let go of my husband and me, or our dog, Reggie. So we set up a "goodnight time." We made a ritual out of everybody saying good-night to each other. We said good-night to Reggie and put him in the kitchen where he sleeps. We had Ben say good-night to Reggie, give him a dog treat, and pat him. Then we said good-night to all our son's stuffed animals and let Ben cover them up so they could "sleep." Finally, we said good-night to Ben. For the first few nights, Ben called out to us. Then one night, as we left his room, we heard him say to one of his stuffed animals, "Good-night. Time to go to sleep."

# Your child's sexuality

Sexuality for a toddler focuses on learning about his body and how it compares to everybody's else's. His exploration of body parts is not sexual—it's purely scientific. Continuing into his preschool years, his curiosity will expand to include not just his body but yours and the bodies of his playmates. Here are some things to know about your child's sexuality.

**Self-touching is normal.** It's not uncommon for toddlers to spend much of their day with their hands down the front of their pants. This is especially true once they are out of diapers and have more freedom to explore their genital area. It's not sexual interest, per se, that causes them to explore their genital area; it's curiosity in general. Just as they have explored their fingers and toes and elbows, toddlers want to explore the penis and vagina. Then when they notice that touching genitals feels good, they want to do it again and again.

Because sticking hands down into the pants is not socially acceptable in public, you may be tempted to make your child stop his exploration. But insisting that he not touch himself will only make him more determined and create a power struggle. It will also cause him to think that the good feeling he gets from touching his genitals is bad or forbidden. Instead, you'll have a better chance of curbing genital touching if you start to teach your child the difference between private and public activities. Explain that some things are okay at home (and then ignore the behavior at home), but are not okay out of the house—not because there's anything wrong with it, but because it's a private activity. By the age of 3 to 4, children should have internalized the concept that genital play is not a public activity.

Some children will hold onto their genitals to comfort themselves, much as they attach themselves to security blankets or pacifiers to help them feel secure and calm. If your child seems to stick his hands down his pants during most of his waking hours, you might look to see if he is experiencing any stress. The same circumstances that can trigger regression—stress or changes in his environment—can also make him look for a new source of comfort. If you can relieve the stress, you may be able to keep him away from the habit of handling his genitals for comfort.

## Family Nudity

Children often learn about mature sexual anatomy and opposite-sex anatomy from seeing their parents naked. Shared nudity with the same-sex parent can help a child develop positive feelings about his own sexuality. The issue of cross-gender nudity is more controversial. Most child-development experts agree that there is no reason to avoid cross-gender nudity during the toddler years if you feel comfortable and calm about it. When your toddler begins to ask questions, points to your genitals or even tugs on them, this is the appropriate time to take cover and introduce the idea of modesty and privacy. By the age of 3, when strong gender identity is forming, cross-gender nudity should be forsaken.

**Erections are normal.** When the diapers come off, a little boy is bound to notice that when he handles his penis, it gets hard. His natural curiosity isn't going to let this go by unnoticed. Some boys find this funny; others find it frightening; and still others think it's no big deal at all. If your son wants an explanation for his erection, be brief and casual. This isn't the time to jump into an explanation of human reproduction. Simply explain that sometimes his penis gets hard; it's perfectly natural and it happens to all boys and men.

**Disrobing is natural for young children.** Many toddlers love to undress and run around naked. Many become quite adept at getting out of diapers or pants faster than you can catch them. This preference for nudity is not related to their dawning sexuality. It is a sign of things much more practical: being nude is more comfortable; taking clothes off is a new skill they enjoy practicing; and your shocked reaction is fun to watch. You can help this phase pass more quickly if you don't make a big deal out of it. In the privacy of your own home, let your child run naked if he insists, explaining that it is not okay to be naked in public. Don't laugh at his in-the-nude antics; you'll only encourage him to do it for attention. Don't scold or punish; you don't want him to learn that his body is bad. In your home, try to ignore the show. In public, calmly and quietly re-dress your child while giving a reminder of the rule against undressing in front of other people. By the age of 3 or so, you can insist that your child at least wear underpants around the house. Instead of allowing him to play naked regularly, give him more socially acceptable naked play by expanding his bath time, for example, if he enjoys nudity.

**Children are curious about anatomy.** Eventually, your child will see other children naked. It may be younger or older siblings. It may be children changing at the beach. It may be a baby getting a diaper change. It may be at nursery school in the communal toileting area. Whoever and wherever it is, another child's nakedness may bring up questions or concerns from your child. Little girls who see boys may get upset that they don't have a penis. Little boys who see girls may worry that they will lose their penises. If your child expresses these concerns give reassurance and a couple of key facts. Explain that boys and men have penises, and that girls and women have vaginas. Boys and girls are different—they're supposed to be. A simple picture book written at a child's level that illustrates the physical differences between little boys and little girls will reinforce your words.

**Playing doctor is not a sexual game.** Young children not only explore their own sexual anatomy, they are also curious about what's in the pants of other children. This is just an outgrowth of their natural curiosity about everything—it is not sexual. If you find your child playing "I'll show you mine if you show me yours," don't overreact. Toddlers, particularly, have no idea that showing their genitals is any more daring than showing their elbows—at least not until they see the shocked reactions of adults. Discovering your child discovering another child's genitalia creates a perfect opportunity to matter-of-factly comment on the situation: "I see you're showing each other your penises" (or vaginas, or both if the show is between opposite-sex friends). Use the moment as an opportunity to encourage modesty: "This part of your body is private and you shouldn't let your friends see it or touch it." And then distract: "Let's play with these brand new blocks." Never ridicule or punish your child for playing doctor. You'll instill shame into something that started out very innocently and naturally, and you'll lose the perfect opportunity to discuss modesty and privacy.

**Teaching your child about sexuality** As the explorations of sexuality begin in toddlerhood and continue through the preschool years, remember:
• **Set boundaries.** Let children know that self-stimulation and nudity are things we do in private, not in public.
• **Answer questions.** Be as matter-of-fact as you can and answer only those questions your child asks; don't get involved in long scientific lectures that will only serve to confuse your child. Be aware of your tone and body language when talking to your child about sex.
• **Use age-appropriate and socially appropriate language.** Teach your children the correct terms for parts of the anatomy, but

don't go overboard with describing and naming sexual apparatus. You may also have to share with your child the social restrictions on publicly naming his sexual organs, perhaps suggesting that he refer to his "private parts" in public.

• **Look at books together.** Read age-appropriate picture books to teach a younger child what a boy's or girl's body looks like.

• **Encourage curiosity.** Praise your child for asking questions about sex; let him know you're glad he asked. Your calm and matter-of-fact attitude that will give your child a positive definition of sexuality.

### Mom-and-son baths

*"I still bathe with my 2-year-old son. At what point should a mom stop taking baths with her boys?"*

In the near future, your son will begin to ask you questions about your anatomy. If you answer his questions about your breasts as casually as if he pointed to your elbow, you will help him learn about anatomy without associating it with guilt or shame and can still continue to bathe with him. Then, some time between his third and fourth birthday he will begin to develop gender identity and realize that you are a girl and he is a boy, and that you are physically different. This is an appropriate time to discontinue bathing together and to teach the concepts of modesty and the mutual need for privacy.

# *Emotional development*

The world of a 2-year-old is full of contradictions and uncertainty. One minute he is a bossy tyrant, sure of his dictates; the next he's a clinging whiner, unsure of what he wants and needs.

## Your child's feelings

In the course of one day, you may see signs of all of the following feelings:

**Insecurity** The 2-year-old hasn't yet figured out exactly how the world works or what he can expect to happen each day. This sense of insecurity leads him to develop inexplicable fears of things like the dark, or thunder, or even a particular room. He now resists any change in his routine because routine helps him keep things in order and gives him a feeling of control. He will also remain very possessive of his things and is not yet ready to share willingly. Your 2-year-old constantly seeks praise for his accomplishments.

**Frustration** Two-year-olds have not yet developed a tolerance for frustration. When things don't go their way, when you don't successfully read their minds or when their fingers won't cooperate with what their brains want to do, they will melt into tantrums. These emotional fits will peak during this year and give way slowly to a more stable reaction to frustration and to fewer violent mood swings.

*For ideas on handling tantrums, see **pages 398–99**.*

**Willfulness** Your 2-year-old will begin to resist your help. He will insist on putting on his coat by himself; he will scream when you won't let him comb his own hair. This willfulness is a sign that he is growing up and that he is beginning to feel secure enough to try to manage things for himself. This persistent defiance is tiring for parents, but it is a positive step toward independence. He will assert his "me-ness" with others, too, often bossing friends and others around.

**Affection** Now is a wonderful time for hugs and kisses. Your child enjoys showing great affection toward you, other family members, and even some other children. A 2-year-old can also be standoffish and refuse to be held; it all depends on his mood.

**How your 2-year-old develops secure relationships** Your toddler is ready to move from relationships based purely on physical sensations to ones that engage his body, mind, *and* emotions. You can see this most clearly in pretend play in which he can try out and learn about new emotional ideas in his relationships. Your two-year-old will not only comfort his "injured" stuffed animal, but will also look for ways to ease the pain with bandages or a trip to the pretend doctor. He will give food and drink to weary toy soldiers. He will take note of another child's tears and laughter and may cry or giggle, too, just because he feels what others are feeling. By examining others' feelings, he can think further about his own needs in relationships.

**Helping your child grow** Your 2-year-old needs your steady and calm influence to make it through this emotionally rocky time. Here's how you can help:

• **Create predictable routines.** Ease his insecurities by creating daily routines that give a predicable quality to his day.

• **Praise his efforts.** When he accomplishes what he's set out to do, let him know you've noticed. Don't go overboard, however, since you don't want him to equate every effort with lavish praise.

• **Reduce his load of daily frustrations.** Offer lots of age-appropriate toys and activities rather than letting him struggle too much with things beyond his capabilities. Recognize that tantrums may be a sign of overload and deal with them in a consistent and calm manner.

*See page 188 for more information about encouraging independence in toddlers.*

• **Encourage independence.** Leave enough time in your schedule for your 2-year-old to do things himself. Recognize defiance as a natural step toward independence and ease his discomfort in this tyrannical role with lots of hugs and kisses.

• **Help him recognize feelings and thoughts.** Promote secure relationships by encouraging your child to think about feelings and ideas, not just physical actions. When he sees a picture of a dog and remarks, "I see dog," take the discussion further by asking your child how he feels when he plays with a dog. Give him words such as "happy" and "sad" to express emotional ideas.

## Routines that help your child feel secure

Daily routines help a toddler in many ways. They offer a sense of security and allow her to feel she has some control over her environment at a time when she often sees the world as a big, scary place. They give her a framework in which to master new skills. Routines ease your child's natural feelings of vulnerability by giving order to her world and offer a feeling of empowerment by letting her know what to expect next. Routines also help young children manage impulsive behavior by assuring them of what is expected of them, reducing the temptation to do something outside the ordinary. And the repetitious aspect of routines helps children develop the habit of self-discipline they need to become self-reliant.

Your 2-year-old may meet this need for sameness by setting up elaborate rituals. She may insist, for example, that her coat goes on before the hat; breaking this order is reasonable cause, to her, for a tantrum. She may demand that everyone sits in the same place at the dinner table at each meal; a change makes eating impossible for her. She may notice if you change the car route to the baby-sitter's and react with fear and confusion. As rigid as this may appear to you, try to appease your child's need for order.

Predictable routines also ease your interactions with your child, making transitions such as going to nursery school, eating family meals, and settling down for bedtime less fertile ground for a power struggle.

The earlier routines are introduced, the better, and initiating them now (if you haven't already) will give your child the feeling of safety she needs to explore the world. Don't expect your child to accept new routines immediately or entirely. She may cry and complain, but if you remain firm and calm, she will accept the routine. Persistent repetition will help her understand that this is what happens at this time of day. The sameness of a sleep routine, for example, carries comfort, security, and a promise that the nightly separation is predictable and temporary.

Whatever routines you create, make sure they're ones you'll want to repeat and can pass on to your child's other caregivers. This continuity of care eases the transitions that confuse and scare young children. If you don't want to kiss *all* your child's stuffed animals and read five books every night, don't start. Once a routine is established, it's very hard to change it. Also, make sure that a baby-sitter knows about the routine and can perform it. If you go out for a quick night at the movies and forget to tell the baby-sitter about the bedtime routine, toddler may be wide awake waiting for you when you come home.

Life is not always as orderly as we'd like it to be, of course, and every family's normal routine is occasionally broken. Vacations, illness, visiting relatives, or even a spontaneous decision to do something different will upset the norm. Although it's bound to happen, try not to change or interrupt your child's daily routines too often or without warning. Explain in advance when you know the schedule will change. Assure your child that the change is temporary and that tomorrow (a word she is beginning to understand) her routine will return to normal. Try to keep the weekends as much like weekdays as possible. Give your toddler snacks, lunch, and a nap at about the same time she has them during the week. Also, try to put her to bed at the same time every day of the week.

Throughout this year, routines will give your child a secure anchor. They promise that home is one place where events and activities are guaranteed, secure, and stable.

**Dealing with the pacifier habit**  Your child may be using a pacifier to help her through the transition from total parental dependence to independence; the comfort derived from sucking gives her a self-directed way of handling stress without looking to you for help. If she's developed an attachment to a pacifier, you needn't try to force your child to give it up just yet.

Most children voluntarily drop the pacifier habit well before the age of five. By this time, they have developed other sources of pleasure and security. Peer pressure and fear of appearing "babyish" also encourage children to discard the habit as they enter the preschool years. Although you shouldn't try to break the sucking habit at this stage of your child's development, you can use preventive measures that weaken your child's reliance on her pacifier.

• **Limit boredom.** Many toddlers want their pacifiers when they're bored. You can reduce their daily sucking time by keeping the pacifier out of sight and keeping them actively involved in play or games.

• **Keep her mouth busy.** When she reaches for the pacifier, ask her a question, encourage her to sing a song, request a kiss.

• **Deal with her other needs.** Don't use the pacifier as a baby-sitter to keep your child quiet and calm. If she's whining or demanding, deal with the situation that's upsetting her without reaching for the pacifier.

• **Don't translate communication garbled by the pacifier.** With a pacifier in her mouth your child may speak words you can't understand or she may get in the habit of pointing and grunting at objects she wants. Explain that she'll have to remove the pacifier if she wants you to understand her. Less frequent use of the pacifier will encourage greater language development.

• **Limit sleep-time use.** It's not really a good idea to let your child sleep with a pacifier because losing it during the night or during naps can awaken her and interrupt her sleep. If she's already in the sleep-time pacifier habit, however, she's now old enough to find it again on her own and may be able to soothe herself back to sleep with a minimum of interruption. If waking up to find her pacifier has become a problem, help wean her from this use of it. Be aware that there will be a few nights of problems. Give your child an extra dose of love and attention to ease the transition. You might also institute a special nighttime ritual to substitute for the pacifier.

These measures may reduce the need for the pacifier, but they probably won't end it. If your child needs it for comfort, she will give it up when she learns other coping skills. In the meantime, check with your pediatrician to be sure you're using a pacifier that won't cause damage to the mouth or teeth, keep it clean, and replace it when it gets worn.

**Easing separation anxiety in toddlers** A toddler is a demanding and egocentric little person who has no reason to believe that you have anything else to do in life but look after his needs. At the same time, in his struggle for independence, he wants to be separate from you—until you leave the room. Then his fear of losing you becomes the overwhelming emotion that brings on feelings of anxiety. When separating from your 2-year-old, whether you're going off to work or simply leaving your child with a Saturday-night sitter, you will likely witness a protest. But now your toddler is capable of understanding more of what you say to him than he was as an infant and is more easily convinced that you will return. The separation is also made a bit easier than during infancy because your child can now keep a picture of you in his mind that assures him you haven't disappeared just because he can't see you.

Taking advantage of your child's need for routine can make life easier for both of you since separation problems are often rooted in a fear of the unpredictable rather than the fear of actual separation. Children who are regularly being cared for by others need to know where they're going, when they'll go, who will take them, what they'll do while they're there, and who will pick them up. The more predictable this routine is, the less it causes concern for your child. If your child goes to Grandma's some days, and to a baby-sitter on other days, and stays home another day, and these changes vary from week to week, this schedule will fill her with separation anxiety because she'll be unsure of what to expect. If such a schedule is necessary, you can ease your child's confusion by marking a large calendar with symbols to show her where each day will be spent. For instance, she could put stickers with stars on the days she'll be with Grandma, flowers on the days she'll go to the baby-sitter's, and

*See **page 654** for handling other stress-reducing habits.*

*For more on handling separation when your child is in childcare, see **page 377**.*

happy faces on the remaining days at home. This takes the surprise and trauma out of each morning.

## Encouraging empathy

Although still quite egocentric, your 2-year-old is beginning to learn that her feelings, which she can now label with names like "happy" or "sad," sometimes are felt by other people too. In her daily quest to explore her world, your child now extends her search to exploring feelings: She wants to know why her playmate is crying. She wants to know why you look sad. This curiosity leads her to a new-found sensitivity toward others.

You can watch your 2-year-old's emotional response to others develop gradually. Love is expressed with more tenderness now as your child realizes that sharing hugs and kisses make you feel happy, too. You may see your child pat the head of a playmate who has hurt himself, showing that not only does she feel for her friend, but wants to do something to help. If another child is crying, your 2-year-old may start to cry, too. These empathetic responses show that your child's perspective of the world is widening; she is starting to put herself in another person's shoes and is learning to recognize and respect the feelings and needs of others.

There's generally no need to push your child into empathetic acts of kindness. Being empathetic is as natural a reaction for her as crying or being angry when she's frustrated. However, you can encourage her altruistic inclinations through your own example and with praise. In the life you share with your child, she experiences your thoughtfulness and sensitivity firsthand. By letting your child know that you listen to her, understand her, and respect her needs, you offer her a living example of how to treat others generously. When you catch your child acting with sensitivity—when she gently hugs a crying playmate, for example—be sure to praise her. This lets her know that empathetic actions are valued and appreciated by others.

## What sharing means

Learning to share is a social skill that takes a certain degree of readiness. Two-year-olds are not ready. In fact, your 2-year-old will defend to the death his right to hold onto any toy he has played with, is playing with, or might play with rather than share it with a playmate or a sibling. He views his possessions almost as a part of himself and is not willing to let them go.

At this age, there are several roadblocks to sharing. Your 2-year-old is just learning the concept of ownership and the word "mine." He is not ready to recognize the ownership rights of others—everything that anybody has is "mine." It's perfectly natural for your child to grab another child's plaything and want to take it home, and yet he'll protest loudly if anyone touches his own toys.

Unfortunately, the concept of ownership comes before the concept of sharing in your toddler's emotional development. Your toddler needs to enjoy the feeling of total possession for a while, then, at around age 3, he can move toward the idea of sharing. Your 2-year-old also resists sharing because he can't grasp the concept of "borrowing." He assumes that if he gives something away, it's gone forever. These beliefs make it impossible for toddlers to share willingly.

**Helping your toddler learn to share**  Though you can't label a 2-year-old who refuses to share as selfish, or uncooperative, or even ungenerous, you can introduce the idea of sharing and offer your child at-home opportunities to give it a try.

• **Introduce the concept of other people's ownership.** Toddlers need to learn that some things belong to others. This desk is Mommy's. This doll is yours. This coat is Daddy's.

• **Show how give-and-take works.** Give your child something; take it back. Roll a ball back and forth. Show that when you give something away, it comes back.

• **Take turns.** Help your child learn that she must wait in line for the slide; she must wait her turn for an empty swing; she must not grab something out of another child's hands. These social conventions don't come easily to a toddler, but by your insisting and reinforcing them regularly, your child will begin to see that other people have rights, too. This idea makes sharing easier.

• **Acknowledge your child's feelings.** Tell her, "I know it's hard to share your favorite things." Letting her know that you understand her reluctance may help her overcome her possessiveness sooner.

• **Don't involve playmates at first.** Don't take something away from her and give it to her playmate. If you do, you'll find that your child will more fiercely guard her possessions for fear that not only her friend but you, too, will take them away.

- **Use example to show her how to share.** Make a habit of sharing and talk about what you're doing. You might say, "These sunglasses are mine, but I'll be happy to share them with you."
- **Role play sharing situations.** You might say, "I'll let you play with my magazines if you let me play with your truck."
- **Praise any move toward sharing.** Children tend to repeat acts that earn them applause.

**Preventing sharing battles** You can avoid many major outbursts if you don't force your child to share. At this age, children have a strong need for stability and security. They need to know that some things are theirs and theirs alone and that their needs are just as important as another child's needs. Still, when 2-year-olds play together, there will be inevitable sharing battles. You can reduce the tension of these get-togethers if you plan ahead:

- **Have duplicate toys.** Ideally, plan to have at least two of each toy during playdates. Or, plan activities that use toys that let everyone be involved at the same time—clay, crayons, and sand, for example. Ask the other child's parent to bring some toys in case your child refuses to share anything. This will prevent the playdate from being a total disaster for your guest. It could also allow each child to practice trading a toy for a time.
- **Put away toys you know are very special** to your child and will cause an outburst if anyone even touches them.
- **Be reasonable in your expectations.** On special occasions, don't expect the concept of sharing to develop suddenly. Your child won't share his new birthday presents with his party friends, so put them away immediately after opening.
- **Make special allowances for older siblings.** Don't expect your child to share anything if a new baby has just joined your family. It's hard enough having to suddenly share your attention; don't compound this by insisting that your child share his "baby" toys.

After you prepare to avoid sharing battles, the best thing to do is stand back. If your child still grabs and covets, don't despair. The tug-of-war that results when one child wants to "share" and the other doesn't isn't a sign of selfishness or aggression. It's a forum for learning to stand up for one's rights. Let your child engage in the struggle, stepping in only when one of the children is in danger of being hurt.

# Your child's social style

This year you'll really see your child's inborn personality direct how she interacts with others. You may discover that she is naturally shy, or confidently outgoing, or persistently aggressive. As your child begins to find herself and venture out into the world, you may find that she needs help to fit in and act in a civilized, socially acceptable way. She needs your good example; she needs your encouragement, and she needs you to show her where the limits and boundaries are.

**The shy child** Many toddlers appear to be shy. They hold back before venturing into a new situation. They hug their parent's leg as they approach a birthday party. They won't get off their parent's lap at the restaurant. They hide during introductions.

If these actions describe your child, you might worry that this shyness will have some negative effect on her future. You may worry that by clinging to you she may miss out on having fun with playmates or may lack the confident and independent personality needed to make her way in the world. The truth is, if your child is holding back from venturing into the world on her own right now, you can stop worrying.

Most toddlers are shy to some extent, whether it is with other children, or with adults, or with any stranger. This reticence is simply an expression of caution in a world that is still new and sometimes a little overwhelming. When your child won't leave your leg, she's telling you, in a non-verbal way, that she needs your support. A shy or bashful child is often considered to be lacking in self-confidence. However, she actually may be quite confident in familiar situations and places, such as at home, when she doesn't have to deal with unfamiliar surroundings and people. By age 6, most children grow out of their shyness. But about 15 percent of children are born with temperaments that make them shy throughout their lives. These children are inner-focused and need time to process their experiences. They hide or show signs of discomfort around strangers; they cling to their parents and are reluctant to try new games. These children never completely shake their shyness, but most learn how to cope with it.

At age 2, it's impossible to tell whether your child's shyness is inborn or developmental, though if you or your spouse is particularly shy, your child is more likely to have inherited the trait. To help her at this stage, it's best not to look for a cure, but rather to find ways to help her to feel confident about herself and to have positive feelings about her interactions with others. These actions can help:

• **Don't label her as shy.** This label will become a handy shield to hide behind and will become a self-fulfilling prophesy. Children learn they don't have to be sociable because "I'm shy." If other people call her shy, quickly note that she's not shy; she simply likes to take her time getting to know people.

• **Don't compare her to other, more outgoing children.** Your child is not other children; comparisons of any attribute will hurt her feelings and damage her self-esteem. This is especially true in the area of shyness because low self-esteem perpetuates the problem.

• **Don't push.** If your child needs time and space to warm up to people, pushing her out in front of you will only make her more determined to hide. If you know she feels anxious in certain situations, give her reassurance and comfort, not ridicule. Build in time to relax when you take her into new situations by arriving early. If you go early to a birthday party, for example, she won't be rushed into the center of attention as everyone looks to see who has just arrived; nor will she be as overwhelmed by the high activity level of a crowd. Arriving early gives her time to adjust to her new surroundings.

• **Practice socializing during playtime.** Your child's stuffed animals or puppets can help her practice feeling comfortable with other people. You might pretend that her teddy bear has just arrived at a friend's house to find that there is another teddy bear visiting. Help your child describe how the teddy feels. Maybe she can suggest something for the bear to say or do. Giving the bear the confidence to make a new friend will give your child an idea of how she too can react to new people.

• **Rehearse greetings.** Before a birthday party or family gathering, practice shaking hands and looking someone directly in the eye. Make it into a game.

• **Prepare for social situations in daily activities.** When company comes to your house, let your child be with you to greet the guests. Let her show them into the house and stay nearby to watch how you interact. Look for opportunities to give your child a chance to practice talking to others. Encourage her to talk to the grocer, the doctor, the mail carrier, and neighborhood children. Each of these experiences will teach her how loudly she needs to speak to be heard and how others will respond positively to her.

- **Give your child "warm-up" time.** Many children who are initially uneasy in a social situation will warm up and join the action if they're given enough time to adjust to the place and the faces. If your child shies away from others, don't immediately take her home. Stay where she can see you, but give her a chance to venture out as she becomes more at ease.
- **Offer reinforcement.** If you see that your child is holding back from a situation that she would like to be active in, help her find a comfortable way to join in. You might suggest that she show the other children her new toy. If she still won't go, you might offer to go along with her. If she draws courage from your presence, lead her over to the group. Stay as long as she needs you and then gradually retreat, letting her know exactly where you will be if she should need you.
- **Be understanding.** Usually it isn't people themselves who make your child act shy; it's the way they behave toward her. Some rush up to children and hug and kiss them or tweak their cheeks and expect a warm response. Most people, even adults, like to get to know people before they have physical contact like this. Let others know that your child prefers a more hands-off approach. If your child prefers to peek out from behind your legs at first, let her; this is a place where she can hide from unwanted endearments and have time to size up the situation. This is her way of getting to know people. Eventually she will come out and voluntarily move toward the action.

**The aggressive toddler** Many toddlers are surprisingly aggressive, and can inflict harm on others if their behavior isn't contained. Fortunately, physical aggression usually represents a developmental stage that children soon grow out of as they learn other, better ways to express themselves.

Young children act aggressively for many reasons:
- **Lack of verbal skills.** Your child doesn't yet have the verbal skills he needs to express his feelings or needs. For him, aggressive actions speak louder than words. You can help him learn to communicate with words by patiently showing him how words can be used to work through a problem. At first, speak for him: You might say, "You must feel very angry right now." Repeat the rule that "hitting your friend is not allowed." Until your child's verbal skills improve, you can also help avoid aggressive acts by providing opportunities for safely venting pent-up frustration and energy. Once

in a while, give him the freedom to run and yell and punch pillows.

- **Lack of restraint.** Your child hasn't yet learned how to control his impulses, so when he feels like hitting someone, he does. It takes time for a child to learn the restrictions society puts on aggressive behavior. You can help him by consistently making it clear that the use of physical force to get what you want is unacceptable. Teach him through word and example that it is wrong to hurt another person. This isn't a lesson children learn quickly, but if you're persistent, your child will learn it eventually.

*For more about the frustrations of 2-year-olds, see **pages 244–45**.*

- **Frustration.** When your toddler hits and throws, he may be acting out his frustrations. Remember, 2-year-olds are quite egocentric and when they want something another child has, they want it *now*. When they play with a puzzle, they want it to work *now*. When they want your attention, they want it *now*. When things don't happen quickly and easily, they become frustrated and often aggressive, pushing, shoving, hitting, and biting. You can reduce daily frustrations by helping your child learn the skills he needs to feel competent and by making sure his toys are age-appropriate.

- **Looking for attention.** Your 2-year-old may have already learned that he gets more attention when he is aggressive than when he is more mildly behaved. Make a habit of giving praise and attention when he is being calm and cooperative. Don't overreact to his aggressive moments. Ignore them unless he is hurting himself or another child. This change in attitude will soon show him that he doesn't need to hit or throw to get your attention.

- **Satisfying physical needs.** Your child may act aggressively when he is tired, hungry, or bored. This is his way of showing you the frustration he feels at not being able to meet his own needs. The next time he pushes over a playmate, check to see if there may be an unmet physical need.

*For more information on handling aggression, see **pages 394–96**.*

- **A play habit.** Do you or your spouse play rough with your child? If you laugh when he pushes you, or if you playfully wrestle him to the ground when he grabs your arm, you may be teaching him to act aggressively for fun. Even in play, always let your child know that hurting other people is not allowed.

If, despite your efforts, your child continues to act overly aggressive and seems unrepentant you should talk to his pediatrician about it. Persistent aggression is a cause for concern. An evaluation to discover the causes of the behavior as well as early intervention are needed to help your child learn other ways of expressing himself.

**Planning the perfect playdate** By the age of 2, most children are ready and eager for some regular play time with others their age. During her time together with another child, your 2-year-old can develop a sense of personal identity by comparing herself and her family to others. She can begin to learn the push and pull of friendship as she sharpens her communication, conflict-resolution, and empathy skills. And, of course, she'll have fun.

Here are some ways you can help:

• **Prepare in advance for the playdate.** Make sure your child is well rested and not hungry. If the date is at your home, double check that the play area is childproofed for your young visitor, not just your own child who may know what's touchable and what's not. Plan for your constant supervision, since wide-awake 2-year-olds should not be left alone for even a few moments.

• **Make sharing easier.** Provide multiple toys and toys that are easy to share.

• **Make your playdate guest feel comfortable.** Most 2-year-olds still want their parents or regular caregivers to stay with them on a playdate, even if they are very familiar with you, your child, and your home. If it raises the comfort level of the get-together, encourage the visiting grownup to stay. If squabbles threaten to disrupt the playdate, step in to change the activity. If that doesn't work, don't punish your child for not playing "nicely" but remove him from the fun for a few minutes so he can calm down and then go back and try again.

• **Step back.** When your 2-year-old becomes familiar with her new playmate, it's time to step back a bit. As long as no one is getting hurt either physically or emotionally, let the children play and engage in some squabbling without constant hovering and intrusion. This tells your child that you trust her to solve minor disagreements by herself and that she doesn't always need to look to you to intervene in her growing social life.

• **Broaden the range of friendships.** From time to time, invite an older child to play with your 2-year-old. While two 5-year-olds would likely balk at having to entertain a 2-year-old, one-on-one mixed-aged playdates offer something positive to each child. Your

## 2-year-olds at Play

Unlike older children who interact openly and consistently with their chosen playmates, your 2-year-old is more likely to interact only sporadically with another 2-year-old with whom you have arranged some play time. Similar to babies and toddlers, 2-year-olds' play will be parallel—side-by-side—as they gladly share space but not necessarily toys or game plans. Now, however, they are ready to begin the meaningful interactions that will mark their later years of play.

*For more on sharing, see **pages 236–38**.*

younger child gets to learn more of the ways of the world of play, and the older child gets to show off his advanced abilities and to hone his nurturing skills. Just as with same-age playdates, it's important for an adult to be ever present during these get-togethers.

• **Evaluate the good and the bad.** After each playdate, take time to think over the event. What activities should you repeat next time? Which ones should be dropped? Do the children enjoy coloring and painting or running and jumping? Plan to structure your next playdate accordingly.

## Fears and frustrations

With his limited experience and growing imagination and abilities, fears and frustrations enter your 2-year-old's life in a new and more complex way. As an infant, your child may have had an intense fear of separation from you or a pronounced fear of strangers. Now his growing imagination allows him to entertain idea-fueled worries and concerns. The bath he loved just a few months ago may suddenly be met with terror because now he can wonder what happens to the water that goes down the drain. He may worry that he, too, could disappear so simply and yet so dramatically. If a friendly dog slobbers on him unexpectedly, he may become frightened of all dogs. If a very real and frightening incident occurs, such as an injury at the playgound or being knocked over by a big wave at the beach, he may become clingy in a way you haven't seen for months.

Experiences and imagination will also fuel his frustrations as he attempts to accomplish things that he cannot yet do. While you encourage him to enjoy the toddler swings at the playground, he becomes angry when he isn't allowed to run into the big-kid swing area. When you praise his three-block tower, he howls because he wants to build with ten blocks. While children need to experience some frustration in order to learn how to deal with it, too much frustration is overwhelming and can trigger tantrums. To ease your child's fears and frustrations and make them more manageable:

• **Don't set the bar too high.** Your child is having enough trouble living up to his own expectations; if you compound this with constant criticism of his fears or set overly high expectations for his achievements, you'll thwart his own internal motivation to succeed.

• **Offer encouragement and praise.** If your child insists on trying and trying to do something, don't discourage him with warnings that he'll never be able to do it. If he takes one small step toward overcoming his fears, don't overlook its importance. Tell him you're proud that he doesn't give up and that he tries so hard.

- **Choose age-appropriate entertainment.** Select toys that challenge your child but that promise eventual success. Even the most confident child will fall to pieces trying to complete a puzzle that's too difficult for his age. Select TV, movies, and books that will not frighten or confuse your child.
- **Teach independence.** Instead of always doing things for your child, give him the skills to do things for himself. When your child is frustrated by his inability to dress himself, don't jump in and finish the job; instead take the time to teach him how to do it and let him practice under your supervision. If your child is afraid of bugs, don't always whisk the bug away; occasionally take time to show him that most bugs are not harmful and that he doesn't need you to protect him. Many of your child's frustrations and fears can be eased if he's given the time to work things out.
- **Accept your child's feelings.** Sometimes your child will not want to overcome his frustrations and fears; he'll want to quit or cry. These are perfectly acceptable ways of handling an overload of emotion when you're 2 years old. Assure him that maybe he'll feel like trying again another day.

## Handling nightmares and night terrors

Nightmares and night terrors can frequently interrupt your rest as well as your child's sleep. Young children have nightmares ten times more frequently than adults because they spend almost 80 percent of their sleep time in the "dream" sleep phase, while those in middle-age, for instance, spend only about 8 to 10 percent of their sleep in this deep phase.

**Nightmares**  It is not known what causes nightmares. Your child's imagination and creativity make her especially vulnerable to vivid dreams. Emerging strong emotions can also surface in intense dreams. Because of the fuzzy boundary between reality and fantasy, these dreams seem all too real to your child. Anxiety and stress can also be factors.

If your toddler has an occasional nightmare, don't worry. But if these bad dreams are persistent, take some time to look for any

## Easing Nighttime Fears

No matter how many times I assured my 2-year-old son that there were no monsters in his room at night, he still insisted that they were there, and that I just couldn't see them. One night I helped him pile all his stuffed animals onto his bed. We lined them up and down the blanket, atop the pillow, under the sheets, and put some securely tucked under his arms. I told him that all these animals loved him and that they were brave and strong and enjoyed protecting sleeping children. I also told him that it was impossible for monsters to get past them and that he was safe. That did it! This army of friendly protectors gave him the security he needed to fall asleep without worry.

sources of anxiety. Something in his experience or environment may be making him feel unable to cope with the demands of daily life. He may need time to adjust to recent changes in his life—the birth of a sibling, a move, a new care provider. He may be responding to family distress or to frightening images he may have seen on television or elsewhere. Or, simply because he is maturing, he may be more alert to the dangers in the world but not be mature enough to handle his fears by talking about them. To help avoid and to calm bad dreams:

• **Plan quiet evening activities.** Don't read scary picture books or allow your child to watch scary movies or TV before bedtime.

• **Leave a light on and keep the bedroom door open** if she wants you to do so. Now is not the time to talk about being a "big kid," since embarrassing your child about her fear or dismissing it without respect to her feelings will only serve to deepen it.

• **If your child wakes up crying, sympathize with his fears.** Stay with him until he calms down.

• **Avoid talking about the details of the nightmare.** Talking about it will only serve to remind your child of the scary details. If he wishes to, you can talk about the dream or draw a picture about it in the daylight.

• **Stay in your child's room rather than invite him into yours.** By letting your child regain her composure in her own room, you help her to see that her own space is quite safe after all.

**Night terrors** Sometimes young children experience night terrors, which usually occur within 90 minutes of going to sleep and are quite different from nightmares. In fact, they don't appear to be associated with dreams at all. No one knows what causes night terrors. Sleep-deprived kids are more prone to night terrors, and missed naps and delayed bedtimes may trigger them. Another cause may be a loud noise—a car horn blasting, for example—which disrupts the deep sleep without waking the child.

During a night terror, which may last from a few minutes to a half hour, your child will wake up screaming and thrashing. He will probably push you away and scream if you attempt to comfort him. Throughout the terror, you may think he is awake because his eyes are open and he may be speaking. Nevertheless, he is deeply asleep and will have no memory of what happened in the morning. The only thing you can do is to protect him from accidentally hurting himself. Also, if you think your child isn't getting enough sleep, that he's skipping naps or going to bed too late, establish fixed bedtimes and nap times.

As frightening as they appear to you, night terrors do not harm your child, nor are they indicative of any deep-rooted problem. Night terrors, which can begin as early as 9 months of age and usually peak at age 3, nearly always disappear by the age of 6. Most children have very few night terrors—just two or three throughout their preschool years. Some kids, however, have them frequently. If your child has recurrent night terrors, discuss the situation with your pediatrician.

## Regression

What's going on when your 2-year-old begins crawling and talking baby talk? Or when, after showing an interest in toilet teaching, he insists on diapers only? Regression, going back over comfortable terrain, is perfectly normal. Children's development does not move straight forward from one stage to the next. It is more often a case of two steps forward, one step back. That explains why your 2-year-old "I-can-do-it" kid may suddenly start acting younger and less capable than he is.

Although it's often difficult to pinpoint the exact reason for a regression, if you see your child reverting to "babyish" behaviors, take some time to see if you can figure out why. If you can uncover the cause, you can deal with the situation with greater sensitivity and take steps to relieve his stress.

Sometimes regression is a form of communication, so try to listen to what your child's behavior is saying to you. If you have a new

> **"IT WORKED FOR ME"**
>
> ### *Have a Monster Hunt*
>
> To ease my daughter's fear of monsters lurking in the shadows, she and I conduct a nightly "Monster Hunt." We use a flashlight and check under the bed, in the closet, even in the dresser drawers. It's become such a game that her fears of monsters have pretty much disappeared.

## Why Kids Regress

Any change in a 2-year-old's life can cause him to take a step backward. Among the most common triggers are a family vacation; the arrival of a new baby; seeing a younger sibling hit a developmental milestone, such as crawling or walking; entering a new nursery school or playgroup, or having a new caregiver; a move to a new house; an illness in the family; a change in the family routine, such as a parent starting work or staying home. Even a growth spurt that increases your child's need for sleep and food can trigger regressive behavior.

baby in the house, your 2-year-old may want more attention. If he reverts in behavior at the same time he starts complaining about going to nursery school, visit the school to find out what's going on. If you are distracted with a family illness or crisis, you might hire a caregiver for your child since your attention and energies are divided. Realize that your child might feel insecure or resentful about this change in routine. If you are experiencing tension at work, be aware that you may be bringing it home and upsetting your child.

If you can't find any direct reason for the regression, your child may be taking a step back just before he takes a developmental leap forward. Two-year-olds are learning so much so quickly that a few steps back once in a while are inevitable. In fact, regression is an integral part of development for virtually all toddlers. Going back to a more comfortable spot is a way of gaining the momentum needed to keep moving forward. Children move forward to master a new physical, emotional, or intellectual skill, and then retreat a bit. Temporarily reverting to crawling, for example, gives a child the confidence to perfect the new and more complex task of running and jumping.

**Handling regression**  Whether or not you can determine the cause of your child's regression, rest assured it is bound to be short-lived. All humans—and especially 2-year-olds—are programmed with an innate drive to move forward. You can get your child back on track if you follow these strategies:

• **Don't give your child a hard time about taking a step backward.** Two-year-olds are more likely to get stuck in a regression when parents make a big deal about it and turn it into a power struggle.

• **Stress the joys of being older.** Praise and encourage the part of your child that wants to be grown up. Encourage him with reminders like: "How nice it is that you are big enough to play on the slide; I'll bet your baby sister wishes she could do that, too." Point out the special toys and privileges that come with maturity.

• **Give some special, uninterrupted attention.** Plan special excursions for just the two of you. The security of your love and attention will give him the courage to move forward.

- **Play along.** If your child wants to sit in the high chair and drink from a bottle, acknowledge his feelings and let him. But let him know you're playing by saying, "Oh, you want to pretend you're a baby. Sometimes that's fun." Emphasize the word "pretend" and keep a relaxed attitude.
- **Set a time limit.** Gently let your child know that he won't be playing this game forever. Agree, for example, to prepare a bottle for this game for the next five meals if he likes. As you give him each bottle, remind him how many more are left in the game. If you can do this with a cheerful attitude, your child can give up his backsliding without feeling embarrassed or shamed.

# Cognitive development

Two-year-olds are consumed with the desire to figure out everything. Because their verbal and intellectual skills are growing by leaps and bounds, they ask lots of questions. "Why?" becomes their mantra.

## What your child knows

The cognitive skills of 2-year-olds are further developed than their physical skills. This causes toddlers much frustration. They may clearly see that the square block fits into the square hole, but their fingers may not have the dexterity needed to make it happen.

Your 2-year-old is developing a sense of time. She can see beyond the very present NOW and use words to indicate the past, present, and future. The phrase "in a minute" now begins to make some sense to her. "Later" is also beginning to have meaning. She can put events in the past, but can't differentiate between yesterday, last week, or last month. The idea of sequence is also developing, making it possible for her to understand what you mean when you say, "First we'll have juice, then we'll go out." She can think ahead and realize that first Mommy comes home, then we have dinner.

Two-year-olds show rapid cognitive growth in many areas, especially in language (see opposite). If you look closely, you'll see changes in the way they think almost daily. Watch for these signs:

• **A sense of self and others.** Your 2-year-old begins to understand separateness from you; when you walk out the door, for instance, she's aware that you, not a part of herself, is leaving. She begins to understand family relationships and she is becoming aware that people have different points of view.

• **The ability to name.** Your child is growing intellectually in her ability to recognize and name items, and to compare a picture of an item to the real thing. At about 2, some children begin to name a few colors correctly.

• **An understanding of symbols.** Your child's ability to represent things symbolically is improving. In imaginative play, you'll see shoeboxes being used as cars, and houses, and blocks.

• **Following directions.** Your 2-year-old is becoming aware of opposites. The concepts of *yes* and *no*, *come* and *go*, *fast* and *slow* are beginning to take shape, making it easier for her to follow directions. She understands physical relationships; for example: *on, in,* and *under*. She can also understand that actions have consequences, and she begins to develop a sense of responsibility.

**How your 2-year-old learns**  Up to this point, your child has learned primarily through her senses. She needed to feel and touch and manipulate. She watched closely and listened intently. Now her learning style begins to mature to include mental processes. She can form mental images of things, actions, and concepts. She will think before she acts, imagining what will happen, rather than having to see it happen. Rather than needing to physically handle an object to see if it will fit in a box, she can now use thoughtful problem-solving powers.

**Helping your child grow**  You can help your child practice mental problem solving by providing her with toys and activities that push her to think about how things work. Give her mechanical toys that move after she winds them up. Supply her with lots of toys and objects that can be sorted by size and shape and color. Buy her large-piece puzzles that she can now complete by thinking about how the shapes of the pieces match the shapes of the spaces. Offer her lots of items for make-believe play: dolls and action figures and dress-up clothes. Encourage her to create scenarios that include problems to be solved.

## Your child's language development

Shortly after your child turns 2, she will suddenly seem to understand everything you say. This year, her speaking vocabulary will grow to about 1,000 or more favorite words. She is probably using two-word combination "sentences" that you'll understand about 50 to 70 percent of the time. By the end of the year, she will be speaking four- or five-word sentences. She also begins to use pronouns this year.

A 2-year-old's approach to language is quite inventive and usually does not yet follow the standard rules of grammar. You will hear your child use words like "comed" or "goed" instead of "came" or "went." These "mistakes" are really a sign of progress. They show that your child has made a discovery about language—that most past-tense verbs end in "ed," and that words have related meanings. She may also say "yucky" for "lucky," and "mell it" for "smell it," and "pido" for "pillow." These mispronunciations are a natural part of language development. Don't correct them; simply pronounce them correctly in your own conversations.

Toddlers want to have two-sided conversations. If told "Please, get your coat," your child may ask, "Why?" simply to get a discussion going. This give-and-take of ideas is exciting to your child even though it's not always easy to understand what she is saying. While your child is talking, just nod your head, look interested, and respond with whatever comes to mind rather than getting too caught up in her pronunciations, which will only frustrate her. Soon enough, you'll understand her words.

You can help her improve her pronunciations by building on the early language skills she already has. When your toddler says, "Me down," rephrase the statement into a full sentence. Say, "Yes, you fell down." Echoing your child's ideas helps her learn how to put her thoughts into language.

As the year progresses, your 2-year-old will be using more and more complete sentences of increasing complexity. Request for help may still involve pulling an adult by the hand, but may also involve two or three words: "Wanna get down." Your child may ask for the name or location of an object, "What's dis?" or "Where baw?" There is still little conversation with other children. Most verbal communication tends to be directed toward protecting property: "No," "Don't touch," "Mine!" Your child will also figure out how to use pronouns. Her plea, "I carry you," when she wants to be held will eventually turn around to, "you carry me."

This is the year you'll watch your child grow from the little person who points to what she wants, pulls you to where she wants to go, and "talks" with a simple word or two, into a chatterbox who will dictate orders, express feelings with words, and carry on lengthy monologues and dialogues. You can stimulate language development if you:

- **Maintain eye contact** with your child when conversing.
- **Try to keep a dialogue going;** this requires genuine listening on your part.
- **Create scenarios** to encourage dialogue; play "doctor's office" or "airport," and use play phones.
- **Read** books and listen to tape-recordings of stories.
- **Establish special talking times,** such as before bedtime.
- **Be patient** with yourself when you don't understand, and with your child when she can't explain herself well.

### What speech says about hearing

*"My 2-year-old doesn't pronounce words the way his peers do. Could he have a hearing problem?"*

Possibly. If you are concerned about your child's hearing, consult your pediatrician. Your child may need to see a speech/language pathologist. Local school systems, hospitals, and community clinics often offer the services of speech/language pathologists. You can also consult a pathologist in private practice. Before age 2½—and as early as 12 to 18 months—a speech/language pathologist can work with parents to get a sample of their child's vocalizations in a play setting. If the child doesn't vocalize or produces only vowel-like sounds, the pathologist will refer the child for a hearing test. Kids older than 2½ can be given a standardized test for speech development.

## Reading to your child

By now, you've discovered the joys of reading to your child. But what you may not realize is that your 2-year-old is developmentally ready to truly discover the pleasure of books. When he was younger, he liked the colors and shapes of the pictures; he enjoyed hearing the sound of your voice, and he loved the intimacy of snuggling at storytime. But now he has the attention span necessary to follow a basic story line. He is also aware of the different characters in a story; he can pick out the details in a scene, and he has a more sophisticated ear for language. Your toddler now uses books to learn more about the world he lives in.

To ensure that you and your toddler get the most out of storytime follow these simple guidelines:

• **Choose the right time.** Traditionally bedtime is storytime, but don't get stuck on this idea if it doesn't work for you. If you're harried or tired at your child's bedtime, you won't feel much like enjoying a good book. Use any time of the day that lets you relax and have fun with reading —maybe after breakfast or when you, or your spouse, return home from work.

• **Follow your child's lead.** Don't make storytime a battle of wills over what book to read and how long to read it. Let your child choose the book, even if it's the same one five days in a row. Let him stop you to ask questions or comment. Let him stop listening when he's tired. Remember your goal is to have a good time with reading.

• **Be dramatic.** Don't let your dignity get in the way of your fun. Give each character in the story a different voice. Act out their parts with gusto. Have some fun with each book and pass that joy on to your child.

• **Ask questions.** Take time as you read to stop occasionally and engage your child in the story by asking him some questions. You might ask, "Can you find the ball the little boy wants to play with?" "Where is the girl's brother in this picture?" "What kinds of things do people usually see when they go to the zoo?" Children develop their imaginations and reasoning abilities by responding to these kinds of questions.

Books are a great place to encourage a love of reading, but they're not the only reading material that will fascinate your child. Use magazines for "picture hunts" in which you and your child hunt for pictures of babies or dogs, for example. Give your child your junk mail to open and look through. Point to signs in the store and

### Reading Is Fun!

Be enthusiastic when you read to your child—it's contagious. If the time you spend reading is playful and animated, your child will catch your love of books, your enjoyment of a good story, and your attitude that books are fun. This is your goal right now.

read them to him. Show him that reading material is everywhere and plays an important part in everyday activities.

All these reading adventures will enlarge your child's speaking vocabulary and help him learn to use language to express thoughts. These are the skills he needs to develop right now before he can learn to read himself. Your 2-year-old isn't ready yet to tackle the symbolic abstractions of the written word because comprehension of spoken language must come first.

## Boosting creativity

Creativity can mean different things to different people. To a scientist it might involve finding something never known before. To a painter it could mean creating a unique image. To a dancer it is self-expression through movement. To a poet it could be the production of emotion through words. To a 2-year-old it means all of these things wrapped in spontaneous energy that bursts open when given the slightest opportunity—and it's fun. It is, in essence, passionate problem solving.

Creative activities are enjoyed by all children — not just those with "artistic" temperaments or skills. At this age, you'll never see a child turn down an opportunity to create. He is not hindered by that inner voice that speaks to adults saying, "I'm not at all creative." All children do have the potential to be creative in some facet of their lives; they just need someone to give them the tools, the place, the freedom to create, and honest encouragement.

**The tools**  There's no need to spend a fortune on creative play things; the tools of the trade are all around you. Start a collection of throwaway items like thread spools (for rolling, stringing, and stacking), boxes (for making houses, cars, and apartment buildings), styrofoam packaging pieces (for collages, gluing, and making "snow"), paper bags (for painting and mask making), and empty paper towel tubes (for telescopes and musical horns). Use your own creative eye to find the creative potential in everyday things.

In addition to the fun of making "projects," you can encourage your child's creative abilities by thinking of ways to use his creations for practical purposes. Show him a placemat and invite him to make one by coloring or painting a piece of construction paper. (If he likes the idea, let him make one for everyone in the family!) Don't buy thank-you cards for holiday or birthday presents; ask your child to make them by coloring a piece of plain paper; then you can write the thank you message on top of the colorful design. Putting his masterpieces in envelopes and sending them out to family and friends will show your young Picasso that you really are proud of his work. Rather than giving store-bought Mother's Day or Father's Day presents, let your child make a gift like a paperweight sculpted from clay or a picture frame made of decorated cardboard. Box it and wrap it carefully (perhaps in wrapping paper made of painted grocery bags). When your child invests his own time and talent, pride and joy become part of the package.

Make sure his toys include items he must figure out with built-in problems to solve. Let him struggle to solve everyday problems, too. When his ball rolls under a chair, give him time to consider ways in which he might get it. Can he move the furniture? Can he use a stick or other tool to push out the ball? Don't jump in to solve the problem for him. If he asks for your help, and if he's not particularly tired or frustrated, ask him to help you find a solution to the problem.

**The place** There's no getting away from the fact that creativity is messy. If you ban the use of fingerpaints and make your toddler keep all the crayons in the box, he'll never know the joy of free creative expression. But at the same time you don't have to turn your house over to the creative impulses of a 2-year-old. Set aside an area specifically for creative ventures. The kitchen is a good spot because it has lots of easy-to-clean surfaces. The bathtub can be a place where messes can be made and clean up is lots of fun. When the weather is good, outdoors is even better. If you know your child relishes the chaos of spilled paints, gluey fingers, scattered clay, and splattered flour, take some precautions before the fun begins. Cover the floor with newspaper or a plastic tarp. Have your child roll up his sleeves and cover up with a smock or one of your old T-shirts, or dress him in his own old clothes. When the fun is finished, encourage your child to help with the clean up.

**Freedom** All day long you show your children how to do things: how to use a spoon, how to climb the stairs safely, how to kick a ball. It's your natural inclination to guide and help. That's why it's understandably difficult to use a hands-off approach to creative projects— but you should.

When you bring out the snap-together blocks, it's always tempting to show your child the "correct" way to use them. But if you can resist the urge, you'll see your child jump right in to experiment through trial and error. He'll create an unusual structure if no one alerts him that he's doing it "wrong." When he's drawing or painting, he doesn't need to be told that trees are green, not blue and pink. He doesn't care that finger paints usually aren't applied with elbows. And he'll happily march to his own tune as long as no one tells him that an empty paper towel roll isn't a very good horn. Your job is to enjoy, not direct.

Of course, you can always be of assistance if you see your child getting frustrated or confused. You can also join in the fun (if invited), and your child may learn by watching you. But be careful not to set your own work up as the model to copy. It's frustrating and defeating for a 2-year-old who judges his work by comparing it to adult drawings of perfect faces and beautiful houses. Bring your work down to his level. Draw a bunch of straight lines. Use the clay to make abstract clumps. Make a free-form collage of scattered leaves and sticks.

**Encouragement**  Don't judge your child's creative efforts; just enjoy and support them. At this age, your child is more interested in the process of creating and in exploring color and texture than he is in the finished product. You will stifle his enthusiasm if you suggest that next time he draws two eyes on the face and makes the hair black instead of purple. Don't say, "The house should have a window and a door"; instead say, "What a big house. Is it ours?" Don't say, "That's not how the song goes. Let me teach you"; instead say, "I never heard that version. Teach me the words." Find something positive to comment upon in each of your child's creative works. Even if you see nothing more than a mass of scribbles, comment on his use of color.

On the other hand, don't overdo false praise. If you insist "that is the most beautiful picture I've ever seen," your toddler may feel your praise is insincere or he may feel pressured to live up to this standard of excellence all the time. Pick out something specific to praise. You might say, "I love the way you used a lot of red." Or, "I can see you worked very hard on this sculpture." Or, "Those sticks add a nice touch to your picture."

Show respect for your child's judgment. If he doesn't like his creation and crumples it up and throws it away, don't rush to rescue it saying, "I think this is a great picture." Instead, ask him if he would like to try again. You might point out something about the discarded project that you liked, but don't insist that he like it, too.

The value of creativity extends far beyond the fun of putting scribbles on a paper. It allows children to think intuitively; it lets them use a flexible approach to problem solving; it is a vehicle that gives voice to their thoughts and emotions. Creativity will boost almost every area of your child's life, from his professional success to academic achievement to social interaction. It is often the key ingredient in a sense of personal fulfillment and in leading a happy life. These things are certainly worth the mess it takes to get there.

---

## Encouraging Creativity

**The spark of creativity comes from within. To help it burn brightly:**

### Do...

be open to creative answers or solutions instead of labeling every response as "right" or "wrong."

allow downtime during which children can daydream freely.

stimulate creativity by making up new words to old songs, by using mirrors to let children be both actor and audience, and by finding creative uses for everyday household objects, such as letting an empty egg carton stand in for a keyboard.

encourage the process. All steps of the creation process are important, not just the final product.

support your child's creativity by displaying his creations and showing them to others.

### Don't...

be overly restrictive in terms of the way things should and shouldn't be done.

compare your child's efforts with anyone else's.

take over for your child when he bails out in the middle of a project. Also, don't insist that he finish what he's started.

offer rewards for creative efforts. The drive needs to come from within, not from without.

worry about messiness.

---

# Great games for 2-year-olds

Your 2-year-old is ready for lots of games and toys that will help her learn more about herself and her world:

**Imaginary play** Dolls, plush toys, and character figures are a big hit now because your child's imagination allows her to make up storylines and adventures. Dress-up items, costumes, and pretend-professional gear (such as a doctor's bag, firefighter's hat, police officer's badge) are also a toddler's delight because she can now imagine herself in these roles. Hand and finger puppets also give a toddler freedom to imagine, fantasize, and explore.

**Grown-up play** Your 2-year-old wants to be just like the grown-ups she admires. She loves using toy computers, cash registers, shopping carts, tool chests, baby carriages. These things cater to her interest in learning about what grown-ups do.

**Round pegs in round holes** Matching shapes is a challenge to toddlers that they are now ready to tackle. Give your child simple wooden puzzles with four or five pieces, shape-sorters with a wide range of shapes (such as ovals, hexagons, and octagons). Also, look for peg boards with pegs of varying shapes and sizes.

**Artistic adventures** With her improved fine motor skills, your 2-year-old is ready to tackle more complex art projects. At this age, you can add poster paints, brushes, play clay, and glue sticks to her art box.

**Hi-tech fun** Your child will love any of the many preschool computers on the market. They are interactive, fun, and can be educational, especially if not overused. Although they can't take your place as your child's first teacher, they are a nice addition. A toddler-sized tape recorder, cassette or CD player, and/or radio is another electronic baby pleaser.

### *Musical Madness*

Your child is growing out of passive musical toys that create a song at the push of a button. Now she wants to be the composer and performer. There are many inexpensive toy instruments, such as drums, horns, tambourines, and keyboards, that you can buy that give young children the chance to experiment with the creation of musical sound. Your child will also enjoy creating her own musical instruments out of pots and pans, cardboard boxes, and empty paper towel rolls.

## Helping your child learn math

"One, two, buckle my shoe" and your child is on his way to learning mathematics. This kind of sing-song approach to memorizing numbers is fun for kids and it gives them the correct names of numbers; so sing away. But rote number counting should not be confused with true mathematical knowledge. Genuine numeracy comes very gradually through experience and is not something you should expect your 2-year-old to master.

If you want to help your child understand and learn math, he will need to grasp the basic, underlying numerical concepts first. Your role in this process with your 2-year-old is to show him, without pressure, how numbers are relevant in his daily life.

Your 2-year-old is developmentally ready to understand the one-to-one relationship between the number of objects he is counting and their numerical identity. This is what he learns as you play "this little piggy" and count on his fingers and toes one by one. Counting toes, ears, and noses, and stairs as you climb them is an excellent way to illustrate the one-to-one correspondence between objects and numbers because toddlers are very attuned to their bodies. They learn quickly through their senses.

Sorting also lays the groundwork that leads to an understanding of why certain numbers are assigned to certain groups of objects. When folding the laundry, show your child one blue sock and ask him to help you find the other blue sock. When he finds the sock, put them next to each other and count: "one, two socks!" When setting the table, ask your toddler to give each person a napkin. This will help him see the relationship of one place setting to one napkin. When he's finished, count aloud the number of napkins: "one, two, three napkins!" These simple games will show your child that numbers represent concrete things.

Numbers are not the only mathematical concepts your child is ready to explore. There's lots to be learned about the basic geometric shapes such as circles, squares, and triangles. You can encourage your child to learn about shapes by making a game out of finding shapes in your daily travels. Point out familiar shapes in the kitchen, in the stores, and in the car. Stop while reading a story and ask your child to find a circle in the picture. Once you start looking for them, you'll find shapes to talk about and explore all around you.

Spatial relationships is another mathematical concept your child is ready to learn about now. Every time he pours his bath water into a plastic container or fills a bucket with sand, he is learning about quantity and volume. Give your child the tools and the opportunity he needs to explore this mathematical realm. For example, putting things into containers and taking them out and figuring out how much stuff will go into a certain amount of space are great math lessons for your 2-year-old.

## What pretending teaches

The pretend play that your child began in earnest as a 1-year-old becomes even more a part of his play at age 2. Now there is a wider circle of people to imitate as he becomes more aware of those outside his immediate circle. There are more experiences to integrate and more ideas to work with. Language is more developed. He has a greater understanding of his impact on his surroundings and of the world's effect on him. At age 2, your child's pretend play builds on and expands the skills he's been learning so far.

In pretend play, your 2-year-old learns to explore his emotions without fear of displeasing you. He can freely express anger, for example, by hitting a doll rather than a playmate. He can transfer his own fear of the dark to a teddy bear, making it cry instead of crying himself. Your child may also experiment with feelings of tenderness by rocking and feeding a favorite stuffed animal. Or he may deal with his budding sense of right and wrong by scolding an imaginary friend. You may even see signs of empathy as he soothes his toy rabbit's boo-boo.

Pretend play also helps 2-year-olds take a giant step forward in their cognitive skills. When, for instance, your child makes a clothespin stand in for an action figure, he is demonstrating his developing ability to make one thing stand for another, to create symbols. Knowing how symbols work is a key factor in learning letters and numbers later on. Imaginary play is also helping your child practice his growing language skills. You may hear the high-pitched voices of stuffed animals conversing with the low-pitched sound of their "parents." During private moments of pretend play, your child will take linguistic chances that he may not be ready to try out in public.

Make-believe also teaches your child how to problem solve. If your child invites four stuffed animals on a picnic, but has only three cups for juice, what can he do? If he snaps his train tracks together to make a circle and finds out that he doesn't have enough tracks to make the two ends meet, what will he do? If he wants to be a teacher, he may have to think of ways to turn his bedroom into a classroom. The ability to think logically and devise solutions throughout life has its origins in this form of play.

During this stage of your child's life, you can help her imagination develop in the same ways you did when she was younger. It's particularly important at this stage not to be too helpful in directing the course of the play. Be careful not to rewrite the script. If your child offers you a spot of tea from her toy teapot, don't correct the way she's holding the cup. If she is pushing a box around pretending it's a train, don't direct her to her real train set. If she asks you to play school, don't automatically assume the role of teacher. Venture into this world of make believe only if invited, and even then, do it humbly.

# Toilet Teaching and Toileting Routines

L earning to use the potty or the toilet is a major event in the lives of children—and their parents. Most children are ready to take this big step sometime between the ages of 2 and 3. The average age is 2 years and 8 months. Exactly when *your* child is ready for this step depends on both physical and psychological factors. Physically, the child must be able to control her sphincter muscles voluntarily. There is no way to rush this development. Psychologically she needs to feel in control of the situation. That's where you can help.

## Signs of readiness

Take your cues from your child to judge the right time to begin toilet teaching. Your child is probably ready to be introduced to the idea of toileting if you see some of these signs:

- She wakes up dry in the morning or after naps and stays dry longer when awake.
- She has bowel movements on a fairly predictable schedule.
- She has the coordination to pull clothes up and down.
- She indicates a dislike of being in a wet or soiled diaper.
- She can follow directions.
- She understands the words that apply to toilet teaching such as "wet" and "potty."

## Getting ready

In the initial stage of toilet teaching, you can prepare your child by helping him gain sensory awareness of the elimination process.

Change your child's diapers as soon as they are wet or soiled to help him develop a preference for being dry and clean. During each day, emphasize the concepts of "wet" and "dry." Let him feel a washcloth that is soaking wet, for instance, and say "wet"; then let him feel a dry washcloth and say "dry." When juice spills on the table, put his finger in the puddle and say "wet"; after you clean it up, let him touch the spot and say "dry."

Then you can begin to help him realize when he's urinating or defecating by watching for the signs such as grimacing, grunting, a reddening face, or a sudden stopping of other activity. Say, "You're making BMs in your diaper," or, "Do you feel your diaper getting warm and wet? That's caused by your urine." Toilet teaching will be easier if your child understands that urine and bowel movements come out of his body and he has some control over when and where it happens.

The next step focuses on a gradual introduction to the toileting process through pretend play. This will help you gauge your child's readiness for toilet teaching and it will also help your child anticipate the challenge facing him and calm any fears he may have. Read books to your child about the toilet training experiences of storybook characters. Buy a potty chair, but don't expect your child to use it correctly right way. You can allow your child to use the chair to train his dolls and stuffed animals. This will allow him to consider the steps involved in this new activity—going to the potty chair, taking down his pants, sitting on the chair, and patiently waiting for a few minutes. This game also gives your child an opportunity to talk about the toileting process, to think about it, and to fit it into his growing realm of experiences. After a while, you can ask, "Would you like to try to use the potty, too?" presenting the idea as an opportunity to do something new and exciting.

**Choosing the time to start teaching**  Toilet teaching is best accomplished during a quiet time in your toddler's life, when there is little undue stress. A new sibling, a new school, a new home, a new sitter, or a new schedule can drain your child's store of emotional energy and make the process of toilet teaching more difficult and will take longer than it would otherwise.

For practical reasons, toilet teaching should begin at a time of year when the weather is mild and clothes are less cumbersome, which makes it easier to dress and undress over and over again.

Mild weather also makes it possible for your child to spend some time naked or in thin underwear while playing in the yard or indoor area. Then if he urinates or has a bowel movement, he can understand very quickly the connection between his bodily feelings and the result.

In addition to the weather, check your own calendar before introducing toilet teaching. If you are a working parent, consider introducing toilet teaching during your vacation time. If this isn't possible, at least look for a time when you won't be going out of town or working overtime. Also avoid times that are hectic or stressful for you, such as during a holiday season when you might be too rushed and busy to give your child the attention he needs.

## Beginning actual potty practice

When your child is ready to sit on the potty himself, don't be surprised if he chooses to do this with his diaper still on. This gives him a sense of security, while allowing him to venture into a new experience. You can schedule regular potty sitting times, such as after a nap, when you're fairly certain he will need to urinate or have a bowel movement. If you see him eliminating while sitting on the potty with a diaper on, don't rush in to interrupt him in the hopes of getting the diaper off to use the potty successfully. Instead, point out to him what's happening and let him experience the sensation of urinating or having a bowel movement sitting down. Praise his efforts without going overboard.

Most likely, your child has seen you use the toilet. Continue to allow this practice, since your child will learn from watching you.

**Successful daytime toileting**  The next step in the toilet-teaching process is to ask your child if he would like to try putting his BM (or whatever term you like to use) right into the potty. When he's willing to try, let him to do so without great fanfare. This is a natural process, not a circus event. Although there are many methods of toilet teaching, it is generally agreed that it is best to focus on daytime bowel training first and then on daytime bladder training. (Hold off on attempting nighttime dryness; that may not happen for a while after daytime dryness occurs.) You can do this by keeping track of when your child is most likely to have a bowel movement each day and then scheduling a potty sitting time during this period. With persistence and patience, eventually you'll hit the right moment and your child will put his BMs into the potty. These early successes will encourage him to do it again the next day. However, don't expect your child to tell you when he has to go just yet; instead, keep up your scheduled sittings.

Your child will often pass urine when having a bowel movement, so bladder training, after bowel training, will be an easy concept for him to grasp. For bladder training, however, you'll need to bring your child to the potty every two hours or so. If your child resists at any point, back off. Let him know you are proud of his accomplishments and that he can try again on another day.

### Potty or toilet?
*"Is it better to teach a child to use the big toilet or to get him his own potty?"*

Many parents find that toilet teaching is easier and that their children are more cooperative if they have a potty chair of their own. This is probably because a potty chair feels safer and is more comfortable than a full-size toilet. A good potty chair has a high back and side arms for support. It has a secure broad base with rubber tips to prevent sliding. A potty chair is also preferred for toilet teaching because it reduces many of the toilet anxieties that children sometimes have. Some children are afraid of the height of the adult toilet; others are afraid of falling through the adult seat into the bowl, and some are afraid of the noise that flushing makes. Potty seats are more "user friendly."

Toileting with a potty seat should not cause too much of a problem when you're away from home—if you plan ahead. You can purchase a foldable potty chair that can travel with you. Or, at home, you can occasionally use an inflatable (and portable) toilet seat that fits on the adult toilet and helps your child feel more secure. Once he's used to this idea, you can bring it with you when away from home.

### Teaching children to wipe themselves
It's important to teach children to wipe themselves independently, which they can usually accomplish by age 3. When your child knows how to wipe himself, he will be more comfortable when in school and when visiting others and you or a family member or his regular sitter are not available. Be sure he also knows that he must always wash his hands after using the toilet.

To help prevent urinary tract infections (UTIs), teach your child—especially girls—to wipe from front to back after urinating or after a bowel movement.

**Cleaning practices for uncircumcised boys** Hygiene for uncircumcised boys will also involve teaching them to gently retract the foreskin when they wipe after urination.

### Teaching boys

*"Should I try to teach my son to urinate into the potty from a standing up position? Or should he urinate sitting down?"*

Most boys feel more secure and find it easier to urinate into a potty from a sitting position. As he gets a bit older, your son can experiment with standing up. He'll learn best if he can watch other males, particularly his father, do it.

### Using pull-up diapers and/or training pants

*"I thought pull-up diapers would be preferable to training pants, but, since they are so absorbent, my daughter isn't at all bothered by wetting them. Should I switch to training pants?"*

Pull-up varieties of diapers can be a real help in toilet teaching, allowing your child to practice using the toilet without the fuss of regular diapers while not worrying too much about accidents. For some kids, of course, the super-absorbency of these diapers eliminates the discomfort of wet diapers and thus reduces a child's motivation. A child who is not highly motivated will, of course, be less likely to use the toilet regularly.

If your child is not quite ready for toilet teaching, the choice between pull-up diapers and underpants is not the issue. In that case, it's simply best to wait a few weeks or months until she's more interested in the process. If you believe that she is ready for toilet teaching, be prepared for some accidents while you make the switch to training pants.

**Handling daytime accidents** Accidents are just that—accidents. They don't require any punitive response, even if your child has been using the potty for a long time. Sometimes children become so involved in what they're doing that they forget to respond to the bodily signals.

When your child forgets to use the potty, keep your cool and

## Safe Potty Seats

After purchasing a potty seat for your son, toss the cuplike urine guard, which can catch on and injure your child's penis. Look for smooth-molded models or those without a urine guard and teach him to aim his urine into the potty.

simply state that you and she need to clean up. Have her help you gather her clean clothing. Let her assist wiping up any urine from the floor if she's had her accident indoors. (It's not a good idea to have her help clean up bowel movements, however, because feces is laden with bacteria.) When the job is accomplished, just say, "Next time, tell me when you have to use the potty, so you can get there on time."

**Help for older daytime wetters** If your child is a daytime wetter over the age of 3½ or so, an exercise to strengthen her pelvic muscles may help her stay dry. Called the Kegel technique, the exercise tightens the urinary sphincter muscles, which control urination. Researchers at Duke University Medical Center in Durham, N.C., taught the techniques to 79 daytime wetters between the ages of 4 and 15. Half also wet their beds at night. The children were taught to contract or "tighten" their bottoms for 5 to 10 minutes. They also learned to stop urination midstream. The kids were asked to do the contractions three times a day, to routinely stop their urination midstream, and to urinate every hour or two—even at school—during the first several weeks to keep their bladders empty and easier to control. After about two months, 60 percent of the kids with daytime incontinence were cured. Most were able to stay dry at night as well.

If your child wets herself during the day, ask her doctor whether she might benefit from Kegel exercises. Be patient: Progress is slow, and ongoing guidance and support from her doctor—and from you—are essential. But not all children with incontinence are helped by the Kegel technique.

If your child is a daytime wetter, you can also try the following:
- **Eliminate all caffeinated beverages from her diet.**
- **Suggest that she try to hold her urine for a few minutes before going; this may help stretch her bladder over time.**
- **Prevent constipation.** Firm stool filling a child's rectum can press on her bladder.

*For more information on constipation, see **page 577**.*

# Working toward nighttime dryness

By the age of 3, most children are toilet trained during the day. Girls generally have an easier time with bladder control at night. However, being able to stay dry through the night may take a little longer for boys. In addition, some children may have immature bladders or may not have developed sleep patterns that will alert them that they need to get out of bed and use the toilet. If your 3-year old regularly wets the bed, you may want to check with his health-care provider to rule out urinary problems or an infection before beginning to focus on nighttime dryness.

You can help your child work toward nighttime dryness by respecting her need to develop her own schedule. Loving patience will bring success much faster than pressure and criticism for lack of control. Praise nights that are dry, while giving support to try again when the bed is wet. Listen to her feelings and encourage a good self-image. Also try to help your child understand why she has not yet succeeded in staying dry through the night. Reassure her that as soon as her body is ready, she will do it. Don't be too quick to stop using diapers at night if the bed is more often wet than dry in the morning. As dry nights accumulate, try making the switch to underpants. Just be sure the bed is covered with heavy-gauge waterproof sheeting under the regular sheets.

Support and patience will help your child want to succeed. Ask if you can wake her when you go to bed to see if she needs to use the toilet. Put a night-light in her room, the hallway, and the bathroom. Try not to emphasize a deadline or any particular age when the goal must be reached.

## Can the process be hurried?
*"My 3½-year-old continues to wet the bed every night. When will he stay dry all night?*

When a child's bladder is mature enough to hold urine for eight to ten hours at a time, he will stay dry through the night. For most children this happens at its own pace without any effort on your part. Most children achieve nighttime bladder control within one year of attaining daytime bladder control; the average age is 33 months. Statistics aside, the nighttime bladder control of children between the ages of 3 and 5 is often an on-again, off-again situation. It is expected that nighttime control will be achieved by most children by the time they are 6 years of age.

*For more on urinary-tract conditions, see **page 658**.*

# Handling toileting difficulties

Toilet teaching, like other forms of learning, is often two steps forward and one step back. And because urinating and having bowel movements is a bodily occurrence, your child is likely to have strong emotions attached to urine and BMs.

**Regression**  Your child may take a step backward in her toileting abilities when she becomes absorbed in learning something else. If she becomes excited about her new level of talking, she'll forget what he's learned about bladder and/or bowel control. Or, if your child feels emotionally stressed, nervous, tense, or under pressure, she may be unable to concentrate on the sensory cures that signal the need to get to the bathroom on time. Or, she may simply be learning, forgetting, and learning again. Whatever the reason, don't overreact and don't punish an accident. In a matter-of-fact manner,

## Successful Toilet Teaching

### Do...

make sure all the people involved in the care of your child know how you are toilet teaching your child.

remember that there is no one right method of toilet teaching. Be willing to experiment to see what works best for your child.

demonstrate tolerance, patience, and warmth throughout the process.

be calm and casual about toilet teaching. Treat it as a natural event.

use precise language. Phrases such as "Go to the bathroom" can confuse your child. Say what you really mean: "Put your BMs into the potty."

### Don't...

expect your child to train at the exact same age or pace as other children. All children are different in their ability to attain mature toileting habits.

allow anyone involved in the care of your child to use punitive toilet-teaching methods.

associate moral values with success or failure at toileting. Avoid calling your child a "good" girl if she uses the potty and "bad" girl if she soils her pants. This instills guilt and undermines self-esteem.

change your child into dry clothes as soon as possible with assurances like, "Next time, I'm sure you'll remember to use the potty."

### Refusal to have bowel movements in the potty

*"My 2½-year-old easily learned to use the toilet to urinate, but she refuses to have a bowel movement in her potty. Any suggestions?"*

Although you shouldn't worry too much about a 2½ year-old who isn't completely toilet taught yet, there are some things you can do to encourage the process. Consider why your child is holding back. Bowel-control delay is often caused by emotional fears connected to the toilet-teaching process itself. For some children, the sensation of letting go of BMs for a free fall into the bowl is an experience they're unfamiliar with and try to avoid. Other children are possessive of their bowel movement because they feel it's a part of themselves they don't want to lose. To avoid causing your child any anxiety about his BM, don't flush it away immediately or even in her presence.

You can help your child get over her fears by establishing a daily routine of potty sitting. If you know the time of day your child is likely to defecate, plan your toileting practice at that time. Or you can create a regular schedule of potty sitting after meals and naps. Have your child sit on the potty for five minutes. This is a good time to read to her and relax her. If she doesn't pass her BMs, allow her to leave the room for five minutes and then bring her back to the potty for another five-minute try. Do this on a regular schedule throughout the day. A few weeks of consistent potty sitting followed by praise and small rewards for successes should encourage your child to complete this part of the toilet training process.

Watch for signs of constipation. If you notice that your child is not moving her bowels at all during the training period, contact her health-care provider, who may recommend a stool softener or other method for reducing her constipation.

*For more information on constipation, see **page 577**.*

# When bedwetting continues

Bedwetting is common in children between the ages of 2 and 4. About 10 percent of children still bedwet at 4, 5, 6, and even older. It's important to be supportive and to find ways to avoid embarrassment until the underlying condition changes. Nighttime wetting usually occurs because the child's bladder simply isn't big enough to hold a large amount of urine. Also, some kids are such deep sleepers

## Handling Bedwetting

My son, Eric, continued to wet his bed right up to age 6. He was frustrated and embarrassed by this and refused to sleep over at friends' houses because of it. My husband was a late bedwetter, too. One day, when Eric was very upset about the problem, his dad told him that he had wet his bed at Eric's age. He told Eric he had been embarrassed, too, but that it was something he outgrew. That made our son feel better.

As for sleepovers, we bought a sleeping bag and sewed an absorbent lining in it. Before he went to a friend's house, I alerted the friend's mother about Eric's problem. As soon as Eric and his friend woke up, "Mom" rolled up the bag and put it in the garage for us to pick up when we collected Eric. I just popped the sleeping bag in our washing machine when we got home—Eric's friend was none the wiser.

that they don't wake up when they need to go to the bathroom.

Certain children continue to wet the bed past age 5. This is referred to as "nocturnal enuresis." About one out of every ten children 5 and over is a nighttime wetter, and boys are more frequently affected than girls. Often, there's a family history of bedwetting. Studies have shown that if one parent was a bedwetter, a child has a 44 percent chance of being one, too; if both parents were bedwetters, the child's risk soars to 80 percent. Also, researchers have discovered a "bedwetting gene," confirming that older bedwetters have a genetic—and not a behavioral—problem. Nobody knows why boys are more prone to nocturnal wetting than girls, but experts feel girls' earlier physical maturation accounts for their earlier bladder control. If your child wets his bed at age 5 or older, don't shame or punish him. Instead, work to solve the root cause of the problem and be patient.

A handful of kids over age 5 experience daytime wetting, and an even smaller number are unable to avoid involuntary wetting during both the day and night. Some children who are prone to day- and nighttime wetting may have a urinary tract infection or other medical condition.

### Help for kindergarten-age bedwetter

*"My 5-year-old recently turned down an invitation to a friend's house for a sleepover because she's afraid that she might wet the bed. Her fears are well-founded. I don't want her to feel bad, but I don't want to push her—what should I do?"*

If a child is not nighttime dry by the age of 5, it makes sense to do something about it. Age 5 is old enough to feel "bad" about oneself for having this common problem. Also, bedwetting is beginning to interfere with your child's social life. Before beginning any program to help your child, talk with her doctor to rule out any medical condition, such as a urinary infection, that could be causing or contributing to the problem.

Realize that your daughter wants to be dry; therefore, any intervention is likely to have a good chance of success. Start by keeping a record of dry or wet nights on a pretty calendar. Seeing dry nights accumulate can make a child strive for more.

*For more information on urinary-tract infections, see **page 658**.*

## Bedwetting

### Do...

encourage your child to empty his bladder just before bedtime.

awaken your child so he can use the toilet again just before you go to bed.

offer praise or rewards for dry nights.

try a moisture alarm. A metal strip worn in underwear sets off a wrist alarm with the first trickle of moisture

ask you child's doctor if she recommends medication. DDAVP (desmopressin acetate), a nasal spray, and imipramine can provide a short-term solution, though the medications have side effects.

### Don't...

allow him to drink large amounts of liquid within two hours before bedtime.

let him drink caffeinated beverages, like colas, which irritate the bladder and promote frequent urination.

punish your child if he has an accident.

# CHAPTER 10

# 3 Years

At the age of 3, your child moves from toddler to preschooler. Now he can talk about his feelings and ask you what he wants to know. Along with an ever-expanding vocabulary comes a growing imagination. The stories you may hear from him now show that your child is experimenting with his new skill of putting thoughts into words. By listening closely, you'll discover what ideas he thinks are important, funny, or confusing.

His attachment to you is strong, though he now sees you as a separate person who has feelings just as he does. He may feel sorry when you're sad and even want to help you solve your problems. He can also identify his own feelings and let you know when he is sad, angry, or happy. Since problems can now be talked about rather than acted out, your child will be less aggressive and more social. Now, having friends becomes important.

Physically, your child begins to lose his baby look and shape. With better control of his body and movements, he will likely become more interested in showing off his skills, even enjoying sports and organized games . You can join in the fun by watching his delight at being able to run faster and jump higher than ever before.

# *Physical development*

This year, your child's baby appearance and uncertain toddler steps and movements are beginning to disappear as your 3-year-old grows and gains increased physical control over her body. Now she can join in organized physical activities, playing Ring-around-the-rosy with new ease. Although at 3½ your child may briefly experience some clumsiness and lack of physical control as she goes through another growth phase, you will probably find that very little slows her down this year.

## Physical changes

Although remaining steady, your child's growth noticeably slows from the ages 3 to 4. The greatest changes you may see are in your child's appearance. She will look more and more like a young child rather than a baby as her proportions change and she loses baby fat. As her muscles become stronger, her arms and legs lengthen and her upper body becomes more slender. Facial features are larger and more distinct as her upper and lower jaws grow and widen to allow for her permanent teeth.

**What your 3-year-old can do** Between the ages of 3 and 4, your child's coordination improves so that she no longer has to work so hard at standing, walking, running, or jumping. The motion of walking becomes more grown-up as her steps become regular and her feet are more steady. However, standing on tiptoe or on one foot may still take concentration. Increased coordination also allows her to ride a tricycle, while better balance makes it possible for her to go up and down stairs without assistance, hop or stand on one foot, and move backward and forward with agility.

At this age, the fine-motor skills of boys and girls differ substantially. Boys will develop the ability to control their hand movements much more slowly than girls. Many precise movements now become possible for a 3-year-old girl as she gains more muscle control of her hands and fingers. Because she now can handle smaller objects, she will be able to throw a small ball, as well as catch a larger one. She will be able to hold a crayon like an adult and copy or trace different shapes and even letters. She also may be partly or wholly able to dress herself by handling buttons, using a zipper, and snapping snaps. Boys will continue to concentrate on using their large muscles and won't turn their attention to finer hand control for a year or more.

**Helping your child grow**  As much as possible, plan physical activities in which your child can test the limits of her growing abilities. Supervised outdoor play, trips to a playground, or rides on a tricycle will help her develop strength and coordination and use her energy productively. Because movement is still an important way for a 3-year-old to express emotions and ideas for which her language skills are still limited, encourage her to demonstrate what she wants to say. Although all of this movement can be distracting, remember that it's fun for your child and an important form of communication. Also provide the tools and the opportunity to practice hand coordination.

## Activities to promote fine-motor skills

To help your child develop manual dexterity, provide art and building materials, such as blocks of different sizes, clay, crayons, and paint. Here are some suggestions for activities that will help to develop your child's fine-motor skills:

- **Putting together jigsaw puzzles** of five to twelve pieces.
- **Stringing large beads** on yarn or thick string.
- **Pouring water** from one container into a different-size container.
- **Dressing dolls and herself** in clothes that have large zippers, snaps, and laces.
- **Building** with blocks, pipecleaners, and other materials.
- **Making shapes** with wet sand or with clay. Clay and dough are great finger and hand exercisers. These materials can be squished, rolled, flattened, pounded, and poked, with each action resulting in a wholly new shape. Don't expect your child to sculpt any recognizable figures or forms just yet; simply let her experiment with the feel and texture and a masterpiece will follow.
- **Using child-size tools,** such as child-size scissors or a toy hammer and screwdriver, under your close supervision. He can then progress to lightweight adult-size tools, such as an eggbeater and a gardening trowel.
- **Coloring, painting, and writing,** using a variety of tools, including crayons, paintbrushes, finger paints, and sticks. While your

3-year-old need not master skills such as writing the letters in his name, some 3-year-olds are anxious to try and can, indeed, do so.

### Basing expectations on age, not size

*"My son is much taller than most other 3-year-olds in his nursery school. I find that the teacher and some parents expect him to act older just because he looks older. How can I make sure that he's treated according to his age, not his size?"*

Some children who are destined to be tall may grow much faster than other children. Because people often judge age by size, many adults may be insensitive to his actual age and maturity level. With the adults your son comes in contact with frequently, such as teachers and friends' parents, it might help to talk with them away from your son before they have a chance to make a thoughtless comment. You might describe some of your worries about him being treated differently. Explain that his size does not reflect his maturity level. If you enlist their support, you may be able to increase their understanding and sensitivity and also help your son.

When it comes to strangers, it's probably better to ignore or forgive their ignorance. You may reply to someone who says, "Oh, he's so big!" with a positive comment such as "Yes, we're so pleased that he's such a big boy."

Because of his size difference, your son may also feel self-conscious. To help him deal with this, consistently try to build his self-esteem by letting him know that how he acts is more important than how he looks. Support and praise what he can do well, and encourage physical activities that will help him gain more control of his body, such as swimming or playing on a gym set.

## Helping your child dress independently

There's no doubt about it—you can dress your child far more quickly than he can himself. Before doing it for him everyday, however, realize that the more you take on this responsibility, the less inclined he will be to learn to dress himself. These ideas will help you step back and give your child the opportunity to dress independently:

• **Give him the time he needs.** It may take him five minutes to put on a shirt. Given the opportunity to practice, he'll soon have that down to just 10 seconds or so.

• **Limit choices.** Your child will be able to accomplish self-dressing long before he's developed any taste in matters of fashion. If you let him dress himself in plaids and stripes but then feel compelled to undress him and redress him "right," you'll undermine any enthusiasm he has for the task. Limit his choices. Perhaps, during the time that he's learning self-dressing and before he can be counted on to choose matching clothes, simply buy a variety of things that can be mixed and matched.

• **Make it easy.** Skip buttons and anything else beyond his ability for now. Opt for big neck holes, elastic waistbands, and even things that look just fine when put on backward. Also, as much as possible, buy clothing that follows the "rules"—tags in the back, rather than the front; T-shirt designs in the front, but not on the back.

• **Teach the basics.** Point out that the seams go on the inside and that tags are usually in the back of a garment and pictures on the fronts of shirts. Flys are in front. So are shirt pockets.

• **Offer encouragement.** Whenever he's gotten dressed independently, congratulate him, and leave off any comments about the strange outfit he may have put together.

# Emotional development

Your 3-year-old lives in a self-centered world of imagination. You may see a blossoming creativity as he engages in fantasy play. He will also be discovering a new independence as he begins to see himself as a person separate from his family. Your goal now will be to give him the safety and security of letting him know you're in charge while allowing him the freedom necessary to explore.

## Your child's feelings

By the age of 3, your child sees himself as a complete person made up of a mind and body with feelings. He experiences a wide range of emotions, including love, anger, frustration, sadness, joy, and fear. He now recognizes emotions in other people as well and now knows that other people may feel differently than he does. He begins to develop empathy for others. He may also assign human qualities and emotions to objects such as toys or the moon and talk to these objects. He easily moves from fantasy to reality and likely has difficulty distinguishing the real from the imagined. From his perspective, the stories he hears and the tales he tells are true. He may believe he becomes the characters he pretends to be, leading him to imagine that he too has special powers and abilities. As a result, he may at times act recklessly with little thought of danger.

**How your 3-year-old develops secure relationships** As your child becomes more independent, he begins to form relationships with other adults and children outside of his own family. Through these friendships, he discovers how people act and think differently than he does, and that he has special qualities, too, that make him unique. He becomes more sensitive to others' feelings and can realize how his actions affect them, even though he may still continue to tease and push others to their limits. Through his interactions with you, other family members, his teachers, and his peers, your child tries out different behaviors and learns safe ways to express feelings in a variety of settings. He also builds self-esteem and a feeling of competence, while learning to rely on and cooperate with others.

**Helping your child grow** Praise your child's imagination and creativity. If invited, join in his fantasy play, but let him control what happens. Encourage regular independent play with one or two playmates so that your child has a chance to get to know them and establish a deeper friendship. If disputes arise over toys or other possessions, suggest that your child solve the problem peacefully with words rather than with aggressive actions. Your 3-year-old won't always be able to share or take turns, but you will see increased cooperation and less competition as the year progresses.

## Raising a can-do kid

Wanting your child to become independent and self-confident and allowing her to become so may create a conflict for you. It can be difficult to let go and to remember that your child eventually needs to be able to handle the world on her own. The only way she can do so is to try out different behaviors and actions while you supervise without trying to do things for her.

There are many ways you can foster independence and self-reliance in your 3-year-old. Demonstrate that her opinions matter by offering appropriate choices. For example, allow her to choose clothing, while making sure an outfit is seasonally appropriate. Don't fret if clothing is mismatched. What's important is that making a choice helps your child develop her own identity and gives her a feeling of control. Food is another area where you can encourage your child to choose from among acceptable options. Just remember to keep choices to a minimum of two or three. Too many choices can be overwhelming for a young child.

Respecting your child's feelings—from happiness and excitement to anger and sadness—also helps her develop a good sense of self. Often, parents try to rush in to "correct" negative feelings that their child is experiencing, but children need to learn to accept those feelings in themselves and to develop the ability to overcome them on their own. For instance, when a child is angry because she can't go out to play on a rainy day, instead of saying, "Don't be upset," say, "I can see you're upset because the rain means you have to play inside. What indoor games can you think of to play instead?"

Be prepared for sudden changes in likes and dislikes as your 3-year-old tries on and discards a number of opinions about a number of things. Even though such behavior can be frustrating, show respect for his viewpoints and changeable ways. And make sure that while you offer choices, your child still feels the comfort of knowing that you are still in charge of the big decisions. He will feel more secure if he understands he can take responsibility for some things but isn't expected to take care of everything.

### Sharing Chores

Now is a good time to share a few simple chores around the house, working alongside you in jobs such as dusting, rinsing vegetables, piling up newspapers and magazines for recycling, and helping you sort laundry. As you set the table, he can be put in charge of placing a napkin at each place. He will feel important and self-reliant while having a new sense of his place in the family.

**Helping your child learn negotiation skills** There's a difference between giving in to your child's demands when you've grown too tired to argue and helping her learn to use her growing verbal and social skills to affect her environment.

Begin to teach your child negotiating skills in matters that are not major issues, such as which video to choose to watch. Suppose she wants to watch an hour-long show, while you prefer that she choose a half-hour-long tape. Ask her her reasons for preferring one over the other. Listen to her arguments. Tell her your reasons for your choice. Then offer her a trade-off, such as "I'll play Candyland with you if you choose the shorter tape." Encourage her to make a good counter argument. Let her "win." Seeing that she has succeeded in striking a bargain will boost your child's self-esteem and sense of having an effect on her world.

Practice sharing toys, trading one you want for one she wants. Share chores: "I will help you clean up your toys and you can help me set the table for dinner." Help her consider friends' feelings as well as her own so that she can put herself in their shoes. Let her see that others have wants and needs that might be at odds with her own. This art of give-and-take will serve her in her dealings with you and others in the future.

A child who can't negotiate for any changes in the rules has limited options. She can have a tantrum, become defiant, or just give up. None of these tactics serves to prod her toward maturity. Negotiation skills signal that your preschooler is aware of what others want as well as what she wants and that everyone's needs can be met.

Although going along with your child's preferences may be difficult at times, you may find that giving your child some choices on how goals are to be reached will result in far fewer battles and increased cooperation. By allowing your child options, you will also help her develop decision-making skills.

## Your child's fears

If your child sees monsters everywhere—under the bed, in the corner, and in the closet—be aware that it's just her vivid imagination turning something unfamiliar into something scary. Even the family car may become a monster whose grillwork and headlights appear frightening to a child who has just learned that there really are dangers in the world.

Fears are a normal part of childhood. Fears of the unknown, of animals, and of danger and death may even be inherited, recent research suggests. You can help your child work through her fears by first identifying the cause, and then working on building her confidence in mastering her fears. Because she may still lack the language to explain what frightens her, try to help her with words to name the fear. Let her know that it's okay to be afraid, and then re-

**"IT WORKED FOR ME"**

### Allowing Experimentation

While I was making dinner, I let Nicholas, 3, mix a concoction of milk, flour, salt, sugar, and some incompatible spices—and then I let him drink it! (He didn't drink much.)

## Pictures Are Scarier than Words

Movies or television programs that your child is watching should be carefully selected because visual images may easily frighten children. Since children under 3 are not as attentive to words as they are to images, a scary story that you read to your child may not cause fear as he will be able to decide just how much scariness he can handle as he listens.

assure her that you will keep her safe. For example, if your child is afraid of the dark, sit together with the lights off and try to name objects in the room. Then turn the lights on and see how many you got right. A night-light will also help dispel fears.

Sometimes fears pop up suddenly, leaving you at a loss to identify or explain them, or how to help. For instance, your child may one day develop a fear of the bath or a fear of rain. At times like these, review family events to see if a change—a birth, a move, an illness or a death in the family, for example—may have triggered your child's fears. You yourself may be fearful of something, which your child senses and turns into her own fear and anxiety. When such a fear develops, acknowledge it and, as much as possible, work around it for the time being. Give your child sponge baths during the time she's afraid of the bath or, if the weather permits, take her swimming in a wading pool or to the sprinklers in the park. During thunderstorms, try distracting your fearful child with a fun project. Some children benefit from learning about the thing that frightens them, so try reading a book about what makes rain and why it's important to help your child see storms as a benefit to her rather than a threat. You can also help if you share some of your own childhood stories, saying something like, "When I was 3, I was afraid of thunder, too. Here's what my mother did to make me feel better." And then offer the comfort your child needs.

Many of the fears that your 3-year-old develops now are transitory, and while he needs your comfort and help, he will likely grow out of these fears quite easily. A fear that persists for months and that isn't easily comforted, however, may turn into a phobia, which will prevent your child from engaging in normal activities. If your child develops phobic behavior, that is, if the behavior interfers with his daily life, discuss the issue with his pediatrician who may recommend therapy to help him get beyond his anxieties. Treatment for phobia is effective and is relatively quick—usually just a few sessions with a behavioral therapist.

Once your child masters a particular fear, she will feel a great sense of accomplishment. Her newfound confidence will allow her to approach her next concern with greater courage.

## *Handling Halloween-Time Fears*

**Preschoolers may not realize that those scary creatures running down the street and coming to their door on Halloween evening are just other kids dressed up in costumes and masks. To help your child avoid being unduly frightened by this annual parade of masked marvels:**

# Do...

plan to go trick-or-treating with one or two friends rather than a large group, which can be overwhelming. Limit the outing to about an hour.

make your Halloween rounds in the late afternoon or at dusk. Even children who aren't afraid of the dark are not used to being out at night, especially when there are spooky sights.

limit your stops to known neighbors' or friends' houses. Seeing friendly faces will help your child enter into the fun of Halloween. This will also prevent confusion around your "don't talk to strangers" rule.

talk about what is real and what is not real to help your child distinguish between real and make-believe threats. You can base your talk on stories you read together or television programs you watch together.

let your child practice putting on and taking off a non-scary mask in front of a mirror.

# Don't...

overwhelm your child with scary images. If, for instance, a neighbor has decorated his house in a particularly scary fashion, take a different route for your Halloween outing.

involve a young child with legitimate fears about the holiday, such as fears of tainted goodies. Instead simply trick-or-treat among friends, delay eating anything until you have examined it at home, and state simply, "We don't eat Halloween candy until we get home."

Remember that Halloween can help your child work through fears by being able to treat them playfully. By putting on the costume of something they fear, children can gain a sense of control of their fears.

## Your child's frustrations

Even though 3-year-olds love to build and create, they may become easily frustrated when they are unable to accomplish what they want to do. Most parents feel the urge to rush over and help their children solve the problem. However, in most cases, leaving your child alone to work out a solution encourages self-reliance and independence.

So, where is the fine line between giving too much help and feeling that you have abandoned your child to sink or swim on his own?

Try to remember that you can support your child while not "fixing" his every problem. You may be surprised at how creative and resourceful your child can be when given the freedom to work out his own solution to a problem. When your child is frustrated, you can offer emotional assistance:

- **Let your child know that it's okay to feel angry and frustrated** and that you understand and respect his feelings.
- **Allow your child to be unhappy.** Let him struggle a bit to find his own solace.
- **Let your child know that you will help if you're needed,** but don't intervene until you give your child a chance to find a solution.
- **Listen to your child's explanations** of what he feels went wrong. Then ask simple questions to help him think about what else he might do.
- **Remember that learning from mistakes is a necessary part of growing up.**
- **Be aware of your child's abilities.** Don't push him to solve problems or handle situations he's not ready for or capable of handling just yet.

## Friendships

Friends are becoming increasingly important to your 3-year-old. You may notice that he now plays and interacts with other children rather than just doing his own activities nearby. This year, his play is far more elaborate than when he was a toddler.

While your 3-year-old is becoming more cooperative and better able to share with others, you may notice that he and his friends constantly test each other during their time together. They may tease one another and make each other cry. Your child may be fiercely happy to see another child, and then suddenly become angry at his playmate and want him to go away. In just a few minutes, however, they're best friends again. All of this pulling toward and pushing away from friendship is very important to your child's development. As he works out his feelings about being an individual, he practices seeing his friend as a rival for toys and attention and as a compatriot who enhances the pleasure of his toys and his playtime. All of these conflicting behaviors are your child's experiments in developing an identity, trying out different roles, learning patterns of behavior in a safe way, and discovering his strengths and weaknesses.

You may be surprised to discover that your child's friends—those with whom he chooses to play when there are a number of peers from which to choose—are very much like him. Studies have shown that young children generally choose companions who are the same sex, the same size, the same age, and have many of the same interests. Girls will usually pair with girls and boys with boys, even if you have tried hard to avoid gender stereotypes.

**Helping your 3-year-old learn to share** One of the hardest skills for a 3-year-old to master is learning to share with others. A reason for this difficulty is that a young child can't understand that sharing is not the same as giving something away. She doesn't believe that the object will be returned, or that it could be traded for another valued object temporarily. As a result, parting with a treasured toy even for a moment is like giving away a piece of herself.

If your child continually has difficulty sharing with other children, try to focus on the value of sharing rather than on her negative behavior. For example, point out how she enjoys playing with her friends' toys. Reassure your child that her toys are still hers even though another child plays with them. Before a playdate, allow your child to put away any special toy that she doesn't wish to share. Play sharing games with her to give her practice, since she is far more likely to allow you to share her toys than another child.

When your child has a friend over for playtime, make sure that available toys have parts that can be shared. These might include dress-up clothes, building blocks, tea sets, and games that provide the most fun when played with a friend. You might suggest an activity that involves playing with two toys at the same time with each child taking a special role. For example, one child could use blocks to build a roadway for the cars that another child is enjoying. One child can serve tea to the children's stuffed bears while another serves pretend food. Also give children the opportunity to play side by side, doing an activity such as coloring, so that they can practice simply enjoying each other's company without having to share.

As much as possible, try not to interfere with your child's interactions with her friend. However, if your child and a friend begin to fight seriously, step in before they hurt each other. Help them work out their disagreement in words and to express the feelings that led to the altercation. Calmly ask each what she needs to say to the other to get what she wants. Praise the children when they demonstrate solving a problem by themselves. Above all, remember that sharing is not a skill that develops quickly. Your child may be generous one day and extremely selfish the next. Take comfort that any sign of generosity is a sign that your child is on the right track.

**Helping your 3-year-old deal with rejection** It's not uncommon for a 3-year-old to come to you in tears with the heart-wrenching story that his best friend has just refused to play with him. To you, such rejection may seem cruel. And you may be at a loss as to how to explain what happened or even comfort your child. Sudden rejection is quite normal among preschoolers, and it often occurs for no other reason than that the other child is out of sorts at the moment. Learning to deal with unwarranted rejection is one of the ways your child can develop a strong sense of self-esteem. If your child has been rejected through no fault of his own, you can help him feel better by simply reassuring him that he is a good friend and that his friend is having a hard time seeing that right now. The best approach you can take is to be sympathetic, while not being overly concerned. "Best friends" may change daily and upsets often pass even more quickly. The same child who just told another he won't play may be ready to play at almost the next instant. Soon, they are happily playing together again as if nothing has happened. If you become too involved or too emotional about the rejection, your child will decide that it's a bigger deal than he'd first thought. He may also conclude that he's unable to handle playing with his peers without your intervention. If the other child is unready to get on with playing, invite your child to join you in another activity for a short time and then give him a chance to reconnect with his friend a little while later.

On occasion, however, a child's overly aggressive or whining behavior or his inability or unwillingness to take part in his friend's chosen activity leads to rejection. Young children don't always see the connection between their own negative behavior and a negative reaction to their actions by their friends. Work with him calmly and sympathetically to help him understand that, for instance, if he shoves another child that child won't want to play with him. To help him learn to treat others with compassion, take some time to talk about how hurtful such behavior is. At the age of 3 your child is just beginning to understand another person's point of view, so he may be ready to talk about such issues. Help him learn to verbalize his feelings, including learning to apologize for his misbehavior to his friend. Kids are quickly forgiving and it's likely that your child will be reinvited to play immediately.

**Your 3-year-old's imaginary friends**   A 3-year-old's emerging imagination and desire to have friends commonly results in the creation of an imaginary friend. You will find that a pretend friend often has special powers or behaves in all the ways your child knows are not acceptable. Sometimes your child will ask you to join in her adventures with this imaginary playmate, perhaps insisting that you set a place at the dinner table for him. Other children prefer to keep their make-believe friends to themselves and the "friend" will suddenly disappear when you or another adult wants to talk to or about him.

Your child's having an imaginary playmate is nothing to worry about and is not a sign of any emotional disorder. Some children invent a friend simply because they feel too shy to make real friends or are isolated from other children in some way. An imaginary friend is always there, and is always ready to do whatever a child wants. If your child shows reluctance to play with others, try setting up some playdates with children you know are like your child — not too aggressive, creative, and verbal. However, don't push the issue. Let your child decide when she is ready.

If your child uses an imaginary friend to avoid taking responsibility for a misbehavior, such as drawing on the wall, acknowledge that you understand that he would *like* to change what happened and you understand that he wishes his friend had done it. Then point out that since his imaginary friend isn't there to clean up the mess that he will have to help you. Also reassure him that you love him even when his behavior is not acceptable.

If your child wants you to become involved with her friend or not, respect her wishes, but don't go overboard in acknowledging the make-believe child's presence. Your child needs you to keep the door to reality open. Simply realize that she is using her imaginary playmate to test her own new emotions and feelings and, through this playmate, is learning skills she can use for future, real friendships.

**Helping the lonely child**   There is a great difference between a lonely child and a child who enjoys being alone. Every child has his own temperament. If your child seems to be perfectly happy to play by himself, don't be concerned that he is lonely. Try to arrange ways for him to spend time with one or two other children, but don't push the issue. If your child is in a nursery or preschool, you may want to discuss with caregivers how your child interacts with other children while at school. Ask that he be given chances to play one-on-one with other children instead of with the entire group for at least a part of the day.

For the child who truly yearns for a friend and seems to be unable to find one, you can help. Arrange a playdate in your home and observe how your child interacts with another child. You may notice that your child needs some help in developing social skills. He may need to learn how to share toys and how to let another have a turn. In other words, he may need to learn how to be a friend.

If your child is lonely because there are no children nearby with whom he can play, or if you recently have moved to a new neighborhood where you don't yet know other children, you will have to do some advance planning. Look in newspapers and community bulletins for activities tailored to children your child's age. Find out where there is a local playground that is popular with parents and children, and spend some time there. If your child is enrolled in a nursery school or day care, make a point of getting to know the parents of other children to enlist their help in expanding your child's social opportunities.

Remember, all it takes is one friend to ease your child's loneliness. You don't have to try to round up a group of playmates. And, given time, most children do find that one special friend.

## Make-believe violence

It is not at all uncommon for a child, even one whose parents don't allow toy guns and other violent toys in the house, to turn anything at hand—from a stick to a half-eaten sandwich—into a make-believe weapon. Seeing your child pretend to shoot 'em up can be disturbing, particularly if this form of play overrides all other activities.

Don't be worried that occasional, even regular, violent play acting means that your child will indeed become a violent person or that he has a great deal of pent-up anger. Such pretend violence is most often a way for your child to express and deal with his own anxieties and fears. Being able to destroy "the enemy" allows your child to feel power over his fears. If the violent play overtakes all other forms of pretend play, however, look at other areas of your child's life to uncover any stresses that may be behind his need to act aggressively and work toward reducing those stresses. Also give your child lots of opportunity to be involved in other, gentler pursuits. But don't forbid this form of fantasy play entirely.

### Superhero play

*"I'm at my wit's end over my son's constant superhero play. How can I help him enjoy other forms of play? "*

At 3, your child is beginning to realize he is separate from the rest of his family. He may begin to realize that he is in charge of himself, which can be frightening as well as exciting. Pretending to be a superhero is a way for him to deal with his fear and to feel powerful and in control. It's also a way for him to express his ideas about good and bad. While this form of play serves your child well, you are right to try to help him find other forms of play to enjoy as well.

To direct him away from superhero play, you can begin to set limits. Explain where he can and cannot act or dress like his favorite superhero, such as in a restaurant or in a store. Help him take credit for what he can do himself, without the help of his superhero apparel. Point out, for example, that he jumped from a chair to the floor as himself and not as a superhero. Introduce real-life heroes through stories and discussions. Also concentrate on other activities you know your child likes.

**Toning down toy weapons** Along with superhero play comes the fascination with toy guns and other toy weapons. A child's fascination with weapons is often supported by action figures and toys tied to cartoon characters on television.

You can discourage toy gun play and limit war games without diminishing your child's active play. Since he has little comprehension of death and how real guns and weapons can hurt people, he will not understand your concern about this form of play. There's no need to go into details about real violence. Instead, simply explain that you don't allow any game or toy that hurts or scares other people.

If you react too negatively to toys that mimic real-life violence, you may actually increase his interest in them. Even without the toys, your child may fashion a gun from a stick or use a finger in place of a toy gun. Instead of an outright ban on this form of play, you might ban toy weapons while allowing your child to use a finger or another toy as a substitute. By doing so, you will be encouraging your child to use his imagination. If your child's interest in guns is

*For more on aggressive play, see **pages 241** and **393–96**.*

## "Bad Guys"

Ask your child what a bad guy is and which bad guy he is after in a particular game. Ask him how the guy got so bad. Then talk about how the bad guy could be changed into someone else who isn't so bad. In this way, you can help him eventually understand that although some people do bad or unsafe things, using a gun on them takes away their chance to change.

primarily an interest in target practice, encourage other target games. If children want to play with water outside on a hot summer day, you might set up a game with a hose, cups of water, or a sprinkler, rather than water pistols or guns.

Also make a point of giving your child information about the dangers of real guns. Make sure that children don't play outdoors with toy guns, which have been mistaken for real guns, with tragic results. Express your own feelings about guns, too, if you feel uncomfortable around them and don't want them in your home. If you have hunters in your family, make sure that any guns in the home are locked and securely stored and are not accessible to your child.

## Teaching children about differences

At 3, your child knows that she is separate from others. She is also beginning to know that she is different physically, mentally, and emotionally. Through interaction with her family she is already learning the rules and customs of the culture in which you live.

At the age of 3, your child also beings to categorize people, according to hair color and texture, skin color, and body size and shape. As she notices these differences and compares herself to others, she may begin asking why she is different from others and why others are different from her. For example, she may comment on a friend who celebrates a different holiday, wonder why a friend whose parents are divorced does not live with both a mom and a dad, or comment on how boys act differently than girls do. Your responses are important in helping her identify these differences and understand the diverse world in which she lives. These questions can also prompt you to think about your own views and to solidify or alter those views based on how well these ideas will serve your child best.

You can help your child learn about her place in the world by teaching her about your family history and your culture as well as teaching her about the larger culture in which your family lives. Talk about why you follow certain customs. If some family members speak a second language, explain why. Talk about other cultures too, helping your child to see them in a positive light.

Your discussion of differences may also extend to the kinds of places in which people live, the different foods people eat, and the various kinds of families that exist in your community.

When you present this diversity as something positive, your child will adopt that viewpoint. Focus on what different people can do rather than on what they cannot do. Talk about positive role models of all kinds. Help your child feel comfort in her family and culture while learning to appreciate the differences in others. When it comes to your child's evaluation of her own abilities against what other children can do, focus on what she *can* do well. Point out that everyone has different interests and skills.

## Handling kids' questions

*"My daughter loudly asked me to explain why another child was using a wheelchair in front of the child and her mother. I didn't know how to handle the situation. Any suggestions?"*

If your child comments aloud on another's appearance or behavior, remember that she didn't say something with the intent of hurting that person's feelings. She just wanted to understand the world better. If the person has heard the comment, you may find that he is not embarrassed or upset and may want to respond himself. Don't assume that, however. Be sensitive to what the other person wants to do and take your cues from him.

If you are surprised by your child's comment and don't feel prepared to reply right away, acknowledge the importance of the question, then say that you can talk about it later. When you do have a chance to talk, use descriptive rather than judgmental words. For instance, instead of saying, "Yes, that poor child can't walk," which focuses on the child's disability, say, "Sometimes people have been injured or were born with a part of their body that doesn't work. The wheelchair helps him travel." Also point out that the person with the disability is not responsible for his disability, that your child cannot catch it, and that there are many things that the child can do, even though his legs don't work. In this way, you can help your child learn that being different doesn't mean the person is less of a person because of the difference.

## Teaching Tolerance

Children naturally notice differences. They don't, however, naturally develop prejudices or form stereotypes about differences. They learn them through social cues and imitation of the adults who matter to them. Your 3-year-old will follow your lead as you comment on the differences among people, learning either to celebrate diversity or to fear it.

## Gender and gender roles

At the age of 3, your child is developing a clearer self-concept of her identity as a girl or a boy. Your daughter may take delight in being a girl and your son be glad he's a boy, even if you have carefully avoided encouraging any stereotypical behaviors. However, many children still may be confused about their sexual identity and are not entirely convinced that his or her gender won't change over time.

Although this focus on gender may not intensify until the age of 4, this year you may notice that your child is becoming more interested in gender-specific toys and activities. Girls may become interested in dress-up, hairstyles, and dolls, while boys turn to sports and want trucks or action figures to enhance their play. By adopting stereotypical pursuits, your child begins to solidify his or her sense of self as a male or female. While being drawn to gender-specific activities, children still need the freedom to pursue lots of gender-neutral and opposite-gender activities so that their emotional boundaries are not limited to stereotypical expectations. Girls still need encouragement to be active and assertive and boys to be verbal and nurturing.

Don't dismiss your child's interests even if you don't consider them gender appropriate. This is a try-out period for your child. The more a girl or boy is allowed to pursue what interests him or her at the moment, the more likely it is that the child will discover his or her own talents and build on them.

# *Cognitive development*

Your 3-year-old can now grasp more abstract ideas, and he understands what his mind is and what it means to think. He is beginning to make the transition from dealing with the world in only physical ways to seeing the world in symbols as well. For example, he understands that one thing can stand for another, such as a doll representing a person, that a word names an object or a person, and that a word as well as an object can be part of a larger category.

# What your child knows

Your child's rapidly expanding vocabulary will vividly show how much he is learning. He can probably name some colors and use some number names to count. His sentences also are becoming longer and more complex, so he can describe and express what he can imagine as well as what he is doing and what he can see. However, because your child still has a literal and self-centered view of the world, reality and fantasy are often indistinguishable to him. For example, he may believe you really have a frog in your throat when you try to explain a hoarse voice. Story characters are real to him and objects have feelings just as people do.

Knowing his daily routine enough to anticipate, for instance, that sunset signals that a certain television show comes on, shows that he is beginning to understand time. While periods of time such as an hour or a number of minutes still mean little, he can make and talk about plans to do something in the future, and he knows that things have happened in the past. He remembers special events such as birthdays and holidays that occur once in awhile, and can probably tell you how old he is, although the concept of a year will still be confusing. Besides events he's actually experienced, he also can now remember and retell parts of a story that he's heard.

Your child is also showing increased skill in solving problems. His reasoning remains one-dimensional, however, and can usually handle no more than a single fact when solving a problem. For example, he will probably believe a taller narrow container holds more water than a shorter wider one even if he's watched you pour the same amount of water into each. He perceives that the taller container is bigger simply because height is more apparent to him than width.

**How your 3-year-old learns**  Your 3-year-old's intense curiosity about the world has no doubt resulted in an endless chain of "Why" questions. His many questions are his window to learning about the world. His questions may also point out his need simply to practice language by engaging you in conversation.

Play and fantasy also play a big role in your child's learning. With his new language abilities, he may talk to imaginary friends or to his toys as though they could respond. He may even narrate whole stories that he makes up to go along with what he is doing. As he nears 3½, his conversations become more directed at real people, especially at other children. He will use language to work out ways to share and solve problems among his friends.

## Smart Play

To stimulate learning, you might provide building and combining toys, such as interlocking blocks and puzzles. Finger paints and crayons will spark an increasing interest in color and design. Clay will give your child a chance to explore how he can make and change things. Encourage him to experiment with many different materials. Ask him to describe his creations.

**Helping your child grow** Talking with and to your child, as well as actively listening to what he has to say, are the best ways to stimulate your child's interest in the world and help him develop his growing language skills. Welcoming his many questions and responding patiently will help him learn and reassure him of the worth of his own mind. Realize that not every question requires a lengthy answer. Don't go overboard explaining the science behind each natural phenomenon he questions. Keep your answers to the level of his understanding, occasionally asking, "What do *you* think?" His replies may give you a fascinating look at how your child views the world. When he appears to lose interest, move on to another topic.

Through regular talks and reading, you can also anticipate some of his questions and give him a framework to make sense of things. For instance, on a walk you might discuss the different colors in nature. You can choose some nonfiction books to read that are written at your child's level of understanding.

Also allow your child plenty of time just to play and explore, both indoors and outdoors. Include time alone, with other children, and with you and other adults. However, be sure to maintain a balance between the new and the familiar in her daily routine. Children exposed to too many new experiences may feel overwhelmed.

## Understanding your child's intelligence

While watching your child learn and grow intellectually, you may wonder if she is on track for her age, or if she needs more formal instruction or some remediation to help her develop to her potential or if she has a superior intelligence that needs special attention. During your child's regular physical exams, her health-care provider should assess her cognitive development as well as her physical growth to ascertain if she's progressing as she should. Be sure to arrive at office visits with any questions you have about your child's intellectual development as well as physical and emotional concerns. If your child is attending preschool, her teacher is also a resource who can help you assess wherther or not your child is progressing cognitively, as well as socially.

At home, you can observe her to see how she approaches learning. While you watch her engage in play and move from one activity to the next, you will see her mind in action. Note how she builds with blocks. Does she use her experiences to create new and different structures? Does she combine building materials to add details to her structures? Does she discuss what she is doing and experiment to find solutions to problems that the activity presents? Pay attention to what she draws and paints. At 3, she should be able to draw simple shapes like circles and triangles, as well as renderings of people, though not all 3-year-olds will include all facial features in these drawings. Watch how she plays with her toys to see if she creates stories to enhance her play and if she can enjoy a variety of different roles in her make-believe play. Note if she is curious about the world and how things work and are put together.

Besides being an observer, you can also spark your child's creative thinking by making suggestions or asking questions as she plays. Guard against taking over and directing her play or testing your child on what she knows, however. Instead, ask her to describe a picture, or tell you what she likes about a color or toy. If she comes to you with a problem, ask her what she might do to solve it, then give her some ideas. Discuss stories, both realistic and fanciful. In these ways, you can help your child think about how she can meet challenges and solve problems.

While 3-year-olds share many common traits, they do not all progress intellectually at the same pace any more than they would be expected to all be the same height. Their different styles of learning and different interests need to be respected. One child may know all of the letters of the alphabet at age 3, while another excels in physical dexterity. One 3-year-old may have a particular talent for making friends while another shows remarkable prowess in counting. The same child who shows an early talent for recognizing letters may, at some later date, lose interest for a time in this activity while he focuses his attention on learning to ride a trike. Like other forms of development, intellectual growth will occur in fits and starts. Early achievement may not signal superior intelligence just as early lagging may not signal a future deficit. The most important

## Avoid Rote Teaching

It's important to remember that normal intellectual development of young children is varied and is not limited to academic achievements. In fact, learning letters, numbers, and facts are not important at present and expending energy on rote learning at this point in your child's life can take away from other more appropriate activities, such as running, climbing, and pretend play.

thing you can do is to support your child's efforts and make him keenly aware that your love for him is not tied to achievement.

**Assessing your expectations** If your child senses that you don't expect too much of him intellectually, he will learn not to expect much either. Expecting too much also has a negative affect and can make your child anxious if he feels he cannot meet your needs for him to achieve. Gentle encouragement, along with exposure to a variety of activities and lots of opportunity to play goes a long way to helping him work to his best ability.

Also be careful of congratulating his every achievement. If you overpraise him, he may become fearful of making a mistake and falling from your good graces. If you label him a terrific artist, for example, he may become far more careful and less creative rather than risk becoming a "bad artist." He may also limit his activities outside of art since this is the area where he knows he will get your approval. Instead, when he shows you a lovely drawing, praise the drawing itself without going overboard praising him.

### Formal lessons

*"What's the right time to begin formal lessons? I've enrolled my 3-year-old in music and gymnastics classes. He seems to love all the stimulation, but I'm concerned about pushing him too much."*

As long as an activity is organized in the spirit of play, your child will probably enjoy as many opportunities as possible to learn new things and use his energy. If he seems to be having fun, these programs are probably fine. However, a 3-year-old should not be pushed into formal programs or forced to learn something that does not interest him. At this age, the most important learning experiences for your child are in play activities. Young children also benefit more from their parents' strong interest than from any organized learning.

Classes can be great fun for children, provided they offer open-ended activities in which there is no right answer or single right way to do something. Carefully observe any program you'd like your child to join to make sure it is age-appropriate and does not induce stress.

## Your child's imagination

Imagination plays a large part in your child's learning at the age of 3. Through imaginative play, by himself and with others, your child builds self-confidence, masters skills, and prepares for more formal learning at a later age. Make-believe role playing also helps him work out internal conflicts; if, for instance, he's angry with a playmate or with you, he can play the part of a knight slaying a dragon, thus letting him settle his inner conflict.

Through play, your child works hard to figure out who he is and how the world works. By trying on different roles, he learns to solve problems through experimentation and invention, and how to express his emotions, worries, and wishes. For example, by pretending to be a superhero or a police officer he feels powerful and in charge. By pretending to be a storekeeper, he experiments with numbers and words that are symbols of the real world. Playing with other children also gives him a chance to learn social skills and to compare his imaginative ideas with others.

You can spark your child's imagination and creativity by providing plenty of space for active and fanciful play. Allow your child to organize his play space in his own way. Focus only on limits that really matter to you. Also give your child plenty of time to play. You may be surprised by how long your child will occupy himself when allowed to set his own pace.

Sometimes, he may want to play privately. But other times, he will want someone to share his activities. By all means join in and play with your child when he wants you to. Just be sure to let your child direct playtime. You may be expected to take a part in role-playing or in making or building something. Or, your child may just want you to actively watch, listen, admire, and perhaps make suggestions. You can enrich playtime by asking questions about the activity and guiding conversation without telling your child how to do something or trying to impose your own logic. Because the distinction between reality and fantasy is still fuzzy at age 3, it's better that your child be the monster in scary play, rather than you, which could frighten him.

One of the most obvious ways your child plays with her imagination is through storytelling. Sometimes you may find yourself a reluctant audience to endless wild stories. At other times, you may discover your child telling stories out loud

## Encouraging Storytelling

Always listen actively, ask questions and respond, but don't correct or "improve" your child's storyline. Three-year-old's stories are usually wildly illogical. You might begin a story and ask your child to make up an ending. Pick out an object, a pet, or a place in the neighborhood and ask your child to make up a story about it. Also get your child involved in drawing, painting, and dramatic play to encourage narration and fantasy. Consider writing down some of these tales so that you will have a wonderful keepsake to share with him later.

when he is playing with his toys by himself. He might even resent your interrupting him in the middle of his narrative because in his imagination, he's not alone at all.

# Building your child's vocabulary

The many stories your 3-year-old tells and the questions she asks are evidence of her rapidly expanding vocabulary. Between the ages of 3 and 4, she will acquire thousands of new words—as many as nine new words per day. In just a few months, she will progress from sentences of five or six words to longer, more complex sentences that express abstract ideas. You are encouraging this growth in vocabulary just by talking to your child and by listening her.

Provide new experiences that you and your child can talk about. For example, go for a walk in the neighborhod, visit a garden and a zoo, find a new park or play area, walk by a construction sight. As you come to each new place, discuss what you see and hear. Compare new sights and experiences to activities you have already done. Use time words when you talk about events past and present, such as *before, after, yesterday*, and *tomorrow*.

Play games with words, especially rhyming games. For example, try to come up with all the words you both can think of that rhyme with *hat*, then make up silly sentences with the rhyming words. Say a sentence with a missing word and let your child think of a word to complete it.

**Handling language delays**  If your child does not seem to be talking as much as other children his age, or if you're worried about how many pronunciation or grammar errors he makes, remain calm. Most 3-year-olds are not entirely proficient as speakers and most develop more advanced conversation skills during this year. If by the age of 3½ your child has difficulty speaking or being understood, or earlier if your child's pediatrician or teacher suggests it, have a speech and hearing evaluation done. If the assessment confirms a hearing problem or a true language delay, begin therapy at once since early intervention can make an enormous difference in your child's ability to learn. If the assessment shows that your child is simply taking a bit longer to reach proficiency, try these ideas to spur his development:

• **Don't overly correct.** As you listen to your child talk, don't worry about correcting pronunciation or primitive syntax. For a 3-

year-old, speech sounds for the letter *r* and letters *th* are difficult to master. Correct pronunciation will come in time, often in just a few months. Likewise, resist the urge to change "He goed" to "He went" when your child is relating a story to you. Such correction at this stage will only frustrate him. Misusing an irregularly formed verb or plural, such as *feets* or *foots* instead of *feet* is actually a sign that your child is absorbing the rules of syntax, as he correctly puts an "-ed" ending onto a past-tense verb or adds an "-s" to a singular noun to make it plural.

- **Model the speech patterns you want.** When your child says something such as, "He goed home," repeat his observation using the syntax you want him to learn. You might, for instance, respond to the above sentence with, "Yes, he went home."
- **Keep talking.** Even if your child doesn't seem to be holding up his end of the conversation, keep him engaged in language development. When, for instance he points to a toy airplane he wants, rather than simply hand it to him, say, "Do you want your airplane?" Give him a chance to respond verbally, but don't insist that he speak in order to communicate with you. You might add, "I like it when you use words instead of pointing," while handing it to him.

**When your child stutters** If your child hesitates between words and appears to be repeating sounds now and then, that is not any cause for concern. About one in 20 preschoolers stutter occasionally, usually more boys than girls. No one knows what causes stuttering, but some children may have difficulty with the normal timing and rhythm of speech. Stuttering is more common when a child is nervous, excited, tired, or not feeling well. A child also may stutter when he tries to talk too fast, or if his ideas get ahead of his ability to express them.

Most stuttering is a transitory event. When a child is stuttering, it usually takes 20 to 30 seconds to say the word on which he is "stuck." Most stuttering goes away within three months. However, for some children, the repetitions and hesitations continue for several months and become a block to communication.

Chronic stuttering is very frustrating for a child, particularly if others rush in to correct him or disengage from conversations with him because of his speech patterns. It's also very frustrating to parents and other listeners. It's important not to show any annoyance or impatience. If your child begins to stutter, don't try to correct him and don't focus on the problem. Slow down your own speech, talking calmly and correctly, and using simple language. Find quiet times to talk together when he will be more relaxed. Also praise him for the things that are not related to speech that he does well.

Severe stuttering may require speech therapy. If your child's stuttering is persistent and interferes with his daily social interactions, early intervention can prevent a speech problem from causing social and emotional problems, too.

# Reading to your child

One of the best ways to boost your child's vocabulary is by reading to her. By reading stories aloud, you help your child enjoy words, learn how to pronounce them, and what meanings to attach to them—all prerequisites in learning to read herself later on.

Reading to a 3-year-old allows her to connect the fanciful stories that fire her imagination with the logic of the storyteller. She grasps cause and effect by seeing how a character's actions lead to certain results. She learns to anticipate outcomes, based on the facts of the story thus far. She learns that certain characters behave in certain ways. You can enhance her sense of the story during reading time by stopping now and then to ask questions about the tale, such as "Why did that happen?" and "What do you think will happen next?"

Reading aloud also helps your child understand the connection between spoken language and written symbols. Point to the words as you read to let your child see that the letters make words and that the words tell the story and that the symbols are read from left to right and from the top to the bottom of the page. Research shows that this simple activity can have a very positive effect on your child's ability to connect letters, sounds, and words when learning to read. Encourage her to study the pictures and to turn the pages. Invite her to "read" to you, making up a story as she turns pages or recounting the story she has memorized from repeated readings.

Let your child set the pace when it comes to reading. She may be content to listen to the whole story as she looks at the pictures with you. Or, she may interrupt frequently to ask questions about the

## Reading Time

Making reading a soothing part of the bedtime routine is one of the best ways to encourage a love of books. But reading should not be limited to bedtime. After naps, when your child is alert, offers a different kind of reading pleasure. Visit a library together to choose books to read. A children's librarian will be able to recommend books geared to your child's interests and age. Join scheduled story hours for preschoolers.

story or about individual words. For most 3-year-olds, 20 minutes is a good limit for reading aloud at each sitting. If she becomes bored, put the book aside for now. Some kids, of course, will want more. It's okay to stop when you've had enough so reading remains a pleasurable part of your routine with your child.

Besides books, also read outdoor signs and other materials to your child, particularly words that are meaningful to her, such as the words on her favorite cereal box or on a recipe that she's helping you prepare. Let her watch you write a letter that she dictates to a family member. Or, ask her to name some items she would like at the grocery store, so she can see you add these important words to the list. Get a set of magnetic letters for the refrigerator and put together names of family members or words your child finds interesting. Label her toys, clothing labels, and bedroom door with her name, which will likely be the first word your child actually learns to read. When your child expresses interest in knowing what certain letters say, offer the answer, but don't push your child to read at this early age.

## Dealing with television and videos

Television and videos have their place in your child's development. The key to making these have a positive affect, of course, rests with you. It's important to limit television to no more than two hours a day so that your child has time for other more active and engaging pursuits.

Watching age-appropriate children's shows, in which the subject matter as well as the language are geared to your child's age, can enhance his language and his social development. Fast-paced cartoons with loud noises rather than dialogue are less helpful. Well-designed programs also can stimulate the imagination and provide information on subjects in which your child is interested.

Television and videos are best enjoyed by your child when you watch alongside him. Comment on the action and ask questions about what your child is viewing. Even if you sometimes rely on TV to engage your child while you shower or cook dinner, be very selective about what programs you turn on or what videos you choose. Decide ahead of time what is worth watching on a given day, then give your child a choice of two programs. Avoid allowing young children to watch adult-oriented programs with you, since much of the content can be frightening and otherwise inappropriate.

# CHAPTER 11

# 4 Years

Extreme, energetic, boastful, bossy, joyful, silly, and ready for anything is how many parents describe their 4-year-olds. What they, and you, are probably dealing with is a little person whose ability to express herself is growing by leaps and bounds and who is discovering the power within herself.

As your child refines his coordination and balance, you may also find that he moves from activity to activity in a blur. Everything is done speedily in an effort to move on to the next interesting project.

Along with the desire for new adventures, children this age also experience emotional highs and lows: Where one minute you are dealing with a confident child, you may suddenly be confronted with a child who is insecure and whiny.

She may also take a sudden like or dislike to various foods or the way some people look and act. She may hate anything that changes a parent, especially Mom, in any way, such as a new hairstyle or clothing. You may never know what sparks these loves and hates, but it's important to try to respect her feelings.

Throughout this year, you'll probably notice a gradual change to a more self-disciplined, calm child. Remember, of course, that your child is unique. Not every 4-year-old will develop and change at the same rate. As a parent of a 4-year-old, you'll have to be ready for almost anything, and to set the limits that your child needs.

# *Physical development*

At the age of 4, your child begins to move like an adult. You will see this change in his way of walking with long, swinging steps as adults do. You may also see your child becoming more athletic and taking a greater interest in sports. At the same time, you'll notice a great improvement in fine motor skills in his ability to use his fingers. Along with these abilities comes a greater attention span which will allow him to concentrate longer on an activity he enjoys. You will probably need to be more attentive to possible reckless behavior. Beware that his improved physical abilities also mean that your child may unknowingly take risks as he climbs, jumps, runs, and learns to ride a tricycle or small bicycle.

## Physical changes

Your child's growth will probably continue at about the same pace as it has for the past year. He will continue to mature in his looks as muscles and bones develop and strengthen. Many preschoolers wonder if they are really getting bigger. If you are regularly measuring your child, you can point to changes since the last measurement, since having evidence of growth is important to him at this age. If your child has visibly grown out of an article clothing, note how big he is getting. If you have kept any smaller clothes he once wore, you can compare sizes to show him how much he has changed.

The age of 4 is a good time to have your pediatrician check both your child's vision and hearing. At this age, your child can describe different sounds and is able to follow directions well enough to take test for vision and hearing. Vision should be about 20/40 or better, and should improve to 20/30 by age 5.

**What your 4-year-old can do**  Both large and fine motor skills are developing rapidly at this age. At some point during this year, your child should be able to stand on one foot for up to ten seconds, swing and climb, do hops with both feet off the ground, jump from a two-foot height with both feet together, and do somersaults. He may even be able to skip. Because his balance has greatly improved, he should be able to go up and down stairs with one foot to a step. He will also begin using his hands more than his arms to catch a ball, and he will be better able to throw a ball overhand.

Your child's hand coordination should be almost completely developed at this point. He should be able to dress himself, even tie shoelaces, as well as brush his teeth and use a fork, spoon, and sometimes a table knife. Better coordination also extends to his creativity. He should be able to build with many blocks, model clay, and cut and paste. His ability to hold and use crayons improves so that he is able to trace and copy geometric shapes such as a star, print some letters, and draw a person with a body. He should also be able to finger-paint and hold a paintbrush.

**Helping your child grow**  To help your child make the most of his developing physical abilities, provide lots of outdoor physical activity as well as opportunities to use his hands in precise movements, drawing, writing, and building things. You can even turn your child's exuberant energy toward helping you in practical ways, such as joining you dusting or washing the car. Whatever physical activity your child enjoys, be sure he is well-supervised, however. His judgment of safe versus reckless behavior will be way behind his developing motor skills, so you'll have to remind him to be careful on playground equipment, and to hold your hand when crossing a street. Attention is especially important near water, where his mix of impulsiveness and daring can be dangerous.

To encourage the development of fine motor skills, provide crayons, pencils, plenty of paper, modeling clay, blunt scissors, puzzles, blocks, and other building materials. Providing a variety of activities will encourage your child to use his new abilities. You may even notice emerging talents. However, at this age, don't focus on any one activity. It's important at this stage for your child to explore a broad range of activities and follow the direction of what he enjoys.

# Your child's handedness

By now, you will have a good idea if your child is right- or left-handed simply by observing which hand she favors when holding a spoon, drawing a picture, and throwing a ball, even though handedness is not entirely fixed until age 5 or 6. About 10 to 15 percent of the population (usually more boys than girls) is left-handed naturally while the remaining percentage favor the right hand. A few people are ambidextrous, which means they are comfortable performing a number of tasks with either hand.

If your child appears to be left-handed, don't try to change her. Until the early part of the twentieth century, teachers and parents usually tried to force a left-handed child to write with the right hand. Experts now agree that this is a bad idea. Constant correction might also cause a child embarrassment and uncertainty.

Even though a percentage of left-handers do develop learning disabilities, many of them also are better at math than right-handers. Learning problems can usually be corrected. If your child is a lefty, look for signs of special talents in art, engineering, or architecture. You'll find a high percentage of left-handers in these professions.

### Are lefties clumsy?

*"Are left-handed children more clumsy than righties?"*

Left-handers have to learn to live in a right-handed world. Many of the tools people use, such as scissors, are made for right-handed people. So, not only is a left-handed child learning basic tasks such as writing or throwing a ball, he is also learning how to use tools that don't feel comfortable or natural. This difficulty can cause more accidents, but it doesn't mean that the child is more clumsy.

Because children learn by imitation, many left-handers also are faced with learning certain skills, such as throwing or batting a ball, from people who perform the skill from the opposite side. So, a lefty must visualize the action in reverse before he can attempt to try it out. As a result, he may seem more physically inept and slower to learn. But, in fact, lefties use great imagination and perception to learn and are in no way more limited because of their hand preference.

**Make sure your lefty has the proper tools**  Most well-equipped toy stores will have a variety of materials for your left-handed child. You might also try stores that specialize in educational materials for young children, which are most likely to have toys especially designed for lefties. Many of the larger malls now have a left-handed store.

# *Emotional development*

At the age of 4, your child is likely experiencing emotional highs and lows. These extremes are a result of your child's vivid imagination, high energy, and desire to learn new things. Much of the time she may feel she can do anything and definitely wants to do so. Although she is probably no longer deeply confused by what the difference is between fantasy and reality, she is able to move between the two with great speed and creativity. Pretend games have now become more complicated and often involve some kind of violence—an acting out of her conflict between good and evil. Her self-confidence is also growing as seen in the way she can carry on a friendly conversation with adults and in her relationships with other children.

### When Your Child Is Rude

New behavior you may encounter is your child criticizing you, being rude, even swearing. Although you may be shocked, it's important to remember that she is trying to get a response from you or just see what happens. She is also testing the limits of her independence and seeing how it feels to question authority. So, while you can set limits on her behavior, it's best not to overreact.

## Your child's feelings

You have probably noticed that your child has no problem expressing how she feels. Sometimes she may be bossy and belligerent. At other times, she will be dramatically loving, then suddenly hate something that was just fine yesterday. She will be confident one minute and fearful the next. Sometimes she will want to try anything new, then go through a period of resisting all change. All of these unpredictable variations usually make a 4-year-old's feelings difficult to deal with. She'll need an extra dose of understanding now.

Your child may show a fascination with bathroom talk, particularly about bowel movements. You may notice this interest in nouns and adjectives that refer to elimination, such as calling someone "a poo-poo." This will probably extend to an increased interest in sexuality. You may be asked where babies come from and what the differences are between girls and boys. For sexual questions, respond with simple, but accurate explanations. Also make your conversation brief without appearing embarrassed or overly serious. If your child's curiosity extends to playing with her own genitals or showing interest in other children's genitals, don't scold or punish.

*For more on children and sexuality, see **pages 227–30.***

Just make sure she knows what you consider unacceptable behavior.

She will probably be sympathetic to others' feelings and want to fix a "hurt" so a friend or an adult will be happy again. In addition to practicing empathy, her kindness is also an expression of how she wants to be treated when hurt and unhappy.

**How your 4-year-old develops secure relationships** Your 4-year-old's love for going out-of-bounds is coupled with the desire to have limits. Even if she resists, she wants to be told just how far she can go and be reminded of rules. The sense of "always" when it comes to routines and rules helps her feel secure. Even when she is acting out with a friend, she may suddenly criticize extreme behavior by saying, "That's not nice."

Typically, some 4-year-olds may become extremely possessive of one parent, especially the parent of the opposite sex, and in turn will probably reject or view the same-sex parent as a rival. Then suddenly, her intense affection will be transferred to a friend her own age. Little by little she is discovering the importance of friends. She may even have a "best" friend.

It's important to remember that besides being playmates, friends can actively influence your 4-year-old's thinking and behavior. She is finding out that other people may have opinions and values that are different from yours. This may result at times in actions that go against your rules and standards.

**Helping your child grow** Because your 4-year-old no doubt enjoys being with other children, especially a group of children, it's important for you to give her opportunities to make new friends. If she cannot find new friends in your neighborhood, and she is not enrolled in a nursery school or a preschool, you should try to arrange play sessions frequently. These can be informal get-togethers at a park or playground or, more formally, in preschool activity programs.

When it comes to your 4-year-old's misbehavior through swearing or rudeness, it's important to separate your child from her behavior. Clearly state why the behavior is bad, while being careful not to give your child the idea that she is "bad." Remind her of your rules and what you expect. For rude remarks, you can make a game of insulting each other to release feelings. For example, if your child calls you a "doo-doo head," you might say a foolish name back, such as "You're a corn on the cob." Another good way to deal with your

*For more
on handling
misbehavior,
see **page 400**.*

4-year-old's wild behavior is to simply ignore her. This will quickly dampen the thrill of what she was doing.

If she is acting silly or telling exaggerated stories about herself, you may want to just join in. You might want to even tell a wild exaggeration of your own. Let your child know that you, too, value the fun of a tall tale.

If your child ever seems overwhelmed by her emotions, especially sadness, it's best to let her have her feelings. Sympathize, without trivializing or ridiculing her emotions in any way. Realize that even 4-year-olds can feel great distress. Your job at this vulnerable time is to acknowledge the emotion and help her identify what she is feeling and to discover ways of soothing herself, including going to you for comfort.

## Building your child's self-esteem

Self-esteem has long been believed to be the basis for healthy emotional and intellectual growth. However, many teachers and parents have misconceptions of how best to instill self-esteem. Simply praising your child, especially if it's superficial or definitely not deserved, does not help him develop good feelings about himself. He probably knows what he can and cannot do well, and if an adult praises him for something he knows isn't wonderful, he will sense the insincerity and may question whether the adult knows what a good job is or that the adult doesn't expect much. Praise can also backfire by undermining your child's motivation. He may come to rely on someone else's approval for everything he does.

Infants and toddlers develop self-esteem just from being loved, accepted, and valued. By the preschool years, self-esteem often becomes connected to achievement. If your child is able to learn a new skill or accomplish a task, he will feel more confident and want to try other things. You can also look for simple responsibilities he can take on around the home, such as setting the table or cleaning his room. When he finishes a task, your praise will let him know he has contributed to maintaining your home and is a valued part of the family.

**"IT WORKED FOR ME"**

### *Helping Children Develop Positive Self-Images*

In our house, we celebrate little things as well as big things. Learning a new skill, making a good grade in school, getting a good dental checkup are all reasons to congratulate someone. I bought a dinner plate that says "You're special." On those days when we have something to celebrate in our family, the person of honor has her dinner on that plate.

A good way to help your child develop self-esteem is to compliment him on accomplishing something specific. Acknowledge what he has been able to do instead of just giving general praise, such as "Aren't you wonderful!" To encourage motivation, you can also help your child evaluate his own work by asking him, for example, to describe what he has done and to tell you what he likes about it. Don't be afraid to criticize your child in a constructive way. If your child never hears critical feedback, he will never learn how to benefit from his mistakes.

Another mistake people often make is to confuse self-esteem with a child's preoccupation with himself. Focusing your child on his wants and desires is not the same as finding ways to help your child feel worthy and competent. Spending too much time on self-celebration will take away from fostering curiosity, cooperation, and caring for others. Instead, encourage your child to explore the world and to cooperate with others. Also focus on persistence by encouraging him to try to come up with his own ways to handle problems and to work hard to achieve goals. While being a supporter, it's also important to resist the temptation to do the task or solve the problem for your child. By doing so, you will take away his sense of accomplishment in knowing he did something himself.

How you acknowledge your child as a person will also help him build self-esteem. Listen respectfully and seriously consider his opinions and suggestions. Treat him as someone who is capable and intelligent. When you follow through on some of his ideas, he will find that his ideas have value, and that he matters.

### Preschool bragging

*"My preschooler is always bragging about things he can do. Is this behavior normal?"*

Your son's behavior is normal for his age. Preschoolers love to exaggerate, show off, and boast. If they don't feel they are praised enough, they will praise themselves. The important thing to remember is that 4-year-olds love attention and they love to talk. Be sure to acknowledge his efforts and accomplishments. When the boasting and exaggeration become too extreme, one approach is to ignore it. An alternative, of course, is to join in the fun by countering his bragging with some obvious exaggerations of your own.

# Children's play styles

At 4, your child is probably interested in a wide variety of activities. Her energy at this age no doubt propels her from activity to activity in an effort to experience as much as possible. While most 4-year-olds are often happiest playing with friends outdoors where they have the space to be as energetic and imaginative as they wish, each child develops her own favorite way to play.

Pretend or fantasy play is probably a big part of your 4-year-old's playtime. Her approach to fantasy play may take one of three forms. She may enjoy being an actor and take on different roles in her own stories. Or, she may have more fun creating imaginary scenes with toys and small action figures. Thirdly, she may want to use different materials, such as blocks and clay, to build and create different designs.

You may find that your child gravitates to more active, physical play and so needs equipment and a large space to move in. Conversely, she may prefer a more quiet playtime with dolls or other toys. She may always want to play with other children, ask you to join in, or spend time playing by herself. What's important is that she enjoy what she is doing.

To identify your child's own play style, observe and follow her lead. Provide a variety of play materials and see what happens. As part of their active fantasy play, most 4-year-olds love to dress up in different costumes. They also love to play with water, build things, put together puzzles, dance and sing, and play games.

Don't worry if your child appears to play in a much quieter or more rambunctious way than other children her age. Some children are natural loners, while others will always be more social and active. Each child has a particular temperament, which expresses itself in the play activities she enjoys. It's important to look for and support your child's individuality while encouraging her to try a variety of activities.

**Exclusionary play** Your 4-year-old is probably much like other children his age in that he loves to play with other children. However, a typical play behavior that emerges around the age of 4 and 5 is two children excluding a third child from playing with them. The two bluntly tell the third that they don't want to play with him and he should go away. If you hear such an interaction, you may worry that your child is turning into a bully if he is one of the rejecters, or that he will become a child who is regularly picked on and excluded if he is the one rejected.

At this age, it's important to know that children aren't sure why their play works, but if two children are heavily involved in something, they may fear that the addition of a third will change or ruin their play. Because they can't figure out how to include another, they will simply tell the child to go away.

Your child also understands that he plays differently with different people. If he is busy stacking blocks with a friend, he will hesitate to include a doll-playing friend. He may also wonder how decisions on what and how they play will change if a third is added.

Another reason behind exclusionary play is simply exploration of feelings. Your child may feel that a current playmate is his friend, while someone he is not playing with is not a friend. As a result, he may say to another child, "You're not my friend now" when what he really means is "We can't play together right now." He may also feel a bond with his current playmate because they agree on rejecting a third child who wants to play.

Rather than forcing your child and a playmate to include another child, help the children—the excluder and the one excluded—understand the conflict. Acknowledge that two children are already playing. Ask them to tell about the activity in which they are involved. Then invite them to think of ways another child might be included. Also allow the child who is excluded to express her feelings. Finally, respect your child's right to choose. You may need to help the third child find something else to do. In addition, you may want to set some rules which include no name calling or other acts of meanness.

### Gender-specific play
*"Our 4-year-old daughter is not stereotypically girlish in any way. She hates dolls and dress-up clothing. She only wants to play rough games with boys. Is this normal?"*

Many experts point out that there are wider differences among people of the same sex than there among people of different sexes. Traditionally known as a "tomboy," your daughter may not yet understand that gender identity is stable and may believe that she can be a girl or a boy depending on the games she plays. She may become more girlish as she grows, especially when she enters puberty, or she may continue to prefer toys and games generally reserved for boys. It's important not to make her feel guilty for her interests. Rather, she should be encouraged to believe that she isn't limited to what in the past have been considered "girl" things and activities. These interests may later lead her into sports and possibly into a career that in the past was considered more male oriented.

## The sensitive child

For no clear reason, a child may be extremely sensitive to his own and others' emotions and to his environment in general. He is easily upset by what seems to be the slightest bump or bruise or insult while playing. Loud noises, changes in routine, or even uncomfortable clothing may set him off. Some sensitivities seem to be genetic. A sensitive baby will startle easily, be bothered by bright lights, and may be agitated by a change in the detergent that you use to wash his clothes. As he grows older, he will probably exhibit his sensitivity in positive as well as more negative ways. He will often show well-developed empathy for a friend who is upset or for a character in a book who is in trouble. He also will laugh more easily and quickly than other children the same age. However, what you may notice more than anything is his tendency to burst into tears at the slightest difficulty and his long struggle to compose himself.

Sometimes parents encourage extreme sensitivity by showing extreme reaction themselves when their child is upset. If concern is out of proportion to the hurt, a sensitive child may feel more uncomfortable than comforted by his parents' concern. He may believe that the hurt is really worse than even he thought it was. As a result, he looks more and more to the parent for protection and support. For some preschoolers, easy crying may be the only way they know to get attention from a parent. If a parent is normally critical and demanding, but shows support when a child is distressed, then the upset will come more frequently.

For a sensitive child, asking him to check his tears and hide his emotions won't help him learn to handle the stress he's feeling. You need to help him find other ways to express his very real upset. For example, keep your own emotions in check while acknowledging your child's emotions, give extra support when he is not crying, and work on other ways to cope. Practicing coping skills, such as helping your child put the reasons for feeling upset into words rather than crying. For example, if he cries when another child gets ahead of him on the line to the slide, teach him to say, "I'm next." The sensitive child does not need to be taught how not to feel his feelings. Instead he needs to learn to gain control over his sensitivities by gaining more control over his environment.

### Handling sensitivity to social problems

*"My daughter is very disturbed by seeing homeless people. I worry that she feels she has to fix the world. She's only 4!"*

Children this age are worried about themselves. When they see a homeless person, it concerns them that they, too, might become homeless.

The most important thing you can do is to reassure your child that homelessness will not happen to her, and that you and other family members will take care of her. Tell her that there are people and organizations that help those in need. Give your child a chance to be helpful by contributing a gift to a children's center at holiday time or to donate money to a shelter. If you donate your own time or money to a charity, be sure to let her know. Don't, however, take her along with you to visit a soup kitchen or other place just yet. The experience could be frightening, and make her feel uncomfortable.

## Your child's anger

Everyone feels anger. But when a 4-year-old expresses anger, it can be upsetting for a parent. You may be tempted to focus on finding ways to make your child feel better. Some parents focus on controlling their child's anger as an aspect of discipline. However, what a child needs most is to be given permission to feel anger and help in expressing it constructively.

One of the first things you can do is to help your child understand when she is angry. Once she begins to calm down, help her describe how she feels physically and emotionally, then tell her that she is angry. Then you can work on giving her the skills to describe what she is angry about. Before talking, however, your child may need some quiet time with you or alone. If you feel your child needs to be alone, don't make the time seem like punishment. By contrast, your child may be the sort who needs some physical release, such as hitting a pillow or running around the playground.

### Useful Anger

Anger used effectively can be a good tool for problem solving. Anger suppressed can often lead to acting out in other ways, such as hurting someone else or even becoming depressed. Anger can also be scary. You need to be a steady presence to help your child understand that even though she feels out of control, the world is still okay.

Within a short period of time after the anger has subsided, bring up the incident again. You might begin by telling your child what you saw that made her angry. If her anger resulted in someone or something being hurt, reinforce that everyone feels anger, but that her way of expressing it was not acceptable. Point out also that such behavior didn't solve the problem.

As you talk about the incident, you may discover that your child actually became angry because she was sad or frustrated. In this case, you may be able to suggest to your child alternative reasons why she felt the way she did and let her choose which makes the most sense. In this way you let her know you acknowledge her feelings while helping her figure out what happened. Then she can begin to identify situations that make her angry, which will help her think of ways to prevent it happening again.

In order to help your child think ahead, show her ways to slow down her anger so she can think before she's out of control. You might suggest she pretend she's a turtle who, with her head down and arms crossed, can't hit or call others names. Even learning to say "I'm mad" will help your child diffuse her anger.

For more on handling your own anger, see *page 401*.

It's also helpful to share with your child how you handle your own anger. You might talk about what you do when you feel angry, such as going for a walk or counting to ten. If you do lose your temper and become angry at your child, walk away, take a deep breath, then go back to your child and talk about what happened. The way you handle anger is a powerful teaching tool, one your child is sure to emulate.

## Handling stress-relieving habits

Does your son constantly nibble on his nails? Does your daughter seem to twirl her hair—almost unconsciously? Don't despair. Such habits are common and even normal. From infancy throughout adulthood, most people find ways to calm their nerves, from sucking on a pacifier to chewing on pencils to cracking knuckles.

Children who are nervous or restless are more prone to self-soothing habits. So are kids who

**"IT WORKED FOR ME"**

### *No More Hair Twirling*

My 4-year-old daughter constantly twirled her hair. Sometimes she even pulled out a few strands. She refused to have her hair cut short, so I took her to a "99 Cent Store" and let her pick out a bag full of barrettes, headbands, and "scrunchies" to keep her hair off her face and out of twirling range. She likes the look of all her new hair accessories and tends to keep her hands off her hair now.

are facing the stress of starting school, moving to a new home, or other disruption in the routine. Some experts also feel that nervous habits are an outlet for kids' unchanneled energies.

How should you respond to nervous habits—especially the most annoying ones like nose-picking? In general, it's best not to interfere, unless the habit poses a physical or psychological threat—if your daughter's hair-pulling is causing her to develop bald patches, for example, or if your son comes home from school crying because his thumb-sucking has made him the object of ridicule by his preschool classmates. If your child has a habit such as nose-picking or nail-biting, make sure he's washing his hands frequently during the time that he's working at curbing the habit, since putting his hands in his mouth or nose can spread infection. For habits that

## Help for Curtailing Habits

The following suggestions can help you help your child cut down or eliminate a variety of habits:

| If your child... | Try... |
|---|---|
| twirls hair excessively | giving her a long-haired stuffed animal or doll, whose hair she can tug on. Consider getting your child a shorter haircut or styling in braids or a pony tail to give her less access to it. |
| bites nails | offering a small squishy ball to squeeze whenever you notice him doing it. This will help him release his tension. He can keep the ball in his pocket and when he catches himself biting his nails he can squeeze the ball instead. Some highly motivated children respond to vanity: Seeing their nails manicured pleases them and reminds them to keep their nails out of their mouths. |
| chews on his clothing | having him wear short sleeves if he chews on cuffs and collarless shirts if collars are his preference. |
| sucks her thumb or fingers (beyond the toddler stage) | offering a toy to keep her hands and mouth busy. Or suggest that your child play with her building blocks or draw a picture. Give her something to hold. Get her talking (it's hard to keep her thumb in her mouth when she's chattering). |
| picks her nose | offering a tissue and a reminder to blow. Suggest that he pick his nose in private. |
| bangs his head | giving him a toy drum or a punching toy to play with to release his excess energy. |
| rocks back and forth | playing music and encouraging her to dance to it . |

you'd like to help your child break, there are strategies you can use.

The first step is to find other, more acceptable or constructive ways for your child to relieve his tension.

# Teaching manners to your preschooler

Manners are simply acting on the realization that other people have needs and deserve consideration. So teaching manners to preschoolers involves the values you instill and the example you set as well as outward displays of prescribed behaviors. Teaching the outward displays of manners without instilling the underlying values is impossible, at least in the long run. For your teaching to be meaningful, your child must himself feel respected.

Begin teaching manners in small bits and appeal to his self-interest. Let him know that both adults and other children will like him better and find him more pleasant to be around if he shows consideration. Above all, stress that good manners are not just a list of rigid do's and don'ts. They involve being kind to the people you meet everyday and are a way to make others feel good. These practices will make your teaching easier:

• **Model the behavior you want.** Your child actually learns more about manners by observing your behavior than by following your instructions. When your child notices other people behaving rudely, acknowledge the behavior, but don't speak rudely in turn about the person. Work on teaching your child that he doesn't have to be rude just because someone else has behaved rudely.

• **Be realistic in your goals.** Like all forms of teaching, you need to tailor instructions in manners according to your child's level of development. Your preschooler's nature is more frank and spontaneous, coupled with a desire to be first, rather than to be considerate. Nevertheless, he is ready to begin the process of absorbing social rules.

It is realistic to expect your preschooler to say, "please," "thank you," and "excuse me" with only occasional prompting and to be able to speak quietly in public, and to wait until someone has finished speaking before he begins to talk. When meeting someone, he should know that it's polite to say "hello" and make eye contact. He should not be expected to remember all the rules all the time, especially if he is excited or tired. Nor can he be expected to behave for overly long periods of time or at functions, such as adult-oriented parties, for which he is little prepared.

Your preschooler will slowly begin to absorb what good manners mean and will find that they have their own reward as people return the favor of treating him respectfully.

- **Don't get involved in power plays.** Don't insist that "please" and "thank you" accompany every request, which turns manners into a power struggle instead of an act of consideration. When your child makes a request without the "magic words," simply say that you would have been happier if he said "please" as you fulfill his request, if you would have fulfilled it anyway. Your child's interest in pleasing you is even greater than his need to assert his independence by resisting using his best manners. Give him the chance.
- **Explain your expectations.** Make your instructions specific, show him what you want, and give reasons for why manners are a good idea. Your child may have no idea when he is doing something impolite or how he looks to others when he chews with his mouth open. When teaching your child to speak politely, you can help by giving him the right words to say. For instance, if you're taking your child to your place of business where he will meet your coworkers, rehearse the script ahead of time, showing him how to shake hands and how to say, "Nice to meet you."
- **Keep criticism to a minimum.** When reminding your child to mind his manners, state the rule without criticizing. For instance, you can say that elbows don't belong on the table rather than demanding that he remove his elbows.
- **Make manners fun.** Try to make tasks that are mannerly, yet difficult, more fun. For example, when it's time to write thank-you notes, have your child draw a picture showing how much fun he is having with a gift rather than struggle to sign his name repeatedly if that task is difficult for him.
- **Consider others' feelings.** You also need to teach your child to respect others' rules and preferences, even when they may be different from your own. For example, you may feel very comfortable having your preschooler address your adult friends by their titles. If a person feels uncomfortable with that form of address and asks to be called by her first name, it's important for your child to show respect in this way by acknowledging that person's preferences.

**Teaching table manners**　Good table manners serve your child in a number of ways. They are likely to make your child a more acceptable guest at another's home and earn him lots of compliments.

This, in turn, enhances his self-esteem. Good table manners are also linked to better health, since they're less likely to cause choking, swallowing too much at once, or gagging. Your 4-year-old is now able to use utensils with ease and is developing the maturity to sit through the family meal as well as enjoy being a guest away from home. It's definitely not too soon to help him with his table-time manners. Like other skills, acquiring good table manners takes time, practice, and patience. To help your child develop table-time skills:

- **Model the behavior you want.** Saying "please pass the milk" is something your child will learn best by hearing it from you first instead of hearing demands.

- **Make a game of it.** Practice manners long before your child will need them in public, perhaps with a teddy-bear tea party or other fun event.

- **Concentrate on just one or two skills at a time.** If you're working on your child learning to eat with his mouth closed, don't spend a lot of time and energy going over lesser requirements. If he's able to eat a meal without displaying the contents of his mouth, congratulate him. Don't pick that moment to say something like, "…If only you could learn to swallow more quietly." Save that lesson for another day.

- **Correct gently.** When your child engages in less-than-model table behavior, especially for rules that are new to him, remind him once—calmly—that he should, for instance, remove his elbows from the table. Phrase your corrections positively, saying, for instance, "It's polite to keep your elbows off the table," instead of "Don't be a slob" or "Get those elbows off the table now!"

- **Don't expect perfection.** When at home, work consistently on instilling polite table behavior, but don't expect your child to have an adult's sense of decorum. When he learns to burp, remind him that it's not polite at the table, but don't act too shocked or surprised. If he's really enjoying this new skill, tell him that it's okay once in a while, but that it's important that he not do it in public or when company is over.

- **Make it easier for him.** Cut his food into small bites (for safety's sake as well as good manners) so that he's not tempted to stuff his mouth. Serve him small portions, which simply gives him less food to play with. Refill his plate only if he's hungry. Pour small glasses of milk or water rather than giving him a large glass that will make a bigger mess if knocked over and that will supply a bigger temptation to blow bubbles into. Avoid mealtime straws if blowing bubbles into drinks is a behavior you'd rather not have. Don't ask your child to sit through long, adult-oriented dinners or to behave impeccably at fancy restaurants. Most young children simply can't sustain their best behavior for long stretches of time while confined to a table.

## Developing a conscience

Learning what is right and wrong and becoming aware of and respecting others' feelings develops slowly and in stages. Before the age of 4, most children have little understanding of morality. They are egocentric, which means they think only of what they want and how they feel. By age 5, children begin to develop a conscience and can begin to understand that their actions might hurt another, and remember that it's important to treat people nicely and that they should not lie, steal, or cheat. However, they don't yet understand *why* this is important. They will try to be "good" because their parents and teachers tell them to do so and because they know they will get in trouble if they aren't. By age 7, fairness becomes important, and children know that other people have different needs and think differently than they do.

So, what do you do to help your child develop a conscience, even though you know it will be years before your efforts really sink in? The best thing you can do is to set a good example. Your child will learn a great deal from watching you do things, such as helping an elderly neighbor do her shopping, or making a donation of money or goods for a relief effort. When performing a civic act, you can explain why your actions are important. For example, if a cashier gives you too much change when your child is with you, you can show him what happened and make a point of correcting the mistake. However, if you try to pass off your child as younger so as not to pay a higher admission price at an entertainment park, for instance, you will not be providing a good model of moral behavior.

You can also use situations in television programs, in books, and in real life to make short, firm statements about moral behavior, such as "Ask before you take something," "Don't hit other people," "Pet the cat gently," "You can have a turn when she is finished." When you catch your child in a lie, remember that he can't fully make the distinction between reality and fantasy and will still use the truth creatively to suit his own purposes. Ask for explanations of

## Encouraging Empathy

One area of moral behavior that your child may exhibit at an early age is empathy. If he is bystander to someone else's distress, and neither the aggressor or victim, you may see that he is quick to react to try to make the person who is hurt feel better. When your child shows empathy toward others, make a point of telling him how nice he is and how proud you are that he cares.

inappropriate behavior, and reward truthfulness. It's important for you also to be truthful with your child.

As often as you can, find ways for your child to help others and give of himself. For example, you might ask him to help you water plants or put away groceries. He can help you gather canned foods to donate to a shelter, or gather newspapers for recycling.

When setting rules, make sure they are fair and are based on good reasons. Elicit your child's ideas so that he has a say in how chores can be divided and what he and siblings can do to share, for example. This will help him begin to think of other's needs and perceptions. Also help him learn ways to respond when treated unfairly by others. He can learn to tell another that he is still playing with a toy, or that it's not nice to hit.

Remember to be patient as your child moves through the different stages of developing a conscience. Don't lecture, as you'll discover that your child will begin to tune you out. Don't use shame or anger as punishment. Your child will likely feel resentment rather than moral understanding. Be careful also not to attack your child's character. Focus on his actions and behavior that you want changed. You might say, "You did a bad thing," rather than "You're a bad boy."

As your child grows older, you can help him face moral dilemmas, such as defending someone else, telling the truth when lying is easy, and taking care of obligations they would rather forget. Be sure to explain that he will always have mixed feelings when faced with a moral dilemma. For example, he may want to help another child against a bully, but will also feel afraid to do so for fear of getting hurt. He may weigh getting in trouble with telling the truth about something. Point out that courage and fear often go hand-in-hand, and that there are different ways to be courageous. You can help him think about how another person feels in different situations. And you can talk about some of the dilemmas you faced as a child, and share your feelings about what happened.

# Cognitive development

During his preschool years, your child is learning language in leaps and bounds. Your child's thinking is now maturing into the ability to think symbolically in which one thing stands for another, such as a word representing an object, or a stuffed animal representing a real animal. Symbolic thinking allows her to use fantasy and play in new and creative ways. At this point she is also forming the foundation for her future learning in school. She enjoys remembering and reciting what she learns now, and is able to generate ideas of her own, as well as understand cause and effect, and solve problems.

## What your child knows

Although, fantasy is still a big part of your 4-year-old's view of the world, she is increasingly able to distinguish between what is real and make-believe. This knowledge doesn't take away from her enjoyment of fantasy play. She may enjoy pretending to be a real person as much as a fantasy character.

Your child now takes pleasure in communicating with people of all ages. However, she still generally believes the world centers on her wants and desires.

Concretely, your child can generally count ten or more objects and name most colors, is gaining an understanding of time, and knows about the uses of everyday objects, such as appliances and money. She should also be able to recite her name and address.

Her communication skills blossom as she learns to pronounce most all of the sounds in the English language with the exception of the letters *f, v, s,* and *z*. She may also still have problems with *sh, l, th,* and *r*. Her vocabulary is now in the thousands of words, and she is able to use fairly complex sentences of up to eight words to tell stories. She is also able to talk in terms of the future.

**How your 4-year-old learns** Generally, your child learns through endless questions, exploration, and personal experience, particularly play. You may find some of her questions to be quite profound, such as curiosity about death and dying, what makes the sun warm, where rain comes from, who God is, and how the stars stay in the sky. Through hands-on activities she can explore what happens when, for example, she pours water from a large container into a small container, and how it feels to jump from a chair to the floor. She also learns through experimenting with various materials she can shape, design, and change, such as clay, paints, and dress-up props. She learns how to interact with others through her family and through play with other children. Social skills are also learned from television, which can be positive or negative, depending on the programming watched.

**Helping your child grow**  Rather than try to introduce your child to any structured learning, offer her a variety of free-form learning opportunities. These may include trips to a zoo and museums, especially those that have exhibits especially tailored to children. Encourage your child's special interests and talents, but don't push him to achieve particular standards. At this point, it's important your child realize how much fun it is to learn so she will be motivated to learn when she enters school. You can use books to help answer her many questions and introduce new ideas. She will probably want to look through books by herself and even pretend to read. Encourage her interest, but don't push her into reading before she's ready.

# Your preschooler's problem-solving skills

By providing many opportunities to practice, plenty of patience for inevitable errors, and lots of feedback, you can help your child learn to solve problems, consider consequences, and make choices. These skills will be invaluable for your child in many areas, including success at school and in choosing friends and activities.

Even in the preschool years, your child will be able to apply different kinds of thinking to solving problems. He is capable of figuring out a principle by seeing one or two examples. He can deduce that he will like doing something because he enjoys related activities. He can also begin to understand how his decisions affect others.

One way you can foster problem-solving skills is by asking questions. Instead of telling your child how to do something, help him see through questions what will happen if he does something, such as leaving a favored toy outside in the rain. Then you can ask how he would feel if the toy was ruined and what he might do to prevent this from happening.

By letting him make some of his own decisions, you will also be fostering sound judgment. These decisions can include choice of breakfast and clothes to wear, within limits and with your guidance. Then you can use these decisions to solve problems. For example, if the day will be warm, your child can use this fact to decide what to wear. If he seems to have trouble solving a problem or making a decision, you can give hints, but be sure to leave room for his own ideas.

Providing plenty of materials for experimentation will also help your child develop problem-solving skills. For example, if your child wants to make a ramp to run his toy trucks down, provide the materials, such as blocks and a piece of sturdy cardboard, and let him experiment with ways to make the ramp. He may go through several attempts before he finds a solution that satisfies him. Showing him the "right way"—your way—could get him to the same result faster, but would undermine his future ability to trust his own hard work and abilities.

Problem-solving skills can also extend to learning how to cooperate. If you need your child to cooperate at certain times, such as wearing a slicker when the forecast is for rain, you could use problem-solving skills to work through the situation. Could he carry the slicker in his backpack so that it's there if he needs it? Will he be playing close enough to home to come and retrieve it if he doesn't want to wear it now? Let him make a reasonable decision on his own. He may surprise you with a solution you hadn't considered.

## Preschool math and science

Your preschooler's natural curiosity about the world makes her a natural scientist. Her enjoyment of organizing things, her fascination with shapes, numbers, amounts, and patterns also makes her a natural mathematician. Although many play activities appear to be just play, you may be surprised at how much math and science she is learning.

Nature is a great place to encourage your young scientist to explore and learn. A backyard garden, a patch of grass, a bug, flower, or tree are all opportunities for your child to investigate the natural world. Digging in the dirt and looking closely at leaves, rocks, and a

### Early Knowledge

Once you start looking for science opportunities to explore with your child, you may be amazed at how many everyday things relate to science. Dropping a ball to the ground demonstrates gravity. Making and flying a paper airplane or a kite illustrates the power of the wind. Looking at the stars and the moon at night opens up a universe full of possibilities.

## Life Lessons

At home, growing bean plants, helping you in a garden, and helping take care of a pet are all ways your child will learn about growth and the needs of living things. Talk about the seeds you find in fruit and vegetables. Point out where these foods come from. Do they grow on trees or bushes, or are they underground?

creeping caterpillar is as much fun for her as it is educational. So that she can explore safely, find an outdoor space that's free of hazards. Help her notice and avoid natural dangers such as poisonous plants and deep water. Be sure to enjoy her discoveries along with her.

The kitchen can be a source of other scientific wonders as well. Water play is always popular with a 4-year-old. Allow her to experiment with pouring a set amount of water into different-sized containers. Appoint her your lab assistant, then, under your supervision, let her see what happens when water is heated or placed in the freezer. Show her how salt and sugar dissolve into water, but vegetable oil doesn't. Place a few drops of vinegar in a small a bowl with a bit of baking soda and watch the fizz. As much as possible, let her direct what you might try next.

Exploring math with your child can be just as much fun. At this age, basic mathematical concepts will make sense. Again, following your child's lead while providing material to investigate is the best approach.

Give your child a variety of different shapes and colors of blocks. Encourage her to stack and build, or make patterns with the shapes or colors. You might set out a simple pattern and ask her to continue it. Look for patterns in music, rhythms, clapping games, finger plays, and stories that repeat words. Blocks are also handy for learning about and naming geometric shapes, such as squares and circles, even octagons and pyramids. As your child learns shapes, look for them wherever you go. For example, you can find a square in a window pane and a circle in a bicycle tire.

When you are doing laundry, ask your child to help you sort by colors and type of clothes. Talk about how various items are alike and different. If she knows numbers, ask her how many socks there are, then count them with her. If she sorts a group of objects on her own, help her name the categories she used.

Compare sizes of objects with your child. Ask her which of two shoes is bigger, which of three bowls is the smallest, and which of two books is heavier. Talk about who is the tallest in your family. Provide boxes of different sizes and allow her to find out how many things or what shapes of things will fit in each box. Make a game of measuring different objects with all kinds of materials such as straws, pencils, paper clips, yarn, and anything else your child suggests. If your child likes to help you in the kitchen, let her measure a cup of flour or sugar and stir up the ingredients. You might even talk about how many cups of flour will fill a small bowl.

Basic number concepts can be introduced by counting fingers and toes. Then count people and objects. Match numbers of objects such as five fingers to five buttons. At dinner time, she can count the number of forks as she sets the table, then make sure there is the same number of spoons. Compare groups of things to see which has more and which has fewer. If your child likes to collect things such as rocks, shells, or toy figures, she can sort them into groups and count them. This is also the age when children get a real kick out of huge numbers, such a trillion or a zillion. While you can't help her actually count items to a quadzillion, it's fun for your child to learn the words that mean "a lot."

Math can even be a part of stories as your child tells you what happened first, next, and last, or first, second, and third. You might also ask her to tell you how to do an activity she enjoys and encourage her to talk about each step as "The first thing you do. . ." Help her understand that stories, events, and activities all follow a sequence or order.

At this age, don't be especially concerned with having your child read and write specific numerals. Written numbers are symbols, and it's important for your child to understand the concepts of numbers before she can move on to symbols that represent numbers. Common misunderstandings of numbers include thinking that five large dogs are more than five little kittens, or that five pennies are worth more than one dime. Don't try to correct your child's mistakes at this point. If you do, she may begin to doubt her abilities. She will learn what is correct soon enough. The important idea now is to allow her time to explore, experiment, and make mistakes with support rather than judgment from you.

## Your preschooler's artwork

By the age of 4, your child's artwork will become more exciting to him as his coordination improves. He should begin drawing shapes, such as circles and squares, and be able to trace or copy a star or diamond. If he draws a picture of a person, he should now be adding

## Homemade Play Dough

Play dough can be purchased or made from equal parts of flour and salt, mixed with a little water to a pastry texture. Plain dough can be painted with poster or finger paints, or you can color the dough with food coloring or mix the flour with powder paint. If you keep the dough in the refrigerator, it will last for a long time. Provide your child with cookie cutters and a small rolling pin as well.

from four to six parts, including the body, all limbs, facial features, and hair. He will also enjoy painting, finger-painting, clay modeling, and cutting and pasting.

To encourage your child to explore his artistic creativity, provide a variety of materials. You can mix nontoxic wallpaper paste with dry powder paint and water to create finger paints. If you don't want to waste sheets of newsprint or drawing paper, give your child materials that can be washed and reused, such as a large square of white Formica-covered board, a square of glossy linoleum, or a sheet of white oilcloth. To make patterns in the paint, give your child a comb, a plastic fork, or a butter curler.

When using brushes and poster paints, you can show your child how to make folded paintings by dropping paint on one side of a paper, then folding the paper in half. Air painting can be done by dropping paint on paper, then blowing on it through a straw. Drip patterns are created by dropping paint on shiny cardboard, then tipping the board in different directions. Paint and ink stamps can be bought or made from squares of soft wood on which objects have been glued, cut from sponges, or carved from potatoes.

To make an art treasure box, you can fill a cardboard box with different colors of construction paper, round-ended scissors, a glue pen, colored tissue and foils, colored cardboard, stickers, pipe cleaners, crepe paper streamers, cotton balls, old magazines for cutting out pictures, tape, and small pieces of fabric. You might also include other objects such as buttons and plastic beads of different shapes, along with yarn, colored string, or ribbons.

## Reading with your preschooler

By now, your child can probably recognize that certain letters, when strung together, form his name. Your child may surprise you when he recognizes the name of his favorite juice drink or "reads" the name of a character from a book page. You may wonder if he is ready to read or if he isn't already "reading." If your child is interested in letters, enjoys looking through books and magazines on his own, practices "writing," and listens attentively to stories, then he may be ready to learn reading basics. However, it's important not to push your child into any formal instruction until he is absolutely ready. Children who are forced to try to read at an early age do not become better readers later. And if they don't meet their parents' expectations, they might also have such a sense of failure when they reach school, they will resist learning. They may be more withdrawn and apathetic about learning if the possibility of failure looms too large.

Your goal at this point should be to encourage a love of learning. The best approach you can use to build this foundation is to provide your child with plenty of enjoyable books and other reading materials to explore whenever he wants to. Be available to read with him and to answer questions. Identify a letter or a word that your child wants to know. You might even ask him if he can find another letter that is the same. Remember to keep such lessons short and informal.

Also provide him with a variety of learning experiences. If available, play with a computer program together, watch a children's program on television and talk about what you've seen. Sing songs and play games. You might also provide materials such as refrigerator magnets in the shape of letters. Allow him to move the letters around and feel their shapes. Always follow his lead as to what he wants to do, and allow him to advance at his own pace. Although it's important that you be involved, too, work with him only as long as he is enjoying an activity. If you notice any frustration or drop in enthusiasm, move on to something else. Successful learning can only take place when you respect and support his individual interests and rate of progress.

## Ready to Read?

If you feel your child is not ready to read, wait a year until he has further developed language skills, memory, and visual maturity that will help him learn to read. A benchmark for visual readiness is to see how well he can track a flashlight beam from left to right. If he can easily stack blocks, he will be able to recognize patterns and sequences. But remember, the desire to read must be his, not yours.

## Language and learning

Language development and the ability to learn go hand-in-hand. We think with words; we communicate with words; we read and we write with words. As your child's mastery of words advances so will her ability to learn.

At each stage in her development, you will see your child's

## If a Child Won't Read

If you try to push your child into learning to read before he is ready, he may lose his enjoyment of books and resist learning later. Just be patient and encourage him when he does show interest in reading words.

understanding of language grow and expand. At 2, your child was finally able to have a conversation that let you know her thoughts and feelings. She discovered the power of words and frequently used a favorite—"no." At 3, she used plurals, saying "boys" when there was more than one boy and she generalized this rule to all words, saying "mans" for "men." At 4, your child has become the teller of wonderful yet chaotic stories that jump from event to event and leave out key pieces of information. At each stage, your child explored and mastered the challenge of thinking with words.

When your child was still a toddler, there were times when you could actually watch the relationship developing between language and thinking. He learned then that asking a question made other people talk back to him. As a 3-year-old, he may have talked out loud when he was planning his actions: "I go outside now," he might have said to himself as he put on his coat. That may continue this year. "I'm making Mommy a card," your 4-year-old might say aloud as he draws you a picture. Using words to describe actions helps preschoolers accomplish the task and stay on track.

Language development, even for your verbal 4-year-old, proceeds every day. It now includes practicing pronunciation, building vocabulary, experimenting with sentence constructions, and learning to tell stories. Learning the tricks and turns of our language is a long, ongoing process that requires many years and much patience. For a few more years yet, your child will work on the pronunciation of words and speaking with correct sentence structure, building his vocabulary along the way. All of this happens on a schedule that allows for considerable individual differences because children do not acquire language skills at exactly the same time or even in the same way. Some children speak in one-word "sentences" until the age of 3; others speak in paragraphs before they reach the age of 2. Some children are lively storytellers; others keep their stories to themselves. Some preschoolers speak clearly and distinctly, others mumble and hesitate. All of these differences are well within the range of normal. Whatever path and timetable your child uses to learn language, one thing is certain: all children need a solid understanding of language before they can learn to read or write.

# CHAPTER 12

# 5 Years

Sunny and happy, with a smile on her face, your 5-year-old greets the world with enthusiasm. She wants to be good, strives to cooperate, and seems to be ready to go along with whatever you say.

Your child also becomes more attached to her family and seriously wants to take on responsibilities in the home. She also loves to learn new things, talking with you, being read to, and wanting to show you what she can do.

She gets along well with children her own age and plays easily with others. She is also generally polite and friendly with adults. You may find that going to the grocery store or visiting a restaurant with your child has become a pleasant experience.

At some point during this year, you may decide that your child is ready for kindergarten. Most 5-year-olds are ready for the demands of school, and she will likely get along well with her teacher and her classmates.

As your child nears 6, however, her sunny disposition may suddenly swing to the opposite side. Where you once heard Yes!, you will soon hear No! Your confident, willing child may suddenly becoming demanding, indecisive, and reluctant to cooperate. Children naturally move from balance to imbalance and back again in stages as they grow. In the meantime, this will be an age you can greatly enjoy with your child.

# *Physical development*

During the fifth year, your child should continue growth at about the same rate as earlier preschool years. If he has been generally calm and quiet, he may now be more restless. Physical changes may also make him more awkward and less sure of his movements. These changes are normally just the next stage in growth.

## Physical changes

While he is 5, your child may grow a couple of inches and gain five or six pounds. Both large and fine motor skills advance as your child's balance and eye-hand coordination improve. At the beginning of the year, your child will probably show confidence in his physical abilities. He now stands straighter with his arms near his body and moves with purpose. If you weren't already sure, you will find that your child is now firmly right- or left-handed. He can direct his hands to move precisely and accurately to do simple tasks. In the second half of the year, this physical self-assuredness may lessen as growth may reduce the control he has over his movements and make it difficult for him to sit still. As a result, he may then feel insecure about what he can do.

Visual changes also occur in the second half of the fifth year. When writing, he may reverse letters and numbers. This is normal and not a sign of any learning disability. Eye and hand coordination may slow and become awkward. Although these changes may appear to be problematic, they really represent changes in orientation brought about by growth. Your child should soon regain some of his balance, at which point you will see more mature behavior and an increase in abilities.

Teeth also change during the fifth year. At first, you will probably notice little difference. But, by the end of the year, new molars will begin to emerge without displacing any baby teeth. As your child moves into the sixth year, his baby teeth will begin to loosen and fall out to be replaced by permanent teeth.

Your 5-year-old may also experience an increase in colds and other minor illnesses due largely to the increased socialization that takes place in kindergarten, if he hasn't been in school before.

**What your 5-year-old can do** Some of the physical changes that generally occur during the fifth year affect eye-hand coordination. He can move eyes and head together and approach things more directly. He may not yet be able to smoothly move eyes from left to right and focus on different things. As a result, he will be better able to focus on one stationary thing than follow something that's moving. You may see evidence of this in longer periods of time spent on one activity, and a determination to color within the lines, for example.

Because he can use his hands with greater control, he will usually be able to lace his shoes and fasten buttons by himself, provided he's been given the opportunity and encouragement to master these skills. If he is interested in playing a piano, he will now be able to place his fingers on the piano keys and play a chord.

He can walk in a straight line, skip, and go down stairs with one foot on each stair. This ability to alternate his foot movements can be seen in learning to ride a tricycle, then moving up to a two-wheel bike. He may want to try roller-skating and even be interested in walking on stilts. You will also find he can climb and swing with ease.

**Helping your child grow** To help your child take advantage of his new skills, try to provide art materials, such as crayons, coloring books and paper, and modeling clay. He might also have fun stringing beads, making pictures with bits of cloth and colored paper, cutting, and tracing. Also provide blocks and other building materials such as snap-together cubes. A tricycle or a two-wheel bike will be greatly enjoyed. If your child wants to learn to ride a bike, training wheels may not be necessary if you supervise closely and see that he is balanced and has control. Roller skates and a jump rope are also items your child can actively use. You'll see him take to equipment for climbing, sliding, and swinging at local school and park playgrounds with increased zest.

## Saying good-bye to baby teeth

By the time your child turns 5, her smile will probably reveal a mouth full of small, white, evenly spaced primary teeth. But beneath the gum surface, permanent teeth are growing and beginning to exert pressure on the roots of her baby teeth. This process doesn't happen rapidly, though, and as a result a baby tooth may loosen,

## TIMELINE *Permanent Tooth Eruption*

**At 5 or 6 years,** a child's first permanent teeth—the first molars—emerge in a space next to the baby molars. (Baby molars are eventually replaced by other permanent teeth.)

**Around age 6 or 7,** a child's teeth begin to loosen—starting with the bottom front teeth—and fall out, commencing a process in which lost baby teeth are replaced by permanent ones. This process continues until age 11 or 12.

**Between ages 11 and 14,** a second set of permanent molars emerges, giving your adolescent 28 teeth.

**At age 15 or older,** one to four wisdom teeth—also called third molars—may emerge giving teens 30 to 32 adult teeth.

then tighten, then loosen again. Once its roots have dissolved, the primary tooth hangs on by a little gum tissue and will come out quite easily.

Let your child wiggle her loose tooth if she wants to. If she's determined to get the tooth out (and under her pillow for the tooth fairy!), place a clean, dry washcloth or a piece of gauze or tissue over the tooth and gently rotate it. When the tooth comes out, have your child bite down on a thick piece of gauze to stop the bleeding. If your child accidentally swallows a tooth, don't worry. The tooth will pass safely through her digestive tract.

**Teething problems with permanent teeth** Occasionally, a permanent tooth will grow behind or, more rarely, in front of, a primary one. This is more likely to occur among the lower front teeth because the gum holding them has only a narrow strip of bone from which they grow. If the bone becomes overcrowded, a permanent tooth might be forced to grow out of position, and it isn't able to put pressure on the primary roots. In most cases, the baby tooth will eventually fall out on its own, but if it hasn't by the time the permanent tooth has reached the same height, the baby tooth should be extracted.

Teeth don't always fall out in the proper order. The correct sequence is for lower incisors (the two center teeth) to come out first, then the upper two or the two teeth on either side of the lower incisors. Tooth loss should also occur bilaterally—first the left, then the right, or vice versa. If there's delay of longer than six months between the loss of a tooth and the loss of the corresponding one, check with your child's dentist. Also, if your child's primary teeth haven't loosened, not necessarily fallen out, by the end of her fifth year, ask her dentist to look at earlier dental X rays or to take new ones to see if permanent teeth are coming in normally.

**Upper Jaw**

Gums ————

Adult Tooth Bud

Baby Tooth Root
(dissolved)

Baby Tooth

## 5-year-olds and sports

Participation in sports is beneficial and rewarding for children in many ways. It can improve physical fitness and motor coordination, promote self-discipline, and increase self esteem. Team sports also hone social skills. An emphasis on performance, however, can rob your child of the joy of participation.

**Good sports for your 5-year-old** Five-year-olds are most interested in playing with others and having fun, just as they did when they were preschoolers. Though now ready for more social activity with their peers and able to handle one-on-one competition with a friend, they are not ready to compete in groups. Imposing competition into your child's sports play may just confuse him and open the door to hurt feelings and bruised self-esteem. Therefore, any sports you encourage your child to take part in should be done with a sense of play and activity rather than competition. Learning to ride a bike or swim, and playing ball games in which she follows directions to accomplish an action, are all good sports she will probably enjoy. Good choices for organized sports are T-ball and soccer programs that are designed for the age group and that are coached by leaders who promote fun over winning.

*For information on choosing sports gear and following safety guidelines in sports, see **page 846**.*

**Organized sports** Most 5-year-olds are not ready for organized sports that expect strict adherence to formal rules. Even when playing an organized game such as soccer or basketball with an adult coach, your child and her teammates are likely to revise the rules at a moment's notice. What they really want to do is have fun, not necessarily win. By emphasizing the win-lose part of the game, your child may end up feeling like a loser if her team doesn't come in first.

Some kids, however, do like the idea of the uniform and the big-kid feeling of being on a team. If your child would enjoy and is interested in an organized sport, here are some tips for evaluating a sports program:

- **Pay close attention to how the program is matched to her developmental and emotional needs.**
- **Find out how the program is structured.** Any instruction should be done in short time periods. Children should be playing most of the time, although not always the sport in question.
- **Make sure the children have help to learn the skills required.**
- **Check that there is good, safe equipment** and enough of it for all players.
- **Observe the program** to see that all the children have a chance to play regardless of their skill.
- **Once your child starts a program, pay attention to how she is doing.** If she stops having fun, then she shouldn't remain in the program.

## Gymnastics Classes

Healthy preschoolers can take part in gymnastics programs, but make sure the program is run by a reputable organization or school and that the instructors are licensed to teach gymnastics to young children. The teachers should be very knowledgeable about the types of activities that are age appropriate and should not urge kids to do more than they are personally capable of doing. They should also have a good understanding of a child's musculoskeletal system and choose activities that won't put undue stress on bones and joints.

**Keeping safety in mind** When kids participate in sports, injuries can happen. In fact, each year more than 775,000 children ages 14 and under are treated in hospital emergency rooms for sports-related injuries. Most of the injuries are due to falls, being struck by an object, and overexertion. The National Safe Kids Campaign estimates that half of all organized sports-related injuries among children could be prevented and recommends that sports injury prevention programs include proper physical and psychological conditioning, use of appropriate safety equipment, a safe playing environment, adequate adult supervision, and safety rules that are enforced. Another important factor in injury reduction is matching or grouping kids according to similar skill level, weight, and physical maturity. If your child is participating in sports activities, make sure he has appropriate, well-fitting shoes and protective equipment, especially head gear. Make sure he drinks enough fluids to prevent dehydration and that there are first-aid supplies nearby. Outdoors, he should wear sunscreen with a protective factor of 15 or more.

**Helping kids be good sports** Every child likes to win. Learning to lose gracefully is a skill that needs to be taught. If your child is often upset over losing a game, he may need to quit playing until he is older. Instead, you might try a cooperative board game or other game in which all the players work together to overcome some obstacle. This will help him learn the concept of winning and losing, and he will be able to share with other players in the satisfaction of winning. However, don't be surprised if interest wanes faster than it does with competitive games. Children like their games to be a little risky and scary, which competition provides.

Be careful not to push your child too hard to learn more complex games before he is ready. This will just increase the possibilities of losing and the chances of frustration. With a young child, start with games of luck, then progress to games of skill as his abilities improve. For example, Candy Land and Old Maid are good for a 5-year-old because they are short and based on luck. By the time he is in the first grade, he may enjoy Parcheesi and Uno.

Don't be surprised when your child cries sometimes when he loses. And, if he loses too frequently, you may find that he changes the rules to suit himself, or cheats in order to win.

The same principles apply to sports. Be sure to choose appropriate sports that fit your child's maturity and skill level. He may still experience frustration at losing, and be tempted to change the rules mid-game in order to win. But if given the best chance possible for winning as often as losing, he will learn that sometimes he is a winner and sometimes a loser. You can help by showing him that you don't value him more or less when he wins or loses, especially when his loss results from his own mistakes.

You can also be a good sport model for your child by saying, when you lose a game, that everyone loses sometimes and that you enjoyed playing the game more than winning or losing it.

*For information on bicycle safety, see* **page 846**.

### Riding two-wheelers
*"Is 5 years old too young to ride a two-wheel bike?"*

Most five-year-olds should have little trouble riding a two-wheel bike, with or even without training wheels, if their sense of balance is generally good. The key is having your child use a bike that is the correct size. A big bike that she'll "grow into" is not a good choice. To know if the bike is the right size, check to see that your child can touch the ground with her feet while seated. Coaster brakes are generally a better choice for a child making the transition from a trike to a two-wheeler. Hand brakes generally require greater hand size and hand strength than most 5-year-olds have. If your child is starting out on a bike without training wheels, opt for practicing on a soft surface. For all bikers, be sure they wear safety helmets.

## Why children show off their skills

"Look what I can do!" "Come watch me!" You are probably hearing these words frequently these days. Your 5-year-old is trying out skills that you take for granted, but that are new and challenging to him. And he just loves to show them off.

Showing off is normal for your child because he believes wholeheartedly that everyone is as interested as he is in the daring things he can do. You might wonder if your child is becoming too self-centered. He's not. This kind of watch-me-centeredness is a normal part of a 5-year old's growth. In fact, he can actually learn valuable social skills because he must consider what others are doing and how they feel as he seeks their attention.

The way to handle this show-off behavior is not, as many parents may feel, to ignore it. In fact, it's better to pay attention to what your child is doing so that you can help him benefit from his self-promotion. Let him know that you're impressed with and proud of what he can do. Even though the accomplishment may seem small to you, being able to swing from a playground bar for example, is new to him. Compliment the effort as well as the achievement. The important thing for your child is his willingness to try something new, to push himself to new heights, both literally and figuratively. In this way, you'll encourage his enthusiasm for improving his skills.

As well as praising your child for his effort and accomplishments, it's also important to set boundaries against constant interruptions. Be clear about the kind of behavior that you will reward with attention. For example, you might point out that speaking quietly will be more effective in getting you to watch.

If your child constantly shows off, however, you may want to look for some other, underlying cause. This would be especially true if he tries ever more risky things to get your attention. You may want to review whether you really listen when he speaks and wants your attention. You might also consider if there have been any recent big changes in your child's life, such as a move, the arrival of a new sibling, or divorce, that's making him especially need your attention and approval now. If there is, your child may need to provide extra reassurance that he is valued and wanted.

# Emotional development

When your child first turns 5, you may feel blessed by her sunny outlook and willingness to please. She may be brimming over with love for everything and everyone and approach whatever she does with self-confidence and enthusiasm. A major change, however, generally occurs around 5½ to 6 years old. During that time, your child may switch from compliance to defiance. She may rarely be calm now, and may be teary, restless, resort to tantrums, and dawdle when she doesn't refuse outright to do something. Emotional development rarely happens at a steady rate. So, your 5-year-old's changes are normal moving forward, then backward in order to progress to the next stage.

## Your child's feelings

Whereas your child may have been intent on trying anything new at the age of 5, she may feel more comfortable now with what she knows. She is likely to feel secure in what she knows how to do and won't go beyond her own identified boundaries. She may also be able to state quite clearly why she feels the way she does. She feels proud of what she can do and beams when praised for something. By the middle of the year, this self-confidence is likely to be shaken as the next stage brings uncertainty.

While 5 is generally a pleasant age, you may encounter some

*For more information on handling misbehaviors, see **pages 393–99**.*

troublesome areas. For example, your child may not easily admit she did something wrong and will fib about what happened. This behavior is typical of her age and does not point to any deep-seated moral lack. She may also feel tempted to take things that belongs to others. This is generally because she has not yet made the distinction between her own and others' property.

**How your 5-year-old develops secure relationships** At the beginning of the fifth year, your child will probably demonstrate great attachment to her mother or the primary caregiver. She feels secure that her mother will be there whenever she wants her and so rarely worries about an absence. In fact, she may feel and boast about how wonderful her parent or parents are. This attachment also extends to the rest of the family. She focuses now on who is a part of the family, including any pets. Grandparents are especially important. Relationships with siblings may achieve a balance now as your child acts kindly toward older children and protective toward younger children. This evenness extends to playmates as well.

### Relating to Mom

By the time your child nears 6, her attitude toward family may seem to change somewhat, especially toward her mother. Whereas before, she felt her mother could do no wrong, she now may be quick to blame her for anything that goes wrong. This change is all a part of the more general changes she is going through at this age, and it's important not to take it personally.

At the age of 5, your child may be expanding her world by going to kindergarten. At this point, a teacher becomes an important person in her life along with family members. She will likely get along well with and benefit greatly from an attentive, friendly teacher. If there seem to be any complaints about the demands of school, you might invite her teacher to visit at your home. Even a short visit will help your child develop a more personal relationship and a sense of being valued by someone who is important to her.

Friendships deepen at the age of 5. Friends provide companionship, allies, and someone to share with. They also provide a way to try out and learn social skills. Your child may feel the need to have lots of friends, or she may be the type of child who is content with one or two friends and who also likes to spend time alone.

**Helping your child grow** When it comes to your child's changing attitudes toward you or another parent during the fifth year, the best approach is not to get too upset when she switches from "I love you" to "I don't like you" and moves from obedience to disobedience. When you have problems with her behavior, a good technique is to talk to her about the feelings behind her actions. For example, say, "You must be very angry to have slammed the door. But slamming the door is not allowed." By acknowledging her feelings along with restating the rules, you let her know that while her actions are not acceptable, her feelings are okay.

Try to anticipate possible discipline problems by thinking how you might prevent them. Focus on what will happen if she is good rather than on the consequences of being bad. If you do feel the need to punish for behavior such as lying and stealing, do so calmly. Remember that at 5, your child strongly wants to do what is right.

## Introverts and extroverts

Many 5-year-olds are talkative and ready to share themselves and whatever they're doing. Yet, you may discover that your child doesn't fit this description, and, in fact, seems unwilling to tell you much about what he did in school. There is no need to worry if your child does not seem to be very outgoing. His temperament may be more that of an introvert than an extrovert.

An extrovert gets his energy from other people and outside events and stimuli. You know what he is thinking because he tells you. Your extrovert likes, even needs, company. Introverts on the other hand gather their energy from within. They like to reflect on their experiences and take the time to understand what they have been doing. Time alone or time spent with one or two other people is how your introvert recharges himself.

Most children have elements of both the extrovert and the introvert, but lean more toward one style or the other. Both have their strengths. However, it is important that you understand who your child is, especially when he enters school, in order to help him successfully negotiate the world.

You can tell if your child is an extrovert by these characteristics:
- He always wants to have friends over to play. He will become bored and whiny if left too much to himself.
- He demands immediate attention when he comes home from school. He is always eager to tell you about his day.
- He learns best by talking and doing.
- He immediately answers questions and finds it hard to wait for his turn.

If your child is an introvert, he will display these characteristics:
- He needs time alone, especially after being with a group. If he doesn't get this time, he may act out in order to force a time-out.
- He thinks before answering questions.
- He's more open at home and with relatives than he is with strangers or at school.
- He has a strong sense of personal space.
- He learns best by watching, reading, or listening.
- He dislikes being pushed into things.
- He is protective of possessions and is easily frustrated when forced to share.

You can help an introverted child by giving him the time alone that he needs. When he is ready, he'll enjoy communicating with you. You might even set a regular talk time when you can talk about his day. He will then have a chance to organize his thoughts before he shares them. If your child is about to start school, consider taking him to the classroom for a visit before the first day. Help him figure out how to get to the room and where the bathroom is. If possible, meet his teacher. If he wants to talk about what he has seen, be ready, but don't ask him too many questions.

A visit to the school beforehand will also help your extrovert. He will want to talk about what he has seen and will probably have many questions. After he starts school, be ready to talk about his day as soon he gets home. Also be prepared to answer questions. This will help him sort out his day. Then he will be ready to move on. If you have more than one extrovert, ask them to take turns with you or be ready to talk to all of them at the same time.

Whichever type of child you have, remember to accept him for who he is. Give attention when needed, but also retreat when you should. You will then give him the freedom to communicate when he needs and wants to.

## The perfectionist

If your child becomes impatient when he can't accomplish what he set out to accomplish right away, he may be a perfectionist who is overly critical of what he tries to do. With this type of temperament, he may set impossible goals for himself, which guarantees that he will fail. He will end up constantly frustrated and may become unwilling to try anything new with the confidence that he will succeed.

You will know if you have a perfectionist if he spends a long time on a project, then takes little pleasure or pride in what he has done because it is not good enough. Even if his results are perfectly adequate, the perfectionist child will still be frustrated and upset. The perfectionist child may also give up on a project just after starting it if he feels his initial efforts aren't leading to the perfect results he wants. This child may, after one failed attempt at bike riding, toss the bike down and declare, "I'll never ride a bike!"

> ### Handling Mistakes
>
> Let your child see you make and recover from mistakes. If your perfectionist sees that its okay to mess up, he may go easier on himself for his own mistakes. Be sure to acknowledge that even though you failed you plan to try again.

To help a perfectionist deal with frustration, first take a look at your own expectations of your child. If you discover you are being overly critical, try to adjust your standards to a more comfortable level for your child. If your child becomes overly anxious when having to start something new, talk about what the new activity requires and what he can expect. Let him know that no new skill is acquired immediately and that everyone needs to practice to learn new things. Remind him, too, of the progress he has made in other endeavors.

Also take a look at any stressful situations your family might be experiencing. A major change can mean extra pressure on your child to behave too well. He might translate this pressure as a need to be perfect.

## Building self-confidence

Some children just seem to be naturally self-confident. They move through life ready to tackle anything because they feel sure they will succeed. However, even the most self-assured children need some help at times to become independent. This applies especially to girls, as our society tends to encourage girls to be more passive and dependent.

To help your child become more resourceful, teach her skills that she can use in her daily life. For instance, teach her how to use the telephone and then encourage her to call a friend for a playdate instead of your making the arrangements. She can also choose a snack that she can make herself. Choices are also important in deciding what book to check out from the library, and what acceptable televisions shows to watch. You might also ask her to help you and

## Self-Sufficiency

Another effective way to boost your child's self-confidence is to demonstrate your own self-sufficiency. A 5-year-old will gain an important model for behavior if she sees you calmly handling a problem and taking charge when necessary.

others in worthwhile ways. She can assist with household tasks, help the family during travels by looking for specific signs or landmarks to get you where you're going, and make presents to give as gifts. Showing her how to take action will help her build a sense of power in dealing with events and people.

When learning new skills, give her a chance to make her own mistakes and solve her own problems rather than stepping in to show her how. If you do need to help, provide hints rather than telling her directly what to do. When she has worked on a project without asking for help, compliment her efforts and tell her how proud you are. She will feel a greater sense of accomplishment, her self-confidence will increase, and she'll be more ready to face new challenges.

Remember that self-confidence and self-reliance don't appear quickly. Don't push your child toward independence before she is ready. What she needs from you is gentle encouragement and a secure base from which she can venture out and return to if she needs to.

**Is your child ready for sleepovers?** You may be surprised if your preschooler asks to sleep over at a friend's house. Though many 5-year-olds and some 4-year-olds are mature enough to handle a night away from their familiar bed and usual routine, you might be awakened by a late-night call asking you to come get her.

To help assure that a sleepover is successful, observe your child's signals and make preparations. If your child still gets up at night and is not yet completely independent in going to the bathroom, brushing her teeth, and getting herself dressed and undressed, she will probably not be ready to spend the night away from her family. If you're not sure, try practice runs by having your child stay at a relative's house or having a relative or other known adult stay with your child in her home while you're away. The familiar setting will allow your child to make an easier transition from sleeping at home with her family to sleeping away without you.

When she is ready to leave for her first away-from-home overnight, remind her specifically about expected behavior, such as going to bed when her friend's parents say it's time. Don't overdo your good-bye discussion, however. For instance, refrain from saying that you'll really miss her, and that if she wants to come home she should call.

If you don't feel she's ready for a sleepover but still claims to want one, you can try accompanying her if the destination is one at which you'll be comfortable, such as a relative's home. Or you can invite your child's playmate to your house, if that child is ready for a sleepover. On the other hand, there's no need to give your child the sleepover or pajama party experience just yet if you'd rather not.

> ### *Friendly Sleepovers*
>
> Make sure that your family and the other child's family are comfortable with each other. This will greatly reduce any worries you might have of entrusting your child with other adults for the night. You'll need to feel comfortable calling late at night and also know that if your child needs to call you her wishes will be respected.

## Handling disappointment and frustration

Seeing your child disappointed and frustrated because a greatly anticipated event does not happen or turns out differently than expected can be heartbreaking. It's also difficult not to step in and immediately fix something if your child becomes frustrated with what he is doing or becomes frustrated when having to wait for something.

Always remember that your sense of time is different from your 5-year-old's. You may feel that a planned event can be easily rescheduled if something happens to change your plans. However, to your child, the idea of tomorrow may seem very far away. All he cares about is that a much-anticipated event is not happening *right now*. Besides disappointment, he may feel frustration at the delay. Because his world is still fairly self-centered, he may feel that the loss was something done to him on purpose.

One mistake that parents often make in dealing with a child's disappointment is to dismiss his feelings, saying, "We can do it another day." This does little to help him deal with his feelings or make him feel less sad. Another mistake is to be overly anxious to mend the hurt or try too hard to make up for the disappointment. By doing so, your child will never learn to cope with disappointment on his own. You may save the day, but your child may get the idea that you don't think he can or is not expected to handle frustration on his own.

To help your child face disappointment, acknowledge his feelings, including sadness, anger, and frustration. Then help him turn his thoughts to other things. You might make suggestions for alternate activities, but don't go too far. Keep your suggestions simple. If your child can't be comforted, you may need to leave him alone for a while to experience his feelings. Make sure he knows though that feeling upset is not a license for acting out.

Impatience is another outgrowth of frustration. You may discover that your child becomes anxious and then angry when he can't do something he wants to do right away. To help your child learn patience and so lessen frustration, help him identify situations in which he becomes most impatient. If it's when he has to wait for something, talk about techniques for making the wait go by faster. This might include thinking of a fun activity with a friend, for example. Then practice waiting, increasing the wait by a few seconds each time. When the next need-to-wait situation occurs, you can remind him of his new skill.

## Relieving your child's stress

*Also see **page 654** for more on stress and children.*

Disappointment, challenges, too-full days, and demands from school and parents can lead to stress—even in children as young as 5. This stress may be exhibited in a series of physical symptoms, such as stomachaches, headaches, anxiety, and depression. Although you can't—and shouldn't—shield your child from all stress, there are things you can do to help reduce undue stress.

• **Make sure that your child is not overscheduled with activities.** Allow her unstructured time just to dream and enjoy her own games.

• **Encourage her to talk about her feelings.**

• **Teach your child appropriate ways to vent her strong emotions.** You could attach a large sheet of paper to the wall and encourage her to draw pictures with big, dramatic strokes. Or provide her with a pillow to punch or toss.

• **Have fun together.** Surprise your child with a special trip to some place fun, such as a movie or just set aside some time for playing a board game or cuddling up with a good book together.

• **Make a date with your child.** Schedule time together on a regular basis so your child knows she can count on having you all to herself for a set period. This time might include walks or running errands together, for example.

• **Try a warm bath.** Forego the bathtub toys, which often provide additional stimulation, and make this bath a thoroughly relaxing one. You might read her a story or even play music during her bath.

• **Play music or a tape** of your child's favorite story to help her tune out distractions for a while.

• **Do some silly things together so you both can laugh.** Funny poems or talking in nonsense syllables are possibilities.

• **Prepare ahead of time for possible stressful situations,** such as a visit to the doctor or the first day of kindergarten. If your child has some idea of what to expect, the experience will be much less stressful for her. Be careful, however, not to prepare too far in advance. Otherwise, she could get anxious anticipating the event.

Besides one-on-one time with you, set aside time, such as one evening a week, in which the whole family slows down and does something together. Try not to let outside demands interfere with this time.

**The need for quiet time** At the age of 5, your child is probably enjoying some exciting challenges; the greatest of which may be kindergarten and the start of her formal education. Although her enthusiasm and curiosity may be at a high level, she is likely not to have the skills for planning and decision-making that will help her understand that she can't do everything that interests her. As a loving parent, you might also want to expose your child to every worthwhile activity. But before signing your child up for an array of formal lessons in addition to school, realize that too much of a good thing may not be in your child's best interests. Instead, give her unstructured time in which she can simply lie on the grass and examine the clouds, time when nothing at all is expected of her, when the TV is off and she can listen to her thoughts and hear the sound of her own heartbeat. Time for dawdling and daydreaming can be far more instructive than learning how to operate a computer or taking ballet lessons.

If your child has a chance to do nothing for a while, she is unlikely to miss out on anything important. In fact, such quiet time will allow your child to explore her own creativity and imagination, and learn how to amuse herself. She may have nothing tangible to show for her

## After-School Rest

Quiet time, especially after school, is also important to allow your child a chance to recharge, sort through the day, and make sense of it all. If she is confused or upset about something that happened during the day, time to think about it may lead to questions she can ask or comments she can share with you.

## A Needed Break

Respect your child's need to skip a class or cancel a planned activity once in a while. This will enable her to take a break without actually quitting an activity she may enjoy. Now and then, she may even have to take a day's break from school when she's healthy but worn out from her schedule.

time, but she will have had a chance to get to know herself. Self-reliance and independence are additional skills that she'll gain from quiet time and time alone.

If you wonder whether your child is getting enough quiet time, watch for complaints about going to an activity or a planned playdate. She may also come up with a headache or a stomachache to avoid doing one more thing. Another sign is if her usually high energy and smooth actions are replaced by nearly frantic activity. If she's showing any sign of overload, give her some time without plans.

You can help your child have downtime by scheduling up to a half hour every day as free time. She also may need to drop one or two activities in order to have a whole day per week for doing nothing. If your child shows great interest in trying new activities, you might schedule a trial class or sign up for just a few classes. Then you will have a chance to see if additional activities will produce an overload without committing yourself and your child to something long-term.

Managing unstructured time may be difficult at first. Above all, resist the temptation to start filling that unplanned time with television or another activity. Although TV can help a child unwind, it may backfire if a program is too stimulating. Try to provide a variety of materials such as books and art materials that your child can use to explore her imagination, but don't insist that she stay busy producing.

## Fifth-year friendships

Between the ages of 5 and 6, you will no doubt notice how much more important friendships are becoming for your child. While friends may change frequently during the fifth year, you may see your child holding on longer to certain friendships as he nears the age of 6. At this point, your child may be more interested in having and keeping one or two friends rather than a whole group of friends. More than ever before, your child bases his friendships upon shared interests, not simply on proximity.

There are several reasons why friendships begin to deepen during the fifth year. One reason is your child's improved ability to talk with his peers. He and his pals can now share real information about their lives and their feelings. Entering school is also a reason why your child may choose a special friend. Even if your child has been in daycare and a nursery school, kindergarten presents a new experience, which is easier to handle with a friend at his side. In addition, because your 5-year-old is just beginning to learn what it means to be a friend, he may find it easier to interact with just one or two friends.

Your child will probably look for a friend who shares his interests and has a similar personality and play style. However, he may also be attracted to another child who is quite different from him in some way. In this way, he gets a chance to see what's its like to do new things and act in different ways.

**When friends have disagreements** Just as most friendships do, 5-year-olds' friendships have their ups and downs. If your child has an argument with a friend, he may suddenly announce that the friendship is over. Most likely, however, they will soon patch things up. Part of each child's ability to forgive is based on his sense of time: *Now* is always paramount, and a friend who annoyed him yesterday is still a friend today—until today's argument.

As long as no one is getting hurt, it's important to let children work out their own disagreements. You can suggest that they spend a few minutes apart from each other so that each has a chance to calm down if things become too heated. Instead of refereeing arguments, ask them to suggest solutions to their problem. You can set up a house rule that there's to be no tattling unless you need to hear a report involving actions that are dangerous or otherwise wrong. Make it clear that in matters such as who gets to play with what, you're out of the picture and you trust them to work out these kinds of disagreements.

What if you don't approve of one of your child's friends? For example, you may feel that a particular playmate encourages your child to misbehave. You will have to set clear limits when the children are together, but don't try to end the friendship unless your child seems to undergo drastic changes. Some things to watch out for are:
• Your child seems to be dominated by his friend. If the friend makes all the play decisions, talk to your child privately about how he can stand up for himself. Rehearse dialogues in which each of

you take turns being the other child, so that your child learns a repertoire of responses to bullying.

• Your child doesn't seem to know what to do by himself if that particular friend isn't available for playing. This is a sign that he has becoming overly dependent on this one friend. However, rather than tell your child that he can't see that friend anymore, try to help your child expand his horizons and meet new friends in addition to this one.

• Your child's friend encourages him to get involved in unacceptable behavior. In this case, you need to step in and let them both know what behaviors are not acceptable. You may need to tell your child that his friend will not be allowed to come over if the bad behavior continues. If the friend engages in behavior of which you disapprove, even if your own child is not drawn into that behavior, you have a right when that child is in your home to state your house rules to him and insist that he abide by them.

• Your child and his friend tease or mistreat other children. Ganging up on others often makes children feel powerful. To prevent your child from taking part in this bullying, make sure your child and his friend are well supervised. Explain why this is necessary. You can help your child develop more empathy for others by leading him to the understanding that real power comes from being liked, not feared, by others.

If your child does not seem to have a best friend, don't worry. A great number of 5-year-olds don't show particular preferences for certain children. Some children prefer time by themselves. Others are perfectly happy to play with whomever is available.

If your child seems to be having trouble making friends, take a look at whether your child needs to learn more about important social skills, such as taking turns and following rules. Make sure, of course, that he has enough access to other children, through school, swim lessons, Sunday school, and the local playground. You might also look for after-school programs that have activities your child enjoys. Here he would have a chance to meet other children who share his interests. If your child is in school, his teacher will be helpful in letting you know areas he needs to work on or suggest a classmate with whom he plays well for a possible at-home playdate.

**Differing opinions on clothes**
*"Since her fifth birthday, my daughter has developed an extreme fashion consciousness, wanting only to wear certain colors and refusing to wear age-appropriate things, which she considers 'babyish.' Any suggestions?"*

It's important that your child feel like one of the gang among her playmates. It's also important that she not wear clothing that you consider inappropriate. Explain to her that part of wearing big-girl clothing means that you need some big-girl cooperation from her. Be willing to compromise. If she's into lime green, there's nothing wrong with buying her appropriate styles in her favorite color. Don't be afraid to hold the line on items that you consider truly offensive or inappropriate. At the same time, allow her to forego frills that she finds inappropriate.

# Your child's spiritual life

For many people, having children often brings up the issue of religion in a new light. How should you as a parent approach religion and spirituality? For parents who are comfortably within a formal religion and/or who have a deeply held belief system, introducing their child to their beliefs is a natural process. Other parents have to work out a new relationship with religion. Do you want your children to be a part of an organized religion? If you and your spouse don't share the same religious background, how will you deal with your differences and pass both traditions on to your child? If you're not a member of an organized religion, should you join one? What spiritual values do you want your children to learn?

All of these questions point to what is a complicated decision for many parents, especially those who may have turned away from their religious upbringing. You may have felt forced to attend religious services as a child and don't want to do the same to your child. However, you may also not want to raise him without any kind of religious or spiritual experience.

Spirituality is not necessarily linked with a specific religion. People can be spiritual without being religious. However, because spirituality is highly personal and cannot easily be explained, you may wonder how you can talk about it with your child. The idea of religion and morality simply as abstract concepts will make little sense to him. However, you can talk about the connections among

## Finding Answers

Like all children, your child no doubt has a basic sense of wonder about the world, including spiritual issues. Religion can provide a structure and a language for expressing this wonder. Spirituality can also be a source for security and self-esteem to help your child through the unavoidable disappointments that he will encounter in life.

all people and living creatures that need to be respected. Understanding these connections can help your child go beyond his needs and understand the needs of others and develop a sense of morality. These connections are also important in building a sense of belonging for your child. He can draw comfort from knowing he has relationships with other people, God, and the natural world. These connections help give meaning to life and encourage a child to reach out to others.

You can begin to help your child build these connections even when he is very young. Even toddlers are capable of understanding other people's basic feelings. As your child grows, you can involve him in family volunteer efforts to help others, such as donating clothes to the homeless and joining projects to clean up the neighborhood. If your child sees you actively involved in a spiritual life, he will be more inclined to develop his own. If you do not have strong religious beliefs, don't try to develop them for the sake of your child. You can still take part in spiritual acts that have meaning, but aren't religious.

Tolerance for other religious beliefs is also an important part of spirituality you'll need to share with your child. You can point out that people have different ways to talk to God. You might emphasize the richness of your own spiritual traditions without giving the impression that there's something wrong with other people for having differing beliefs. If your child asks you spiritual questions, first try to find out what he means. You might be surprised at the deepness of his thinking. Then answer directly and simply.

If you want to make spiritual values a strong part of everyday life, set aside time for spirituality. Saying grace before meals, planning a weekly Sabbath dinner, and taking time to pray together are ways to bring spirituality into your home. If you're searching for a religious aspect to your family's life, don't feel that you have to return to the patterns of your childhood. Look for a group that fits your family's needs and personality. Make sure that you and your children are welcome. You may need to visit more than one house of worship to find a community in which you feel at home.

Many churches, synagogues, and mosques offer Sunday school for young children, which is often a good way for your child to learn the basics of a religious faith. You may find your child is enthusiastic about attending Sunday school because he gets to be with other children. However, he may also resist going after the novelty wears off. Whether or not he has to continue depends on how strongly you feel about the importance of formal religious training and any requirements of membership to that community. To help your child more readily accept religious school, you can make the time a little more appealing by creating your own special rituals, such as going out to breakfast after services, or planning some other enjoyable family activity.

One of the basics to remember when establishing a spiritual life for your child is the importance of taking part in the experience with your child. If your child is the only one in the family who is participating, the experience will mean little to him.

**Talking about death with your child**    Spirituality becomes vital when your child's questions death. Your child's questions may be sparked by attendance at a religious service, the death of a family member or a pet, or the death of a character in a loved story. The questions also may be accompanied by fear and sadness, as well as curiosity.

Although you may feel uncomfortable with talking about death, it's important to be truthful with your child while keeping your explanations as simple as possible. You might start with simple analogies such as explaining that death is like breaking a toy that can't be fixed. However, be careful in your choice of images. If you say that death is like sleeping and never waking up, your child may suddenly develop a tremendous fear about going to bed and to sleep. The same may be true if you say that people die who are so sick they can't get well. Your child may interpret this into a great fear of even minor illnesses.

Ask your child what he thinks death is. It's likely that he has heard things about death before. Try to explain simply what happens to people's bodies after they die. Depending on your beliefs, you can say that people are put in box called a coffin, which is put in the ground. Or, explain that cremation is a process where a person's body is made into ashes. However, avoid telling your child that cremation involves burning and fire. You might then explain that when a person dies, his soul leaves the body and goes to live with God. In addition, you might want to say that even when people die their

PARENTS RESOURCES

## Books about Death

Try to bring up the subject of death with your child before you have to face it at the death of a close relative or friend. You might read children's books together that deal with death, such as:

**Nana Upstairs & Nana Downstairs** by Tomie dePaola (Puffin)

**Badger's Parting Gifts** by Susan Varley (Lothrop, Lee & Shepard)

**Jim's Dog Muffins** by Miriam Cohen (Picture Yearling)

spirit stays with us because we remember them. If you're not sure what you believe about death, it's all right to express this to your child as well.

Until the age of 5, most children are not able to grasp the permanence of death, especially because their time sense is not well developed. Your child may ask you the same questions over and over again, saying for instance, "Yes, I know Grandpa died, but when is he coming back?" Try to be as patient as possible, remembering how hard the concept of death is for a young child to understand. Remember also that one of the greatest fears children can have is that their parents could die and leave them alone. If your child wants to know when you might die, you could tell him that most people don't die until they have lived a long time. You could add that you won't die until long after he is grown up and has children of his own. In addition, tell him that you expect him to live for a very long time.

When someone dies, whether it be a person or a pet, recognize that your child will probably grieve. He will feel sad and numb just as you might even if he doesn't fully understanding his feeling. Try to find a way to involve your child in mourning rituals. If you don't feel comfortable bringing him to the funeral, you might visit the cemetery with him afterward. Be aware, too, that seeing a parent or grandparent out of control can be very upsetting to a child. If mourners are going to be highly emotional, it may be better to leave your child home rather than take him to the funeral or burial. Realize, too, that your child might seem blasé about death, and may not act in ways that would be appropriate for an older person. For instance, he may want to play as usual, even in the middle of a funeral. It's important that you allow your child to mourn in his own way and time.

As much as possible, confront your own fears about death. This will help you speak with your child about the subject.

**Raising a charitable child** Teaching your child compassion for others helps deepen her sense of community, builds her self-esteem, and allows her to see herself in a positive light. It also helps the entire community when each member, even very young ones, works for the greater good. A way to help your child mine her charitable impulses is to get her involved in small acts of kindness. Teach her to hold the door for the person behind her. With her, help carry a package for an older neighbor. Invite her to go with you to take donations of food and clothing to a local shelter or food pantry, or to deliver groceries or meals to the homebound. If you allow her to participate as much as possible, she will gain a sense of her own importance as well as enjoy the rewards of helping others.

As your child begins to understand that helping others can be a wonderful experience, she may start to worry that she needs to try to help everyone. There's no need for her to feel guilty. Focus on the fact that even the smallest efforts are worthwhile and that you and she are doing what you can. You may only be able to do something once a month or commit to a single worthy cause. Holidays also offer many opportunities to share her good fortune. Helping others, even a little bit, will show your child that she can do something and that people everywhere are a lot like she is.

# Cognitive development

During the fifth year, your child's increased vocabulary and command of language may result in what you may think is nonstop chatter. Five-year-olds love to talk, especially because language is now meaningful. Increased vocabulary also helps him understand more abstract ideas, such as a sense of time in understanding the cycles of years and seasons, and knowing what minutes, hours, days, and weeks are. However, he will still be mainly interested in what is happening in the present. His sense of space is also centered mainly in where he is now, although his world increasingly includes independence in moving about his neighborhood and community as well as his home.

## What your child knows

Your child's developing sense of the meaning of language may bring with it an intense interest in words, especially big words. He probably loves to be read to and may want to learn how to read himself.

## Lisping

Lisping results from an inability to form words correctly that contain the sounds of s and z because the tongue is placed between rather than behind the teeth. Lisping may result from a variety of causes, including physical conditions such as a cleft palate, hearing loss, or dental problems such as too many teeth or improper positioning of teeth. Lisping can also come from a child imitating another lisper or from stressful conditions. If your child lisps, you should have your doctor examine him. You may be advised to consult a speech therapist if your child's lisp could be lessened through treatment.

Some 5-year-olds do learn to read simple text. He may know the letters of the alphabet quite well, and should be able to recognize his written name. He may even be able to print his first name, as well as other letters and words.

His interest in words and reading also shows he understands that words represent objects and ideas, and that things he does have a cause and an effect. His understanding of natural events and objects may still be personal in that he may still think that things have feelings and that everything that moves is alive. In trying to make sense of the world, he often comes up with his own explanations or forms generalizations from what he sees. Although many of his ideas may be scientifically unfounded, they do make sense from his point of view.

A more mature sense of space means that your child can now follow simple directions. He may even become interested in maps and will want to make simple maps to show the way he takes to school or the position of things in a room at home. His sense of space is still usually limited to his immediate community, which means that attendance at a local preschool or kindergarten will be much easier and less stressful than having to travel a distance. If he is interested in faraway towns or states, it's usually because a relative or a family friend lives there.

Your child's sense of numbers has greatly improved since she was 4. She should be able to count from one to ten, and may be able to count much higher. She may understand the concept of adding single-digit numbers. She probably recognizes and can name different coins, though she may not be clear on the difference in value among them. As she nears age 6, she may progress to recognizing and writing numbers to 20 and beyond, and will understand what it means to subtract from a group. However, this knowledge usually comes slowly, with many reversals along the way.

Interest in sex is often less than it was the year before. Bathroom jokes and giggling about bellybuttons decreases. In fact, your child may become quite modest about his body during his fifth year.

Humor has now progressed from giggles and silliness to enjoyment of wordplay, interest in funny stories, and fooling people, such as pretending not to know something very simple when you know that he does.

**How your 5-year-old learns**  Your 5-year-old learns a great deal from exploration and trying to figure things out, although he may not be as adventurous as he was at the age of 4. Jigsaw puzzles and board games are great fun for a 5-year-old. His increased understanding of language means he can get information from others and even from books if he is interested in reading. He also learns from asking questions, from conversation, and by observation.

**Helping your child grow**  You can help your 5-year-old learn new things through talking with him about his interests, and through simple explanations and demonstrations. As much as possible, take short trips in the community to see new places, such as the library and the post office to find out what these places are and what happens there. When you go places together or do an activity with him, you may find he is just as interested in how you get somewhere or make something as in the end product.

You can help increase his understanding of language by introducing and pointing out new words. Because he enjoys the sound of big words, he may enjoy learning the names of dinosaurs or other animals or things that interest him. He will also enjoy rhyming games and wordplay that focuses on the different meanings of words. For example, he will have fun finding out that some words that sound the same, such as blue and blew, mean quite different things. You might even try making up some silly stories with him by asking him to provide parts of the story. For example, you might start with, "This is a story about…" then ask your child to tell you the name of a person or an animal. Then go on to encourage your child to tell you where the animal is and what she likes to do, for example. Some of your child's made-up stories may contain some violence such as accidents as your child sorts through and begins to understand the dangers in the world. Your child will usually tell stories that have happy endings. The violence is often a way for your child to make the real world less scary and to give him a sense of power over events.

To encourage your child to experiment and explore his imagination, provide lots of materials for art activities and for building.

He will probably have great fun making tents with blankets, chairs, and tables. He will also enjoy playing games in which he has to think a little and possibly solve a problem in order to win.

Television is also popular at this age, and children can learn many constructive things by watching. Help him select appropriate programs and limit his viewing time. Your child will also love it if you watch with him and talk about what is going on.

## Your child's learning style

Traditionally, intelligence has been assumed to be the ability to understand language and mathematics. Creativity, ability with music or sports, and good social skills have recently been shown to be aspects of intelligence, too. Based on the research of Dr. Howard Gardner, a professor of education at the Harvard Graduate School of Education, intelligence is now understood to include a multitude of talents—various ways in which each learner learns best. Gardner and others describe these intelligences as musical, linguistic, interpersonal, logico-mathematical, spatial, intrapersonal, and bodily-kinesthetic.

If your child is **musical**, he will, at the age of 5 or 6, be able to sing on key, keep a beat, make up his own songs, and remember music he has heard. He will understand pitch or melody, rhythm, and tone. In his learning, he will understand concepts presented musically. For instance, he may learn to read most easily by studying the words of songs he enjoys singing or may learn to count by saying the numbers rhythmically.

If your child is **linguistic**, she will be able to use spoken and written language to express meaning quite easily. She understands the subtleties of meaning and grammar and enjoys the sound of language. She has fun with puns and rhymes, enjoys reading, and can tell a story that holds together. She learns best through language and will gather information by reading and talking and listening.

If your child is able to tell how people are feeling and understanding why they act as they do, he may be an **interpersonal** child. You will know he is interpersonal if he enjoys friends and group activities and is empathetic. This child learns best in a group, working alongside others.

Being able to think conceptually, to reason in an orderly way, can think well abstractly, and investigate the physical world through experimentation, then, she is **logico-mathematical**. She has skill with numbers and patterns, and an ability to estimate. She might also make up her own ways to count and think up her own experiments. She learns best when given the opportunity to make logical connections between facts. She may, for instance, understand reading through a phonics approach, which involves a more-or-less logical symbol-to-sound relationship.

If your child is **spatial**, he will be drawn to blocks, paints, clay, and other art media. He will also enjoy putting things together and taking them apart. He will be able to recognize shapes in different contexts, and can mentally change an image. He will be able to learn to read maps. He will gain skills by handling materials, perhaps learning his letters by grasping three-dimensional forms of letters.

If your child is able to distinguish her feelings from others, and expresses herself through a combination of gestures, facial expressions, and words, she may be **intrapersonal**. Signs of this kind of intelligence are seen in your child's ability to talk about her own experience, such as telling you what she thinks is fun to do as well as what she finds hard to do. She is also aware of what she loves and fears. An intrapersonal child may grow up to be a poet or an artist. Your intrapersonal child will learn best when the materials at hand appeal to her emotions. For instance, she may learn to read and write by keeping a diary.

If your child is well coordinated and has a natural ability in sports and dancing, he is **bodily-kinesthetic**. He will be able to develop the fine motor control of a craftsperson and the large muscle control of an athlete. A bodily-kinesthetic child learns best when his whole body is involved in the learning process, perhaps learning to count while doing jumping jacks.

Schools are increasing paying heed to the different kinds of intelligences children possess and are finding new ways to teach children according to their personal strengths. Whether or not your child's school subscribes to this form of teaching, you can enhance your child's ability to learn, as well as help him uncover his own special talents, by observing him closely to see what makes him tick and to help him use that talent to pursue a variety of skills.

If, for instance, you feel your child needs help with numbers, you could try a variety of methods to help him grasp mathematical concepts. You can measure items at home, make up songs with numbers, practice addition and subtraction to movements, measure ingredients for a recipe you read together, plan and shop for a party together, talk about how he might spend his allowance, or make plans to save money for a special purchase.

## Boosting your child's pre-reading skills

Before your child can begin to read, she must first master a variety of skills, some of which may not seem to have much to do with reading. For example, being able to locate things spatially, such as *top, bottom, over, under, left ,*and *right* is critical to being able to follow words from left to right and from the top to the bottom of a page. The same holds true for being able to understand the sequence of actions and events and being able to recognize and form patterns. These skills will help your child follow and understand a story, and recognize familiar words. She also must be physically ready. Her eyes and hands must be working in coordination.

In addition to a language-rich environment—a home where language, conversation, and reading are valued and reading materials are readily available—some of the ways you can help your child develop these skills is to play games such as Simon Says in which she identifies the top of her head, the bottom of her shoe, and her right and left ear. For sequence and order, you can use such words as first, next, second, last when you do an activity with her. For example, if she helps make something in the kitchen, you can point to a recipe and say, "The first step we do is…" You can also ask her to describe what she is doing in these terms.

A primary skill, of course, is becoming familiar with language. Your child will naturally be exposed to language in many forms throughout the day. You can boost this exposure by talking with her as much as possible. Encourage her to talk about things she does, to describe what she sees, and to tell you stories. Talk about colors, letters, and numbers. By actively listening and talking, her understanding and use of language will grow rapidly.

If she is curious about letters, you can talk about the letters in her name. You can point out letters in signs, and spell simple words as you use them. For example, you might say, "Here is your C-A-P for your head." You could also label things in

### Keep Reading

Reading to your child is also important. In this way, she will become familiar with the idea of reading and that reading is fun. You could also get a book that uses small pictures in place of many words, and invite her to read along with you. She can read the pictures while you read the words.

the house that have one-syllable names. Give her plastic or wooden letter blocks to play with and let her make pretend or real words to read to you.

## What kindergartners know about time

How often have you said to your child something like, "You have five minutes to get ready for bed," then discovered in five minutes that he has done nothing to get ready. Didn't he take you seriously? Is he being purposely difficult?

No doubt you talk to your child often about minutes, hours, and days, and even years. However, these words are really quite abstract to your child, even when he uses them himself. In addition, you may hear your child read the numbers from a digital clock and think he is telling the time when actually he is just reading the numbers.

Your child first learned the concepts *now* and *not now*, then *yesterday* and *tomorrow*. These concepts became clear as he began to recognize that events come in a certain order, and when he could remember something that happened in the recent past, and wish for something to happen in the future. By the time he enters kindergarten, he should understand how old he is now and how old he will be on his next birthday. However, he will probably not know the days of the week or be able to tell time on a clock with hands.

To tell time, your child may use markers such as whether it is daylight or nighttime. He might also better understand the passage of time by thinking of the seasons. These are natural changes that he can see and so equate with the passing of time. For example, he may say he got up when the sun shone in his window, rather than giving a specific time.

To help your child learn to tell time, establish regular routines so that he knows there are times to eat, to sleep, to play, and to go to school, for example. You might find magazine pictures that show people doing things at different times of the day. Help your child arrange the pictures and talk about the timely order of events.

When you tell your child that something will happen in three

> ### Kid Time
>
> Adults and children experience time in very different ways. What seems like a short period of time to you, say a minute or five minutes, can be practically forever to your child. He doesn't care about time in the same way you do, mainly because he lives very much in the here and now and in whatever he is doing at the moment.

minutes, for instance, also attach some reference to it, such as how long it takes you to brush your teeth. If you are looking forward to an event a few days or weeks away, you could help your child count down the days by marking them on a calendar. To focus on the cycle of seasons, months, and days of the week, you might write them down in a big circle. Say the words together as you go around the circle.

To learn about telling time on a clock with hands, you can start by pointing out the clock's hands move in the same direction. If he asks why, you could explain that the first clocks people used followed the movement of the sun across the sky. Then focus on the short, or hour, hand. Although he won't be able to see it moving, you could say that this hand goes around the clock two times every day, once during the day and once during the night. Show your child the number the short hand points to and tell him that this number tells what hour it is. Once he understands hours, you can move on to the long hand and talk about minutes.

If your child does not seem interested in learning how to tell time, don't push him. He will learn about time in school.

## Your child's listening skills

You no doubt already know that listening is one of the hardest things for your child to do. Even if she says she heard what you said, she may have heard only part of it and will soon be rushing off to do something else. She also may have heard you but will forget in a few minutes what you said.

Listening skills take a long time to develop, mainly because children have short attention spans and are easily distracted by things around them. However, there are some things you can do to help your improve her listening skills. There may be no obvious improvement for quite a while, but persistence will likely pay off.

If your child is generally an extrovert, you can help her practice taking turns listening and waiting for others to finish speaking before she begins talking. While talking to her one-on-one, encourage her to wait if she is tempted to cut you short with what she has to say. After you tell her something, ask her if she can tell you in her own words what you just said. This practice can eventually be extended to sharing ideas at a family meal.

If your child is easily distracted and unwilling to stop long enough to pay attention, you might try whispering. Keep it up long enough for her to notice that you are saying something. She may just become curious enough to want to know what you are saying and stop to pay attention.

When you know you have your child's attention, make what you want to say brief. Ask her to look at you while you are speaking. Then watch her eyes and expression to see if she understands and note when she begins to wander. You may want to ask her what you just said and see if her reply bears any resemblance to your words.

> ### *Focus on Listening*
>
> Use words that get your child's attention and help her prepare to listen. They may include:
>
> **Let me see your eyes.**
>
> **Eyes on me.**
>
> **I need your listening ears.**
>
> **Right now it's my turn.**

## What your child needs to know

By the age of 5, your child should have basic knowledge of certain kinds of information. Following are some of the developmental areas you will want to be aware of.

**Reading** Your 5-year-old may be learning to recognize letters or be reading independently. Most commonly, she will like to identify words she sees on signs, such as *hot, cold, stop,* and so on. She also recognizes her own name and be able to use cut-out letters to form her and other family members' names. By the time she is 5½, she may be familiar with all the letters of the alphabet and be able to read and spell several simple words. She may even be able to read short books, especially if she is attending a kindergarten in which reading is stressed.

**Math concepts** Most 5-year-olds can count to 20 or 30 or higher with some errors, and write numbers 1 to 10. Your child should also be able to do simple one-digit addition, and possibly simple subtraction. She will recognize various coins. Your child should also be able to tell how old she is and have some concept of telling time on a clock.

**Language concepts** At this age, your child knows that words represent objects and ideas, and understands the concept of cause and effect. She should be able to name all common colors, several shapes, objects around the house, and the days of the week even though time concepts are not yet well developed. She should also be able to follow simple directions up to three to five steps.

*Also see **pages 404–29** for more information about early education.*

**Personal information**   Your 5-year-old should know her first and last name, her birth date, and her address. (Some children will also know their phone numbers, but not including area code.) She should also know your first and last name.

**Spatial concepts**   By the time your child is 5, she should be able to tell her right hand from her left, and understand directional words such as *above, below, inside, outside,* and so on. She should also have a conceptual understanding of where she lives and be able to move about her neighborhood comfortably. Size relationships should also be familiar to her. For example, she should be able to distinguish *big, small; tall, short;* and *long, short.*

### Eye-hand coordination

*"My daughter's teacher says that her eye-hand coordination is not well developed yet. What does this mean?"*

The fine motor skills, or the ability to control and use the hands to make small movements, develops along with a child's vision. Children generally develop the ability to focus their eyes as they move them up and down along with their hands. You can see this in a child's ability to stack blocks. The skill of being able to focus while moving the eyes back and forth along with the hand comes later and is an important prerequisite for learning to read and write. What your daughter's teacher is no doubt referring to is the ability of the eyes and the hands to work together to do fine work such as coloring, cutting with scissors, and manipulating small items. In time, you will probably find her eye-hand coordination improves. If you feel you don't see much improvement, you may want to ask your doctor for advice and screening for possible vision problems.

# Part 2

# Through the Years

Certain issues of child raising—childcare, discipline, sibling relationships, for example—are best addressed across a spectrum of ages and stages. While your approach to each of these concerns, of course, takes your child's age and level of development into account, her needs and your responses in these areas will develop on a continuum.

What you may find to be an appropriate response to childcare when your child is an infant may not be your best approach when she's 2 or 4. Some issues, such as the birth of a sibling, while affecting all children in certain ways, require a different kind of response for a toddler than for a preschooler. Likewise, raising multiples or raising a child in a single-parent home require very different approaches to the same issues at each age and stage of your child's development.

# CHAPTER 1

# You and Your Adopted Child

The waiting period for making your family may have taken more than nine months, but, in truth, no amount of planning can prepare you for the awesome changes that your child's arrival brings. In addition to all the concerns that biological parents face, you have some that are unique to you.

## Welcoming your child home

Without the usual countdown through pregnancy, your child's arrival is likely to feel instantaneous, even if you knew the approximate date on which to expect her, and even if you've been waiting years for the event. Like any new parent, you probably don't feel ready. In the swirl of activity surrounding her arrival, your joy may be mixed with a sense of unreality.

In the case of infant adoption, the homecoming you plan will not differ significantly from the joy and panic that any new parent feels. Take advantage of any offers of help that come your way. Carve out quiet times, too, so your new family members can get to know each other. As the months go on, you'll make the transition from parenting this little stranger—which all new babies are—to parenting the child you've grown to know and love.

If your child arrives in your family older than a newborn, you'll need to take special steps to smooth his arrival. Your child may be anxious, missing those who have previously cared for him. He may have strong reactions to changes in his environment and his diet. If he was born in another country, hearing another language, he'll need time to adapt to the sounds and rhythms of your speech. Some children adapt to the overwhelming changes by shutting down for a time and becoming unusually placid. Others act out. You may need an extra reserve of patience and wisdom to make him feel fully a part of his new surroundings. While your family's particular circumstances will dictate how you help your child and yourself, you can ease the transition in these ways:

• **Accept any feelings of disappointment or grief.** Few parents are delighted with every aspect of their child all the time. If your child is behaving in ways that were not part of your fantasy, don't be afraid to recognize that this experience is not all that you bargained for. Your next step is to move on to helping your child and yourself deal actively with any real problems that you are facing.

• **Enjoy your child's unique characteristics.** Birth parents spend lots of time contemplating who their baby looks like and to which side of the family to attribute his bad habits. You and your child are freed from genetic expectations, and your child can develop into his own personhood without having to carry on a particular habit, talent, or lack of talent. The environment in which you're raising him will add much to his development, but you won't have to worry that he'll inherit any of his adoptive family's less-than-admirable traits.

• **Don't feel compelled to tell everyone that your child is adopted.** Some adoptive parents feel that they're "cheating" when they greet an admiring word about their baby with a quick "he's adopted." The simple truth is that this beautiful baby is *your* child now.

• **Do whatever feels right in terms of celebrating your child's arrival.** There are no hard-and-fast rules that dictate a large party or a small intimate gathering. So do whatever feels right for you and your child.

## Special health considerations

In most ways, taking care of your child's health is no different from other parents' concerns. There are a few additional considerations, however. Because your infant does not have the natural immunity to your germs, he may be more susceptible to catching colds and other communicable ailments from you during his first few weeks and months. There's no need to go overboard with protecting him from every germ. Simply make a point of washing your hands frequently before handling him, especially if you've got the sniffles.

Over a few months' time, his immunity will be stronger and the differences in your genetic makeup will have no effect on his health. Likewise an older child from another culture whose immunity was already established in his birthplace may catch a variety of bugs in his new environment because his system has limited tolerance against local bacteria.

## Your child's emotional well-being

In the early months of your child's life, your loving care helps to develop her emotional stability. You may be concerned, even now, about how being adopted will impact on her self-esteem and her relationship with you as she gets older. Research shows that the vast majority of children who grow up in loving homes do not experience any decline in their sense of self or self-worth due to their adoption. Your adopted child may, however, need to explore her biological past at some point in her life. It's important that you not treat her curiosity as a threat to your own strong bond with her.

Experts now believe it is vital that being adopted never come as a surprise to your child. She should grow up knowing about how she became part of your family, but she does not need to hear a daily recounting of how adoption makes her "special" or anything else that makes her feel too unusual. During her preschool years, she will not entirely understand what it means to be adopted. Some young children will be very curious about their backgrounds and will feel anything from a sense of personal loss to sympathy with their biological parents to anxiety. Others will be only moderately curious. A few will seem totally unconcerned. All of these reactions are normal. Your job is to answer your child's questions honestly as they come up.

### Raising a child of another race

*"My adopted daughter is from China and my husband and I are Caucasian. I worry about how to make sure she grows up with a strong sense of who she is and is not troubled by the differences in our appearance and cultural backgrounds. What can we do?"*

### Medical History

Do all you can to learn about your child's medical history. If your child is from another country, you may need additional medical tests and inoculations to detect or protect him from diseases that are common in his place of birth. Be sure to share any information you have about his genetic and cultural background with his pediatrician so the doctor is alert to any health issues that are common in your child's birthplace.

In virtually all matters, children take their cues from their parents. If you are comfortable with the fact that your child is obviously of different ethnic roots than you are, and that this is nothing to cause concern, this will be the attitude your child will develop. It will reinforce her own sense of identity, however, if you give her the means to learn about her own ethnic culture as well as the culture in which you're raising her. Learn as much as you can about China yourself, its history, holidays, and, if possible, the particular locale of your daughter's birth family. Show her that you have genuine interest in her cultural roots, but be sure to allow her to involve herself as she chooses. She may display little—if any—interest in her roots for many years. Children generally want to be like their friends, and they are not always keen to explore anything that makes them different. If this becomes her attitude, let her know that should she someday become intrigued by her background, you're there to help her.

### Talking to your child about adoption

*"What should I tell my baby son about being adopted?"*

Birth children hear many stories about the day they were born. The adoption day has the same importance and impact, and you should share your excitement about the wonderful day you found out that you were the lucky couple who got to adopt your son. Begin your discussion of adoption early, so that the word *adoption* and the concept that families are made in many different ways are part of his thinking vocabulary even before he can talk. At some point in the period between ages 2 and 4, share a more detailed story about his adoption. Let the focus be on how your family came to be. Do not burden him with details about why his biological family was unable to care for him, which could create undue anxiety. Let him know that he can ask any questions about his adoption and that you will answer anything you can. Accept that at times he may mourn for his birth parents; let him know that his feelings—whatever they are—are acceptable to you so that he does not take on the role of protecting you from his strong emotions.

## Understanding your feelings

Your feelings, quite naturally, affect your child's feelings. Coupled with earlier disappointments about not conceiving, you may now feel some trepidation about becoming attached. Many new adoptive parents harbor a concern that, until the adoption is final, their new

## *Getting Baby Pictures*

I adopted my 3-year-old son last year. I don't have any pictures of him as an infant. When his nursery school teacher asked each child to bring in a baby picture for the bulletin board, I didn't know what to do. A technologically savvy friend helped. He used his computer and a current picture of my son to generate an image that shows what Jeremy looked like as a baby. Now we have this wonderful picture framed in his room and I was able to send a copy to nursery school.

family is at risk. It's important that you relax and spend time as you imagined — snuggling close and rejoicing in your baby. Don't let your worries interfere with the happy reality that your baby is indeed yours.

The exhaustion that is part of new parenthood, and the feelings of being overwhelmed, can be particularly difficult for adoptive parents to handle. You wanted this baby so much that you may feel guilty for not feeling maternal or paternal every second. If you're experiencing new parenthood blues, realize that, while they may not be hormonally caused and therefore "acceptable," your feelings are every bit as valid as those of any other new parent. Give yourself permission to feel too tired to feel happy all the time.

Some new adoptive moms worry that they lack a "maternal instinct," and misinterpret their inexperience as parents as something peculiar to them. Rest assured that no parent is born knowing how to care for a child; for everyone, it is a learned art. You may feel, too, a need to make up for lost time in the bonding process because you didn't carry this child in your womb or care for her in her first days, weeks, months, or even years. Bonding does take time. While it can't be rushed, it can't be stopped either.

You may find that having adopted your child grants you a certain freedom that biological parents can't enjoy, and that is the freedom to allow your child to be whomever she is. You won't as readily get caught up in trying to define your child's temperament, her likes and dislikes, her appearance, or any other aspect of who she is according to genetics. Your child won't be limited by being labeled as "looking just like Aunt Nancy" or "having Uncle Jake's musical abilities." Instead, her good looks and talents will be all her own—and that's a birthright that every child should enjoy.

### Helping grandparents accept adoption

*"I was upset to hear my mother tell a friend she has four grand-children and one adopted granddaughter—my child. How can I make her realize that my daughter is as much a part of our family as my sisters' children?"*

Your mother may well feel completely comfortable with your daughter as her granddaughter, but find it interesting that she is adopted and want to share the information with a friend. However, if you sense she is creating a separate niche for your child in her mind, you should discuss the matter with her. Tell her how important it is to you for her to accept your daughter with the same sense of inclusion that she has for your siblings' children. If you are like many adoptive parents, you went through a period of adjustment as you learned to think of and accept your daughter as truly yours. It will probably shift your mother's thinking if you honestly recount the feelings you experienced and how you found resolution.

---

**PARENTS RESOURCES**

***Resolve:*** Provides infertility and adoption education and local support groups.
　1310 Broadway
　Somerville, MA 02144-1731
　(617) 623-0744

**Books for Adopted Children**

There are a number of good books on adoption for children of all ages. Some excellent ones are:

***The Day We Met You*** by Phoebe Koehler (Aladdin Paperbacks), a picture book for very young children.

***Let's Talk About It: Adoption*** by Fred Rogers (Paper Star). Mr. Rogers explains adoption.

***Through Moon and Stars and Night Skies*** by Ann Turner (Econo-Clad Books) describes adopting a child from a faraway land.

# CHAPTER 2

# Childcare

When it's time to return to work, whatever your child's age, you will probably feel at least some sadness and perhaps a little guilt. Added to the mix may be anxiety about how your child will adjust, how safe she'll be in another's care, and how you, too, will feel about the separation. The single biggest way to relieve much of your distress is by finding the right childcare for your child. If you are confident your child is in a safe, nurturing environment while away from you, you will be freed from anxiety that can interfere with your job and your life. Moreover, you'll be able to communicate that confidence to your child.

Finding the care that will keep you and your child both happy and secure calls for careful thought and evaluation. The time and hard work it may take, however, will pay big dividends in the long run for your whole family.

## *Finding the right care*

Your needs, your child's needs, your family's budget, and convenience are the factors you'll be considering when choosing childcare. Each type of care—relative care, hired in-home, daycare centers, and family daycare—has its advantages and possible drawbacks.

When you hire someone to care for your child, whether in your home or elsewhere, you are entrusting this person or persons with your child's safety and well-being. Consequently, you need to check and double-check to be sure the choice you make is sound. Be prepared with insightful interview questions, and call all references. Check with your baby's medical provider and with families you know who have used any sitter or center you are considering. Word gets around quickly when a spot is available in a good center or if a good in-home sitter is looking for a new job. Likewise, asking around will alert you to any problems with a center or sitter. And don't neglect your own instincts. Sometimes a person or a situation just doesn't feel right. If that's your reaction at any time, don't brush it off. Listen to your feelings and evaluate them carefully.

You may also decide that what works best for your child this year isn't the best choice next year. Many families, by the time the children are old enough not to need supervision, have experienced nearly all types of childcare. Finding the right care for your child, as you are about to discover, will be an ongoing challenge in the years to come.

## Group care

There are many choices when it comes to group care, from neighborhood family daycare to corporate childcare centers to for-profit childcare chains.

**Family daycare** "Family daycare" is the term applied to childcare arrangements that take place in another's home, often a mother who has chosen this work as a means of earning a living while caring for her own child. For many parents, family daycare is a perfect answer to their childcare needs. It's a cozier arrangement than traditional childcare centers, and is often more flexible than a large center. It is generally less expensive than either in-home care or daycare centers. Because of mixed age groupings, you may also keep siblings together with the same caregiver. On the down side, the quality of care is not regularly supervised, though a licensed home is inspected from time to time. Also, should the provider become ill or have to leave town for a family emergency, you may not have any backup, and your child may not be permitted to join the group when he's ill.

When looking at a family daycare home, be sure that it is licensed, which means it meets at least minimum requirements of cleanliness and safety. The ratio of caregiver to children is as important in a home as it is in a center.

To make your evaluation, spend some time in the home during the day. Watch the children for their happiness quotient; kids who

*For more
information on
family-daycare
training, see
resources on
page 376.*

are thriving in childcare are busy and contented. If the children seem out of control or are too rambunctious for the caregiver to handle, look elsewhere.

Check into a potential caregiver's background with children, and find out what training she has. In a recent study, researchers found that providers who have 18 to 36 hours of instruction on topics such as child development, discipline, nutrition, and safety offered better-quality care. They were more likely to plan age-appropriate activities for the children, comply with safety standards, and be more committed to their jobs.

Should you decide on family daycare, keep in mind that you may develop a more personal relationship with the caregiver than you would with a center staff; while this can be comforting, don't let it stop you from keeping a critical eye for your child's well-being under her care.

**Childcare centers**  Enrollment at childcare centers is at an all-time high as more and more parents opt for the security and stability they offer. Recent research shows that children benefit cognitively from high-quality center care; their early language skills are actually enhanced by the care provided by trained professionals.

The key here is that the center must be of high quality, something that's not possible to judge by simply looking at the facility. The most well-equipped and physically attractive center might be poorly staffed, or staff members might be overwhelmed by the number of children. On the other hand, a poorly laid out and badly equipped center is not likely to be a good choice. You want a combination of comfortable surroundings and a comforting, competent staff. Therefore, you need to investigate, spending time at the center and talking with other parents, including those who have chosen this site and those who have left it. Look only at licensed centers, and ask to see the certification.

Spend some time observing a typical day at the center. It may look like fun or just plain chaos. Because young children learn in the context of play, the center you choose should give children plenty of opportunities for all kinds of play, including free play; physical play; circle

### *Children to Staffer Ratio*

The recommended number of children for each adult in a child-care center is:

3–4 infants or toddlers
4–6 two-year-olds
7–8 three-year-olds
8–9 four-year-olds
8–10 five-year-olds

time in which children converse with the teacher and each other; art, and story time. Centers often have policies about early education; find out if the views of any center you're interested in are in line with your beliefs about how formally, or otherwise, your child should experience early learning. An even more important issue is the loving nature of staff members. Your own observations, particularly of how the staff handles upset children, should tell you a great deal.

Should you decide on center care, you will most likely need an emergency backup plan for those days when your child is sick. You'll do yourself a great service by determining in advance if a neighborhood baby-sitter can come in, or which spouse will stay home with your child. Never take a sick child to the center, hoping the staff won't notice. It isn't fair to the other children, and it isn't fair to a child who is sick and longs for his own home. Some centers, of course, do have sick-child arrangements, in which your child can rest away from the other children in the care of someone who's supervising only the under-the-weather kids.

**Childcare center safety checklist** Keep in mind this checklist used by the National Association for the Education of Young Children for judging safety and cleanliness:
- Running water, soap, and paper towels are readily available.
- Baby toys are washed daily and disinfected twice a week.
- Diapering takes place at a changing table, never near an area where children play or where food is stored or prepared.
- All electrical outlets are covered with protective caps and all potentially dangerous products, including medicines and cleaning supplies, are stored in original, labeled containers in locked cabinets.
- The center has working smoke detectors, and fire extinguishers are easily accessible to the staff.
- Daily cleaning includes disinfecting bathroom fixtures, removing trash, and cleaning the kitchen area.
- All play equipment is clean and in good repair, with no sharp edges or rusty nails.
- At least one staff person who is certified in emergency pediatric first aid and CPR for infants and children and who knows the Heimlich maneuver is always present.
- Perishable foods are stored in the refrigerator at temperatures low enough to prevent spoilage. Other foods are kept in containers on shelves at least six inches above the floor. Lunches from home are kept in the refrigerator.

## In-home care

In-home care, in which your child's caretaker comes to your home, is in many ways the most convenient for parents. In-home sitters range from trained nannies, who may have training in child development and first aid to women who, although not trained formally, have had many years' experience caring for children, including their own. Or you might opt for an au pair, a young person, usually a woman in her early twenties, often from abroad, who lives with your family.

**The advantages of in-home care**  In-home sitters can care for your child in the comforting familiarity of your home. Your child can be cared for even when he has the sniffles, a condition that might bar him from a group setting. For newborns, whose immunity is immature, in-home care precludes your child spending time with other sniffling children. With care at home, you needn't worry about getting him up and dressed and out the door in the morning, which can be very tension producing for everyone. You won't need to take him out in inclement weather, either. The sitter at home can also help out to some degree around the house; while childcare should always be their top priority, most sitters are willing to tidy up a bit and perhaps even put dinner in the oven. In-home sitters can be day workers or may live in. They may also be available if your work requires some overtime. If you will regularly need this type of overtime, however, be sure to discuss the situation with your sitter and find out if she's agreeable. In-home au pairs, generally hired through an agency, may be barred by their contracts from working overtime.

**The drawbacks of in-home care**  For all the advantages of in-home care, it's important, however, to recognize some drawbacks, too. In-home care is enormously expensive compared to other forms of care. It is not easily monitored, and it's not always possible to determine just how well your child is being cared for in an unsupervised setting. The costs of one-on-one care are generally quite high. And a sitter may quit without much notice, leaving you without the resources of a backup. Also, as your child gets older, in-home care may not offer the social and learning opportunities that a more established center can offer.

If you choose in-home care, the IRS and your state's work rules require that tax returns be filed quarterly, and that taxes, including social security taxes, and other compensation—sick days, vacation time, and overtime—be paid. Additionally, medical insurance is a benefit many families give full-time sitters.

**The interview** When you interview a prospective sitter, be prepared with your questions; have them written down, since it's easy to forget what you wanted to ask. Request proof of identity, current address, and names and phone numbers of references. Check the references, making sure to ask why the sitter is no longer working for that family and whether the former employers would hire the sitter again. Following are questions to ask the sitter that will help you evaluate her as a potential caregiver:

• What kind of childcare experience has she had? Ask her to explain the best and the worst experiences. The details can be telling.

• What is her attitude about working mothers? Does she approve of mothers leaving their infants with others?

• How does she handle issues of discipline? Be specific. Ask her what she would do if your baby cried for an hour or more. What if your toddler was defiant or inattentive to her? What if your child broke her watch or other prized possession?

• How does she feel about TV? Would she watch TV herself while your child was playing or napping? Would she offer television as a regular activity?

• How does she feel about the rules you've set for the children? If her philosophy differs from yours, can she comfortably follow your standards?

• How much does she like to mingle with other sitters, parents, and kids? Does she enjoy taking the kids outdoors to play?

• What does she know about good nutrition? Does she limit snacks to good-for-you-foods?

• Find out what she would do in an emergency such as your child suddenly becoming ill or a fire in the building.

**Au pairs** Au pairs, young women (and some young men) often bring energy and enthusiasm to the job. When hired through an

> ### *Finding a Sitter*
>
> You can advertise for a nanny or sitter in your local paper or on community bulletin boards, or you can register with an agency. Word-of-mouth, however, is often the best source. Ask everyone you meet who has had a sitter; someone whose child no longer needs full-time care may be delighted to have a sitter she values highly go directly to another family. Good sources for finding sitters who are no longer needed by a family include local nursery schools. Many parents post the names and numbers of their sitters who are soon to need new jobs.

agency, as most are, they are committed to spending a year with your family, which allows real bonds to form. However, they may also bring their own problems, leaving you in the role of mothering your au pair, particularly if she becomes homesick. You will probably need to train the au pair in childcare; because of her youth, it's unlikely she has had much experience. There's also a lack of privacy that accompanies any live-in arrangement.

Some families in which the children are past the infant/toddler stage particularly like having an au pair. If she is from another country, the children will have a natural way to learn about another culture and language. Having her in the home also means you can stay at work a few minutes late without undue anxiety about the sitter waiting with her coat on. However, in fairness to the au pair, you should agree on what her regular hours are, and keep to them except under extreme circumstances. Additionally, you must adhere to your contractual obligations with the au pair and her agency regarding her hours.

**Working with your in-home sitter** For many parents, hiring a sitter is their first experience of being an employer, and most are unsure how to develop and strengthen the relationship with someone who is such an important person to the family. It's essential that you and the sitter agree on what the job entails. Have a written agreement spelling out the parameters of the job—the hours, the pay, the benefits, when payments are made, the additional compensation for additional hours, vacations, etc.

To help the relationship run smoothly:
- **Realize that the sitter has a life of her own.** You may think of your sitter as a part of your family, but she's got her own life and, perhaps, her own children, too. Invite her to join any family activities that are not part of her job, but don't feel rejected if she chooses not to join you.
- **Be mindful of your agreement.** Don't expect your sitter to accept additional hours without additional pay or to alter her plans at the last minute to meet your schedule. Plan ahead and check any changes that you may need with her. Likewise, pay her on time and fully, including any overtime due.
- **Respect cultural differences and differences in beliefs and attitudes.** Unless a difference impinges on your child's well-being, realize that exposure to the ideas of others can be a good thing for your child.

- **Act respectively toward her.** Speak to her in the same tones you'd speak to another adult rather than speaking down to her. Don't correct her in front of the children. If an issue needs to be discussed, set aside time to talk to her privately and be willing to listen as well as to speak.

Take the following steps to assure your child's safety and your sitter's safety as well:
- Take her through the entire house including the basement, and explain the security system, if you have one, in detail. Point out the location of anything she may need to know, such as the cabinet where you store extra lightbulbs.
- Write down your address and directions to your home. This is crucial if she has to give instructions to help locate your home in an emergency.
- Discuss your fire and other emergency evacuation plans. Be sure she understands that her first responsibility is the children, and that she should get them out immediately in the event of fire or to the safest place in the house during a storm. Go over the escape route, all exits from the house, and how the locks work, and point out potential hazards.
- Show her the location of key light switches and circuit breakers or fuse boxes in the event of a power outage. Keep a box with a flashlight, battery-operated radio, candles, matches, blankets, and bottled water in the house and tell the sitter where it is.
- Post emergency numbers, numbers where you and your spouse can be reached at all times, numbers of your child's doctor, and the numbers of trusted friends, neighbors, and relatives she can contact in an emergency.

# When it's time for a change

Even the best childcare arrangements don't last forever. The in-home sitter who was perfect for your infant may not be able to keep up with your active toddler. The family daycare center that worked so well for your toddler may not offer the stimulation you want for your preschooler. Perhaps a caregiver needs to move on. Or a new center may open in your neighborhood that's even better than the one you've been using. The reasons for changing childcare arrangements are many, and the change need not be traumatic.

When change comes abruptly—when, for instance, a sitter quits, a center closes, or you discover a good reason to sever the relationship—you're faced with the double task of finding replacement care quickly and helping your child adjust. Don't panic. It may be necessary to put a temporary plan in place, such as you or your spouse taking some vacation days, or calling on a friend or relative to pitch in to give yourself time to find the right longer-term arrangement. It helps to look at this crisis as a reminder that a back-up plan is always necessary, even when you're comfortable with the status quo. The research you do now will serve you if and when you need to make future changes.

Don't feel that you must replicate your current arrangement, or that you must do something completely different. For instance, if your child has been in a center, you don't need to find another center simply because he's used to that. On the other hand, if you've been unhappy with a particular center, you needn't decide that a center is out of the question. The important thing is to look at each possibility with an open mind.

## PARENTS RESOURCES

**Au Pairs.** There are a number of agencies that will place an au pair with you. Among them are:

**AuPair in America**
102 Greenwich Avenue
Greenwich, CT 06830
(800) 727-2437
www.aifs.com/java/us/aifsaup/
index.htm

**EurAuPair**
250 N. Coast Hwy.
Laguna Beach, CA 92651
(800) 333-3804
www.euraupair.com

**AuPairCare**
1 Post Street
San Francisco, CA 94104
(800) 4-AU-PAIR
www.aupaircare.com

**E.F. Au Pair**
1 Memorial Drive
Cambridge, MA 02142
(800) 333-6056
www.efaupair.com

For local referrals, call the **National Association of Childcare Resource and Referral Agencies** at (202) 393-5501 or visit www.naccrra.net.

# *Handling feelings*

Allowing someone else to care for your child—whether it's upon your return to work after a brief maternity leave or when your child is already a toddler or preschooler—can make you anxious. Even though you know you've chosen the best childcare situation, you may worry about how your child will cope without you. In fact, much of that is up to you, though your child's temperament will also play a part.

## When maternity leave ends

No matter how long your maternity leave, you're likely to feel a sense of surprise when it's over. "Where did the time go?" you'll ask yourself. You may be looking forward to getting back to work or you may be wishing that you still had a few more weeks or months to devote entirely to your baby. Or both. Such mixed feelings are normal. Accept that you might feel torn about returning to work, and, if you have the option of changing your mind at a later date, give yourself permission to rethink your decision after you've had some time back in the workforce.

You can make the situation less stressful with a phase-in period. Start your child in his childcare center or with your in-home sitter while you're still on leave, to give yourself time to adjust and so you can feel secure about the arrangement you've chosen. It's also a good idea to return to work mid-week. If you start on a Wednesday, for instance, you've only got three days to go before you're with your baby all day long again.

**TIME FOR YOU**

### *Returning to Work*

**Cook and freeze plenty of dinners in advance.** This eliminates the stress of cooking from scratch during the week.

**Buy yourself a new outfit.** Pick out one that fits well and makes you feel really attractive.

**Buy flowers for your desk.** Or let your husband know that you'd like him to send them.

**Get better acquainted** with some of the other parents in your workplace.

**Make a lunch date** with your spouse or a friend.

**Exercise on your lunch hour.** If going to a gym is impossible, try taking a brisk half-hour walk.

**Get a locket and put a picture of your baby in it** to wear everyday.

**Make the first hour of your return home sacred time.** Don't read the paper or make any calls, and let the answering machine pick up incoming calls.

## Relieving Separation Anxiety

Try the following to ease your child into independence:

# Do...

offer short practice sessions. When your child is absorbed in play, leave the immediate area but stay in sight. When she is comfortable with this, leave the room for a minute or two and then come back. Stay out of sight, but not out of reach, for gradually longer periods of time.

find a capable caregiver or daycare setting. The more confidence you have in your child's caregiver, the less worried you'll feel when you leave; your child will pick up on this sense of security.

give your child plenty of time to get used to a new caregiving situation. If possible, have a sitter come to your house for a social visit before you leave your child in her care. In a childcare setting, arrange to visit with your child a few times before you plan to leave her.

prepare your child before you leave. Explain that you must leave and that you'll see her later.

try to draw her attention to some enjoyable activity before you go. Engage in a brief period of upbeat, smiling conversation with the sitter or teacher. Some experts feel that when your child sees you being friendly to a caregiver, she feels friendly to the caregiver, too.

allow her to bring along any security object that eases her anxiety.

suggest some fun activity you'll do together later on.

# Don't...

sneak out when your child isn't looking. It's easier and faster to duck out the door, but this defeats the purpose of teaching your child to learn to accept separation. It's confusing and upsetting for your child to realize suddenly that you're not around and have no idea where you are or if you'll be back. Let your child see you depart and later see you come back. It won't be long before she is able to realize that leaving is not a forever thing.

communicate your fears to your child through your body language, tone of voice, and facial expressions. If your child detects that you're worried, she'll be worried, too. Don't use a forlorn expression and sorrowful, apologetic tone of voice. Stay calm, sympathetic, yet matter-of-fact. Say good-bye cheerfully and then leave.

prolong your good-byes by rushing back for another and another kiss.

upon your return, detail all the fun things you did while you were away. This will make your child determined to stay with you the next time.

say how sad you were to be away either, which will bring out your child's empathic response—she won't want you to go away for fear that you'll be sad.

stop leaving your child with others because she complains. Children need opportunities to learn they can cope without you. Avoiding separation stunts the growth of autonomy and promotes insecurity.

# CHAPTER 3

# Discipline and Setting Limits

How you choose to discipline your child reflects the values you wish to impart and what kind of person you want your child to be. Your goals in discipline are clearly long-term, but your approach takes place in the here and now. Guidelines cannot wait. Nor can they remain unchanged as your child grows from one stage of development to another. Like all important aspects of child raising, your aim should be to help your child learn to internalize the behaviors that will serve him and those around him best.

## Understanding discipline

Discipline is not the same as punishment, though the two are often confused. Discipline is really about teaching your child appropriate behavior with the goal that she will eventually be able to control her own behavior without outside prodding. You will accomplish that goal of discipline by your example, your willingness to risk her momentary displeasure to assure her well-being and the well-being of others, and your commitment to the long-range goal of raising an independent, thinking, responsible adult.

### Your style as a parent

Your own parental style determines how you discipline your child. You can help your child choose positive over negative behaviors by developing a disciplinary style that is neither too strict nor too permissive. Children raised with inflexible and overly strict rules eventually learn to distrust their own feelings and instincts. Many come to believe that without adult guidance, their choices will always be wrong. These children have developed such a strong desire to please that they need to be told exactly what to do and how to do it, and are thus very susceptible to negative peer pressure later on. Other children raised in very strict households learn to behave according to the rules only when they are being watched. These kids develop little in the way of a conscience and are not apt to grow into self-disciplined adults.

On the other end of the discipline spectrum, a permissive parental style allows children to remain immature and impulsive. Having few rules to follow and limited guidance delays the process of maturity. Children of overly permissive parents don't easily learn to abide by rules or to postpone present pleasure for future gain. Like the children of very strict parents, they become insecure, never sure of what is expected of them or of how to interact with others.

The middle road—often called "authoritative"—is the best route to raising a well-adjusted child who grows into a self-disciplined and self-assured adult. Authoritative parents:

- Initiate open communication between themselves and their children.
- Expect certain behaviors from their children and share these expectations with their children.
- Encourage their children's independence and individuality.
- Set clear-cut rules.
- Firmly and consistently enforce their rules.

Authoritative discipline gives your child a sense of security that will help her grow emotionally strong. As you develop your approach to disciplining your child, aim toward this middle ground. Realize that your child will, at least on occasion, misbehave, and that, as she grows, you'll need to adjust your expectations to meet her changing developmental needs. You'll also have to adapt your style of parenting to work with your child's unique personality.

**Sharing discipline decisions with your spouse** Sharing the responsibility of disciplining your child with your spouse is essential. When both of a child's parents share a similar viewpoint and approach matters of discipline in cooperation with one another, the child feels secure. When, on the other hand, one parent abdicates, leaving all discipline decisions to the other, or when parents argue over discipline in a child's presence, she can feel confused and insecure.

You and your child's other parent do not need to have identical child-rearing philosophies, but you do need to present a shared general outlook and a mutually supportive approach to discipline. This is true whether you're raising your child with her other parent or if you're separated or otherwise not sharing the day-to-day care. While you might differ on the details, your styles can complement without undermining each other's. When you differ on a specific issue, discuss the situation calmly and without resorting to power plays. Your child can adapt to your different styles as long she doesn't sense that there is severe conflict between these styles. If an issue presents itself and your spouse handles it differently than you might have and you cannot discuss how to handle it beforehand, reserve your judgment until you see what happens. Your mate's new approach may work.

Work toward a mutual understanding of what you can expect from your child. If one of you has less experience with childish behaviors, arrange an opportunity for that parent to observe how other children her age act. For example, if you are usually the one who takes your child to birthday parties, have your spouse do so the next time. Seeing how other children of the same age behave often helps in understanding that your child is behaving normally.

## Understanding misbehavior

Children misbehave for a variety of reasons, none of which should be taken personally. Even a generally cooperative child has days when he can't meet your expectations because he's tired, not feeling well, reacting to a hurtful event with a playmate, or adjusting to a change in his life. Sometimes children "misbehave" simply because they don't know what is expected of them. This is particularly true when they're faced with new situations, such as visiting another family.

Because they strive to be "good," young children often attribute "bad" behavior to someone else. This is not so much to avoid being punished as to keep their good feelings about themselves alive. As your child moves from age 2 to 3 to 4 and 5, she is less likely to attribute her own misbehavior to an invisible "other." By the prekindergarten or kindergarten age, she's aware that she

## Timing and Behavior

Your child's sense of time may affect her behavior. You may tell your child that she's not allowed to eat the cookies on the counter before dinner. A moment later, she may take one. Is she being defiant? Not necessarily. She may simply have concluded that what you said five minutes ago doesn't count now. By 5, however, she is capable of retaining the idea of "no cookies" for an entire afternoon.

did behave badly. She may still deny the deed, however, because, to her own logic, she didn't mean to do it and therefore shouldn't be in trouble for it. Four- and 5-year-olds often claim that any misdeed was an accident, which, in fact, it was, since there was no premeditation involved. Your reaction should be similar to your response when she was younger, but can now also include a more involved discussion about the rules and, if the behavior is a repeated one, perhaps a time-out or other reasonable punishment.

**Working with your child's personality**
The discipline strategies that work for one child may not be the best for another child. Each child's inborn temperament must be respected in matters of behavior, and you will have more success if you tailor your demands to your child's special personality. If your child is relatively easygoing, she may need only occasional reminders to behave as you want. If your child has difficulty making transitions from one activity to the next, you need to modify your approach to allow her the time she needs to adjust before considering her slowness to respond or her anger at being interrupted as an act of defiance. If your child is strong willed, you will need to develop a more creative approach to discipline so that you and she will not be locked into a battle of wills which, ultimately, neither of you can really win.

If you've been following a path that has not made disciplining easier on you and your child, try another approach. Let your child know that you are making changes and what you hope the result will be. For instance, if you've been verbally correcting him to pick up his toys to no avail, there's no point in continuing to talk to him about it. It's time to try something else. You can say, "I've been correcting you too much about picking up your toys. I'm going to try something new to help you remember to clean up after yourself. If you leave a toy in the middle of the living room, I will put it away for a while. You can earn it back by remembering to pick up all your toys the next time." Give him a warning before changing your tactics.

**Considering your child's level of development** As your

child's verbal skills and understanding of the world grow, it's tempting to believe that he is more mature than he really is. Conversely, it's also easy not to recognize that a child has matured enough to expect a higher level of cooperation. Adjusting your expectations to your child's level of development is one of your greatest challenges in discipline.

Assessing what you can reasonably expect from your child is an ongoing process. It requires observing your child, noting his unique temperament, any particular stress he may be feeling, and his behavior in relationship to other children his age. Then, as your child matures, you can change your expectations gradually.

# Encouraging positive behavior

Your main goal in disciplining is not to correct misbehaviors that you observe in your child, but rather to encourage the behaviors you want your child to practice.

## Creating routines

Instituting regular daily routines is your surest means of inspiring your child's cooperation. The child who expects certain actions to follow a regular schedule is less likely to balk at events such as dinner time and bedtime. The less reason there is for your child to wonder what is expected of her, the less likely it is that she'll act out her confusion with whining, crying, and demands. Following are some guidelines for creating daily routines:

**At mealtime** As much as possible, try to schedule mealtimes about the same time every day. To involve your child in a mealtime routine, you could give him one or two tasks that he can do regularly to help you get ready. For example, he could set all or a part of the table, or help you prepare one part of the meal. If possible, try to have the whole family sit down together to eat dinner. This will help a routine of getting together at least once a day and will give your child some consistent time with the rest of the family. Cleaning up after a meal can also be a part of routines. Your child may be able to help clear the table and stack dishes. When it comes time to put away clean dishes, he might enjoy sorting and putting away the flatware. Whatever part you ask your child to play in a mealtime routine, make sure it suits his age, temperament, and abilities.

**At toy-cleanup time** Making a room tidy and free of toys and clutter may seem at times to be an impossible task. Your child may resent having to stop playing to clean up, or he may feel that because he's finished with certain toys and moved on to something else, he wants to have nothing more to do with them. Instead of making general commands, such as "Clean up your room," break down the task into steps that you verbalize. To make this chore into a regular routine, try to follow the same steps in the same order each time. At first, show your child what to do while asking him to help. Little by little give him more of the responsibility. To further encourage cooperation, you could. For example, you could say that you will read a story together, or some other activity, after the toys are put away. Also be sure to praise your child for a job well done.

*For more on bedtime routines, see **pages 163–64** and **225–26**.*

**At bedtime** Keep to your routine as firmly as possible, with exceptions only for very special reasons. Even though your child will probably test the routine frequently, if he knows where the limits are, he may not put up as much of a struggle.

First decide when you want your child to be in bed. This decision will be based on your needs as well as your child's temperament and need for a certain amount of sleep. Some children do better staying up a little later than others. Then you might build in a five- or ten-minute cushion by giving a warning that bedtime is near. You could even give him a choice on how he wants to spend the rest of the time. The next step could be helping your child relax and unwind with a bath and a story, a quiet game and a rock in a rocking chair, or a soothing song and a back rub. The key is to be consistent and not to rush through the routine.

If your child consistently tries to get up again after the deadline has passed, you won't be able to force him to stay in bed. However, you can set limits by insisting he stay in his room. Excuses for getting up might be headed off by providing a fun night-light, a plastic bottle or canteen next to the bed for a quick drink, or a small tape recorder for playing a favorite song at low volume until he gets sleepy. If there really is a need to get up, try not to talk loudly or angrily. Quickly handle the problem and lead him back to bed. If he becomes scared, comfort him by going to his bed rather than inviting him into yours.

**In the car** Whether you plan a quick trip to the store, or a longer drive, routines can help make the journey smoother for both you and your child. A car routine should always include getting into a car seat or booster seat and using a seat belt. To make the confinement less difficult for your child, add certain rituals to your routine. For example, you might play some of his favorite songs if you have a cassette player in the car. You could bring certain favorite books and small toys and put them within reach. Play games such as counting trucks or cars of a certain color, or looking for certain letters, numbers, or colors on signs. On longer trips, you might bring along a box containing activity materials. Stop at least every two hours for a stretch, a visit to a toilet, and possibly a snack. Anticipating regular stops will also help your child handle the time better.

## Setting limits

Setting limits helps keep your child healthy and physically and emotionally safe. However, trying to direct every aspect of your child's behavior can just lead to exhaustion. The key to setting limits appropriately is deciding what issues are really important to you and what issues you're willing to negotiate. The nonnegotiable issues usually fall under safety, health, and values categories, such as crossing the street with an adult, being considerate of others, and wearing a seat belt in a car. The issues that you can be more flexible usually involve convenience and personal preferences, such as television watching and food and clothing choices.

Once you've decided on which issues to be firm and which to be flexible about, you can set your rules and stick to them. You can be firm, for example, about the need to wear a hat on a cold day, but you can be flexible about what your child chooses to wear under her snowsuit. Avoid trying to have too many rules. It's difficult for a child to remember and abide by them all. By choosing your battles wisely, learning when to say no and when to say yes, you can exercise the right level of control.

In your day-to-day routines, you'll also want to remind your child of your rules, preferably beforehand rather than as corrections. For instance, before a shopping expedition, you can tell your child that she will be allowed to pick out one treat, but no more. Note if there are any items that are not acceptable as a choice. Then ignore any additional requests. Before bedtime, review the routine to remind your child of what's expected. Throughout the day, try to honor your child's likes and dislikes as much as possible.

The second part of setting limits is enforcing them. It's important that your child know what you expect as well as know the consequences of any misbehavior. It's unfair to scold a child for behavior he didn't know was unacceptable. It's also confusing to fail to correct a misbehavior for which your child knows your rule.

**Teaching patience and delaying gratification** Two of the most important skills you can help your child learn are the abilities to be patient and to delay gratification. Both go against a child's instinct to want things (including your attention) and to want them *now*. The child who does learn these skills is much more likely to succeed in school and to be able to form and maintain good relationships. Here are some ways to teach these important skills:

• **Keep your promises.** Studies show that a child who has learned to expect her parents to keep their word is far more likely to be willing to forego instant gratification because she's secure in the knowledge that her needs will indeed be met.

• **Share the pleasure of success.** Let your child know when you are pleased with yourself for having worked hard at something to see a job through to its completion. Congratulate your child when she struggles to accomplish a task without giving up.

• **Offer practice in saving.** Encourage your child to save her nickels and dimes toward an achievable goal. Match her savings or contribute what you can so that her practice has a payoff within a relatively brief period of time, since a preschooler usually can't wait weeks or months to be satisfied.

## Handling the "Gimmies"

Preschoolers often get an attack of the "gimmies," asking that you "give me this" or "buy me that." The gimmies are not a sign that your child is particularly materialistic or selfish. They can better be described as curiosity run amok. When your child sees something new and interesting, it's natural for him to want to handle it and make it his own. Giving in to the gimmies too readily can dissuade your child from learning to prioritize and limit his needs.

- **Show the benefits of waiting.** You might even make a game out of it by offering your child one treat now or two treats in an hour.

**Avoiding the happiness trap** If you find yourself frequently wavering and letting some of your important rules slide, you might be falling into the "happiness trap." It's sometimes difficult to watch the child you love so much be unhappy. When that momentary unhappiness is the result of her not wanting to follow a rule, it's easy to give in "just this once." If your child senses that she may eventually get to "yes" if she asks enough, you need to stop and evaluate your methods before you find yourself mired in endless demands and negotiations. Ask yourself how strongly you feel about the issue under consideration. Once you decide where you stand, you can work at being an authoritative parent who is able to provide structure and set limits, while still respecting your child's needs and desires. You may even find out that you can maintain your credibility without having to say no all the time.

If, however, your changing a "no" to a "yes" is more a matter of convenience than conviction, you need to consider the long-term disservice that giving in has on your child. She will become much less happy when she is faced with a constant need to test the limits.

## Encouraging cooperation

As important—and perhaps even more important—as correcting misbehaviors is noting episodes of cooperation and congratulating your child for his good behavior. When you see your child sharing a treasured toy with a friend, be sure to tell him you noticed. The good feeling he gets from this verbal reward will make it more likely that he'll continue to display your preferred behavior. Catching a child being good is particularly effective in areas in which your child has had difficulty meeting your expectations. For instance, if your child has had a hard time being patient for your attention when you're on the phone, remind him at the first ring that you need to have a moment to yourself. Then, just 30 seconds or so into the conversation, before his patience has run out, thank him for giving you the time you need. If he interrupts two minutes into the conversation, thank him for waiting so long before interrupting. These incremental rewards help him stretch his patience the next time around.

When your child is especially resistant to what you want her to do, helping her learn to cooperate can be especially difficult. It's tempting to resort to bribes to get her to cooperate. Although offering your child a toy or candy for good behavior may get immediate results, in the long run, such tactics backfire. They say to your child that you have given up and can't control her. You also may be setting up a pattern in which your child expects to be rewarded for her cooperation. At this point, she won't cooperate unless you first promise to buy her something. You might also have to raise the stakes in order to get the same results. If you are already involved in excessive deal-making, breaking the pattern won't be easy. Begin by rephrasing your requests to eliminate the "If you do this, I'll give you that" routine. You might say that by picking up her toys, your child will be able to find them the next time. If she reminds you of a past bribe, simply say that this time it won't happen.

Nontangible rewards, however, do have their place in encouraging cooperation. Unlike bribes, which are promised beforehand, rewards generally come after the fact. For example, you might suggest a fun activity to enjoy with your child as a consequence of her cooperation during a not-so-fun activity. After a trip to the grocery store, you might say, "Since I was able to do our shopping so quickly because of your cooperation, we now have time to make pudding together." This form of reward encourages more good behavior.

# Limiting unacceptable behaviors

No child can cooperate, refrain from dawdling, or simply behave all the time. In fact, a little pushing to see how far the rules stretch is a healthy endeavor for your child. There are times, however, when you need your child to do as you ask and to not misbehave.

## Responding to common childish behaviors

In spite of all your best efforts to teach your child positive behaviors, it is natural for her to engage in misbehavior. Your goal is to limit behaviors you do not want while giving your child room to make mistakes and learn from them.

**Dawdling and inattentiveness**  Children have a different sense of time than do adults. Getting your child to hurry up and adapt to your schedule is a likely cause of friction. There are a number of things you can do to avoid battles about dawdling. Most of them require changes in yourself rather than your child.

• **Identify the parts of the day when dawdling seems to cause particular trouble.** The morning when everyone must be out of the house at a certain time or at bedtime, when your child moves very slowly toward ending his day, are common times. Modify your routine to allow for these regular occasions of dawdling. Give yourself 15 more minutes each morning and arrange all that you can the night before. Set the beginning of the bedtime routine early enough to allow for some dawdling while still getting your child to bed on time.

• **Give your child enough time.** With fewer skills and less experience, your child simply takes longer to accomplish tasks than you do. If your child is accompanying you on an errand, give yourselves enough time so that his naturally slower movements and his easily distractible nature don't put you in a position of having to nag him to keep up. When your child needs to make a transition from one activity or place to another, decide how long you'll let your child dawdle before time has run out. Give five-minute warnings that the deadline is approaching.

> **"IT WORKED FOR ME"**
>
> ### Defeating Dawdling
>
> When I'm in a hurry, and I need my three-year-old son to get dressed quickly, I'll put on a music tape and challenge him to get ready before a certain song is over.

• **Understand your child's motives.** Your child isn't dawdling to drive you crazy. Some dawdling may be in response to anxiety. She may not want to go to bed because it means separating from you and the rest of the family. The same may be true for getting ready to go to the baby-sitter's or a nursery school in the morning. Sometimes what appears to be dawdling is really your child's absorption in an activity. His misunderstanding of time makes it easy for him to believe that he can both finish his project and be outside the door with you at the same moment.

• **Follow rituals.** Rituals help both you and your child operate on "automatic pilot," moving from one activity to another with relative ease. The more attuned your child is to the daily ritual, the less he'll dawdle through it, since each facet of the routine holds its own pleasure. At bedtime, for instance, your routine might include a game, a story, singing a favorite song, or rocking in a rocker chair. Don't rush the routine. When it's over, your child will be more likely to accept the next step—getting into bed.

When I'm in a hurry, and I need my three year-old son to get dressed quickly, I'll put on a music tape and challenge him to get ready before a certain song is over."

Inattentiveness is another form of dawdling. Take a moment to assess your child's motivation for ignoring you. He may be so engrossed in an activity that he's blocked out all disturbances, including you. When you need to redirect your child's attention, move in closer and make eye contact. Acknowledge that he wants to keep doing what he's doing, or that he doesn't want to do what you want him to. Let him know how you feel, too, and why you need for him to listen to you now. Then give him a short limit before the activity has to end. You can also give him choices about how he might want to finish what he's doing, such as offering to help him clean up or letting him do it by himself. If necessary, gently move him away from the activity and redirect him to what needs to be done.

Your child may have learned that if he ignores you long enough, you will stop making demands. If this is the case, work on following through when you need his cooperation rather than developing a pattern of inattentiveness. He may also have learned to ignore you if most of the words you direct at him are corrections or complaints. In this case you need to make sure that you engage him in other, more enjoyable conversations as well as being regularly attentive to his attempts to talk to you.

**Fibbing** All children lie, at least on occasion. The fib your child tells, however, should not be confused with true dishonesty. While a preschooler may lie much as an adolescent would to avoid punishment, a preschooler's reasoning is entirely different. When she denies responsibility for a misdeed, she truly believes that she is not responsible for something she didn't mean to do. She may also exaggerate wildly, which is a reflection of her immature thinking and logic, not a desire to deceive. For instance, she may announce that she can drive a car, fly, or that she is the one who built a nearby bridge because she can easily imagine herself doing so. She may tell others that she will be getting a lavish present for her birthday or the whole family will soon be going to Disneyland, even though no such plans have been made or discussed, because the boundary between reality and wishful thinking is still quite hazy. In your young child's mind, if she wants or wishes for something hard enough, it becomes true.

A good way to respond to such amazing statements is to share the fantasy. Ask your child questions about the gift or the proposed trip. Then help her connect the fantasy to things that are more real. For example, if she says she's getting an elephant for a pet, you might have her act out the fantasy with a stuffed animal. You could also visit a zoo to see a real elephant.

As you discuss the value of honesty to your child, your own behavior is the most potent teacher. Telling your child that there are no cookies in the house because you don't want her to have any defeats your goal. Instead, risk her displeasure by stating that there are cookies, but that she must wait to have them. Making good on your promises is also essential in instilling honesty. If you promise to read your child a story after dinner, don't renege. If your words mean something to her, then she will better understand that what she says matters, too.

## When Your Child Lies

### Do...

remember that lies often come directly from your child's active fantasy life and imagination and may not be intentional. They may be more stories or tall tales than lies, and he may actually believe what he says.

remember that lying is part of being a normal child. Your child will be constantly testing you, and fibbing is one way to do so.

make it clear that lying is not permitted and that you can't be fooled. Then drop the subject.

explain how frequent lying could actually put him in danger or lead you to mistrust him. What if he were really sick or hurt and you didn't believe him?

### Don't...

react too strongly to lies. If you frighten your child by yelling or being overly punitive, he may become even more reluctant to tell the truth the next time.

tempt him to lie by asking if he did something wrong when you know that he has. Tell him that you know what he did. Then remind him not to do it again.

**Interrupting** Young children interrupt. It's their nature to believe that the world centers around them and that everyone else sees the world from this perspective. Your child honestly feels that you have nothing more important to do than pay attention to her. To reduce the disruption and your frustration level:

• **Split your focus when you can.** For example, give your child a hug as you remind her to stay quiet while you talk on the phone.

• **Provide alternatives to your attention.** Keep a box of special toys by the phone for her to play with while you talk. Give her a coloring book while you're busy paying the bills.

• **Make a date.** When you can't be interrupted, set a timer or otherwise indicate to your child when you will be available. Then keep your meeting, remembering to thank her for her patience.

• **Don't interrupt her.** When you and your child are engaged in a conversation or activity and another adult enters the room, don't immediately disengage from your child. In fact, be obvious about needing a moment to allow your child to complete what she has to say or do. This shows her the same respect you want her to show to you.

**Whining** Once your child can talk competently, he'll practice a variety of voices—including whining—to get and hold your attention. When whining doesn't work, most children give it up. Surprisingly, most children learn to whine because so often it works quite well. If you give in to whining, particularly after ignoring your child's well-stated requests, she'll begin her next request with a whine. She may also notice that others, including her parents or other important people in her life, achieve their goals through whining. Fortunately, whining is one of the easiest negative behaviors to eliminate.

• **Identify the problem** behind the whining. Your child may be hungry, thirsty, sick, scared, bored, lonely, sad, or otherwise uncomfortable. If words aren't part of the whine, ask her to explain her problem in words. If the complaint behind the whine is warranted, try to resolve the matter.

• **State your policy on whining** if you feel the whine is less than urgent. Tell your child you can't understand what she wants when she whines. Ask her to tell you clearly and in a more grown-up voice what the problem is.

• **Use humor.** You might pretend to capture the whine and throw it away. Or, in a playful manner, you could whine back. Just be sure your child does not feel that you're making fun of her.

- **Ignore it.** If none of these tactics work, ignore the whining, which of course is easier said than done. Avoid making eye contact, keeping your manner and expression neutral even if you're angry. Give no verbal or other cues in response to the whine.
- **Move it.** If the whining escalates, explain that she'll have to do it another room, or she will have to go home if you are out of the house. If this fails, then take your child to her room or home.
- **Offer praise.** When the whining stops, praise your child and thank her for talking in a big-kid way. Then, if appropriate, give your child what she wants.

## Handling unacceptable behaviors

Sometimes young children act in ways that are clearly unacceptable, such as being destructive or hurtful, taking dangerous risks, having tantrums, or being truly defiant—behaviors that you must correct before your child harms herself or others.

**Aggressive behavior** As your child moves from toddlerhood into her preschool years, she will learn to express anger more peacefully through words rather than violently through actions. You may wonder just how much aggression is normal. For preschoolers, occasional pushing and shoving are common, and most children will respond positively to reminders to use their words and not their hands to settle disputes. If a child is getting hurt, you will need to step in and stop the fighting and try to help your child and her friend negotiate a resolution to their argument without resorting to aggression. What's important is not to determine who started the fight, but to help them state why they are fighting and to emphasize that hurting each other is not acceptable.

---

**"IT WORKED FOR ME"**

### The Father of Invention

My husband pretends that he's a robot called "the Whining Machine" when our 3-year-old twins start to whine. He says, "The Whining Machine is coming to get the whine out! You'd better hurry!" Then the kids laugh and scream, "It's out, it's out!" It works.

### Violent Solo Play

If you notice your child acting aggressively while playing alone, he may simply be trying out a behavior just to see how it feels. This form of play is not necessarily a sign of deep-seated anger or an aggressive personality. Try to react calmly to mild or occasional aggression. Ask your child about his game and let him know you don't like violence, without totally disallowing it. A certain amount of violent play acting, in fact, can help him sort out his feelings. Some violent play also allows your child to refine his sense of right and wrong, by giving him a chance to let good triumph over evil.

However, regular and/or intense aggression needs a different approach. Some signs of unusual aggressive behavior include physically injuring himself or others, attacking others, destroying others' property, acting cruelly toward pets, being sent home and not being allowed to play with others at school and neighboring homes, and being, in general, a danger to himself and others. Allowed to continue, extreme forms of aggression can lead to serious social and emotional problems.

It's important to consider the reasons behind your child's aggressive behavior. If he's being bullied by others—other children or adults—he may be acting aggressively as a way of reclaiming his sense of self. He may be exposed to too much violence, either in life or through the media. In that case, it's essential that he be shown more appropriate ways of dealing with others and handling his feelings. He may not have learned the necessary degree of empathy for others and may have also learned that aggression and intimidation will get him what he wants.

*For more on aggression, see **page 241**.*

Apologizing is very important. A lack of remorse after an aggressive act by a preschooler is worrisome and needs to be addressed. First watch to see if this is a pattern of behavior. If aggression is frequent, professional attention is needed.

**Biting, pinching, and hitting** Because young children often lack the language skills necessary to express feelings, they often resort to acting out their feelings by biting, hitting, pushing, grabbing, pinching, spitting, and kicking. First, remember that such behavior is not a reflection of whether you are a good or a bad parent. Such behavior is actually normal for young children. However, it's important to address the problem so it doesn't become habitual or intensify. As children age, it's also important to watch out for intentional aggression. Any violent action that seems to be carefully thought out or even planned is reason for concern.

Young children are aggressive for a variety of reasons. Aggression can be a way to express anger and frustration, or an attempt to communicate, test social roles, get attention, explore and experiment. Such behavior can be used to express physical needs, anxiety or pain, to feel powerful, or to release tension. Because young children usually can't think through the consequences of their actions, such aggressive behavior is often impulsive and a reaction to something else.

To handle this type of aggressive behavior, review the situation and the impulse that may have led to acting out. You may want to state that you know why the action happened, such as, "I know you are upset that Jason took your toy." Then you can discuss consequences and set limits by telling your child that you won't let him bite (or whatever the behavior is) because it hurts people.

Oftentimes, it's the parent herself who is the victim of this kind of aggression. If your child bites or hits you, don't respond in kind. Firmly hold him and say, "Hitting is not allowed."

The next step could be to try to redirect your child into more acceptable behavior. Explain that you and other people don't like such behavior. Point out that if he is angry, for example, he could growl like a lion, or he could tell a friend to stop whatever is upsetting him. In this way, your child learns that he can stand up for himself against aggressive behavior.

Rather than separating your child from another when aggressive behavior occurs, try talking to the children. Point out how one of them hurt the other. Then ask what the offender was trying to tell the other child. Walk them through safe ways to express themselves. You can help yours and another child understand that they can verbalize feelings and that their ideas are important.

Whatever you do, don't respond in kind by biting or hitting back. Your child won't necessarily equate his hurt with what he has done to another. And, if he sees you behave in the same way, he may feel that it's actually okay. It's important to show your child the behavior you want him to practice. It's also crucial not to label your child as a biter, a kicker, or whatever. You may actually reinforce the behavior.

**Cursing and using inappropriate language** The first time your child uses a word that isn't used in polite company, you may be inclined to think it's funny. Keep that feeling to yourself unless you're willing to have your child repeat the word on a regular basis. Likewise, overreacting in a negative way gives the word more power than it should have and makes it far more appealing to your child.

The best way to keep your child from speaking inappropriately is to make clear in a firm but nonharsh voice that "we don't use that word in our family," assuming, of course, that you don't. If vulgar language is common in your family, your child will pick it up and can expect him to speak in the same way. In that case, unless you want your child to mimic you, it's important to weed out the offending words from your own vocabulary, while you're within his earshot.

**Defiance and talking back** When your child discovered *no*, he also learned just how powerful a word it is. It can make things happen, and usually gets a reaction. It may be the first time he actually felt he had some control over a part of his life. As he explores what he can do with this word, you may find his seeming defiance reaching extreme, almost laughable levels. He may even begin saying *no* to the activities you know he enjoys the most.

## When Dealing with Kids' Aggression

### Do...

separate children who are physically fighting until they have calmed down.

supervise your child when he has an argument with a playmate so that you can quickly step in if the disagreement becomes physical.

help your child learn ways to handle anger without violence. For example, talk about the power of words in settling differences.

help your child to understand how it feels to be bullied by others. Talk about how bullies lose their friends and have trouble making new ones.

praise your child when he is able to refrain from aggressive behavior in situations when you might expect an outburst.

look at how you and other members of your family express anger and resolve conflict. By controlling your own temper and expressing anger in peaceful ways, you can provide a good example.

### Don't...

permit any conflicts at home to be settled in physical ways.

wait to reprimand your child when he breaks a rule about aggressive behavior. Deal with the situation immediately so he can better understand what he has done wrong.

forget to have your child apologize for his behavior. If property has been destroyed, find some way he can work to replace what has been broken.

be intimidated by your child's aggressive behavior to the point where you are unable to take charge.

feel guilty about having to punish your child for aggressive behavior.

lose hope that aggressive behavior can't be changed. If you doubt that your child can learn to control himself, then he will have a harder time learning to do so.

hesitate to find outside help if you feel your child's aggressive behavior hasn't improved.

To handle the "no's," the first thing you have to remember is that your child will not always be agreeable. He may say no just to say no, or he may really not want to do something. He usually doesn't intend his no's as a personal affront to you.

Give your child choices. Making a choice gives him more of a feeling of control, so he will feel less of a need to be defiant. Limit the choices to two or three and to appropriate situations. For example, if he doesn't want to put on a jacket, you might give him a choice of putting it on himself or having you help. If he refuses to wear the jacket, you could offer to take it along with you.

Give your child more control over his environment by giving him things to do himself. For example, put toys and books within easy reach. Provide clothes that are easy to put on and take off by himself. Create places to put clothes, such as pegs and low drawers, so he can put them away himself. You might even set bowls, spoons, and a box of cereal where he can easily reach them. Even though letting him do certain things himself will probably take longer and may create messes, you will be giving him some independence that will likely head off defiance.

Provide opportunities for your child to help you in ways that make him feel like he is really contributing. Some possibilities include rinsing vegetables, taking books off a coffee table so you can dust, using a sponge to clean up his own spill, piling up newspapers for recycling, cleaning crumbs with a hand-held vacuum, putting letters in a mailbox, and unpacking light, unbreakable things from a grocery bag. Be sure to praise him for his help.

Another form of defiance is excessive demands and dissatisfaction with much of what you do. Your child may be unwilling to wait even a brief time for you to provide something and end up demanding everything "Now!" The word *Now* is nearly as powerful as *no*. When your child discovers this word, he may honestly believe that using it will make things happen immediately. When it doesn't work, he may use it again and again out of frustration. When you try to explain that you are getting whatever it is ready and that he will have to wait a few minutes, he will likely respond with " no!"

If possible, involve your child in the process of whatever he is waiting for. If you are cooking a meal, find ways to have him help, so he doesn't just sit and brood over how long it takes. He could possibly pour in ingredients, stir something, or get you a spoon.

Sometimes it will seem that you can't satisfy your defiant child.

It's important at this point to remember that defiance generally comes from his feeling powerless over what happens in his world. Often, it helps to say calmly that you can't talk to him or do anything for him when he uses certain words or a certain tone of voice. By helping him see that he will have more control by using different words and tone, you will find his defiance lessening.

**Destructive behavior** Young children cannot be expected to handle others' possessions with great care and will, quite naturally, break fragile items. Sometimes, however, children destroy others' property—often a playmate's toys—deliberately. It's important to respond firmly, stating that the behavior is not acceptable. Removing your child from playing with her friend can help bring the lesson home. Important, too, is helping your child make amends. She can be reminded to apologize. She can also offer a replacement toy or a picture she's drawn or other token in return.

**Tantrums** Young children are constantly struggling for control— of their own impulses, of your schedule, of the world around them. The ultimate loss of control is a temper tantrum. A typical tantrum involves a child throwing herself on the floor while kicking, screaming, crying, and sometimes holding her breath. Some children may even faint. The first time you witness your child having a tantrum, you may be frightened as well as frustrated, angry, and, if the tantrum takes place in public, embarrassed.

Tantrums are rarely dangerous to your child, nor are they usually a sign of any severe emotional disorder. They usually first occur around the age of 2 or 3 and diminish by age 4 or 5. During these years, your child is beginning to gain independence and looking for ways to control the events in her life. However, when she is thwarted in her desires or when she reaches beyond her skill level to try to do something she can't yet do, she becomes frustrated and angry. When words don't come as quickly as the emotions, she falls apart. Furthering her upset, she resents and tries to push away your attempts to calm her. How can you help her regain control?

Although you can't prevent every tantrum, you may be able to diminish their frequency by watching that your child does not become overly frustrated, anxious, or tired. Quiet times or naps will help your child recover flagging energy before she goes beyond her limits. Also review the limits you have put on her. If they are too severe, she may fight them at every turn. If you relax some of her rules while firmly keeping to those you consider most important, you won't have to be saying no so often. She will get her own way once in a while and you can't reserve the no's for when they are most important.

When a tantrum does occur, try to remain calm. If you yell, you will probably make the tantrum worse. Try gently but firmly holding your child. Physically restraining your child may be necessary to keep her from hurting herself or others. Be sure to check your own feelings before physically joining her, however. If you feel you're about to go over the edge, you may need to remove yourself from the scene for a moment to calm down. If you're able to restrain her gently, move her away from the scene of her anger to give her a chance to recover. Or try distracting her if she's able to shift her focus for a moment to something other than her anger. For a mild tantrum, humor might defuse the situation as long as the humor is shared and is not perceived as your making fun of her.

Once she is calm enough to hear you, you can offer to help her succeed with the thing that has frustrated her, such as helping to put on her shoes or showing her how to throw a ball. When she's frustrated over a safety issue, such as wanting to use a real hammer and nails to build something while you are unable to supervise, you can agree to help her at another time while reiterating your rule about not using your tools on her own.

Do not let a tantrum cause you to feel defeated and don't let a tantrum lead you to give in to demands, which will only encourage further outbursts. If the tantrum takes place in a public place, where your child is trying to force you to give in to her desires, it's best to abandon your plans and head home rather than give in to gain a quick peace. Whether at home or away from home, react firmly but calmly. Say, "You will not get what you want by crying and kicking your feet. When you calm down, we'll talk about the problem." Then create some calming-down time, either in the comfort of your arms or in a special time-out place. Your taking control helps your child feel she is safe while she regains her self control.

## Breath-holding

When a child holds her breath, even to the point of fainting, parents are understandably alarmed. In spite of your feelings, it's important not to show how upset this behavior makes you. To do so demonstrates to your child that she has enormous power over you—and that's terrifying to her. She needs you to be in control. Handle breath-holding incidents as you would any other aspect of tantrum throwing: Remain calm, remove your child from the scene, give a time-out. Let him know that "Holding your breath will not get you what you want."

# Discipline strategies

Children need help to live within the limits you've established. Consequences that help your child understand his behavior and learn to control himself work best, beginning in toddlerhood.

**Verbal corrections and removal** Young toddlers, kids from age 1 to 2, often need only consistent verbal reminders to discontinue a misbehavior or to follow a preferred behavior. Often, a firm, "No," along with a change of scene, is all it takes to get a toddler to understand what is expected. For instance, the 1-year-old who tosses sand in the playground needs to be reminded of the rule and, if the misbehavior is repeated, to be removed from the playground. This routine may have to be repeated before it becomes effective.

**Time-outs** Time-outs involve removing your child from a situation in which he is misbehaving and giving him the opportunity to calm down. Used wisely, time-outs can be very effective, from the age of 1½ or so through the preschool years.

Time-outs are most effective when used to help an overexcited child regain self-control. By removing your child from the source of stimulation, you give him a chance to refocus his energy away from the misbehavior to a more positive behavior. In most situations, only a few minutes or even seconds are enough for your child to calm down. Time-outs do not have to mean banishment. You can designate a corner of the room you're in as a time-out location. It doesn't have to be the same place every time. Set an alarm clock or oven timer for a few minutes, telling him that when the buzzer sounds, the time-out is over. Make sure your child understands the reason for the time-out. Speak calmly so that your child knows you're serious, but not angry. He is likely to respond more to your tone than to your words, so yelling may make the situation even worse. Reassure him that you still love him.

Longer time-outs are less effective as they give your child time to become resentful and for his anger to fester instead of abate. Short time-outs also give you a chance to calm down. Then you can be a model for your child on how to get back on track.

Time-outs can also be used as a preventative measure. Sometimes you can tell when your child is about to lose control by the tone of her voice or the look in her eyes. This is the ideal time to call a time-out. Then take your child to a more peaceful environment. When he calms down, acknowledge that you notice the difference in his attitude. Tell him he's doing a good job, and ask if he's ready to go back to what he was doing.

When used too often and for every infraction, time-outs lose their effectiveness, so use this teaching tool judiciously.

**Enforcing reasonable consequences** Helping a child connect a misbehavior to a consequence is effective with children age 3 and older. When possible, choose consequences that are related to the misbehavior so that your child learns to connect the "crime" to the punishment. If your child balks at wearing his seat belt, arrange for him to stay home while you go out. When he's hurtful to a friend, help him find ways to make amends and teach him to apologize.

Be sure your child understands how a misbehavior is linked to a consequence and to follow through. If, for instance, the issue you're responding to is wearing a helmet when riding a trike, your child needs to know that you require him to don a helmet each time he takes his tricycle for a spin. If he forgets, simply remind him. If he balks, tell him what the consequences will be, such as not allowing him to ride his bike for the remainder of the day. If he then rides without his helmet, follow through and put the trike away without further discussion. Speak firmly and clearly and without anger.

# Handling your own anger

When your child has a temper tantrum or otherwise acts out, you may find that your own equilibrium is threatened. Loving your child is no protection against feeling incredible anger toward him at the same time. In fact, the intensity of your love makes anger more likely, because if you didn't care so much, you wouldn't have such strong feelings of anger either.

It would be foolish to try to not feel anger. Anger is a normal emotion. Just as you accept that your child is sometimes angry, you need to accept this feeling in yourself. And just as you work toward directing your child's anger, you need to put your own anger in perspective and not to let it overtake you. Each time you handle your own anger effectively, you give your child a role model for dealing with his own angry feelings. To keep your anger in check:

• **Recognize and name it.** Let your child and yourself know that you are angry. When your child has upset you to the point of anger, tell him. Say, "What you are doing is making me very angry." This gives him a chance to learn about your feelings as well as his own and gives him the language to express those feelings. Stating your anger plainly also signals to your child that negative emotions are normal. Use this technique judiciously, however, as your child may begin to tune you out if he hears "I'm angry" too often. To avoid being tuned out, vary your words. You might use a word he's never heard before in place of "angry," such as "aggravated" or "aghast." Taking the time to think of new words will also give you a few more seconds to regain your self-control.

• **Give yourself a moment to calm down.** One of the best solutions for dealing with your own anger with your child is to walk away before you say or do something, such as make threats or call your child names, that you'll later regret. When you feel your anger rising and you're afraid of losing control, say, "I need a time-out so that I can calm down." Don't leave the house or go out of your child's line of vision, however, since this can frighten him tremendously if he thinks you're abandoning him.

• **Resume normal interaction as soon as possible.** If you tell your child you will talk about the matter when you feel better, then make sure to do so within a fairly short period of time. If you give him the silent treatment for most of the day, you are letting him know that you think he's so awful you can't stand to be around him.

• **Apologize.** When you've misplaced your anger at your child's feet, don't hesitate to say you're sorry. Even if you're justifiably angry at your child, if you've said or done something hurtful, apologize. This gives your child the model of behavior to apologize for his own hurtful words or actions. Don't worry that apologizing will undermine your authority. Your child needs to know that everyone can be wrong at times, and that it's okay to admit so.

• **Limit the opportunities for becoming angry.** Look for ways to change the routine to avoid situations that regularly result in confrontation. For example, if your household is rushed in the mornings, identify things you can do the night before to eliminate this usual stress.

## When Disciplining

### Do...

be consistent. When your child knows what's expected of her and what consequences follow a misbehavior, she is better able to learn to accept your limits.

be firm. Your tone of voice and your willingness to follow through on your expectations sends the message that you mean business.

remember there is no one "correct" way to discipline your child. Take advantage of different methods, selecting the one that works best in a particular circumstance.

empathize with your child by trying to put yourself in her place. Think of times when you may have been overtired, stressed, felt helpless, or upset. Let your child know that you understand why she is upset, which will show her you are on her side even when you have to say no.

try to be flexible and keep your perspective. Remember, there are some battles that are not worth fighting if they are not crucial to your child's safety and well-being. Decide ahead of time which rules you absolutely won't negotiate and which ones can be bent now and then.

state clearly and specifically what behaviors are not acceptable rather than making general statements.

try to find the humor in a situation.

keep in mind your child's age, temperament, and abilities.

### Don't...

threaten to do something that you cannot or will not follow through on, such as saying that you'll throw all of his toys away if he doesn't pick them up. Such threats and failure to follow through weaken your credibility.

react overly harshly, which serves most to frighten rather than teach your child.

spank. Although spanking may appear to stop the misbehavior and make a child more obedient, the results may be deceptive. Spanking generally scares a child and makes her feel defensive. Neither of these emotions help her learn from her mistakes. Spanking doesn't encourage her to think about why she got in trouble. Most of all, spanking may give her the message that it's okay to hit and be hit.

# CHAPTER 4

· · · · · · · · · · · · · · · · · · · · · · · · · · · · · · · · · · · · · · · · · · · · · · · · ·

# Early Education

Though all of childhood is an exciting learning experience, the beginning of formal education—whether a part-time nursery school program or a full day of kindergarten—is a momentous occasion. The best preparation is emotional in nature. The child who feels secure and loved and who has had experiences with developing positive relationships with adults and other children is well equipped to venture forth.

## *Nursery and preschool*

Nursery school and preschool are educational environments for preschoolers from age 2½ to 4. Unlike childcare, which may also include appropriate educational experiences for preschoolers, nursery school and preschool are not full-day, 8 a.m. to 6 p.m. programs. Most involve half- or full-day schedules that fall within the hours of a regular school day, or approximately 8:30 a.m. to 3 p.m. Some nursery school and preschool programs, however, do offer extended days to accommodate the schedules of working parents, and include such childcare routines as lunch and naptime.

Nursery schools emphasize the teaching of social skills and, for 4-year-olds, kindergarten preparation. The terms "nursery school" and "preschool" are usually used interchangeably, although programs for 4-year olds are generally called preschools or pre-K programs.

*For information about childcare, see **pages 368–78**.*

### Is nursery school necessary?

There's no hard and fast rule about the need for nursery school, though most kids who attend nursery school do benefit from the experience. A good nursery program allows children to learn a great deal from peer interactions and from teachers trained in early-childhood development. Kids in preschool programs also have fun.

On the other hand, children who have lots of positive interactions at home with adults and other children may gain many of the same benefits without attending a nursery school program. For some kids—those with language delays, with phobic separation anxiety, or behavioral problems—the neighborhood nursery school is probably not be the best place to begin their formal educational experience. Your child's age and temperament, your feelings about preschool, and the options available in your area are also factors to consider as you decide if nursery school is right for your child.

# What children learn in nursery school

A nursery school program provides your child with more opportunities to meet and play with other children and to form attachments to other caring adults. Although 2-year-olds may normally play alone even when they are with other children, they usually do enjoy watching and imitating each other as long as a loving and responsive adult is present to help prevent grabs for one another's toys and to soothe hurt feelings and hurt knees. Three- and 4-year-olds seek out children to play with, and if your child doesn't otherwise have many playmates available, a preschool is a great resource for widening his social circle.

Nursery schools provide children with new experiences and activities they can't enjoy at home. Most families do not have the physical space or the equipment to allow a child to run, jump, climb, and play, whereas a good preschool is designed for such activities and has the right playground equipment right outside the door. A preschool generally has a wider variety of creative materials available than you have the resources or the space at home for.

In addition, a nursery school teacher, trained in early childhood development, can guide your child in his social interactions and his use of play materials in appropriate ways. The preschool experience can also help prepare your child for the more formal setting of a kindergarten.

Nursery or preschool is usually the place where 2- to 4-year-olds get their first real experiences interacting with other children and with adults outside the family. More than academic skills, the social skills learned at this age are the skills that are essential for future success in school and elsewhere. The classroom actually becomes like a community where each child should have a voice and a re-

## Learning Through Conflict

Even arguments between children in a nursery-school setting can provide an opportunity for learning social skills. Supportive teachers will help children express their thoughts and emotions with words rather than by acting out. They will also help children reach a solution together, such as taking turns to use a favored toy. Learning how to identify, express, and control their emotions is often the biggest accomplishment of children in nursery school.

sponsibility appropriate to his age for helping to make the school a nice place to be. This is also a place where children can learn to be aware of and take care of others. In fact, you may find your child forming a strong attachment and identification with his preschool group. He may be eager to contribute to parties by bringing in food to share. He may also want to invite classmates and even his teacher to your home for a visit.

**Nursery school goals** Nursery school can help build a child's confidence and increase his motivation. If children can feel good about themselves and their ability to learn, they will have a great chance to do well when they start more formal schooling. In a good nursery-school program, your child will be encouraged to learn:

• **Appropriate social behavior,** such as waiting for his turn, sharing, participating in group activities, following directions from his teacher, settling disagreements verbally, making his needs known, and recognizing the needs and rights of others.

• **Language skills,** such as asking and answering questions, listening to a story, retelling a story or describing an event, and making up a story.

• **Community functions,** such as the roles of different people in the school and neighborhood, the purpose of various shops and other places in the community. He should also learn about his own role in the classroom community, such as being responsible for putting away toys he has taken from the shelves.

• **Appropriate uses of materials,** such as art supplies, toys, and other items in the classroom.

• **Freedom of expression and creativity.** Children should be encouraged to create drawings without having to follow a particular model, making the grass purple, if they wish, for instance. Children should be encouraged to find divergent uses for materials, such as using a twig for a paintbrush or a box for a racecar, rather than only using materials in predictable ways.

• **Cultural literacy.** For preschoolers, this means learning popular songs and rhymes, group games that will enhance their ability to play with others, and learning about holidays and other celebrations.

- **Increased independence.** Putting on her own coat, placing her belongings in her own cubby, working on a project—these things give a child a sense of her own abilities to accomplish tasks without the help of a parent.
- **Academic skills.** While there should not be an emphasis on learning to read or do math, children will learn the names of colors and shapes, how to grasp a writing or drawing tool and use scissors, some letter and number recognition, and sequence and time concepts, such as first and last and today and yesterday.

**Learning language in nursery school** The burst of language learning that takes place between the ages of 2 and 4 can be enhanced in a nursery-school setting. In addition to using words while playing with other children, your child's use of the materials provided in nursery school encourages further experimentation and practice with language. Toys and dress-up clothes that encourage pretend play promote thinking and talking about the various roles they are playing. With their imaginations in gear, most preschoolers will offer a running commentary on the action, describing their every movement. ("I am a dragon! I have a long tail. I am running through a forest.") Children also strengthen their language skills as they learn negotiation and cooperation. For example, your child may offer a toy to the other child, saying, "You can play with this now, if you'll let me play with that," or "Let's play with this together and pretend that…"

Language skills also involve listening, and your preschooler will learn a great deal by listening to the teacher give directions and read stories. Rhymes and silly words are especially popular with preschoolers, which is one reason why Dr. Seuss books are a continual favorite. A clever teacher will even use silly language and rhyme to encourage cooperation.

## The right age to begin

If your purpose for sending your child to preschool is to give her a jump on her education, don't forget the valuable education she has already been getting at home. It's also important to remember that young children should not be "pushed" into formal education until they are ready. A good program for

### Learning Through Questions

A good preschool program will be open to children's frequent questions. A teacher may even be able to use many of these questions to construct activities so that children can have the experience of finding out the answers themselves.

2- and 3-year olds will focus on play, not on academic skills such as reading or counting. A program for 4-year-olds will emphasize play as well as offer instruction in basic academic skills, such as identifying shapes and colors and the letters in your child's name. You need to match your child's level of development with the programs available.

The right age at which to begin nursery school depends, of course, on your child, your family's needs, and community standards. If your 3-year old has been satisfied by frequent playdates with neighborhood kids, and most of his friends are beginning nursery school, it might be better for him to enroll, too, if now he suddenly has no playmates available during the day. If you find yourself unable to meet his needs for play and learning, the nursery school experience will fill that need.

While nursery schools are suited for most 2- to 4-year olds, the programs need to be tailored for each age. A program for a 2-year-old should involve a small group of children with lots of adult contact and free play, such as running and climbing indoors and outdoors, sharing a snack with the class, and listening to stories. The routine for 3- and 4-year-olds is usually more structured and offers more interaction among the children, including group games and fine-motor skill activities such as art. If your child is 4, she may be ready for a pre-kindergarten program which may be a full day in length and include some desk-time activities.

To determine if your child is ready for nursery school, talk to the teachers and administrators of your local schools to learn about their programs and what they expect in terms of readiness for a child your child's age. Your child's pediatrician can also help you evaluate her readiness and can offer suggestions for intermediary experiences that would be beneficial before beginning school, such as speech therapy for a slow talker or occupational therapy for a child with lagging motor skills. In general, a child is ready for nursery school if she:

- Can communicate her needs to adults outside her family.
- Reasonably takes direction.
- Is potty trained during the day.
- Enjoys other children's company.

**When it's better to wait**  If your child hasn't had much experience with other children, he may not take well to being part of a crowd after being the center of attention. A less formal playgroup might be a better choice as a transition between home and school.

If your child's verbal skills are lagging, preschool may not be the best way to help her catch up. A child who is slow to talk is more likely to learn language from talking one-on-one with you—and perhaps a trained speech therapist. In fact, the child who has difficulty making herself understood may be more hesitant to talk to others she doesn't know well. And if she is with several other children, she may not have as much opportunity to communicate in ways she needs to. A specialized program that includes speech therapy would be more appropriate.

While some separation anxiety is normal in toddlers and preschoolers, extreme, phobic reactions to separation will not be put to rest by attending school. Normal separation anxieties lessen over time; phobic reactions increase. If your child is terrified of leaving you, you need to address this issue before enrolling her in a school. Likewise, issues of antisocial behavior, tantrum-throwing, or excess defiance to adult authority need to be addressed before entering preschool. If your child's behavior will interfere with his ability to participate in school, talk to his pediatrician, who can refer you to appropriate help.

### Shyness and school

*"My 3-year-old is extremely shy. Should I push her to go to nursery school or should I wait for her to get over her shyness?"*

Shyness is a genetic trait, one that your child won't "get over" but, nevertheless, one she can, through experience, learn to live with. If she's moderately shy with strangers but is able to form close attachments to people outside her family, nursery school may be just what she needs to help her handle her shyness and develop some social confidence. However, it's important not to force her into a program that's large and boisterous, which may further intimidate her. She'll be more at ease and adjust more quickly to a small group with a teacher who is understanding and supportive of your child's natural temperament.

If your child is extremely shy and has not, in spite of opportunities to do so, become attached to other children and adults, she may need professional help to allow her to develop the social skills she'll need for school. If it's simply a lack of social experience that makes your daughter feel very shy, give her opportunities to interact with other children in the familiarity of her home before placing her in school. Perhaps you can invite over one or two friends at a time for a playdate. At all times, respect her feelings about situations that make her uncomfortable and encourage her to communicate what she feels. Encourage her steps toward sociability, letting her know that you trust that she will learn to work around her shyness.

## Different methods of teaching preschoolers

When you begin to look for a preschool for your child, you'll notice that most of the schools look the same. There will be teachers and children and small tables and chairs; there will be children's drawings on the walls and toys on the shelves. The critical differences between one school and another may not be in the classroom environment, but in what the teachers and children are doing. In some schools, the children will spend the day playing with whatever strikes their fancy while the teachers watch and answer their questions; in others, the children will spend much of the day seated at the table all coloring in the same shapes and pictures while the teacher guides them explaining what to do and how to do it.

**Choosing a nursery-school program** Once you decide to enroll your child in a nursery or preschool, how do you locate a school? The first step is to ask yourself some practical questions, such as:
- How close to home do you want your child to be? It's usually best to look at schools near your home or near your workplace.
- What hours do you need your child to be in school? This may depend on your work or school hours, or the schedules of other family members.
- What part of your family budget can you spend on school? If you find more than one school within your range, it may be wiser to go with the school that pays its teacher-caregivers more and therefore costs more. Schools that can pay their teachers a little more generally attract a better-trained staff. Keep in mind, however, that the most expensive school you can afford is not always the best for your child. You may want to do some research into how a school you are interested in is funded. Some facilities are subsidized by the state or federal government and can provide excellent programs at lower cost. Others are church or synagogue based and provide high-quality care that may be subsidized by the religious community.

• Do you want a creative activities-based playgroup setting or a more formal educational setting? Again, your child's age and temperament will probably determine the program.

Once you have decided on your criteria, how do you find the school you want? One of your best resources will probably be other parents who have had or currently have children in a preschool program. Ask parents you know in your neighborhood and in your workplace. You could also ask your child's doctor and others who are familiar with local preschools, including librarians and teachers. If you can't get recommendations in these ways, you might start with your telephone book Yellow Pages, under the headings "Nursery Schools" or "Preschools." Talk to the kindergarten teachers in your local school district to see if they have any recommendations.

When you decide on one or more places to consider further, the next step is to actually visit the school. You will need to go when children are there to see some of the activities and how the kids interact with the adult staff. You will also need to speak with the adults who will be taking care of your child. Also make a point of talking with other parents to find out what they like and may not like about the place. You should also take your child for a visit before making a definite decision.

### Evaluating a school

• **Look at supplies and equipment.** Check that there is a variety of art materials, toys, and playground equipment. Children don't need elaborate toys to learn, but they do need a variety of supplies that are in good working order. Be wary if you see toys with broken or missing pieces, limited art materials, or books with torn pages and missing covers, for example. Look for different sizes and kinds of writing and painting paper, whether the crayons and paintbrushes are the right size for small hands, and good supplies of paint and clay. Check that there is space and appropriate materials for creative activities in art, music, blocks, sand, and water play.

• **Talk with the teacher about the program, the type of activities, and the skills taught.** Determine how play figures into the program. Free play should be balanced with organized play activities.

• **Ask the director about her own goals and educational ideas.** Talk about what she likes best about the job. Ask about her training and the teachers' experence. Adults trained in child development or early-childhood education make better preschool teachers.

- **What's the ratio of children to teachers?** There should be one adult for every four to six 2-year-olds, and one adult for every seven to eight 3-year-olds, and one adult for every eight to nine 4-year-olds. Also note whether adults actually spend most of their time with the children.
- **What is the school's policy when a teacher is absent?** Is a substitute provided? Are classes merged? Does the director step in to act as teacher?
- **Observe the classrooms.** While school is in session, observe the children and the teachers and note whether they appear busy and happy or overwhelmed or bored.
- **Watch the children involved in activities.** Note whether each child is engaged, whether everyone is doing the same thing, or whether small groups are involved in different activities.
- **Look at the set up of classroom and play areas.** There should be lots of hands-on projects, such as making simple recipes, working with puppets, planting and tending seeds, and working with finger-paints. If children are expected to sit at desks and do teacher-directed activities, there won't be much time for creative exploration.
- **Interview the teacher about her discipline policy.** Note her attitude when she talks about children. While observing the class, watch the teacher actually discipline a child, if possible. Her interactions should be positive and accepting of both "victims" and "transgressors."
- **How are toileting accidents handled?** A child should never be made to feel ashamed of a toileting accident.
- **Observe how the teacher interacts with your child when you visit the school.** The teacher should be respectful of your child's personality, helping a clingy, boisterous, shy, or wound-up child feel welcome.
- **Try to look at the facilities through your child's eyes.** Are there comfortable spaces for different ways of learning? For example, can the children sit on the floor for a circle time? Are there are also chairs and tables? Is there room on walls for children's artwork? Remember, a place that is too tidy may actually be too controlled and not inviting to children's activities.
- **How are new students welcomed?** What kind of transition-time is allowed? Can parents stay with their children during the first days? It's important to choose a program that will accommodate children's needs—both kids who happily join the class on the first day and those who need more time to adjust.

Don't hesitate to ask for references. And above all, ask yourself: Would you would want to spend time here?

**Checking for safety** In addition to your child's emotional and cognitive development, you need to be sure that the facility is physically safe.

• **What's the ratio of adults to children?** Are there enough adults who would be able to get all of the children out of the building quickly, if necessary?

• **How are emergencies handled?** Pose questions about what is done if a child becomes ill or is hurt. Check to see that the school has working smoke detectors, and fire extinguishers are easily accessible. Check that there is a well-stocked first-aid kit easily accessible. Make sure that at least one person on staff is trained in basic aid, including choking first aid and CPR.

• **Is food preparation done with health in mind?** If meals are served, visit during a mealtime. Try to see how the meals are prepared and what kind of food is served. Note whether staff members wash their hands before and after preparing meals and after assisting children with toileting. Running water, soap, and paper towels should be readily available. Perishable foods should be stored in the refrigerator at temperatures low enough to prevent spoilage. Other foods should be kept in containers on shelves at least six inches above the floor. Lunches from home should be kept in the refrigerator.

• **Are toilets clean and easily accessible?** Check that toilet facilities are clean and designed for children. For example, can children safely reach the sink? Is the thermostat set so that the water cannot reach scalding temperatures? Is the toilet area easily accessible to the children and within sight of the teacher or other adult if your child should need help? Are children taught to wash their hands after using the toilet?

• **Are the facilities childproofed and designed for safety?** Are there safety plugs in electrical outlets? Are breakable materials and scissors, thumb tacks, and art supplies safely out of reach when not in supervised use? If the school has 2-year-olds, are there gates on stairs? Do stairways have child-height handrails? Is there easy access out of the building? Are all potentially dangerous products, including medicines and cleaning supplies, stored in original, labeled containers in locked cabinets? Do windows have guards?

• **Is all play equipment clean and in good repair?**

# Getting your child ready for nursery school

When the time is right for your child to begin a nursery or preschool program, you want him to be ready. How can you help your child prepare? Put away the workbooks—there are no academic skills necessary for entering preschool. But that doesn't mean you can't help your child prepare for this experience in other ways. Being part of a larger group takes some getting used to for children who are accustomed to being the center of your attention. You can help your child learn how to be social by helping him practice the concept of sharing. You might also provide opportunities for being with other children in playgroups or at the neighborhood playground; this will help him learn how to play, take turns, and communicate verbally instead of physically.

To get along with his teacher, your child will have to know how to follow directions. Give him a chance to practice this skill at home by playing Simon Says–type games in which he follows your lead. Move on to more direct forms of instruction by asking him to complete a simple task, such as getting his shoes from the closet. When he has the idea of doing as you ask (when you ask it) help him learn how to clean up after himself; direct him to put away his toys; tell him to clear his papers off the kitchen table and put them where they belong. Be persistent and don't cave in and do it yourself; at preschool the teacher can't clean up after every child. Your child will be better prepared for school if he knows how to follow his teacher's instructions.

Your child will also have a head start in school if he has learned to be aware of his surroundings with all his senses. You can play games at home that will encourage him to really see, hear, smell, taste, and touch. When he looks at a tree ask him what he sees; point out that a tree has leaves, and branches, and bark, and height, and shape. Ask him to describe what he hears when his eyes are closed; learning to listen carefully is a valuable skill.

## Interviewing for preschool

*"In our city, preschool admission requires extensive interviews. Is there any way to prepare a 3-year-old for this process?"*

---

### Everyday Preparation

Preparing for preschool is something you can do in very simple everyday moments. Answer your child's questions. Listen when he talks to you. Ask him questions that help him think about the world. Be available to your child and responsive to his needs—this will give him the confidence he needs to enter preschool ready to enjoy the experience.

Try to schedule the interview for a time of day when your child is most likely to be well rested and not too cranky. Also choose comfortable clothes rather than a new and potentially scratchy outfit. As difficult as it might be for you, don't show any anxiety or communicate any sense that the meeting is overly important. You can familiarize your child with the school beforehand with an informal visit and you can explain some of the things that are likely to occur, such as telling your child that a teacher will meet him and ask him to play with some other children. Don't try to drill him on his knowledge of colors or shapes or any other skill you think will impress the school personnel.

Keep in mind that you're looking for a good match between your child and the school instead of looking to get your child into a particular preschool. The "right" preschool is the one that will welcome your child because the school is well suited to meet his needs.

**Easing your preschooler's fear of separation** Even children who have been used to being cared for by others may, as they enter school, develop a fear of being apart from their parents. Once again, this reaction is not necessarily a sign of regression but can be due to their increased awareness of the world's dangers. Children who have recently undergone major changes in their lives, such as the birth of a sibling or a move, may become even more clingy as they adjust to the change. Some of the ways you can help your preschool child deal with separation are:

- **Develop a ritual for your leave taking.** For example, each morning before you leave your child at school, sing a particular song that your child enjoys. When you say good-bye, develop a special way of waving to each other. In this way, your child has a chance to be a part of and exercise more control over the situation.

- **Talk about something else.** On the way to preschool, don't focus on the time you'll be apart from your child. Talk about the fun things she'll do at school, the weather, or her new shoes. Avoid reassurances that she'll be just fine without you.

- **Offer support, not sympathy.** If your child begins to cry or whine at the preschool

---

**"IT WORKED FOR ME"**

### *Having a Sitter Help Ease Separation Anxiety*

My 3-year-old daughter cried most mornings when I dropped her off at preschool. One morning, when I had to be at work early, I asked her regular baby-sitter to take her. There were no tears at all. I asked the sitter to take her for the next week, so that my child would get used to arriving at school without the routine of crying when I left. It worked. When I went back to taking her, she happily went into her classroom.

## Taking the Surprise Out of the Morning Schedule

My 2-year-old goes to a local nursery school three mornings a week. Although her teacher says she's very happy there, she always seemed startled and confused when I announced it was time to get ready for school. Many mornings we had to struggle through crying tantrums before we could get out the door. It took me a while, but finally I realized that the problem wasn't nursery school, it was the element of surprise. My daughter doesn't adjust quickly to changes in her routine. Because she never knew what days she was going to school and what days she was staying home, she was always on edge in the morning. The problem was easily solved: I gave her a wall calendar and we colored in red the dates that were school days. Then each night we would look at the calendar and she would go to bed knowing what to expect in the morning. Now when I announce that it's time to get ready for school, she laughs and says, "I know that!"

door, don't break down yourself. If you show signs of weakening, the crying will continue in the hopes you'll change your mind and take her home. Be positive and supportive, but remind her that her job is to go to school.

• **Don't get angry.** This is not the time for anger or shaming your child. Calling your whining child a baby will only add humiliation and guilt to the emotional pain she's already feeling. Let her know her feelings are natural and understandable, and then let her know that you'll want to hear about all the fun things she did while you were apart.

### Handling a changed attitude

*"My son started nursery school very enthusiastically, but now, after just six weeks, he says he doesn't want to go anymore. Should I encourage him to stick it out?"*

First, encourage him to tell you why he doesn't want to go any more. Many children love the build-up of excitement as they prepare for school, but then want life to "get back to normal" once they've experienced a few days actually attending school. Too much preparation and talk about how wonderful school will be can actually backfire when the child discovers that school is not a constant fun-filled circus.

The transition to school is stressful, even when your child is enjoying his time in the classroom. The demands of interacting with new friends and teachers may seem overwhelming. Additional time and patience will aid his adjustment. Sometimes an incident at school upsets a child. Perhaps another child pushed him or the teacher corrected him.

For some children, having a good time away from home makes them feel guilty, especially if they think their parents are sad when they're away.

Before removing your child from school, talk with his teacher. Find out how his days in the classroom are going. Is he withdrawn or does he interact with the other children? Has anything happened that frightened or upset him? Has she noticed any change in his behavior? Listen for her suggestions and advice.

If the teacher isn't taking your concerns seriously or can't address them to your satisfaction, talk to the school administrator. Perhaps a change to a different class is in order. If you feel the program has not proven to be adequate for your child, you may want to encourage him to finish the term, then look for another nursery school with a more appropriate program.

Also consider spending some time at the school to observe your son's group. If you uncover anything actually or potentially dangerous—such as teachers being unresponsive to children's needs, children behaving in dangerous ways, or anything else that does not seem right to you—it would be wise to take him out of the program now rather than waiting. More likely, however, if you sense your child is simply having a bit of trouble adjusting to the new routine, urge him to stick it out. Let him know that you trust him to make the adjustment.

# *Kindergarten*

Kindergarten is the first step in formal education. Most kindergartens are part of the local public-school or private-school systems. A few are extensions of nursery schools, designed especially for 5-year-olds. In some localities, kindergarten attendance is mandated, though school attendance is not usually law until a child has reached the age of 6.

Because of the proliferation of nursery-school and preschool programs, kindergarten has undergone a radical change from just a generation ago. Most children today arrive in kindergarten with some experience in a classroom, so this year is no longer viewed as the single, formal preparatory event for first grade. Because of that early exposure, the kindergarten curriculum is no longer focused on introducing social skills, though these remain an important part of the program. Academic skills, increasingly, are working their way into the kindergartner's day, leaving less time for the appropriate play that was once the essence of kindergarten.

# When to start kindergarten

Traditionally, reaching age 5 signaled readiness for kindergarten. In many areas, that has changed, and today parents need to learn about the kindergarten their child will attend before deciding when the time is right. To evaluate your child's readiness:

- **Know the school's cutoff date.** Traditionally that has been age 5 by a specific birthdate, such as June 30, September 1, or December 31, of the year in which the child is to begin school. Children who turn 5 after the cutoff date have to wait until the following year to begin in such a publicly funded program. Some public and many private schools have earlier cutoffs, a few going so far as to exclude those who have not turned 6 by the start of kindergarten.

- **Look at the curriculum.** Traditional kindergarten emphasizes play and sets the stage for more academic learning by introducing letter recognition and early arithmetic concepts, such as simple addition. Class seating is informal, with children gathered around shared tables. These are well-suited to children who are close to age 5 at the start of the year or who may turn 6 before the end of kindergarten.

- **Consider the ages of the other children in the class.** Even a very mature 5-year-old will have difficulties in kindergarten if most of his classmates are 6. If the curriculum has been adjusted to meet the developmental needs of 6-year-olds rather than the traditional kindergarten age of 5, a 5-year-old would have additional pressures put on him. Likewise, a mature 6-year old might do better in a first-grade class rather than spending a year in a traditional kindergarten class of mostly 5-year-olds. Though exceptions certainly need to be made for maturity and other aspects of development, most kids do best with others their age.

## Older Kindergartners

In areas where the entrance age for kindergarten is closer to 6, the kindergarten curriculum itself may resemble what was once the first-grade curriculum. In effect, these older kindergartners are offered a drawn-out first-grade curriculum, in which the academic skills once reserved for first grade are introduced in kindergarten. The academic kindergarten is generally not appropriate for 5-year-olds.

## Older or younger — which is better?

Beginning in the 1980s, there had been a trend to delay kindergarten entrance to age 6. In some cases, school districts instituted an earlier cutoff date for entry. Frequently, however, it was the parents who chose to keep their children (especially those with summer or fall birthdays) at home another year to give them the perceived advantage of being the oldest in the class rather than the youngest.

Increasingly, however, in a reversal of the trend toward delayed admission, age 5 is again being looked at as the appropriate starting age. After reviewing the school records of thousands of children from kindergarten through high school, researchers found no true benefits from being held back a year over the long term. Though the younger kids in a class were found to be at a slight disadvantage in kindergarten through second grade, on average, by the third grade any seeming age benefits disappeared. Moreover, more recent research shows that the younger children appear to do better as they progress through the grades, earning higher grades and having a lower drop-out rate.

Still, age cannot be the only factor in determining the best time to start kindergarten. The educational program at your child's school and the age and development level of the children with whom she will be attending are key. If, for instance, the great majority of your child's classmates will be a full year older, you might want to wait another year or find another school where her classmates will be closer to her own age. If the normal admission date allows 5-year-olds to begin, and there's no particular reason to hold your child back, however, the traditional age is probably the right one for your child.

**Determining your child's readiness** If you're unsure about your child's readiness for kindergarten, consider having him evaluated by an educational consultant who's familiar with the kindergarten curriculum in the school your child will attend. The screening should cover perceptual and motor skills, physical development, social skills, linguistic development, and a grasp of basic "readiness" concepts such as colors and shapes.

Meet with your child's preschool teacher and with a school guidance counselor to discuss your child's progress. Present the results of the screening and ask for their recommendations.

---

**"IT WORKED FOR ME"**

## *Handling Parents' Fears of Separation*

I had to realize that it wasn't just my child who might be affected by our separation on her first day of preschool. I was so tense it was terrible, and I knew my daughter would sense there was something wrong. I talked over my feelings with my husband and a good friend, who were both a big help. In fact, I even went with my friend when she dropped off her son, who is a little older than my child, at kindergarten. I was impressed by how casual they were. I rehearsed in my mind over and over what it would be like for me and my daughter. On the big day, I was fairly calm. What really surprised me was my daughter. She just marched off with the teacher like she had been doing this every day. I knew then that it's not only young children that need a little care and attention when it's time for big changes. Parents need understanding, too.

The following list can give you some idea of the academic and social skills that help indicate whether a child is ready:

- plays well with other children as well as alone
- respects others' possessions
- is able to share with other children
- can resolve small conflicts with another child
- can follow simple directions and rules
- can work independently for five minutes
- is able to listen to a story for ten minutes
- can talk in complete sentences
- can count to ten
- can distinguish and name simple shapes
- is able to identify and name four colors
- can use crayons, paints, paste, and clay
- is able to bounce and catch a ball
- can cut paper with blunt scissors
- is able to run, hop, and jump
- can clap
- can button a shirt and zip a zipper
- is able to build with blocks
- can tell his right hand from his left hand
- knows his first and last name, his phone number, address, and parents' names

## If You Decide to Wait

If you decide your child should wait to go to kindergarten, you will need to explain to her why without making her feel she has failed in some way. This is especially important if her friends are going on to kindergarten, or if she has siblings who started kindergarten at her age.

Don't make apologies or assume that she will feel bad. Simply state that "Mom and Dad decided that this year you will stay in pre-school. We think it will be better and more fun for you."

**Development vs. temperament** The difficulty in making a judgment about your child's readiness lies in determining whether or not a lag in a certain area is a developmental issue (something that will change in time) or a part of his temperament. For example, a shy child may be perceived as needing more time in a pre-K program with the idea that he may become more assertive in a few months time. However, if shyness is an innate part of a child's temperament, he may do just fine in kindergarten. In fact, if held back, his shyness may worsen. If you are uncertain what to do, age may be a deciding factor. If your child is painfully shy and is a young five who is close to the cutoff date, you may want to hold him back another year. This would give him the confidence of being one of the oldest instead of one of the youngest children when he does start kindergarten.

Small size might also be a reason parents hesitate to put their child in kindergarten. Another year in pre-K may give a child a chance to catch up physically. However, another year may not make a difference if the child is genetically destined to be a small person. Again, you will have to weigh his size against his emotional, social, and academic readiness. What it often comes to is trusting your own instincts and knowing your child.

> **PARENTS RESOURCE**
>
> *National Association for the Education of Young Children* **(NAEYC).** This organization offers resources and services to early childhood professionals, parents, and policy makers about child development and early education.
> 1509 16th St. NW
> Washington, DC 20036-1426
> (800) 424-2460
> (202) 232-8777
> www.naeyc.org

## Getting started at school

You can help your child make the leap to formal schooling by preparing her in advance and practicing "school skills" at home.

Talk to the teacher whose class your child will attend or visit the classroom to learn what a typical day in school might be like. Let your child playact a day at school with siblings, friends, or even her stuffed animals. Introduce her to some of the tools she may be using, such as alphabet worksheets. Don't go overboard, however, with academic preparation. Simply assure your child that you trust that she will do fine and that you and the teacher will help her if there's anything she needs.

### Easing first-day jitters

*"My daughter cries every night because all her preschool friends are going to different schools. How can I make her feel more confident on her first day of kindergarten?"*

It's time to make a new friend fast. Ask around your neighborhood or among your friends for the phone numbers of a few children who will be in your child's class. Invite one or two over to your house for a short afternoon playtime. On the first day of school, your child will have someone to stand next to and this kind of social support is sometimes all it takes to ease those first-day jitters.

# The kindergarten year

Your child will be learning a lot more than the ABCs in kindergarten. She will grow socially as she practices her getting-along skills. She will blossom emotionally as she becomes more independent and secure. And she will expand her academic horizons to include skills like reading, writing, math, and problem solving. During this exciting year, watch for signs of the following:

• **Social skills:** Kindergarten children are learning to be cooperative and responsible members of a group. You'll see that children who are ready for kindergarten are less self-centered and begin to accept other children's ideas and incorporate them in play. They like to help each other and the group as a whole. Physical fighting won't happen as often because these children are now able to discuss their problems and are learning to use socially acceptable ways of getting what they want like asking, trading, compromising, or substituting.

• **Emotional development:** Your kindergartner will experience and experiment with a wide range of emotions. She may be giddy and happy one minute and crying hysterically the next, but throughout this year, she will be learning how to express these feelings appropriately and to relieve stress and tension through words, drawing, and physical play. This ability to channel emotions gives your child a sense of self-control so she can better enjoy working with other children. Also during this year, kindergartners continue their quest for independence. If allowed, your child will become more competent at making decisions and doing things for herself. Kindergarten lets her reach out to the world and be a part of it.

**Academic learning** The following skills are a sampling of the academic skills your kindergartner will develop:

• **Oral language skills:** Your child is learning more about listening, speaking, telling stories, and expressing feelings and ideas.

• **Perceptual discrimination skills:** It's important at this age to be able to recognize and identify shapes and colors and to find hidden shapes in pictures.

## Transitional Schools

An alternative to repeating the same preschool program is to find a transitional program in your school that offers more than just a repeat of what your child has already done in pre-K. Some schools offer classes that allow children to complete kindergarten and first grade in three instead of two years. Other schools have special kindergarten classes for children born late in the year.

- **Comparison skills:** Your child will learn to understand and use words that describe time (*before/after*), size (*short/tall/big/little*), position (*over/under*), amount (*most/least*), distance (*here/there/ near/far*); she will also use comparatives (*big/bigger/biggest*) and opposites (*before/after/up/down*).
- **Classification and sequencing skills:** Kindergartners will spend lots of time learning to sort and classify according to size, form, and function. They will also put things in order of amount and according to time.
- **Reading and writing skills:** In kindergarten, your child will learn to recognize letters, say the alphabet, write her own name, and write ideas with pictures, scribbles, and invented spelling. She will also learn to read her own writing, read her name, read certain sight words, and enjoy as many additional reading adventures as her individualized talents allow.
- **Math skills:** The world of math opens up to kindergartners. In addition to recognizing, writing, and counting numbers, your child will come to understand what written and spoken numbers mean; she will use numbers to put pictures in order, to record amounts and measurements, to do simple addition and subtraction of concrete objects, and to use numbers and counting to solve problems.
- **Problem-solving skills:** Kindergartners have many opportunities for flexing their ability to solve problems. They will learn to identify problems and solutions. They will learn to predict outcomes and think about cause and effect. They may even begin to use the scientific method to hypothesize, test, observe, and record results.

**Reading and writing** In most kindergartens, children are not expected to become independent readers by the end of the year. It's a rare 5-year-old, in fact, who can accomplish this task. And children who read at age 5 do not necessarily become better readers at age 6 or 7 than do those children who begin to read later on.

The important thing this year is for your child's interest in books and reading to continue to grow. She also needs to become increasingly familiar with the reading process—learning to look at the words from left to right and from top to bottom of the page. She needs to feel free to take on the role of author herself, having her dictated stories transcribed for her to "read" back to you, drawing pictures to illustrate her ideas, and experimenting with using written words. Spelling should not be a focus of these early attempts at writing.

Become familiar with the teaching methods your child's teacher will be using this year. You may hear terms like "whole language," which describes a method of teaching children to read using exposure to literature and language in a variety of ways. Children are taught to recognize words by context and sight. In a whole-language classroom, students are involved in word games, listening to stories and poems, labeling different things in the classroom, and learning reading skills through following a recipe, for example. If your child can match written words, remember and write some letters, and copy words or a short sentence, she has a good visual memory and will probably learn well with a whole-language approach.

Or, your child's school may emphasize phonics instruction in which children learn the sounds of the letters and are encouraged to sound-out new words; they may use workbooks and other tools to help children learn to decode the written word. Though phonics instruction went through a period of disuse, it is enjoying a resurgence because many parents and educators found that whole-language instruction alone did not unlock the key to reading for all children. If your child can distinguish words by sound, remember and repeat an unfamiliar sentence, and is able to remember nursery rhymes and songs, she has a good auditory memory and may learn well with a phonics-based approach.

Most schools today use a combination of whole-language and phonics instruction. Many also include sensory learning, in which children write letters in the air, in sand, or other materials, play with 3-D letters, and learn songs and plays about letters and words. If your child is artistic, physical, or spatial and can do puzzles and build with blocks, she will probably benefit from this multisensory approach.

### Early readers at school
*"My 4-year-old is already reading. Will she be bored when she starts kindergarten?"*

The typical kindergarten curriculum has so much to offer, that it is unlikely your child will be bored even if she has mastered beginning reading skills. Teachers commonly face a classroom of children who come to school for the first time with a wide range of skills or lack of skills. You might ask your child's teacher how she plans her teaching around children who know how to read along with children who have no reading skills at all. There will also likely be many reading skills that she does not yet know. For instance, some children learn to decode—to sound out words—very early, but need more time to understand the content of a story. Others master the understanding of plot and character early, but don't learn to decode until much later.

Children also develop different skills at different times, and while your child has unlocked the key to reading, a good kindergarten program will emphasize a number of other skills that are appropriate for your daughter to be learning now, such as social skills and art and music.

**Understanding school achievement**  Perhaps not in kindergarten, but definitely by the first grade, parents often run into the issue of their child's achievement. All parents want their child to do things well and to be academically successful. However, each child has different talents, and not every child will be a top performer in every area. It's a hard lesson for parents to learn, but one that will prevent a great deal of suffering in your family—it's okay to be average.

It's important that you focus on what your child can do well while encouraging him to work on the skills in which he needs improvement. While your child may not be the best reader, he may have artistic or musical talent. He might have difficulty grasping mathematical concepts, but he may be a great soccer player.

If you're worried about your child's achievement, meet with his teacher and ask if he is working up to his potential. The teacher should be able to describe to you where your child's strengths as well as his weaknesses lie.

Above all, it's important to remember that some of the greatest achievement comes from the most ordinary beginnings.

# Handling school problems

Larger class sizes, higher expectations, a new environment, and a changed routine can cause even the most even-tempered, confident child some problems. Most problems can be handled with patience and lots of communication. If your child is having difficulties:

• **Talk to the teacher.** Unlike in nursery school where you may have been able to drop by anytime to chat, it's more likely that you'll need to make an appointment. Do so early in the school year before problems grow. Let the teacher know precisely what it is you want to discuss so that she can be prepared to address your concerns. Write down your concerns and bring the list with you to your meeting so that you're sure to cover the necessary information.

• **Develop a partnership with the school.** You and your child's teacher and the school administration share the goal of helping your child succeed in school. Approach the teacher and administrator as partners, not adversaries. Always be on the lookout for ways you can work together.

• **Advocate for your child.** Find out what special programs exist in the school that can address any particular needs your child has.

### Handling behavior problems

*"My 5-year-old son has been acting up in kindergarten. His teacher suspects that he's hyperactive and wants to have him evaluated by the school district psychologist. What can I expect regarding the testing?"*

*For more on ADHD, see* **pages 563–68**.

Many children who are rambunctious and/or easily distracted have difficulties settling in to the routines and rigors of kindergarten. Professional evaluations can help determine if your child is simply naturally active or if he has a condition referred to as attention deficit hyperactivity disorder (ADHD) that could be helped by behavioral and/or drug therapy.

Testing consists of observing your child's behavior both in the classroom and in the psychologist's office. It includes a battery of psychological and educational written and oral tests, doing things that are likely to be familiar to your child, such as building with blocks, drawing, and telling a story. Many of those tested are found to be within the normal range for emotional, physical, and cognitive development. Some are found to have superior intelligence, but lagging social skills, or, indeed, to meet the criterion of ADHD. Early diagnosis and treatment can prevent later school problems.

In addition to discussing the issue with the school personnel, talk to your child's pediatrician about her recommendations.

## School fears

Adjusting to kindergarten may actually take as long as eight weeks. During this period, many children occasionally balk at going to school. Some are simply tired of the routine. Others who may have had a bad day at school decide simply that they'd rather not go back for a while. Children who may resist going to school but who are comfortable in most social situations are not suffering from school phobia. They simply need encouragement to keep going, and assurance that you know they will, indeed, adjust.

**What to do about school resistance** For the child who's having a slow adjustment but is not phobic in general, patience and persistence are called for. Specific changes in the school situation, such as being assigned to a different class, may help. If your school has morning and afternoon kindergarten sessions rather than a full day, consider switching your child to a different session. Some children can cope better with the demands of school when their time there better matches their own biological clock.

School resistance may also be caused by something happening at school. A bully may be picking on your child. If so, involve the teacher in solving the problem so that your child can see that there are solutions as well as problems at school. The teacher herself might be the reason. If you suspect this is so, meet with the school principal or guidance counselor. Try not to see the school as an adversary. You are more likely to get help if the staff sees you as someone who wants to solve a problem rather than someone who wants to accuse.

Whatever you do, don't keep your child at home. Every day he spends away from school is one more day to be anxious about going back. He will also be falling further and further behind. Be sympathetic to his reluctance to go, but be clear that staying away from school is not a choice. Remind him that going to school is his job, just as you have a job.

You can temper the "no choice but to go to school" rule by offering your child other choices, such as what clothing to wear, what food to take for lunch, or whether he would like to take the bus or have you drive him. You might also allow him to call you and check in after being in school an hour, if the school allows it. Addressing school fears directly can keep them from blossoming into true phobias.

# School phobia

If resistance to school is chronic and shows no signs of letting up, however, your child may have developed a school phobia. It's important to realize that school phobia rarely exists on its own.

Kids who are phobic about school almost always suffer from other common emotional disorders, including separation anxiety disorder (SAD) and/or social phobia. Unlike common separation anxiety, which generally abates after a few weeks, a child who suffers extreme separation anxiety is not so much afraid to go to school as he is afraid of leaving home. This child is preoccupied with worries

## Building Friendships with Parents of Your Child's Classmates

The age when your child begins school offers you an excellent opportunity to expand your own circle of friends. After all, your children are embarking on a new adventure and who, other than another parent of a kindergartner, can better understand what you're experiencing? Widening your circle of friendships also serves your child well, as she gets to see you approach someone new with a smile and a few words. To build friendships with other parents:

• If possible, get a list of other children who are going to be attending the same school as your child and call the parents to invite them and their child for a meeting in the playground or your home before classes begin. This will not only give your child a familiar face on the first day of school, but will give you a ready source of information and mutual support as you make the transition from the parent of a baby or toddler to the parent of a school-going kid.

• Be available before and/or after school whenever possible to mingle with other parents.

• Attend all school meetings, where you'll get to know the most active, and involved parents.

• Trade off watching the children of your child's classmates after school or on weekends.

• Volunteer to join the class for trips and at other times when you can.

Friendships formed with other parents often last a lifetime. Even when your children are grown and on their own, you still have the shared experience of raising your families together.

---

about his family and wants to be home to monitor everyone's well-being. In addition to not wanting to go to school, he is likely to show his fear of separation by sleeping in his parents' room and by becoming upset when his parents go out at night, leaving him with a sitter. This may be a long-term disability or one that came about because of a crisis in the family, such as illness or divorce.

A child who has social phobia is one who is pathologically self-conscious and therefore super-shy. Her school phobia is another aspect of her discomfort around people whom she doesn't know well. Unlike a child who suffers occasional shyness, this child doesn't warm up to others eventually.

Occasionally, unaddressed school fears based on real problems grow into phobias. If, for instance, a kindergartner regularly was picked on while on the school bus and no adult—you, his teacher, or the bus driver—helped resolve the issue, his fears would mount and soon overwhelm him.

**Handling school phobia** If your child is truly phobic about going to school, you can best help your child by being sympathetic, but firm. Don't keep him out of class, but listen carefully, find the reason, and address the underlying problem. Professional help may be called for.

A therapist can help a child let go of his inappropriate sense of responsibility for matters outside his control, such as family problems. A therapist can work with a severely shy child to help her develop the social skills she needs to get along in the world. With kindness and understanding, a phobic child is likely to get over a school phobia even if he remains uncomfortable with school.

# School bus safety

If your child is transported to and from school by bus, teach him to follow these guidelines:

- **Stay out of the "danger zone,"** any area close to the bus from which the driver cannot see a child directly or reflected in the rearview mirror. A bus driver can't see objects that are closer than ten feet from the bus. Stay out of that zone—that includes not going back to pick up a dropped item after they leave the bus.
- **Wait until the bus has stopped and the safety lights are flashing before crossing the street to get on a bus.** You should always accompany your child to the bus stop. Have your child look to the left and right before crossing the street. For extra protection cross the street only after the bus driver signals.
- **Practice good behavior on the bus.** Children shouldn't be allowed to scream and yell or jump around on the bus. It's difficult for the driver to hear traffic and sirens if the noise inside the bus is too loud, and distractions can be dangerous.
- **Keep arms, heads, and legs inside the bus at all times.**

### School bus fears

*"My 5-year-old is afraid to take the school bus to school. He's fine at the school as long as I drive him there. How can I encourage him to enjoy the ride?"*

There are two factors that make a school bus ride more enjoyable: familiarity with buses and a buddy. If your child is not used to riding in a bus, give him a chance to see what it's like. Find out if you and your child can climb aboard some time when the bus is not in service; if not, take him for a ride on a city bus. This will let him see how much fun it is to sit up high on a bus. Then find your son a traveling friend. Find out who else rides his bus and invite this little person over for an afternoon of play. Then when your son boards the bus, he will have a familiar face to sit with.

# CHAPTER 5

# Multiples

Multiple births, not long ago an oddity, have been dramatically increasing in the last decade. One reason is that many women are delaying childbirth, and older women tend to release more eggs at ovulation. Additionally, more couples are turning to fertility treatments to increase their chances of getting pregnant—and multiples are the result in numerous cases. The rate of twin births has doubled in the last ten years, from one in every 80 to 90 births to one in every 40 to 45. The rise of triplets has been even more astonishing—one in 1,300 births today, up from 1 in 6,400 in the 1980s. As the parents of multiples, you are assuredly not alone.

## Getting in gear

As a parent of multiples, you'll need additional reserves of just about everything—from baby equipment to patience and creativity. Your home may suddenly be bursting from an abundance of cribs, strollers, and other infant paraphernalia. Before becoming completely overwhelmed, stop to consider how much you really need. Some items can be shared for now. Some are really unnecessary, especially weighed against your need for space and realistic budgetary restrictions. As much as possible, limit the gear.

For the first three or four months, two babies can share a crib. Since you won't be changing two babies at a time, get just one changing table. Invest only in what you really need to have in multiples—car seats, strollers, and bedding. Items don't have to match, so high chairs and other equipment can be gotten at yard sales or through local penny-saver newspapers, provided that they meet current safety standards. Use the money you save to invest in time and energy savers for you—hiring baby-sitters and housekeepers or getting a large-capacity washer and dryer, for example.

Look over catalogs and other printed materials aimed at parents of twins and other multiples for equipment designed especially for your and their needs rather than trying to make do by adapting single-baby items. When purchasing clothing, stick to easy-to-dress and easy-care designs, avoiding anything that needs ironing.

## Taking care of yourself

From the start, the primary caregiving parent is outnumbered. Even when both parents of multiples are on call, there's little room for switching off and trading baby-care duties. Nevertheless, in the early months particularly, it's vital that parents, individually and as a team, carve out some time for themselves to renew their energies and to maintain their own equilibrium.

Fortunately, the world is excited about multiple births so you are probably receiving many offers of help from friends and extended family. Say yes at all times. Those who aren't familiar with baby-care can run errands, prepare a few meals, or straighten the house. Hiring a high school–age "mother's helper" for a few hours a day gives you yet another set of hands. Keep an updated list of what needs to be done so you're ready on a moment's notice to suggest ways in which anyone who offers can be of service. Use some time when others are there to get away from the house for brief periods. A cup of coffee out, by yourself or with your spouse, will do wonders for your spirits when you return home. However busy you are as a parent, you need to be in touch with your own needs as well.

Taking good care of your own health is of paramount importance for all new mothers, but for mothers of multiples, it is critical—and easier to let slip. When you are so busy caring for the babies, you may be tempted to forget regular meals. Getting enough sleep is almost a dream, as is making sure you have some exercise each day. But your health must be a priority. It is virtually impossible to meet the numerous responsibilities you now have if you aren't strong and reasonably rested.

### Cutting Down on Clothing Concerns

I have four children under the age of three—a 2½ year old and 1-year-old triplets—all girls. To keep myself from going crazy with keeping laundry straight, I buy only things that can be mixed and matched. One size of white tube socks fits them all, saving me from having to match pairs. All their bottoms—pants, shorts, and skirts—are denim, brown, or red. All of their tops are solid yellow, blue, red, white, or stripes or patterns that go with any of the bottoms. The only things that are truly individual are their jackets and shoes and, for me, that's enough right now.

**Working out your schedule** Unlike parents of singles who can work their schedules around their baby's schedule, you'll have to help your children develop a somewhat predictable schedule a bit earlier. For instance, when one awakens, wake the other and attend to their feeding and changing needs one right after the other or in tandem. Breast-feeding is possible with multiple babies, although it's obviously more of a challenge. You can feed two babies at the same time using the football hold. You'll need cushions and some help finding the position that works best for you and your babies. If you're bottle-feeding your infants, try feeding them on a quilt on the floor, where you can handle bottles and snuggle close, without any fear of a child falling. Give each one a turn at being enveloped in your arms during meal time, while you stay close to the other(s).

Cut back on other routines. When your infants are newborns, bathe each on alternate days. When they're older, bathe them together. Help them learn some aspects of self-care at an early age. Even a 2-year-old can dress herself as long as you're in the habit of providing easy-on and easy-off clothing and you resolve not to worry about items being on backwards.

Spend time now childproofing your home. Cut back on excess clutter to reduce your housekeeping chores. Create a safe enclosed space where your kids can play freely and you can keep an eye on them without worrying about one wandering off. Establish ownership of each item of clothing, each toy, and private places for each child early to keep sibling battles to a minimum.

*For more information on childproofing, see **pages 762–823**.*

## Helping develop individuality

Gone are the days when multiples were given matching names and matching everything else. The change has been a good one for children who are born part of a team. Wisely, parents of multiples are concerned with seeing that each of their children develops his or her own identity, separate from his or her womb-mates. To help your children develop a healthy sense of self:

• **Avoid referring to them as "the twins" or "the quads,"** and remind others to refer to them by name, not by the condition of their birth.

• **Give them opportunities for privacy.** While not all siblings can have their own rooms, it's especially important for multiples to have the opportunity to be alone now and again.

- **Don't always insist that they be together.** While multiple children can offer each other hours of companionship and can entertain one another, they should not be each other's only playmates. Each needs the opportunity to develop separate friendships outside the family.
- **Plan one-on-one time with each child.** When you're running errands, take one child with you while your spouse takes another. If a grandparent can take one child for an overnight stay, take advantage of the opportunity for that child to have an individual adventure while the child or children at home can enjoy having more of you to attend to them.
- **Make a special point of soliciting each child's opinions and thoughts.** While you don't want to get into the habit of running a short-order restaurant, don't insist that each child eat the exact same meal at each sitting. Keep it simple by offering reasonable choices: "Would you like vanilla yogurt or cherry? Do you want your sandwich cut in triangles or rectangles? Do you want red sauce or cheese on your noodles?"

> **"IT WORKED FOR ME"**
>
> ### Helping an Older Sibling Be a Helper
>
> When my twins, a girl and a boy, were born, my older son was 4 and used to being an only child. I explained to him from the beginning that he would have to help out; he could see even at his young age that I really needed him to pitch in, and I think that boosted his sense of pride. I also took time each afternoon as the babies napped, to sit with him alone. Sometimes we read, sometimes we just talked, but I made sure that he knew he had my complete attention.

## Respecting different personalities

*"One of my twin girls is a particularly strong personality. Although they're only 3, she is overwhelming her sister. How should I handle this?"*

The best approach is to think of your girls not as twins, but as siblings and to treat the situation accordingly. If you feel strongly that you need to ease the dominance of one child over the other, give the girls more time apart and encourage separate activities—even if it is just across the floor from each other with their own books. Teach the more timid one to use her words to express her feelings. Likewise, teach your more dominant child to listen to her sister's opinions.

Don't be surprised, however, if you see more than one flip-flop in personalities as your girls grow. Some children who are aggressive as toddlers become more withdrawn as they enter school, and vice versa. Should this not happen with your daughters, your more retiring daughter will probably learn in time, through interaction with her sister, to stand up for herself effectively.

**IDing identicals**

*"Since my two beautiful twin boys are identical, what can I do to help others tell them apart?*

Your sons will no doubt have to endure many people asking them, "Which one are you?" but you can ease that problem from the start. Dress them differently, and not just in the same outfits of different colors. Consider displaying their initials prominently on each child's clothing. (For safety reasons, don't have their names visible.) Those who know the boys' names will then easily know, for instance, that D on a jacket means David and J means Jake. If each has a favorite color, dress each one according to that preference — at least until he gets tired of it. Also help your boys see the humor in the situation so that neither one develops any sense that there's something wrong with having people mix them up.

Although separate identities are important for your boys to achieve, remember that there is also joy in being a twin. Take pleasure in the special relationship and closeness that comes easily to twins, especially identical ones such as your boys.

# The bonds between multiples

Observors have long noted that children from a multiple birth, especially those who are identical rather than fraternal, have a particular bond with one another. In some cases, they even develop a language of their own. While there is undoubtedly great comfort in such closeness, it carries with it as well, the potential for closing out the rest of the world. To help your children develop their own unique characteristics, be sure that they have ample opportunity to develop relationships with other kids, apart from one another. You can do this by having your children go to separate play groups, at least part of the time. Another way to assure more independent development is to have each child spend time alone with one parent or the other, rather than always being part of a group experience.

**Placing triplets in school**

*"Our school has two kindergarten classes. Is it better to put one of our triplets into a separate class or keep them all together?"*

In general, children who are twins or triplets develop their unique personalities more fully by having separate school experiences. Your school situation, however, calls for careful evaluation. The danger is that the triplet singled out to be in the class alone will see it as some kind of punishment, or will be upset to be the only sibling isolated from the other two. If one of your children seems to enjoy being more independent and would thrive in a separate environment, by all means place this one in the other class. If, as is more often the case, the three children are equally close, it is better to save separate experiences for another year or for other activities outside of school.

**PARENTS RESOURCES**

*For Parents of Multiples*

**The National Organization of Mothers of Twins Clubs:** information on products, facts, and research about multiples, and local chapters.
P.O. Box 438
Thompson Station, TN 37179-0438
(615) 595-0936
(877) 540-2200
www.nomotc.com

**The Triplet Connection:** a resource packet and newsletter for parents of triplets or more.
P.O. Box 99571
Stockton, CA 95209
(209) 474-0885
www.tripletconnection.org

**Twin Services:** a counseling and referral phone service.
P.O. Box 10066
Berkeley, CA 94709
(510) 524-0863
www.parentsoup.com/library/organizations/bpdp020.html

**Mothers of Supertwins [MOST]:** prenatal and postnatal information and support for families with triplets or more.
P.O. Box 951
Brentwood, NY 11717-0627
(631) 859-1110
www.mostonline.org

# CHAPTER 6

# Raising Siblings

Adjusting to life as a sibling is never without stress for a young child who has to learn to share his parents with a squirming, screaming stranger. Instead of the happy event that the birth of a second child signals to the parents, a first-born can be downright traumatized by the arrival of a sibling. Many child-development experts have described the impact of a new baby on the first-born as akin to how you would feel if your spouse suddenly announced that he likes being a husband so much that he's decided to bring in a new wife to add to your happy family. Your child may well wonder why you're choosing to "replace" him with another child.

You can ease the transition by letting your child know what life with a baby is like and by assuring him of his own special place in the family.

## Spacing your children

It is generally believed that the spacing of children has an important impact on well-being, personality, and development. But despite many studies and ongoing research, there is very little agreement about what kind of spacing is best. Should children be close in age so they make good playmates? Should children be far apart in age so they each get a chance to be the family baby? What spacing will maximize mutual respect and companionship between the kids and minimize battles over who has more chocolate chips in her cookie?

While not every family can plan the spacing of siblings precisely, there are pros and cons to different types of spacing.

# One to two years apart

**Potential problems** Having a closely spaced sibling can be tough on both kids. The younger child often feels the stress of competing in an arena in which she is not yet developmentally capable. The older child may feel hampered by a younger sibling's lack of skill. (As time goes on, of course, the younger child may prove to be more adept at certain things than his older sibling.

The assumption that parents are likely to make—that the children should be playmates—may simply not work to the advantage of either child at various points in their development. In addition to the disparate skill levels, they may not be temperamentally well-suited, and may have widely different interests and talents. If they were further apart in age, there would not be the expectation that they should spend a lot of time interacting, but close-in-age siblings have more difficulty getting away from one another. Having similar, but certainly not identical, needs and interests, makes sibling battles more likely. Many child-development experts agree that the closer the age of the siblings, the greater the rivalry. Since it's harder for parents to give each child enough individual attention when they're both still babies. The children naturally compete for parental love and care.

Closely spaced siblings can make life more challenging for parents as well. Having two babies in diapers who both demand (and need) your individual attention and supervision is exhausting. It can also be more costly than further-apart siblings who would be able to use hand-me-down equipment, such as cribs and high chairs. On the other hand, costs can be lowered by having one baby-sitter to watch both children while you work, instead of paying for childcare consecutively.

Two closely spaced babies is also hard on your body and on your emotions, as you care for an infant during pregancy and then for a newborn during the high-needs period of your first child's toddlerhood. You will also have two babies to raise — but each at a different developmental stage with different needs, a challenge that can undermine your best efforts at being a good parent.

## Children and Your Career

Spacing siblings close together may also be best for two-career couples. Having your children closely spaced allows you to get over the more difficult and tiring years of juggling infancy and job demands. Or, you may want to stay at home during your children's infancy and return when they're a bit older. Spacing children close together allows you to do this more easily, with only one break in your career.

**Possible plusses** Having a closely spaced sibling can be a good ego-boost for the older brother or sister, who will, quite naturally, be more adept at most things than the younger one is. Research has found that when the new baby arrives during the sibling's second year he accepts the new baby as just a regular part of life and can't remember a time when he received his parent's undivided attention. This can reduce the psychological and emotional trauma often associated with adjusting to a new family member.

Many parents have found that closely spaced siblings, especially same-sex siblings, do indeed become best friends, drawn together by common interests. As they grow, they may always have a ready playmate, a helper, a confident, and an ally.

## Two to five years apart

**Potential problems** Once an older child's babyhood has passed, it can be physically and emotionally difficult to start all over again. Once you've put away the diapers, high chair, playpen, stroller, infant seat, bottles, and so on, it can be hard to take them all back out. You've just returned to "grown-up" restaurants; you're remembering how nice it is to do things spontaneously without packing up all the infant paraphernalia; you're even sleeping through the night now. A new infant will change all of that—again.

From the older (previously "only") child's perspective, getting a sibling when he's 3 or older makes him acutely aware of the shift in your focus. This child has been the king of the hill for a long time and will not want to give up the crown without a battle. Your older child who was previously quite independent, had a pleasant personality, and was fully toilet taught may suddenly become whiny, clinging, and disruptive and may revert to wetting and soiling. Also, now, instead of fighting over who gets to play with the one truck in the room, the older one will constantly cry "foul" when the younger one goes anywhere near his toys. He wants a definitive split that separates his things, his room, his toys, his everything, from baby things. Don't expect that an older child will fully understand your need to spend more time with the baby. There will be cries for attention and of resentment over having to share you.

Keep in mind that children spaced further apart have different interests and schedules. You will be shuttling the older one to school, friends, and activities, while the younger one is still far more dependent on you for entertainment and attention. As they get older, your children will each have different friends and activities that will pull them—and you—in different directions. Because there's little chance they'll be on the same sports team or in the same ballet class, you'll sometimes have to choose which events to attend and the rivalry that demands you attend each one's activities at the same time will intensify.

For career reasons, some families find it less convenient to space children far apart. Whether parents are waiting for children to be out of babyhood before returning to work or trying to work around infant-care arrangements and childhood illnesses, they find it best to get this stage of parenting behind them. Certainly, having babies spaced closely together is more hectic on workday mornings, but when the children are older, more independent, and settled in school, life gets easier.

**Possible plusses** This range is usually physically and emotionally easier on you and the babies. Your body belongs to you for a while between the two children. The first baby can have all of you until you have steered him through toddlerhood and he can be launched into at least the beginnings of preschool friendships and adventures before needing to share you. Then the new baby has opportunities for your undivided attention as well.

The older sibling is young enough to bond with the baby, but old enough to enjoy spending some time away from you. Juggling an older child's needs with the baby's is far less grueling. The older child is potty taught, can talk about what she is feeling, and can play by herself occasionally. This makes it easier to have a new baby in the house.

# More than five years

**Potential problems** You may have forgotten much of the exhaustion that comes from babyhood and feel like a new parent all over again. Your children will be following very different social calendars and are not likely, during their early childhood years, to have much in common. (Of course, even twins can have widely different temperaments.) Your older child may resent your shift in focus and your younger child may resent his or her older sibling's unwillingness to invite him along for play. Your older child won't be as helpful as you might believe he or she will be.

**Possible plusses** Unlike a closer-in-age sibling, your older child can share in your delight at the antics of the new baby and is much less likely to feel any jealousy. The older sibling may indeed be a help, entertaining the baby for brief periods of time. (Be cautious, however, about giving your older child too much responsibility; the older child needs to be treated as a child, too, not as a surrogate parent.) Both children will likely gain from the devotion that the younger one shows to the elder, enhancing the older child's self-esteem and giving the younger one a big, but not grown-up, ally.

## What birth order means

Over the years, there have been many studies that measure the effects of birth order on children. The results, unfortunately, often muddy rather than clarify the issue. One study says first borns are more popular with peers; another says they are less popular. One study says second borns have low anxiety levels; another says they have high anxiety levels. It's impossible to make an accurate prediction of personality, or abilities, or future accomplishments based on birth order alone.

There are some studies, however, that come to common conclusions that are fun to look at and consider. The following information has been gathered to present some of these findings. None of it is absolute and you should remember that your family dynamics play a larger role in your children's development than the order in which they were born.

### Families Are Unique

Because every family and every child is unique, there is no one right prescription for family planning. Whether your child is 1 or 5 or somewhere older or in-between when the new baby is born, she may not like it—but she'll learn to cope. If you give your children love, respect, and attention, each one will grow up feeling positive about themselves and close to their siblings—whatever the age difference.

**First borns** Regardless of sex, the first born is viewed as the most favored birth position. The first-born position is associated with leadership, independence, and intelligence. Perhaps this is because first-born babies often receive more of the parent's attention and concern. This parental doting might explain why there is a high correlation between being a first born and having higher intelligence and achieving higher professional status than later-born siblings, including the fact that most U.S. presidents were first borns. A recent study out of James Madison University in Virginia lends support to this belief with its findings that first-born undergraduate college students had a significantly higher GPA than later borns. Researchers have noticed that as young as three months of age, first borns are more attentive to their surroundings than latter borns. They are also more oriented toward adults because they are their primary social contacts for at least the first year of life. Even after a second child is born, the first born still patterns her behavior after the parents.

**Latter borns** Latter-born babies seem to prefer watching and mimicking their siblings over their parents. This difference in who they model affects the babies' behavior. Latter borns seem to laugh and giggle more often because their siblings are sillier and more spontaneous with their laughter than their parents. Perhaps because older siblings are there to entertain and respond to their little brother or sister, second-born children receive far less of what's called contingency attention from their parents. This means that although parents give a later-born child plenty of stimulation and attention through bathing, feeding, and general caring, they don't frequently respond to the child's individual behaviors, such as reacting to the baby's facial expressions or new skill with the same intensity they did to their first borns.

It's often said that middle children feel less loved and more lonely. Perhaps this happens because the second child of three often gets squeezed in the middle between the adulation of the first born and the babying of the last born. On the other hand, the middle children of four don't seem to suffer this isolation; the middle two tend to comfort each other and supply the needed attention and love.

The middle birth position is associated with sociability, thoughtfulness, and being insecure and rebellious. The middle birth position is the only position that does not include "spoiled" in its profile.

Being born at the end of the pack seems to have its own advantages. Third borns and latter children tend to receive plenty of stimulation and contingency attention. This may be because parents have learned to relax and enjoy their children. They are no longer worrying over every sniffle and have given up the goal of being perfect parents. They now spend more time laughing, snuggling, and enjoying.

The youngest birth position, like the middle position, is associated with sociableness and thoughtfulness. It is also associated with dependence, irresponsibility, immaturity, and passivity.

An interesting comparison of the ways birth order may affect the problem-solving preferences of children was discovered in a study of scientists who have made outstanding discoveries in their fields. The results revealed that first borns tended to work diligently toward furthering on going studies while latter borns tended to leave the beaten path and find new ways to approach the problem. The important point is that birth order did not exclude anyone from being an accomplished scientist. Although the scientists approached their work from different directions based on their placement in the family, both first-born and latter-born children were contributing to their society and the advancement of knowledge.

## Telling your first-born

If your first-born is older than a toddler, your first decision will be when to tell her that you're expecting. To a young child—under the age of 5 or so—nine months is an inconceivably long period of time to wait for the new arrival. If possible, hold off your announcement at least until the pregnancy becomes noticeable. (This also guards against the possibility of having to explain a miscarriage, which is more likely to happen within the first three months.) On the other hand, your child should hear about the upcoming arrival directly from you. If you intend to tell many people about the pregnancy and talk about it in front of your child, then share the news early on. An aura of secretiveness will only serve to make your older child anxious.

When you're ready to make the announcement, keep it simple. In a pleasant voice, tell your child, "We're going to have a new baby in the family." Don't expect excited congratulations. To some children, this news is about as exciting as hearing that there will be a new supermarket opening down the street next week; it's simply not of great interest. It will take many conversations before your child truly comprehends what's happening.

## Preparing your older child for changes

If there will be changes, let your older child know about them before the baby arrives. Explain, for instance, that she will be sharing her room with the baby. If you will be making major changes such as moving your older child out of her crib, enrolling her in a nursery school, or moving to a larger home, do it at least three months before the due date, if possible, so the change isn't closely connected to the baby's arrival.

As the due date nears, help your child prepare emotionally by letting her know what to expect. Arrange a tour of the hospital where you'll give birth, showing her, if possible, the newborn nursery. Knowing where you'll be when you're away can be very comforting. Prepare for her care with someone she knows well during the period when you and your spouse are at the hospital.

The time surrounding your second child's birth is a perfect time to recount your first-born's arrival. Enjoy looking at pictures of your older child together, retelling the wonderful story of her birth and homecoming. Let your older child choose some of her newborn clothing and toys that you have saved to give to her new sibling. Have her join you on shopping expeditions to pick out some newborn necessities. Help her draw "welcome home" pictures for her new brother or sister. Get her a special doll or doll-care toy so that she can mimic your baby care routine. Help your older child practice gentle behaviors toward a doll or other newborn stand-in, such as a teddy bear, but don't be overly concerned if your toddler-age child is inconsistent about treating this stand-in with great care. Tossing this doll out of her bed does not indicate that your older child has any deep-seated resentment toward the soon-to-be sibling. It simply means that she can't remember from moment to moment that babies need special care or that this doll or bear represents a real, live baby. So don't admonish your older child for failing to have perfect baby-care instincts. She's not supposed to, but, with your help, she'll learn soon enough.

## What Will This Mean for Me!

Remember that young children judge everything from a purely selfish perspective. The number one concern is most likely "Will Mommy and Daddy love me less?" Your best response is to reassure your child by telling her how important she is in the family and to you. Your child also worries about how a new baby will affect her daily schedule. Make it clear that when the baby arrives, you'll still be her parent and that many things will continue just as they always have.

## Introducing new siblings

When the day arrives to bring your new baby home, you may feel a conflict about who to make a fuss over—the new sibling or your first-born. This is, after all, the moment that sharing you begins. If possible, arrange for another adult to hold your newborn as you give your older child some much-needed one-on-one time with you. If your older child seems interested in the new baby, help him have a closer look, letting him compare his own "big" size with the smallness of the newcomer. Again, take the opportunity to recall your older child's homecoming. Don't be surprised, however, if your first born doesn't seem all that interested in his new brother or sister. He may be no more interested in this new addition to your home than he would be in a new dining-room table. Especially if the newborn is sleeping at introduction time, he may not be all that appealing to the big kid. Consider presenting your older child with another gift along with his sibling—such as a new tricycle or a baby doll of his own.

It's important that you not insist that the big brother or sister instantly "bond" with the new baby. If the older child shows little interest for now, let him get involved in other things. Be careful, too, not to launch into a list of rules regarding the new arrival, such as insisting that the older child remain quiet or stay far from the baby. While you certainly need to protect the new baby from overly enthusiatic or curious jabs by his older sibling, you want to avoid giving your older child the message that this baby has more rights and is more important to you than he is.

Rather than cramming the introductions into a short space of time, be content with the knowledge that over the next few days and weeks, your older child will come to know his sibling and to get used to his presence.

**When a child has strong feelings about the upcoming birth**
*"My 5-year-old daughter insists she wants a sister. We do not know the sex of our soon-to-be born second child, but we're worried about how our daughter will react to a brother."*

Five-year-olds have just begun to align themselves strongly with others of their own gender, so it's not surprising that your child wants a sibling of the same sex. This stongly stated preference in no way signals the future relationship of your children.

In talking about the new sibling, be matter of fact, stating that some babies are boys and some are girls. Let her know that you accept the fact that she has a preference and that it's okay to want a sister more than a brother. Help her think of some advantages to having both a sister and a brother, and help her dispel any stereotypes she may have. For instance, let her know that a brother will be just as likely to look up to her as a sister would and will be equally in need of her advice and help. If she thinks boys are not as much fun as girls, help her think of friendships she enjoys with boys. But don't get too involved in trying to convince her that she will be thrilled to have a brother. She may not be at first.

### Handling regression

*"My 4-year-old has been acting like a baby since her brother was born. What should I do?"*

Your daughter's behavior is not at all unusual; many children revert to babyish behaviors after the birth of a sibling. Your daughter has noticed that her brother gets lots of attention because he is so helpless. Simple logic tells her that she will get more attention if she also acts "babyish." Generally, the best thing to do is to tolerate her behavior without comment. You might calmly note, "I've noticed you're doing some babyish things lately, but I'm sure it won't be long before you're feeling like a big girl again." If you can avoid scolding or arguing when regressive behavior appears, you'll find that this stage will subside on its own. You can speed the process by giving your child extra doses of love and attention when she is acting like a "big" 4-year-old.

*For more information about regression, see **page 247**.*

# What siblings gain

The sibling relationship is unique to all others. Sharing the same home and the same parents, brothers and sisters observe one another to learn about their family's rules and rituals, what kind of behavior earns praise, and what warrants a time-out or other consequence for negative behavior. They also teach one another a variety of skills—from talking to block stacking to negotiating for your time and attention. Many of these are things they can't learn from their peers, who don't have the same family, or from their parents, who have an adult perspective.

Siblings also look to each other for life's lessons because they identify with each other in size and age. When a baby is listening to speech and learning to talk, it's easier to learn from someone who uses simple words and sentences. It's also helpful to learn from someone who matches your level of energy and patience. Siblings often don't mind playing the same game over and over or jumping off the same large rock a thousand times. The energy and repetition required for learning is a natural part of children's play.

Sometimes sibling lessons are deliberate, sometimes they're not. Many older brothers and sisters make a conscious effort to teach their baby siblings how to talk or walk. They spend important one-on-one time with them and are very quick to give the kind of enthusiastic involvement that encourages learning. Other times the lessons are not so obvious. Babies are avid learners who watch and listen carefully. They imitate facial expressions, moods, actions, and sounds. They laugh when their older siblings laugh; they cry when they cry. The younger sibling also uses a brother or sister to learn how to be independent from you. With the older sibling in the lead, the baby is more willing to venture away from her parents. She will use her siblings as a secure base so she can explore the rest of the world without feeling completely alone. The young sibling also benefits from trying to keep up with the older kids. Toddlers with sisters or brothers usually mature earlier and learn skills at earlier ages than the first born. They feel more comfortable taking risks because they see their sibling do it and want to keep up.

The older siblings, too, learn a lot about themselves from the younger ones. Because the young child looks up to big sister or brother, older siblings receive daily doses of esteem-building admiration. They feel proud of themselves when they accomplish things that younger siblings aren't yet able to. They also feel important when they are given some responsibility for interacting with the baby.

Whether it's teaching a younger sibling how to use the potty or learning together how to share, the time siblings spend together sets the stage for a very valuable give-and-take, teach-and-learn relationship that will mark children's sociability throughout their lives.

# Playing favorites

"You love him more than you love me!" This cry has been chanted throughout the ages. All children are sure that you gave their sibling the cookie with more chips in it because you favor that child. Because your children are on guarded watch for any inequity of affection, you may decide to handle the problem by diligently trying to treat each of them exactly the same.

Unfortunately, not only is this impossible, but it will tend to aggravate problems with sibling rivalry. Even if you were able to distribute all things equally, your children will find other ways to judge their position in your heart. They will complain that you kissed the baby goodnight first; they'll complain that you kissed the baby goodnight last. There's no winning the favoritism war through equity.

Instead of trying to do the same things for all your children, focus on each one individually and find ways to let each one know that you understand their strengths and weaknesses and admire them for who they are as a person. Respond to them according to their different ages, personalities, abilities, and moods. When your 4-year-old complains that you always carry the baby around, but you never carry him, explain, "I love you both very much. The baby needs me to hold her and feed her and change her. You need me to read you stories and tuck you in at night. But I do want to spend more time with you. As soon as I put the baby down for a nap, let's play a game together."

You can also give each child special attention by arranging guaranteed one-on-one time with each child. Each week, schedule on your calendar an appointment with each child when the two of you can be alone (even if it's only in her bedroom). Promise your undivided attention for a realistic time, perhaps even setting a timer for 15 minutes and when the bell rings, turning your attention to your older child. Let your child choose what to do during that time. She might want to talk, or read, or play a game. It doesn't matter what you do as long as the time together is uninterrupted. This approach guarantees each child all of your attention at some point each week, and it gives you a chance to keep up on what's important in their lives.

Also, be careful not to feed accusations of favoritism by comparing siblings. When one child is running around recklessly and the other is sitting quietly with a coloring book, it's tempting to ask the speedster, "Why can't you be more like your brother?" But this feeds the flames of perceived favoritism. Instead, always address your child's positive and negative behaviors as they relate to her, no one else.

As much as you try to value each child individually, the truth is, many parents do favor one child over the others. Variables such as age, gender, temperament, and birth order all influence the way you feel about your children at different stages in their development. These feelings are natural. Sometimes you can't help but relate better to one child than to another. But try to separate what you feel

### Reducing Daily Squabbles

I have found I can cut down on daily squabbles with a penny and a kitchen timer. When my 2-year-old twins start fighting over who gets to play with a certain toy I flip the penny to see who gets to play with it first. They love the game of calling heads or tails, and then I set the timer for five minutes. When the timer rings, the twin who's playing with the toy knows it's time to give it to her sister.

from how you treat your children. Make sure you notice and express appreciation for all your children's unique qualities and talents. And remember that your personal feelings of favoritism will ebb and flow as your children grow and change. The adorable toddler becomes the demanding 4-year-old; the hard-to-please preschooler blossoms into the confident first grader. The child who grates on your nerves today will be a real pleasure tomorrow.

It's unrealistic to expect that there will be no favoritism in any family at any time, but your goal should be to avoid making it obvious by treating all your children as valued individuals. This sends the message that it is possible to be fair without trying to make everything equal.

### Sharing among siblings

*"How can I help my 5-year-old share his toys with his 2-year-old sister? He gets so upset whenever she touches anything of his."*

Your 5-year-old's reaction is very reasonable, especially considering the harm that 2-year-olds can do to toys. Make every effort to protect your son's belongings from his sister, giving him sealable plastic boxes to store his toys and helping him find a safe, out-of-the way place for other prized possessions. Keeping the younger child away from her big brother's toys is also safer since many of the toys your son plays with are dangerous to a toddler.

To help your son learn to share with his sister in a meaningful, nonthreatening way, suggest that he periodically look through his outgrown toys for things that might be of interest to his sister.

### Bathing siblings together

*"I have a 2-year-old daughter and a 4-year-old son. At what point should they stop taking baths together?"*

There's no doubt that bathing siblings together can be easier for you and more fun for your children. When bathing children of the opposite sex together, let their own behavior and feelings determine your practice of shared baths for now. If either child appears to be uncomfortable — excessively curious or extremely modest — it's time to discontinue the practice. In any case, it's a good idea to begin giving them separate baths once the older child has reached age 5 or so. The same rules apply to bathing same-sex sibs. If either child expresses discomfort with the routine, it's time to change it.

# Handling sibling wars

Sibling wars can be considered a problem-solving classroom. There's so much your children learn when they disagree with each other: how to negotiate, how to argue, how to be assertive, how to test their limits, how to compromise, how to handle anger, how to use words to reason, how to empathize, how to make up. All of these positive skills of conflict resolution are better taught in the heat of battle than at any other time.

Conflict resolution doesn't mean that you as the parent step in to divide and conquer. If you solve your children's arguments, you teach them that problems are solved by adults—they can't do it themselves. All the communication, critical thinking, and decision-making skills that go into problem solving will be practiced by the adult, not the children.

However, leaving sibling wars to your children to solve themselves is easier said than done. First you have to be sure the fighting isn't physical. If it is, this requires immediate intervention and perhaps separation of the dueling warriors. Then you have to have nerves of steel to sit back and listen to the noise. Then you have to have patience. Kids aren't as busy as you are; they have plenty of time to dedicate to making their point.

Once you start to stand back, you find that what seemed like major battles are really little skirmishes that are settled quite quickly—usually within five minutes. But if they are not, then it's time to help your children learn how to resolve their conflicts.

## Problem solving for children under age 3

Young children often don't have the impulse control or the vocabulary to settle their disputes peacefully by themselves. That's why their squabbles quickly erode into physical battering. When this happens, they need you to help them learn the rules of problem solving.

## *Mediation Don'ts*

Don't use your physical strength to break up a fight. It doesn't make sense to yank your child's arm or to spank him to teach the lesson, "You can't hit your sister." If you must intervene, be calm and firm, using words and reason. And don't overreact. Toddlers' battles are usually swift and quickly forgotten. If they drag on, you can generally diffuse the tension simply by distracting your children; offer some juice or a new game and the war is over.

• **Set limits and stick to them consistently.** No hitting, no biting, no grabbing or pushing. Make sure your children know you won't tolerate anyone breaking these rules and explain in advance that there will be a penalty if they do (either a time-out, or the loss of a privilege, or the removal of the object of contention).

• **Teach your children what compromise means.** Suggest ways they can both have what they want. If they both want to play with the same toy, for example, suggest that they use a timer to give each one ten minutes to play. When the timer rings, it's the other child's turn.

• **Help your child give words to his feelings and a reason for them.** Ask, "Do you feel angry because Mara took your toy?" Show your child that he is more likely to get what he wants if he uses words instead of fists. Encourage him to ask nicely for what he wants.

## Problem solving for 3- to 5-year-olds

Three- to five-year-olds are mature enough to verbalize their complaints and solve their problems with some critical thinking skills. The next time they come to you with their problem, explain that you are going to help them find their own solutions. (This should catch their attention because solving problems is usually a highly coveted adult job; you are offering them a lot of power.) Then set down the ground rules: During problem solving, there is no interrupting, yelling, put-downs, or hitting. Then offer this three-part plan:

• **Each child tells his side of the argument** (not to you, to the other child). The other child restates what he just heard the first child say and vice versa. Because they are probably in the habit of bringing their complaints to you, it will take some prompting to get your kids to talk to each other. This is an important step because the goal is to teach them how to solve their problems without your interference. This first step also helps them learn to see a problem from another point of view and to listen to the other's complaint without interrupting. (Let your children speak for themselves unless you see the younger one struggling to find the right words.)

- **The children brainstorm for a solution.** The rules of brainstorming are easy for kids to understand: anything goes and no criticizing. Push your kids to come up with lots and lots of solutions to their problem. You'll find them hesitant at first because kids tend to think there's only one right answer to a problem. When you ask for more, they may think their suggestion was "wrong." Validate their responses by saying, "That's one way; now can you think of a different way?" If they run out of ideas too quickly, prompt them by asking, "What can you say to solve this problem?" Or, "What can you do to solve this problem?" The solutions don't have to be ones they'll actually use, or even ones that make much sense. The idea is to get them to think past the first impulsive solution that comes to mind.
- **The children pick a solution that's agreeable to both of them.** Children are more agreeable to trying solutions they think of themselves (even if you've suggested the same one a thousand times in the past!). They're also more likely to try harder to make the solution work. If the chosen answer to the problem falls apart a few minutes later, go back to step one and start again.

If you consistently use this three step problem-solving approach to sibling battles, you'll soon see your children initiate the technique by themselves. Eventually, you'll hear one of them say, "Let's think of a solution we both like." Although the battles will continue in the future, your children will now have what they need to resolve them using critical thinking skills, rather than their fists.

## Preventing sibling wars

While your children are learning how to resolve their conflicts peacefully, you might try the following preventative techniques:

- **Praise positive behavior.** Have you ever noticed that your kids seem to fight more when you're very busy? It's because some sibling fights are mounted just to get your attention. Kids know you'll stop whatever you're doing to referee. You can break this cycle by giving your kids more of your attention when you catch them being good. When you see them playing together nicely, don't tip-toe past for fear of breaking the spell; stop and praise them for being such good friends. Show them continuously that you're more impressed by friendship than by squabbles and that they can get your attention better with good behavior than with bad.

- **Teach problem-solving skills.**
- **Model good problem-solving behavior yourself.** Listen to how you and your spouse or other family members talk to each other when you're angry. The way you "fight" will teach your children more than instructions in conflict resolution ever will. When adults slam doors, bang fists, and scream, or seethe in silence, children feel scared and vulnerable. But later they use this behavior as a model for their own battles. If you don't want your children settling their squabbles with loud or physical shows of anger, don't do it yourself. Instead, why not try the three-step plan for problem solving yourself; you might be surprised how well it works even for adults.

## When a Child Is an Only

It is a common misconception that only children are lonelier than children who have brothers and sisters. Studies show that only kids don't think of themselves as lonely or unhappy.

It's true that only children often miss out on experiences that children from larger families take for granted. This is especially true for only children in single-parent families. If you have an only child, look for opportunities for her to:

• **Make friends who are a few years older or younger.** Preschoolers have a wonderful time trying to keep up with a child in the first or second grade. Only children also benefit from not always being the youngest person around. Playing with a baby or toddler, for example, can help a child feel more confident in skills she's recently mastered.

• **Take part in activities that build teamwork skills.** Pretend games, in which children respond to one another instead of simply sharing space in a sandbox, help preschoolers develop cooperation skills. Sports are a good choice for kids in grade school.

• **Get together with relatives.** Most children sense without much prompting that relationships with cousins, grandparents, aunts, and uncles are somehow special.

# CHAPTER 7

# Single Parents and Stepfamilies

Raising kids in stepfamilies or alone brings special challenges, both emotional and physical. More than most parents, you need to be aware that raising a family is a process, something you accompish over the long haul, as well as a day-to-day experience. Patience is your greatest ally. And, as do all parents, you need to remember that you are not in this alone and that there are many types of support available to you.

## *Single parents*

Raising a child on your own, whether by choice, death, or divorce, can sometimes seem to be a Herculean feat. But you'll discover that you are capable of doing the job and doing it well. You may often find that besides experiencing more loneliness and money worries, you enjoy greater satisfaction and more independence than parents with partners.

As a single parent, the most important word to remember is "attitude." With a positive attitude, you are more likely to look on your task as an adventure, recognize the benefits of being able to make decisions on your own, and find creative ways to manage schedules and finances. If you are to succeed at rather than just survive single parenthood, you also need to resist looking to the past with regret or anger. Instead, look to the future and be realistic about the present instead of reviewing what could or shouldn't have been. And, first of all, besides taking care of your child or children, you also need to take care of yourself mentally, spiritually, and physically.

# Suddenly single

As a suddenly single parent, you may at times feel overwhelmed by the responsibility. If you're divorced or widowed, grief is likely to be part of the picture. However, if you are single because of a divorce you may also welcome an independent home without the dissension and tension that may have characterized your marriage.

Of course, a foremost concern will be supporting yourself and your child. If you are newly divorced or widowed, you may be faced with finding a job if spousal support and/or child support or life insurance is not enough or if you don't receive any financial support. You might also need to consider going back to school to get the training you need for a job. If you are already working, you may need to expand a part-time or even a full-time job. If you were previously used to having two incomes, you will need to adjust to having less. Whatever changes you may need to make to meet your economic needs, they will more than likely affect your time at home. Your child will probably see less of you and will also have to adjust to less money for buying the things she may want.

Combining work responsibilities with home responsibilities is often a source of great stress for single parents. The job doesn't end when the work day ends as you face the duties of a parent when you return home. Although every working parent needs to also find time to do the laundry, the grocery shopping, housework, and help children with homework, the single parent faces these tasks alone. There is also the worry when you are at work about what to do if your child becomes ill at school or daycare, and how you handle a request to stay late at work when you have to pick up your child at a certain time.

In dealing with these stresses and conflicts, the first step is perhaps to list the problems you face or anticipate as a single parent. You might write these problems as statements or as questions. For example, *What do I do if my child becomes sick while I'm at work? Who takes care of my child between the time school ends and I get home from work? When do I do shopping and housework?* Following are some guidelines that may help you solve some of your concerns:

• **Don't feel guilty or apologize for being a single parent.** Children grow strong in the care of at least one loving parent. Quality is not related to the quantity of parents in your home.

• **Ask for help.** Rather than try to do it all yourself, make sure you have help when you need it. Always have a backup plan in place to cover unforeseen situations.

- **Choose your priorities.** Don't worry about things that can wait. If you can't do housework until the weekend, then don't worry about it. If you feel spending time with your child is more important, have soup and sandwiches for dinner instead of taking the time to cook.
- **Be realistic.** Before you exhaust yourself trying to do everything, take stock of what you can realistically do. Learn to say no when you need to.

**Creating workable schedules**  Many single parents discover that their best resource for managing children and a household by themselves is to develop and write down daily and weekly schedules Be sure to include your child in creating the schedule so he feels he has some control over his world. He will also be able to see where you make a commitment to spend time with him.

To construct a schedule, you may want to start with activities that must be done at a specific time. These may include your job and your child's school or childcare. Then list activities that are necessary but can be done at flexible times. These might include housework and shopping. A third category can be activities that you and your child enjoy such as visiting family or friends or going to a local park.

Now you can create a schedule that takes into account the different types of activities. For example, you may want to list what time you need to get up in order to have breakfast and be ready by the time you have to leave for work and get your child to school or daycare. You can then put down what time you can leave work, pick up your child, return home, and make and eat dinner. For the evening, you can schedule time for cuddling and housework. You can then look for the flexible time that is for you and your child to do whatever you wish. For weekends, you can build in time for other weekly chores. As well as flexible time.

You may want to write your schedule on a large sheet of paper in pencil, then post it in the kitchen.

**Taking care of business**  As you establish new routines, you will probably discover that you need to ask your child to take on more responsibility than she previously had. Depending on your child's age, you might ask that

> **TIME FOR YOU**
> ## *Private Time*
>
> While making your schedule, it's important to remember that you should not spend all of your free time with your child. Be sure to build in time for friends and outside interests. Both you and your child need to develop a life and privacy on your own as well as the time you spend as a family.

she be responsible for keeping her room clean, puitting her laundry in the hamper, watering plants, feeding a pet, or putting her toys away. You can also encourage her to make as many of her own decisions as possible. Be careful not to overload your child, however, in an effort to feel less overwhelmed yourself. Sometimes a single parent can become too dependent on a child. Although your child may prove to be more independent than you thought she would be, don't start expecting her to be more responsible and mature than she is capable of. Remember that she is still a child and needs you as a parent, no matter how caring she may become. While being honest about what needs to be done and your concerns, don't turn her into a confidante or an adviser.

**Solo parents and discipline**  It may seem difficult to always be the one to have make the decision about what your child should be doing and how she should behave. If you are divorced, you may find discipline difficult because you feel guilty over everything your child has gone through. And, with all the responsibilities you face as a single parent, you may be just too tired to discipline your child. It's sometimes easier to say *yes*, than have to deal with the resistance or complaints that *no* brings about.

There are many reasons why you may experience discipline problems as a single parent. Your child may misbehave to get your attention because he feels he doesn't have enough time with you.

If problems persist as you and your child try to adjust to a single-parent household, you may feel that you are losing control. If you are divorced, you may want to call on the noncustodial parent for help, if possible. However, don't let your ex-spouse undermine your authority, but enlist his or her support of your position as an authority figure. If you cannot call on your ex-spouse, you might think of an alternative authority you can use for support, such as grandparents or other relatives.

*For more on discipline, see **pages 379–403**.*

It's also important to set realistic rules and consistently stick to them. If a rule is broken, enforce immediate short-term consequences that fit the behavior.

**Resolving disputes with your child**  Not being able to get along with your child for any length of time can cause a great deal of tension and stress in your household. A possible approach to resolving this problem is to step back from the argument and try to identify what the real issues are. You may be dealing with both your own and your child's reactions to a major life change. You may need to talk again with your child and explain that there is no going back to the family life you had before. Ask again for her help in maintaining new routines and doing the jobs that need to be done to keep your household running well.

You might also be experiencing a sense of failure at not being able to give your child everything she would like. Take stock of your expectations and adjust where necessary what you think your child needs to keep her happy. By forming more realistic expectations you can help to reduce your own stress.

**Building a support system** Being a single parent can often be lonely and isolating. If you were once married, you may enjoy no longer having to please or compromise with a full-time partner. But you may suddenly find yourself no longer included in couple activities. If you have never been married or had a partner, you may find it difficult to establish relationships with couples, and you may no longer feel you have much in common with other single friends who don't have children.

An important part of taking care of yourself as a single parent is to make and maintain connections with other people. Other single parents especially can be a great support and comfort for facing and solving many of the unique problems single parents encounter. They can also be a source for new friendships with people you have much in common

**TIME FOR YOU**
## Taking Care of Yourself

As a single parent, you are responsible for the day-to-day welfare of your child. For this reason, your own physical and mental health takes on increased importance. Following are some tips for watching out for yourself:

• Make sure you eat a balanced and nutritious diet and get at least a little exercise every day. Neglect of your physical needs will turn you into a worn-out, unhappy, tense parent.

• To make the transition from work to home less stressful and frantic, build a few minutes for yourself into your coming-home routine. After greeting your child, you might give him a snack and have him watch something on TV while you unwind. If your child is too young to to be left alone, spend a few minutes sitting quietly, holding her, and talking about your days.

• If your child is old enough to handle some of the daily chores, give her a choice of what she wants to do.

• When possible, take some time for yourself by hiring a baby-sitter or asking a relative, friend, or neighbor to watch your child. Even taking a walk or sitting on a park bench reading a book can give you the breather you need.

• Plan fun things to do with your child, even if they are brief. Make sure that many of these activities are things you really want to do, too, and aren't just planned for your child's enjoyment.

• Get involved in activities you like to do. For example, take a course at a local college on something you have always wanted to explore, such as writing, cooking, or dancing.

with. Where do you find other single parents? You may be surprised how many other parents at your child's preschool are single. You can also find them through such organizations as Parents Without Partners. Look for a local chapter in your phone book or in newspaper listings of organization meetings.

Don't give up on your old friends either. You may discover that single friends enjoy spending time with your child, which will also give her a chance to interact with other adults. Very close friends may even become an extended family of adopted "aunts" and "uncles." Married friends who don't feel threatened by your single state can also be a great resource for support. They can provide their own helpful hints and offer stability and reliability. In turn, you can offer them the benefit of new ideas, a less traditional lifestyle, and what you have learned about becoming a resourceful single parent.

## Single parents and dating

As a parent, you may wonder how you should handle dating. If you are divorced, your children will need some time to adjust to their parents' break up before having to face the idea of their parents becoming involved with other people. A new romantic interest in a parent's life will be especially difficult for children who fantasize about their parents getting back together. Try to wait at least six months before you consider dating. Then talk with your child about her feelings and opinions on your meeting and going out with an adult friend. When you do decide to date someone, make sure your child understands the difference between dating, having a relationship, getting engaged, and getting married. Explain that not all friendships result in marriage.

Don't feel that you have to introduce your child to every date you have. In fact, even if your child is curious about someone you are going out with, it's best to reserve an introduction only to someone with whom you are developing a serious relationship. By doing so, you will avoid your child forming an attachment to someone who may only be in her life for a brief time.

Before your date and your child meet, prepare each of them. Talk with your child about why you like this person. Then suggest that you would like to plan a time to meet. Let her be a part of the arrangements. Also tell your friend about your child.

Don't expect your child and your friend to instantly like each other. Just as you needed time to develop a relationship, so will your friend and your child. In fact, it's best to discourage your friend from trying to impress your child or attempting to get too close too quickly.

If your child expresses an instant dislike for your friend, help her sort out her feelings. If she sees that your friend is special to you, she may feel threatened. She may not want to give up the fantasy that you and her other parent will reunite. She might also believe that her importance to you will lessen if there is someone else in your life. She may even worry that this person will take you away from her. She may express these feelings to you privately or directly to your friend.

With your child, gently reiterate that you and your ex-spouse will not be getting back together again. Explain how important this person is to you and perhaps talk about some of the things you think she will like about him or her. Ask her to give your relationship a chance. Then continue to be aware of your child's feelings and always be willing to listen so she feels that the new person in your life has not taken her place.

As your new relationship develops, it's a good idea to inform your ex-spouse, so your child won't feel she has to keep the relationship a secret, or be the one to tell your ex-spouse.

# *Divorced parents*

Children whose parents divorce are the largest segment of children being raised in single-parent families. Being part of a large group, however, doesn't necessarily make life any easier for kids or parents. Divorce most often involves bitterness and anger, which, if fostered by either parent, can do serious harm to a child. On the other hand, children whose parents divorce retain the opportunity to maintain a good relationship with their other parent, and that involvement will serve your children well.

## Helping children through divorce

If you are soon to become a single parent because of divorce, you are likely worried about how your child will be affected along with how you will cope with this great change in your own life. The first thing you need to do is accept that you will probably not be able to function normally, as a person or a parent, for a while. You and your child need time to adjust to a new way of living your lives. But how do you make the transition as easy as possible for your child, while being as kind as possible to yourself? Following are some guidelines that may help.

• **Talk with your child before any actual separation takes place.** Try to plan your talk for the weekend so that there is time for your child to think about what she is told before having to go back to school or daycare. If possible, both you and your spouse should meet with your child. If this isn't possible, take turns. If you have more than one child, talk to each one separately. As simply as possible, explain what is about to happen. For example, you might say that you and your spouse have decided not to live together in the same house anymore. Point out that this makes you sad and acknowledge that you expect your child will be hurt by this news. Be sure to reassure her that your problems are not her fault and that you both still love her. Then allow your child to express her feelings, whether this be in words, tears, or an angry outburst. Try to stay calm, and be prepared for questions. Depending on your child's age, you may be asked why you are getting divorced, who she will be staying with, and if she will be able to see the spouse who is leaving. You might also be questioned about whether you will be moving, if the family will have enough money, if she will go to the same school and have the same friends. Many of these questions will come from her own fears about what will happen to her. Answer them as directly and specifically as possible. Remind your child that your job and her other parent's job is to take care of her and that she will continue to be cherished and cared for.

• **Recognize your child's emotions during the process and afterward.** While the divorce is in process, and likely for a while afterwards, your child is likely to experience a wide range of emotions. Allow her to express these emotions, including anger, fear, disappointment, sadness, a feeling of betrayal, and loneliness. If she acts out her anger, you should let her know that you understand she is angry, but this doesn't mean you will allow her to misbehave. Depending on her age, she may at times blame one or the other parent and possibly herself for the divorce. You should let her know that the divorce was beyond her control. Explain that this is a grown-up decision and that she did not cause it and cannot change it. Don't force conversation between you and your child about the divorce, but be open to the times she may want to talk about it.

• **Try to maintain normal routines.** As much as possible, keep mealtimes and bedtimes the same as usual. Give your child an idea of what each day's plan is so that the immediate future, at least, is predictable. If you have to move right away, try to find a place as near as possible to your old neighborhood or where there are other children nearby. Bring your child's favorite toys and her own bed and other furniture, if possible, to the new place.

• **Be honest about changes.** While trying to keep your child's routines as intact as possible, also be honest about necessary changes. You may need to explain that there won't be as much money to live on as there was before. To be reassuring, you may need to be specific by saying that you won't be able to buy name-brand clothes or go out to eat. Make sure your child understands that you will have a home and that she will have her favorite things, even if you have to move.

• **Don't put overwhelming strain on yourself** by trying too hard to act normal. You may need to tell your child, even if she is young, that you don't feel like yourself. Reassure her that even though you are feeling or acting differently, you can still take care of her and your sadness is not her fault.

• **Gather support.** Don't hesitate to ask family and friends to help you through the transition. Many friends and relatives may feel awkward talking with you about the divorce, so you may need to make suggestions on how they can help. For example, you might ask a friend to call regularly. You could request that relatives take your child out for some fun. You could also talk to your child's teacher or daycare provider about what is happening and ask for reports on any changes in your child's behavior.

• **Keep your child out of your arguments.** It's important but hard to remember that difficulties and anger with your separated or ex-spouse should be worked on away from your child. You may not want to communicate at all, but you need to make the effort in order to allow your child to have access to both parents. Try to anticipate the situations in which you might have problems with your child present. Then try to minimize these confrontations by changing the situation in some way. For example, if you and your spouse argue when your child is brought home from a visit, you may need to make the exchange elsewhere or find a neutral third party to assist

## Finding New Traditions

After my divorce, I realized that I didn't know what to do during the holidays. All the little things we had done to prepare as a family seemed useless. Also there was the question of how my children would now divide their time between two households. I never did enjoy doing elaborate decorating for Christmas, so, instead of getting a big tree and hauling out all the ornaments, we decided to make our own decorations. These were as simple as cut-paper snowflakes hanging in a window. My ex and I then agreed to rotate Christmas and Thanksgiving. Depending on which holiday we spend together, my children and I may plan a special dinner together, then spend some of the time with my parents. For the holidays on which my children are with my ex, I plan a special dinner with friends who are also single.

you. Be aware also that your child will have her own conflicting feelings of loyalty toward both parents. It's important not to encourage her to favor one parent over another and, in fact, to encourage positive feelings about both parents.

- **Maintain a relationship with the other parent.** Although you will no longer be married, you and your ex-spouse will always be parents. Do all you can to ensure that your child maintains a relationship with the noncustodial parent through regular visits.

### Helping toddlers cope

*"Although my son is just 2 years old, I worry how my recent divorce will affect him. What should I expect?"*

Even though your child is too young to reason out what is happening to his family, be assured that he is attuned to your feelings. So, you may find that he seems to need you more at a time when you may feel least able to take care of him. Remember that he is at a point in his life when he is developing his sense of security about the world. To help him through this time, keep changes to a minimum. This isn't the time to begin toilet teaching. You might also have to explain more than once about the divorce. Be sure to reassure as often as possible the parent who no longer lives with him still loves him. Try not to argue with your ex-spouse when he can hear you. Because he is so sensitive to emotions, he will likely be upset. Be prepared for some regressive behavior. For example, your son may suddenly want a bottle. And, last but not least, find ways to relieve your own stress. For example, ask relatives or friends who know your son to watch him for an afternoon, so you can get a chance to rest or do something else for a while.

## Custody and communication

Traditionally, the mother has usually been the parent who is given sole custody of a child in a divorce. However, in recent years the father is also likely to be awarded custody depending on the court's view of the case, and more and more joint custody is awarded. Custody means that the child lives with the custodial parent who is then responsible for the child's welfare. Some experts feel that joint custody is better for children than sole custody. When parents have joint custody, they must make decisions about their children together. However, this type of arrangement works only if the parents can maintain communication, work together as parents, and tolerate their differences. Developing such a relationship soon after a divorce can be difficult and takes a lot of hard work.

To maintain a parenting relationship with your ex-spouse, you may need to limit communication to just phone conversations at first. However you communicate, make sure you discuss what you expect of each other and how you plan to operate as co-parents. Set up a regular schedule for talking to your ex-spouse so you can handle any parenting issues that come up before they become crises. These conversations should also not deal exclusively with problems. They should include observations about your child's growth, events in his life, his interactions with others, school, and so on.

Another important issue you should resolve as soon as possible is visitations. If you are the custodial parent, you should encourage your ex-spouse to see your child regularly, unless there has been a problem, such as abuse, that might make visitations unsafe. No matter what your feelings are about your ex-spouse, you need to respect your child's relationship with his other parent. Try to be flexible as much you can and, depending on your child's age, try to involve him in planning visits. If the noncustodial parent tries to break off the relationship, you may need to get help, perhaps from former in-laws or a counselor, to keep the contact open.

If you are the noncustodial parent, you have the responsibility of being involved in your child's life on a regular basis without the benefits of daily contact. If circumstances require you to live a distance away from your child, the responsibility becomes even tougher. You may also have to deal with your child's possible resentment that you are no longer living with him, as well as trying to maintain a parental relationship with your ex-spouse. To help reassure your child that he belongs to you and your family, make a point of calling regularly, writing letters, and sending pictures, audio-tapes, or videotapes of yourself and other relatives. Don't, however, fall into the trap of showering your child with adventures and presents.

Maintaining as close a relationship as possible is the best gift you can give. Just because you are not a daily presence in your child's life doesn't mean you aren't an important influence.

# Widowed parents

If your child's other parent has died, you are sharing a grief, but are experiencing the grieving process very differently. More than other single parents, you're apt to cling to your child for solace. That's a natural reaction, but one you'll need to put in its place to avoid overwhelming your child or becoming overprotective.

*For more on talking to your child about death, see pages 349–50.*

Don't be afraid to put your needs for comfort in the foreground because your well-being is essential to your child. Seek professional help to see you through your feelings of loss and, quite possibly, anger, too. If your child is old enough, seek help for her, too, to give her a chance to express her feelings without fear of worrying you.

Be honest with your child about your sadness, but don't burden her with tearful outbursts or sad withdrawal from her. Save your crying for when you're among adult friends. Stick to routines as much as possible to give your child the feeling that not everything is different now. Give her plenty of opportunities to talk with you about her missing parent, and answer her questions honestly according to your beliefs.

# Single parents by choice

The fastest-growing percentage of single parents are those who choose single parenthood through a sexual encounter, medical-assisted insemination, or adoption. Unlike single parents who become single through divorce or death of a partner, you are more likely to greet single parenthood with great enthusiasm, relishing even the solo middle-of-the-night feedings with gusto. There's no doubt that as a single parent by choice you can be a capable and devoted parent, competently handling the day-to-day challenges of raising a child alone. Unburdened by anger or grief, you may be freer to see the joys in parenthood, while downplaying the emotional and physical strain of the job. Your first questioning of your choice may not come until the question comes from your child. With the vast majority of single parents by choice being women, that question is usually "Do I have a Daddy?"

## Helping your child understand your family

No doubt, your child will know other children whose fathers are not a daily presence. But, most likely, these other children do know their fathers and may have regular interactions with them. Sooner than you may anticipate, sometimes as early as age 2, your child will begin to question her family's configuration. How do you respond?

• **Let your child know that she has a father.** Everyone does, even if your child was conceived through artificial insemination. Depending on your child's age and level of understanding, you can offer the details. Some suggested responses are "Yes, you have a father. Everyone has a father. Your father does not live with us." If you are single because you did not marry your child's father, you can add something like, "Mommies and daddies have to be best friends in order to get married. And since we weren't best friends, I chose not to marry." If your child was conceived through artificial insemination, you might say, "I wanted to have you very much so a doctor helped me get pregnant." Similarly, if you adopted your child on your own, say "I wanted you for my child and so I adopted you."

• **Don't downplay the importance of fathers.** No child needs to hear that fathers are superfluous. Be very matter-of-fact to your child about her absent father, refraining from such comments as "You don't need a father." Your child may indeed feel a need for a father. Don't apologize for the choice you've made. Instead acknowledge that you and your child see the event differently: "Yes, I know you wish your father lived with us." You might want to ask in a nonjudgmental way what she would do with her father if he was present and allow her to imagine aloud what it might be like. You can even share her fantasy, saying something like, "Yes, it would be nice to go bike riding with a dad."

### PARENTS RESOURCES

*Support Groups*

**Parents Without Partners** (local chapters throughout the country)
1650 South Dixie Highway
Suite 510
Boca Raton, FL 33432
(561) 391-8833
www.parentswithoutpartners.org

**Single Mothers By Choice**
P.O. Box 1642
Gracie Square Station
New York, NY 10028
(212) 988-0993

**PARENTS RESOURCES**

*Books*

*Talking About Death: A Dialogue Between Parent and Child* by Rabbi Earl Grollman, D.D. (Beacon Press)

*Talking About Divorce and Separation: A Dialogue Between Parent and Child* by Rabbi Earl Grollman, D.D. (Beacon Press)

*Single Mothers by Choice: A Guidbeook for Single Women Who Are Considering or Have Chosen Motherhood* by Jane Mattes, M.S.W. (Times Books)

*Growing Up With Divorce: Helping Your Child Avoid Immediate and Later Emotional Problems* by Neil Kalter, Ph.D. (Fawcett Books)

*Helping Children Cope With Divorce* by Edward Teyber, Ph.D. (Lexington Books)

• **Provide whatever information you have about her other parent.** Your child's curiosity is natural and is best met with honesty and directness. You can let your child know what positive traits she shares with her father, such as saying, "You're good at sports like your father." Let her know that at some time in the future, you're willing to help her find her father if that's what she wants and if it's at all possible.

# *Stepfamilies*

When a dating relationship turns serious and you make plans for marriage, you also face the prospect of forming a stepfamily. You may also be moving from single parenthood into stepparenthood as well if your new spouse has his or her own children. A step- or blended family has its own set of unique advantages and problems and a stepparent enters into a new relationship with a child that is similar to yet greatly different from that of a parent. And, even though blended families are becoming increasingly common, you are likely to have few guidelines on how the members of your new family should relate to each other, what you can do to smooth the transition, and how you should continue to relate to noncustodial parents and to new and old relatives.

## Forming new relationships

As you no doubt have learned, there's no such thing as an instant family. Though you may have hoped that you and your new spouse would immediately love each other's children and that the children would reciprocate, the fact is that the relationships take time and patience to form. Children may, instead of embracing this new family, actually attempt to sabotage the new marriage. You and your spouse, too, may be unprepared for your own possible dislike of your new stepchildren or your spouse's strained relationship with your children.

If you are about to or have recently married and become part of a stepfamily, you can best ease the transition by trying to take the child's point of view, whether it's your natural child's view or that of your stepchild. While you may be swept up in romantic feelings of a new marriage and look forward to making a home together, your child or stepchild may be anticipating this change with great fear and anxiety. How your child adjusts and reacts to these changes will depend on his age, his developmental stage, and whether the marriage follows a death or a divorce, and how soon, or whether it is a first-time marriage. Other factors that can affect your child's adjustment are the quality of the relationship between you and your new spouse and whether or not there are other children involved in the marriage.

Like all children, your child or stepchild needs to feel he belongs and that he has some control in his life. When a parent marries, he will be faced with a great emotional and physical upheaval, which can be especially stressful if it comes on the heels of numerous other changes. He may worry just what his place will be in this new family and whether anyone will be aware of and willing to take care of his needs. In fact, he may not want a new family, especially if he is still grieving over the loss of his old family and now has to give up a dearly held wish that his natural parents will be getting back together.

As you try to understand how your child may be feeling, you'll have to be patient, and help him talk about his feelings. You'll also have to be prepared for different behaviors, depending on your child's age.

If your child is a toddler, he may regress to babyish behaviors, such as giving up any toilet-teaching. If he is slightly older, he may act out by throwing tantrums, refusing to eat, clinging to his own parent, and not being able to sleep. For your young child, it's important to keep routines as stable as possible, be as attentive and loving as possible, and maintain a close relationship with the non-custodial parent if that parent is available.

If your child is between the ages of 4 to 7, he may react strongly to physical disruptions when he becomes a part of a stepfamily. He may become possessive of toys and space. He may feel upset if he is no longer the oldest or the youngest child, or if he has been an only child and suddenly finds he has to share space and parents with one or more stepsiblings. To help your child at this age, try to find small ways to give him some control. Offer as many choices as possible, and allow him to make decisions when it's appropriate. For example, you could give him a turn at deciding on a family activity, which will help him feel like a valued member of the family.

Your child or stepchild may also be angry with his own parent for seeming to divide the love that was once so focused on him. In addition, he may try to test that parent's love by wanting his parent to choose between him and the new partner. If you are the natural parent, you need to reassure your child that you love him just as much and make an effort to spend one-on-one time with him, while making it clear that he needs to spend time with his stepparent, too, and you need private time with your new spouse as well. If you are the new stepparent, you have to allow your spouse to give your stepchild periods of undivided attention.

You also need to make your feelings known to your spouse and talk about how you might handle your child's or your stepchild's possessive or hostile behavior. If you are the stepparent, realize that your spouse may feel caught in the middle between you and his or her natural child and won't want to aggravate the situation by taking one side or the other. You may have to talk with your stepchild on your own and explain your view of the situation and how you feel.

A good way to lessen the feeling that someone in the family is an outsider is for parents to spend special time with their own children and to also find time for stepchildren as well. Even 15 minutes a day will help and could start with doing something together such as shopping or cooking. Sometimes if you concentrate on an activity first, rather than the relationship, the tension will defuse over time. If you feel that after a long time, your stepchild still doesn't accept you, or you believe your own child continues to reject his stepparent, it's important for the stepparent to keep trying. Let your child express his feelings and don't overreact if they are negative. Look for interests you or your spouse have in common and activities the family might enjoy together. Above all, treat your stepchild with fairness and respect. Although it may seem to take a long time, you will eventually be rewarded.

## Becoming a stepfamily

When a stepfamily first forms, one or more members, especially parents, may be blinded to the reality of what it takes to make a family by some of the myths about stepfamilies. Some of these myths include the belief that stepfamilies can function as first-time families do, that everyone in the family will love each other in time, that the parents have learned from mistakes made in former marriages, that if a stepparent treats stepchildren nicely and lovingly they will accept him or her, and that relating to stepchildren is the same as relating to a natural child. In discovering these beliefs to be myths, stepfamilies often go through several emotional stages before they become a real family.

At first, there may be a sense of unreality as new parents dream about a happy family life. They both may be, along with their children, on their best behavior in an effort to make things work and a desire to be liked and loved.

In the second stage, confusion may result as differences surface. One or more family members may deny that any happiness is slipping away even as tension grows. The novelty of the new family has worn off, and there may even be fears that there may be a break up.

In the next stage, conflicts are out in the open as hidden resentments and angers are expressed. In this stage, it's especially important for everyone to realize that such conflict is normal. To get through this time, communication and negotiation skills are crucial.

In the fourth stage, emotions calm down as family members learn more about each other and figure out how to resolve issues. At this point, both parents and children begin to realize that they really are a family that can work together to resolve upsets and restore balance.

In the final stage, the stepfamily again feels optimistic. Everyone is better able to accept each other as they are. Real family ties are formed. As difficult and complex as you may discover a stepfamily to be, you can succeed if you are willing to be patient and understanding as you get to know and learn to live with each other.

## The new home

One of the first issues your stepfamily will have to resolve is where you live. Usually the best decision is for everyone to move into a new place rather than one or the other parent's homes. By doing so, you can avoid power struggles over territory, feelings of being invaded by strangers, and any sense of being unwanted and having no personal space in an unfamiliar place.

After the move, it's important to establish and discuss boundaries as soon as possible. Make sure each child has a personal space, even if she has to share a room with a sibling or a stepsibling. Talk about respecting this space and each other's possessions. This talk may need to happen more than once as disputes and disagreements arise. If you are a noncustodial parent whose child will also be visiting and spending time in your home, he will need to have his space as well. He may feel uncertain at first and perhaps resentful of stepsiblings that get to live with you, so it's important to do what you can to make him feel welcome, to help him understand that this is his home too, and to reassure him that you love him just as much as you always have even though you now will be making room for your new spouse's children as well.

## The need to communicate

Also important to helping children adjust to a new marriage is keeping any conflicts between you and your new spouse at a low level. Discuss any disagreements and criticisms out of earshot of your own child or a stepchild. This also applies to any disputes you may have with a noncustodial parent.

Another important issue you may not think to address when you marry is your own feelings about sharing your child with another adult, especially if you are marrying after being on your own for a long time after a divorce or if you are marrying for the first time. While you love your new spouse, you might experience some conflicting feelings about your child forming a close relationship with another adult who will essentially be his parent along with you. Whereas before you were solely responsible for making decisions regarding your child, now you have to consider another adult who no doubt wants to be involved. You might also find that your spouse's ideas on raising a child differ from yours, which can be a source of disagreement and resentment. If you are a stepparent, you may be sensitive to feeling shut out of parental involvement and decisions. It's important to remember that as individuals you each have your own set of expectations and values. When you both bring your ideas to running a relatively instant family, there are bound to be some conflicts. At these times, it's crucial to communicate how you feel and to give your-

---

**"IT WORKED FOR ME"**

### Accepting a Stepchild

I resented my stepdaughter taking time away with my husband. It helped when I kept reminding myself of how she must feel sharing her Dad with me. Since I decided to let my husband and his 10-year-old daughter spend some time together by themselves, I've felt less threatened, more in control. And I no longer feel left out of their closeness.

self and your spouse a chance to sort out different opinions. Then, for the sake of your new family, you need to work on ways to compromise in situations where you disagree so you can offer consistency to your children.

As you and your new family adjust to each other, remember that building relationships takes time. It took years to form the relationship you have with your child, so be patient with the time it takes for your spouse and your child to get to know each other and the time it takes for you to become acquainted with your stepchild. You might tell children that there will be some rough spots as well as good days, but that you all have to give love a chance to grow.

### Communicating with noncustodial parents

If your new marriage is a remarriage, you are still a parent with your ex-spouse as well as a parent with your new spouse. It's important for your child that she maintain as much contact with her other parent as she had before you remarried by keeping to the same visitation schedule as much as possible. This may feel awkward and upsetting to you as you try to form your new family and think that your child has a new parent and should not be so involved with the old. You may not want to be reminded that you had another family that didn't work. You might worry that your new spouse won't be given a chance to be a good stepparent if your child's other parent is still a major part of her life. If your ex-spouse has remarried, you may resent your child spending time with another family that is equally important to her. However, you need to remember that your ex-spouse will always be your child's parent. It's never a good idea to try to force a child to choose one parent or family over another or be made to feel that one family is better than another.

Stepfamilies can be complicated as a child ends up with three or four parents. It's important that all the parents communicate in

---

**"IT WORKED FOR ME"**

## Relating to an Ex-Spouse

My husband's son came to live us when he was 8, and I had no idea what my role should be. I felt motherly toward him, but I knew I could never claim to be his mother. In fact, I wanted him to call be by my first name, rather than "Mom." I encouraged my husband to maintain a good relationship with his ex-wife and tried to keep a back seat to their parental decisions. But it was hard. I often felt like I was in limbo, both a parent and not a parent. My husband was great. He made sure that his son visited his mother on a regular schedule. He also supported my "light touch" approach while telling his son that I was in charge when he wasn't home. But I still worried that maybe I was letting my own fears prevent me from being more of a parent. I finally knew I had made the right decision when I got a call one Mother's Day from my husband's ex-wife. She said straight out, "Thank you for taking care of my son and letting me be his mother." I was so surprised and relieved, I cried when I hung up the phone.

as civil a manner as possible and be a part of decisions that affect the child. However, making sure a child has contact with both parents can result in some scheduling nightmares, especially if they live a distance from each other. By spending blocks of time in two different homes, your child may feel that she doesn't belong anywhere. There are no easy answers. You and your ex-spouse must work together to make sure your child spends time with you both, yet keep disruptions to a minimum. If you live near each other, a schedule of weekdays with one parent and weekends with the other may work. If you live far away from each other, you may need to schedule vacation times for your child to spend with the other parent. Try to remain flexible. A schedule may not work in your child's best interests, or may need to change as your child grows and her interests and needs change.

If you find yourself overly worried about what you should do, it may help to seek out other stepfamilies who have wrestled with these problems. Ask what worked best for them and how they had to adjust arrangements as problems arose. The best ideas usually come from those who have been there.

## Blending lifestyles

Boundaries also become an issue when two families blend together into one. For example, how do stepfamilies adjust when one parent and child has lived casually while another parent and child are more comfortable with a neat household and set schedules? There's no easy answer to this dilemma because you and your child both may feel uncomfortable and possibly resentful at feeling forced to change your way of life to suit the other side of your new family.

Again, compromise is all important in adjusting to conflicting lifestyles and resolving disagreements. Before you are married and living together, you and your new partner should talk about any differences you have observed in the way you both live and the way you are each raising your children. Look for common points you can agree on, then work on areas where you need to compromise. One parent may need to agree to be more flexible, while the other parent agrees to be less casual. Although this is often a problem in first families, there is the added disadvantage of bringing together more than two people with their own sets of habits, values, attitudes, and rituals in a stepfamily.

When you first begin living together, it's important for everyone to be able to express constructively what bothers them about others in the family and able to handle honest feedback. When complaints are out in the open, it doesn't mean that people should be forced to change. It means that open communication will help family members get to know each other, understand each other's points of view, and look for ways to make changes that will make living together easier. It may take time to get used to someone else's habits, but with practice you can do it. Above all, you should stress the need to accept each other's differences.

Differing attitudes and values can also be a source of disagreement in a stepfamily. Parents may differ in their attitudes toward school, what children should be allowed to do when they play, and what constitutes good manners. Children may differ in their attitudes toward school, play, friends, and family. Again, it's important to discuss attitudes with your future spouse before you get married. If you also can't find common ground in major value areas, it will be difficult for you to hold together as a stepfamily. Think about how you feel about issues of honesty, cleanliness, privacy, sharing, education, diet, personal freedom, holidays, relatives, friends, religion, and so on. Then decide what your priorities are, the quality of your life with your stepfamily or a value that might be stepped on. You may need to suspend your judgment in order to make decisions that are the best for your new family.

Family rituals are another area of possible conflict for stepfamilies. Rituals provide an identity for a family and serve as ways to keep a family together. Consistently observing them can become very important to a family, who will resist changing them in any way. As you and your spouse work to establish your stepfamily, you may find that some of your rituals differ, such as how to celebrate a particular holiday or even daily rituals you have always practiced. Or, you may have rituals you feel are important while your spouse has little to do with rituals of any kind.

Blending rituals and forming new rituals can be a challenge for a stepfamily. You may have to explore different ways to handle rituals before you settle on what's most comfortable. For example, you may decide to celebrate a holiday a certain way one year and another way the next year. Or, you may be able to find ways to compromise by blending parts of two different rituals. To manage rituals successfully, each family member has to be willing to give a little.

# Handling discipline issues in stepfamilies

*For more on
discipline, see
**pages 379–403**.*

One of the thorniest problems you may face as a parent or stepparent is how to develop a strategy for discipline that suits your entire family. Although you know discipline is needed, you may be unsure who should apply it, when it should take place, or how much is enough. If the marriage is relatively recent, you may also feel forced to agree on a strategy immediately because one or more children are acting out any resentments or difficulties they may have adjusting to their new family.

As you may have already discovered, your child or your spouse's child may not be happy having a stepparent discipline her. During the early stage of your marriage, usually for about two years, it's probably best to leave the disciplining to the biological parent, until the stepparent has a chance to develop a solid relationship with a stepchild. This doesn't mean that the stepparent should not take charge when the other parent is not present or shouldn't expect stepchildren to behave in a civil manner. Let a stepchild know when she gets out of line. If she resists with the excuse that you're not her "real" parent, agree with her, but let her know that you expect her to follow the rules of the house. You might also point out that you are the adult in charge, even if you aren't her "real" parent, and that you have to enforce the rules. As you would with your own child, it's also important that you be consistent, focus on the misbehavior and make any punishment specific and appropriate for her age, allow her to experience any natural consequences of mistakes without interfering, choose your battles and are not critical of every little thing that displeases you, praise and encourage good behavior.

It's also important to discuss and establish ahead of time family rules and expectations of behavior you both have. Then you need to communicate these to your children. Allow them a chance to give their opinions, too.

As everyone becomes more comfortable with your new family, you and your spouse might try taking equal responsibility for discipline, which means that the parent who sees a child misbehave should address it. Make sure that you agree or at least reach a compromise on how to discipline so you can support each other if a child complains.

# Stepsiblings

Besides getting used to and living with a new parent, your child and your stepchild are also trying to adjust to the sudden addition of a sibling who alters his place in the family. If your child has been an only child, he will likely miss having all of your attention. If your child has been the younger child and a stepsibling is younger than he is, he will suddenly be faced with the expectations and responsibility that go along with being an older sister or brother. Your child will also be dealing with getting to know and living with a comparative stranger who may have a very different temperament than either of you.

*For more on siblings, see* **pages 436–52**.

For you, it's important not to compare your child and stepchild. Look for positive traits and skills in each child and try to focus on how differences can be fun. You should also resist showing favoritism in time spent together, praise, or disciplinary matters. However, don't feel you have to prove to your stepchild that you can love him just as much as your own child. You may try too hard out of a sense of guilt, which will only cause resentment on both sides. You might also end up treating your stepchild as a guest rather than as a normal child who is part of your family.

Then be patient and allow time for relationships to form. Don't expect your child and stepchild to instantly bond and love or even like each other. Expect some power struggles over territory and parental attentions as they adjust to each other. Make sure they each have their own space and respect each other's possessions and personal places. Stepsiblings may likely be jealous of each other as well and accuse you of paying more attention to one or the other. There may be jealousy and envy over presents received or time a stepsibling spends with a noncustodial parent. All of these issues take time to work out. You will have to handle disputes as they come up and attempt to be fair in all arguments.

# From "yours and mine" to "ours"

A stepfamily goes through another major change and adjustment when the new parents have a child together. A new baby, who is a half-sibling to all other children in the family, may serve to unite a stepfamily or it can pull a stepfamily apart. Having three sets of children—yours, mine, and ours—comes with its own set of pressures.

When you know a new baby is on the way, be positive when you tell your children and relatives. If the pregnancy isn't planned, be honest with relatives and ask for their support emotionally. Help to prepare your children and stepchildren for the new baby by giving them plenty of time to get used to the idea. Talk about what it will be like to live with a baby, but don't overdo it. Try to be understanding of any signs of anger or resentment. The prospect of a new sibling that belongs to you both may be extremely threatening. Reinforce that they will still be very special to both of you whether they are your natural children or stepchildren.

Also include children who don't live with you. Make sure that they have a chance to meet and get to know the new child, even it's just through pictures, videotapes, letters, and phone calls at first.

As the baby grows, evaluate how your methods for raising this child might be different than how you raised your other children. Think about whether you are more lenient or strict. Be prepared for possible jealousy on the part of other children if they feel the new baby is more favored than they were.

For you and your spouse, a new baby can symbolize the connections of your blended family. If you keep your expectations realistic and make yourself aware of problems you are likely to encounter, your stepfamily can develop even deeper relationships than you have already been able to form.

## PARENTS RESOURCES

### Support for Stepfamilies

Because many parents have no idea what to expect or how to form a stepfamily, outside support is important. Talking with other stepfamilies can help you get on track and solve some of the common issues that arise. Here are a few books you might try:

*Families Apart: Ten Keys to Successful Co-Parenting* by Melinda Blau (Perigree)

*Stepfamily Realities: How to Overcome Difficulties and Have a Happy Family* by Margaret Newman (New Harbinger Publications)

*The Family Puzzle: Putting the Pieces Together* by Nancy S. and William D. Palmer with Kay Marshall Strom (Piñon Press)

*Second Chances: Men, Women and Children a Decade After Divorce* by Judith S. Wallerstein, Ph.D., and Sandra Blakeslee (Houghton Mifflin Co.)

# Part 3

# Your Child's Health

**P**robably nothing consumes your attention quite so much as your child's health. While not every aspect of health care is within your power to control, there is much you can do to create a healthy environment, maintain healty habits, and respond to the minor and more serious health issues throughout your child's life. As you teach the basics of good hygiene and provide an example of a healthy lifestyle, you will do much to prevent illness.

# CHAPTER 1

# Healthy Habits

No matter how hard you try, you simply can't protect your child from all the germs with which he can come into contact. Nor should you try. However, by teaching him good hygiene habits and simple germ-avoidance procedures, you can cut down considerably on his (and your) bouts with illness. Teaching healthy habits should include helping your child get the sleep and exercise he needs, as well as dressing for the weather.

## *Staying healthy*

Young children are more prone than adults to viral and bacterial infections because their immune systems aren't mature enough to fight off invading germs. And because your child spends so much time around other germ-carrying kids and often puts her hands in her nose and mouth, she gets sick more frequently than do adults. Healthy habits help prevent the spread of colds and other viruses and reduce the risk of bacterial infections.

### Good hygiene

In addition to the daily grooming routines you practice and teach your child, it's important for you and your child's caregivers to teach — and follow — good household hygiene.

**Wash hands** Because colds and other viruses are frequently spread by hand contact, teaching your child to wash her hands thoroughly before meals, before and after using the toilet, and whenever she has spent time playing with other children is your first line of defense against many contagious diseases. Hand-washing also diminishes your child's risk of lead poisoning if she touches lead dust and then puts her hands in her mouth. If your child has a cold or other contagious illness, *you* must be sure to wash your own hands frequently since you'll touch plenty of things she's handled or sneezed on.

*For more on lead poisoning, see **page 629**.*

Follow these guidelines when teaching your child how to wash her hands:
- **Use warm, not hot, water.**
- **Lather up with soap.** As a further precaution, use a soap that comes in a pump dispenser rather than bar soap, which can harbor germs.
- **Demonstrate thorough washing.** Show that a good hand-washing should take at least ten seconds.
- **Dry completely.** Teach your child to dry her hands thoroughly, since damp hands harbor germs. Each family member should use her own towel to avoid spreading germs. If someone is ill, she should use paper towels to avoid reinfecting herself and others.

**Wash frequently handled items** Wash items your child frequently handles, particularly toys and furnishings he puts into his mouth, especially when he has a cold or other contagious condition. When a family member is sick, use alcohol towelettes, available at drugstores, to wipe off doorknobs, the telephone handle and mouthpiece, the handle on your fridge, and the TV remote—anything that's likely to be touched frequently by many hands. If possible, do so immediately after these items have been touched. At the least, clean daily. Cold viruses can live for several hours on hard, porous surfaces, so regular washing will help reduce the risk of spreading germs throughout the family.

**Teach nose blowing** Your child can also learn how to keep his germs to himself. Once he's around 18 months old, teach him how to wipe and blow his nose properly, using a clean tissue. Have him practice blowing out of his nose in front of a mirror, with his mouth closed. Keep a box of tissues in every room of the house so he can use a new one each time he needs to wipe or blow his nose. Teach him to throw his tissue into the waste basket and to wash his hands when he's finished.

To teach nose blowing, make a game of it by asking your child to imitate you doing the following: First blow air out of your mouth. Hold up a tissue and show him how the air you blow out of your mouth makes the tissue move. Next show him how you can blow air out of your nose, too. Push one nostril closed and blow air out of the other one, making the tissue move. Let him try each of these steps. Once he can direct air out of one nostril show him how you use the tissue to blow your nose. When you happen to blow your nose during the day, tell your child to watch and ask him if he wants to try. If he likes to play the nose-blowing game, you'll have a much better chance of getting him to blow his nose when it's congested.

For more on head lice, see **page 609**.

**Avoid sharing germs and bugs**  Although you work hard to teach your child to share his toys, work equally hard to teach him that certain things are not for sharing. No one in the family should share drinking glasses or eating utensils or personal hygiene products such as toothbrushes. Likewise, teach your child that he shouldn't share hats or combs with others. By doing so he puts himself at risk for contracting head lice. Each person in the family should have his or her own towel and grooming aids, and all should be washed frequently.

Don't share food with your child. Nibbling off another's plate, or drinking from the same glass or through the same straw can spread cold, flu, and stomach germs.

To limit the spread of airborne germs, teach your child to turn his head away from others when he coughs or sneezes and to cover his mouth with the crook of his arm instead of his hands whenever he sneezes or coughs—and then to wash his hands.

**Is some exposure to illness a good thing?**
*"Is it better to expose children to some common illnesses to build their immunity—or should you try to keep them away from infected kids?"*

Daily living will provide your child with plenty of exposure to common germs. It's not a good idea to expose a child to a contagious disease intentionally to "build up his immunity." Illnesses of any kind lower a person's immunity while he is ill and put him at risk for other illnesses. However, it's fine to let your youngster play with a child who is past the contagious stage of certain illnesses even if that child still has some symptoms. For instance, a child with spots from chicken pox was contagious from before the spots appeared to until the sores crust over, but he is not contagious after that.

**Keeping kids safe from pet-borne illnesses**
Pets are a natural and healthy part of many kids' lives. Even if your child doesn't have a pet, she's bound to play with animals at a friend's house or in the neighborhood. To keep your child safe from pet-borne illnesses:

• Be sure the pet has all its inoculations and is treated promptly for any symptoms of illness by the veterinarian.

• Have your child wash his hands after playing with an animal.

• Teach your child not to share food with his pet.

• Instruct your child not to touch his pet's urine or feces or the area where the pet relieves himself, such as a cat's litter box or a hamster's cage.

## Bathing and grooming
Though bathtime and dressing time may be mundane routines for you, they're opportunities for your child to learn a lot about herself.

### Bath frequency
*"Do kids really need a daily bath?"*
No. Especially during the cooler months, children can skip a day or even two or three days, provided that they keep their genital area clean with proper toileting routines. They should also wash their hands a few times a day, before and after using the toilet and before meals and bedtime. Washing their face in the morning and at night will help them feel fresher. In warmer weather, and when kids have been playing outdoors, or have worked up a sweat, a bath before bed is definitely a good idea.

**Bathtime fun** Some kids need a little prodding to entice them into the tub. For them especially, here are some ideas to enhance their enjoyment of bath time:

• **Get some silly soaps.** Soaps shaped like ducks or hearts can encourage scrubbing.

**PARENTS ALERT**

## *Handling Flea Infestation*

Fleas are bound to be a problem if you let pets indoors. To flea-proof your child you must flea-proof your pets. Bathe dogs and cats regularly with a flea shampoo or treat them with other flea-prevention measures. Wash the pet's bedding frequently in hot water. Fleas also deposit eggs in rugs, chairs, and sofas, and if your house becomes infested, you'll need to have an exterminator de-flea the house. Flea "bombs" are available over-the-counter and from veterinarians, but you should use them only when your family (and pets) plan to be out of the home for at least 24 hours, after which, it's safe to return. Keep in mind that someone must keep close watch on the house while you are away, since there have been reports of flea bombs exploding and causing fires.

*For information on bath time safety routines, see page 832.*

### *After-Bath Warm-ups*

To ease the chill when stepping out of the tub, I warm my son's towel and terry-cloth robe in the dryer right before he gets out while my husband watches him in the bath. He loves the toasty warm feel of it.

- **Paint the town.** Or at least the inside of the tub. Nontoxic water paints and specially designed bath paints can bring out the artist in your little bather. Clean up is easy.
- **Invest in bath toys.** Toys specially designed for the bath—floating islands with pirates or mermaids, water wheels, and other toys that won't be damaged by submersion—are good bets.
- **Make washcloth puppets.** Or purchase commercially made ones.
- **Offer a messy treat.** Popsicles that you might not allow to be eaten in the living room can be a real treat in the bath, especially on a hot summer night.

**Bathing products for toddlers and preschoolers** Baby soaps or nonsoap cleansers like Cetaphil lotion are ideal for a young child's sensitive skin. Steer clear of harsh deodorant soaps and those with lots of fragrance, which could irritate your child's skin. In fact, no matter what kind of soap your child is using, it's only necessary to soap hands, feet, and the genital area. Soaping the whole body, especially the face, will dry your child's skin.

**Keeping bath toys clean** Soap scum build-up and humidity can cause bath toys to become havens for germs and mildew. After each use, rinse bath toys under the shower spray and store them in an airy container, such as a colander or hanging basket. Every few weeks, wash the toys with an antibacterial detergent or vinegar and water and rinse them thoroughly.

**PARENTS ALERT**

### *Bubble Bath*

An occasional bubble bath that doesn't contain fragrance is fine. But avoid frequent bubble baths, particularly ones with perfumes, because they can dry out skin and trigger urinary tract infections.

## Hair care

If your child perspires a lot, she may need a daily hair washing. Otherwise, every other day or even just twice a week may be enough, especially in good weather, when neither heat nor hats build up sweat on the head. Despite what the shampoo label says, lathering once is usually enough. There's rarely a need to lather, rinse, and lather again. Rinse thoroughly, since soap left on the hair can cause itching and flaking. Work with your child to find the easiest ways to rinse in order to avoid soap and water in the eyes, which can be frightening as well as painful to kids. Here are some possibilities:

• **Put a picture on the ceiling** or simply direct your child to look up, which makes pouring water over his head, not his face, easier.

• **Try a shampoo guard.** This is a product that sits on your child's forehead like a halo and which directs the water away from his face.

• **Let your child do it.** It may take longer, but if he's the one pouring water over his head, he's less likely to be frightened by it.

**Hair care products**  Children's shampoos really are better for kids since they are gentler and cut down on eye sting. Cream rinses and spray detanglers can help unsnarl long hair, which will make your child more comfortable, but they aren't necessary for most kids.

### Dyes in shampoos

*"I've noticed that most baby shampoos contain dyes. Can these be harmful?"*

No. Baby shampoos are formulated to meet a baby's needs; they are gentle on the skin and less irritating if they get into your baby's eyes. Many generations of babies have been shampooed with these products without any problem. If you prefer to avoid these chemicals, however, health-food stores generally stock dye-free products. Just be sure to find a formula that is designed specifically for kids.

**Getting out tangles**  You'll find special cream rinses and sprays formulated just for kids for detangling wet hair at your local drug store. Use a wide tooth plastic comb with blunt tips to comb your child's hair. Don't untangle too vigorously. If your child's hair is long and tangled, start at the bottom and work your way up. To minimize broken ends, a main cause of tangles, don't use rubber bands in your child's hair or braid her hair too tightly. To keep tangles from forming overnight, loosely braid long hair or use a satin pillowcase.

**Haircuts**  Whether you take your child to a professional or do it yourself, haircuts are a big deal to your child. Most toddlers and

---

**"IT WORKED FOR ME"**

## Easy Sun Showers

During the summer, instead of the usual evening baths, I let my two children, ages 3 and 4, put on their bathing suits and take their showers with a hose attachment in the backyard. They wear water shoes so that I don't have to worry about stray rocks and other things hurting their feet. The water is a bit cooler than it would be in the indoor bathroom, but the kids love it. They don't even mind having their hair washed.

### Removing Gum from Hair

I have two tricks for getting gum out of hair: One is to put an ice cube on the gum to freeze it. When it's hard, it's easier to chip off. The other trick is to put peanut butter on the gum, which causes it to slide right off the hair.

many preschoolers balk, which isn't surprising when you consider how they must experience the situation: Someone's coming at them with a sharp object and removing part of them, while telling them to sit still!

To make haircutting time less frightful, choose a barber who's experienced working with children. If you do the cutting yourself, make your child more comfortable by giving him something to hold as a distraction. Change his clothes soon afterward because the little cut hairs feel very prickly. You may want to consider cutting your child's hair in the bath, where you can wash the little hairs away immediately.

## Getting Rid of Ear Wax

### Do...

realize that ear wax isn't "bad." It does a good job of protecting the ear canal and eardrum from foreign bodies such as dirt, bugs, and fungi. It usually falls out on its own, but sometimes you have to wipe it away.

use a clean, soft, wet washcloth and a little soap to gently clean the outer ear and opening of the ear canal every day.

### Don't...

use a cotton swab to clean the inside of the ear. You may push wax deeper into the ear. If your child has a buildup of wax, his doctor can use a little instrument to safely remove it. The doctor may also recommend wax-softening drops, to be used at bedtime

insert any object into the ear, such as a bobby pin, to remove wax.

## Ears

For an illustration of the middle and inner ear, see **page 586**.

Use a damp washcloth to wipe dirt away from the outer portion of your child's ear. Never insert an object—such as a cotton swab, hairpin, or other tool—into your child's ear. The object could pierce the eardrum and cause damage.

### Ear piercing

*"Is there any reason not to get a toddler's ears pierced?"*

It's okay to have your toddler's ears pierced, provided you follow certain precautions: Have the procedure done by a pediatrician or a reputable jeweler using a sterile "gun." Use only 14K gold-post earrings at first. After piercing, turn the earring every day, dab alcohol on the opening and use an antibacterial ointment daily, until the holes completely heal, usually in about six weeks. Afterward, you can get your daughter either 14K gold posts or surgical steel-post earrings. (Other metals, could corrode.) Also avoid hoop earrings, which could get caught and tear your child's lobes.

## Nail care

Dirty fingernails are a perfect breeding ground for germs. To cut down on grime buildup, keep your child's nails trimmed short. Then, at bath time, gently scrub each finger with a soft nail brush to remove accumulated dirt. Toddlers are notoriously resistant when it comes to having any part of their body "cut off," be it their hair or their nails. When grooming your toddler's nails, you may want to do the job when she's sleeping, especially if she tends to struggle and pull away from you. Older children often feel quite grown-up when it comes to getting manicures, and therefore offer no resistance. If she allows you to cut her nails when she's awake, try these methods to make the job easier:

- **Use a soft-bristle toothbrush or soft nail brush** and soap and water to gently scrub under her nails to clean away dirt.
- **Use blunt-tip safety scissors or nail clippers.**
- **Cut nails after she's been playing in the tub.** They will be softer and easier to trim.
- **Trim nails just to the tip of the finger.**
- **Gently file ragged edges with an emery board.** Look for a super-soft one.

### Nail-care products
*"Is it safe to let a young child wear nail polish? I worry about my 4-year-old daughter ingesting toxins from polish."*

If you and your daughter want her to wear polish, buy nontoxic

---

**"IT WORKED FOR ME"**

### *Mini Manicure*

My 3-year-old hated having her nails trimmed and screamed and pulled away from me every time I tried to cut them. However, she was always fascinated by my own home manicures. One day, I asked if she would like me to do her nails when I did mine, and she hesitantly agreed. We both soaked our fingertips in bowls of "bubble bath" water for a few minutes. I cut my nails first, and then I trimmed hers. I gave her a chamois nail buffer and let her buff her nails. She was extremely pleased with herself! Now she insists we do our nails together.

varieties designed especially for kids. Refrain from using polish, however, if she frequently puts her fingers in her mouth. Be very cautious when using nail polish remover on your child's nails. The acetone vapors should not be inhaled and the remover itself is dangerous if ingested. After using remover, thoroughly wash her hands. Always store these products where your child can't reach them.

# Daily care of teeth

*For more information on teething, see **page 121**.*

Caring for your child's teeth should begin even before her first tooth erupts. It involves not only dental hygiene and regular professional care, but good nutrition. Like all aspects of your child's health, good dental care moves from your total responsibility to your child's responsibility very gradually.

**Caring for your child's teeth and gums**  Although baby teeth are eventually replaced by permanent ones, you need to make sure that your child's "milk teeth," as these first teeth are often called, are well cared for. In addition to the discomfort and cost involved in repairing cavities and removing diseased teeth, the premature loss of your baby's teeth can negatively affect the way her permanent teeth come in.

Your primary concern in the early years is preventing cavities. Cavities are caused by a combination of things: a bacterium called *Streptococcus mutans*, which lives in almost everyone's mouth; sugary or starchy foods; and time for the bacteria, sugars, and starches to get together to do their dirty work. This combination of nature, diet, and hygiene can cause an invisible acidic film called plaque to form on the teeth. If the plaque isn't removed, it bores microscopic holes into the tough surface enamel of a tooth, eventually eating through it—and a cavity is born. In addition to making sure your child receives regular dental care, you'll need to teach him daily dental hygiene.

During infancy and early toddlerhood, you'll be doing all the brushing and flossing. Don't introduce toothpaste until your child is old enough to learn not to swallow it, usually about age 2. Then, gradually, you can turn the responsibility over to him.

**Teaching your child to brush and floss**  At around age 2, most children are ready to begin brushing their own teeth with your supervision. By age 5 or so, a child should be able to brush independently. Although it's best for kids to brush their teeth several times a day, primarily after meals and snacks, if your child brushes only once a day, make sure it's at night, right before bedtime. Plaque-causing bacteria build up in the mouth overnight, and brushing before bedtime helps get rid of the bacteria.

*For information about professional dental care, see **page 533**.*

Don't be afraid to ask your child's dentist for advice on instructing your child in the art of brushing. These tips should also help:

• **Choose the right brush.** Choose a soft- to medium-hard bristle brush.

• **Use the right amount of toothpaste.** Don't overdo it. About a pea-size dollop is enough. Too much fluoride-based paste can cause tooth discoloration.

• **Hold the toothbrush properly.** Your child should hold the toothbrush at a 45-degree angle to the gums and guide it along her front and back teeth.

• **Use the right strokes and cover all areas.** Using smooth, circular strokes, teach her to brush the outer portion of the upper teeth, then the lower. Show her how to position the toothbrush vertically and use an up-and-down motion to clean the inside surfaces of the top and bottom teeth and to scrub the chewing surfaces of all teeth.

• **Spend time.** Encourage her to brush for about two minutes at each brushing and than make sure she rinses well with water.

**Flossing** Pediatric dentists recommend daily flossing for kids in addition to brushing. By removing food particles from between the teeth, flossing curbs the buildup of plaque, which can lead to cavities and the premature loss of baby teeth. While children 7 and older may be taught to floss their teeth properly on their own, parents need to do the work for kids 6 and under. Daily flossing is a major commitment on the part of parents *and* kids. If you start flossing your child's teeth when his first molars erupt, he'll become used to the process over time. To make flossing more appealing, let your child choose a flavored floss. To make the process easier:

• **Find a comfortable position.** Try having your child lie on the couch, with his head on your lap.

• **Be thorough.** Starting at the back of the mouth, wrap a piece of floss halfway around the tooth at the gum line and gently work the floss up and down the tooth for a few seconds.

• **Repeat the procedure** on the other side of the tooth.

### Fluoride

*"Our water supply is fluoridated. Should our children have additional fluoride treatments to prevent cavities?"*

Supplemental fluoride is most beneficial to children 6 months and older, but not all kids need fluoride supplements. To determine if your child needs additional fluoride, you need to know how much fluoride is already in your water supply, which you can learn from your local water company or health department. Your child's age is also a factor, as is the amount of fluoridated water she drinks daily. If your water has less than 0.3 parts per million (ppm) of fluoride, your children will benefit from fluoride supplements or treatments with fluoride. If your water has 0.3 to 0.6 ppm fluoride, children 6 months to 3 years don't need supplements or treatments; from 3 to 6 years they require supplements or treatments. And if your water has more than 0.6 ppm, no supplements are needed at any age, provided that your child drinks 12 or more ounces of water per day.

## Daily Dental Care

| Do... | Don't... |
|---|---|
| make sure your child eats a balanced diet, especially the calcium and vitamins D and C, which are essential for building and maintaining healthy teeth. | let your child drink excess amounts of juice. The sugar and acid in juice are prime triggers for plaque buildup. |
| offer cheddar cheese as a snack or as part of a meal when kids can't brush. Some studies suggest that an ingredient in cheddar cheese helps fight decay. | force your child to brush his teeth every time he has eaten, which can make brushing an unpleasant experience.<br><br>threaten your child with a visit to the dentist if he doesn't follow all correct hygiene procedures. |
| try to coax your child into brushing for two minutes after each meal and snack (if possible), and at bedtime. | let an older child have more than one snack between meals, if possible. Each time a person eats, cavity-causing bacteria leap into action, mounting a 20-minute "acid attack" on teeth. The more often a child eats, the more her teeth are exposed to a buildup of plaque. |
| make sure your child gets regular dental checkups. | |

It's important not to overprotect with fluoride. If children ingest too much fluoride while first or permanent teeth are forming, mild fluorosis—a mottling that causes small white spots or brownish-gray stains—can appear on permanent teeth.

## Dressing and clothing routines

It can be great fun to dress your child in cute little outfits, but appearance is only one factor to consider when choosing appropriate clothing for her. The right clothing can also help protect your child's health and enhance her safety.

**Choosing children's clothing** The best children's clothes are easy-care, comfortable, and hazard free. In addition to style, you'll need to add these criteria to your shopping list:

- **Check for safety.** Examine clothing for hazards—loose buttons and/or decorations should be repaired. Drawstrings should be removed. Sleepwear should be well-fitting and fire-retardant. Shoes should be well-fitting, with the right soles for their walking and running ability.
- **Choose easy-on-and-off.** A young child, especially one in the midst of toilet teaching, needs clothing that she can negotiate herself. Easy-on-and-off bottoms, elastic waistbands, wide-enough neck openings, and a minimum of fussy decorations make self-care easier.
- **Get the right size.** A good fit is vital for comfort and safety. While it's certainly okay to choose items with "room to grow," too much room can present hazards—too-long pants' legs or footed-sleepwear could cause falls, for instance. Simply choosing a garment by the size on the label is not a good method of determining fit. Various manufacturers size clothing differently. Your best bet is to become familiar with a brand you like and build your child's wardrobe around it. Or, bring your child or a well-fitting outfit along on your shopping expeditions to assure a good fit. If ordering from a catalog, ask if the sizes run "true to size" or smaller or larger than usual. Then order one item from that catalog and check the sizing before placing a larger order.

**PARENTS ALERT**

## Drawstring Dangers

Beware of drawstrings on children's clothing. Since 1985, at least 12 children 15 months through 11 years have died and 27 have nearly strangled when drawstrings on their jackets, sweatshirts, hooded T-shirts, or capes got caught on playground equipment, cribs, escalators, or fences. For optimum safety, remove drawstrings from children's clothing or cut them very short. If necessary, replace them with velcro fasteners, elastic, or snaps.

**Sleepwear** Sleepwear should be fire retardant. In addition to checking for fire retardancy labels, be sure to follow the manufacturer's washing guidelines to maintain the retardancy. Also sleepwear should be well fitting—no frills or baggy arms and legs that can much more easily catch fire than snugly fitting items.

**Choosing shoes** What types of shoes should you buy for your child as his or her feet grow? Follow these tips:

- **Prewalkers.** Infants and crawlers need only booties or socks to keep their feet warm. Baby feet don't need extra support. Baby shoes are fine as long as they are flexible. Make sure the sole is shaped like a foot. The soles should toe in slightly and not be straight from front to back.

- **Toddlers.** As soon as your child starts walking, he should be fitted for shoes at a reputable children's shoe store. Leather and canvas shoes let young feet breathe and allow freedom of movement. For new walkers, avoid thick or rubbery soles that can grab the floor and cause falls. Toddler feet grow quickly, so have your child's feet sized every two to three months.

- **Preschoolers and up.** Active kids need flexible shoes that are made of breathable leather or canvas. Once walking becomes routine, switch to skid-resistant rubber soles. Toe boxes—the front part of the shoes—should be roomy. Children 4 to 9 should have their feet measured every four to six months.

*For information on your baby's first shoes, see **page 150**.*

# Sleep needs

By age 1, babies typically sleep around 14 hours per day, including two daytime naps. By 18 months, most children sleep 13 to 14 hours daily, with only one midday nap. By age 4, kids reduce their sleep needs to an average of 11 to 12 hours a night, usually forgoing naps entirely. As children grow, they simply need less sleep, and a typical 5-year-old needs only about 11 hours of shut-eye a day. Keep in mind, though, that like adults, kids vary in their sleep needs, and some 5-year-olds may need to take an occasional cat nap after a day at kindergarten, especially if they've had lots of physical activity or aren't feeling well. Others may do fine on an hour or so less than is usual for a child that age.

Getting enough sleep is essential for children to function normally and learn at their optimal levels. However, many children, like adults, are sleep deprived. The reasons for this are varied. Oftentimes, working parents allow their children to stay up late so that they will have enough time to spend with them in the evenings. When children are enrolled in childcare, nursery school, or kindergarten, they are often required to be up and out of the house before they've had their full dose of sleep. Signs of sleep deprivation include lethargy or, conversely, excessively energetic behavior. Children who need more sleep than they are getting may be mislabeled as having attention-deficit disorder, may be difficult to control, and may be extremely moody.

> **"IT WORKED FOR ME"**
>
> ## *Winding Down at Bedtime*
>
> I sit on the edge of the bed with Alec, who is 4, and help him send good wishes to every family member by saying, "God bless Daddy, God bless Jonathan, God bless Aunt Harriet, God bless Cousin Timmy," and so on. Then I say, "May you have a very, very good night's sleep and be refreshed for..." and then I fill in whatever is coming up the next day.

**Getting enough sleep** If your child is not getting the sleep he needs:

- **Establish a bedtime routine.** Following a set order of evening rituals leading to bed helps a child feel sleepy enough to fall asleep when he gets into bed, instead of lying awake.
- **Adjust your child's daytime sleep schedule.** If your child has difficulty getting to sleep because of long daytime naps, shorten the naps. If you need to have your child awake in the evening so that you can spend more time with him, lengthen his daytime naps, and/or ask your sitter or his childcare center to arrange for extra daytime rest periods.
- **Adjust your own schedule.** Begin your time with him earlier in the evening, perhaps bringing home work to do after he's asleep.
- **Dim the lights.** Though you needn't make a child who's frightened of the dark sleep in a dark room, research shows that sleeping in a brightly lit room reduces the quality of sleep. If your child's emotional needs require some lighting, opt for a night light or keep the door ajar until he's asleep.
- **Let your child's sleep needs lead the way.** Help your child adjust to the schedule that suits your family gradually. Put the night owl to bed and let him play in bed until he falls asleep. Wake him when you need for him to get up. His own sleep needs will soon reset his clock. Likewise, keep the early bird up later, which will make him more likely to sleep later in the morning.

*See page 384 for tips on establishing bedtime routines.*

### Night-lights

*"Are night-lights a good idea in my child's room?"*

Absolutely. Many children pass through stages of being afraid of the dark. Often they outgrow such fears by age 5 or 6, but in the meantime a simple, dim night-light can go a long way toward alleviating their fears. Don't worry about a little bit of light keeping your child awake at night. Her own fears would be much more likely to prevent her from sleeping.

Night-lights that guide the ways to the bathroom, down stairways, and to exits (in case of a fire) are also a good idea from a safety point of view. In rooms where bunk beds are used, a night-light is essential to help the child in the top bunk climb down should she need to do so.

In choosing a night-light make sure that it is UL (Underwriter's Laboratory) approved. Plug it into an outlet away from flammable materials such as drapes or bed coverings. Use a very low wattage bulb, preferably one that does not get hot, such as a compact fluorescent light. An overhead light on a dimmer switch will also do the trick.

### Nighttime room temperature

*"Is it better for a child to sleep with the windows open or closed? What about air conditioning?"*

Healthy babies weighing at least eight pounds are pretty adept at regulating their own body temperatures and they do well in rooms with comfortable temperatures between 65° and 68°F. Ideal room temperature for sleeping is around 65°F, although 60° for sleeping in cool or cold weather is adequate. Many parents worry that their houses are too cool for their young children and hence, overheat them. The dry air of overheated houses can parch the skin and harden the mucus in the nose, irritating air passages and lowering resistance to infection, so it's actually healthier to set the thermostat a bit lower.

Although it's good for children (and adults) to get a daily dose of fresh air, it's not necessarily healthier to sleep with the windows open or shut. If a more comfortable temperature is achieved with the windows open, or the room is stuffy, then feel free to open them. Be cautious, however, with young children, and make sure window guards are in place to prevent accidental falls. You can also use locks that allow the window to open only a few inches, or open double hung windows from the top only.

Air conditioning is fine, too, if a comfortable temperature can be maintained. Most units today have thermostats which allow for steady and fairly accurate climate control. If your unit does not, it may make the room uncomfortably cool if left on all night, in which case it might be better to cool the room first with air-conditioning then use a fan once your child is tucked into bed. In either case, never place a cooling device so that it blows right on a child. It should, rather, circulate the air around the room.

## Making exercise a part of the day

Regular aerobic exercise—the kind that gives the heart and lungs a good workout—is essential for your child's current and future health. Kids who get regular exercise have better appetites, grow physically stronger, and tend to sleep better. What's more, exercise helps calm stressed-out children. The long-term benefits of exercise include a re-duced risk of cardiovascular disease in adulthood.

Kids as young as age 2 are capable of learning and very willing to learn the basics of sports skills, such as running, jumping, and tossing and catching a ball. In fact, it would be difficult to stop a child from having physical fun. It's also important for your child to limit seden-tary pastimes like watching TV and to see you keeping active. A worthwhile family routine of taking brisk walks together after dinner can accomplish both goals.

**Encouraging "couch potatoes" to exercise** For kids who've developed a habit of lazing in front of the TV, try these ideas to get them moving:

• **Invite your child to join you in an activity.** Playing with you is always more fun than watching TV.

• **Make commercial time, exercise time.** When you're watching together, use station breaks and ads as opportunities to do some jumping jacks.

• **Don't put out snacks during TV time.** Eating and watching is a bad combination that could lay the foundation for a lifetime of unhealthy habits.

---

**"IT WORKED FOR ME"**

### Working Out with Kids

When I do my daily workout, my two sons, ages 4 years and 18 months, join me. Mostly they mimic whatever I do, whether it's leg lifts or aerobics. They think exercise is fun time with Mommy, so I get to fit regular exercise into my schedule while they burn off extra energy.

---

**"IT WORKED FOR ME"**

### Creative Walks

To increase my 4-year-old son's interest in walking, I try to turn our walks into scavenger hunts: I encourage him to look for a leaf with five veins, a pink flower, and other things.

# Seasonal health concerns

As the weather changes and seasons transform the outdoor environment, you will need to take appropriate measures to adapt to the climate. Both hot and cold conditions require special attention, whether it means gearing up for the cold and guarding against frostbite or preventing heat stroke and protecting skin from the harmful rays of the sun.

**Winter weather concerns**  Winter's chill can be both invigorating and hazardous. Dressing for warmth is a key concern. Following are a few cold-weather safeguards to follow:
- **Dress your child for wintry weather.**
- **Apply sunscreen to his face.**
- **Warn children against touching cold metal;** their skin might stick to the surface.
- **Have your child remove wet garments,** especially socks, boots, and mittens, because they make skin more sensitive to frostbite. Check for frost nip (skin is red and stings) or frostbite (skin may be pale, numb, glossy, and hard).
- **Give your child a snack.** Food provides energy to help keep kids warm. Good choices are warm cocoa or soup. They'll keep him hydrated as well as heated.

*For first aid for treating frostbite, see **page 686**.*

**Frostbite prevention**  Prolonged exposure to cold, wind, and moisture can increase a child's risk of frostbite, which occurs when skin and underlying tissues freeze, turning skin pale, numb, glossy, and hard to the touch. Frostbite primarily occurs on parts of the body that are exposed to the elements.

To prevent frostbite:
- **Dress your child warmly.**
- **Monitor his condition.** Keep tabs on him when he's playing outdoors on a cold or windy day. If his face looks very red or chapped, take him indoors. If the skin on any part of his body turns from red to white and is very cold and numb, bring him indoors immediately.
- **Watch the temperature.** Keep your child inside when the temperature approaches 5°F and/or 0°F windchill.
- **Feed him.** Give your child plenty of fluids and a hearty meal or snack before he heads outdoors. This will help blood carry heat to his extremities.

**Winter sun protection**  Although the sun's rays aren't as strong during winter, they can still damage the skin. If your child spends a lot of time in the snow, or you live in an area where the sun's rays are strong all year round, you need to pay extra attention to sun protection. Ultraviolet (UV) radiation increases 4 to 5 percent every 1,000 feet above sea level. For example, the sun in the Colorado Rockies in January is just as potent as the sun on a New York beach in June. Also, sun exposure almost doubles when rays reflect off ice and snow, according to the Skin Cancer Foundation.

No matter where you live, if your child will be outdoors for more than 20 minutes, even on a cloudy day, apply sunscreen with a sun protection factor (SPF) of 15 or higher to all exposed areas, including his nose, the back of his neck, tips of ears, and the backs of hands, if he is likely to take off his mittens. Also apply a lip balm with an SPF of 15. Choose a PABA-free sunscreen for kids.

**Dressing for cold, winter weather**  Toddlers and older kids may seem impervious to cold, shedding hats and mittens on even the coldest days. Despite their seeming resilience, they *do* need protection from the elements. Try these smart cold-weather dress tips, especially in snowy or cold, damp weather:
- **Dress your child in layers.** Start by dressing your child in long underwear made of a lightweight, breathable fabric like cotton, polypropylene, silk, or any of the new insulating fibers. Layer on a light cotton button-up shirt, long-sleeved T-shirt, or a turtleneck. Add a heavier top made of wool, cotton flannel, or polar fleece. The layers will trap air, creating insulation. Add a jacket and pants that are waterproof and insulated with down, fleece, or polyester fiberfill.
- **Keep your child's head covered.** Have your child wear a knit hat, lined cap, or snug-fitting hood that covers his ears. Avoid long, dangling scarves that can pose a safety hazard.
- **Keep hands and feet toasty.** Choose mittens that are lined and waterproof. Mittens are warmer than gloves because the fingers give off and share heat. If your child will wear only gloves, look for ones that are lined and waterproof. Elasticized wrists help mittens and gloves stay put. Keep feet warm with thin cotton socks topped with thicker socks made of wool or heavy cotton. Look for waterproof, lined boots, with a low, flat heel and a treaded sole for traction. A waterproof cloth top with a drawstring seals out snow and keeps boots on.

• **Protect your child's face.** Shield your child's face from wind-burn or frostbite with a knit face mask or turtleneck neck warmer, not a loose-fitting scarf. If your child does wear a scarf, make sure it is tucked into his jacket securely, rather than having the ends hang loosely.

### Encouraging hat wearing

*"What can I do to get my 4-year-old son to wear a hat during the winter?"*

Ask your child what style of hat he'd like. Kids 4 and up are fashion-conscious—and if your child picks out a hat he likes, he'll be more likely to wear it. Be sure the hat isn't scratchy. Kids who are allergic to wool need knit caps made out of soft, but heavy-weight, cotton or acrylic (look for ones with double layers). Or, choose a cloth or wool hat that's lined with a soft, non-itchy material. Also, steer clear of hats that fit so tightly they give the child a headache.

If your son still refuses to wear a hat, invest in earmuffs, a wide head band (the kind worn by skiers), or a jacket with a hood—one without a drawstring. Some kids tend to lose hats, or consider them a "hassle" to put on. Hoods are easier to keep track of, and your son may be more apt to pull on his hood if his ears get cold than to search for his hat.

**Warm-weather concerns** Hot weather brings its own set of concerns, such as sunburn, heat exhaustion, and sun stroke. During hot summer months:

• **Keep your kids indoors in an air-conditioned or fan-cooled room between 10 a.m. and 4 p.m.,** when the suns rays are strongest. If your child must go outdoors, have her stay in the shade. At the beach or park, have her sit under an umbrella.

• **Dress kids in lightweight, breathable fabrics,** such as cotton. Light colors will reflect the heat; darker ones absorb heat.

• **Never leave a child in a hot car,** even if the window is partially rolled down. The intense heat can lead to heat exhaustion, heat-stroke, or death.

• **Provide plenty of liquids** if your child is playing outside. Ideally, he should drink eight ounces of noncarbonated fluid every half hour. Water is best and juice is okay—but juice contains a lot of sugar, which can slow fluid absorption, so dilute the juice with water. Avoid salt pills, which can interfere with fluid absorption.

• **If your child takes any medications, ask her doctor if the sun or heat will interact adversely with the medicine.** Antihistamines, for example, slow down sweat production, raising the risk of heat stroke. Some antibiotics and cortisone products can make a child more susceptible to sunburn.

**Sunburn prevention** A number of studies suggest that just one severe burn in childhood significantly raises the risk of skin cancer in adulthood. The key is prevention. To sunproof your child:

• **Opt for shade, when possible.** Encourage play under sun umbrellas and other sources of shade. Use a stroller canopy when taking a walk.

• **Avoid reflected light.** Remember that sunlight bounces off sand and water, so even if your child is guarded by an umbrella at the beach, reflected rays can still reach him, making sunscreen a must for kids over 6 months of age. For infants, cover them with clothing or a lightweight sheet.

• **Dress kids in sunproof clothing made of tightly woven fabric,** like cotton. Long sleeves and pants offer good sun protection, and a hat with a three-inch brim isreommended. At the very least, have your child wear a baseball cap with the bill pointing forward, to protect his face.

• **Use sunscreen with a sun protection factor (SPF) of 15 or higher,** even on cloudy or hazy days. Don't forget areas like the back of the neck, backs of hands, nose, and tips of ears. Reapply according to the label directions. If the sunscreen is not waterproof, reapply after swimming. Keep sunscreen away from the eyes and mouth. Apply an SPF 15 lip balm, too, and reapply it every couple of hours.

**PARENTS ALERT**

*Heat-related Illnesses*

Children who are overheated can develop dehydration, heat exhaustion, heat cramps, and/or heat rash. When your child's ability to withstand heat shuts down, he may develop potentially fatal heat stroke or sun stroke. It's essential that children who have experienced too much heat be cooled immediately and given plenty of water to drink. (For first aid for these conditions, see page **690**.) The best way to prevent heat-related illnesses is by keeping kids cool and well hydrated.

• **Try to schedule outdoor play and beach time for early and late in the day,** avoiding the hours between 10 a.m. and 4 p.m., when the sun's rays are strongest.

**Sunglasses for kids** Most kids don't need sunglasses. The natural lens of the eye has a built-in UV filter, and it's only as people get older—into adulthood—that the filter stops working well and sunglasses become necessary.

A handful of kids do need sunglasses, however, including those who are prone to migraines, since the bright light can trigger a headache. Children who have a history of herpes simplex in or near the eyes also benefit from the extra protection that sunglasses offer since UV rays activate the virus. Also, if your child constantly squints or uses his hand to shield his eyes when he's outdoors, he may need sunglasses simply for comfort. When buying, choose ones with brown or green plastic lenses that block both UVA and UVB rays.

*See **page 668** for symptoms and treatments for bee stings and bug bites.*

**Keeping kids safe from summer bugs and bees** Whenever there's a likelihood of coming into contact with ticks, bees, and other insects, have your child:
• Wear light-colored long-sleeved shirts and pants outdoors, if possible. Tuck pants cuffs into socks.
• Avoid infested woods or waters or other areas where insects gather.
• Use a repellent containing no more than 10 percent DEET.
• Avoid using products, such as soaps, that have a flower-like scent.
• Know the signs of serious allergic reactions to bites and stings and first-aid treatments for all forms of insect and bee bites.

**Preventing tick-borne illnesses** Unlike other insects that bite and move on, ticks burrow into the skin. Since they harbor a number of illnesses, including Lyme disease and Rocky Mountain spotted fever, they need to be identified and removed as soon as possible. Fortunately, a tick must be attached for 36 to 48 hours before it can transmit disease, so daily tick checks can reduce your child's risk for a tick-related illness. When checking your child for ticks, pay special attention to areas along the hairline, in the groin, under the armpits, behind the knees, and in eyebrows, where ticks can easily hide.

If you have a furry pet, check it regularly for ticks and remove them promptly. Ask your vet to recommend a safe tick shampoo or dip for the animal. Put a tick collar on your pet whenever it's outside.

Spraying your property with a tick pesticide also helps. Just be sure to follow the package safety directions explicitly.

**Using DEET safely** When used as directed, an insect repellent containing DEET (diethyltoluamide) can keep bugs, including ticks, at bay. The American Academy of Pediatrics recommends that it be sprayed very sparingly on children, and not to use it on babies younger than 1 year. When choosing a product that contains DEET, be sure the concentration of DEET does not exceed 10 percent. Read the product labels carefully; some contain 100 percent DEET.

Apply repellent to exposed skin on legs and onto the pants cuffs, shirt collars or socks. Don't spray it on hands or faces or on any irritated skin. Apply the repellent just before your child enters a wooded or bushy area, and reapply it every two hours, as long as your child remains outdoors. When your child comes indoors, have him wash or bathe thoroughly to remove all traces of the repellent.

*See pages 631 and 646 for information on treating tick-related illesses.*

**PARENTS ALERT**

### Recognizing the Tick

A baby or "nymph" deer tick is about the size and color of a poppy seed or a pencil dot. An adult deer tick is about the size of a small apple seed and has a black head with a rust-colored back and abdomen. Ticks have 8 legs. Ticks engorged with blood can swell to nearly one-quarter of an inch. If you aren't sure that an insect is a tick, take it to your area veterinarian or county cooperative extension association for identification.

# CHAPTER 2

# Diet and Nutrition

**F**eeding your child right should begin with introducing her to healthful choices and making sure that most of the food you serve suits her nutritional needs, though there's nothing wrong with allowing your child an occasional treat. The best way to ensure that she eats a well-balanced diet, of course, is to set a good example yourself.

## *Eating right*

**E**ating right is easy for infants, whose choices are limited and who are not influenced by television commercials or their friends' preferences. Beyond infancy, however, your child will need your help making appropriate choices. There's more to developing good eating habits than simply choosing one food over another. By learning to eat to satisfy hunger rather than merely for pleasure or out of boredom, your child will develop a healthy attitude toward food, which is essential for maintaining a lifetime of healthful eating.

Like adults, children need a variety of foods. In many ways, however, children's nutritional needs differ from adults'. Certainly, your child needs less total food than you do, but because he is growing, he'll need more food in proportion to his body weight than you do. He'll need more frequent meals—as many as six a day. Some foods that are good for you may not be right for him yet; other foods that you limit for yourself—such as whole milk—may be the best choice for him. And because he's still working out his relationship to food and eating, he may develop some quirky eating habits. These behaviors are perfectly normal and need to be respected.

*For information about the nutritional needs of infants, see **pages 21–31**.*

## Dealing with Picky Eating

Picky eating involves a variety of behaviors. To help your child develop a more tolerant attitude toward food:

### Do...

serve your child age-appropriate portions. Give toddlers portions that are one-fourth to one-third the size of adult portions. A toddler faced with both a plateful of food and a parent who expects him to eat it all, is likely to become fussy and finicky at the table. Increase portion sizes for preschoolers and kindergartners, but don't expect your 5-year-old to eat the same amount of cooked carrots as you do. By scaling down portion sizes, you give your child the opportunity to ask for seconds, which will help him feel in control.

offer new and unfamiliar foods, but do so in small portions and don't insist that your child eat everything. In fact, when a food is served for the first time, let your child know that you only expect him to sample it and that he may spit it out if he doesn't like it.

serve your child's old favorites—or at least a familiar, acceptable food—at each meal. If you want to add a dish that your child has not shown much interest in before, pair it with something she likes. For example, if you are encouraging her to enjoy green beans, serve them with her favorite macaroni.

serve a small dessert with dinner. It's likely your child will down her dessert first, but that's okay. The dessert will stimulate her appetite, making her more willing to move on to more nutritious fare.

### Don't...

worry if each meal is not nutritionally complete. Though your child may eat only starchy foods one day, his natural desire for variety will motivate him to nibble on a piece of fruit or a vegetable later on and to try a small serving of meat the next day. During a week's time, he'll consume a variety of foods and get the majority of the nutrients he needs.

use food as either a reward or a punishment. If you bribe your child to eat her spinach so that she can have a "yummy dessert," you inadvertently reinforce the idea that sweets are better than nutritious food. If you reward good behavior with a treat, you teach an unhealthy association between food and positive feelings. Likewise, if you threaten to withhold a food treat for any unacceptable behavior, you teach that food can be used as a weapon, an idea that even a young child can internalize and use at future meals.

prepare separate meals for your picky eater. Most parents simply don't have time to be short order cooks. Also, if your child gets into the habit of eating only specially prepared meals, she may never want to dine on foods the whole family is enjoying.

make enticing foods your child sees others enjoying completely off limits. Allow her the occasional candy or soft drink that's served at a birthday party, for instance, to avoid making these foods seem even more enticing. (If you disapprove of the menu at a party, feed your child well beforehand so that she won't be too hungry.) Likewise, having a sweetened breakfast cereal on occasion will not ruin your child's health. Consider allowing her to mix a restricted cereal with an approved one, showing her that you value her opinion, while helping her to maintain a healthful diet.

**Family meals**

Try to sit down as a family for at least one meal a day and use the opportunity to talk. The time you spend at the dinner table also teaches your child table manners, the pleasure of communicating, and the sense of closeness and belonging that will nourish him as much as the food.

# Handling dining dilemmas

Children go through phases when they refrain from eating food of a particular color. Or they panic when one food on the plate touches another. Some kids subsist for weeks on end on nothing but macaroni and cheese. A few won't eat food that's "broken," such as a cut-up piece of cheese or a half of a cookie. All of these behaviors are normal and all will disappear as abruptly as they began, provided that you don't make too much of a fuss about it. There's no need, during your child's picky stage, to go overboard with serving him only what he wants. But accommodating him somewhat—offering a spoonful of macaroni and cheese, along with the rest of the family meal—can keep food quirks from turning into mealtime battles.

# Adding fun—and nutrition

Though you don't want your child to expect you to carve every sandwich into a cute shape, adding a little fun and fancy to meals and snacks can help interest your child in new foods. Try these strategies to perk up young appetites:

• **Enlist kids' help in the kitchen.** They're more likely to eat foods they've helped prepare. Even toddlers can wash and tear lettuce for salads and help stir ingredients. Older children can also help make up the menu.

• **Serve cut-up fruits and vegetables** to children age 4 and up with dips featuring low-fat salad dressing, yogurt, or even ketchup.

• **Decorate casseroles or baked pasta dishes with "faces" made of cut up veggies.**

• **Serve foods in unusual containers.** For example, serve small fruits and vegetables in a muffin tin; turn clean Frisbees into picnic plates.

• **Substitute a bagel, pita pocket, or hamburger bun** for regular bread. Make two-tone sandwiches, using a slice of white bread on top and whole-wheat on the bottom.

• **Grate or finely chop zucchini, carrots, mushrooms, or broccoli and add** to spaghetti sauce, soups, and casseroles. Add grated zucchini and carrots to homemade breads and muffins and serve as a snack, breakfast, or dessert.

# Feeding your 1-year-old

With teeth come far greater menu possibilities for your child. By age 1, his ability to chew and his continuing need for calories should make solid foods the bulk of his diet.

Between ages 1 and 2, most toddlers need about 900 to 1,400 calories a day, though counting calories is not necessary. What's important is to offer a variety of healthful options and to encourage, but not push, your child to eat at regular meal times. He may also need three to four snacks each day. While considering the recommended daily portions from each food group, don't worry too much if your child gets most of his calories from one group one day and from another group the next day. As long as he regularly eats foods from each category, he'll achieve the balance he needs over the course of a few days.

## Recommended Servings for 1-Year-Olds

**Grains:** 4–6 servings a day
**Fruits and Vegetables:** 4–6 servings a day
(including at least 1 serving citrus fruit)
**Dairy Products:** 4 servings a day
**Protein (Meat, Fish, Poultry, Eggs):**
2–4 servings a day

### Recommended Serving Sizes

**Grains, beans, and legumes:**
½ slice of bread
¼ bagel
1 ounce cereal
¼ cup cooked rice, pasta, mashed peas, or beans

**Fruits and vegetables:**
¼ cup broccoli, peas, spinach, carrots, corn, yellow squash
½ whole fruit, such as a pear, or ½ cup chopped or cooked fruit

**Dairy products:**
½ cup whole milk
½ cup yogurt
1 oz. cheese

**Protein:**
1 egg
2 oz. meat, fish, poultry
2½ oz. tofu

# Feeding your 2- or 3-year-old

By age 2, your child's abilities to chew and to form strong opinions about food are well established. Since his rate of growth slows considerably during this period, his appetite may diminish for a time. After all, 2- and 3-year-olds have far more interesting things to do than eat! It's important not to express too much concern if your child suddenly cuts down on his food intake. Rest assured that he'll eat when he's hungry. (Of course, some 2- and 3-year-olds develop

## Recommended Servings for 2- and 3-Year-Olds

**Grains:** 6 or more servings a day

**Fruits and Vegetables:** 6 or more servings a day (including at least 1 serving citrus fruit)

**Dairy Products:** 4 servings a day

**Protein (Meat, Fish, Poultry and Eggs):** 4 servings a day

### Recommended Serving Sizes

**Grains, beans, and legumes:**
1 slice of bread
½ bagel
½ cup cereal or pasta ½ cup mashed peas, pinto or kidney beans, or chick peas

**Fruits and vegetables:**
¼ cup broccoli, peas, spinach, carrots, corn, yellow squash
½ whole fruit, such as a pear, or ½ cup chopped or cooked fruit

**Dairy products:**
½ cup low-fat milk
½ cup low-fat yogurt
1 oz. reduced-fat cheese

**Protein:**
1 egg
2 oz. meat, fish, poultry
2½ oz. tofu

bigger appetites when their growth rates demand more calories.) Children this age generally consume anywhere from 900 to 1,700 calories a day.

During these years, continue to provide lots of variety and to allow frequent snacking along with regularly scheduled meals. Finicky eating may become an issue at this time. Most 2- and 3-year-olds simply are not very adventurous when it comes to eating and may find new foods intimidating or scary. They are also becoming more independent, and by saying "No!" when you offer them a food—even a favorite one—they gain a needed sense of control. You can help by respecting their choices and not insisting that they eat every offered food and by regularly offering familiar foods as part of your family's meals.

Age 2 is the time for your child to begin the transition from the higher-fat diet of a toddler to the lower-fat, lower-cholesterol diet that will become part of his lifelong habit of healthy eating. It may be time to switch from whole milk to 2 percent and then to 1 percent, gradually reducing fat to no more than 30 percent of his total daily calories by age 5. Also limit eggs to two to three per week. Note that some pediatricians and nutritionists prefer, however, that children continue to consume whole milk unless there's a reason not to. Continue to avoid offering foods that are potential choking hazards since he's still learning to chew properly and is likely to stuff more food into his mouth than he can safely swallow.

# Feeding your preschooler

Your 4- and 5-year-old should be consuming between 1,000 and 1,800 calories a day, depending on her height, weight, and level of activity. Offer her a variety of foods from the basic food groups, but be prepared for some continued pickiness; kids in this age group still have strong food preferences and their tastes can vary from day to day. At this age, many kids develop a dislike for mixed-up foods such as casseroles. Many prefer to have each food completely separated, which makes compartmentalized plates very popular with preschoolers. It's wise not to insist that your child eat a combo that she finds truly disgusting. The phase will soon pass. Four- and 5-year olds are now able to consume just about all foods, including the crunchy fruits and vegetables that you wisely restricted earlier.

## Recommended Servings for 4- and 5-Year-Olds

**Grains:** 4 servings a day

**Fruits and Vegetables:** 6–7 servings a day (including at least 1 serving citrus fruit)

**Dairy Products:** 2–5 servings a day

**Protein (Meat, Fish, Poultry and Eggs):** 2 servings a day

### Recommended Serving Sizes

**Grains, beans, legumes:**
1 slice bread
½ bagel
½ cup cereal
½ cup rice, pasta, or beans, chickpeas, or lentils

**Fruits and vegetables:**
½ cup asparagus, broccoli, peas, spinach, carrots, corn, yellow squash
1 small or ½ large whole fruit
½ cup chopped or cooked fruit

**Dairy products:**
½ cup low-fat milk
½ cup low-fat yogurt

**Protein:**
1 egg
2 oz. lean meat, fish, or poultry
2½ oz. tofu

As many preschoolers enter kindergarten, they will have their first "big-kid" exposure to other kids' eating habits and to school lunches, either of which may undermine all your conscientious attention to a balanced diet for a time. Your child will still do most of his eating at home where you can oversee the content of meals and snacks. If his school lunch is not as nutritionally sound as it should be (many are high in fat), pack him a nutritious lunch from home if possible. Don't overreact to your child's curiosity and his desire to experiment with foods you may not have made available to him at home. Except in cases of food allergies, don't label any foods as off limits, since this may increase their appeal. Also, this stance works

## Fast Foods at Home

My 4-year-old daughter insisted on foods that tasted like fast-food restaurant fare at every meal— things like hamburgers and tacos—and refused to eat vegetables. Her idea of a serving of vegetables was a plate of French fries! Finally, I started adding grated vegetables to hamburgers before I broiled them. I also mixed corn, grated carrots, cut-up string beans, and chopped broccoli with ground beef and taco mix and spooned the concoction into taco shells, which I then sprinkled liberally with grated low-fat cheddar cheese. My daughter loves these nutritious treats!

To further boost her intake of vegetables, I make "fake" French fries, dipping quarter-inch strips of zucchini into a batter made of flour, water, and just a little salt— and baking them at 400° for about 15 minutes.

*For information about milk substitutes, see* **pages 517–18**. *For a list of non-dairy foods that are high in calcium, see* **page 514**.

against your continuing efforts to get your child to try new foods.

Since children this age are very interested in growing bigger and stronger, your best strategy for helping your child choose healthful foods over empty calories is to emphasize the fuel-aspect of food, saying something like, "Apples help you grow big and strong, but candy bars don't help build your muscles."

## The basic food groups

The Food Pyramid on page 507 shows the optimum proportion of each food group in your child's daily diet. If possible, offer your child items from each group every day.

**Grains** Foods such as cereal, bread, potatoes, rice, and pasta, provide carbohydrates, which are essential for energy, and fiber, which promotes good digestion and may prevent cancer later in life. Though butter and creamy sauces do not pose a health problem for toddlers, you may want to limit these flavor enhancers when you introduce grains so that your child doesn't develop a lifelong habit of enjoying them only when they're smothered in fat. Choose grains that are fortified with vitamins and minerals and whole-grain varieties.

**Fruits and vegetables** Produce offers fiber and numerous vitamins, especially C and A. Most children prefer the sweet flavors of fruits to the more bitter taste of vegetables, so don't worry if yours spits out his spinach and opts for bananas. Introduce vegetables more slowly if your child prefers it that way. Fruit juices do not offer the same nutritional value as whole fruits. Children who drink more than 12 ounces of fruit juice a day are more likely to become overweight or fail to reach their potential height than kids who drink less. With few molars in place, toddlers should steer clear of crunchy fruits and vegetables.

**Dairy products** Dairy, which includes milk, yogurt, cheese, and some puddings, provides calcium, protein, and, in some instances, vitamin D. Though children over the age of 2 should switch to low-fat milk products, children under 2 need the fat and cholesterol that whole milk contains to ensure proper growth.

**Meat, poultry, fish, and eggs** These foods provide protein and zinc. Your primary concerns when serving them should be to make sure that they are thoroughly cooked and to prevent choking by offering small, well-cut pieces and making sure that all bones have been removed. Eggs, which are a good source of protein, need not be limited for toddlers, though you'll want to cut back to fewer servings as your child gets older. One concern with introducing eggs to your child's diet, however, is that they may trigger an allergic reaction.

**Sweets and fats** small amounts

**Protein** 2–4 servings

**Dairy** 2–4 servings

**Vegetables** 2–3 servings

**Fruit** 2–3 servings

**Breads & Grains** 4–6 servings

### Is it safe for a child to be a vegetarian?

*"Our family has gradually switched to a vegetarian diet. Is such a diet okay for our child, who will soon be weaned?"*

You will have given your child a good start if you have breast-fed him though his early months—and, in fact, continue to do so throughout the first year. When you do wean your baby, it is far preferable for your child to include milk products in his diet. Milk contains not only calcium and protein, but also a number of vitamins, all of which are important to your baby's health and development.

Toddlers and older children can eat a vegetarian diet, as long as they eat other foods and food combinations that provide all the nutrients they need for proper growth and development. Children who eat dairy products and eggs can easily get their daily quota of protein without further adjustments to their diets. Those who eat no dairy products or eggs also run the risk of consuming too little protein unless they eat protein-rich alternatives such as tofu and protein-enriched pasta. Parents can create "complete" proteins by combining two "incomplete" protein foods, such as rice and beans, macaroni and peas, or chickpeas and green beans. Kids also may need a vitamin $B_{12}$ supplement. (Check with your doctor before giving your child supplements.) You also need to make sure that your child gets an adequate amount of calcium as well as vitamins A and D if he doesn't drink milk. Try soy milk fortified with calcium and vitamins.

Children on a meatless diet may be deficient in iron, which is why they should consume plenty of iron-rich foods (see chart). Eating vitamin C-rich foods at the same time can boost iron absorption. Some vegetarian children, however, may need to take an iron supplement.

It's generally a good idea to give vegan kids a daily children's multivitamin and mineral supplement just to be safe.

### Do kids need vitamin supplements?

*"Should I give my 4-year-old vitamins to make sure he's getting all his nutrients?"*

Because most children get the nutrients they need from the foods they eat and the milk they drink, a daily vitamin-and-mineral supplement is not necessary for healthy kids who eat a varied, well-balanced diet. But it's fine to give kids age 1 and older a children's multivitamin and mineral supplement three or four times a week, especially if they are in a picky eating stage. However, some kids—

particularly those who consume more than 32 ounces of milk a day—may need extra iron since milk and milk products can interfere with the proper absorption of iron. Such children should eat plenty of iron-rich foods, such as slightly mashed kidney beans, potatoes (baked in the skin), prunes, eggs, tuna, and bananas. If your child's health-care provider suspects that he isn't getting enough iron and is anemic, he or she may recommend an iron supplement rather than a multivitamin.

## Heart-smart eating for the whole family

The roots of heart disease begin in early childhood. Studies have shown that some children as young as age 5 have "fatty streaks" in their arteries, which may lead to atherosclerosis (hardening of the arteries) in adulthood. Researchers feel these fatty streaks are caused by a diet high in saturated fats and cholesterol. Saturated fat is found is butter, cheese, whole milk, ice cream, meat, and, to some degree, poultry and fish. Cholesterol is found in egg yolks, dairy products, meat, poultry, fish, shellfish, and many commercially baked products.

To ensure that your child develops a heart-smart diet early on, limit her fat and cholesterol intake after the age of 2 by following these suggestions from the National Cholesterol Education Program:

- Limit consumption of saturated fats (butter, whole milk, and whole-milk products, fatty meats, high-fat shortenings and lard, many prepared frozen dinners, and chocolate) to 10 percent of her total daily caloric intake.
- Limit total fat consumption to no more than 30 percent of the daily diet and cholesterol to less than 300 mg of cholesterol a day.

**PARENTS ALERT**

### *Hazardous Foods*

*A few common foods and spices can be poisonous or harmful to children:*

**Salt.** The salt, or sodium, found in baby foods, baby formula, and most other foods is not a problem for healthy children. Kids with high blood pressure may need to cut back on sodium, however. Any child who consumes an extraordinarily large amount of salt, sodium bicarbonate, or soy sauce may suffer from salt poisoning and may experience seizures.

**Nutmeg.** Normal amounts of nutmeg contained in cookies and cakes pose no hazards. But if a child swallows a very large amount of nutmeg, she may suffer hallucinations. This is very rare.

**Cooking extracts.** Extracts such as vanilla that contain alcohol pose a poisoning risk. If a child drinks a large amount of vanilla, he may suffer central nervous system damage, experience seizures, lapse into a coma, or even die.

**Bay leaves.** The sharp edges of bay leaves have been known to cause damage to the gastrointestinal tract. If you cook with bay leaves remove all the leaves and any parts that have broken off before serving.

*Other foods can cause allergic reactions in susceptible people. For more on food allergies, see **pages 515–20**.*

You can accomplish this by substituting low-fat or skim for whole-milk products; substituting sunflower or safflower oils for high-fat cooking oils, limiting egg yolks to no more than three or four a week; choosing trimmed, lean red meats or by replacing meat with leaner fish; and removing the skin from poultry

• Eat a greater quantity and variety of fruits, vegetables, grains, and legumes.

## Diet and weight

While chubby children are often considered cute, excess pounds may put them at risk for future health problems, including high cholesterol, diabetes, and heart disease. You can help your child maintain a healthy weight by offering lower-fat foods and by encouraging exercise.

**Feeding overweight kids**  Most experts do not recommend stringent, low-fat diets for overweight kids. By reducing total fat intake to below 30 percent of total calories, your child is at risk of missing important nutrients such as protein, vitamins, and minerals, which are essential for his growth and development. And by declaring all fats and sweets "off limits," you may inadvertently cause him to overindulge in tempting treats at friends' houses. Instead, you can help your overweight child shed extra pounds or simply slow down his weight gain by following these guidelines:

• **Limit your child's TV viewing time,** and don't let him snack on fattening foods such as potato chips when he does watch. Instead, offer fresh fruits, low-fat yogurt, or other healthful treats.

• **Increase his physical activity.** See that he gets at least 30 minutes of strenuous physical activity daily. Very chubby kids need about 60 minutes of intense exercise a day. Jumping rope, riding a tricycle or bike, playing running games, roller-skating, or swimming are all good options.

• **Limit but don't eliminate fats and sweets.** If your child is over 2, tailor his diet to include low-fat foods, substituting skim milk for low-fat milk and turkey for ham, for example. Eliminate creamy sauces and other high-fat foods from the family's diet. Also limit his intake of sweets, but don't ban them completely.

• **Serve foods in portion sizes.** Instead of placing serving bowls of food on the table, portion out food on each person's plate. Allow seconds of lower-calorie, highly nutritious foods such as greens or fruits.

- **Encourage lots of water drinking.** Or offer no-calorie fruit-flavored seltzers.
- **Eat a healthful diet yourself.** Kids mimic their parents, and if your child sees you enjoying a hot fudge sundae he'll want one too. But if he sees you snacking on pear or orange slices, he may ask to share that treat.
- **Never shame or embarrass your child about his weight.** Also don't allow others to do so. If your child is teased by his peers about his weight, teach him strategies for dealing with it, such as telling the teaser, "I don't tease you, and I don't like it when you tease me."

**Feeding underweight kids**  If your child's doctor determines that your child weighs less than she should and there is no physical cause for her low weight, simply encourage more frequent snacking, allowing some higher-fat foods such as ice cream. Don't encourage her to overload on empty calories, however. Nor should you insist that she finish everything on her plate, which could cause eating problems.

See **page 617** for information about height and weight.

See **page 493** for information about exercise.

## Healthy Substitutions

Many favorite foods are available in lower-fat, lower-calorie versions.

| Instead of... | Serve... |
| --- | --- |
| French toast | pancakes (using a reduced-fat mix) |
| scrambled eggs | poached eggs |
| banana | pear |
| ice cream bar | ice pop (or frozen fruit bar) |
| pudding | gelatin |
| chocolate-chip cookie | graham cracker |
| American cheese | part-skim mozzarella |
| bologna | turkey |
| lasagna | macaroni with low-fat cheese |
| apple juice | flavored seltzer |

## *The Nutrients Kids Need*

Eating a balanced diet — choosing a variety of foods from each of the four food groups — generally ensures that your child is getting all the vitamins and minerals she needs to fulfill her minimum daily requirement (MDR) over the course of the week. Use these charts to check that your child's diet does indeed include all the necessary nutrients:

| NUTRIENT | MDR (Ages 1–3/Ages 4–6) | WHAT IT DOES | GOOD FOOD SOURCES |
|---|---|---|---|
| Protein | 16 grams/24 grams | Builds new body tissues, helps make antibodies that combat invaders like disease-causing bacteria, transports oxygen and nutrients in the blood, aids in clotting of blood. | Meat, poultry, fish, milk and other dairy products, eggs, potatoes, tofu, protein-enriched pasta, beans and rice (combined to form a complete protein). |
| **Vitamins** Vitamin A | 400 IU*/500 IU | Helps build strong bones and teeth. Essential for normal vision, healthy cell structure. Also keeps skin healthy and protects the linings of the mouth, nose, throat, lungs, and digestive and urinary tracts against infection. | Eggs, dairy products, orange and yellow vegetables and fruits (carrots, squash, sweet potatoes, apricots, peaches, cantaloupe), and dark green leafy vegetables (spinach, kale, broccoli). |
| Vitamin D | 400 IU/400 IU | Essential for bone and teeth development. Also needed for absorption of calcium and phosphorus. | Eggs, butter, fish (and sunshine). Children are not likely to get enough vitamin D from diet or outdoor play alone, and therefore should eat foods that are fortified with vitamin D, such as fortified grains and milk. |
| Vitamin E | 6 mg**/7 mg | Vital for healthy cell structure. Protects the lungs and other tissues from damage by pollutants. Helps form red blood cells, and produces energy in the heart and muscles. | Vegetable oils, green leafy vegetables, whole-grain cereals, and wheat germ. |
| Vitamin K | 15 mcg†/20 mcg | Helps blood clot properly. | Leafy green vegetables, fruits, cow's milk, and yogurt. Most people get an adequate amount of vitamin K in their diets and do not need supplements. |
| Vitamin C | 40 mg/45 mg | Vital for growth and maintenance of healthy bones, teeth, gums, ligaments, and blood vessels. Helps the body absorb folic acid and iron. Necessary for normal immune responses to infection. Promotes wound healing. | Citrus fruits, strawberries, cantaloupe, tomatoes, potatoes, and green leafy vegetables. |

## The Nutrients Kids Need

| NUTRIENT | MDR (Ages 1–3/Ages 4–6) | WHAT IT DOES | GOOD FOOD SOURCES |
|---|---|---|---|
| **Vitamins, cont.** Thiamin (Vitamin $B_1$) | 0.7 mg/0.9 mg | Helps body break down and use carbohydrates. Important for a healthy nervous system, healthy muscles, and normal heart function. | Pork, whole-grain or enriched cereals and breads, brown rice, pasta, meat, fish, beans, eggs, wheat germ, and most vegetables. |
| Riboflavin (Vitamin $B_2$). | 0.8 mg/1.1 mg | Helps to break down carbohydrates, fats, and proteins. Aids in the production of energy in cells using oxygen. Needed for utilization of other B vitamins and for hormone production by adrenal glands. | Milk, cheese, eggs, leafy green vegetables, whole grains, and beans. |
| Niacin (Vitamin $B_3$) | 9 mg/12 mg | Helps body produce energy. Essential for proper functioning of the nervous system, for a healthy skin and digestive system. | Lean meat, poultry, fish, whole-grain products, nuts, and dried beans. |
| Vitamin $B_6$ | 1.0 mg/1.1 mg | Helps break down protein, carbohydrates, and fats from food. Helps the body produce energy. Necessary for production of red blood cells and antibodies that fight infection. Essential for normal nervous system functioning. | Chicken, fish, whole-grain cereals, wheat germ, eggs, bananas, avocados, and potatoes. |
| Folic acid | 100 mcg/200 mcg (50 IU/75 IU) | Vital for formation of red blood cells and the development and proper function of the central nervous system. | Leafy green vegetables, mushrooms, oranges, dried beans and peas, egg yolks, and fortified grain products. |
| Vitamin $B_{12}$ | 2.0 mcg/2.5 mcg | Crucial for production of red blood cells. Helps the body use carbohydrates and folic acid. Necessary for maintaining a healthy nervous system. | Kidney beans, lean meats, fish, chicken, eggs, and dairy products. |

## The Nutrients Kids Need

| NUTRIENT | MDR (Ages 1–3/Ages 4–6) | WHAT IT DOES | GOOD FOOD SOURCES |
|---|---|---|---|
| **Minerals** Calcium | 800 mg/800 mg | Essential for formation and maintenance of strong bones and teeth, blood clotting, transmission of nerve impulses, and muscle contraction. | Milk, cheese, yogurt, calcium-enriched orange juice or enriched soy milk, sardines, canned salmon, dark green leafy vegetables, and dried beans. |
| Magnesium | 80 mg/120 mg | Essential for healthy bones and teeth, the transmission of nerve impulses, and contraction of muscles. Helps convert blood sugar into energy and regulates body temperature. | Leafy green vegetables, whole grains, soybeans, and seafood. |
| Iron | 10 mg/10 mg | Critical in formation of red blood cells; carries oxygen in blood. Helps store oxygen in muscles for use during exercise. Helps convert blood sugar into energy. | Liver, meat, eggs, chicken, fish, green lefty vegetables, dried fruit, enriched or whole-grain cereals, breads, and pasta, dried beans. |
| Zinc | 10 mg/10 mg | Helps body manufacture protein and the genetic material of cells. Necessary for normal rate of growth, development of reproductive organs, and healing of wounds and burns. | Lean meat, seafood, whole-grain breads and cereals, and dried beans. |
| Potassium | MDR has not been established | Works with sodium to control the body's water balance, conduction of nerve impulses, and maintenance of a normal heart rhythm. Helps in storage and breakdown of carbohydrates to produce energy. | Green leafy vegetables, oranges, potatoes, bananas, lean meat, beans, and milk. |
| Iodine | 70 mcg/90 mcg. | Essential for normal thyroid functioning, which regulates the body's energy production, promotes growth and development, and helps burn excess fat. | Seafood, bread, dairy products, and iodized table salt. |

*IU=international units  **mg=milligrams  †mcg=micrograms)

# Food allergies and sensitivities

Occasionally, children develop a sensitivity or allergy to a particular food. A food allergy occurs when the body's immune system mistakenly views a food as harmful and produces antibodies to help fight off the "invader." The antibodies release chemicals that trigger an allergic reaction minutes to hours after the offending food has been eaten.

If you or your spouse has a history of food allergies or suffers from eczema, which often accompanies food allergies, your child is more likely to develop allergic reactions, too, though food allergies may show up even among children with no family history of such sensitivities. Waiting to offer the foods that commonly cause allergic reactions gives your child's immune system the time it needs to mature enough to withstand the offending substance, thus preventing an allergy from developing. And once an allergy has been confirmed, eliminating exposure to that food until the child is older can prevent the allergy from becoming a lifelong condition. Many children do outgrow their allergies, provided that they are not regularly subjected to the offending substance.

The most common culprits in causing allergic reactions are milk protein, egg whites, soy, citrus fruits and juices, corn, wheat, peanuts, and shellfish. It's a good idea to introduce these foods to your child gradually and in small amounts. Wait until your child is 12 months old before offering him cow's milk, wheat, soy, corn, and citrus; wait until he's 24 months old to introduce him to egg whites. Hold off on

**PARENTS ALERT**

## *Food Choking Hazards*

Choosing foods wisely, making sure they're cut small enough for little mouths, and supervising whenever your child is eating will help minimize his risk of choking. Don't let your child eat on the run. He is more likely to choke if he does. Encourage him to stay seated while eating and supervise him whenever he eats. Also teach him to take small bites and to chew well before swallowing. Before the age of 5, do not serve:

- Spoonfuls of peanut butter (Even peanut butter smeared liberally onto bread or a cracker can be problematic for all children.)
- Hot dogs or meat sticks, especially when cut into circular pieces
- Raw vegetables such as carrots that are cut into circles, rather than thin strips
- Uncooked peas
- Celery, which is too "stringy" for kids to swallow easily
- Nuts of any kind (Children should not eat peanuts before age 7, when they are more able to thoroughly chew them.)
- Popcorn
- Seeds in apples, watermelon, and other fruit
- Whole-grain breads or muffins that contain seeds or nuts, including sesame seed and poppy seed bagels
- Hard candies
- Any hard, round food item that could be accidentally swallowed whole, such as grapes.
- Gum

## *Pregnant and Nursing Moms' Diets*

If you're pregnant or nursing, you should avoid eating peanuts and shellfish since ingesting these foods raises the risk of your child developing allergies to them. And if you're nursing and your baby has symptoms of gastrointestinal distress, you should systematically eliminate suspect foods from your diet to see if this change results in less discomfort for your child.

introducing shellfish and any products containing peanuts until age 3.

Children who are allergic to milk protein, egg whites, soy, citrus, corn, and wheat may develop symptoms such as a runny or stuffy nose, diarrhea, vomiting, a skin rash, or localized hives minutes or hours after eating the food. Allergic reactions to peanuts and shellfish tend to be far more severe, including anaphylactic shock, which is life threatening and requires immediate emergency medical care. Symptoms of this severe reaction include wheezing, noisy breathing and/or difficulty breathing, extreme flushing of the skin, itching (especially body-wide), generalized hives, swelling of the face, lips, and throat, abdominal cramps, dizziness, and fainting. It's important to note that the first exposure to the allergen may not produce symptoms. The allergy, however, will trigger symptoms the second or third time your child consumes the offending food.

To diagnose a non-life-threatening food allergy, experts usually suggest that parents eliminate the suspected allergen from the child's diet for a few weeks to see if symptoms disappear. The food is then gradually reintroduced to the diet to see whether symptoms return. Allergies can also be detected through a skin-prick test, in which traces of suspected allergens are injected into the child's skin to see if a tell-tale rash develops. In some cases, blood tests also may be ordered in an attempt to identify substances that cause allergies, though these tests are not thought be as reliable as skin-prick tests. If, however, a child experiences a severe allergic reaction to any food, that food must be eliminated from the diet completely. Additional exposure through testing should be avoided.

If your child suffers symptoms of a severe allergic reaction, his health-care provider should refer him to a pediatric allergist. If the allergist feels that your child might have a life-threatening reaction to a particular food, he will probably recommend that you keep an epinephrine kit on hand at all times. (Epinephrine is a chemical that counteracts anaphylactic shock by boosting blood pressure and opening airways in the respiratory tract so the child can breathe.) The kits contain penlike instruments, which you use to inject epinephrine as soon as the child shows any symptoms of a severe allergic reaction. If such precautions are necessary, you should make sure that your child's teacher, baby-sitter, grandparents, and any others who may be responsible for his care are instructed and comfortable with the proper procedure. After the drug has been administered, take your child to his doctor or to a hospital emergency room for follow-up treatment.

| Substitutions for Allergic Kids | |
|---|---|
| **Instead of...** | **Offer...** |
| wheat, corn | rice, barley, oats |
| citrus fruits | cantaloupe, tomatoes |
| whole egg | egg yolk |

*For information on first aid for allergic reactions, see **page 666**.*

Children sometimes outgrow food allergies. In the meantime, if your child is allergic to a particular food, you can substitute other similarly nutritious foods in its place.

**Lactose intolerance**  Rarely, children are born without the ability to digest lactose, the sugar contained in cow's milk, a condition called "lactose intolerance." This sensitivity is usually diagnosed when an infant or older child has repeated bouts of diarrhea or other sign of gastrointestinal upset. Basically, the child's digestive system is deficient in the enzyme lactase, which aids in the digestion of lactose. Sometimes, children who have had a gastrointestinal ailment temporarily develop lactose intolerance. In either case, sensitive kids experience symptoms such as bloating, gas, cramps, and diarrhea when they drink milk or consume other dairy products. The diagnosis and treatment of infants with lactose intolerance is determined by the child's pediatrician.

For older kids whose doctors have determined that a lactose intolerance exists, a simple switch from regular to lactose-reduced milk and other lactose-reduced dairy products, readily available at most grocery stores, solves the problem. Liquid lactase drops, which are available at drug stores, also can be added to regular milk to make it more easily digestible. Some lactose-intolerant kids are able to handle a small amount of dairy products; for example, one-third glass of milk may not upset their stomachs, while a full glass of milk will. And, a few are able to digest yogurt that contains active cultures, with labels reading, "contains live *Lactobacillus*." Serving dairy products at mealtimes, along with other foods, also aids in digestion for many children. If your child is unable to handle lactose-reduced milk or milk treated with liquid lactase, offer him calcium-fortified soy milk and orange juice enriched with calcium as well as calcium-rich foods.

## Hidden Allergens

Avoiding food allergens, particularly those that bring on severe reactions, requires vigilance since many allergens are hidden ingredients in other foods. For example, hot dogs contain milk; eggs are included in some noodles and most baked goods and bake mixes. Peanut oil is used in many foods, including spicy dishes such as chili. When dining out, ask the waiter to find out if an offending food is an ingredient in the dish your child has ordered. Be sure your child is taught to avoid all offers of foods that have not been approved by you or another responsible adult. If your child suffers from an allergy that could be life-threatening, have him wear a Medic-Alert bracelet at all times.

Likewise, if you're nursing and need to eliminate dairy products for your child's sake, include such calcium-rich foods as canned salmon with the bones, sardines with bones, broccoli, or calcium supplements in your own diet.

**Milk and dairy allergy** Less frequently—in about 1 to 3 children out of a 100—a child may develop an inability to digest the protein in milk and dairy products. Breast-fed babies who are unable to digest milk may show symptoms whenever their mothers consume dairy products. More often, a milk allergy surfaces when a baby first receives infant formula or a breast-fed infant or a child who has received soy formula starts drinking cows' milk, usually at about age 1. Though most outgrow their milk allergy at around age 2, a handful of kids continue to have trouble with milk for years. Symptoms of a milk allergy may include vomiting, diarrhea, constipation, asthma or wheezing, a stuffy or runny nose, cough, eczema, hives, irritability, poor appetite, and fatigue. Occasionally, a milk allergy triggers bleeding in the digestive tract. Symptoms can occur anytime from a few minutes to several hours after the child consumes milk or another dairy product.

If your child shows signs of a milk allergy, call his health-care provider. If symptoms include difficulty breathing, extreme paleness, turning blue, extreme weakness, generalized hives, swelling in his head or neck regions, or bloody diarrhea, take him to the doctor or a hospital emergency room immediately. The doctor will probably recommend that you eliminate milk and all other dairy products from his diet for a time to see if he improves. Meanwhile, be sure that he gets the nutrients found in milk—calcium, protein, and vitamin D—from other food sources.

# Foods to avoid or limit

In addition to avoiding foods that can cause an allergic reaction, it's a good idea to eliminate or strictly limit the following from your child's diet:

**Fake fat**  Olean, sold under the brand name Olestra, is an artificial fat made from sugar and vegetable oil. It has been approved by the Food and Drug Administration and is an ingredient in a variety of snack foods, including crackers, cheese puffs, and potato and tortilla chips. Though the food has been deemed safe for adults, research concludes that some people cannot tolerate it, especially in large amounts. As it travels through the gastrointestinal tract, Olean absorbs the fat-soluble vitamins, A, D, E, and K. It may also cause gastrointestinal problems, such as gas, bloating, and diarrhea. Since it prohibits vitamin absorption and, in any case, is contained primarily in foods that offer little nutritional value, it's best to steer children away from it.

**Artificial sweeteners**  Almost every "diet" product on the market today, from sodas to gelatins to chewing gum, contains aspartame, marketed as Nutrasweet and Equal. Because scientists don't know what long-term health effects aspartame may have, you may want to see that your child avoids products containing this sweetener. Also, foods containing artificial sweeteners tend to be products that do not provide essential nutrients.

**Caffeine**  Caffeine is a drug that can lead to nervousness, irritability, agitation, heartburn, diarrhea, upset stomach, and difficulty sleeping in some children. Many beverages and foods that kids love contain caffeine. Avoid giving most caffeinated beverages to children under 5; for kids aged 5 to 9, limit caffeine intake to 50 milligrams (mg) a day. When introducing any caffeinated food or beverage to your child, offer a small amount. If she displays any of the symptoms listed above, switch to a caffeine-free version of the product.

## Caffeine in Common Snacks

| Snack | Caffeine |
|---|---|
| Coca-Cola (12 oz) | 46 mg |
| Mountain Dew (12 oz) | 54 mg |
| chocolate milk (8 oz) | 8 mg |
| hot cocoa mix (1 oz package) | 5 mg |
| Reese's Peanut Butter Cup (1.8 oz) | 6 mg |

Sugar There's been a tremendous amount of debate about whether sugar causes hyperactivity in some children. Studies have both corroborated and challenged these claims, and much more research needs to be done before a conclusive answer is found. That debate aside, however, there are still many reasons why you'll want to limit your child's sugar intake. Sugar has no nutritional value. Also, items that contain sugar are frequently loaded with other nutritionally empty ingredients, such as saturated fats, which also need to be limited. In addition, sugar contributes to tooth decay and can cause obesity in kids who fill up on sugary snacks while shunning more nutritious fare.

In order to cut back on the refined sugar in your child's diet, while satisfying his natural preference for sweets, offer him sweet-tasting substitutes, such as whole fresh fruit or dried fruit, which contains sugar, but is also packed with vitamins and fiber, or home-made muffins made with a minimum of sugar. Also, beware of hidden sugars in foods. Sugar comes in many forms and may be listed on food labels as fructose, glucose, honey, corn syrup, corn syrup solids, maple syrup, turbinado sugar, dextrose, and sucrose. To avoid sugar overload without being overly restrictive at special events such as a birthday party, feed your child a meal consisting of complex carbohydrates, protein, and a little fat a few hours before the party. (Reduced-fat cheddar cheese on whole-grain bread is a good option.) Such nourishing foods will help his body process sugar at a slower, more stable rate.

Refined carbohydrates These are the white-flour grains contained in foods such as bagels, many pastas, white rice, and white bread, from which the bulk of the fiber has been removed. Though serving these foods, particularly if they are enriched with nutrients, such as thiamin, riboflavin, and iron, is fine on occasion, it's also important to offer your child complex carbohydrates, which are made from whole-grain flours, such as whole-grain cereal, breads, and pastas and brown rice.

# CHAPTER 3

# Medical Care

**B**y the time your child reaches adulthood, you will have met with many health-care professionals. You'll need to rely on the expertise of doctors, dentists, and eye-care experts as well as any specialists your child may need to see. You'll also have to rely on and trust your own instincts.

It's important not only to know your child's medical history, but also to understand how to work with medical professionals and insurers, and dispense medications properly. As a team, you and your child's doctors can enhance your child's well-being.

## Medical history

**I**ncreasingly, researchers are finding genetic links to various health conditions. The more you know about your family's medical history, the more this new information can serve you.

### Charting your family's medical history

Your family medical history will help your child's doctor provide the right care. If you haven't already done so, research your family's medical history. Note any serious childhood and adult illnesses or conditions, childhood allergies, chronic conditions, hospital stays, and operations that family members have had. Note whether your parents, grandparents, or siblings suffered from conditions such as asthma, juvenile diabetes, etc. If there is an unusual pattern of illness among aunts, uncles, and cousins—such as juvenile rheumatoid arthritis—include that as well. Use the checklist to help you record your findings. And use the following charts to track your child's personal medical history.

## Our Family Medical History

|  | MOTHER | FATHER | NOTES |
|---|---|---|---|
| Serious childhood illnesses |  |  |  |
| Allergies: childhood<br>　　　　adult |  |  |  |
| Immunizations |  |  |  |
| Chronic conditions |  |  |  |
| Hospital stays |  |  |  |
| Operations |  |  |  |
| Known exposure to any<br>harmful substance |  |  |  |
| Negative reactions to medications |  |  |  |
| Medications taken during pregnancy<br>and while nursing |  |  |  |
| Chronic conditions that any<br>family member has had and<br>their relationship |  |  |  |
| Causes of death in family |  |  |  |

## *Charting Your Child's Medical History*

Your child's medical history begins with his family history and includes information about his birth, his own growth and development, illnesses, immunizations, accidents, and any other pertinent information. Keep this reference up-to-date and available to share with his physician.

_____'s Medical History

**BIRTH INFORMATION**

Date of Birth: ____ / ____ / ____

Weight at Birth: ____ lbs. ____ oz. (or ____ grams)

Length at Birth: _____ inches or _____ centimeters

Delivery Complications, if any: _____

_____

**RECORD OF ILLNESSES**

| | Dates/Duration | Symptoms | Medications |
|---|---|---|---|
| _____ | _____ to _____ | _____ | _____ |
| _____ | _____ to _____ | _____ | _____ |
| _____ | _____ to _____ | _____ | _____ |
| _____ | _____ to _____ | _____ | _____ |

**ALLERGIES**

| | Reactions/Symptoms | Treatment |
|---|---|---|
| Foods: _____ | _____ | _____ |
| Animals: _____ | _____ | _____ |
| Environmental/ Seasonal: _____ | _____ | _____ |
| Other: _____ | _____ | _____ |

**Medications Taken/Reactions** _____

_____

**Operations**_____

_____

**Accidents**_____

_____

## CHECK-UP RECORDS

| | Height | Weight | Special Notes |
|---|---|---|---|
| First office visit | | | |
| Six-month visit | | | |
| 1-year | | | |
| 2-year | | | |
| 3-year | | | |
| 4-year | | | |
| 5-year | | | |
| 6-year | | | |

## RECORD OF IMMUNIZATIONS

Hepatitis B: ____  ____  ____  ____

DTaP: ____  ____  ____  ____  ____  ____

HiB: ____  ____  ____  ____

Polio: ____  ____  ____  ____

MMR: ____  ____

Chicken Pox: ____  ____

Other: _____

# Health-care professionals

Your child's health-care team includes his primary-care physician, a dentist and, periodically, an eye specialist. If accident or illness strikes, he'll also need care by a specialist. Along the way, you may consider alternative medical care.

## Working with your child's physician

While it's critical that your child's doctor give him the best care possible—and that the two of them get along—it's just as important that you develop a pleasant, trusting relationship with your child's physician. If you have any problems with the doctor, speak up. If she seems too authoritarian or doesn't listen to your concerns, tell her you want to work with her, to develop a true partnership. If she talks too fast or uses medical jargon you can't understand, ask her to clarify her points in lay person's terms. After major checkups and visits for serious ailments, ask the doctor to summarize what she has told you in writing or to speak slowly and clearly enough for you to record what she says. Whenever the doctor's comments and instructions are written down, you'll be more likely to remember them.

Be sure that you supply the doctor with all the information she needs to treat your child, including your personal and family medical histories and your child's medical history. Come prepared for your child's office visit. Write down any unusual symptoms your child has had recently, as well as any questions you have. Give the physician a copy of the list. Also, be truthful about anything that may affect your child's health. For example, if your son has developed symptoms of asthma and someone in the household smokes, it's vital that you share this information with the doctor.

Sometimes, doctors and parents disagree about treatments. For example, if you feel your child's doctor prescribes medications too liberally, express your concerns and ask her to explain her reasons. You may find that she does have a good reason even though she may share your view that medication should be prescribed conservatively in most cases. Take advantage of your doctor's expertise in areas such as nutrition, exercise, sleep needs, and disease prevention, but don't be afraid to use your own judgment, too. Usually, pediatricians and parents can work out their differences and learn how to communicate more effectively with each other. But sometimes, the fit just isn't right and you'll need to make the decision to switch doctors.

*For information about choosing your child's health-care provider, see **page 5**.*

# Your child's routine checkups

See **page 82** for
information
about first-year
medical visits.

See **page 547** for
a quick guide to
immunizations.

Between the ages of 1 and 6, your child requires medical checkups at regular intervals. Many pediatric and family practice clinics send reminders to parents, but some don't, so note on your calendar when it's time to take your child in for an exam. If your child is enrolled in a preschool, nursery, or kindergarten program, you'll need written proof that his immunizations are up-to-date and that he's able to participate in the class or a notation from the doctor about required restrictions on his activities. Use the chart on the next page as a guide to preparing for each major scheduled visit.

**The first school checkup** Until now, you may have found your child's checkups pretty routine. But at around age 5, and possibly during your child's fourth year, he is ready for his prekindergarten checkup, which includes a number of new assessments. His doctor will probably discuss kindergarten readiness with you and can help guide you in making the decision to enroll him now or to give him another a year in preschool. Discuss development issues privately with the doctor, or schedule a phone conversation later on, since it may be difficult for you and the doctor to talk freely about developmental concerns if your child is in the room.

Prepare your child for the visit. With his increased maturity, certain aspects of the exam that didn't trouble him before may bother him now. Being asked to undress and be poked and prodded by his doctor can be unnerving for a child this age. Help him relax by letting him know what to expect. A children's book about going to the doctor's office may prove helpful. Also, encourage your child to use a toy doctor's kit to examine himself, you, and his stuffed animals so he can familiarize himself with some basic procedures. Explain before the visit that it's the doctor's job to examine all parts of his body, even private parts. This can be upsetting and confusing to a child who has been taught never to let someone touch him. Assure your child that you'll be there for the whole visit and that he can hold your hand during it if he wishes.

For information
on preparing for
immunizations,
see **page 543**.

Immunizations and skin-prick tests are a part of the routine fifth-year checkup, and your child may be distressed at the thought of being stuck by a needle. Ease your child's anxiety by being as honest, straightforward, and reassuring as you can.

# What to Expect at Scheduled Visits for Toddlers and Preschoolers

(For an explanation of individual immunizations, see pages **543–47**)

| Age | Immunizations | What to Bring | What to Expect |
|---|---|---|---|
| 12 months | MMR, Hib, DTaP, and OPV. (Some doctors wait to give the DTaP and the OPV until the 15- or 18-month checkup); HbOC-DTP, a combination vaccine, may be given instead of the Hib and DTP. The chicken pox vaccine may be given. | A list noting concerns you have, any unusual symptoms your child exhibits, and recent skills he's developed. | General questions about your child's health and development. Height, weight, and head circumference assessments. Observation to assess development, hearing, and vision. Blood tests to check for anemia and lead poisoning. A tuberculin test may also be given. |
| 15 months | MMR , Hib, Chicken pox, DTaP and OPV (if not given at 12 months). HbOC-DTP, a combination vaccine, may be given instead of the Hib and DTP. | Same as 12 months. | Same as 12 months. |
| 18 months | DTaP and/or chicken pox, if not given at 12 or 15 months; OPV or IPV if not given at 12 or 15 months. | Same as at 12- and15-month checkups, plus questions about nutrition or sleep habits. | Assessment of growth; observation of child to determine developmental skills, hearing, vision. Blood tests for lead and/or anemia. Possibly a tuberculin test. |
| 2 years | None, unless a particular immunization has been missed. | Same as previous, plus questions about your child's development, eating and sleeping habits, etc. | Assessment of growth. Physician observation of child to determine intellectual and physical development. Hearing and vision tests. More clinical blood work. |
| 3 years | None if vaccinations are up-to-date. | Same as previous, plus info on toilet-teaching progress, speech, etc. Be sure to mention new skills, like riding a tricycle, feeding self, etc. | Growth assessment. Physician observation to check physical and intellectual development. Vision, hearing, and speech checks. Clinical work, if necessary. |
| 4 years* | Polio booster. Some states require a MMR booster for school entry; check with your child's preschool. | Same as previous. | Growth assessment. Possible test of hearing, visual acuity. Blood work if necessary. |
| 5 years* | OPV or IPV; the DTaP booster; an MMR booster (if not given at 4 years for preschool admission). | Same as previous, plus list of kindergarten-readiness skills to discuss. | Growth assessments, blood pressure check, hearing and vision tests,  cholesterol test, skin-prick test for tuberculosis and urinalysis. |

# What about alternative care?

Alternative therapies are moving more and more into mainstream medicine. By the end of 1996, more than 40 percent of Americans had turned to alternative or nonconventional therapies, everything from acupuncture to herbalism. The U.S. government is funding studies to determine the effectiveness and safety of some of these new approaches to healing and health.

Certain procedures have already become widely accepted, based on years of practice. Biofeedback, for instance, has been found to help children prone to migraines control the pain of these headache attacks. Similarly, relaxation, or deep-breathing, exercises can reduce the pain from migraines, arthritis, and stress. Acupuncture has been shown to reduce post-operative pain.

If you are considering taking your child to an alternative practitioner of any kind, it's important to review the treatments with your child's medical practitioner. Be sure to consult with your child's doctor before giving her any herbal medication. Just because herbs are natural and may have no or few side effects for adults, they are not necessarily safe for children.

If your child's doctor feels that seeing an alternative therapist might be helpful, find a qualified practitioner. Ask your child's doctor for a referral or consult with a teaching hospital in your area. Be wary of any practitioner who makes grandiose claims, such as a chiropractor who claims to be able to cure your child's asthma by manipulating her spine. There's little medical evidence to support such a claim.

---

**PARENTS RESOURCE**

## *Alternative Medicine*

*Manifesto for a New Medicine: Your Guide to Healing Partnerships and the Wise Use of Alternative Therapies* by James S. Gordon, M.D. (Perseus Press). The author is a clinical professor in the Departments of Psychiatry and Family Medicine at the Georgetown University School of Medicine and Director of the Center for Mind-Body Medicine in Washington, D.C.

---

# Handling emergency room visits

Visits to the emergency room are usually traumatic for everyone. Whenever possible, have your child's injuries and illnesses treated by her own physician in an office rather than a hospital setting. Save visits to the ER for life-threatening emergencies or those times when it's not possible to make an unscheduled office visit. If, for instance, your child's tooth is knocked out on a weekday, a trip to her dentist is better than rushing to the ER. The dentist will probably see her right away, while ER doctors may keep her waiting, since her injury is less serious than other ER cases. Keep in mind, too, that many insurance providers won't pay for ER visits for conditions that could have been handled in a doctor's office.

In some instances, a trip to the ER is a must. If your child has a severe asthma attack, is in shock, has suffered severe trauma such as head or abdominal injuries, has a certain type of seizure, or a diabetes-related attack, get to an emergency room at once, or call for an ambulance. Pediatrician's offices usually lack the proper emergency equipment, such as oxygen tanks and masks, intravenous catheters and fluids, and certain drugs required for some emergency conditions. If time allows, call your doctor so she can meet you at the ER or can at least be in touch with the ER medical team. If possible, bring your child's health-insurance card, record of immunizations, and containers of any medicines he is taking.

Since nobody has an appointment in the ER, be prepared to wait in all but the most serious of cases. A triage nurse will ask you questions about your child's condition, take a brief medical history, and do a blood-pressure check, and then decide whether his condition warrants immediate attention. If you've checked in with the triage nurse but feel your child is becoming sicker, speak up. You may want to ask to see a patient advocate if the ER staff is not responsive enough.

Be prepared to explain as calmly as possible what brings you to the ER. Be precise. Explain, for example, that your child hit her head when she fell off her trike two hours ago, felt dizzy for an hour earlier, and is now complaining of a severe headache and says she can't see well. The triage nurse will quickly recognize any serious change in condition and get immediate attention for your child.

If your child does not need to be admitted to the hospital, ask that all instructions about care and medication for your child be written down for you to take home before you leave the ER. Send or fax a copy to her pediatrician and plan to consult with the doctor later.

**PARENTS ALERT**

## The Right ER

Find out which ER in your area is best equipped to handle pediatric emergencies. Surprisingly, some ERs do not have child-size instruments on hand.

**Are X rays safe for kids?**
*"My 4-year-old injured her thumb recently and the doctor ordered an X ray. Is it okay for kids to have X rays?"*

Yes. The amount of radiation that is emitted by an X-ray machine isn't dangerous. Repeated X rays over the course of a year could cause problems in the future, but most doctors are careful to monitor the dosage of radiation a patient receives.

There is a difference between diagnostic radiation (used for X rays) and therapeutic radiation (used to treat cancerous tumors). Diagnostic radiation is given in small doses and poses little risk. Therapeutic radiation is given in higher doses and is not used on children under age 2.

**Kids' casts**  If your child fractures a bone, his doctor will order X rays to determine the severity and exact area of the break. If the fracture is complicated, the physician may ask an orthopedist—a doctor who specializes in the care and repair of bones—to take a look at the X rays and to examine your child.

Minor fractures call for a plaster or fiberglass cast or a splint. If your child suffers a more serious fracture, an orthopedic surgeon may need to realign the bones—a procedure that is done under general or local anesthesia.

Call your doctor immediately if your child has a cast and develops any of these symptoms:
• An increase in pain or numbness in the injured limb.
• Blue or very pale fingers or toes.

If these occur, the extremity may be swelling, putting pressure on nerves and blood vessels. The cast will need to be readjusted immediately to prevent permanent damage.

# When your child is hospitalized

For both parents and kids, the prospect of a hospital stay can be overwhelming and scary. Although your child may never be hospitalized, you should arm yourself with a few facts and strategies in the event that he is.

You will have to act as your child's advocate if he is hospitalized, making certain that he receives the best care possible. You'll also want to help him stay calm. If your child is having an operation or tests, talk privately with the doctor who will be performing the procedure. Ask any questions you may have.

**Helping your child cope at the hospital**   To allay your child's fears about a hospital stay, do your best not to show any fearful or negative emotions yourself. No amount of reassurance that everything will be okay will mean much if you're falling apart. If this is to be a long stay, arrange time for yourself to restore your energy. Eat right and try to get enough sleep. Get whatever help you can for yourself so that you can help your child.

If your child is over age 3, try to tour the hospital beforehand so that he can see what the various rooms look like. If the hospital has a child-life advocate, he or she will serve as your— and your child's—best resource for easing anxieties. The child-life specialist will be with your child throughout procedures, but does not perform medical functions. Thus your child learns to associate the specialist's presence with support instead of with pain. This advocate will also help your child work through any emotional upset caused by his hospital stay.

Whether or not there is an advocate assigned to your child's case, ask about hospital protocol. Can you be with your child in the operating room while anesthesia is being administered or while he's getting X rays? Can you sleep in his room? It's essential that you or some other trusted adult be there overnight in case your child awakens, and during the day whenever procedures must be performed. Find out about your needs, too. Are there shower facilities for parents? Will the hospital supply you with a fold-out cot? Is there a chaplain, social worker, or therapist with whom you can talk?

Allow your child to cry and offer him comfort. Don't ask him to put on a brave face if he's not feeling brave. Nevertheless, gently but firmly insist that he cooperate in his medical care as much as he is able to. Distract him from painful and uncomfortable procedures,

---

**PARENTS RESOURCES**

### *Preparing for Hospital Visits*

Books and videos about going to the hospital may be helpful. Check your area library or bookstore for the following:

***Curious George Goes to the Hospital*** by Margaret and H.A. Rey (Houghton Mifflin), for ages 4 and up. When Curious George swallows a jigsaw-puzzle piece, an educational adventure follows.

***Going to the Hospital*** by Anne Civardi and Stephen Cartwright (Educational Development Corporation), for preschoolers. Ben Bell has to have an operation because he gets so many earaches.

but don't lie to him. Instead of allowing a medical professional to inflict pain in a furtive way, say, "This is going to hurt, but I'm going to hold you and do my best to make you feel better soon." If warranted, ask that he be given a sedative in a suppository, nasal spray, or oral form before the procedure. Be honest about what's happening, but don't offer more information than your child requests or can understand. For example, if your child is over the age of 4 or so and is going have a general anesthesia before an operation, explain that the doctor will put a mask over his face that contains air that smells. If possible, arrange to have your child handle a mask beforehand. Assure him that you'll be there as soon as the operation is over. Tell him he may expect to feel a bit sick afterward, but that he'll feel much better soon. Children who are particularly sensitive and fearful probably won't be able to handle a lot of information, and hearing too much will further overwhelm them. So judge how much information you give based on your own knowledge of his personality.

Many children view a hospital stay as punishment for some real or perceived misdeed. It's very important to reassure your child that he did nothing wrong and that the illness or the accident that brought him to the hospital was not his fault.

If this is a scheduled stay, read him books about the hospital experience before he's admitted. Bring comforting items from home—his favorite blanket or stuffed animal, for instance—to make the hospital seem less foreign. If he's able to, have him join other children in the pediatric ward playroom. Focus his concentration on something other than the hospital routine, such as by teaching him a new card game or the words to a silly song. Talk about things you'll do together when he goes home.

**What to know about anesthesia**　If a procedure involves anesthesia, you'll need to find out all the important details. "Will a general, regional, or local be used? What are the side effects?" If your child is to be given a general, she won't be allowed to eat or drink for up to 8 to 12 hours prior to the procedure, so ask that surgery be scheduled for first thing in the morning so she won't have to wait for hours on an empty stomach. Ask how the general anesthesia will be administered. Will your child inhale gas through a mask or will she be given the medication intravenously, through an IV, or both?

Ask if the anesthesia will be administered by an anesthesiologist, a medical doctor, by a nurse anesthetist or a technician, and find out if the anesthesia expert is board-certified in his or her specialty.

# Professional dental care

Your child should make her initial trip to the dentist around the time her first tooth erupts. Taking care of her "baby" teeth helps to ensure healthy teeth and gums for a lifetime.

## Choosing and working with a dentist

In addition to practicing good dental hygiene at home, your best defense again tooth decay is regular dental checkups. The American Academy of Pediatric Dentistry recommends that a child have his first dental appointment by 18 months of age at the latest, and ideally, within 6 months after the arrival of his first tooth. Yearly checkups are a good idea for anyone over the age of 2. Your child's dentist will not only check to see that teeth are emerging properly, but he or she can offer advice on proper brushing techniques as well as provide any needed fluoride or sealant treatments, which can further help prevent decay.

It is not necessary to take your child to a pediatric dentist, especially if you're pleased with your family dentist. However, pediatric dentists are trained in treating kids, and if yours has any anxiety about dental visits, a dentist skilled in caring for children's' teeth (who's also more likely to have a kid-pleasing waiting room) may be your best bet.

### Preparing your child for a dental visit

Dental care continues to become less painful and more efficient. If you've experienced truly unpleasant dental visits, you might inadvertently pass that anxiety on to your child. Be careful not to talk of your own dental visits with a sense of dread. Never threaten your child with a dental visit, such as telling him that if he doesn't brush, the dentist will have to do something.

Prepare your child for her dental visits as you would for any new experience: Talk to her about what she can expect. Perhaps read a book or two about dental visits. Visit the dentist's office before the actual appointment, so that she can see and become comfortable with the place. Schedule the first appointment for a look only,

---

**"IT WORKED FOR ME"**

## Planning for Later

My 4-year-old always gets nervous before dental visits, so on our drive to the office I ask him what he'd like to do after his exam. Would he like to stop for an ice cream cone on the way home? Or should we go to the park playground for a while? During the visit, I remind him several times of the fun activity we have planned. This helps him focus on something other than the dental exam.

### Bringing Along a "Friend"

Before I took my 2-year-old, Lisa, to the dentist for the first time, I suggested that she bring her stuffed dinosaur, Benjy, with her so he could have his "teeth" examined-too. To prepare Benjy for the experience, Lisa brushed his pretend teeth, then checked to make sure his teeth were white and sparkly. My daughter asked her new dentist to take a look at Benjy's teeth before he examined hers. The dentist spent several minutes carefully checking the toy's mouth, then congratulated Lisa on taking such good care of her friend's teeth. By the time he started the actual exam, my daughter was relaxed—and actually enjoying the visit!

foregoing any treatment if possible. Then be matter-of-fact about the upcoming visit.

If she appears anxious, reassure her, but don't remind her not to worry if the idea hasn't crossed her mind. She may even be looking forward to the experience.

### Novocain

*"My son needs to have a tooth removed, which the dentist will do using Novocain. How safe is this procedure?"*

Novocain is safe for most kids. Novocain is often used with or without epinephrine. Novocain numbs the tooth, gum, and part of the check and lip; epinephrine curbs blood loss. Note that a child with asthma can be given Novocain but should not receive epinephrine if he is using a bronchiodilator.

### The right time for braces

*"My daughter's dentist has recommended that she get braces. She's only 5. Isn't it better to wait until all of her permanent teeth come in?"*

Braces not only correct the position of teeth but also adjust improper jaw alignment, which, in many cases, is better done while the jaw is still forming. Certain conditions of tooth eruption also benefit from the earlier application of braces.

# Professional eye care

An ophthalmologist is a medical physician specially trained in the care of eyes; an optometrist is not a physician but has received training in diagnosing and treating certain eye conditions. And an optician is a technician who fits lenses. All children should have periodic eye tests performed by their pediatricians. If a problem is suspected or if there is a family history of eye disorders, you should have your child examined by a pediatric ophthalmologist.

## First eye exam

*"When should children have their first eye exam? Are exams part of regular doctor checkup, or should I go to an eye specialist?"*

The American Academy of Pediatrics has released guidelines calling for pediatricians to check a child's eyes at birth and at each well-child visit thereafter.

If the doctor notices anything amiss, she should refer your child to an ophthalmologist for further screening. Three to 5 percent of babies have visual problems, such as strabismus, amblyopia, glaucoma, or cataracts as well as near- or far-sightedness. The earlier such problems are diagnosed, the more successful treatment will be.

If your family has a history of early-childhood eye disorders, your child should be checked several weeks after birth by a pediatric ophthalmologist. A child without a family history of an early vision problem and who doesn't show symptoms of an early vision disorder should have his eyes examined by his physician at each visit and, at age 5, by an ophthalmologist. If his vision is normal, annual vision screenings at school and by his pediatrician should suffice.

**Age-by-age eye checks** Your child's physician will perform certain eye tests at each stage of his development. Here's what to expect:

**Birth to 3 months** The doctor will use a penlight to view your baby's eyes, making sure they are structurally normal and react correctly to light. She will also check for signs of eye disorders.

**3 months to 3 years** The doctor will repeat earlier visual tests, and as soon as your child is able to track objects, she may use a brightly colored toy to make sure his eyes focus and see together and that each eye sees properly on its own.

**3 years and up** The doctor will use tools, such as picture and letter cards, to test your child's vision. When your child turns 4, she'll use an ophthalmoscope to examine the optic nerve and retina.

**If your child needs glasses** Your child's ophthalmologist can recommend an optometrist or optician who is comfortable working with young children and who can recommend the sturdiest frames and safest lenses for kids. Let your child choose the style of frames she wants, within the doctor's guidelines, of course, since liking the frames will ensure that she will wear them willingly.

*See **page 66** for symptoms of eye problems in infants.*

*For information on common eye conditions, see **pages 591–97**.*

• Select a frame that correctly fits the child's face and corresponds to the prescription. A strong prescription calls for a smaller frame front so lenses aren't too thick.

• Bridges (nose pieces) come in different sizes. Choose a frame with a bridge that keeps the glasses from slipping down on the nose or wiggling. The bridge should prevent the glasses from resting on your child's cheeks.

• Choose frames with spring hinges connecting the frame front to the temples (ear wires); the springs help keep the frames from being damaged when bent.

• Choose frames with "comfort cables," ear wires for toddlers. These mold around the ears and stay put. Babies need special frames designed with a headband.

• Polycarbonate lenses, which are lightweight and shatter-resistant are a must for kids. If your child has a strong prescription, check out aspheric and high-index polycarbonate lenses, which are thinner.

**TLC for glasses** Tell kids 4 and up to try to remember to put their glasses in their case whenever they take them off, or to give them to you for safe keeping. Caution them not to put glasses in pockets, or to scrunch them into book bags.

# *Medications*

**PARENTS ALERT**

## *No Teaspoons for Dosing*

Using a regular kitchen teaspoon instead of a calibrated spoon can be very dangerous. Flatware spoons can vary from less than half to double the recommended "teaspoon" dosage. Always use a calibrated teaspoon.

As valuable as medications are in treating common illnesses, their misuse can cause more harm than good, so you need to make sure your child receives the correct medicine, at the right time, and in the proper dosage. Because of their small size, children are more likely than adults to suffer an adverse reaction to an overdose of an over-the-counter (OTC) or prescription medication, or to a dose of the wrong medicine. Adult-strength medicines are not for children, and certain common adult medications, such as aspirin, should never be given to kids without a doctor's recomendation.

# Forms of children's medicines

Children's medications, like adult medicines, come in a variety of forms—pills, tablets, and liquids. Because young children can't swallow pills whole, children's medications, particularly OTC pain medicines, are available in chewable form. Most children's medications, however, are given in liquid form. There are three types of liquid medicine. Syrups and elixirs are most often OTC medicines, such as cold remedies. Suspensions are more often medicines your child's doctor has prescribed.

- **Syrup.** A sugar-based liquid that helps improve a drug's taste.
- **Elixir.** An alcohol-based liquid that helps to dissolve certain drugs. Alcohol content may vary, so carefully check age guidelines on the label before giving to your child.
- **Suspension.** A cloudy liquid that helps maintain uniform concentration for certain powdered medications. For optimum effectiveness, you must shake the bottle well before use because the potent portion of the drug can settle at the bottom.

Unless otherwise noted on the label, keep liquid medicines and vitamins in the refrigerator.

# Giving liquid medicines

A number of tools are available to help you judge the correct dosage of liquid medications. These devices will also make it easier for you to gain your child's cooperation in taking her medicine. Always rinse the measuring device with warm water after each use.

- **Nurser (for infants).** Use as you would a bottle. When your baby finishes, fill the nurser with water, and let him suck on it to finish any remaining medicine.
- **Oral syringe.** This is also for infants and toddlers. To use, place your child in a semireclining position. Aiming for the side of her mouth, slowly push the plunger down. Lightly stroke front of child's throat to help her swallow.
- **Oral dropper.** This is designed especially for infants and toddlers. To use an oral dropper, place your child in semireclining position in her infant seat or in your arms. Place the dropper bulb between her bottom molars or rear gum and cheek, and squirt the medication to the inside of her cheek. (Don't squirt it

down her throat, which could cause choking.) Lightly stroke the front of her throat to help her swallow.

- **Calibrated spoon** Use with children toddler age and up. Have your child sit, and slowly pour the medicine into her mouth or let her sip it.
- **Dosage cup.** These are designed for children age 3 and up. Make sure the medicine is flush with the calibrated line on the cup. Allow your child to sip the medicine. Then, fill cup with water and have him drink it to finish any medicine remaining in the cup.

### How to give your child other medicines

- **Ear Drops.** Have your child lie on his side. For a child 3 or under, gently pull the outer ear down and back. For a child over 3, pull the outer ear up and back. Squeeze the dropper so that the liquid slides slowly into the ear canal, but don't let the dropper itself enter the ear canal. Place a small cotton ball in the outer ear for five minutes, until the medicine is absorbed.
- **Eye drops or ointment.** Have your child sit or lie down and tilt her head backward. Gently pull down her lower lid to form a small pocket between her lid and cheek. Insert the drops or apply a thin strip of ointment in the pocket (see illustration opposite). Or, squeeze a small amount of ointment onto a sterile gauze pad and apply it to her lower lid, starting at the inner corner. Instruct your child to close her eyes for one minute or so, and don't let her touch them. Clean the ointment tube with rubbing alcohol after each use.
- **Nasal drops.** Remove any mucus by gently twirling a cotton swab in your child's nose or by using a nasal aspirator. Have your child lie down with his chin up, and slowly insert drops. Try not to insert the dispenser into his nose, but hold it just outside his nostril. Have him lie still for ten seconds and then instruct him to breathe in through his nose two to three times. If the dispenser does come into contact with his nasal passages, clean it with hot, soapy water or rubbing alcohol before storing it.
- **Nasal spray.** With your child sitting and his head tilted slightly back, insert the sprayer into his nostril and have him inhale slowly as you gently squeeze. Continue squeezing as you remove the sprayer to keep nasal mucus and bacteria from being sucked into the dispenser. Clean the applicator with hot, soapy water or alcohol after using.

- **Rectal suppository.** Have your child lie on his side with his knees drawn up to his chest. Spread his buttocks gently and insert the suppository about one-half to one inch into his rectum. For a child 3 or younger, use your pinkie finger to insert the suppository; for an older child, use your index finger. Hold his buttocks together for one minute or so after inserting the medication.

### Baby aspirin

*"I've heard that aspirin can cause a serious condition known as Reye syndrome in kids. Why is it still available at drugstores?"*

Always give your child ibuprofen or acetaminophen for treating fever or aches and pains rather than baby aspirin unless specifically instructed to do so by your child's physician. Baby aspirin is most commonly used by adults who cannot take or do not need full-strength aspirin. It is recommended for children in rare instances to treat a few specific childhood illnesses, but it should only be given under strict supervision by the child's doctor. The benefit of using aspirin in these few cases outweighs the small risk of contracting Reye syndrome, a serious liver disease.

## Antibiotics

When penicillin was discovered in 1940, it was considered a "miracle cure" for almost every bacterial infection imaginable. It wasn't right for everyone, of course, and overuse caused it to lose its effectiveness for some people, but new and better-targeted antibiotics were easily prescribed and often taken. This overuse has had some serious negative side effects. One result is that wholly new antibiotic-resistant strains of bacterial infections have emerged. As a result, some commonly prescribed antibiotics are no longer reliable defenders against such common ailments as ear and sinus infections, tonsillitis, pneumonia, and tuberculosis.

**PEDIATRICK**

### Administering Eye Drops

Cold eye drops can cause pain, dizziness, or vomiting. Before using, roll the bottle between your hands or run it under warm water until it's slightly lukewarm. Also, if you must treat both of your child's eyes, even when only one is infected, medicate the uninfected eye first. Wipe the dropper with alcohol and rinse with plain water before putting it away. If your child won't keep his eyes open when you administer drops, ask him to close both eyes. Place a drop of medication in the inner corner of each eye and then have him blink. The drops should easily enter his eyes.

*When administering eye drops to a baby, hold his head still.*

## Helping the Medicine Go Down

If your child absolutely refuses to take a medicine, mix it into a tablespoon of applesauce and see if he'll eat it. But check with your doctor or pharmacist first; some medications shouldn't be taken with food, and certain pills aren't supposed to be broken (especially enteric-coated ones). Avoid mixing medicines in juice or other liquids because your child may not drink all the liquid and won't get the entire dose.

**Using antibiotics wisely** Children who contract these illnesses frequently and who have taken many courses of antibiotic treatments may be at risk for developing resistance to the drugs. Children can also develop a resistance to an antibiotic if they stop taking their prescribed antibiotic before completing the full dose. This allows infectious bacteria that have not been killed to produce antibiotic-resistant offspring, and the child may suffer a relapse that does not respond to the medication.

Increasingly, physicians are rethinking the need for antibiotics for every ear infection. Many children recover just as well without the medication. Because strep is a potentially life-threatening bacterium, however, antibiotics remain the medication of choice. To ensure that antibiotics will work for your child, take these precautions:

• **Follow dosage instructions to the letter.** If your child's doctor has prescribed an antibiotic for ten days, make sure your child takes all the medication for the full length of time prescribed. If you inadvertently miss a dose, call the doctor to learn what to do.

• **Choose an antibiotic that requires fewer administrations.** Ask your pediatrician if he can prescribe an antibiotic that can be given less frequently if you aren't able to, or are likely to forget to, dose your child at prescribed intervals over a 10-day period.

• **Don't keep leftover antibiotics.** Since antibiotics are prescribed for a single illness, there really shouldn't be any leftover medication. Also antibiotics can lose their potency over time.

• **Limit your child's intake.** Don't ask your doctor to prescribe antibiotics for a common cold or other viral infection. Antibiotics do not kill viruses. Discuss other ways to soothe your child's illness.

• **Follow good hygiene and first-aid procedures.** Limit exposure to infections whenever possible. Wash hands frequently to reduce the spread of colds and flu. Treat skin wounds immediately to prevent an infection from taking root.

### Allergies to antibiotics

*"How can I tell if my son is allergic to an antibiotic?"*

The more a child takes a particular antibiotic, the more likely he is to develop an allergy to it. Allergy is a learned response, so it's rare to have an allergic reaction on the first exposure to an antibiotic. An allergic reaction to an antibiotic usually begins with a rash, especially hives. At first a child may develop bright red cheeks; then itchy raised welts will appear all over the body. Another rash, erythema multiform, resembles hives, but is characterized by blotches that look like bull's-eyes.

If your son develops either of these rashes, call his doctor immediately and discontinue the medication. In extremely rare cases, an allergic reaction to an antibiotic can be fatal.

## Your family's medicine chest

Your family's medicine chest must be off-limits to children. Ironically, the best place to store medicines is not in the traditional bathroom medicine cabinet. This is not only too accessible to kids, but the heat and humidity of the bathroom may decrease the effectiveness of some medicines.

**Medicine chest musts** Every family with young children needs to have certain medical tools and medications available at all times. Make sure that all items with expiration dates are current and safely discard and replace expired items. Keep the following staples in a locked medicine cabinet or locked cupboard, out of children's reach:

• **A rectal thermometer.** The glass "bulb" types provide most accurate readings and is the "gold standard" for children under 4. Digital ear thermometers are okay for children over the age of 1.

• **Adhesive strip bandages.**

• **Sterile gauze pads and adhesive tape** to secure the gauze pads.

• **Small, round-tip scissors,** for cutting bandages and tape.

• **Rubbing alcohol,** for cleaning thermometers and other medical tools.

• **Ice pack,** for use on bruises and sprains. Store refreezable packs in freezer. For travel, buy "instant cold packs," available at most drugstores. A bag of frozen peas or a frozen washcloth also makes a good ice pack. Always be sure to wrap any "ice pack" in a towel or other cloth.

• **Calibrated medicine spoon, dropper, and/or oral syringe.**

• **One-half percent hydrocortisone cream** for bug bites and itchy rashes.

• **Acetaminophen or ibuprofen** in infant and/or children's strength, depending on your child's age.

## Medicines in Handbags

Storing medicines in handbags is a convenience for adults but may be deadly for children who like to explore grown-up belongings. Remind grand-parents and others with whom your child may come in contact to keep all medicines safely out of reach. When guests visit, store their handbags in an out-of-the-way place, such as a closet shelf.

• **Syrup of ipecac** to induce vomiting in case your child ingests a toxic substance; call your local poison control center or your doctor before giving syrup of ipecac to a child. Also, replace this medication every year since it loses its potency over time. In some locations, a prescription is needed for this medication.

• **Oral electrolyte solution** for use if your child has diarrhea; call your doctor before administering. Frozen popsicles made from electrolyte solution are also available.

• **Antibacterial ointment** for cuts and scrapes. Ointments containing neomycin can cause allergic reactions in some susceptible kids.

• **Saline nasal spray or drops** to relieve stuffiness due to colds.

• **Antihistamine** to counter for allergic reactions.

• **Sunscreen,** having an SPF of 15 or higher. Choose one that's PABA-free and replace it every year.

# Immunizations

Immunizations against diseases have dramatically improved the health of generations of children. Availability alone offers no protection; you must make certain that your child receives her vaccinations on schedule. Negative reactions are rare today and are less dangerous than the disease for which the inoculation is intended.

## What to know about immunizations

According to the Centers for Disease Control and Prevention, one-quarter of all children in the United States have not been fully immunized against common childhood diseases. A compelling reason why children should receive the recommended immunizations is that major outbreak of disease tend to occur when the immunization schedule is interrupted. For example, in the early 1990s, a failure to immunize large numbers of 12- to 15-month olds against measles resulted in an epidemic infecting more than 55,000 people; 11,000 of these were hospitalized, and 120 died.

Here's an overview of what a vaccine does, what, if any, reactions you can expect your child to have, and special precautions you can take:

**DTaP.** The letters D, T, and P stand for diphtheria, tetanus, and pertussis. Pertussis is another name for whooping cough. DTaP vaccines are part of your child's 2-month, 4-month, and 6-month exams. At age 15-to 18 months and again at age 4 to 6 years, your child will receive the DTaP.

**Possible reactions:** Within 24 hours after the shot, you child may display irritability, lack of energy, pain and redness around the area where vaccine was injected, and/or a fever of less than 102° F. These symptoms should clear within 24 hours. To relieve discomfort, give your child the appropriate dose of children's-strength acetaminophen every four hours.

**When to call the doctor**: If, after his immunization, your child displays constant crying
for more than 3 hours, high-pitched crying, excessive sleepiness or difficulty waking up, limpness or paleness, a fever of 105°F or higher,
and/or a convulsion, call his physician. Very
rarely, the vaccine causes a severe neurological reaction. But overall, it is very safe.

**Who should not have DTaP vaccina-
tions?** Children who have had a severe reaction
to the first immunization, and those with a history of convulsions or a nervous system disease
should postpone or forgo this immunization.

**Sabin (OPV) and Salk (IPV) Polio Vaccines.** The polio vaccines protect against polio, a viral disease that can cause partial or
body-wide paralysis. It is available in either an oral form (the Sabin
vaccine) or as in injection (the Salk vaccine). The polio vaccine is
given at 2 and 4 months and at age 15 to 18 months and 4 to 6 years.
Because of an intensive polio vaccination program launched in the
1950s, cases of polio in the United States are rare, though the unimmunized remain at risk. The most common polio vaccine is the oral
polio vaccine (OPV), a liquid that contains live polio virus. IPV (in-
active polio vaccine) is given by injection and does not contain a live
virus. For many years, the OPV was given at 2 and 4 months, and
the IPV given later. The IPV is now available for the first two vaccinations. Some experts prefer this vaccine because it lessens the
chance of spreading the virus to non-inoculated people and eliminates the rare, but possible, occurrence of polio itself being transmitted by the vaccine. Other experts prefer the OPV vaccine to the
IPV vaccine because it is painless and because it provides more permanent immunity than the Salk vaccine. There are no strict guidelines about which vaccine to choose. Parents and physicians should
weigh the benefits of each and decide which one they prefer.

**Possible reactions:** It's very rare that a child will experience
any side effects from either form of the polio vaccine. A very small
number may develop redness and soreness at the injection site when
taking the IPV. Others may experience fussiness, crying, and loss of
appetite following either vaccine. Symptoms last less than 24 hours.

**Who should not have the OPV?** Children whose immune

systems are compromised by conditions such as HIV or because they are receiving chemotherapy for cancer are usually given the injectable vaccine in place of the OPV. For these children, the live vaccine could actually cause polio.

**Additional cautions:** You should be aware that live polio virus can be passed to others through the baby's stools for several days after the live polio vaccination is given. A nonvaccinated person who comes into contact with the feces, such as a caregiver from a country where the vaccine is not readily available, can be infected by contact with your child's feces. Likewise, anyone whose immunity is suppressed by HIV, AIDS, or chemotherapy is at risk. In these cases, it's best that they avoid contact with your child's feces. If they should come in contact with fecal matter, they should wash their hands thoroughly.

**MMR.** The MMR provides immunity against measles, mumps, and rubella, all of which can have serious medical complications. It is given between the ages of 12 and 15 months. A booster dose is recommended between the ages of 4 and 6 or between 11 and 12.

**Possible reactions:** Seven to ten days following an injection, your child may experience slight swelling of the lymph nodes in his neck or groin, a mild rash, a low-grade fever, and/or sleepiness.

**Who should not have the MMR?** Children who are allergic to eggs may suffer a reaction since the vaccine is grown in chicken embryos. Tell your child's doctor about any prior allergic reaction to eggs to determine if your child should postpone this vaccination.

**Hepatitis B Vaccine.** This protects against hepatitis B, a virus that can lead to severe liver damage. It is given at birth, at 1 to 4 months, and again at 6 to 18 months. Although hepatitis B is transmitted primarily through sexual contact, chronic carriers who are pregnant can pass the infection on to their unborn child. The virus can also be passed in mother's milk. Children under 5 who are infected have a 30 to 60 percent chance of becoming lifelong carriers of the disease or of developing liver failure. A series of three hepatitis B shots is believed to provide lifelong immunity. Both the American Academy of Pediatrics and the Centers for Disease Control and Prevention strongly recommend that children be inoculated against hepatitis B.

**Possible reactions:** Some children experience irritability and redness, swelling, or pain at the injection site. Symptoms can last for up to 24 hours.

**Who should not have the Hepatitis B vaccine?** Children who are allergic to yeast—a component of this vaccine—should not receive the shot. Also, kids who have an active illness, other than a minor cold, should postpone getting the shot.

*For information on epiglotitis, see page 590.*

**Haemophilus B Conjugate Vaccine (HiB).** This vaccine protects against the haemophilus flu bacterium, which can lead to epiglotitis and some types of meningitis . It is given at 2, 4, and 6 months, and again between 12 and 18 months.

*For information on meningitis, see page 634.*

**Possible reactions:** Side effects are rare.

**Who should not have the HiB vaccine?** There are no known risk factors.

## Chicken pox (Varicella).

A chicken pox vaccine, marketed under the brand name Virivax, was approved by the Food and Drug Administration in 1995. Virivax is considered safe for most children, and the American Academy of Pediatrics and the Centers for Disease Control and Prevention advise that all healthy children have one dose between the ages of 12 and 18 months. An older child can be inoculated at the earliest convenient opportunity. Even though the vaccine is very effective, about 10 to 30 percent of those who receive it will still develop chicken pox. But they may suffer fewer than 10 pox sores instead of the usual 300 to 400. The vaccine is believed to protect kids for at least six years; boosters may be needed thereafter.

**Possible reactions:** Side effects are mild and may include redness and swelling at the injection site, as well as fever, nausea, and a rash. Intermittent low-grade fevers can occur for up to 42 days. A few children develop poxlike blisters within 8 to 18 days after the shot. An extremely small number develop generalized chicken pox rash within 5 to 26 days, but aren't very sick.

**Who should not have the chicken pox vaccine?** Any child who has a weakened immune system, who takes steroids (such as prednisone), who has received immune globulin or other blood products during the previous five months, or who is allergic to the antibiotic neomycin or to gelatin should postpone this vaccination. Also any child who has an active illness, other than a mild cold, should postpone the shot.

**Additional cautions:** Salicylates—such as aspirin, which should not be given to children and adolescents without a doctor's approval in any case—must be avoided for six weeks after the vaccination is given.

## A Quick-Reference Guide to Immunizations

| | DTP/DTaP* | Polio | MMR | Hepatitis B | HiB Haemophilus |
|---|---|---|---|---|---|
| Birth | | | | X | |
| 1-2 months | | | | X** | |
| 2 months | X | X | | | X*** |
| 4 months | X | X | | | X*** |
| 6 months | X | | | | X*** |
| 6-12 months | | | | X** | |
| 12-18 months | X | X | X | | X*** |
| 4-6 years | X | X | X | | |

*The DTaP, the acellular version of the DTP vaccine, is the preferred vaccine; the DTaP is an acceptable alternative.
**May be given a few months later.
***Depends on which Haemophilus influenza type B vaccine was given previously.

# CHAPTER 4

# Symptoms and Treatments for Childhood Illnesses

Though most kids are affected by only a handful of relatively harmless and easy-to-treat illnesses, parents need to be aware of the more potentially dangerous conditions to assure early and correct treatment. For children over 3 months of age, symptoms can usually be handled at home, under your doctor's guidance. Severe symptoms should always be addressed immediately by your child's physician. Whenever you're in doubt about the severity of an illness or the meaning of symptoms, call the doctor. Don't be bashful about calling your pediatrician when you've got any question or if you're worried about some aspect of your child's health.

## When to call the doctor

Call the doctor for any symptoms in your newborn. If your child is 3 months to 12 months, call the doctor for:

• **Changes in appearance.** If your baby just doesn't "look right" to you, this could be a sign that something is wrong.
• **Changes in behavior.** Behaviorial changes include lethargy, excessive sleepiness or wakefulness, excessive or high-pitched crying, and/or the appearance of pain. Your child may be in pain if he recoils when you touch him in a certain spot, or if he appears to be holding himself still to avoid discomfort.

- **Bloated or tender abdomen.**
- **Blue coloration or paleness.** This could indicate that your child is experiencing a breathing or circulatory problem or allergy.
- **Changes in bowel habits or urine output.** A distinct change in the frequency, consistency, or color of your child's feces or urine could indicate diarrhea, dehydration, constipation or blocked intestines, jaundice, injury or other serious condition.
- **Breathing difficulty.** Difficulty breathing is signaled by any gaps in breathing, rapid breathing, shallow breathing, wheezy or raspy breathing, paleness, or blue coloration. These symptoms could indicate asthma or other allergies, apnea, a cold or other virus , pneumonia, an injury, or other medical emergency.
- **Bruising or injury.** Bruises, particularly those that have no apparent cause, and injuries to the head or torso, as well as possible breaks and dislocations should be examined by a doctor.
- **Convulsion or seizure.** This could indicate a fever, a seizure disorder, or other condition.
- **Fever.** A temperature of 101.4°F or higher.
- **Fontanal changes.** Any bulging or depression of your baby's "soft spot" on your baby's head. This could indicate dehydration or other serious condition.
- **Skin rashes, excess sweatiness or clamminess, or salty sweat.** Minor rashes such as diaper rash or other common skin conditions may not need a doctor's attention. However, excessive sweatiness or clamminess could indicate juvenile diabetes. Sweat that tastes salty could indicate cystic fibrosis.
- **Difficulty swallowing.**
- **Vomiting.** See page 74 for determining the difference between spitting up, which is normal, and vomiting, which needs a doctor's attention. Projectile vomiting, while relatively common, must be addressed by the doctor to rule out pyloric stenosis, a rare but serious condition.
- **Yellowing of the whites of the eyes and/or the skin,** which could indicate jaundice.
- **In boys, tenderness and/or swelling in the scrotal area.** This could indicate a hernia or undescended testicles, as well as conditions that require emergency evaluation.

Nonemergency conditions that need your doctor's prompt attention include:
- **Indications of hearing or vision problems.** If your child

*For information about handling symptoms and illnesses in newborns, see **page 58–74**.*

doesn't respond to audio and visual stimuli or if his eyes show any clouding or other abnormality.

• **In girls, a closing of the labial tissues.** This could indicate labial adhesions.

If your child is over 12 months, review the symptoms detailed below and call the doctor as indicated and whenever you have concerns about your child's health.

# Conditions and illnesses

Below are the most common conditions and illnesses that can affect children. If you or your child's doctor suspects a particular condition or illness, review the entry for information about the possible causes and treatment options. If your child is experiencing symptoms, review the lists of symptoms included in each entry for help in identifying the condition or illness. Discuss any unfamiliar or severe symptoms with the doctor before providing home treatments.

Note: The following entries are listed alphabetically and include, in most cases, information about causes, symptoms, and treatments for the various illnesses and conditions. In cases in which the symptoms alone are not sufficient to make or confirm a diagnosis, the entry also includes information about tests and other means of determining a diagnosis.

## Adenoiditis and tonsillitis

The adenoids and tonsils are made up of immune-system cells that help fight off invading bacteria and viruses. Large tonsils or adenoids are not an automatic cause for alarm.

**Causes of adenoiditis and tonsillitis** Some kids' tonsils and adenoids are simply larger than others and never cause difficulties. Sometimes the adenoids or the tonsils or both become inflamed due to infection or allergy, conditions known as adenoiditis and tonsillitis. Often, they return to normal size, but sometimes they remain inflamed or become inflamed repeatedly.

### Symptoms of tonsillitis and adenoiditis

• Swelling. If you think your child has enlarged tonsils, look at the back of her throat. In extreme cases, the tonsils may touch each other. The adenoids are out of sight, so enlargement is harder to identify.

• Difficulty breathing or swallowing. Chronically enlarged tonsils or adenoids may interfere with airflow through the nose or throat, causing the heart to beat faster or slower than usual. Also, if enlarged tonsils make swallowing difficult, a child may be discouraged from eating.

• A sore throat .

• Fever of 101°F or higher.

• Tender or enlarged lymph glands in the neck.

• A coating of white or yellow pus or green or yellow nasal secretions at the back of the throat.

• Frequent ear infections.

• Mouth breathing rather than nose breathing.

• Chronically stuffy nose.

• Chronic nasal speech. For instance, the word *money* may be pronounced "buddy."

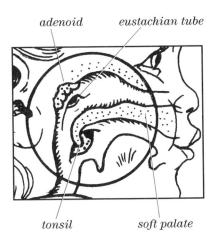

adenoid     eustachian tube

tonsil     soft palate

enlarged tonsil     normal tonsil

*The adenoids and tonsils are part of a barrier of soft tissues that ring the back of the throat and nose. The adenoids form the top of the ring; the tonsils form the sides. (The lingual tonsils— which are located at the base of the tongue and rarely cause problems— ring the bottom of the throat. )*

*For information on treating mild sore throat, see **page 650**.*

**Treating mild tonsillitis or adenoiditis** See treatment for mild sore throats.

**Treating severe or chronic tonsillitis or adenoiditis** The treatment is surgical removal of the tonsils and/or adenoids, known as tonsillectomy and/or adenoidectomy. The two procedures are often done together and are commonly called T & A.

**Who should have a T & A?** Although doctors no longer routinely remove children's adenoids and tonsils, tonsillectomies and adenoidectomies remain among the top childhood surgeries. Which kids are good candidates for the procedures? Each child's problems need to be evaluated individually, but there are guidelines for determining whether a child is likely to benefit from having his tonsils and/or adenoids removed.
• Severe and/or chronic symptoms. The American Academy of Otolaryngology–Head and Neck Surgery recommends T & A if a child has four severe tonsil and/or adenoid infections during the course of one year. The American Academy of Pediatrics (AAP) guidelines are more conservative, stating that surgery should be considered only if the child has had seven infections in one year, five in each of two consecutive years, or three in each of three consecutive years. Airway obstruction, difficulty swallowing, obstructive sleep apnea, and peritonsilar abscess are the only problems that make surgery absolutely necessary.
• The child is over the age of 2. Doctors are reluctant to perform T & A's on kids 2 and under since it can take several years to develop enough of a medical history to justify the surgery for reasons of chronic infection. The exception is extreme airway obstruction, for which doctors will operate on a child as young as 9 months.
• Chronic mouth breathing. The procedure is also often recommended for a child whose condition makes him always breathe through his mouth. Mouth breathing may cause children to develop facial or dental abnormalities.
• A single, severe infection. Occasionally, a single tonsil and/or adenoid infection, including peritonsilar abscess, warrants surgery if the infection doesn't respond to antibiotics.

**When your child needs a T & A** If your doctor decides that your child needs a tonsillectomy and/or adenoidectomy, the procedure(s) will be done at a hospital under general anesthesia. Most kids leave the hospital 24 hours after surgery. A T & A takes only an hour from administration of anesthesia to arrival in the recovery room. After the operation, 5 percent of kids experience complications such as infection, bleeding, and dehydration. Infection is treated with antibiotics. Most often, any postoperative bleeding occurs before a child is discharged from the hospital, though you'll have to monitor your child once she's home to make sure bleeding does not occur, which would require a trip to the ER. Dehydration can usually be prevented by making sure the child drinks enough fluids when she comes home from the hospital. If your child must have her adenoids and/or tonsils removed, don't worry that she'll become more susceptible to illness: Her lymphatic system has a backup supply of similar infection-fighting tissue.

> ### TLC after T & A
>
> To ease your child's recovery:
>
> • Offer lots of fluids to moisten the throat and reduce the risk of dehydration.
>
> • Let your child eat whatever he wants. He'll avoid any foods that irritate his throat, and will probably ask for cool, bland foods like ice cream or gelatin.

## Allergies

Allergies are an unpleasant and sometimes dangerous physical reaction to the environment or to a particular food or venom.

**Causes of allergies** Allergies occur when the body's immune system mistakes a harmless substance—such as pollen, pet dander, or a food—for a toxic one and mounts an attack on it by releasing substances called "histamines." A tendency toward allergies is often hereditary, and a child whose parents both have allergies has a 50 percent chance of developing an allergic condition. If one parent is allergic, the child's chances of developing allergies are one in four. But while members of the same family may be allergy-prone, each person may have his own special allergy: One might be allergic to wheat, another to pet saliva or dander, and another to pollen or mold, for example. An allergic reaction can be immediate or may occur hours after contact with the offending allergen. It may last just a few seconds or may last for days.

For most children, allergic reactions are not life threatening and can be treated at home. Sudden onset and chronic conditions require medical care.

*See **page 793** for information on reducing allergens in your home.*

**Diagnosing allergies** If you suspect your child has an allergy, have her evaluated by her physician and/or an allergist. Doctors diagnose allergies by taking a family and personal medical history and by examining the child. The exam may include skin tests in which allergens are injected into the child's skin to see if a reaction—such as hives—occurs. Some evaluations involve blood tests. Test results should be interpreted by a pediatrician who has a specialty in allergy, or by an allergist.

## Symptoms of mild allergies
- Occasional sneezing and/or coughing
- Tearing of eyes
- Mild runny nose
- Mild itching

## Treating mild allergies
- Limit or eliminate exposure to the allergen.
- Wash your child's hands and face if he has been in contact with something to which he's allergic.
- Administer OTC medications. Your child's doctor may recommend a nasal spray, such as Nasalcrom or Becenase, that reduces the likelihood of an allergic reaction. He may also suggest that your child use a saline nasal mist daily to keep her nasal passages moist.

## Symptoms of severe sudden-onset allergies
- Breathing difficulty, including rapid and/or noisy breathing and/or wheezing.
- Swelling, particularly of the face, lips, tongue, or throat
- Hives, generalized rash, and/or severe generalized itching
- Flushed skin, paleness, and/or clamminess
- Gastrointestinal distress, including vomiting, cramps, and/or diarrhea
- Lightheadedness, dizziness, and/or fainting

*For first aid for an allergic reaction, see **page 666**.*

## Symptoms of severe chronic allergies, including asthma
- Recurrent runny nose and/or sneezing
- Chronic coughing, with or without other cold symptoms, particularly at night
- Repeated sneezing, with or without other cold symptoms
- Frequent itching

- Hives or a rash
- Black circles around the eyes, a look of sleepiness or sleep deprivation
- Stomach cramps
- Wheezing

### Treating severe and/or chronic allergies

- Seek emergency treatment for life-threatening allergic reactions. Administer first-aid, if needed.
- Medicate, if warranted. For more on allergy medications, see below.
- Be prepared. If an allergy specialist determines that your child has a life-threatening allergy to a particular food or insect bite, she will recommend that you keep an epinephrine kit handy at all times. If your child is diagnosed with asthma, you will be advised to treat the underlying condition and to keep emergency medications and/or equipment readily available. If your child is diagnosed with a food allergy, you'll need to investigate the ingredients in the foods he already eats as well as any new foods he wants to eat; you'll also need to teach him to decline foods that you or another responsible adult has not inspected. For environmental and seasonal allergies and asthma, you'll have to take precautions, including changes in housekeeping and other routines.

### PARENTS ALERT

## When Allergies Are a Matter of Life or Death

Some allergies are life threatening. Sudden onset reactions to bee stings and to certain foods and medications can prove fatal in a handful of susceptible children and require immediate medical attention. Chronic conditions, such as asthma, can become life threatening if early symptoms are not recognized and treated properly. If your child develops any symptoms of severe allergic reaction, call 911 or take him to an ER immediately.

## Allergies to animals

Animal dander and saliva bring on allergy attacks in many susceptible children. Fur often harbors allergens. Kids are more apt to be allergic to cats than to dogs. Cats frequently groom themselves by licking, and they then shed dander—scales of skin—that are covered in their saliva. Children can also be allergic to farm and ranch animals, such as horses. A handful of kids are allergic to bird feathers or the mold in fish tanks.

**Handling mild allergies to animals** It's important to treat even mild allergies seriously, since regular exposure can turn a mild case into a severe one. It's probably best that your allergic child not have a pet or spend time in the company of animals. Some physicians, however, believe that keeping a pet should be permitted, provided certain precautions are taken:

• Limit exposure. Make sure a pet doesn't sleep in the child's room; this includes keeping birdcages and fish tanks in another location. Always have your child wash his hands and face after petting the animal. Do not let him sleep in clothes in which he has held or cuddled the pet. Train your pet to stay off beds, chairs, and the sofa.

• Groom the animal frequently. If possible, bathe a furry animal once a week and brush it outdoors daily to remove dander and fur. Also, wash the pet's bedding every week. If fish tank mold is an allergen, use a good filter and clean the tank frequently. Likewise, clean birdcages often. In all cases, do not allow the allergic child to assist in the grooming and cleaning.

• Do frequent housecleaning. If an animal lives indoors, vacuum with a HEPA-vacuum and damp-mop floors and other surfaces a few times a week. Consider replacing wall-to-wall carpet with throw rugs that can be washed once a week.

**Handling severe allergies to animals** If your child is severely allergic to animals or has asthma—and all the above strategies fail— you will need to find a new home for your pet. Some local newspapers offer free or low-cost advertisement space to owners who can't keep their pets. Veterinarians post adoption notices on bulletin boards in clinic waiting areas. It's vital not to expose a severely allergic child to any animal that can trigger an allergic reaction.

## *Allergies due to the indoor environment*

Allergies to dust mites and mold are common, and these allergens are present at home and other places your child frequents; you will not be able to eliminate them, but you can lessen their effects. Children can also be allergic to certain fabrics, metals, upholstery fillings, and fragrances.

### Handling indoor environmental allergies

• Reduce dust. While dust itself doesn't cause allergies—microscopic insects called dust mites are the actual culprits—reducing dust will lessen the dust mite population. Dust mites live virtually everywhere indoors, on counter tops, in bedding, carpeting, and curtains, and in the "fur" of stuffed animals.

You can't totally eliminate dust mites from your child's environment, but you can protect him to some degree. Your best move is to eliminate as many dust-collecting surfaces as you can in your child's room, to reduce the need for constant cleaning. Choose bare floors over carpeted ones, vinyl shades over drapes or curtains, closed closets instead of clothing racks and bureaus, and enclosed rather than open bookshelves. Make sure your child's room isn't overpopulated with stuffed animals. Let him keep two or three out and store the rest in a closet or chest and wash or use a wet cloth to wipe them down every week.

Damp-mop the floor and furnishings in your child's room once a week. Wash your child's sheets, pillowcases, and blanket once or twice a week in hot water. Choose synthetic over natural fabrics because mites thrive in cotton and wool. Put heavy-gauge plastic covers on mattresses and pillows. (Contact the American Lung Association for a list of retailers in your area who specialize in items such as especially designed bedding to reduce dust mite exposure.) In warm weather, use an air conditioner in your child's room, but don't use fans, which just stir up the dust. Air conditioners have the added benefit of filtering out dust and pollens. If possible, install a central or room dehumidifier; dust mites thrive in moderate to high humidity.

When cleaning the rest of the house, use a HEPA-filter vacuum, and vacuum rugs and upholstery when your child isn't home or is out of the room, since vacuuming can "stir up" dust mites.

• Curb mold growth. Mold frequently triggers allergies in kids. Older houses are prone to an overgrowth of mold, especially in the bathroom where there's lots of moisture. A dehumidifier can help curb mold growth. Also, provide good ventilation throughout the house by installing exhaust fans in the bathroom, kitchen, and laundry room—any place where steam is likely to build up. Dry the shower curtains or glass shower doors after use. A car squeegee is great for removing moisture from glass doors. When cleaning the bathroom, use an antimold cleanser or a mixture of chlorine bleach and water. If there's any moisture or mildew elsewhere in the house,

## *What to Know About Allergy Medications*

If your child suffers from frequent allergy attacks despite your best efforts to allergy-proof his environment, his doctor may recommend medication or a series of desensitization shots. Prescription and OTC allergy medicines can be given in a number of ways: orally, by injection, or in the form of nasal drops and sprays, inhalers, eye drops, and skin creams. Allergy medications can have side effects, though, so your doctor will ask you to keep close tabs on your child, checking for adverse reactions. The most common allergy medications are:

• **Antihistamines.** These block the effects of histamines which are released by the body in an allergic reaction. Antihistamines make some kids drowsy or irritable. Switching from one product to another may alleviate side effects.

• **Cortisone.** This powerful drug curbs sinus inflammation and is sometimes prescribed for kids with severe or chronic allergies, usually in a nasal-spray form; occasionally a child needs oral cortisone. Oral cortisone therapy must be carefully monitored by a physician since these medications may impair growth as well as affect immune functioning.

• **Allergy shots.** Doctors sometimes prescribe desensitization or "allergy shots" for very allergic kids. For a period of time—usually several years—the doctor gives the child weekly shots containing a diluted amount of whatever substance triggers the allergy, until he gradually becomes less sensitive to the offending agent. Allergy shots don't always work, though, and can be time consuming and expensive as well as uncomfortable for your child.

Note: Nasal sprays such as Nasalcrom and Beconase can, with regular use, help prevent allergic symptoms. However, they can trigger throat irritation, nasal irritation, and sneezing in some kids.

particularly in your child's room, use an antimold cleanser or chlorine bleach mixed with water to wash down the walls. Trade house plants that release moisture into the air, such as coleus, for cactuses, which "drink up" moisture. Paint instead of wallpapering your child's room, since mold can grow behind wallpaper where you won't see it until it has already caused a reaction in your child.

• Replace irritating fabrics and metals. Wool can irritate some kids' skin, causing a rash and/or itching. For kids who are sensitive to wool, opt for blankets made of cotton or synthetic fibers. If a child is allergic to dust, choose synthetic bedding. Kids with a wool allergy are also usually allergic to lanolin, a moisturizer that's derived from wool, so check skin lotion labels carefully to avoid using any products containing lanolin.

Feathers can cause sneezing and other allergic symptoms in certain children, who should not wear down-filled coats or use feather-filled pillows or comforters. Choose foam or polyester-filled pillows and comforters, and coats lined with Thinsulate or another synthetic, hypoallergenic insulation.

• Keep the air clean of odors and contaminants. Perfumes and other fragrances may cause sneezing, watery eyes, a runny nose, and skin rashes or itching. For sensitive children, use fragrance-free laundry detergent, bath soap, and shampoo. Also steer clear of scented bubble baths and avoid fabric softeners. Avoid wearing perfumes yourself and ask others who care for your child to do the same. If commercial cleaning products irritate your child, use alternatives, such as vinegar and water in place of chemicals. Tobacco smoke may cause eye irritation, sinus congestion, and coughing in children, and can trigger asthma attacks.

*For more on reducing airborne allergens in your home, see page 793.*

## Allergies due to the outdoor environment

If your child develops itchy, watery eyes; sneezing; a stuffy nose; dark circles under his eyes; or postnasal drip every spring, late summer, or fall, he may be one of the 35 million Americans allergic to the pollen on flowers, weeds, and grass. This condition is commonly known as "hay fever" or seasonal allergic rhinitis.

**Handling seasonal allergies**  To minimize your child's discomfort:
- Limit outdoor play during prime allergy times. Keep your child indoors when the pollen count is highest—usually in the morning and on windy days.
- Bathe your child. After he's played outdoors, have him bathe and shampoo to remove pollen that's accumulated on his skin and hair. Wash his play clothes after each wearing.
- Keep indoor air pollen-free. Use an air-conditioner in his bedroom at night and in other rooms during the day, when he's home. Keep windows shut, especially on windy days.
- Keep your lawn mowed short. Also be sure to mow and remove the clippings when your child's not in the area.

## Anemia

Anemia occurs when the concentration of hemoglobin, the oxygen-carrying pigment in the blood, drops below normal. Hemoglobin molecules are carried inside red blood cells and transport oxygen from the lungs to the body's tissues. Under normal conditions, stable hemoglobin concentrations are maintained by a strict balance between red cell production in the bone marrow and red cell

*See page 741 for information about Sickle-Cell Anemia.*

destruction in the spleen. If this balance is disrupted, and anemia devlops, there won't be enough hemoglobin to carry oxygen to all the cells in the body.

**Causes of anemia** Anemia is caused by insufficient iron in the diet. Infants get the iron they need in breast milk or iron-fortified formula. An infant may develop anemia if he starts drinking cow's milk too early, especially if he doesn't take an iron supplement or eat enough iron-rich food. That's because cow's milk can irritate the bowel and trigger intestinal bleeding in very young babies, especially those under 6 months.

Older children who don't eat iron-rich foods or who drink huge quantities of milk may be at risk for anemia, since the calcium in milk can interfere with proper iron absorption.

**Symptoms of anemia**
• Pallor—or unusual paleness of the skin. The child's lips look less pink than usual. There's also a decrease in pinkness of the lining of the eyelids and the nail beds.
• Tiredness. Anemic children tire easily and may feel weak and irritable.

**Symptoms of severe anemia include:**
• Shortness of breath
• Rapid heartbeat
• Swelling of the feet and hands

**Diagnosing anemia** If you suspect anemia, schedule a visit to the doctor, who will perform blood tests that detect anemia and possibly prescribe iron supplements.

**Treating anemia** The American Academy of Pediatrics recommends that babies under 1 year of age consume breast milk or iron-fortified formula, not cow's milk. Children 6 months and older should consume iron-rich foods, including meat and iron-fortified cereal. If your child is diagnosed with anemia, the doctor may recommend iron supplements. Never give iron supplements without a doctor's recommendation.

**Iron supplement how-to's** If her doctor recommends that your child take an iron supplement, follow these tips:

• For a child over 1 year of age, give the supplement at the same time he eats citrus fruit or drinks citrus juice. The vitamin C in citrus boosts iron absorption.

• Give the iron supplement several hours before or several hours after the child has consumed milk or other dairy products. Dairy products block iron absorption.

• If your child is taking a liquid supplement, brush her teeth and gums afterward. Liquid iron can turn teeth a grayish color.

• Increase your child's intake of high-fiber foods and water. Iron supplements may cause constipation.

• Don't be alarmed if your child's poop looks black! Iron darkens stool.

• Don't overdose. Iron can be toxic, so follow the dosage prescribed precisely. Keep supplements locked away with other medications to avoid accidental overdose.

**PARENTS ALERT**

## *Iron Supplement Poisoning*

If your child does need iron supplements, keep them in a locked cabinet. Iron supplements are toxic to children when taken in large amounts. In extremely rare cases, overdoses can be lethal.

# Apnea (sleep apnea)

*Sleep apnea* is the term used when a person stops breathing during sleep. It's not uncommon for healthy babies, especially preemies, to experience brief periods—20 seconds or less—of apnea. Apnea episodes are only considered problematic when they last longer than 20 seconds or if the baby turns pale, blue, or limp, or has a decreased heart rate. Any of these additional symptoms calls for immediate medical involvement.

In older children, apnea occurs when the upper airways become blocked during sleep, possibly by enlarged adenoids or tonsils, which leads to momentary lapses in breathing.

**Causes of sleep apnea** Apnea can be caused by physical problems, such as allergies, colds, and other upper respiratory ailments, tonsilitis and adenoiditis, as well as exposure to cigarette smoke. In many cases, the cause is unknown.

**Symptoms of sleep apnea** In infants, the only symptom might be a prolonged gap in breathing. In older children, symptoms include:

- Loud snoring or snorting during sleep, interspersed with periods of silence. Breathing resumes when an involuntary reaction reopens the airways. Snoring alone, however, does not indicate apnea.
- Restless sleeping. Kids who have sleep apnea are often restless sleepers.
- Fatigue. Children suffering from sleep apnea are often tired or drowsy during the day and have trouble concentrating due to interrupted sleep.

*See **pages 675–76** for more on CPR.*

**Treating apnea in infants**   If your infant under the age of 1 year appears to be having an apnea episode, gently shake her, which may arouse her sufficiently to resume breathing. Then, notify her doctor.

If your child turns blue, call 911 or your emergency number for assistance. Perform CPR if necessary while another party calls for help.

**Monitoring and treating apnea in older children**   If you suspect that your child has apnea, talk to his doctor. Though apnea in older children can cause a loss of sleep, it is not a medical emergency.

The doctor may recommend that your child stay overnight in a sleep laboratory for proper diagnosis. You'll be able to stay with him throughout the night. Once your child is in bed, the staff will attach electrodes to his skin which are connected to a monitor to record his breathing and heart rates, as well as oxygen levels. If the monitor detects a disturbance in the breathing and heart rates and a drop in oxygen intake, your child probably has sleep apnea.

Children with sleep apnea usually undergo a tonsillectomy and adenoidectomy to allow them to breathe more normally.

# Appendicitis

This serious condition is an inflammation of the appendix, a narrow, hollow structure attached to the large intestine. Though more common in kids over 6 and adults, it can occur at any age. Appendicitis can be difficult to diagnose, because so many of its symptoms mimic a stomach virus.

**Causes of appendicitis**   Though the cause of inflammation is not always known, it can happen if a piece of food or stool gets trapped inside the appendix.

### Symptoms of appendicitis
- Abdominal pain, usually around the navel, at first. The pain then spreads to the lower right portion of the abdomen. (If the appendix isn't located in the usual place, the child may feel pain in his back or somewhere else in the abdomen.)
- Worsening and/or moving pain. After a few hours, the pain worsens and may move to the lower right side. A child will have trouble walking or standing erect.
- Loss of appetite
- Vomiting a few hours after pain starts
- Fever over 100°F, in some, but not all, cases

### Diagnosing and treating appendicitis
- Seek medical advice immediately. Tests may confirm or rule out this diagnosis.
- Surgery. In the majority of cases, the appendix must be removed surgically to prevent it from bursting.

# Attention deficit disorder (ADD) and attention deficit hyperactivity disorder (ADHD)

ADHD appears to be an inborn behavioral condition that affects up to 5 percent of all children under 13 in the United States, with boys more prone to the disorder than girls. Children with ADHD have difficulty focusing their attention—and, as a result, find it hard to concentrate on ordinary tasks or schoolwork. Some, but not all, are hyperactive as well. Those with focusing difficulties but without hyperactivity are said to have attention deficit disorder (ADD). Most ADHD and ADD kids have normal or above-normal intelligence, but sometimes appear mentally deficient because their attention span makes learning so difficult. ADHD and ADD can continue into adulthood, affecting personal relationships and job performance—but when the condition is diagnosed in early childhood, the child can learn to improve his attention span and control his impulses effectively. Approximately 40 to 60 percent of children with ADHD or ADD have one or more of the specific learning disabilities described below.

### For Learning Disabled Children

***National Center for Learning Disabilities (NCLD).*** The NCLD's Information & Referral Service provides a wide array of information to parents of learning-disabled children. The service maintains a list of more than 3000 schools, colleges, diagnostic centers, support organizations, information services, and special programs throughout the nation for people with learning disabilities.

381 Park Avenue South, Suite 1401
New York, NY 10016
(888) 575-7373
(212) 545-7510
www.ncld.org

***Learning Disabilities Association of America***

4156 Library Rd.
Pittsburgh, PA 15234-1349
(412) 341-1515
www.ldanatl.org

**Symptoms of ADD** Children with ADD can have one or more of these symptoms:

- Difficulty following through on tasks and understanding instructions
- Quickly losing interest in games or tasks
- Frequently losing belongings
- A tendency to be unusually disorganized
- Difficulty doing projects or tasks that require long-term attention and effort
- Forgetfulness
- Tendency to be easily distracted

**Symptoms of ADHD** ADHD children have many of the symptoms of ADD, along with the following symptoms:

- Restlessness, fidgeting
- Inability to remain seated
- Running or climbing inappropriately
- Talking excessively
- Difficulty playing quietly
- Blurting out answers or frequently interrupting parents, playmates, and teachers
- Impulsiveness

**Causes of ADD and ADHD** Several decades ago, experts felt that kids with ADD or ADHD had suffered some type of brain damage. But researchers now feel that the problem lies in the brain's chemistry. People with ADD and ADHD may have short supplies of one or more neurotransmitters, such as serotonin or dopamine. Other experts suggest that in some children, the disorder is caused by maternal alcohol abuse or smoking, or by early-childhood illnesses such as meningitis. There's no conclusive proof that these factors cause ADHD, though.

ADD and ADHD do seem to be inherited disorders, and between 30 and 40 percent of kids diagnosed with the condition have relatives with the same problem. The rate of ADHD in identical twins is greater when one twin has the disorder than among fraternal twins.

**Diagnosing ADD and ADHD** Making a correct diagnosis can be tricky. There's no blood test or single psychological test for ADD or ADHD. If you suspect your child has a problem, his doctor should do a complete physical exam to rule out other possible causes of his seeming inattention, testing, for example, for a vision or hearing disorder. If his doctor rules out other causes, your child should then see a psychologist, child psychiatrist, or neurologist who has had a great deal of experience diagnosing and treating children with ADHD. But even if that professional makes a diagnosis of ADD or ADHD, you'd be wise to get a second opinion: Many children who have behavioral or learning problems—but not actual ADD or ADHD—have been misdiagnosed with the condition.

### Judging activity levels

*"How can I tell if my 4-year-old daughter is 'hyperactive?' She rarely sits still."*

To help you determine if your child might be hyperactive, ask yourself these questions: Does her energy seem never to run out? Is she impulsive to the point of disregarding her own safety? Is she rambunctious to the point of violence? Is her attention span extremely short? Does she move from one thing to another without being able to concentrate on any one thing? Is she disruptive to the family and to others? Do you get many complaints about her behavior? If your answer is yes to a number of these questions, your child may be hyperactive or just normally overactive. For a definite diagnosis, your child will need to be assessed by a professional who will be able to distinguish between normal and hyperactive behavior. If she is hyperactive, physical problems will first need

## Books

*Every Child Is Learning: A Training Program for Teachers and Parents.* The kit includes a guided video program and resource manual that helps identify, understand, and plan activities that promote school success. It also identifies behaviors that place preschool children at risk for later learning problems. Available from:
   NCLD
   381 Park Avenue South, Suite 1401
   New York, NY 10016

*No Easy Answers: The Learning Disabled Child at Home and at School* by Sally L. Smith (Bantam Books).

*The Misunderstood Child: Understanding and Coping With Your Child's Learning Disabilities* by Larry B. Silver (Times Books).

*No One to Play With* by Betty B. Osman (Academic Therapy Publications).

to be considered. Then psychological causes will be explored. Ask your family doctor for advice.

**Treating ADD** Treatment consists of:

• **Educational help,** in which specially trained teachers work with the child to increase his attention span and overcome any learning disabilities.

• **Medication** to heighten attention by stimulating the nervous system. Three medications, Ritalin, Dexedrine, and Adderal, which has been in use and have been studied for over 60 years, help many children with ADHD. These medications seem to kick in quickly, and certain kids experience noticeable improvement in attention span and self-control. Ritalin, Dexedrine, and Adderal don't work for all kids, though, and they can produce nuisance side effects, such as loss of appetite, nervousness, trouble sleeping, and rapid heartbeat. They must also be taken several times a day.

**Treating ADHD** The most effective treatment for ADHD is medication; other treatments that have shown some effectiveness are:

• Behavior modification techniques at school and at home
• Parent training because parenting a child with ADHD is more difficult than parenting an average child
• Social-skills training, usually in a group setting, using behavior therapy techniques to strengthen the child's listening and social-interaction abilities
• Organizational skills training helping the child "learn" how to get more organized
• Educational training (tutoring)

**Managing your child's condition** Parents are often overwhelmed and frustrated by a child who has ADD or ADHD. It helps to realize that the child is just as frustrated by his condition—and that he isn't able to easily control his focus or his more negative behavior. You can help your child by doing the following:

• Try to establish a routine—or structure—for your child. If he knows what to expect—when dinner will be served, when snacks are offered, what time he's supposed to study, when bedtime is—he'll feel more in control.

• If your child is very active, don't try to get her to sit still or to stop running around unless she's putting herself or others at risk. When you reprimand her, try to take a positive tone. For example, say, "Jumping up and down on Grandma's couch isn't a good idea. Go outside to jump."

• Don't overwhelm your child with tasks that he's bound to fail at. Instead, give him projects that require a short attention span. When he's mastered a project, give him a slightly harder one.

• When your child is working on a project, even something as simple as playing with blocks, make sure he isn't distracted by other things—such as the TV. (Music, however, may be helpful.)

• Some kids with ADHD become so frustrated they lash out at others, hitting their parents, siblings, or friends—or knocking over a playmate's toys. Help your child learn to vent his anger in other ways. For example, he can scream into a pillow or punch an inflated plastic clown or punching bag. Getting rid of excess energy will also help. Suggest that he run or jump in the backyard or take him to the playground for a good workout.

• Don't put your child in situations he isn't ready for. If he has a hard time sitting still, a two-hour movie isn't a good idea. And, he may be more comfortable eating takeout food than spending an hour or more sitting in a crowded restaurant.

### Diet and ADHA

*"I've heard that sugar and food additives can trigger episodes of ADHD in children. Will putting my son on a special diet help cure him of the disorder?"*

There's no proof that sugar or food additives cause or worsen ADHD. However, you can easily cut back on the sugar your child eats, and avoid processed foods that contain additives. If, within a couple of months, your child's symptoms improve, he can safely continue such a diet. However, he will still need behavioral and educational therapy, and will also need drug therapy.

# Bowlegs and knock-knees

Between the ages of 1 and 2, many toddlers appear bowlegged, with their legs curved outward at the knees. Children between the ages of 3 and 6 are often knock-kneed, with their knees seeming to hit together. Usually, kids' legs straighten over time.

**Causes of bowleggedness or knock-knees**  Most often, these conditions are simply the result of immature muscle tone. Very rarely, bowlegs and knock-knees are caused by arthritis, a fracture of the growth plate around the knee, or a tumor. If your child has bowlegs or knock-knees and is unusually short for his age, he may have a growth problem and should see a doctor who specializes in metabolic disorders.

**Symptoms of problematic bowleggedness or knock-knees**  If your child has any of the following symptoms, her doctor may refer her to a pediatric orthopedist for a workup:
- Very pronounced curving of the legs
- Only one leg is affected. Your child's gait will be off as well, and she may appear to have a limp.
- Bowlegs worsening after age 2
- Knock-knees persisting beyond age 7

**Treating bowleggedness or knock-knees**  In most cases, the treatment is time: As your child grows, the conditions will diminish and disappear on their own. The American Academy of Pediatrics does not recommend braces, corrective shoes or orthotics, or special exercises as treatments for bowlegs or knock-knees, noting that these can be harmful to a child's physical development and cause emotional distress. Problematic bowleggedness and knock-knees, however, require treatment of the underlying condition.

# Bronchiolitis

This is an inflammation of the lower respiratory tract that hampers breathing. It's prevalent between November and April and primarily affects infants and toddlers, though older kids can get it too. It's most serious in premature babies and in children who have a chronic condition such as heart disease, lung disease, or Down syndrome.

**Causes of bronchiolitis** It is almost always caused by the respiratory syncytial virus (RSV). Bronchiolitis is contagious and is passed around from person to person in much the same way as a cold virus—through contact and by inhaling droplets released by sneezing.

*For more on RSV, see* **page 642.**

**Symptoms of bronchiolitis** Cold symptoms progress to:
- Wheezing
- Shortness of breath and rapid breathing that makes eating and sleeping difficult
- Occasionally, low-grade fever and runny nose
- In severe cases, a child gasps for air and/or develops a bluish tinge around his lips and fingertips, indicating that his airways are so blocked that he's not getting enough oxygen into his blood.

**Treating mild bronchiolitis**
- Call your child's doctor. All cases of bronchiolitis should be evaluated.
- Run a cool-mist humidifier in your child's room to ease breathing.
- Offer plenty of fluids and frequent feedings to make sure your child doesn't become dehydrated.

**Treating severe bronchiolitis** Take your child to the ER or call your doctor immediately if your child has difficulty breathing. Treatment includes:
- Oxygen and bronchodilating drugs to ease breathing
- In some cases, the drug ribavirin to kill the virus
- In some cases, hospitalization so the child can be fed intravenously

# Bronchitis

Bronchitis is an inflammation of the larger branches of the bronchial "tree," which lead to the lungs; the windpipe is often inflamed, too. It is sometimes confused with brochiolitis, which is an inflamation of the smaller branches of the bronchial tree. In some susceptible kids, bronchitis can lead to an ear infection. The condition usually lasts for a few days or a few weeks at the most.

**Causes of bronchitis** The ailment is usually caused by a virus, most often one of the many that trigger colds, and is spread by inhaling droplets that have been coughed or sneezed into the air by an infected person.

**Symptoms of bronchitis**
- Fever, sometimes of 102°F or higher
- A harsh or hacking cough that may worsen at night
- Vomiting
- Greenish or yellow-tinged sputum
- Wheezing

**Treating bronchitis**
- Bed rest
- Plenty of fluids
- Nasal suctioning (for infants, to remove mucus from the nose)
- Expectorant cough medication to bring up bronchial secretions
- Acetaminophen to lower fever
- The use of a humidifier to ease nighttime breathing

If a secondary bacterial infection of the bronchi develops, your child's doctor will probably prescribe antibiotics. However, most cases of bronchitis don't involve bacterial infections and do not require antibiotics.

# Bruising

Most childhood bruising is caused by accidents. Unless a bruise is severe and accompanied by bleeding and/or loss of consciousness and/or a bone injury or concussion, it is no cause for alarm.

However, unexplained bruising and frequent bruising could signal a serious illness, such as leukemia, and should be evaluated by a physician.

# Canker sores

These common sores, which appear in the mouth, are painful, but they aren't contagious. Canker sores occur singly or in groups and can crop up anywhere in the mouth—on the roof, inside the cheeks, on the gums, or on the tongue. The canker sores can last for more than ten days and may recur.

**Causes and triggers of canker sores**  No one knows the underlying cause of canker sores, though some experts speculate that an autoimmune response, in which the body develops antibodies that attack its own tissues, may be the culprit. Triggers of canker sores include:
• Fever, usually accompanying a cold
• Fatigue, emotional upset, or stress
• Foods. Some kids get canker sores after eating a particular food, especially citrus fruits.

**Symptoms of canker sores/identifying canker sores**
• Mouth pain at the site of the sore or sores
• Small blisters anywhere in the mouth. The blisters break and ulcers form and get bigger until there's a bright red sore surrounding a whitish-yellow cavity.

**Treating canker sores**
• For children over the age of 3, encourage mouth rinsing. Have your child swish ice-cold water around in her mouth to curb pain. You can also try rinsing the mouth with a solution of antihistamine elixir, such as Benadryl, and an antacid suspension, such as Mylanta or Maalox, before meals and at bedtime—no more than four times a day for no more than three days. (For a child 5 or younger, use ¼ teaspoon of each product; for an older child, use ½ teaspoon of each.) Encourage your child not to swallow the mixture, although it won't hurt her.
• For younger children, apply a topical ointment. OTC topical medications like those used to relieve teething pain may also help canker sores. Squeeze or pour a little onto a cotton swab and dab onto the sores.

# Cat-scratch disease

Cat-scratch disease, also called cat-scratch fever, may develop after a child is scratched or bitten by a cat, especially a kitten. Mild symptoms usually last two to four months.

**Causes of cat-scratch disease**  The illness is caused by *Bartonella henselae*, which is transmitted by cats via their claws or saliva. Only cats who harbor this bacterium can transmit the disease, so a scratch or bite from an uninfected cat, while still requiring first-aid to heal the wound and prevent any other form of bacterial infection, is not a risk factor for cat-scratch disease. If your cat is infected with *Bartonella henselae*, it should be treated by a veterinarian.

**Symptoms of cat-scratch disease**
• Red pimples at the site of the wound. These show up about 7 to 12 days after being bitten or scratched.
• Swollen glands. One to four weeks after being scratched, glands in the neck, jaw, or armpits may become tender.
• A rash
• Fever
• Fatigue
Less frequent symptoms include:
• Loss of appetite
• Headache
• Abdominal pain and/or vomiting

**Treating cat-scratch disease**  After any cat scratch, you must wash the wound thoroughly with soap and water. Call the doctor if your child's skin has been broken by a bite or scratch. If your child develops mild symptoms, no further treatment is needed. Severe infections are treated with antibiotics.

# Chicken pox (varicella)

*For information on vaccination, see **page 546**.*

Chicken pox is a common and extremely contagious childhood illness that occurs most often in late winter and early spring. Symptoms are usually slow to appear. A child may not develop full-blown chicken pox for 20 days after exposure. Infected persons are contagious from 24 to 48 hours before symptoms appear until the pox crust over. The chicken pox vaccine can prevent or lesson the severity of the illness.

**Cause of chicken pox**  Chicken pox is caused by the varicella-zoster virus, a member of the herpes family. It is spread when an infected person sneezes, coughs, spits, or drools, releasing germ-laden droplets into the air, which are inhaled.

### Symptoms of chicken pox

- A rash. Pox—from just a few to hundreds of itchy, fluid-filled sores—may appear anywhere on the body, even in the throat and mouth. Active lesions begin to fade after a few days, but scabs may linger for up to 20 days.
- Slight fever
- Lethargy
- Headache and/or muscle aches

**Treating chicken pox** If your child is especially uncomfortable, try the following:
- Baths. Let him sit in a tepid bath containing colloidal oatmeal or Aveeno oatmeal to soothe itching.
- Calamine lotion. Using a cotton swab, dab lotion on sores.
- Oral antihistamine. Benadryl (diphenhydramine hydrochloride) is often given to kids over age 2 to ease itching.
- Fever-reducing medication. If your child is over age 2, give acetaminophen to reduce fever if it's making him uncomfortable. Call the doctor if your child is under age 2 before giving this medication. Do not give aspirin; it has been linked to Reye syndrome, which can damage the liver and brain.
- Fluids. Offer your child plenty of fluids if he has a fever.
- Comfortable clothing. Dress your child in loose cotton clothing that doesn't irritate the skin.
- Keep nails trimmed. Trim your child's fingernails to minimize scratching and thus, the risk of infection or scarring.
- Soothing foods. If your child has sores in his mouth or throat, give him gelatin, ice cream, or other soft, easy-to-swallow foods.

## Colds, cold symptoms, and coughs

The typical child catches five or six colds a year. Most colds last about a week to 10 days. Coughs may linger for a couple of weeks.

**Causes of colds** Colds are triggered by a variety of viruses. In fact, more than 200 viruses, all highly contagious, are suspected of triggering the combination of symptoms—achiness, congestion, coughing, and sniffles—that define a cold. An infected person may cough or sneeze the germs into the air for another person to inhale, but most cold germs are spread by hand contact with items that an infected person has touched.

## When to Call the Doctor

Call your child's doctor if he develops any of the following symptoms. His cold may have turned into something more serious:

• **A marked change in behavior;** for example, your active, playful son becomes listless or unresponsive.

• **Fever that lasts for more than three days or rises sharply and suddenly.** While any rise in temperature means you should be alert for problem, a sudden "spiking" fever is an alarm signal. If your child's temperature merely creeps up a little, his behavior is your best clue as to whether or not you should worry. Keep in mind that everyone's temperature rises during the day and is a little higher in the evening than in the morning.

• **Signs of an ear infection.** Symptoms include: fever that rises suddenly, increasing fussiness or restlessness, increasing problems sleeping, and rubbing an ear or turning the head from side to side. Older kids may complain of ear pain or discomfort.

• **Nasal discharge that becomes thicker and is yellowish or greenish.** Thick yellow-green secretions are fairly normal toward the end of a cold, but these symptoms are cause for concern if other symptoms, such as a spiking fever, are also present, and may indicate that the child has developed a sinus infection.

• **Labored or difficult breathing, wheezing, or raspy breathing.** Heaving of the chest in order to breathe is a signal of distress.

• **Inflammation of the mucus membranes around the eyes** or any discharge from the eyes, which may indicate conjunctivitis.

• **Swollen glands in the neck, armpit, or groin.**

• **The cold lasts longer than 14 days.**

**Symptoms of colds** Typical cold symptoms include:
• A runny nose
• Nasal congestion
• Sneezing
• A non-phlegm-producing cough
• A sore throat
• Fatigue, and a general "out-of-sorts" feeling
• A loss of appetite
• Fever, occasionally

**Treating colds and symptoms of colds** While you can't cure a cold, you can treat its symptoms to make your child more comfortable.

• Run a cool-mist humidifier in your child's room, especially at night, to help him breathe more easily. Clean the humidifier daily to keep molds and other organisms from accumulating, using a mixture of white vinegar and water, or equal parts bleach and water.

• Have your child blow his nose, or remove nasal secretion with drops and/or swabs and/or a nasal syringe. Use saline nasal drops if stuffiness is interfering with his eating and sleep. Use just a couple of drops in each nostril before feedings and sleep. Saline drops are nonmedicated and available at drugstores. Avoid using decongestant or medicated drops without checking with your doctor. You can also use a bulb nasal syringe, available at drugstores, or twirl a clean cotton swab in the lower part of each nostril, to remove nasal secretions if your child cannot blow his nose and the mucus is especially thick. Suction or swab secretions just after using saline nasal drops; the drops thin the secretions, making them easier to remove.

• Offer plenty of fluids. Fluids help thin nasal secretions. Anecdotal evidence indicates that chicken soup helps ease cold symptoms. Avoid giving your child milk products, which may increase mucus secretions.

• Give your child a warm bath. Let him play in a slightly warm bath to ease breathing and help lower fever.

• Give your child a pain reliever/fever reducer. Ask your doctor if she recommends acetaminophen or ibuprofen to reduce fever and relieve achiness.

• Elevate your child's head during sleeping. Place a pillow or several towels under the head of your child's mattress to raise his head slightly and aid in draining mucus from his nasal cavity. Do not use pillows directly under your child's head under the age of 2.

### *Colds vs. Flu*

While hundreds of viruses are suspected of causing colds, only a few lead to flu. Typically, cold symptoms come on slowly, starting with a sneeze and progressing to a runny nose and stuffiness, cough, and low-grade fever. Flu symptoms hit suddenly and are associated with more body aches and pains and a higher fever.

### Vitamin C and colds

*"Can regular doses of vitamin C keep my child from getting a cold?"*

Though vitamin C is important for wound healing, its cold-fighting role is unproven.

## *Coughs*

A cough is the body's way of protecting the lungs from invaders — anything from noxious fumes to a buildup of mucus. Most coughs are triggered by throat irritation and are nothing more than an annoying symptom of an upper respiratory infection, such as a cold or the flu, or dryness of the throat caused by overheated homes or air conditioning. But they sometimes signal more serious conditions, such as bronchiolitis or pneumonia.

**Nonproductive coughs** Coughs caused by viral infections, like a cold or the flu, are usually non-productive. That is, the child doesn't cough up much sputum — a mixture of mucus, pus, and cellular debris that has pooled in the bronchi, the airways leading to the lungs. Instead, the cough is typically triggered by nasal secretions that trickle into the throat (postnasal drip) and cause irritation.

## When to Call the Doctor

Call the doctor if:

- Your child has difficulty breathing.
- Your child develops a chronic cough after choking on food or a small object. Children who have inhaled food or small objects may have long-lasting coughs.
- A cough lasts longer than a week.
- Coughing is painful, intense, or persistent.
- Your child also vomits or turns blue while coughing.
- A cough comes on suddenly and is accompanied by fever.
- Your child coughs during or after exercise or on most nights.

Allergies, as well as minor upper respiratory infections, often lead to non-productive coughs, as does exposure to second-hand smoke.

**Productive coughs** If your child has mucus in the bronchi—typical in cases of pneumonia—he'll have a productive cough. This mucus is harder to bring up than postnasal drip secretions, and requires long, hard coughing episodes from deep within the chest. A child who coughs at night—but not during the day—may have a mild form of asthma.

**What to know about cough remedies** There are many OTC cough remedies available for children. However, avoid giving your child OTC or prescription cough remedies, especially cough suppressants, without first consulting your doctor. He needs to determine the cause of the cough and treat the underlying problem. For example, if your child has asthma, she'll need special asthma medications, and a cough medicine could mask more serious symptoms. If your child has a bacterial infection, she'll need antibiotics. Coughs due to colds or allergies may respond to cough medications, including antihistamines and decongestants. Keep in mind that these and other cough remedies can cause adverse reactions in children, including extreme drowsiness, excitability, and irritability. The most common cough remedies are:

- Expectorants, which thin mucus in the bronchi so it can be coughed up more easily. The most effective ingredient is guaifenesin.
- Cough suppressants, such as dextromethorphan, which inhibit the cough reflex in the throat and windpipes. Suppressants are rarely recommended for children.
- Decongestants, which shrink blood vessels in the walls of breathing passages. This curbs the amount of mucus produced. Pseudophedrine and phenylephrine are common ingredients.
- Antihistamines, which decrease allergy-related mucus membrane secretions and curb swelling of the membranes. Chlorpheniramine and brompheniramine are common ingredients.

# Constipation

Constipation is marked by hard stools or an inability to move the bowels frequently enough for health and comfort. Diagnosing constipation in kids can be tricky since bowel patterns vary. While one child may have one or two movements a day, another child might move his bowels every other day or even every few days, and not be technically constipated.

**Causes of constipation**   Most cases of childhood constipation are "idiopathic," which means no one—including your child's doctor—can figure out why the child is constipated. Heredity sometimes plays a role. Foods are a common cause. A lack of physical activity, a change in routine, or the stress of toilet teaching can also cause constipation.

Some chronically constipated kids avoid having a bowel movement in order not to aggravate anal fissures, tiny cracks around the anus that split open and bleed when the child forces out stool. Children may realize that it hurts when they have a movement, so they hold in the feces—which causes it to become even bigger, harder, and more painful to pass.

Less frequent causes of constipation include lead poisoning, hypothyroidism, and, in infants, Hirschsprung's disease. In some cases, the cause is bowel obstruction, a very serious condition.

*See **page 629** for information on lead contamination.*

## Symptoms of constipation

- Stools are hard and difficult to move.
- There's a reduction in the frequency of movements. For instance, a child who usually has a bowel movement every day or every other day will go three or four days between movements.
- Blood appears in or on the outside of the stool, due to tiny fissures that form in the rectum because of straining.
- Abdominal pain is relieved after having a large movement.
- Your child soils his diapers or underpants with a brownish liquid that seeps out around hardened stool.

## Treating occasional constipation

- Adjust the diet. For infants who are eating solids, add one or two of the following high-fiber foods to his diet: mashed or strained prunes, apricots, peas, beans, or diluted prune juice. For babies over 6 months, offer mashed bran cereal. For toddlers and preschoolers,

add fresh fruits and vegetables to the diet. Cut back on binding foods, such as rice, rice cereals, bananas, and fresh apples.
• Offer your child plain water. Infants over 6 months of age can have up to 8 ounces a day. Toddlers and older children can have 16 or more ounces. Keep a pitcher of water in the refrigerator so your older child can help herself to extra liquids.
• Encourage exercise. Motion helps relieve constipation—and gravity will help the stool move more easily through the child's digestive tract.
• Set a schedule. When you begin toilet teaching, suggest that your child sit on the toilet after breakfast for 5 to 10 minutes each day. Likewise, encourage your older child to spend a few minutes at the same time each day on the toilet. Give him a book or toy to play with while he waits for something to happen. By sitting on the toilet at the same time daily, he may be able to achieve regular bowel movements.

### Treating severe or chronic constipation
• Have your child evaluated by a physician. The pediatrician may recommend a mild laxative, stool softener, enema, or glycerin suppository. These remedies should be used only on a physician's recommendation. Chronic use of laxatives or other aids may cause dependency on those products. Also have your child tested for lead poisoning and/or hypothyroidism.
• If your child is suddenly and painfully constipated, have him evaluated immediately for a possible bowel obstruction.

## Coxsackie virus (hand-foot-and-mouth disease)
Coxsackie virus is most likely to strike babies and young children in the summer and fall. Most cases of coxsackie last about a week and cause no complications.

**Causes of Coxsackie infection** Coxsackie is spread via mouth-to-mouth and hand-to-mouth contact. The virus also lives in feces, and a child may touch his anus or diaper, pick up the virus, and spread it to another child.

### Symptoms of Coxsackie virus
• Fever.

- Mouth blisters and loss of appetite. The child will have difficulty eating and swallowing as painful blisters form in the mouth and throat.
- Blisters on the fingers, soles of feet, and, sometimes, on the legs, buttocks, arms, and face.

**Treating Coxsackie virus** You can ease your child's discomfort by:
- Offering soft, cool foods, such as gelatin, ice cream, and cooled mashed potatoes.
- Avoiding spicy foods. They can irritate the sores.
- Offering fever-reducing medications.

# Croup (viral croup)

Croup is an inflammation of the upper-respiratory tract and is most common in kids under age 3. It generally occurs in the winter. With treatment, symptoms usually clear after three to six days. Severe croup, however, requires medical attention.

**Causes of croup** Croup is caused by a variety of viruses.

**Symptoms of croup**
- A deep, raspy, "barking" cough
- Hoarseness
- Difficulty breathing
- Fever

**Treating mild croup**
- Use a cool-mist humidifier, or take your child into a steamy bathroom to ease breathing.
- Give a fever-reducing medication, such as acetaminophen.
- Offer fluids to prevent dehydration.

# Dehydration

Dehydration is a loss of body fluids.

**Causes of dehydration** Dehydration is usually the result of diarrhea and/or vomiting; occasionally, it is caused by extreme heat exposure.

---

### When to Call the Doctor

Call the doctor if:
- Your child has long coughing spasms
- He has difficulty breathing
- He develops a bluish tinge around his lips
- He gets no relief from a humidifier or bathroom steam
- He thrashes around or seems unusually distressed

## Symptoms of dehydration

- Listlessness. The child doesn't want to play, even with a new toy. He doesn't make good eye contact, and may have a "dazed" look.
- Decreased urination. Fewer than four wet diapers or four trips to the potty for urinating a day show that a child's kidneys are not processing enough urine.
- Dry mouth and cracked lips
- Few or no tears when crying
- Increased heart rate
- Poor coloration. His nails aren't as pink as usual and his skin looks pale.
- Sunken eyes

In addition to vomiting and/or diarrhea, the following may accompany dehydration:
- Fever that persists for more than 24 hours
- Blood or mucus in the stool
- Any kind of rash
- A bloated or extremely tender abdomen

### Playing "Teatime" to Encourage Drinking

When my daughter had moderate diarrhea, her doctor recommended oral rehydration therapy liquids, but she refused to drink them from her regular cup. Finally, I got out her dolls' "tea set" and we had a tea party. She drank her rehydration liquid out of the tea cups, while I drank my iced tea.

### Treating mild dehydration: oral rehydration therapy (ORT)

Call your pediatrician if your child shows any symptoms of dehydration. The doctor may suggest oral rehydration therapy (ORT). Most children who do not have any other symptoms and who have mild dehydration may be rehydrated at home. Infants under 6 months of age and children who are experiencing additional symptoms may be hospitalized.

Although some doctors tell parents to give juice, chicken broth, or water to rehydrate children who have mild to moderate symptoms, these liquids do not contain the electrolytes the body needs. The American Academy of Pediatrics recommends that dehydration be treated with oral rehydration therapy (ORT), over-the-counter electrolyte fluids sold under brand names such as Pedialyte, Infalyte, Naturalyte, and Rehydrate. These are available in liquid form; some brands are available in ice pop form as well.

Even when a child is vomiting, he usually can keep some rehydrating solution down. If it's difficult for your child to eat a popsicle or to drink from a cup or a bottle, use a medicine dropper or spoon to give him rehydration liquids. Follow the dosage recommendations based on your child's weight and age on the product label and your doctor's instructions. Be persistent. It's essential that your child be rehydrated promptly.

### Treating moderate to severe dehydration

For moderate to severe dehydration, your child should be treated in a health-care facility, where he can receive intravenous fluids, if necessary.

## Dermatitis/eczema

Doctors use the term *eczema* to describe various skin conditions. The two types of eczema that affect children are atopic dermatitis and contact dermatitis.

In 50 percent of cases, atopic dermatitis clears up by the time the child is 2 or 3, though it can persist into adulthood. Contact dermatitis can affect people of any age.

**Causes of dermatitis**    Atopic dermatitis is usually hereditary and occurs in children with a family history of allergies or eczema. Contact dermatitis is caused by substances that irritate the skin. Almost anything can trigger contact dermatitis in kids who have sensitive skin, including bubble baths; scented or harsh soaps; certain foods, such as citrus fruits and juices; and rough fabrics, such as wool. Some children develop dermatitis only when they come into contact with a particular substance to which they are allergic, such as dyes used in clothing, especially dark blue dyes; nickel, a metal in most costume jewelry; plants, including poison ivy and poison oak; and glues that attach soles or toe coverings to shoes, which can produce a rash on the child's feet.

**Symptoms of atopic dermatitis**    In infants and children under the age of 4, atopic dermatitis may look like diaper rash and appear in the diaper area. In children 4 and over, the symptoms are:
- Circular, raised, itchy, scaly bumps on the face, arms, trunk, or legs. The bumps may be more prominent behind a child's knees and on the insides of his elbows.
- Very dry skin

**Treatment**    Have a physician evaluate the condition. While there is no cure for atopic dermatitis, the following may recommend:

**PARENTS ALERT**

### Discard Opened Rehydration Liquids

Because bacteria grow rapidly in rehydration liquids, use opened bottles or mixed (powdered) preparations within 24 hours and discard leftovers immediately.

- Have your child take short baths in lukewarm water. He should avoid baths that last more than 10 minutes, as well as baths in hot water, both of which can dry out his skin.
- Use moisturizer. Ask your doctor to recommend a non-scented, gentle moisturizer. Apply it after your child bathes, when his skin is still damp.
- Avoid clothing made of wool or other itchy fabrics, which can irritate his skin.
- If your child's skin is very itchy, apply lukewarm compresses to the affected area. Your doctor may recommend that you follow this with a medicated cream or lotion, usually a cortisone preparation.
- Consider an antihistamine. Ask your child's doctor if she recommends an oral antihistamine to help relieve itching.

**Symptom of contact dermatitis** An itchy rash that may blister, typically appearing a few hours after contact with an irritating substance.

**Treating contact dermatitis** If your child has symptoms of contact dermatitis, her doctor will want to find out which substance is the culprit. She may do allergy tests in which she places a small sample of the potential irritant on your child's skin. If redness and itching occur, she will advise you to avoid that particular allergen. If your child has a severe itchy rash, she may recommend a topical cortisone cream or lotion to provide relief.

**PARENTS ALERT**

### Be Careful of Costume Jewelry

Nickel, a metal in most costume jewelry, can trigger skin rashes, redness, and irritation in sensitive kids. For them, choose plastic jewelry; use real gold or stainless steel for pierced ears.

### When symptoms prevent sleep

*"My 4-year-old has had eczema for most of his life. As a result, he has trouble falling asleep and sleeping through the night—even when his skin isn't acting up. Any suggestions?"*

Itchy skin can definitely make sleeping difficult. To help your son fall asleep, try keeping his skin moist. Before bed, have him soak in lukewarm water for ten minutes or less. Pat him dry and smooth an ointment, such as petroleum jelly, onto affected areas. If your child's eczema is severe, his doctor may recommend a prescription steroid cream and a long-lasting oral antihistamine to curb itching through the night.

Researchers at the University of Pittsburgh School of Medicine

*For more on sleep routines, see **page 384**.*

have found that youngsters with chronic skin problems may have difficulty falling and staying asleep even when their eczema is under control simply because they're used to staying awake at bedtime as well as waking up frequently during the night. To end this "programmed" wakefulness, establish a regular bedtime schedule, with time for soothing diversions, such as reading a story. Such routines help kids fall asleep. If your son wakes up, comfort him briefly, then leave his room. Eventually, he will learn to put himself back to sleep.

# Diarrhea

Diarrhea, which is marked by a soupy or watery stool, is a symptom of an underlying problem. When a child passes large amounts of food, especially from diarrhea—but sometimes from vomiting—he loses essential substances like potassium, chloride, and sodium (electrolytes). If the body's electrolytes aren't in the proper balance, many organs, including the heart, cannot function properly. Although short-term diarrhea poses little risk for a child, moderate to severe diarrhea can lead to extreme dehydration and shock.

*For treating dehydration, see **page 580**.*

**Causes of diarrhea** Systemic viral or bacterial infections are a primary cause, and diarrhea is sometimes a tip-off that the child has an ear infection, urinary tract infection, or even pneumonia). Certain drugs, including antibiotics and anti-seizure medications, can cause loose stools. "Juice-bingeing" is another major cause; the sugar in fruit juice draws water into the bowel, creating loose stools. Lactose intolerance—a sensitivity to the lactose (sugar) in milk or milk-based formula—can trigger bouts of diarrhea in some kids. Milk allergy is a less frequent cause.

**Symptoms of diarrhea** Diarrhea is characterized by loose, watery stools.

**Treating mild diarrhea** For a child who has a loose bowel movement every hour or so, but who has no signs of dehydration:
• Don't give your child antidiarrheal medications. While they curb diarrhea, they can also prevent the bacteria or virus that may be causing loose stools from being washed out of the system.
• Avoid giving your child high-fat foods, sugar, juice, cola, or sports drinks, which may aggravate the condition.

- Rehydrate. Offer small amounts of liquid every half hour during waking hours. Or, on your doctor's recommendation, offer a course of oral rehydration therapy.
- Once she feels well enough to eat, offer your child easily digested foods like rice, potatoes, breads, and unsweetened cereal.
- As she improves, gradually offer foods such as chicken, lean beef, yogurt, produce, and milk.
- If diarrhea persists for more than 24 hours, alert her doctor.

### Milk and diarrhea

*"Should I avoid giving my child milk when she has diarrhea?"*

*For more on lactose intolerance and milk allergy, see page 517.*

It was once thought that cow's milk could worsen diarrhea, but recent evidence indicates that, except in severe cases, it's fine for children to continue to drink milk during bouts of diarrhea. In studies, researchers have found no significant difference in the recovery time of children who were allowed to drink milk, those who were given milk diluted with water, and those who were given no milk. A small number of kids with severe diarrhea did develop temporary lactose intolerance—which means they could not digest the sugar in dairy products—and they, therefore, got worse from drinking milk. Additionally, there's no evidence that breast milk aggravates diarrhea, so sick children who are nursing should continue to do so.

**Treating moderate to severe diarrhea** Call your doctor. She will probably recommend that you restore the fluids your child has lost with an electrolyte solution to prevent dehydration.

# Diphtheria

*For information on vaccinations, see page 543.*

Diphtheria is a potentially fatal bacterial illness. Until the advent of mass immunizations in the 1930s, diphtheria was one of the leading causes of childhood death worldwide. Today it is extremely rare in developed countries. Diphtheria is, however, still a risk for nonimmunized people traveling to developing countries and for unimmunized children who come into contact with travelers or immigrants from countries in which immunizations are not readily available. (Adults with the disease may be asymptomatic.) Serious complications occur when the bacteria release a toxin into the bloodstream. Penicillin kills the diphtheria organism, but is ineffective against toxin in the blood. If the disease is suspected, an antitoxin, derived from the blood of immunized horses, must be given as soon as possible, in addition to penicillin. Your child's best protection against diphtheria is the DTaP vaccination.

**Causes of diphtheria** Diphtheria bacteria are spread by cough and physical contact with an infected person.

**Symptoms of diphtheria** Note that the symptoms of diphthereia and strep throat are the same. Either condition must be tested for and treated by a physician.
- Sore throat
- Fever

**Treating diphtheria** The doctor usually prescribes an antitoxin; antibiotics may also be prescribed to prevent and/or treat secondary infections.

## Dislocations

Dislocations are the separation of the bones at the joints. Dislocated elbows, shoulders, and hips are more common in infants and young children than in older children and adults because the ligaments that support these joints are less developed.

*For first aid for dislocations, see **page 671**.*

**Causes of dislocation** Dislocations are caused when a young child's arm or leg is pulled in a jerky motion or is twisted.

**Treating dislocations** Dislocations need to be examined and treated by a physician.

## Ear infections (otitis media)

Otitis media—an inflammation of the middle ear more commonly known as an "ear infection"—is the second most common childhood ailment, following upper respiratory infections. By age 6, almost all children have had at least one episode of otitis media. Ear infections account for 24.5 million doctor visits each year. Kids under 3 are most susceptible, possibly because their eustachian tubes, which allow fluids and bacteria to drain from the ear into the nose, are narrower than those of older kids. This may lead to a buildup of fluid in the middle ear, which can provide a breeding ground for bacteria and infection.

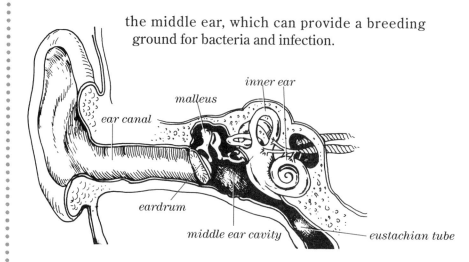

**Causes of ear infections** Otitis media is caused by bacteria or viral infection and frequently follows a cold or the flu. When these upper respiratory illnesses strike, the lining of the eustachian tube and/or middle ear can become inflamed, trapping the fluid that's naturally there. A child may go on to develop one of the four types of otitis media or may develop labyrinthitis, an inflammation of the inner ear:

*Acute otitis media* develops when bacteria or a virus invades the middle ear and multiplies. The inflammation worsens, and as fluid builds up, pressure develops behind the eardrum, causing pain. Left untreated, acute otitis media can lead to permanent hearing loss.

*Recurrent otitis media* refers to repeated bouts of the acute form. Typically, the child will suffer a relapse once or twice every month.

*Otitis media with effusion* (OME) also involves an accumulation of fluid in the middle ear, and although infectious bacteria may be present, the child suffers no symptoms of infection. In fact, many kids don't have any pain or discomfort. Also, OME can occur on its own, rather than on the heels of acute or recurrent otitis media.

*Chronic otitis media* is OME that doesn't clear up after three months or more. Untreated, the fluid buildup thickens and may change the shape of the eardrum, possibly causing temporary hearing loss. If your child has this condition, he may need reconstructive surgery to correct the problem.

*Labyrinthitis* is an inflammation of the fluid-filled chambers of the inner ear, which may cause an earache. It needs to be diagnosed by a physician, who will recommend appropriate treatment.

**Symptoms of otitis media**  OME generally has no symptoms; chronic OME can result in temporary hearing loss. Acute otitis media symptoms include:
- Pain and irritability. Your child may cry and tug or rub at his ear or the side of his face.
- Unwillingness to lie down because a prone position worsens the pain.
- Fever ranging from 100 to 104°F.
- Balance problems. The child stumbles and falls.
- Short-term difficulty hearing or long-term hearing loss, which is evident from speech delays.

**Treating ear infections and easing ear-infection pain**
- See the doctor. If you suspect that your child has an ear infection, take her to her doctor for proper diagnosis.
- Use antibiotics if they are prescribed by your doctor (see below).
- Don't put OTC ear drops or water in your child's ear. These can cause more harm than good. Warm oil may be useful for treating pain, however.
- Have your child sit up as much as possible. Sitting up relieves pressure against the eardrum.
- Keep the ear warm. On windy days, have your child wear a hat with ear flaps. Do not apply warmth to the ear unless your doctor has assured you that there is no abcess in the ear. If there's an abcess, the warmth could cause the abcess to burst.
- Encourage your child to swallow. This will help open his eustachian tube, relieving pressure.
- Offer pain relievers. Give children's-strength acetaminophen to relieve pain.

**What to know about antibiotics for treating ear infections**
Because OME infection may clear up on its own, antibiotics may not be necessary as long as the condition isn't chronic. If a regular exam reveals OME, your child's doctor may recommend a wait-and-see approach. Antibiotics will be necessary only if your child's hearing appears to be affected and he's experiencing speech delays, if he has a fever, if he's in pain and the pain is not eased by ear drops prescribed for the pain, or if the condition does not clear on its own. Since nearly 90 percent of OME cases do clear up on their own within 90 days, this approach often makes sense.

---

**"IT WORKED FOR ME"**

### *Easing Pain*

When my 2-year-old had an ear infection I used a potato to ease his pain! I microwaved the potato on high for 5 minutes, then put it in a thick sock and gently held it against his ear.

**Ear tubes, adenoid surgery, and steroid treatments** If your child suffers from recurrent or chronic OME, her doctor may recommend a surgical procedure called myringotomy, which involves drilling a tiny hole in the eardrum, removing fluid, and inserting a small, pressure-equalizing tympanostomy tube, which is smaller than the tip of a cotton swab. The tube keeps the eardrum open, allowing for more normal pressure in the middle ear and preventing the buildup of fluid. Once the fluid has drained out, the infection usually clears up. The tube usually falls out on its own within 3 to 18 months. But some kids need a new tube inserted because drainage isn't complete. Myringotomy is performed under general anesthesia at a hospital. Because any surgery is risky, the myringotomy should be performed only for children who have had the infection for 4 to 6 months and have suffered significant hearing loss.

Research is currently being done to determine if laser surgery can replace ear tube surgery. The laser surgery involves burning a small hole, which quickly heals, into each eardrum to relieve pain and allow drainage. Major advantages of this procedure are that it provides immediate relief and that it does not require anesthesia.

Another study has found that a treatment combining antibiotics with prednisone (a steroid drug) may reduce the need for ear tubes. Researchers found that in most kids between 6 months and 1 year who received the combination treatment, middle-ear fluid cleared up within a month. Those who took the steroid for 7 days along with an antibiotic for 30 days showed the best results. However, this type of therapy should be given only to children whose infection hasn't cleared up within six weeks after an initial course of antibiotics.

In some kids with chronic fluid buildup, the adenoids may be obstructing drainage through the eustachian tube. Removal of the adenoids, a mass of soft tissue behind the nasal passages, is sometimes recommended for kids 4 and older who have had OME for three or more months, because bacteria in infected adenoids can travel to the middle ear. The American Academy of Pediatrics advises that adenoids be removed only if they are repeatedly inflamed.

### Preventing ear infections
• Don't allow your child to drink in a lying-down position. Generally, that means no bottles or sippy cups. Drinking in a prone position allows fluids to back up into the ear canal.

- Breast-feed your child for up to a year, if possible. Researchers have found that antibodies in breast milk help prevent ear infections.
- Keep your child away from cigarette smoke. Studies show that smoke can trigger OME in children.

### Swimmer's ear (external otitis)
This is a bacterial or fungal infection of the ear canal or outer ear.

**Causes of swimmer's ear**  As its name implies, swimmer's ear occurs when a child gets water in his ear—while swimming, bathing, or washing his hair, or even from profuse sweating. If sweating causes the problem, suggest that he wear a baseball cap with an absorbent brim or a sweat band. Make sure that the sweat band does not fit too tightly, which could cause a headache, and that it has snap or Velcro closures, which make it less likely to cause a choking hazard than a full-circle style.

**Symptoms of swimmers' ear**
- Pain
- Itch
- A plugged-up feeling in the ear, which the child will indicate by poking a finger into the ear or rubbing it
- Low-grade fever
- Redness and swelling around the ear

**Treating swimmer's ear**  Though swimmer's ear usually isn't serious, call the doctor if your child shows symptoms. The doctor may recommend acetaminophen for pain or medicated ear drops, containing an antibiotic and an anti-inflammatory agent.

# Encephalitis
Encephalitis is an acute inflammation of the brain. In some cases, the illness causes only mild symptoms, such as a headache and nausea, and passes quickly. In others, serious neurological symptoms and impairment can occur. Severe encephalitis may lead to coma and death.

**Causes of encephalitis**  Encephalitis is triggered by a variety of viruses. There are two types of encephalitis: primary and secondary. Primary encephalitis is often caused by mosquito bites. Carrier mosquitoes feed on animals or birds that are infected with the disease, then transmit the virus to other animals and birds and, rarely, to humans. (Carrier mosquitoes usually are not the type that bite people, but, occasionally, human-biting mosquitoes become infected with an encephalitis virus.)

*Primary encephalitis* outbreaks occur during warm weather—when mosquitoes are active—particularly at dawn and dusk. To protect your child, make sure she wears a long-sleeved shirt and long pants when she is in a mosquito-infested area. Spray her clothing with bug repellent containing no more than 10 percent DEET. Encourage her to play indoors during dusk and evening. When taking your baby outside, cover his carriage with mosquito netting. To keep mosquitoes away from your home, don't allow stagnant water, a breeding ground for the insects, to collect in gutters, driveways, birdbaths, or wading pools. Install snug-fitting screens on your windows.

*Secondary encephalitis* is a complication of another disease, such as measles, German measles (rubella), chicken pox, or mumps. The herpes virus can also lead to encephalitis, and an infant who picks up the herpes virus on his trip through the birth canal may develop the illness.

### Symptoms of encephalitis
- Fever, sometimes of 103°F or higher
- Headache
- Nausea
- Vomiting
- Stiff neck
- Drowsiness
- In infants, bulging of the fontanel

**Diagnosing encephalitis** Laboratory studies of cerebral spinal fluid are made to obtain an accurate diagnosis.

**Treating encephalitis** Call 911 or your local emergency number or take your child to the ER immediately.

## Epiglottitis

An extremely serious inflammation of the epiglottis—the upper part of the larynx or voice box—epiglottitis can be fatal if not treated as soon as symptoms appear. Children between the ages of 2 and 4 are at greatest risk for epiglottitis, which is most likely transmitted through infected droplets coughed into the air. The *hemophilus influenzae* (Hib) vaccine prevents most cases of epiglottitis, though some immunized children will develop the condition.

**Causes of epiglottitis** Bacteria trigger the condition, and most often the culprit is Hib; rarely, group A streptococcus leads to the illness.

**Symptoms of epiglottitis** Symptoms may come on suddenly, and include:
- Severe difficulty breathing. Your child may make a high-pitched squeak when she inhales and may insist on sitting up with her nose in the air as though she were sniffing. Her tongue may protrude and her nails and lips may turn blue, signaling that she's not getting enough oxygen.
- Drooling
- Fever of 102°F or higher

**Treating epiglottitis**
- Call 911 or your local emergency number or take your child to the ER immediately.
- Don't try to force your child to lie down. Encourage and enable her to stay in a position that allows her to breathe. Make sure she remains calm and in the most comfortable breathing position.

Children with epiglottitis are hospitalized. Tubes are inserted into their airways to promote easy breathing, and they are given antibiotics to fight the infection.

# Eye concerns

Eye concerns run from the relatively inocuous, such as nearsightedness, to potentially sight-threatening conditions, such as cataracts. If you suspect that your child suffers from an eye condition, have her examined by her pediatrician or an opthalmologist.

**Symptoms of visual problems** Symptoms of vision problems in toddlers and preschoolers include:

*For information about raising a child with a visual impairment, see **page 757**.*

*For first aid for eye injuries, see **page 684**.*

- Looking closely or at an angle. The child puts her face right up to a book page or frequently turns her head to see. She sits very close to the TV.
- Lack of interest in picture books or colorful toys.
- Tendency to be startled. If a child doesn't have good peripheral vision, she will not have seen someone or something heading her way.
- Lack of interest in finger painting, coloring, or drawing.
- Frequent rubbing, blinking, or squinting of the eyes.
- Frequent headaches.
- Poor eye-hand coordination.
- Apparent clumsiness. The child is much more prone to bumping into things or people than other children her age.

## Amblyopia

This partial or total loss of vision in one eye can occur from birth until age 7 or 8; most cases develop by age 5. Amblyopia is usually detected only through vision screening by a pediatrician, an ophthalmologist, or an optometrist. If amblyopia isn't diagnosed and treated before age 9, the condition may not be correctable and the child will have permanent partial or total vision loss in that eye.

**Cause of amblyopia** Experts believe that there is a failure in the linkup of nerve connections between the retina and the brain. Because of this, the eye doesn't send the correct signals to the brain.

**Symptoms of amblyopia**
- One eye may appear glazed
- Favoring one eye when reading
- Regularly bumping into objects on one side of the body

**Treating amblyopia** Your child's eye-care practitioner will probably recommend that he wear a patch on his normal eye, forcing him to use and thus strengthen his "lazy" or weak eye. The length of treatment varies, depending on the seriousness of condition.

## Astigmatism

Astigmatism causes blurred or wavy vision and is a common cause of nearsightedness in children.

**Symptoms and treatments of astigmatism** Same as nearsightedness.

## Blepharitis

A common inflammation of the eyelids, this condition is rarely contagious, but it often is chronic.

**Causes of blepharitis** Most often, the staphylococcus bacterium causes this condition, though some cases are triggered by seborrhea, a chronic oily, scaly condition that can affect the eyelids as well as the scalp and face.

**Symptoms of blepharitis**
• Redness around the eye
• Eye irritation
• Discharge from the eye
• Scaly skin around the eye. There may appear to be "dandruff" along the lid margins.

**Treating blepharitis**
• Washing. Twice a day, put a drop of baby shampoo onto a clean, damp washcloth and smooth across the lids, then rinse with lukewarm water.
• Antibiotics. Stubborn cases call for prescription antibiotic drops or ointments.

## Blocked tear duct

This condition occurs in newborns when one or both tearducts don't open properly and is marked by excessive tearing or mucus in one or both eyes. In rare instances, a duct may be blocked by a tiny cyst.

**Treating a blocked tear tuct** Usually, the condition clears up on its own within 6 to 12 months with the following home treatment: Using a clean damp cloth, gently cleanse the mucus from lid by wiping it from inner to outer corner. Don't touch your baby's eye directly.

If the blockage doesn't disappear by 12 months, an ophthalmologist may massage the duct or pass a probe down the duct to clear it, or may surgically correct the condition.

## *Color blindness*

Color blindness is an inability to differentiate between certain colors. Some kids can't tell the difference between red and green; others have trouble distinguishing blue from yellow. Some have both a red-green and a blue-yellow deficiency. Boys are more prone to color blindness than are girls. As many as 1 in 8 boys and 1 in 230 girls may be color blind.

**Causes of color blindness** Color blindness is an inherited condition.

**Symptoms of color blindness** When the child starts learning colors, at around age 2, he has difficulty telling them apart. His doctor can test his color "sense" with special charts.

**Dealing with color blindness** There's no cure for color blindness, but as children grow, parents can help kids adapt by:
• Marking clothes with symbols or words, so kids can select color-coordinated outfits.
• Labeling crayons, markers, and pencils with the color name once children can read.
• Teaching kids where the red, yellow, and green traffic lights are located and showing them how to tell when each one is lit. (Your eye-care professional can provide you with helpful tips.)

## *Conjunctivitis ("pink eye")*

This is an inflammation of the conjunctiva—the thin, transparent layer of mucus membrane that lines the eyelid and a portion of the eyeball. Viral conjunctivitis often accompanies a sore throat or cold.

**Causes of conjunctivitis** Viruses, bacteria, or allergies.

**Symptoms of conjunctivitis**
• Yellowish or clear discharge or watering of one or both eyes
• Sensitivity to light
• Itchiness
• Redness of the conjunctiva and "whites of the eye"

**Treating conjunctivitis** If your child develops symptoms of conjunctivitis, she should see her doctor or an opthalmologist. Only a physician can determine which type of conjuncitivits the child has, whether it's contagious, and what the proper treatment is. Viral and bacterial conjunctivitis can be spread from child to child via the hands, so children who have these conditions must wash their hands frequently to avoid infecting others and reinfecting themselves.

- A cool compress eases itching for all forms of conjunctivitis.
- For viral conjunctivitis: Viral conjunctivitis will clear up on its own in about a week.
- For bacterial conjunctivitis: Ointment or antibiotic drops clear up bacterial conjunctivitis in three to four days.
- For allergic conjunctivitis: Prescription anti-inflammatory medication helps allergic conjunctivitis.

## Farsightedness (hyperopia)

Hyperopia, better-known as farsightedness, makes it difficult for a child to see clearly at close distances.

**Causes of farsightedness** Babies and young children have a tendency to be slightly farsighted, but as they grow older their vision becomes normal. Kids who remain hyperopic may have inherited the condition from their parents. Farsighted children have a somewhat flattened eyeball. As a result, images are not clearly focused on the retina.

**Symptoms of Farsightedness**
- Holding books or pictures far away from the face
- Difficulty doing close work, such as coloring or writing, and a lack of interest in puzzles or toys that require close-up vision
- Rubbing the eyes
- Headache

**Treating farsightedness**
- Visit an ophthalmologist for a diagnosis.
- Corrective glasses may be prescribed.

## Nearsightedness (myopia)

Kids who are myopic, or nearsighted, see things fine up close, but they have trouble seeing objects or figures in the distance. A handful of kids develop myopia as early as age 3, but most cases of nearsightedness don't show up until the age of 9 or 10.

**Causes of nearsightedness**  Most nearsighted kids inherit their myopia from one or both parents. People are nearsighted because their eyeballs are too long from front to back. This causes light to focus in front of the retina instead of on it.

**Symptoms of nearsightedness**  If your child exhibits these signs of eye trouble, have her examined by a pediatric opthamologist:
- Sitting too close to the TV
- Holding books and other objects very close to the face
- Squinting to see better
- Inability to see faraway objects that others can see

**Treating nearsightedness**  There's no way to prevent myopia, but it can be corrected with glasses and, when the child is in her early teens, with contact lenses. If your child is nearsighted, she should have her eyes checked every six months or so; her sight may change so quickly that she'll need frequent changes in her prescription.

## Ptosis

Ptosis is a condition marked by a droopy eyelid or lids.

**Causes of ptosis**  Some kids are born with the condition, while others develop it during early childhood. Ptosis is usually inherited, but is occasionally caused by other conditions, such as glaucoma or cataracts.

**Symptoms of ptosis**
- One or both lids are enlarged and droop.
- Sometimes the lid covers the entire eye, curbing vision or causing amblyopia. If the drooping lid puts pressure on the cornea, astigmatism can occur.

**Treating ptosis**  Your child will need to be monitored by an ophthalmologist to make sure she doesn't also develop amblyopia or astigmatism. Surgery to strengthen weak eyelid muscles is sometimes performed, usually at age 3 or older. When another eye problem, such as glaucoma or cataracts, is the cause, the underlying condition is treated.

## Strabismus ("wandering eye" or crossed-eyes)

Strabismus is a misalignment of the eyes. It may be present at birth, but it can occur later, usually developing before the age of 5. Strabismus can affect depth perception and eye-hand coordination. If strabismus isn't detected and treated before the age of 10, the child may favor one eye in order to prevent "double vision." If this happens, the abnormal eye won't develop properly and the child's vision can't be corrected to a normal or near-normal level. Strabismus may cause amblyopia.

**Causes of strabismus** This condition is caused by a muscular imbalance or miscommunication between the brain and eyes.

**Symptom of strabismus** One eye turns in or out or floats up or down, making it difficult for the child to focus both eyes.

**Treating strabismus** Corrective lenses help some children. More serious cases call for surgery by an ophthalmologist to "straighten" the abnormal eye. If the child has strabismus and amblyopia, the normal eye is also patched to improve vision in the weak eye.

## Stye

A stye is an infection in a hair follicle of the eyelashes.

**Causes of a stye** A stye is caused by ordinary germs that a child rubs with her hands onto the eyelid. Most styes come to a head and break open, sometimes releasing pus. Left untreated, one stye may lead to others. If your child frequently develops styes, she should be examined by her doctor to rule out an underlying condition that is lowering her immunity to infection. To keep your child from spreading germs to you or to other kids, encourage her to wash her hands after touching her eyes. Also, if you develop a stye, keep your hands clean so you don't transmit germs to your child.

### Symptoms of a stye
- A pimple-like sore on the eyelid
- Pain when the child closes her eyes or rubs them

**Treating a stye** Soaking the eye with a warm, clean cloth may promote quicker healing. Also, your child's doctor may prescribe an antibiotic ointment to heal the stye and prevent its spread.

## Fainting

Fainting can be a symptom of heat exhaustion, a heart condition, stress, or other conditions. Always have your child evaluated by her physician if she faints.

## Febrile seizures

*For information about seizure disorders, see **page 717**.*

When abnormal electrical impulses occur in the brain, a seizure can result. About three to four percent of all children experience a "febrile" seizure at some point.

**Causes of febrile seizures** Febrile seizures are triggered by rapid rise in temperature and occur most commonly in kids between 9 months and 5 years of age. There seems to be a genetic component to this type of seizure. If either you or your partner or your child's siblings had febrile seizures, your child may be more prone to them. These seizures do not harm the child in any way. Typically, a febrile seizure lasts anywhere from a few seconds to four or five minutes.

**Symptoms of febrile seizures** During a seizure, the child may arch her back and roll her eyes. Some kids twitch and shake.

**Treating febrile seizures** No treatment is needed. Once the seizure ends, the child's behavior quickly returns to normal, though she may seem groggy or disoriented for a few minutes.

## Fever

*For information about fever in newborns, see **page 67**.*

Fever is a symptom of a wide range of illnesses. While a high fever—over 101.4°F in a child under age 1 or over 104°F in a child over age 1—should always be discussed with your child's doctor, high fever, in itself, is not necessarily a sign of severe illness. Likewise, a low-grade fever does not always indicate the absence of serious illness. Kids may run a fever of 104°F during the course of a minor ailment, or they may have a temperature of only 101°F and have a serious illness, such as meningitis. Parents often fear that a high fever will cause brain damage, but for that to occur, a child's fever would have to reach 107°F or greater, and fevers caused by infection or illness virtually never get that high. Only heatstroke would cause a child's temperature to soar to 107°F.

Fever is usually a positive sign that your child's body is fighting off a viral or bacterial infections, typically a cold, croup, or a sore throat. Occasionally, a fever signals the presence of non-infectious conditions, such as a reaction to an immunization, particularly the DTP shot. More rarely, a fever is triggered by a serious condition such as an auto-immune disorder; an inflammatory disease; an endocrine disorder, such as hyperthyroidism; or childhood cancers, including leukemia.

### When to Call the Doctor

Call the doctor if your child under the age of 1 has a temperature over 101.4°F. For a child over the age of 1, call if his temperature reaches 104°F or higher. Also call if, in addition to fever, he has any of these symptoms:

- Cries inconsolably or whimpers or cries whenever you move or touch him.

- Has slept longer than usual and you have difficulty waking him

- Isn't able to swallow and drools saliva

- Vomits

- Has trouble breathing

- Has a stiff neck. (While a preschooler can tell you about this, a baby or toddler with a stiff neck will usually lie very still to avoid painful movement.)

- Is unusually listless or has a vacant stare

- Has a seizure

- Has a fever for more than 48 hours but no signs of infection, such as a runny nose, rash, or upset stomach

### Treating a mild fever that is symptomatic of another illness

- Offer fever-reducing medications, such as acetaminophen or ibuprofen. Do not offer aspirin.
- Offer plenty of fluids to avoid dehydration.
- Dress your child in cool, comfortable clothing. Do not overdress or use blankets to cover a child with a fever.
- Keep the room a comfortable temperature and free of drafts.

### When to treat a fever

*"Which is better—letting a low-grade fever run its course or treating it with fever-lowering medication?"*

PARENTS
ALERT

## No Alcohol Rubs or Baths

Alcohol baths, once used to reduce fevers, are no longer recommended for children. The alcohol and water solution creates a rebound effect in which the infant's temperature drops quickly but rebounds higher almost immediately. Alcohol rubbed on the skin can be absorbed and cause poisoning. Also, breathing the fumes in an alcohol bath can have a slightly toxic effect on a child.

*For information about Reye syndrome, see **page 643**.*

Because a fever causes the heart rate to accelerate and saps energy, children who are already debilitated by cardiac problems or chronic conditions such as severe asthma usually require fever-reducing medications whenever they contract a fever-causing illness. These medications prevent a fever from putting an added strain on a child's heart or help conserve energy that the asthmatic child needs for breathing. Children with a history of febrile seizures may also benefit from fever-reducing drugs.

But an otherwise healthy child who has a simple viral infection does not necessarily require treatment with an OTC fever preparation.

Fever medicines don't "cure" an illness. They simply help lower the child's temperature so he feels more comfortable. In general, if your child is playing, eating, and sleeping well, he probably doesn't need medication. But if he's cranky, uncomfortable, and doesn't want to eat or play, a fever-reducer is probably in order.

Doctors usually recommend infant- or children's-strength acetaminophen or ibuprofen. You can alternate these medications instead of choosing one over the other. This will lower the amount of either type of medication that your child receives, while still reducing symptoms. When using any OTC medication, follow the label dosage recommendations precisely. Be aware that various formulas require different dosages. If you switch brands or formulas of the same brand, you must check the label. Do not assume that an older child requires a larger dose of a medication. Also, fever medications should not be used by children under the age of 2 without a doctor's recommendation. If your child is unusually small or large for his age, ask his doctor how much you should give him. Never giver your child aspirin, since aspirin has been linked to a severe condition called Reye syndrome.

**Treating a high fever, a fever unrelated to another illness, or a long-term fever** Call your child's doctor. The physician will want to examine her to rule out serious disorders.

**Choosing the right thermometer** There are a number of different types of thermometers, which vary in their effectiveness:

• **Rectal thermometer** If you want to know exactly what your newborn to 4-year-old's core body temperature is, use an old-fashioned glass bulb rectal thermometer. Keep several rectal thermometers in the house. Inevitably, one will be misplaced or dropped and broken. A rectal thermometer for a baby under 3 months of age is a must since the doctor needs to know the precise temperature.

In a pinch, with an older child, you can use an oral thermometer in place of the rectal version, but remember that the "bulb" on the end of an oral thermometer is narrower and may slip out of a child's rectum more easily. Once you've used an oral thermometer in your child's rectum, it should not be used orally, even after cleansing it with soap, water, and alcohol. Digital rectal thermometers are available, but since they require batteries, they may not work when you need them. If you use a digital rectal thermometer, be sure to keep fresh spare batteries readily available.

• **Oral thermometer** When your child is around 5 and can hold a thermometer under her tongue, you an switch to an oral glass thermometer or an oral digital thermometer. If you choose the digital variety, be sure that the battery is properly charged to assure an accurate reading.

• **Forehead strip thermometer** Although easy to use, these won't provide an accurate temperature reading.

• **Digital ear thermometer** Electronic ear thermometers can be used for children over the age of 1 year. Babies' ear canals are too small for the thermometer tip to fit into properly. Digital ear thermometers do not always give accurate readings, however. It's not unusual to get a reading of 101°F on the first try and a reading of 102° a few minutes later.

• **Pacifier thermometers.** Designed as a pacifier, these digital thermometers are accurate within 0.2°F. Readings take about 90 seconds to register and the device plays a lullaby to indicate that the peak temperature has been reached. Although more expensive, they are easy to use with infants and toddlers.

---

## When Fever Medications Don't Work

Fever medications take about 45 minutes to work. If your child still has a fever 45 minutes after taking a medication, try giving her a sponge bath if she seems uncomfortable. If she's acting fine, however, don't worry about lowering her temperature. Just keep an eye on her. If the fever persists or rises or if she is very uncomfortable, call the doctor.

*For information on how to take your child's temperature rectally, see* **page 67**.

- **Underarm temperature** with an oral glass or digital thermometer. An armpit reading is only accurate if the thermometer is held in place for at least five minutes.

## Fifth disease

Fifth disease is a common viral infection that usually affects kids ages 3 through 14, mostly in the early spring. Its name derives from the simple fact that it was the fifth common childhood illness defined by doctors. (The first four are measles, mumps, chicken pox, and rubella.)

**Causes of fifth disease** An infected child can spread the virus by coughing or sneezing one or two days before the rash appears. Once the rash develops, the child is no longer contagious.

**Symptoms of fifth disease**
- Bright red cheeks that look as though they've been slapped.
- A lacy-looking rash can appear on the child's arms, legs, and trunk, and may intensify if the child is exposed to sunlight or is especially active.
  - Runny nose
  - Headache
  - Sore throat
  - Fever under 101°F
  - Joint aches

**Treating fifth disease** Fifth disease tends to run its course in five to ten days, though the rash can recur for weeks or months, especially with exposure to sunlight.
- Treat symptoms to make your child more comfortable.
- Avoid exposure to sunlight.

**PARENTS ALERT**

### Dangers of Fifth Disease

The fifth disease virus can interfere with the production of red blood cells in children and adults who have immune-system deficiencies or blood diseases, such as sickle-cell anemia. The virus can also cause fetal complications during pregnancy, especially the first half, so if you're pregnant and have been exposed to fifth disease, call your obstetrician.

# Flat feet

If your child's arches appear to touch the ground instead of curving, she may have flat feet, a very normal condition of preschoolers. Some babies' feet look flat because of the "fat pads" on the bottoms, even though their arches are raised.

**Causes of flat feet** Kids can be born with a tendency toward flat feet or they can develop the condition due to weak foot and leg muscles or overly stretched and strained foot ligaments.

**Symptom of flat feet** A lack of visible arches charecterizes flat feet. By age 2 or 3, a child's arches should be becoming visible; by age 6 most children have visible arches. In about 10 percent of the population, flat feet persist into adolescence and adulthood.

**Treating flat feet** Podiatrists (non-MDs who specialize in the treatment of foot disorders) often recommend that kids get custom-made plastic orthotics which can be inserted into shoes to help the feet "develop normally," but the American Academy of Pediatrics notes that orthotics may cause more problems than the flat feet themselves and will not help your child's feet develop an arch. The best "treatment" is time. The normal exercise of walking and running will develop a child's arches naturally.

In very rare instances, a child will have extremely rigid flat feet and will have difficulty moving her foot up and down or sideways at the ankle. This type of flat feet can cause pain in the teen years and may lead to arthritis of the foot if left untreated. If your child's foot is stiff and she has foot pain, sores, or pressure spots on the inner side of a foot, tell her doctor. She may refer your child to a pediatric orthopedist for corrective surgery.

## PEDIATRICK

### Testing for Flat Feet

To find out if your child has flat feet, do this simple test when she's 2 or 3 years old. Place your child's wet bare feet on a piece of dark-colored construction paper or on concrete. A foot with a normal arch will leave spots at the heel, outside border, and toe area— but none in the arch area. If your child's arch leaves an imprint, her feet are flat.

# Food poisoning

Food poisoning is a bacterial infection of the intestinal tract. Proper hygiene, food handling, and cooking can prevent food poisoning. Depending on the amount of bacteria present in the food eaten and

*For more information on preventing food poisoning, see **page 825**.*

the age, weight, and general health of the person, food poisoning may cause only mild stomach upset. In other cases, it can be life threatening.

**Causes of food poisoning** Food poisoning occurs after a person eats food contaminated with bacteria. The source is often undercooked meat, poultry, fish, or eggs, or foods or hands that have been in contact with these undercooked foods. Food that has been sitting out too long and food that has been contaminated by improper handling are also sources. A number of organisms can cause food poisoning:

- *Botulism* is caused by the bacterium *Clostridium botulinum*. The bacterium grows in improperly canned food. *Clostridium botulinum* is also contained in some honey; while it doesn't adversely affect adults and older children, it can cause severe poisoning in children under age 1.
- *Clostridium perfringens* is a bacteria found in soil, sewage, and some human and animal intestines. It can be transferred to food by the hands of an infected person. It thrives in unrefrigerated food that has been left out for a long time, as well as in food warmed by a hot plate or a steam table that has been sitting out for hours.
- *E. coli* bacteria may contaminate raw or undercooked beef, though the organism has also been traced to salami and the skins of fruits and vegetables. High cooking temperatures (achieved through pastuerization) kill *E. coli*. Thoroughly scrubbing produce before cutting it can curb the risk of poisoning.
- *Hepatitis A* virus is often transmitted by food that has been contaminated with human excrement. (For example, someone who is infected with the disease fails to wash his hands after going to the bathroom—then touches food that others may eat.) Also, shellfish, which have been exposed to human waste, can harbor the virus. Other common food sources of hepatitis A are produce such as lettuce and strawberries. You can help protect your child against the disease by thoroughly scrubbing fruits and vegetables. You may want to peel fruits and veggies before serving them to your children. Also, be sure to cook shellfish thoroughly; de-vein and completely cook shrimp before serving.

*E. coli can also be transmitted by person-to-person contact; see **page 825**.*

**PARENTS ALERT**

## Shrimp Safety

Check shrimp served in restaurants to make sure the vein—the little gray/black strip that runs down the back—has been totally removed; if it hasn't, send the dish back.

- *Salmonella* bacteria contaminate raw or undercooked meat, poultry, and fish, eggs, and unpasteurized milk. High cooking temperatures kill salmonella bacteria.
- *Staphylococcus aureus* is transmitted to foods by unwashed hands of infected people. If the temperature of the food rises to 100° F, the staph bacteria multiply and produce a toxin that ordinary cooking cannot destroy.

**Symptoms of food poisoning** Symptoms of most forms of food poisoning occur within hours or a few days of ingesting bacteria and include one or more of the following:
- Nausea
- Vomiting
- Diarrhea, including bloody diarrhea
- Abdominal cramps
- Headache
- Fever
- Inflammation of the intestinal tract

**Symptoms of botulism include:**
- Double vision
- Difficulty in swallowing and breathing

Hepatitis A symptoms usually appear within 30 days of infection.

**Treating mild food poisoning** If symptoms aren't severe:
- Call your doctor if you suspect your child has food poisoning.
- Restrict food and liquid intake for two to four hours after symptoms first appear.
- Offer ORT if recommended by your doctor.

**Treating severe food poisoning** If your child shows signs of dehydration, has bloody diarrhea, passes a large volume of water with his stool, becomes confused, weak, restless, feels a tingling sensation in his arms and legs, has hallucinations, or finds it hard to breathe:
- Seek medical help immediately. Take your child to the ER. If you do not know the source of the infection, try to save a sample of his vomit for analysis to help speed diagnosis.
- Treatment may range from an at-home course of antibiotics to hospitalization for intravenous antibiotic treatments.

*Salmonella can also be transmitted by certain animals; for more on animal-borne salmonella, see **page 647**.*

*For symptoms and treatment of hepatitis A, see **page 618**.*

*For information on ORT, see **page 580**.*

# Gassiness and flatulence

*For information on colic, see* **page 61**.

A child with gas has a bloated feeling and minor abdominal pain or discomfort, usually accompanied by burping or the passing of gas. In infants, this condition is often called "colic."

**Causes of gassiness**  Food commonly triggers gas. The culprits often include onions, broccoli, cauliflower, beans, and bananas. Lactose intolerance can also cause gassiness in sensitive kids.

**Symptoms of gassiness**
- Burping
- Passing gas
- Abdominal pain, usually relieved by passing gas or by having a bowel movement

**Treating gassiness**
- Exercise. Encourage your child to take a walk with you. Motion often causes gas to dissipate more quickly.
- Changes in the diet. Cut back on gassy foods.
- Constipation relief.

*For information on constipation relief, see* **page 577**.

# German measles (rubella)

*For information on vaccination, see* **page 545**.

German measles is a highly contagious disease. Any child or adult who hasn't been immunized against the disease is susceptible, particularly in the late winter and early spring. The MMR (measles, mumps, rubella) vaccine provides immunity. Most kids with German measles are sick for one to five days. Very rarely, German measles can lead to encephalitis.

**Causes of German measles**
German measles is caused by the rubella virus. The virus is spread when an infected person coughs droplets into the air; it can also be transmitted via person-to-person contact.

**Symptoms of German measles**  Although some infected children show no symptoms, others will have the following symptoms:
- Fever of 100 to 102°F
- Swollen glands
- A rash consisting of flat reddish/pink spots that starts on the face

and sometimes spreads to the neck, chest, and the rest of the body. Occasionally, the rash spreads to the roof of the mouth.

**Treating the symptoms of German measles** If your child contracts German measles, give him extra fluids. Acetaminophen can ease the discomfort of fever. Keep him away from other children or adults, especially pregnant women, unless you are certain they've been immunized againt rubella or have previously had it.

## Giardiasis

This is a gastrointestinal infection.

**Causes of giardiasis** This infection is caused by the parasite *giardia*. Giardia grows in the stool of infected people. If proper hygiene isn't followed, this organism can be passed via the hands to children, particularly in daycare settings.

**Symptoms of giardiasis**
- Diarrhea that may come and go and often has a green, greasy appearance
- Poor appetite
- Weight loss
- Abdominal pain

**Diagnosing giardiasis** A stool sample must be tested to determine if the symptoms are caused by giardiasis.

**Treating giardiasis** A course of antibiotics is the standard treatment.

## Growing pains

Around age 4, your child may complain of leg aches, often called "growing pains."

### PARENTS ALERT

### *German Measles During Pregnancy*

When the German measles virus infects a woman during the first three months of her pregnancy, it can cause irreversible damage to the fetus. Infants born with "congenital rubella" are more prone to eye disorders such as cataracts and glaucoma, heart problems, deafness, and severe mental retardation.

Before you conceive, your doctor can test your blood to see if you have antibodies to German measles. If you aren't immune, get vaccinated immediately. Then wait three months before trying to conceive. If you are already pregnant and you have never had German measles or been vaccinated, avoid anyone who has, or is suspected of having, the illness as well as anyone who has come into contact with an infected person.

**Causes of growing pains**  Most often, these aches are caused by sore tendons in the thigh and calf. Tendon pain is usually triggered by physical activity, most often jumping, and tends to occur at night.

**Symptoms of growing pains**  The only symptom is the pain itself, which can be quite severe.

**Treating growing pains**  The best treatment is to rub your child's leg for 5 to 20 minutes or until the pain subsides. If your child can't sleep because of leg pain, acetaminophen or ibuprofen may help ease his discomfort and ensure a good night's sleep.

## When to Call the Doctor

If the leg pain occurs during the day or interferes with your child's normal activities, call the doctor.

## Headache

Headaches can affect children as young as age 3. By 7 years of age, 40 percent of kids have experienced at least one.

*For more on meningitis, see **page 634**.*

**Causes of headaches**  Most headaches are caused by a lack of sleep, hunger, or tension. Injuries to the head can also cause headaches. Recurring discomfort may signal vision trouble, sinusitis, allergies, a more severe illness, including meningitis, or, very rarely, a tumor.

**Treating headaches**  Most mild headaches go away when the underlying cause is treated, which usually means getting enough sleep, eating, relaxing, reducing allergens, and treating underlying conditions such as sinusitis. The pain usually subsides sooner with acetaminophen or ibuprofen. If the pain persists, seek medical advice. Persistent or overwhelming pain, which tends to start at the back of the head and worsens as the day goes on or that affects just one side of the head, may indicate a tension headache or migraine. In these instances, an analgesic or massage of the temples or back of the neck may bring relief.

## When to Call the Doctor

If your child has severe head pain that awakens her, occurs only in the morning, or is accompanied by a stiff neck, weakness, or numbness in any part of the body, or seizures, call her doctor. These symptoms could signal meningitis or another serious disorder.

**Relief for migraines**  Stress, odors, and some foods—such as pizza, hot dogs, peanut butter, and chocolate—can trigger a migraine, a pounding pain on one or both sides of the child's head. Migraines are usually accompanied by nausea, vomiting, or vision disturbances. To prevent migraines, have your child avoid possible triggers. If a food is suspected, for example, your child's doctor may advise you to eliminate it from your child's diet, then reintroduce it gradually in small amounts to see if the symptoms recur. To relieve pain, the doctor may recommend acetaminophen or ibuprofen or a prescription medication. Frequent migraines may require a daily preventive drug.

# Head lice

Some six million cases of head lice—or pediculosis—occur annually among U.S. children ages 3 to 12, according to the National Pediculosis Association (NPA). Head lice are tiny, beige-colored insects about the size of a sesame seed. They live on the scalp and lay eggs—called nits—that stick to the hair shaft. Head lice are more common among children with fine, straight hair, though any child can be affected.

**Causes of head lice**  Contamination is caused by contact with another person who is infested and/or contact with items such as hats, hair accessories, combs, pillows, headphones, and collared clothing of an infested person.

**Symptoms of head lice**
- **Head-scratching** This is the primary symptom of infestation.
- **Scratch marks and/or tiny red bite marks** near the hairline, particularly at the forehead, behind the ears, or at the back of her neck may indicate that your child has been scratching.
- **Visible bugs and nits** Some kids seem totally unaware that something is crawling on their heads and show no symptoms. You may notice the insects on your child's hair, though. Unlike dandruff, which can be brushed out, lice stick tenaciously to the hair.

**PARENTS RESOURCE**

## The NPA

For more information about head lice prevention, call the **NPA** at (800) 446-4-NPA or visit them online at www.headlice.org.

**"IT WORKED FOR ME"**

## Using a Fine Tooth Comb

After repeated bouts with head lice, I hesitated using strong chemical shampoos again. I found that twice daily combing with an ultra-fine-tooth comb—the one that came with a lice shampoo—along with daily search for and removal of nits did the trick.

**PARENTS ALERT**

### Lice Shampoos May be Harmful to Asthmatics

The chemicals in lice shampoos may cause breathing difficulty or trigger an asthma episode in children or adults who have asthma. Consult with your child's doctor before using.

**Treating head lice** Ordinary shampooing and brushing won't dislodge lice and nits. Your child's doctor can recommend a lice-killing shampoo and/or cream rinse. These are not usually recommended for children under age 2, who are usually treated with lice removal and nit-picking only, a laborious process. If using an insecticide shampoo and/or rinse on your toddler or older child, follow package instructions carefully and avoid getting the product on any other parts of the body. Wash your child's hair over a sink, rather than in the tub. After shampooing and rinsing, you'll need to remove any remaining lice and nits with a fine-toothed nit comb. The treatment usually needs to be repeated after 10 days. If infestation is not eliminated with this round of treatment, talk with your doctor before repeating the process.

**Preventing reinfection** After your child has been treated, wash all combs and brushes he may have used in disinfectant, bleach, or lice-killing shampoo, or replace them with new ones. Wash bed linens, towels, pillows, hats, clothing, and stuffed animals with which your child has come into contact in hot (130°F) water. Stuffed animals and other items that cannot be washed can be tumbled in a dryer set at "high" for about 20 minutes. Or, you can put them in a tightly closed plastic bag for 14 to 16 days; doing so will kill the lice and eggs. Thoroughly vacuum sofas and chairs, mattresses, and car seats, especially head rests.

If one family member has lice, you need to check everyone else for symptoms. You needn't worry about "de-licing" family pets, like cats, dogs, hamsters, and guinea pigs. For unknown reasons, head lice aren't attracted to these animals.

## Hearing concerns

Hearing loss can be difficult to detect in young children. Early detection and treatment can prevent long-term language impairment.

*For newborn hearing concerns, see **page 68**.*

**Causes of hearing loss** Ear infections are the most common cause of temporary and long-term hearing problems. Some hearing loss is congenital.

**Symptoms of hearing loss**  To determine if your child has a possible hearing loss, review the following criteria.

**3 to 6 months:**
- Your baby doesn't look up or turn toward a new sound.
- She doesn't respond to changes in your voice.
- She doesn't imitate her own voice.
- She doesn't play with rattles and other toys that make sounds.
- She fails to repeat sounds like ooh, aah, and ba-ba.
- Loud voices don't frighten her.

**6 to 10 months:**
- Your baby doesn't respond to sounds that are not loud, including his own name, a ringing telephone, or someone's voice.
- He doesn't seem to recognize words like "bye-bye."
- He doesn't make babbling sounds when alone.
- He doesn't start to respond to requests such as "come here."
- He doesn't look at things or pictures when someone talks about them.

**10 to 15 months:**
- Your baby doesn't experiment with her own voice, enjoying the sound of it.
- She doesn't point to or look at familiar objects or people when asked to.
- She doesn't imitate simple words and sounds.
- She doesn't enjoy games like peek-a-boo and pat-a-cake.

**15 to 18 months:**
- Your baby fails to follow simple directions, such as "give me the cup."

## SOUND LEVELS

### Not harmful

30 dB (whisper)
40 dB (quiet room)
50 dB (chirping birds, moderate rainfall, refrigerator)
60 dB (normal conversation, dishwasher, air conditioner)
70 dB (coffee grinder, busy restaurant, vacuum cleaner, television, food processor, sewing machine)
80 dB (heavy traffic, alarm clock, blender, hair dryer, whistling kettle, garbage disposal)

### Dangerous

90 dB (lawn mower, subway, motorcycle, tractor, busy video arcade)
100 dB (personal cassette player on high, snowmobile, boom box)
110 dB (baby's cry, shouting in ear, car horn, squeaky toy held close to ear, leaf blower)
120 dB (thunder, rock concert)
130 dB (jack hammer)

### Very dangerous

140+ dB (airplane taking off, gunshot, cap gun, firecracker)

## *Turn Down The Sound!*

Hearing impairment caused by exposure to noise can occur at any age, including early infancy. Very loud sounds, like an explosion or gunfire, can produce immediate, severe, and permanent hearing loss. Longer exposure to less intense noise can also impair hearing.

Sound level or strength is measured in decibels (dB). The sound level of conversational speech is between 65 and 70 dB. The Occupational Safety and Health Administration offers these guidelines for maximum safe exposure to sound: 8 hours at 90 dB; 4 hours at 95 dB; 2 hours at 100 dB; 1 hour at 105 dB; 30 minutes at 110 dB; 15 minutes at 115 dB, and 7½ minutes for 120 dB. Listening to music with earphones can be harmful to a child's hearing.

- He doesn't use new words often.
- He doesn't use 2- to 3-word sentences to talk about or ask for things.
- He doesn't know 10 to 20 words.

### 18 to 24 months:

- Your baby doesn't understand "yes/no" questions, such as "Do you want the ball?"
- She doesn't understand simple phrases, like "on the table."
- She doesn't enjoy being read to.

### 24 to 36 months:

- Your child doesn't understand phrases like "not now" and "no more."
- He doesn't choose things by size (big, little).
- He doesn't follow simple directions, such as "eat your cereal" or "bring your shoes."
- He doesn't understand actions words such as "run" and "jump."

### Other signs of hearing disorders include:

- Your child frequently tugs at one or both ears.
- He has difficulty hearing when a sound comes from behind him or from outside his range of peripheral vision.
- He understands words only when facing the person who is speaking to him. (Some kids learn a crude form of lip reading and can make out basic words by studying lips.)
- He doesn't respond to his name or loud sounds.
- He appears startled when approached from out of his range of vision; an older child with a hearing deficiency will have delayed speech.
- He doesn't respond to music by smiling, clapping, singing, or dancing.
- He has difficulty distinguishing between words that sound alike, such as "for" and "door."
- He tends to favor one ear when listening.
- He turns the volume too high on the TV or tape or CD player.
- He frequently complains about ear pain or a ringing sound.

**Diagnosing hearing problems** When hearing loss is suspected in children, they are tested by an audiologist, a specialist who tests and measures hearing by using various sound frequencies, game-like activities, and other techniques.

# Heart conditions

Heart murmurs and arrhythmias are the two most common heart conditions affecting children.

## *Heart murmurs*

Approximately 80 percent of all children develop a heart murmur between birth and adolescence. In the vast majority, the condition is harmless. Technically, everybody has a murmur: it's the "whooshing" sound made by blood as it runs through the heart, much like water rushing through pipes. Usually, this whooshing is so faint a doctor can't hear it with a stethoscope. But when turbulence in the blood flow makes the whoosh audible, it's an official murmur and needs to be checked out.

Most murmurs are known as "normal" or "functional" and are frequently detected in kids between ages 2 and 6—probably because children that age are more likely to sit still during an exam, allowing the doctor to hear the murmur. A heart murmur is easiest to pick up in a preschooler, because a 3- or 4-year-old's heart rate is slower than that of a younger child, making the murmur more audible. Also, because a preschooler's chest wall is thin, the doctor is more able to detect sounds inside the chest.

*See **page 729** for information on congenital heart conditions.*

**Causes of murmurs** The cause of most functional murmurs is unknown. Occasionally, a heart murmur is caused by rheumatic fever, a disease that can damage the heart valves. (Strep throat can trigger rheumatic fever; that's why doctors are quick to treat strep with antibiotics.) One out of 100 children who has a murmur is diagnosed with a congenital abnormality, such as a hole between the upper or lower chambers of the heart or a faulty valve. A family history of heart problems and/or diabetes can also be linked to murmurs in children.

**Diagnosing murmurs** If your child's doctor suspects that he may have a heart abnormality, she'll refer him to a pediatric cardiologist, a doctor who specializes in diagnosing and treating heart conditions in children. Don't be too alarmed if this occurs; sometimes pediatricians and family-practice doctors simply can't tell whether a murmur is functional or signals a serious condition, and they want a specialist to make the diagnosis.

A cardiologist will listen to the child's heart to determine how loud the murmur is, where it occurs in the heart's pumping cycle, where it can be heard, and what type of sound it makes. The cardiologist may order an electrocardiogram (EKG), which measures electrical activity controlling the heartbeat, or a Doppler echocardiogram, which provides video images of the heart. She'll also check the child for physical signs of a possible heart defect, such as a tendency to tire easily.

**Treating functional murmurs** A child with a functional or normal murmur doesn't require any special monitoring, and he can play, exercise, and function normally. Many children outgrow their murmurs sometime during adolescence, though a murmur may persist throughout adulthood.

**Treating serious murmurs** The treatment will depend on the cause and will be determined by a pediatric cardiologist.

## Arrhythymia

An arrhythmia is an irregular heartbeat that occurs when there's a problem in the electrical circuit that runs through the nerves in the heart walls. Normally, your child's heartbeat will speed up and slow down somewhat throughout the day. If he has been crying or playing hard, his heartbeat will be faster than usual and when he's calm or resting, his heartbeat will slow. A true arrhythmia, on the other hand, can be harmful, causing fainting or, in some cases, heart failure. If your child's doctor diagnoses an arrhythmia, it may mean that his heart is beating faster than normal, slower than normal, or that it is beating with no regularity.

**Causes of arrhythmia** Some children are born with abnormalities in this circuiting. Others develop an irregular heartbeat after an infection or because of a chemical imbalance in their blood.

**Symptoms of arrhythmia** If your child has an arrhythmia, his doctor will probably discover it during a regular exam. But if you notice any of the following, call the doctor immediately:
• Rapid heartbeat. Your child complains that his heart is beating fast, even when he's not exercising or isn't angry or upset.
• Sudden paleness, limpness, or listlessness
• Weakness or dizziness
• Fainting

**Diagnosing arrhythmia** If your child's doctor suspects an arrhythmia, she may refer him to a pediatric cardiologist, who will perform an EKG (electrocardiogram) and other tests.

**Treating arrhythmia** Arrhythmias can be successfully controlled with medication.

# Height and weight

During each of your child's regular checkups, her doctor will measure her height to make sure she's within the upper and lower limits for her age and weight. The doctor will use special charts that determine which percentile she's in as a way of determining where your child "stands" in relation to her peers. For instance, if your 3-year-old's height indicates that she falls in the 50th percentile, that means that she is taller than 50 percent of children her age and shorter than 50 percent. In other words, she's right in the middle. If she falls in the 95th percentile, she's taller than 95 percent of the girls her age and shorter than 5 percent. If she lands in the 5th percentile, she's shorter than 95 percent of her female counterparts and taller than the other 5 percent.

*For information on infant height and weight, see **page 84**.*

**When kids are overweight** A child who is larger than average is not considered overweight as long as his height and weight are proportionate to one another. Nor is a child who is slightly chubby prior to a growth spurt considered overweight. A child is considered obese when his weight is in or above the 95th percentile for his age, sex, and height—in other words, when he's heavier than 95 percent of his peers who are the same height. Some chubby kids can blame their excess pounds on heredity; a child who has a heavy parent is more likely to become obese. But many kids are over-

*For information on feeding an overweight child, see **page 510**.*

weight due to a lack of physical exercise and a diet laden with fat and empty calories. Since an overweight child is more likely to become an overweight adult, you shuold focus on helping your child maintain a healthy weight.

*For information on feeding an underweight child see page 511*.

**When kids are underweight**  Being underweight may have a genetic component. Your child's doctor will rule out any health problems as the cause for low weight. The doctor may suggest feeding your child high-calorie nutritional supplements if he's seriously underweight. More likely, the doctor will conclude that if your child is otherwise healthy, there's no need to be concerned about his weight.

**When children are shorter than average** There are many reasons why a healthy child might be short. If you and your partner are small, it's reasonable that you will produce smaller children. If there are lots of short people in your family, your child may be small even if you are average-height. But there are some serious conditions that can result in slow growth—including chronic kidney problems, hormonal disorders, and gastrointestinal complications from chronic illnesses—that inhibit proper nutrition, so it's important for you to discuss your concerns with your child's doctor.

**When children are taller than average**
In rare instances, extremely tall children may have a medical condition that is causing their unusual growth. Doctors expect kids to follow closely a given percentile curve line as they grow in height. When a child shoots up rapidly more than a few years before puberty, her doctor may do tests to check for a chromosomal abnormality or a problem with bone and connective tissue. She may also test pituitary gland function to see if it is producing too much growth hormone. If a physical illness is the cause, it can be treated. Usually, however, tallness has a genetic cause.

# Growth Charts For 1 to 6 Years

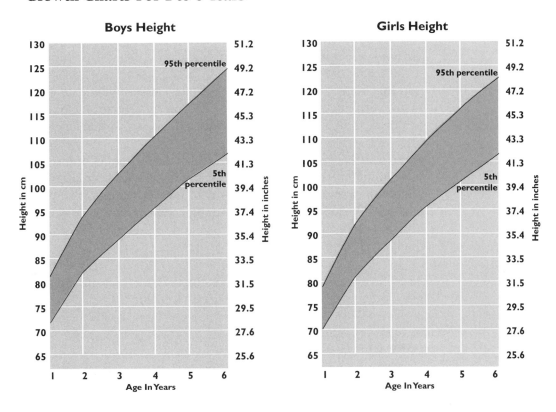

### Boys Height

Height in cm / Height in inches

| 130 | 51.2 |
| 125 | 49.2 |
| 120 | 47.2 |
| 115 | 45.3 |
| 110 | 43.3 |
| 105 | 41.3 |
| 100 | 39.4 |
| 95 | 37.4 |
| 90 | 35.4 |
| 85 | 33.5 |
| 80 | 31.5 |
| 75 | 29.5 |
| 70 | 27.6 |
| 65 | 25.6 |

95th percentile

5th percentile

Age In Years: 1 2 3 4 5 6

### Girls Height

Height in cm / Height in inches

| 130 | 51.2 |
| 125 | 49.2 |
| 120 | 47.2 |
| 115 | 45.3 |
| 110 | 43.3 |
| 105 | 41.3 |
| 100 | 39.4 |
| 95 | 37.4 |
| 90 | 35.4 |
| 85 | 33.5 |
| 80 | 31.5 |
| 75 | 29.5 |
| 70 | 27.6 |
| 65 | 25.6 |

95th percentile

5th percentile

Age In Years: 1 2 3 4 5 6

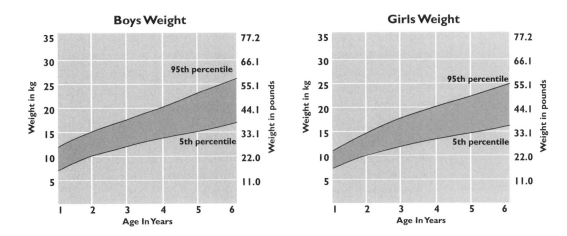

### Boys Weight

Weight in kg / Weight in pounds

| 35 | 77.2 |
| 30 | 66.1 |
| 25 | 55.1 |
| 20 | 44.1 |
| 15 | 33.1 |
| 10 | 22.0 |
| 5 | 11.0 |

95th percentile

5th percentile

Age In Years: 1 2 3 4 5 6

### Girls Weight

Weight in kg / Weight in pounds

| 35 | 77.2 |
| 30 | 66.1 |
| 25 | 55.1 |
| 20 | 44.1 |
| 15 | 33.1 |
| 10 | 22.0 |
| 5 | 11.0 |

95th percentile

5th percentile

Age In Years: 1 2 3 4 5 6

# Hematuria

Hematuria is the presence of blood in the urine.

**Causes of hematuria** Hematuria can be caused by a variety of factors and your child should be checked by her doctor as soon as possible if blood is detected in her urine. Causes include an inflammation or infection of the urinary tract, or a more serious medical problem, such as a defect in the body's ability to regulate clotting.

*For information about urinary tract infections, see **page 658**.*

**Symptoms of hematuria** Urine that is red, orange, or brownish may contain blood. Occasionally, urine takes on a reddish tint if a child has eaten red food like beets, or taken a certain medication, such as a laxative containing phenolphthalein. But if you cannot definitely link the color change to a food or medicine, your child's doctor will need to examine her.

**Treating hematuria** Since hematuria is a symptom, not an illness, the underlying condition must be treated.

# Hepatitis A and B

Hepatitis is a viral infection that causes an inflammation of the liver. There are various types of hepatitis, but the two most common forms are hepatitis A and hepatitis B.

**Preventing or limiting the severity of hepatitis** Make sure your child is vaccinated against hepatitis B; a full series of shots is believed to provide lifelong immunity to the disease. A hepatitis A vaccine should be given if your child has been exposed to the disease and as a preventative measure if your family plans to travel to areas such as Mexico and parts of the Caribbean where the disease is prevalent.

Hepatitis cannot be transmitted by simple contact, such as touching or talking with an infected person. Because both the hepatitis A and B viruses can live in saliva, tell older kids to avoid sharing eating utensils, and try to keep babies and toddlers from mouthing other children's toys. If your child is in daycare, make sure staff members wash their hands thoroughly between diaper changes and clean changing tables and pads after diapering each child.

**Causes of hepatitis A** Hepatitis A can be transmitted through contaminated food and water. Because human feces may contain the virus, it may also spread when a person fails to wash her hands between diaper changes. Raw or undercooked shellfish, drinking water contaminated with human feces, and improperly handled produce can also harbor the virus. Rarely, hepatitis A is transmitted by contaminated blood, semen, or saliva. If your child becomes infected, she'll start to show symptoms from two to four weeks after exposure. Hepatitis A is rarely fatal and often causes only mild illness.

**Symptoms of hepatitis A**  Many children with hepatitis A show only minor signs of illness, including mild fatigue for a few days. But others have more tell-tale symptoms, including:
- Fever
- Malaise
- Loss of appetite
- Nausea
- Abdominal discomfort
- Dark urine

These symptoms may be followed within a few days by jaundice (a yellowing of the skin and eyes). While hepatitis A can be mild, lasting only a week or two, some kids and adults suffer from fatigue for several months.

**Causes of hepatitis B**  Hepatitis B is much more serious than hepatitis A. The hepatitis B virus, which is transmitted by contaminated blood, semen, and saliva, can cause chronic liver damage, and in some cases, complete liver failure. Also, 10 out of every 100 people infected with hepatitis B become chronic carriers of the virus and can transmit it to others, primarily through sexual intercourse. Women infected with hepatitis B can pass the virus along to their children during delivery.

**Symptoms of hepatitis B**  Children with hepatitis B are less likely to have a fever, but they are more prone to nausea, vomiting, abdominal pain, and extreme fatigue. They may also develop jaundice.

**Treating hepatitis A and B**  A child who has been exposed to hepatitis A should receive a gamma globulin injection within 14 days of the exposure. Gamma globulin can prevent infection or shorten the duration of the illness and minimize symptoms. In 1995, the

Also see
*hydrocele, or
infant hernia,*
**page 624.**

## PARENTS ALERT

### Medications and Hepatitis

If your child has hepatitis, don't give him acetaminophen or ibuprofen to lower his fever. His liver may not be functioning well enough to process these medications; also, if your child is taking any medication at the time of diagnosis, his doctor may want to adjust the dosage to prevent a toxic buildup in the liver.

Food and Drug Administration approved a hepatitis A vaccine—Havrix—for use in kids over 2; most people are protected from infection for 15 days after receiving the injection, which is recommended for those visiting foreign countries where hepatitis A is prevalent.

If a child contracts either hepatitis A or B, rest and a good diet are the two most common treatments. Unless your child is very ill or extremely tired, he doesn't have to stay in bed. Simply monitor his activity so he doesn't become overly fatigued. If your child is vomiting a great deal or loses his appetite, call his doctor, who will want to make sure he isn't becoming dehydrated. Occasionally, kids who can't keep down any food or who have no appetite are hospitalized and fed intravenously. If hepatitis B leads to liver damage, that condition must be treated.

## Hernia (inguinal)

About 5 in every 100 children—most commonly boys—are diagnosed with an inguinal hernia.

**Causes of inguinal hernia** Inguinal hernias occur when a portion of a child's intestine slips through an opening in the lower abdominal wall.

**Symptoms of inguinal hernia** If your child has an inguinal hernia, you'll probably notice a small lump or bulge in his groin, or an enlarged scrotum. Most children who have inguinal hernias don't feel any discomfort.

**Treating inguinal hernias** An inguinal hernia must be surgically corrected in order to prevent a piece of intestine from getting trapped in the abdominal wall. If this occurs, the groin and/or scrotal area will become red, swollen, and painful; a trapped intestine requires immediate surgery.

# Herpes simplex

Herpes simplex is a virus that infects most people at some point during childhood or adolescence. It appears as a sore on the mouth, and is often called a "cold sore" or a "fever blister." Herpes simplex should not be confused with genital herpes, a similar virus contracted primarily through sexual contact.

**Causes of herpes simplex** Herpes simplex is transmitted via person-to-person contact through kissing or touching the lesions. If your child has a cold sore, have him wash his hands frequently and tell him not to kiss playmates or family members. You should also avoid kissing him on the mouth until the lesions are healed. Take care to wash your own hands after touching your child.

Once the initial infection clears up, the virus remains dormant until something causes a flare-up. Triggers include exposure to sunlight, physical stress from colds, the flu, teething, emotional upset, and sometimes, fever.

**Symptoms of herpes simplex** Children who are infected with the herpes simplex virus (HSV) have sores, which may appear in the mouth, on the lips and the area around the lips, as well as near the eyes. HSV can also affect the facial nerves. A first-time infection is often the most severe, with painful sores appearing on the gums, sides, and roof of the mouth. Fever—often as high as 105 or 106°F, irritability, sore throat, swollen glands, and loss of appetite may also occur.

Later infections usually start on the lips. Your child may feel a tingling or "tugging" sensation a day or so before a pimple-like bump erupts. The lesion then turns into a painful blister that oozes a whitish or yellowish pus. The blister may form an itchy scab that will fall off within two to three weeks. Flare-ups occasionally cause headaches. Children who develop herpes sores in or near the eyes are at higher risk for conjunctivitis.

*For information about conjunctivitis, see **page 594**.*

**Treating herpes simplex and preventing flare-ups** If your child is prone to cold sores, make sure she uses a lip balm with a sun protection factor (SPF) of 15 whenever she plans to be outdoors for more than 10 or 15 minutes, even during the winter months. Kids who are prone to herpes simplex of the eyes should wear sunglasses that screen both UVB and UVA rays whenever they are outdoors during sunny weather for more than 15 minutes. They should always wear sunglasses at the beach or other sunny places. If stress seems to trigger flares, teach your child relaxation techniques.

If your child has sores in his mouth, offer him bland, nonspicy, nonacidic foods until the sores heal. You can soothe the discomfort by wrapping an ice cube in a paper towel and holding it against the sore or by letting your child suck on an ice pop. To prevent a bacterial infection, gently cleanse the sores with soap and water, and pat dry. Then use a cotton swab to dab an antibiotic ointment onto the sore.

If your child has lots of sores and has lowered immunity because of another illness, your doctor may prescribe the oral antiviral drug acyclovir to halt the infection.

## Hiccups

*For information on hiccups in babies, see **page 69**.*

Hiccups are harmless, though they can be annoying and even interfere with sleep if they persist. A typical hiccup attack lasts about 15 to 20 minutes. Hiccups generally occur in groups of fewer than 7 or more than 64, so once your child reachers her seventh hiccup, she will probably keep going.

**Causes of hiccups** In older babies and children, hiccup attacks are often brought on by overeating, drinking carbonated beverages, sudden excitement, emotional stress, and the giggles. Activities that cause a sudden change in your child's body temperature—such as hopping into a chilly wading pool or eating ice cream quickly—may also bring on a case of the hiccups.

**Treating hiccups** Fill a glass with water and have your child drink from the far side of the glass. She should bend her head forward until her chin is almost in the glass. Then she should take 10 to 15 sips. She may have to do this two or three times before the cure occurs. During the hiccups, it's important that your child not attempt to eat, since doing so could increase her risk of choking.

> **"IT WORKED FOR ME"**
>
> ### Handling Hiccups
>
> Whenever my 4-year-old daughter gets overly excited or starts giggling she begins to hiccup. I calm her down with a trick my own mom used with me. We sit at the kitchen table, facing each other. I take her hands in mine and look into her eyes and say, "Okay, hiccup. That's good. Now, I want to hear another one. Come on. Bet you can't hiccup." I do this for about 4 or 5 minutes and her hiccups disappear. I think she's concentrating so hard on trying to hiccup that she calms down and the spasms stop!

# High cholesterol

Cholesterol is a fatlike substance in the blood that can, over time, lead to atherosclerosis—the number one cause of heart attack and stroke. The National Cholesterol Education Program and the American Academy of Pediatrics recommend that a child 2 or older have his cholestorol level tested if he has any of these risk factors:

- A parent or grandparent who developed heart disease, suffered a heart attack or stroke, or died from a heart attack before age 55.
- A parent who has a cholesterol level of 240 or higher.
- A parent or grandparent whose medical history cannot be obtained, especially if the child has other risk factors, such as obesity, diabetes, or inactivity.

In adults, a healthy cholesterol level is less than 200 milligrams (mg) per deciliter (dl) of blood. In a youngster 19 and under:

> 170 mg/dl is considered "acceptable."
> 170 to 199 mg/dl is considered "borderline."
> 200 mg/dl or greater is considered "high."

**Causes of high cholesterol** Eating foods high in saturated fat is the primary dietary cause of high cholesterol in kids and adults. Eating foods rich in cholesterol is the secondary cause. Some children also inherit a predisposition toward high cholesterol.

**Diagnosing high cholesterol** The only way to learn your child's blood cholesterol level is to have her blood tested. Your child's doctor may want to test her cholesterol levels if she has high blood pressure or regularly eats foods loaded with total fat, saturated fat, and cholesterol, or if there's a family history of high cholesterol.

**Treating high cholestoral** If your pediatrician finds that your child's total cholesterol is borderline high or high, he may order a complete cholesterol profile to determine his levels of low-density lipoproteins or LDL (the so-called "bad" cholesterol), high-density lipoproteins or HDL (the "good" cholesterol), and triglycerides, which carry and store fatty acids. Since a child should not eat or drink anything for 12 hours before the test, try to schedule it early in the morning so she doesn't have to go without food for too long.

Most cases of high cholesterol can be treated by modifying the diet and increasing physical activity. If a child's cholesterol is ex-

*See **page 509** for information on cholesterol-controlling diets.*

Also see
*inguinal
hernia,*
**page 620**.

## PARENTS ALERT

### When Hives Indicate a Life-Threatening Allergy

Very rarely, hives will be accompanied by swelling of the inside of the mouth and throat. This often happens after a child who is allergic to bee stings is stung, or a child with a severe food or drug allergy consumes an offending substance. If swelling occurs, or if your child begins to wheeze or has trouble breathing, seek medical help immediately. If you have an epinephrine kit, administer the shot, then call 911 for help or rush your child to the nearest emergency room.

tremely high and cannot be lowered by diet and exercise alone, she may need cholesterol-lowering drugs. However, drugs are rarely given to kids, and children under the age of 10 should not take cholesterol medications.

## Hives

Hives are itchy, raised welts. Usually the raised area is pale and the surrounding skin or bottom of the hive is red.

**Causes of hives**  Hives are usually a symptom of an allergy or a sensitivity to certain foods or medications. A hive may erupt after the child has taken a medication to which he's sensitive, such as an antibiotic, or eaten a food—especially eggs and shellfish—to which he's allergic. Certain infections may trigger hives in susceptible kids.

**Treating hives**  Since a hive generally signals an allergic reaction, and may be the first symptom of an allergy, it's important to avoid the allergen in the future, since a second exposure may cause a more severe reaction. If your child develops one or more hives, keep a careful eye on him to see if a severe allergic reaction occurs. Call the doctor if the hives are particularly bothersome, even if a severe reaction does not occur. If the hives are simply itchy and annoying, talk to your doctor about giving your child an over-the-counter medication, such as Benadryl, to curb the itching and swelling. You can also ease itching by applying cool compresses or letting your child soak in a cool bath.

## Hydrocele (infant hernia)

In the male fetus, the testicles develop in the abdominal cavity, and then move down through a tube—the inguinal canal—into the scrotum just before birth. The testes pull the lining of the abdominal wall along with them to form a sac that connects the testicles to the abdominal cavity. Ideally, the opening into the abdominal space closes, but the passage may remain open. When that happens, fluid that normally surrounds the abdominal organs will flow through the opening and build up in the scrotal area, creating a communicating hydrocele, or infant hernia. According to the American Academy of Pediatrics, about half of all newborn males have a hydrocele, and, in many, the condition clears up within the first year of life.

**Diagnosing hydrocele** A child with this type of hernia may not feel any pain, but you may notice a swelling on one side of his scrotum. Your child's doctor can make a definite diagnosis.

**Treating hydrocele** If the condition persists beyond the first year, your child's doctor may recommend simple surgery to drain the excess fluid from the scrotal area and close the opening into the abdominal cavity.

If your son has a hydrocele, contact his pediatrician if he experiences tenderness in the scrotal area or has unexplained nausea and/or vomiting. Abdominal fluid may have pushed a section of your child's intestine into the scrotal area. If the intestine is trapped there, his doctor will immediately perform surgery to release the intestine and close the opening between the abdomen and scrotum.

# Hypertension (high blood pressure)

A child's blood pressure can change based on her age and height. Therefore, what's "normal" for each child must be determined by the child's regular physician.

Children who have high blood pressure may develop hypertension during adulthood. When researchers took blood pressure readings of more than 1,500 children between the ages of 5 and 14 and retested the children 15 years later, they found that those whose childhood readings were in the top 20 percent of the group were up to three and a half times more likely to have high blood pressure as adults. Adults with high blood pressure are at increased risk for stroke and heart attacks.

**Causes of hypertension** Hypertension can be inherited. Obesity also leads to an increased risk. Congenital heart abnormalities, such as atrial and ventricular septal defects, can sometimes lead to high blood pressure.

**Diagnosing hypertension**  The doctor uses a blood-pression cuff to perform a painless test, routinely performed at regular office visits.

**Treating hypertension**  If your child's blood pressure is on the high side, his doctor may recommend that you:
• Reduce the fat in your child's diet. Kids 2 and up should get no more than 30 percent of their daily calories from fat.
• Cut salt (sodium) intake. Limit the amount of high-salt processed foods, such as luncheon meat, that your child eats, and avoid adding salt to foods you cook.
• Serve potassium-rich foods, like bananas, apples, and strawberries. Potassium may help control sodium levels.
• Make sure your child is physically active for about 30 minutes a day. Physical activity helps keep blood pressure in check.

# Impetigo

Impetigo is a contagious bacterial infection of the skin.

**Causes of impetigo**  The bacteria that trigger impetigo usually enter the skin through a sore, scratch, or cut. An infected person can spread the bacteria by touching the sores and transferring the organisms to another part of her body or to others. A child with impetigo should be separated from other children until her rash improves—about 48 hours after she starts taking an oral antibiotic or using a topical antibiotic cream.

**Symptoms of impetigo**  This infection is marked by brownish/honey-colored scabs or crusty areas on the face—especially around the nose, mouth, or ears. The infection usually begins with a pimple that has a yellowish or white blister on top. An infected child usually rubs the blister off, and a scab forms in its place.

**Treating impetigo**  If you suspect that your child has impetigo, have her examined by her doctor. If she has a mild case, the doctor may recommend a topical prescription antibiotic. For more severe cases, an oral, broad-spectrum antibiotic is usually prescribed. Hot soaks and hot compresses can also help. Just be sure that the water isn't so hot that it causes discomfort.

# Infection

Like adults, kids are susceptible to both bacterial and viral infections.

**Causes of bacterial infections** Bacteria, such as staphylococcus, streptococcus, and the hemophilus influenza B bacterium, can trigger many different types of infections, including boils on the skin, bacterial pneumonia, the very common strep throat, and epiglottitis.

**Treating bacterial infections** Bacterial infections are usually treated with oral antibiotics. Bacterial infections of the skin are most often treated with topical antibiotic creams.

**Causes of viral infections** Viral infections are caused by viruses, a vast variety of organisms that are responsible for everything from the common cold and the flu to measles.

**Treating viral infections** Antibiotics are ineffective against viruses, but if a viral infection, such as a cold, leads to a bacterial infection, such as bronchitis, your child's doctor may prescribe an antibiotic.

# Influenza (flu)

The flu is a viral infection. Though your child may get the flu anytime from mid-fall through early spring, peak flu season runs from December through March in most parts of the country. Two varieties of the flu are common in the United States: Type A and Type B. Type A flu, which is usually accompanied by fever, can cause febrile seizures. Type B infections are marked by severe gastrointestinal discomfort and may mimic appendicitis.

Symptoms of flu come on suddenly. Within a week, most kids start to feel better, though their coughs can linger for several weeks, and they may continue to tire easily for as long as a couple of weeks.

**Causes of flu infection** The flu spreads when an infected person coughs germ-laden droplets into the air. The virus is also transmitted by nose and throat secretions on kids' hands.

*See **page 598** for information on seizures.*

*See **page 574** for information about the difference between the flu and a cold.*

**Symptoms of flu**
- A fever that's usually 102°F or higher in children
- Muscle aches and headache
- Extreme fatigue
- A persistent cough
- A severe sore throat
- Some children also suffer gastrointestinal symptoms, including a stomach ache, nausea, and vomiting.

**Treating the flu** You can ease your child's achiness and help lower her fever with acetaminophen. (Ibuprofen may be too hard on her tummy during a bout of flu.)

Also, offer her lots of liquids and make sure she gets plenty of bed rest. If your child's symptoms worsen, call her doctor, who may want to examine your child to rule out pneumonia, which is an occasional complication of the flu, an ear infection, strep throat, or another bacterial infection.

In a child age 1 or older who has severe symptoms or a lung, heart, or other serious medical condition, symptoms can be eased with the antiviral medication Amantadine. Because Amantadine has side effects, such as nausea or insomnia, it is not recommended in most cases.

# Jaundice

Also see infant jaundice, on **page 69**.

Jaundice is the result of an abnormal increase in blood levels of bilirubin, a yellow-orange pigment.

**Causes of jaundice** A number of conditions can trigger illness-related jaundice, including liver disease, blocked bile ducts, bowel obstruction, hypothyroidism, and certain infections, such as rubella, hepatitis A and B, mononucleosis, and herpes.

**Treating illness-related jaundice** Children with illness-related jaundice may be hospitalized for weeks and treated for the underlying condition.

# Labial adhesions

In the majority of newborn girls, the labia—or "lips" of the skin—surrounding the opening to the vagina are separated. Occasionally, though, they adhere, blocking the opening partially or completely. This condition, known as "labial adhesions," usually occurs during the first few months of life, but can occur during early childhood and even as late as puberty.

**Causes of labial adhesions** It is not known why some girls are born with this condition. However, doctors know that later onset adhesions may occur if the genital area is frequently irritated and inflamed—usually because of diaper rash, harsh detergents used on diapers or panties, or constant perspiration or moistness in the genital area.

**Symptoms of labial adhesions** Girls with labial adhesions may have difficulty urinating and may be more prone to urinary tract infections (UTIs). If the vaginal opening is completely blocked, urine or vaginal secretions can pool behind the obstruction, leading to infection.

**Treating labial adhesions** If you notice that the opening of your daughter's vagina appears closed or partially closed, ask her doctor to examine her. The doctor may try to spread the labia gently, which often is all that's needed. But if the connecting tissue is strong, the doctor will probably prescribe a cream containing the hormone estrogen, which will help open the labia over a period of time. Once the labia are separated, you will need to apply the cream for three to five days until the skin is healed. Very rarely, the labia will need to be separated surgically.

# Lead poisoning

Lead poisoning affects an estimated 1.7 million children age 5 and under. The U.S. Centers for Disease Control and Prevention lists lead as the leading environmental hazard to American children, affecting children of all socioeconomic backgrounds. Even low levels of lead contamination can result in lowered intelligence, learning disabilities, and behavioral problems. Children with moderate levels can, in addition to learning difficulties, suffer from anemia and colic. At high levels, a child also develops neurological problems and becomes critically ill. Children under age 3, whose brains and nervous systems are still developing, are at the greatest risk, though exposure at any age can keep a child from reaching his full potential.

*For information on reducing the risk of lead in your home, see **page 800**.*

**Causes of lead poisoning** Lead poisoning is caused by ingesting paint chips, dust, or soil contaminated with lead. A lack of visible paint or plaster chips does not mean that the environment is free of lead hazards. The main risk factor is living in a home or attending a school built before 1978.

**Symptoms of lead poisoning** Lead poisoning is most often detected through a routine blood test taken during a child's regular well-child checkup. A level of 10 micrograms per deciliter of blood (mcg/dl) is considered "elevated." Many children who have lead poisoning show no symptoms initially or the early symptoms—behavioral changes and irritability—are mistaken for signs of other conditions, such as colic in infants and attention deficit disorder in older children.

Additional symptoms, which usually don't occur until lead levels surpass 45 mcg/dl, may include constipation, abdominal cramps, diarrhea, vomiting, anemia, increased or decreased sleep, over- or under-activity, irritability, and observable learning problems. Some infants stop eating. Very high levels (over 70 mcg/dl) can trigger seizures, nerve paralysis, deafness, encephalopathy, and, in some cases, death. Cases of severe lead poisoning are very rare, however.

**Testing for lead poisoning** Babies should be tested for lead exposure between 9 and 12 months of age, according to the American Academy of Pediatrics. Children this age are crawling to explore their environment and are, therefore, more apt to eat lead-paint chips or suck on lead-contaminated surfaces, such as toys exposed to lead dust. Thereafter, all children should be tested annually until age 6, according to the Centers for Disease Control and Prevention. If an environment is known to contain lead, everyone in the home should be tested, including newborns. Preliminary testing may require a simple finger-stick, although some doctors prefer to draw blood for analysis.

If your child has a serum lead level of 10 or higher, have your home tested to find the source of the lead. Although over-the-counter home kits are available for testing for lead in paint and water, they may not provide accurate readings. The National Safety Council recommends professional testing.

**Treating lead poisoning** Treatment of mild lead poisoning involves keeping the child away from areas that contain lead and removing lead from your home. Doctors also recommend dietary changes involving increasing your child's consumption of calcium and iron (which inhibit lead absorption) and, in children over the age of 2, decreasing consumption of fat (which speeds up absorption). Over time, the child's serum lead level will drop. Severe cases are treated by chelation, a process in which doctors inject the child with medications that help rid the body of lead.

# Lyme disease

Lyme disease is the number one tick-borne illness in the United States. It is named for Lyme, Connecticut, where the illness was first identified. May through August are the prime months for Lyme disease infection, though the bacterium carried by infected ticks can spread anytime the temperature is above 35°F. Nymph ticks cause most of the cases of Lyme disease that occur in late spring and summer, but adult ticks can transmit it, especially in the fall.

*For information on preventing Lyme disease, see **page 499**.*

*For information about removing a tick, see **page 667**.*

**Causes of Lyme disease**  The Lyme bacterium, *Borrelia burgdorferi*, is transmitted by ticks, which are borne by deer, field mice, chipmunks, and birds.

In the Northeast and Upper Midwest, the culprit is the deer tick, which is no bigger than the head of a pin. Its cousin, the western black tick, spreads the disease in the West.

**Symptoms of Lyme disease**  Many people infected with Lyme disease develop a circular "bull's-eye" rash, known as *erythema migrans*, 2 to 40 days after being bitten. The rash can occur anywhere on the body, not just the site of the bite, and often shows up in dark, moist areas such as the groin, the back of the knees, or the armpits. Some people develop rashes in several areas. Others, however, don't develop a rash.

Other symptoms, which tend to mimic those of the flu, may include:
- Headache
- Fatigue
- Pain in the muscles and joints
- Fever
- Sore throat

- Chills
- Nausea
- Vomiting
- Swollen lymph nodes

Most symptoms disappear in a week or so, but if not treated, more serious symptoms, including arthritis, neurological disorders such as menengitis, and heart disorders can occur weeks, months, or even years later.

**Diagnosing Lyme disease**  A blood test can confirm Lyme, but because the blood test can yield false-negative results during the first month after infection, the test may need to be repeated in four to eight weeks for a definitive diagnosis.

**Treating Lyme disease** Most pediatricians can treat early Lyme disease adequately with antibiotics. A child under age 9 usually receives a course of oral amoxicillin. Older children are often prescribed amoxicullin or doxycycline. Only one percent of children who are treated with antibiotics go on to develop more serious symptoms. In these instances, doctors may prescribe the antibiotic ceftriaxone or cefotaxime, given intravenously for up to 30 days.

## Malabsorption

Malabsorption is the body's inability to absorb essential nutrients into the bloodstream. This can lead to malnutrition.

**Causes of malabsorption**  Occasionally, a child isn't able to digest a certain nutrient, for example, milk sugar, or lactose, resulting in malabsorbtion. In some kids, chronic infection or inflammation of the digestive tract can lead to malabsorption. Children with cystic fibrosis often suffer from malabsorption because they lack enzymes necessary for proper digestion.

**Symptoms of malabsorption**
- Abdominal pain
- Vomiting
- Frequent, diarrhea-like stools with a very foul smell

- Poor growth and slowed weight gain
- Lowered resistance to infection
- Dry or scaly skin

**Diagnosing malabsorption** When a child shows symptoms of malabsorption, his pediatrician may run a number of tests as well as ask the parent to keep a food diary, listing everything the child eats.

If initial tests do not yield a cause, the doctor may screen for cystic fibrosis or may biopsy a small part of the intestinal wall to check for inflammation or infection.

**Treating malabsorption.** Treatment depends on the results of the tests, and may include dietary changes. If infection is present, antibiotics are prescribed. Children with cystic fibrosis are given enzymes that help them to digest essential nutrients.

*For information on cystic fibrosis, see **page 734**.*

# Measles (rubella)

Measles is a highly contagious viral infection. Children who have received the MMR (measles, mumps, rubella) vaccination are immune to the disease. If your child hasn't been vaccinated, he's most prone to the virus during the winter and spring. Most cases last for about a week, and the child is able to resume normal activities a couple of days after his temperature has returned to normal.

*For information on vaccination, see **page 545**.*

**Causes of measles** The disease is spread when a child inhales the droplets that have been released by an infected person's cough or and sneeze.

**Symptoms of measles** The initial symptoms resemble those of a cold—fever, runny nose, red, tearing eyes, and a dry cough. Some kids also develop diarrhea and swollen glands. After three or four days, the child develops a rash—pink spots that may start behind the ears, then gradually spread over the face and body, becoming bigger and darker.

**Treating measles** If you suspect your child has measles, call his doctor. Unvaccinated children who have been exposed to measles may be given a gamma globulin injection, which can prevent the illness or produce milder symptoms. If light bothers your child's eyes, a common condition associated with measles infection, dim the lights in his room. Although your child probably won't have much of an appetite, encourage him to consume plenty of fluids to prevent dehydration. If his fever causes discomfort, give him acetaminophen. If his cough worsens or his fever goes down and then rises again, alert the doctor. Occasionally, measles can lead to pneumonia, bronchitis, middle ear infections, ear abscesses, and encephalitis, and the doctor may want to see your child to evaluate his condition.

## Meningitis

Meningitis is an inflammation of the tissues surrounding the brain and/or the spinal cord. It can be fatal.

*For information on vaccination, see **page 545**.*

**Causes of meningitis** Both viruses and bacteria can cause the illness. Viral meningitis tends to be less severe and is caused by a variety of viruses. Bacterial meningitis is caused by the hemophilus influenza B, or Hib bacteria, and strikes most often during the winter. Hib bacteria are transmitted via person-to-person contact or through germ-laden droplets that are coughed into the air. Bacterial meningitis can lead to neurological damage and is sometimes fatal. Although there's no vaccine to prevent viral meningitis, you can protect your child from Hib meningitis by seeing that she receives the Hib vaccination.

**Symptoms of meningitis** In infants, the fontanel, or soft spot on the skull, may bulge. Additional symptoms for all children may include:
- Fever
- Lethargy
- High-pitched crying
- Irritability
- Vomiting
- Loss of appetite
- Stiff neck
- Sensitivity to light
- Blurred or fuzzy vision

**Treating meningitis** If your child develops any symptoms of meningitis, even if she has received the Hib vaccine, call the doctor immediately. If you can't reach the doctor, take your child to a hospital emergency room. Children with viral meningitis are usually hospitalized and treated with acetaminophen, bed rest, and oral rehydration therapy if vomiting is severe enough to cause possible dehydration. Children with bacterial meningitis are also treated with antibiotics.

# Mononucleosis

Mononuclsosis, commonly referred to as "mono," is a viral infection. It usually affects children and teens and lasts about two to three weeks, but, if severe, can last weeks to months.

**Causes of mono** It's often called "the kissing disease" because of the belief that it is transmitted orally. Mono is actually spread by inhaling droplets from a cough or sneeze of an infected person.

**Symptoms of mononucleosis**
- Fever
- Headache
- Sore throat
- Swollen glands
- Fatigue
- Sometimes a rash and jaundice

**Treating mono** If your child develops symptoms, call the doctor. Mono is treated with bed rest, lots of fluids, and acetaminophen to relieve headache and reduce fever. Antibiotics are not helpful in treating mono. If an exam reveals that the child's liver enzymes are elevated and/or that the spleen is enlarged, the child must be monitored over time.

# Motion sickness

Motion sickness is queasiness brought on by passive movement, such as a ride in a fast-moving car, boat, plane, or amusement-park ride.

**Causes of motion sickness** Motion sickness occurs when the motion-sensing areas of the body—the eyes and ears, in particular—don't receive the same signals from the brain simultaneously. For example, a child riding in a car sees trees and houses rushing by, but his ears don't sense that movement. This, in turn, throws his sensory system off balance.

### Symptoms of motion sickness
• Queasiness, nausea, and stomach pain
• Sometimes, vomiting and a cold sweat

### Treatments for motion sickness
• Food. Give your child a light snack before car, train, plane, or boat trips, since an empty stomach is more prone to upset.
• Decreased visual stimuli. Don't let your child read or look at picture books during travel. Instead, suggest she play a word game with you, or listen to music.
• Focus. Have your child look toward the front of the car at the horizon, not out the side windows.
• Fresh air. Keep a window cracked or the car air conditioning on, since stuffiness and heat can trigger queasiness.
• Exercise breaks. If your child starts to feel sick, stop the car and let her walk around for 10 to 15 minutes.
• Medication. If your child is very prone to motion sickness, her doctor may recommend an anti-motion sickness medication that she can take an hour before travel.

**PARENTS ALERT**

## *Mumps Are Dangerous in Adolescent and Adult Males*

While mumps-related complications are rare during childhood, mumps may cause sterility in adolescent males who have passed through puberty, and in adult males.

If your young child gets the mumps and male adult or teen-aged friends or relatives haven't had them, or haven't been vaccinated, they should stay away from the child during an outbreak and for at least 10 days after his symptoms have disappeared.

# Mumps

A viral infection, mumps may begin with an earache and fever, and usually runs its course within seven days and occurs most often in late winter and spring. Rarely, the mumps can lead to meningoencephalitis, a serious inflammation of the brain. You can protect your child against mumps by making sure he gets his MMR (measles, mumps, and rubella) vaccinations.

**Causes of mumps** Mumps is spread through tiny droplets from coughs. An infected person is contagious for as long as ten days after his symptoms have disappeared.

**Symptoms of mumps** After the first day of infection, the glands around the ear and jaw swell. Some kids suffer such mild symptoms their parents aren't aware that they have the mumps. Others lose their appetite and feel pain when chewing or swallowing or when they eat acidic or sour foods.

Call your child's doctor if he experiences any of the following symptoms:
- Vomiting
- Headache
- Unusual drowsiness
- Stiffness of the back or neck

These symptoms could indicate that your child has meningoen-cephalititis, a rare complication of the mumps. Treatment may require hospitalization.

**Treating mumps** If your child gets a mild case of the mumps, give him acetaminophen to ease his pain. Also offer him bland, nonacidic foods and plenty of fluids. Cool compresses applied to the swollen area may help relieve pain.

*For information on vaccination, see **page 545**.*

## Papular urticaria

Papular urticaria commonly afflicts children ages 2 to 7 who haven't yet developed an immunity to flea venom. By age 7, a child has usually outgrown the likelihood of contracting the condition.

**Cause of papular urticaria** Flea bites.
**Symptom of papular urticaria** Itchy, hive-like bumps turn into solid knotlike eruptions, which can last from a few days to several months. An experienced clinician can make the diagnosis by physical exam. The condition can be confirmed by examining blood and tissue samples from the child.

**Treating papular urticaria**
- Antihistamines (OTC or prescription)
- Cortisone cream, and/or anti-itch agents

## Pertussis (whooping cough)

Pertussis, commonly called "whooping cough," is a serious upper respiratory disease that occurs when the air passages become clogged by mucus. Untreated, whooping cough can lead to pneu-

**PARENTS ALERT**

### *Risk for Apnea*

Infants with pertussis may require hospitalization, intravenous feeding, and monitoring since they are also at risk for apnea.

monia and may be fatal. DTaP (diphtheria, tetanus, pertussis) vaccinations protect kids against this contagious illness.

**Symptoms of pertussis** Whooping cough begins with a cold and a dry cough. After about ten days, the child develops intense, explosive fits of coughing that prevents him from breathing easily. At the end of each coughing spasm, the child takes a big breath, which is accompanied by a "whooping" sound. Infants, however, may simply have a spasmodic cough, without the "whoop" sound. Other symptoms may include fever and vomiting.

**Treating pertussis** Call the doctor if your child develops symptoms of whooping cough. The doctor may recommend:
• Antibiotics
• Suctioning mucus from nasal passages
• A cool-mist humidifier to ease breathing
• Fluid oral rehydration therapy to prevent dehydration
• Frequent small feedings

## Pigeon toes (intoeing)

This condition occurs when a child's foot-, shin-, thigh-, or hip-bones rotate in, causing his feet and legs to turn in when he walks. In rare instances, a bone may remain rotated, but it doesn't affect the ability to walk or cause pain. Intoeing, which is common among young children, usually disappears by age 8 without the need for casts, braces, or special shoes. If intoeing starts to affect your child's self-esteem, however, talk with his pediatrician about treatment options.

### *How to Spot Intoeing*

| Problem | Usually Disappears By |
|---|---|
| Infant's flexible feet curve in at middle; related to the baby's position in the womb. | 6 months |
| Shinbones rotate in, causing feet and lower legs to turn in. | 2 to 3 years |
| Upper thigh bones rotate in, causing feet to turn in when child walks or runs. Child is able to sit in a W position, with knees bent and legs angled to the side. | 4 to 8 years |
| Shins and hips rotate in; knees appear to point in. | Shins straighten by age 3 or 4; hips, by age 8 |

# Pinworms

Pinworms are a relatively harmless intestinal infestation.

**Causes of pinworms**  The tiny pinworms are spread by hand-to-hand, hand-to-mouth, or hand-to-food contact. When a person is infected, the mature worm lays its eggs on the skin around the anus and buttocks. If a child or a caregiver touches that area and gets the eggs on his hands, he can pass them on to another person through the objects he handles, or by direct contact. If that person puts his hands in his mouth or touches his food before thoroughly washing his hands, the eggs can travel to his small intestine where they hatch and travel to the end of the intestine. The mature worms mate, and the female deposits new eggs around the host's anus, continuing the cycle of infestation. Pinworms can also be transmitted by pets. While cats and dogs don't harbor eggs in their feces, an infected person can transmit pinworm eggs to the animals, who carry them in their fur and infect others with whom they come in contact.

**Symptoms of pinworms**
* Rectal itching, especially at night.
* Redness and irritation in the anal area.
* Vaginal discharge in girls, if the worms crawl into the child's vaginal area.
* Visible presence. Some kids have no symptoms. In these cases, pinworms are detected only by visual inspection. (Pinworms are thread-like, whitish worms, about ¼ to ½ inch long).

**Treating pinworms**
* Oral medication. This causes a child to expel the pinworms during bowel movements.
* Good hygiene, especially washing hands after using the toilet or playing with pets, and before eating, can prevent infestation.

# Pneumonia

Pneumonia is an inflammation of the lungs.

**Causes of pneumonia**  Pneumonia is caused by a number of organisms, including viruses, bacteria, and fungi. The condition most often occurs during cold and flu season, but can occur during the summer months as well.

**Symptoms of pneumonia** Pneumonia's early symptoms mimic those of a cold or flu. These symptoms are followed by a rising fever; a productive, phlegmy cough; rapid breathing and wheezing; difficulty breathing; heavy mucus; and, sometimes, abdominal distension and pain.

**Treating pneumonia** Call the doctor if your child has any symptoms, including a cold or flu that suddenly worsens. Take her to a hospital emergency room if her skin turns blue or she has difficulty breathing.

Bacterial pneumonia is treated with antibiotics. Antibiotics are not used to treat viral pneumonia, unless the virus leads to bacterial pneumonia or another bacterial infection. Both types of pneumonia require bed rest and fluid replacement. To speed along the drainage of mucus from bronchi and lungs, resting in a sitting up position is preferable to lying down. Young children are often hospitalized.

## Pyloric stenosis

Pyloric stenosis is a congenital condition in which the valve leading from the stomach into the intestines won't open up enough to let food through. As a result, the baby may vomit with force, a phenonemon known as projectile vomiting. Vomiting may occur during or shortly after feeding. Affected babies are often constipated as well. It is more common in boys than girls.

**Diagnosing pyloric stenosis** Pyloric stenosis is usually detected when a baby is a few weeks old. A doctor will consider this diagnosis in babies who have experienced projectile vomiting and will confirm the diagnosis by examining the baby's abdomen for thickening or lumps in the area and/or by taking an ultrasound. Left untreated, the condition can cause malnutrition and dehydration.

**Treating pyloric stenosis** Pyloric stenosis is corrected surgically.

## Rabies (hydrophobia)

Rabies is a deadly form of viral encephalitis. About 20,000 Americans are exposed to rabies each year. This disease can be carried by any warm-blooded mammal, including dogs, cats, horses, raccoons, skunks, foxes, rabbits, ferrets, prairie dogs, hamsters, gerbils, guinea pigs, goats, and cows. Bats are also carriers. If you own a pet that can be innoculated against rabies, keep its innoculations up to date. (Dogs, cats, and ferrets can be vaccinated against rabies; hamsters, gerbils, and guinea pigs cannot, but because they are kept in cages indoors, it isn't likely that they will contract the disease.) When not treated promptly, rabies is almost always fatal.

**Causes of rabies** The virus is found in an infected animal's saliva and is transmitted to humans through a bite, lick, or scratch. Even petting an infected animal that has licked its skin can transmit the disease.

**Preventing rabies** After a child has been bitten or scratched by an animal, follow first-aid procedures, washing the wound thoroughly with soap and water, and have your child evaluated by her physician. Try to locate the owner of any dog or cat that has bitten or scratched your child to make sure that it has been inoculated within the past three years. If the animal has been inoculated, there is no possibility of rabies.

*For more information on cleaning wounds, see **page 620**.*

If your child was bitten or scratched by an uninocuated or unidentified pet or a wild animal, and if there is any possibility that the animal is infected, your child will have to be treated. Also, if the saliva of any infected animal could have entered your child's system by mouth or through an open wound, she will need treatment.

**Symptoms of rabies** The incubation period can vary from as little as five days to as much as eight months, so it's possible for a pet or child to be bitten by an infected animal, and not show any symptoms for some time.

- Pain
- Cold, itching, or tingling at the site of the wound
- Fever of 101 to 102°F
- Loss of appetite and nausea
- Sore throat
- Cough
- Irritability
- Unusual sensitivity to light and noise
- Rapid heartbeat
- Excessive drooling, tearing, and/or sweating

By the time the following symptoms appear, it's generally too late for treatment and the disease is fatal.
- Anxiety
- Vision problems
- Drooping of the facial muscles
- Fever of 103°F or above
- Frothing at the mouth
- Paralysis

**Treating rabies** It's vital to treat rabies before any symptoms occur since the disease is almost always fatal if not treated early. Treatment for suspected rabies is essential, even when infection cannot be confirmed. Treatment consists of a single injection of immune globulin on the day of possible exposure. This is followed by a series of five vaccinations, administered on the day of exposure, and on days 3, 7, 14, and 28 following exposure.

## Rashes

*For information on reducing allergens, see page 793.*

A variety of ailments cause rashes, and the underlying condition needs to be treated. Most rashes are not cause for alarm. If your child develops a sudden rash, especially after eating or after being bitten by an insect, monitor her closely. If she doesn't appear uncomfortable or in distress, simply keep an eye on her. If she develops hives and/or appears to be having breathing difficulty or develops facial or neck swelling, seek medical help immediately.

## Respiratory syncytial virus (RSV)

This is an upper-respiratory infection. It is extremely common among babies and children under age 3. Children over 3 rarely become infected. Though most infected children recover completely, it is fatal to more than 4,000 annually.

**Causes of RSV** Respiratory syncytial virus is spread by close contact with respiratory secretions of an infected child or things an infected child has touched. Its spread can be limited by avoiding infected children, practicing careful hygiene, and avoiding smoke. RSV is most prevalent in winter. It can lead to bronchiolitis, pneumonia, asthma, and/or sudden breathing difficulty.

**Symptoms of RSV** RSV first appears as mild to severe cold symptoms. Other symptoms include:

- Wheezy breathing
- Sore throat
- Fever
- Lethargy
- Rapid and/or strained breathing
- Apnea in infants, particularly in preemies

**Treating RSV** If your child's cold symptoms appear severe or if she appears to be having any difficulty breathing, call the doctor. In most cases, the symptoms are treatable, and the illness runs its course in about a week. In cases in which a child's immunity is compromised by prematurity or by another illness, a child may be hospitalized and treated with antiviral drugs.

## Reye syndrome

Reye syndrome is a very rare but serious illness that most often occurs in children between the ages of 3 and 12. Reye syndrome can damage the brain and liver, but may affect other areas of the body as well. While many children who contract the disease don't have long-lasting complications, a few do develop permanent brain damage or even die.

**Causes of Reye syndrome** A viral infection, such as chicken pox or the flu, precedes the onset of Reye syndrome. Experts don't know why most kids who get viral illnesses don't also come down with Reye syndrome, but they speculate that chemical changes or a toxin released in the child's body may make a child more prone to the syndrome. Also, children who take aspirin—especially for chicken pox or the flu—are more apt to get the virus.

**Symptoms of Reye syndrome** Call the doctor immediately—or take your child to the nearest hospital emergency room—if your child shows any of the following symptoms.

**PARENTS ALERT**

### Avoid Aspirin

To reduce the risk for Reye syndrome, the American Academy of Pediatrics urges that parents never give aspirin or products containing aspirin to children under age 16. Aspirin therapy is sometimes prescribed for children who have illnesses like juvenile rheumatoid arthritis, rheumatic fever, or Kawasaki's disease, but only under a doctor's strict supervision.

- She seems to be improving following a bout with the chicken pox, flu, or other viral illness and then suddenly starts vomiting frequently—every one to two hours— over a 24 hour period.
- She also exhibits behavioral changes, becoming lethargic, then suddenly agitated, angry, confused, or delirious.

**Treating Reye syndrome** If your child develops Reye syndrome, he must be hospitalized for treatment. If the child doesn't receive medical treatment immediately, he may have seizures or go into a coma. In some instances, a child is transferred to a medical center that specializes in treating the disorder.

# Rheumatic fever

*For information about strep, see **page 653**.*

Rheumatic fever is a reaction to strep. Though rheumatic fever most commonly strikes kids between the ages of 8 and 12, it can occur in younger children. Serious attacks may damage the heart muscle and cause severe joint pain. To lower your child's risk of rheumatic fever, call her doctor if she develops symptoms of strep throat.

**Causes of rheumatic fever** Rheumatic fever occurs when strep throat isn't treated. Rheumatic fever is not contagious.

**Symptoms of rheumatic fever**
- Inflamed, tender joints
- Headache
- Stomach ache
- Fever

If the heart has been affected, a child will also be pale and listless and will tire easily.

**Treating rheumatic fever** If your child develops rheumatic fever, his doctor may treat it with aspirin to curb inflammation and pain. Since rheumatic fever isn't a viral illness, the risk of Reye syndrome brought on by aspirin is very small; antibiotics are generally prescribed to prevent a second attack.

# Rhinitis

Rhinitis is an inflammation of the mucus membrane that lines the nose.

**Causes of rhinitis** There are several types of rhinitis, but the most common ones are viral (commonly accompanying a cold or sinusitis), and allergic (triggered by pollens, house dust, molds, and pet dander and saliva).

**Symptoms of rhinitis**
- Nasal stuffiness and discharge of mucus
- Sneezing
- Facial pressure and pain

**Treating rhinitis** Treatment will depend on the type of rhinitis your child has. If it's caused by a cold virus, you'll need to treat the cold. If it's caused by allergies, you'll need to reduce the allergens. If the rhinitis accompanies sinustitis, you'll also need to treat that condition.

# Ringworm (tinea)

Ringworm isn't caused by a worm. It's actually a common fungal infection of the skin and/or scalp.

**Causes of ringworm** Ringworm on the skin is transmitted by person-to-person contact and by pet-to-person contact. The fungus can also live on items that have been handled by an infected person. Ringworm of the scalp is usually transmitted by person-to-person contact and from hats, brushes, and combs that have been used by an infected person. Occasionally, scalp ringworm is transmitted by an infected pet. You can help guard your child from ringworm infection by keeping her away from infected children. Also, check family cats and dogs for signs of infection—scaly, hairless areas—and have your veterinarian treat them. Throw away any hairbrushes, combs, or hats an infected person in the family has recently used, and wash pillowcases and bed linens in very hot, soapy water.

**Symptoms of ringworm**
- Round or oval red patches with rings that surround a smooth center. The patches may or may not itch and can sometimes resemble chapped skin.
- Balding patches on the child's head or thinning hair if the scalp is affected. Flaking and itching of the scalp may also appear.
- The affected areas may become inflamed and tender.

**Diagnosing ringworm** Your child's doctor may diagnose ringworm by viewing the rash under a special violet-colored lamp called a Wood's light, or by taking a scraping from one of the lesions.

**Treating ringworm** Ringworm on the body is usually treated with a topical antifungal medication. If your child's rash doesn't clear up within a few weeks, or large parts of her body are affected, the doctor may prescribe an oral antifungal medication.

Scalp ringworm is harder to treat than ringworm on the skin and usually requires four to eight weeks of oral antifungal medication. Your child's doctor will probably also prescribe a shampoo containing selenium sulfide.

## Rocky Mountain spotted fever

Rocky Mountain spotted fever is caused by an organism called *Rickettsia rickettsii.*

**Causes of Rocky Mountain spotted fever** This disease is transmitted by the bite of a tick—most often, the common dog tick. Rabbits and other small mammals can also carry the tick. If you have a dog, regularly check it for ticks and remove them immediately. If not treated promptly, Rocky Mountain fever can lead to shock and death. With treatment, the infection usually runs its course within three weeks. In rare cases, the nervous system, heart, lungs, digestive system, and kidneys may be affected.

**Symptoms of Rocky Mountain spotted fever** Symptoms usually appear one to 14 days after the bite and may include:
• Flat, red spots on the palms and soles of the feet. These appear approximately five days after infection, but sometimes earlier. These spots then spread to the wrists, ankles, legs, arms, and trunk. Occasionally, the spots turn into pimplelike bumps. Some children experience no rash.
• Headache
• Fever
• Muscle pain and weakness
• Nausea, vomiting, and, occasionally, abdominal pain

**Treating Rocky Mountain spotted fever** Doctors treat the illness with antimicrobial drugs. Acetaminophen may also be recommended to reduce fever and muscle pain.

*For information on removing a tick, see **page 667**.*

# Roseola

Roseola is common infection caused by human herpes virus 6 and possibly human herpes virus 7. It typically affects kids between 6 months and 2 years of age and is most common during the spring and summer.

### Symptoms of roseola
- A sudden high fever, which can soar to 106°F and usually lasts three days
- Reddish-pink spots on the trunk, face, arms, and legs that last from 24 to 48 hours
- A loss of appetite
- Sometimes, swollen glands or a runny nose

**Treating roseola** If you suspect your child has roseola, call the doctor. Call the doctor again if your child's fever lasts more than three days or he is lethargic, especially cranky, or has a convulsion. Treatment includes acetaminophen for fever and lots of fluids to prevent dehydration.

# Salmonella (animal-borne)

Salmonella is a bacterium that can be transmitted through cold-blooded animals such as lizards, iguanas, and turtles, as well as tainted food. Young children are particularly susceptible. About 75,000 cases of salmonella infection per year are traced to contact with reptiles.

*Also see **page 603** for information on food poisoning.*

**Causes of animal-borne salmonella** A person can become infected by touching an infected reptile's feces, usually while cleaning its cage. Simply handling an infected reptile can also transmit the disease. Because of the likelihood that turtles, particularly, can spread the bacterium, the sale of these animals in pet stores has been banned in many places. The Centers for Disease Control and Prevention strongly recommend that no reptiles be kept in a home with children under the age of 5, even if the children never come in direct contact with the animal.

*For information on treating diarrhea, see page 583; fever, see page 598; vomiting, see page 661.*

### Symptoms of animal-borne salmonella
- Diarrhea, which is sometimes bloody
- Fever
- Stomach cramps and vomiting

**Treating animal-borne salmonella** If your child has symptoms of salmonella after being in contact with a lizard, iguana, or turtle, call the doctor. In adults and children over the age of 1, the infection usually runs it course in five to seven days. In babies, salmonella can spread to the bloodstream and nervous system, and will require treatment by a physician. In older children, treat the symptoms accordingly.

## Scabies

Scabies is a contagious skin condition.

**Causes of scabies** Scabies is caused by a tiny mite that burrows under the skin. It occurs most often on the wrists, the backs of hands, the area between the fingers, the pubic area, and on the abdomen. It is usually transmitted by person-to-person contact.

### Symptoms of scabies
- The appearance of groups of pimplelike eruptions topped with scabs
- Many scratch marks from constant itching

**Treating scabies** If you suspect that your child has scabies, schedule an appointment with her doctor immediately for proper diagnosis. If your child is infected, the doctor will recommend that she—and everyone else in the home—be treated with a special mite-killing topical medication.

## Scarlet fever (scarlatina)

Scarlet fever is a bacterial infection, characterized by a reddish, sandpaper-like rash.

Left untreated, scarlet fever can lead to ear, sinus, and lung infections as well as to rheumatic fever. Very rarely, it results in an inflammation of the kidneys.

**Causes of scarlet fever** Scarlet fever is caused by the streptococcus bacteria, the same bacteria that causes strep throat.

**Symptoms of scarlet fever**
- A bright, red rash on the face, under the arms, and in the groin area, which may spread to the rest of the body
- Rough and peeling skin
- Sore throat
- Fever of 101 to 104°F
- Headache

**Treating scarlet fever** Call the doctor if you suspect scarlet fever. Treatment includes antibiotics. Acetaminophen may be used to lower fever.

# Sinusitis

Sinusitis is an inflammation of the sinuses. Complications from sinusitis are rare, but because the sinuses are so close to the brain, it is possible for bacteria from a severe infection to spread to the brain, triggering meningitis.

**Causes of sinusitis** Sinusitis results when the sinuses become inflamed due to an allergy or infected as a result of a cold.

**Symptoms of sinusitis**
- Swelling of the lining of the nose and sinuses
- Headache
- Pain behind or over the eyes.
- Clear, thick, and yellowish or whitish nasal discharge
- A cough
- Swelling around the eyes upon awakening.
- Sometimes, persistent bad breath
- A fever, if the sinusitis is caused by a cold
The following symptoms indicate complications that require immediate medical care:
- Swelling of the eyes that lasts all day
- Very severe headache
- Sensitivity to light
- Irritability

*For information on removing allergens, see* **page 793**.

**Treating sinusitis** Call the doctor if your child has symptoms of sinusitis.

Allergy-related sinusitis usually clears up when the allergen is removed. Occasionally, allergy-related sinusitis requires antibiotic treatment because the child's nasal passages are so blocked that bacteria-breeding fluid has accumulated in the sinuses.

Because cold-related sinusitis is caused by a buildup of bacteria in the sinus area, it is usually treated with oral antibiotics. In some cases, antibiotic treatment isn't effective and the infected sinuses have to be drained. Very rarely, surgery is necessary.

## Snoring

All children snore on occasion. However, snoring can also be a symptom of adenoiditis or tonsilitis, allergies, or apnea. If snoring interferes with your child's sleep or is particularly pronounced, discuss the condition with his physician.

### When to Call the Doctor

If your child's sore throat is accompanied by any of the following symptoms, call her doctor immediately:
- Drooling
- White spots on a reddened throat
- A rash, which could signal scarlet fever, triggered by a strep infection
- A fever of 102°F or higher
- Pain when swallowing
- Swollen or tender glands in neck
- Hoarseness

Also call if a sore throat persists for more than 2 weeks.

## Sore throat

A sore throat in a child shouldn't be taken lightly since it can signal a strep infection or infected tonsils or adenoids.

**Causes of sore throat** Often, a sore throat is caused by colds or other viruses, postnasal drip from an allergy, which irritates the tissues in the throat, or overheated, dry rooms.

**Diagnosing a sore throat** All sore throats that last more than one day need to be cultured to determine the cause. Infections, left untreated, could cause serious complications.

**Treating a sore throat** The underlying condition must be treated. In cases of simple irritation due to overheated dry rooms or over-air conditioned rooms:
- Give the child plenty of fluids.
- Place cool-mist humidifiers in rooms where the child spends most of her time.

- Lower the thermostat to 68°F during winter. In summer, aim air-conditioning vents upward so they don't blow air onto a child's face.

# Stomach ache

A stomach ache is a symptom of a gastrointestinal or other illness or may be the result of an injury.

**Causes of stomach aches**  Childhood tummy turbulence can be caused by a host of things—indigestion, a mild stomach virus, a gastrointestinal parasite, food poisoning, or appendicitis. Illnesses not directly related to the stomach or intestines, including urinary tract infections, strep throat, and colds, can also trigger tummy troubles in children. A child who has asthma or pneumonia may complain of an upset stomach, since he has to work his stomach muscles very hard to breathe. A chronically constipated youngster will suffer frequent stomach pain that's relieved once he has a bowel movement. Sometimes, a child gets a tummy ache because he is upset or fearful about something. A blow to the abdomen can also trigger a stomach ache, which could be a sign of internal bleeding.

**Symptoms of mild stomach ache**
- Complaints of pain, though sufferers will basically act like themselves
- Paleness or looking flushed, but not looking seriously ill
- Ease of movement. A child does not complain of worsening pain when she moves.
- Ease of breathing. A child does not appear to be struggling for breath or to be breathing rapidly.
- Vomiting. A child with a mild stomach upset may vomit a few times over a 24-hour period. The vomit appears to be undigested food.
- Decreased appetite
- Diarrhea. No blood appears in the stool.
- No signs of dehydration

**"IT WORKED FOR ME"**

## Comfort Foods

When my 3-year-old had a stomach virus, she didn't want to eat solid food, even after she stopped vomiting. I remembered that when I had severe morning sickness I was hungry for only three things—watermelon, frozen lemonade "cubes," and potato chips—so I gave my daughter cut up chunks of watermelon (with the seeds removed), lemonade pops, and a few potato chips. These foods stimulated her appetite and within a few hours she asked for some cereal, and later, mashed potatoes. The next day, she was ready for baked chicken.

### Treating mild stomach upsets

• Try to determine the source of his discomfort and treat the source. Could he be constipated? Does his tummy hurt when he urinates? Has he recently eaten something that may not agree with him? Is he feeling stressed? Is he hungry?

• Ask how he feels about eating and/or drinking. Offer him any bland food that interests him. If he doesn't want to eat, don't force him to. Offer small amounts of an over-the-counter electrolyte solution to infants and toddlers and a high-sugar, no-fizz liquid to older children. A tablespoon every 15 to 20 minutes will usually help the child feel better.

• If your child vomits, let the stomach rest for an hour before offering these solutions again.

*For information about deydration, see **page 579**.*

• Avoid giving your child OTC or prescription medications for indigestion, gas, diarrhea, or constipation without consulting her doctor. Also, don't give a child Pepto-Bismol; it contains an aspirin derivative, which can cause Reye syndrome.

• Avoid giving ibuprofen if your child has a fever or headache, because this medication can cause further tummy upset. Give acetaminophen instead to reduce fever and headache pain.

If your child's tummy ache continues for more than 8 hours or gets worse, call his physician.

**Signs of severe stomach upsets** A child with a serious tummy ache needs prompt medical attention to rule out appendicitis or other life-threatening medical conditions. Symptoms of severe abdominal/gastrointestinal distress include:

• Unusual behavior. A child may be listless, extremely irritable, or exhibiting great pain.

• Paleness. A child may appear flushed and may feel clammy.

• Increased pain with movement. A child may walk in a crouched, tummy-holding position.

• Difficulty breathing. A youngster's breathing may be labored or very rapid.

• Frequent vomiting

• Vomit may resemble bile or may contain blood.

• No appetite. A child has no interest in food and may be repelled by the sight of food.

• Excessive sleepiness. He may fall into a deep sleep, awakened only by pain or vomiting.

- Signs of dehydration
- Excesssive diarrhea

**Treating severe or chronic stomach ache** Call the doctor or take your child to the ER.

# Strep throat

Strep throat is a contagious bacterial infection. Left untreated, it can lead to rheumatic fever or scarlet fever.

**Causes of strep** Strep throat is triggered by group A streptococcus. Most kids contract strep from other infected kids. The bacteria are transmitted by respiratory secretions on hands, toys, and other objects. Strep can occasionally be passed between dogs and humans, so if your child has frequent bouts of strep throat that can't be linked to a particular cause, ask your veterinarian to test your dog for strep. If the dog is infected, he'll need to be treated.

**Symptoms of strep**
- White spots on a red throat are the most tell-tale sign, but sometimes the spots are hard to see.
- Fever
- Difficulty swallowing
- Sometimes, swollen glands in the neck

**Diagnosing strep** Call your child's doctor if your child develops even a mild sore throat and a low-grade fever lasting longer than 24 hours. Because of complications that can arise if left untreated, it's essential to call the doctor if you suspect your child may have strep. The doctor will take a throat culture.

**Treating strep** Strep is treated with antibiotics, which will curb pain and other symptoms within about 24 hours. Your child must take the full course of antibiotics to completely cure the infection. The doctor may also recommend acetaminophen to reduce pain.

Offer your child nonacidic foods and beverages. Mildly warm liquids, including chicken soup, and cool ice pops may soothe irritated throat tissue.

**PEDIATRICK**

## *Preventing Strep Reinfection*

If your child has strep throat, changing his toothbrush may prevent reinfection. Give him a new toothbrush 48 hours after he starts taking antibiotics, then a second one after the course of treatment ends.

# Stress

A child, like an adult, can feel stressed by tensions in the home, by changes such as a move or the arrival of a new family member, busy schedules, and many other causes. Since stress lowers immunity and puts your child at greater risk for other illnesses, it's important that her stress levels be reduced. The best remedy is to eliminate or reduce the sources of stress. When the stress is brought on by external factors such as a busy schedule, simply offering your child more downtime can do the trick. However, not all stress is so easily eliminated. In those instances, it's important to limit a child's exposure to the stress, when possible, and to allow the child to talk freely about household tensions, such as illness in the family, so that she understands that she is not the cause of any family difficulties. Your reassurance and care can go a long way to helping to reduce stress. A child can also learn stress-relieving routines to lower her anxiety levels.

### Stress-relieving exercises

• Have your child lie on her back and slowly inhale on a count of four, hold her breath for a count of two, and then, when you say the word "relax," exhale to the count of four. Have her pretend her stomach is a balloon and she's blowing it up; this will help her breathe with her diaphragm, rather than her chest muscles. Suggest she whisper "relax" when she exhales. Eventually, just saying "relax" to herself will evoke a warm, relaxed feeling.

# Swollen glands

Lymph glands—which are located in the neck, the armpits, and the groin—are part of the body's natural defense system against disease. Swelling indicates an infection somewhere in the body.

**Causes of swollen glands** Swollen glands can be triggered by a variety of ailments, including mononucleosis, German measles, mumps, and strep throat.

**Symptoms of swollen glands** You may notice a slight swelling in one or more of the lymph areas. The gland will feel somewhat hard and will move around slightly when you touch it.

**Treating swollen glands** Call your child's doctor if she develops swollen glands. The treatment will depend on the source of the inflammation.

# Tetanus (lockjaw)

Tetanus is a serious bacterial infection, which triggers a toxic reaction. In rare instances, tetanus can be fatal.

**Causes of tetanus** The bacterium *Clostridium tetani* is responsible for a tetanus infection. The bacterium can enter the body through a puncture wound, a cut or deep scrape, or a burn.

**Symptoms of tetanus**
• Muscle spasms near the wound
• Involuntary muscle contractions that can cause the jaw to lock in place. An infant has difficulty nursing or sucking on a bottle because her jaw has locked.
• Twisting of the neck and arching of the back
• Convulsions
• Rapid heartbeat
• Low-grade fever
• Profuse sweating

If your child suffers a puncture wound, cut, scrape, or burn—and hasn't received a DTaP (diphtheria, tetanus, pertussis) vaccination—call her doctor. If she develops any symptoms of tetanus, take her to a hospital emergency room immediately. Doctors will administer tetanus antitoxins, antibiotics, and muscle relaxants.

To guard your child against tetanus, make sure she receives her DTaP immunizations on schedule and that she wear shoes when outdoors (she should wear rubber-soled swimming shoes at beaches and lakes).

*For information on vaccination, see **page 545**.*

# Tics

A tic is more than a nervous habit. A habit is a behavior a child can control—if he decides to—but a tic is an involuntary muscle movement, such as eye blinking or tongue clicking. Some kids can't help sticking their tongues out, almost as if they need to stretch them. Others open their mouths wide, shrug their shoulders, or shake their heads. Vocal tics include clearing the throat, sniffing, coughing, or saying words out of context.

**Causes of tics** Although a tic may signify that your child is experiencing stress, it isn't necessarily a direct response to a stressful situation; it can sometimes happen randomly. Some experts feel there's a gene that makes a child more prone to developing tics. The good news is that most tics disappear after a few weeks or months. They may never recur, or they may come back for a little while and then disappear again. Because a tic is difficult to control, don't tell your child to stop his tic.

**Treating tics** If the tic is especially noticeable, explain to your child's teachers and other adults who see him frequently that his behavior is involuntary and that talking with the child about the problem could increase his anxiety and make the problem worse. If a tic worsens or your child is being ridiculed by other kids, tell his doctor. She may be able to prescribe a medication that can help control the condition.

# Toe-walking

It's not unusual for a child to tiptoe as she learns to take her first steps. Walking on tiptoes may make a child feel more "balanced." Occasionally, walking on tiptoe—or toe-walking—becomes a habit, but it usually subsides within a few months.

If your child toe-walks for longer than this, the doctor should examine her to rule out an underlying problem. Occasionally, toe-walking is caused by a shortened Achilles tendon—the cord that attaches the heel bone to the leg bone. This makes it difficult for a child to put her foot down flat.

# Tuberculosis (TB)

TB is a chronic bacterial infection of the lungs.

**Causes of TB** TB is spread when an infected person coughs and others inhale the germs. In rare cases, TB is spread via unpasteurized milk. Children under 2, and those whose immune systems are compromised, are at highest risk for contracting TB since their immune systems are less developed than those of older kids. Rarely, the TB bacteria spreads through the person's bloodstream, affecting many organs in his body.

**Symptoms of TB** An infected child may have no symptoms. Some children can harbor the bacteria for years and show no symptoms until adolescence or adulthood. If symptoms do appear, they include:

- Fever
- Persistent cough
- Weakness
- Rapid breathing
- Swollen glands
- Irritability
- Night sweats
- Weight loss
- Poor growth

**Diagnosing TB** TB exposure can be detected by a skin test—the Tine Test—in which killed TB germs are injected into the skin. If the child is infected, or has been infected at some point during his life, the site of the injection will swell and turn red at the injection site within 48 hours. If your child's test is positive, his doctor will probably order a chest X ray which can show signs of current or past infection. The doctor may also test your child's sputum (cough secretions) for signs of TB bacteria.

**Treating TB** If the child doesn't have symptoms of active infection, the doctor will usually prescribe the oral antibiotic isoniazid, to be taken daily for six to nine months. Active TB infections require a combination of two or more medications given for as long as a year and a half. Though some kids are hospitalized initially, most of the treatment can take place at home.

If your child has come into contact with someone who has TB, he and anyone else who has been around the person may need to be treated with the antibiotic isoniazid for several months—even if they test negative for the disease.

# Undescended testicles

The testes develop in the abdomen of boys before birth. As the child nears birth, the testes descend into the scrotum, the small sack that houses them. But in a handful of boys, especially those who are born prematurely, one or both testicles fail to descend properly. In some boys, the descent will occur during the first nine months of life; in others, one or both testicles may sit just above the scrotum or lie in the inguinal canal, the tube that leads to the scrotum. In some boys, the testicles are sometimes present in the scrotum, but at other times—when the child is cold, for example—they move back up above the scrotum. In this case, the testicles are said to be "retractile."

**Causes of undescended testicles**  The cause of undescended testicles isn't clear, though insufficient hormones during gestation or a blockage in the inguinal canal may be to blame.

**Treating undescended testicles**  If your son has an undescended testicle, the doctor may test his response to hormones, though hormone therapy itself, a controversial treatment, is unlikely.

Surgery is the standard treatment and should be performed between 10 and 12 months of age. The procedure is done under general anesthesia on an outpatient basis. If an inguinal hernia (a small bulge in the groin; see page 620) is also present—which happens in about 50 percent of cases—both conditions may be treated surgically at the same time.

When undescended testicles aren't corrected within the first two years of life, a child has a higher than average risk of infertility as well as an increased risk of testicular cancer in young adulthood.

# Urinary tract infections

Urinary tract infection (UTI) is actually a catch-all term doctors use to describe several types of infections. *Cystitis* is the most common and is more likely to affect girls than boys. Other types of UTIs are *urethritis* and *pyelonephritis*.

**Causes of UTIs**  UTIs are usually caused by bacteria, especially the notorious *E. coli*, which enter the urinary tract through the urethra, the tube that leads up to the bladder. An infection that's confined to the bladder is usually referred to as cystitis. Girls (and adult women) are especially prone to *cystitis*, since *E. coli* and other bacteria that live in the rectum can easily travel to the urethra, then up to the bladder. Most often, this occurs when a child wipes from back to front after a bowel movement. Boys rarely get cystitis, primarily because their urethra is located so far away from their rectum.

A child with cystitis may also suffer from *urethritis*, an inflammation of the urethra. Urethritis can develop separately from cystitis—and is often triggered by a substance that irritates the urethra, including bubble bath, scented soaps, and scented or rough toilet paper.

Occasionally, cystitis can lead to a serious kidney infection, called *pyelonephritis*. This occurs when bacteria that have multiplied in the bladder travel up the ureters, the two tubes that connect the bladder to the kidneys. Sometimes, a bacterial infection in the bloodstream can lead to pyelonephritis.

### Symptoms of cystitis
- Discomfort or pain when urinating
- A need to urinate frequently
- Blood in the urine
- Fever
- Possible lower abdominal pain and tenderness

### Symptoms of urethritis
- Burning pain during urination
- Sometimes, increased urination

### Symptoms of pyelonephritis
- High fever
- General abdominal pain
- Back pain, just below the rib cage

This UTI is less likely to trigger frequent or painful urination.

**Diagnosing UTIs** If you suspect your child is suffering from a UTI, take her to the doctor as soon as possible. If she has symptoms

---

## Preventing UTIs

Teach your child—especially your daughter—to wipe from front to back after urinating or after a bowel movement. If your child is prone to UTIs, have her switch from synthetic to cotton underpants and don't let her sit around for long periods in a wet bathing suit. If your child is prone to urethritis, she should avoid anything that may irritate the urethra, including scented toilet paper, bubble bath, and harsh or scented bath soaps. Research suggests that drinking cranberry juice may lessen the risk of recurrent cystitis.

of pyelonephritis, call her doctor immediately.

Because a young child has a greater risk of developing kidney damage from UTIs than an adult, it's essential that she receive prompt treatment for any UTI. The doctor will take a urine sample for culturing. If your child has a serious UTI, her doctor will probably do further tests, such as an ultrasound to check her kidneys.

**Treating UTIs**  If your child has an infection, the doctor will prescribe an antibiotic, which will usually clear symptoms in two or three days. Make sure she takes the entire course of medication (often she may need to take it for as long as 10 days); otherwise, the bacteria may regrow and she could suffer a relapse.

# Vaginal infections

Although a thick, mucousy, creamy white or bloody vaginal discharge is normal in newborn girls, any discharge—other than a clear one—after the first few weeks of life could signal an infection. Vaginitis and vulvovaginitis are inflammations of the vagina and/or the vulva, the external female genitalia, which includes the labia or lips of the vagina.

**Causes of vaginal infections**  Vaginitis and vulvovaginitis may be caused by harsh or scented bath soap; sitting for prolonged periods in bubble bath or wet diapers; and the use of strong laundry detergents, particularly on underwear. Occasionally, an object that a girl has inserted in her vagina will trigger vaginal inflammation and a foul smelling, bloody discharge. Other causes of vaginal infections are yeast, an infectious fungal organism, and strep, which can be transferred to the vagina from a strep infection of the throat. The latter can happen when a child picks her nose and wipes herself after using the toilet, without washing her hands in between.

**Symptoms of vaginal infections**
• Vaginal itching
• A smelly discharge
• Occasionally, some bleeding, due to irritation of the delicate tissue

**Treating vaginal infections**  If your child has any symptoms of vaginal irritation or infection, the doctor should examine her to determine the cause and appropriate treatment. Depending on what the doctor finds, your child may be prescribed topical and/or oral antibiotics or fungal medications. If the infection has been triggered by a foreign object, the doctor will remove it.

# Vomiting

Vomiting isn't an illness—it's a symptom of a variety of ailments.

**Causes of vomiting** A viral gastrointestinal infection is the primary cause of vomiting in a child. However, a bacterial infection, food poisoning, and nongastrointestinal ailments such as ear and urinary tract infections, colds, flu, pneumonia, meningitis, allergies , and appendicitis can also trigger vomiting. Vomiting occurs when a child's abdominal muscles and diaphragm contract so strongly that the stomach contents are forced up through the esophagus and out through the mouth, and, sometimes, the nose.

**When vomiting signals a mild illness** Vomiting is not considered serious if the vomit is made up of undigested food particles; the vomiting lasts less than 24 hours; and the vomiting is not accompanied by other serious symptoms.

**Treating mild bouts of vomiting**
• Prevent choking. Keep your child upright to prevent him from inhaling the vomit. If he's sleepy, position him on his side, rather than on his back.
• Rehydrate. One hour after your child has vomited, offer him about 2 ounces of cool water to restore liquids he has lost from throwing up. Give him 2 ounces of water every 30 minutes or so after that. If he's vomited a

## When to Call the Doctor

• Projectile vomiting. Sometimes a child throws up so forcefully that she spews the vomit across the room, a symptom known as projectile vomiting. A single incident is no cause for alarm, but repeated episodes of projectile vomiting may signal more serious conditions.

• Vomit contains blood, which may signal internal bleeding.

• Vomit is green-colored, indicating the presence of bile.

• Vomiting is accompanied by severe pain, which could indicate appendicitis.

• Vomiting is accompanied by fever.

• Vomiting is accompanied by signs of dehydration.

• Vomiting continues for more than 24 hours in a child over the age of 1 or for more than 8 hours in a child under age 1.

• Vomiting is accompanied by lethargy.

• Vomiting is accompanied by seizures.

• Child can't keep down any fluids.

lot, ask your doctor whether you shuld give him an electrolyte solution. Do not give any milk or dairy products for 24 hours. Let him suck on popsicles if he finds that easier than drinking.

- Withhold solid foods for about 24 hours. Gradually return him to his normal diet, unless he continues to vomit.
- Don't give OTC or prescription medications to prevent vomiting unless your doctor recommends them.

*See **page 74** for information on projectile vomiting.*

# Warts

A wart is defined as a hard bump that is usually brown, yellow, or gray. Warts may occur singly or in clusters anywhere on the body. When they appear on the bottom of the feet, they're known as "plantar warts" and are often painful.

**Causes of warts** Warts are caused by the human papilloma virus, which thrives in moist environments and can be transmitted through person-to-person contact. Children are especially prone to plantar warts because they tend to walk barefoot in public areas, such as pools and locker rooms.

**Treating warts** Warts on the hands and other areas of the body are often treated with topical medications, freezing, burning, or laser surgery. But they tend to recur. Researchers have discovered that an oral drug that is typically used for ulcers, cimetidine, given three times daily may cause the warts to become flatter and less visible. Two months into the study, the warts had disappeared in 80 percent of the children. Cimetidine seems to be safe for children and doesn't seem to cause side effects. If your child is prone to multiple outbreaks of warts, ask her doctor about cimetidine treatment.

Doctors treat plantar warts with OTC medications containing salicylic acid; cryotherapy (freezing with liquid nitrogen); cauterizing (burning the wart); or surgical removal. Another form wart-removal treatment involves the use of pulse-dye lasers.

If your child has plantar warts, discard her shoes, unless they can be thoroughly washed with a disinfectant, and wash socks as soon as she starts treatment. During a flare-up, regularly clean your bathroom, including the tub floor and rubber tub mat, with a disinfectant to keep other family members from getting infected.

# *Caring for sick kids*

Taking care of a sick youngster can be stressful. Often, a child's ear infection or bout with the flu bug means that Mom or Dad has to take a day off from work, cancel prearranged activities, or track down another caregiver who can stay with the sick child. When this occurs, the best you can do is to concentrate on helping your child to feel better. If your child hasn't learned to talk yet, he won't be able to tell you what he needs. You'll simply have to guess at what remedies will ease his discomfort. If he's older and able to voice his needs, ask what might make him feel better. An ice pop for a sore throat? Gelatin for a tummy ache?

Make sure your child is comfortable—and isn't bored. If your son has a cold, he needn't stay in bed. He might feel more comfortable on the sofa, where he can watch a favorite video. Or offer to let your child spend a sick day in your bed for a change of pace. Often, kids find Mom and Dad's bed more comfortable than their own, and there's plenty of space to spread out books and games.

A child who is sick often has a poor appetite. Take your cues from your child when it comes to food. If her throat is sore, serve "slippery" foods, like pudding. If she has an earache, she won't want to chew very much, so offer softer items like cooked cereal, bread, or mashed potatoes. To stimulate her appetite, serve food in an appealing or novel way: decorate her place setting with flowers, action figures or little plastic animals, and fun straws.

Since you and your child are stuck at home, make the most of your time by reading or playing games together.

# First Aid

## Handling medical emergencies

It's important to learn how to deal with an emergency before it happens. Now is the time to educate yourself, your children, and those who care for your children in first aid and to gather the necessary materials you need to handle an emergency effectively.

### Emergency preparedness

- Know who to call for help. Post community emergency numbers prominently near each phone. Know which hospital in your area has the best pediatric emergency room.
- Post your home address and phone number near your phone for use by your child's caregivers or other visitors who may need to report this information to emergency personnel. When traveling, always have the address of where you're staying readily available.

*See **page 697** for information on creating your family first-aid kit.*

- Keep a first-aid kit ready at home, in the car, and on vacation. Be sure that others who care for your children know where it is.
- Keep medical records and the names and numbers of your child's physicians in a handy file that you can take with you to an emergency room. If you don't have such a file easily accessible, do not waste time gathering this information on your way to the ER.

*See **page 621** for information on keeping medical records.*

- Learn rescue breathing, CPR, and the Heimlich maneuver, and special rescue techniques for infants. Knowing how to perform these routines can save your child's life if she stops breathing, her heart stops beating, or if she's choking. The American Red Cross and the American Heart Association offer comprehensive child-rescue courses. See the white pages of your phone book for the location nearest you. All parents and caregivers are strongly urged to take these classes.
- Keep your child's tetanus boosters up to date.
- Prepare your child for an emergency. As soon as she's capable of understanding, usually by age 4, teach your child how to use the phone to call for help. Also instruct her in the following emergency procedures.

**Teaching emergency procedures to your child**   Make sure your child knows what to do in case of an emergency:
- Teach her how to use the telephone to call you, a neighbor, a relative, or a close friend in an emergency. If you have a phone with speed dialing, you can preprogram it so your child will only need to press one button. (In this case, even a preschooler can learn to use it.)
- Place emergency numbers next to the phone. If you have a 911 service in your area, make sure your child understands what the service is for and knows the information she needs to have if she calls.
- Make sure she knows her full name, your full name, address, and phone number as early as possible. Many 5-year-olds are capable of learning some or all of this information. When outside, consider having her wear an ID bracelet or putting your business card or other ID in her pocket.
- Rehearse making emergency calls and talking to appropriate strangers.

## Quick Guide for First Aid

Allergies (severe), 666

Back injuries, 667
Bee stings, 669
Bites, 667
Bleeding (external), 669
Bleeding (internal), 670
Blisters, 671
Bone and joint
    injuries, 671
Breaks and
    sprains, 671
Breathing difficulties, 674
Bruises, cuts,
    scrapes, 670
Bug bites, 669
Burns, 678

Choking, 676
Concussion, 688
Convulsions/seizure, 682
CPR, 675

Drowning, 682

Ear injuries, 683
Electrical shock, 684
Eye injuries, 684

Fainting, 686
Frostbite, 686

Hand and finger
    injuries, 687
Head and neck
    injuries, 687

Heat cramps, 688
Heat exhaustion, 688
Heat rash, 689
Heat stroke, 690

Mouth/tooth injuries, 690

Nose injuries, 692

Poisoning, 693
Poison ivy, etc., 694

Rescue breathing, 674

Shock, 695
Splinters, 696
Stings, 667
Sunstroke, 690

## Assessing and treating injuries

**When to seek emergency medical care**  Call 911 (or your local emergency number) and/or take your child to the ER (emergency room) immediately for treatment if your child:
- Has difficulty breathing
- Has swelling in the face or throat
- Is bleeding profusely
- Has a head or neck injury or injury to his eyes
- Is unconscious
- Has a near-electrocution or near-drowning experience
- Has a seizure

## Allergies

*For treating non-life-threatening allergies, see **page 553**.*

Most common allergies will not require first aid. However, severe asthma attacks, severe allergic reactions to foods, insect bites, or bee stings can require quick action to save your child's life.

**Assessing allergic reactions**  If your child develops any of the following allergic reaction symptoms, call 911 or take him to a hospital emergency room immediately:
- Wheezing or noisy breathing; difficulty breathing
- Difficulty swallowing
- Swelling of the face, lips, throat, or penis
- Lightheadedness, dizziness, fainting

If your child develops any of these non lifethreatening symptoms, keep a close eye on him to ensure that his condition does not worsen:
- Hives
- Flushed skin
- Generalized itching
- Vomiting
- Diarrhea
- Abdominal cramps

**PARENTS RESOURCE**

For more information about **Medic Alert**, call (800) 825-3785 or visit www.medicalert.org.

### Treating severe allergic reactions
- Provide first aid immediately for any breathing difficulty
- Keep an epinephrine kit handy at all times if your child has a potentially life-threatening allergy.

• Have your child wear a Medic Alert bracelet that describes his allergy.

# Back injuries

Seek medical help for all serious back injuries. Do not move your child, if at all possible. Allow trained medical personnel to transport your child to the hospital.

# Bites and stings

You'll need to seek medical help if:
• An animal or human bite breaks the skin.
• Your child is bitten by a wild animal or one suspected of carrying disease.
• Your child is stung by any marine animal. Most marine stings are relatively harmless, but a handful of children suffer a severe reaction, including shock and cessation of breathing.
• The victim exhibits any signs of allergic reaction or shock—such as difficulty breathing, extensive hives, swelling, or a loss of consciousness.

*Also see rescue breathing, **page 674**, and shock, **page 695**.*

### Treating animal or human bites
• Wash the bite area immediately with soap and warm water. Run the water over the bite for about 10 minutes, if possible. Don't worry if the wound bleeds a little. Avoid antibiotic ointments because the ingredients won't kill many of the bacteria present. Cover the cleaned wound with a sterile gauze dressing.
• Get information about the biter. If a neighbor's pet was the culprit, find out if the animal has been vaccinated against rabies. Ask to see the vaccination certificate, or check with the animal's vet, if possible. If the animal is a stray dog or is wild—a raccoon, squirrel, bat, or fox, for example—your child's health-care provider will determine whether your child needs to be treated for rabies. If the bite is from a human, determine if the person has any infectious diseases for which your child should be treated.
• If the skin has been broken, follow up this first aid with a visit to your child's health-care

**PEDIATRICK**

## *How to Remove a Tick*

Using fine-tipped tweezers, grasp the tick as close to its mouth and as close to your child's skin as possible. Firmly but gently pull the tick up and out. Don't squeeze or twist the tick's body—bacteria could be released into your child's bloodstream. Also, don't use nail polish or a lit match to remove the tick.

Once the tick is out, apply alcohol or antibiotic ointment to the bite site.

# Symptoms and Treatments for Bee Stings and Bug Bites

The following is a guide to recognizing and treating some common bites and stings. For information on tick-borne illnesses, see Lyme disease, pages 499 and 631, and Rocky Mountain spotted fever, pages 499 and 646.

| BUG BITE | SYMPTOMS | TREATMENT |
|---|---|---|
| **Bee, wasp, yellow jacket, hornet** Swelling of skin with a puncture, caused by stinger, in center. | Burning sensation; pain. Itching may occur one to two days later. | Remove the stinger. Cleanse sting site in warm soapy water for five to ten minutes; apply OTC steroid cream.* If stings are numerous or very itchy, a prescription topical or oral steroid. |
| **Chigger, mite, red bug** May start as a tiny red dot; may later be surrounded by a flesh-colored or reddish swelling. Chiggers attach to exposed skin, but may burrow under waistbands, sock cuffs, and straps. | Intense itching. | Cool oatmeal bath; OTC or prescription steroid cream.* For severe itching oral steroids or antihistamines. |
| **Flea** A hive-like bump, about ¼ inch in size, which may swell to ½ inch. Bites may occur in threes. Ankles and legs are prime sites, but bites can occur anywhere. | Itching, sometimes followed by tenderness and burning. | Calamine lotion; OTC or prescription steroid cream.* |
| **Freshwater fluke** Clusters of hive-like bumps, usually on skin not covered by swimsuit, appear 10 to 20 hours after the tiny parasite, which lives in salt- and freshwater lakes, burrows into the skin. | Prickly sensation, itching, burning; can last up to two weeks until immune system destroys the parasite. | OTC or prescription steroid cream.* |
| **Horsefly** A hive-like bump that ranges from ⅛ to ¼ inch in diameter; can last for a few hours to several days. | Itching, possibly accompanied by pain. | Calamine lotion; OTC or prescription steroid cream.* |
| **Mosquito** A hive-like bump, about ¼ inch in diameter. May last a few hours to a week or longer. | Itching. | Cool compress; cool oatmeal bath, calamine lotion; OTC or prescription steroid cream.* |
| **Red "fire" ant** Resembles a mosquito bite; usually occurs on buttocks or legs after a child sits on ant-infested ground. | Itching; sometimes pain and tenderness. | Cool compresses; OTC or prescription steroid cream.* |

*Check with your child's doctor before using any topical steroid cream.

provider, or, if there's a deep wound, take your child to the ER. The physician will probably prescribe oral antibiotics (both animal and human mouths are full of bacteria that can cause infection), and may recommend a tetanus booster and/or rabies shots. Some deep bites require stitches.

## Bee stings and bug bites

Few kids make it through spring and summer without an occasional bug bite or sting. Fortunately, most bites and stings cause only minor discomfort and clear up within a few days. A parent's most difficult problem is identifying which bug caused the bite.

## Bleeding (external)

Seek medical attention if:
• A cut or blow leads to profuse external bleeding, or your child complains of pain or is vomiting blood, signaling possible internal bleeding.
• Infection appears.
• The cut is deep or is more than ½-inch in length or is on your child's face. You'll need to determine if the wound requires cosmetic treatment, stitches, and/or if your child needs a tetanus booster.

**Assessing and treating bleeding wounds on the head** If your child suffers a blow to the head that breaks the skin, expect lots of bleeding because the scalp has many small blood vessels. Sometimes, what appears to be a great gush of blood actually stems from an insignificant wound. To treat a bleeding head wound:
• Clean the cut gently with soap and water.
• Apply firm, uninterrupted pressure with a clean cloth for at least five minutes. Bleeding may take up to ten minutes to stop.

**PEDIATRICK**

### How to Remove a Stinger

Cleanse the sting site with soap and warm water. Using a stiff object, such as a credit car, gently scrape the stinger off. Don't press on it or try to pull it out, which could release more venom. After removing the stinger, cleanse the area again to remove surface venom and bacteria. Apply antibacterial ointment.

### How to Apply Pressure to a Bleeding Wound

• **Use a clean folded towel, clean diaper, or a washcloth.** If no cloth is available, use your bare hand; if possible, wash your hand in warm soapy water or rub it with a premoistened alcohol towelette before applying it to the open wound. (Don't apply an alcohol towlette directly to the wound.)

• **Leave the original towel or pad in place** even if it becomes soaked with blood. Removing the pressure of the towel for even a moment could increase blood loss. Just place a new towel over the soaked one.

*See page 627 for signs of infection.*

- Call your child's doctor if the cleaned wound appears deep or continues to bleed for more than ten minutes.

### Treating minor cuts and scrapes

- Wash the area thoroughly, but gently, with antibacterial soap and water to remove dirt.
- If the wound is bleeding, apply gentle pressure by holding a clean wet washcloth or paper towel on the wound.
- Apply a spray or lotion antiseptic and an antibiotic ointment.
- Cover the wound with a bandage or gauze pad secured with tape.
- After 12 hours or if the bandage gets wets or dirty, rewash the area, apply antiseptic spray and antibiotic ointment, and cover with a clean bandage or gauze pad.
- After 24 hours, remove the bandage or pad. If the wound is still raw, wash and rebandange it. If a scab has formed, leave the wound uncovered.
- Observe the wound for signs of infection.

**Treating profuse external bleeding:** For any severe external bleeding, you should seek immediate medical attention. While you're waiting for help, follow these procedures:

- Have your child sit or lie down.
- Apply pressure to the wound.
- Elevate the injured area above the heart, to help curb blood flow to the wound.
- Don't apply a tourniquet unless a doctor or the emergency operator advises you to do so.

## Bleeding (internal)

Seek medical help if there's any possibility of internal bleeding. Though internal bleeding is not obvious like external bleeding, it poses a very serious threat. A blow to the abdomen or head can trigger potentially dangerous internal bleeding that requires emergency medical assistance.

### Assessing abdominal injuries for signs of internal bleeding

The symptoms of abdominal injuries are:

- Bruise marks on the abdomen
- Blood in vomit, or coughed-up blood that is either bright red or dark, or has the consistency of coffee grounds
- Blood in the stool or urine

- Signs of shock, including cold, clammy, pale skin, a rapid, weak pulse, confusion, chills or "shakes," and sometimes, nausea

### Treating possible internal bleeding
- Call 911 immediately.
- Withhold all food and drink.

## Blisters

Children sometimes develop blisters on their feet—most often on and above the heels, on the sides of their feet, and on the tops of their toes—because of shoes that don't fit properly. These "friction" blisters are caused when shoes rub against tender skin. Unlike calluses, which are hard and develop over time, blisters erupt fairly quickly and are soft. Blisters can also result from finger sucking and from burns.

### Treating Friction Blisters
- Gently cleanse the area with mild soap and water.
- Cover it loosely with a bandage or sterile gauze pad.
- Keep the blister clean and dry.

Do not use a pin or other tool to break a blister. This could could cause the lesion to become infected. If a blister does break open, trim away the loose skin with a pair of sterilized nail scissors. Do not pull any skin that remains firmly attached, which would only enlarge the wound. And cover it with a bandage.

If at any point the blister develops pus or redness around the edges, it may have become infected, so call your child's doctor.

## Bone and joint injuries— breaks and sprains

Seek medical help for any possible broken, sprained, or dislocated bone.

**Assessing breaks** For most breaks to the arm, fingers, or toes, you can take your child to the hospital yourself. However, wait for an ambulance if the break is to the neck, back, hip, or leg, if the bone

---

**PEDIATRICK**

### Relieving Blister Pain

If your child develops a blister because a shoe is too loose and rubs up and down on his heel, have him wear two pairs of socks until you can get to a store to buy shoes that fit properly. The double layer of material will cut down on the friction between his shoe and his skin, as well as provide padding between his shoe and the blister.

*For treating burn blisters, see page 678.*

protrudes, or if there's additional serious injury. The emergency medical personnel will be able to move your child properly so that there's less risk of further damage.

### Treating breaks
• Don't give your child anything to drink or eat without first getting medical advice.
If a bone is protruding:
• Apply pressure to curb profuse bleeding.
• Don't try to move the bone back under the skin.
If you absolutely must move your child to take him to the hospital:
• Immobilize the injured limb or joint by splinting it.

**Assessing dislocations**  Have your child seen by her health-care professional if she dislocates any bones, even if you are able to replace the joint yourself.

**Treating a dislocated elbow**  If your child will allow it, you can try gently rotating his wrist to the palm-up and palm-down positions; this may release the trapped tissue between the elbow joints. But if his pain continues or he can't use his arm normally within a few minutes, support the arm with a sling made from a towel or cloth and seek medical attention.

**Treating a dislocated shoulder**  If your child has a dislocated shoulder, she'll feel pain in the shoulder and upper arm and you may or may not notice a deformity of the shoulder. The pain worsens with movement.

If you suspect your child has a dislocated shoulder, take her to a hospital emergency room. There, a doctor will probably X ray her shoulder to rule out an accompanying fracture. She will then maneuver the head of the humerus back into the shoulder socket. Your child will have to wear a sling for several weeks to make sure her shoulder is immobilized. The doctor may suggest giving acetaminophen or ibuprofen, as well as applying ice packs to the shoulder, to ease her pain.

**Assessing sprains**  Sprains are a stretching or tearing of the ligaments that hold the bones together at a joint. A sprain occurs when the ligaments in the ankle, wrist, or another joint are pulled suddenly. Sprains are fairly un-common in young children be-cause their ligaments are generally quite strong, but ac-tive toddlers and preschoolers occasionally suffer sprains—in part because they are always on the go and they are still rela-tively uncoordinated and apt to stumble frequently. The most commonly sprained joint in both kids and adults is the ankle. If your child has a sprain, she'll feel pain and the injured area will swell and eventually, bruise. She'll be able to move the injured limb fairly normally, though.

## Treating sprains

• Elevate the injured limb as much as possible, by placing the sprained leg or arm on a pillow.
• Apply ice packs. Do not apply ice directly to the skin.
• Support the sprained joints or muscles with an elastic ban-dage. Don't wrap the bandange so tightly, though, that you cut off circulation to the limb.
• Call your child's doctor, es-pecially if the sprain seems se-vere or pain continues for more than a couple of hours.

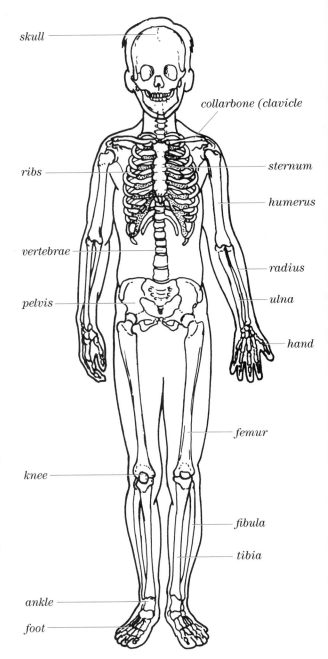

skull

collarbone (clavicle

ribs

sternum

humerus

vertebrae

radius

ulna

pelvis

hand

femur

knee

fibula

tibia

ankle

foot

# Breathing difficulties

The following instructions are best used as a reminder of the emergency procedures you have learned in a formal class. Before beginning any of these procedures, assess the situation carefully. Seek medical help if:

- Your child is unconscious.
- Your child turns blue.
- Your child cannot cough up an object.

**Assessing breathing**  Is your child conscious or unconscious? Is she breathing? Does she have a pulse? Do not administer rescue breathing or CPR if your child is breathing on her own and her heart is beating. If your child is not or appears not to be breathing, you must first perform rescue breathing. This may or may not be followed by CPR. If your child is choking on food or another object, you first need to clear her airway before performing rescue breathing and/or CPR.

**Performing rescue breathing**
Rescue breathing, which is manipulating an injured person's respiration when she cannot breathe on her own, should be performed if your child is not breathing as a result of a near drowning, an injury, or a severe allergic reaction. If your child is not breathing as the result of choking on an object, first apply the Heimlich maneuver.

If your child appears to be unconsious:
- Call your area emergency number or have someone else do so.
- Try to rouse her by shouting her name or tapping her shoulder. Do not shake her. She may have a head or neck injury which could be worsened by shaking.
- Check for breathing. If your child doesn't respond, place your ear over his mouth to listen for breathing. If he is breathing, take him to a hospital ER, or, if an ambulance is on its way, wait for the paramedics to arrive.

If your child has stopped breathing:
- Place him on a flat surface, such as a table or the floor. *Caution:* If you suspect he may have suffered a neck or spinal injury, move him very carefully, without bending his neck. If he is lying facedown, use one hand to support his head so that his neck doesn't twist when you roll him over.

- Tilt your child's head back slightly to open his airway. Do not tilt his head back too far, which could block the airway in an infant or toddler or worsen a neck injury in any child.
- Lift his chin up gently with one hand while pushing down on the forehead with the other hand. This will move his tongue from the back of his throat.
- Use your thumb and index finger to pinch your child's nose shut if he is over the age of 1.
- Place your mouth over his mouth to form a seal. For babies under the age of 1, place your mouth over his nose and mouth.
- Give your child two slow rescue breaths, each about 1½ seconds long, every 3 seconds. With infants, be careful not to breathe too forcefully.
- Take a deep breath between each rescue breath.

After giving two rescue breaths:
- Check to see if the child's chest is rising and falling, or place your ear by his mouth or nose to listen for breathing.

If he still isn't breathing:
- Gently tilt his head back again and repeat the rescue breathing process.Continue giving one rescue breath every 3 seconds, or about 20 breaths per minute until he begins breathing on his own.
- After two rescue breaths, check your child's pulse. For babies under 1, place a finger (not your thumb) on the artery in front of the elbow. For children age 1 and up, check the artery in the neck under the ear and behind the jawbone.

If you cannot detect a pulse:
- Assume that the child's heart has stopped beating and initiate CPR.

**Performing CPR for infants under 1 year of age** Perform CPR if your child has no pulse and he's not breathing:
- Place two or three fingers on her breastbone, about one finger-width below the nipple line, just below the sternum. Do not apply pressure to the tip of the sternum because it can cause internal damage.

**PARENTS ALERT**

## Vomiting During Rescue Breathing

If your child begins to vomit at any point during rescue breathing, turn her onto one side to prevent her from inhaling vomit. Use your finger to "sweep" vomit from her mouth. Reposition her on her back and continue rescue breathing. If you suspect that she has sustained a head or neck injury, be especially careful when turning her, using your hand to support her head and neck so that they don't twist, roll, or tilt forward or back.

- Press down about ½ to 1 inch. Do not exert too much pressure.
- Stop pressing, but don't remove your fingers. Allow your baby's sternum to return to its normal position.
- Continue chest compressions at a rate of at least 100 per minute.
- After completing compressions, give the child one long, slow breath. (See above.)
- Continue with 5 compressions, then one breath; 5 compressions, then one breath, until you can detect a pulse.
- If you haven't already called 911, do so as soon as your child begins breathing.

**Performing CPR for toddlers and older children** Perform CPR if your child has no pulse and he's not breathing:
- Place the heel of one hand over the lower third of the breastbone.
- Press down 1 to 1½ inches.
- Continue chest compressions at a rate of about 100 per minute.
- After completing 5 compressions, give the child one long, slow breath. (See rescue breathing above.)
- Continue with 5 compressions, then one breath; 5 compressions, then one breath, until you can detect a pulse.
- If you haven't already called 911, do so as soon as your child begins breathing.

## Choking

When a child breathes anything other than air into his windpipes, choking can occur. Kids, especially infants and toddlers, are prone to choking when a liquid goes down the wrong way. They will typically cough, gasp, and gag until the windpipe is cleared. Happily, inhaled liquids rarely cause any real harm since they are usually coughed up fairly quickly. Choking can be life threatening when a child swallows or inhales an object or food that blocks his airways and prevents air from getting to his lungs. Seek medical help if:
- Your child is unconscious and/or turns blue.
- He cannot dislodge the object on his own.
- If there is any possibility that the successfully applied first-aid treatment caused internal injuries.

**Assessing the situation** If your child can cough, let him continue to cough so he can expel the object. Do not pound on his back; this could cause whatever is obstructing the throat to lodge in the airways.

If your child is seriously choking on food or small object:
- He will not be able to talk.
- He will have difficulty breathing.
- His face will become red, then blue.

**Treating a choking condition** If your child experiences symptoms of life-threatening choking, stay calm and take the following steps immediately. Do not take time to call your local emergency number, but if someone else is available, have him or her do so.

**Dislodging foreign bodies in the airways of infants**
- Gently place the baby facedown on your forearm or lap. Her head should be lower than her trunk.
- For an infant under 20 pounds, stabilize her head and neck with your hand by resting your forearm against your leg or body.
- For a larger infant, you can lay the baby facedown over your lap. Use your hand to support his head.
- Using the heel of your free hand, give four rapid back blows between the shoulder blades to dislodge the object.

If your infant still can't breathe:
- Place her on a firm surface on her back.
- Using two fingers, give four rapid thrusts over the breastbone.
- If she still isn't breathing, open her airway using the tongue-jaw lift technique (described below) and look for a foreign body.
- If you see an object, use your finger to try to sweep it out.
- If your child still can't breathe on her own, start rescue breathing (see above).

**Performing the Heimlich maneuver for children over the age of 1**
- With your child in a sitting or standing position, stand or kneel behind him.
- Make a fist with one of your hands, with your thumb pointing toward your child's stomach.
- Place your fist just above his belly button.
- Using your other arm, reach around his body and cover your fist with your other hand. Keep your elbows pointed out.

- Deliver 6 to 20 abdominal thrusts, pulling your fists in and upward, until he coughs up the item he's swallowed.

If the object isn't dislodged:
- Lay your child on his back and kneel at his feet.
- Place the heel of one hand in the center of his body, between his belly button and rib cage.
- Place your other hand on top of the first hand.
- Press into his abdomen with a rapid, upward, but gentle thrust.
- If your child doesn't cough up the item, use the tongue-jaw lift (described below) and look into the back of his throat for the object. If you see it, sweep it out with your finger.
- If your child doesn't begin to breathe, start rescue breathing, (see above).
- If he still doesn't begin to breathe, repeat the Heimlich maneuver with a series of 6 to 10 abdominal thrusts.
- Alternate the Heimlich maneuver with rescue breathing, described above.
- Call for emergency help if you haven't already done so.

**Performing the tongue-jaw lift**
- Grasp your child's tongue and lower jaw between your thumb and forefinger to open the child's mouth.
- Use your thumb to press down gently on the tongue as you lift up the jaw.
- Look into the back of the throat for a foreign object.
- Use your finger to sweep the object aside. Be careful to use a gentle side-to-side motion to avoid pushing the object further into the airway.

# Burns

Burns larger than the size of a quarter, that blister immediately and/or that ooze require emergency medical attention.

Also seek medical help:
- For any burn that is more than superficial (small with slight redness).
- For all electrical burns (see below.)
- For a chemical burn, especially if the child has also inhaled noxious fumes or the burn is more than superficial or is large (see below).

- If any burn is on the hands, face, feet, or genitals.
- If redness or pain from a superficial burn continues for more than a few hours.
- If a burn that has been treated becomes infected. (An infected burn will become increasingly red and swollen despite treatment; there will probably also be increased pain.)

**Assessing burns**  Burns are divided into three categories, depending on severity.
- First-degree burns are the least serious. These burns cause redness and, sometimes, minor swelling of the skin.
- Second-degree burns cause blistering and significant swelling.
- Third-degree burns may appear charred or whitish. A third-degree burn is the most serious type and usually leads to severe injury of not only the surface layer of the skin, but the deeper tissues as well. Because a third-degree burn destroys nerve endings, the victim may feel little or no pain initially.

**Treating minor burns**
- Run cool water over the spot.
- Do not apply an ointment.
- Keep uncovered.

**Treating second- and third-degree burns**  If your child has a deep burn or a burn over a large area:
- Call your local emergency number immediately or rush the child to a hospital ER.
- Have your child lie flat while waiting for help.
- Remove clothing from the burned area; don't try to pull off clothes that are stuck to burned skin.
- Apply cool compresses to burned areas if possible. Do not apply pressure to burns.
- Don't use ointments, antiseptic sprays or lotions, creams, butter, or powder.
- Place a loose, clean sheet over your child if he seems cold.
- If the child's arms or legs are burned, place them on a pillow or any other object so that they are slightly higher than his heart.

**Treating chemical burns** If your child is burned by drain cleaner, lye, or any other caustic acid:
- Read the label on the chemical container and follow the steps for treatment.
- If the label explaining emergency treatment is not available, call the poison control center for instructions.
- If burns are extensive, or to the face, or if your child has trouble breathing from inhaling noxious fumes, seek medical help immediately.

While awaiting help:
- Gently brush off chemical matter from the skin using a dry towel, washcloth, clean diaper, or your own clothing. Do not risk spreading or activating the chemical by allowing contact with water.
- Remove any contaminated clothing. Be careful not to spread the chemical.
- Douse the affected skin area with cool water. If possible, wash gently with soap.

**Treating contact burns** If your child has been burned by contact with a hot material, such as a radiator or a playground slide, wrap the injury in a cool compress.

*For first aid for electrical shock, see **page 684**.*

**Treating electrical burns** If your child is burned by an electrical appliance or by lightning:
- Disconnect the power source or pull your child away from the source using a dry, non-metal object, such as a wooden spoon, broom handle, or chair leg; don't use your bare hands.
- Begin CPR if your child isn't breathing or his heart has stopped beating.
- Seek immediate medical attention for all electrical burns.

*See **page 675** for information on CPR.*

**Treating fire-caused burns** If your child has been burned by contact with fire, seek medical help immediately.

**Treating friction burns** If your child has been burned by friction, wrap the injury in a cool compress.

**Treating scalds** If your child has been burned by a hot liquid over an area larger than a quarter, call the doctor. If burns are extensive, take your child to the emergency room. If the burned area is oozing pus, cover very loosely with a sterile gauze pad and seek medical attention immediately.

If the scald is limited to a small area:
• Soak the area in cool water or gently run cool water over the area for 10 or 15 minutes to relieve pain, or apply clean, cool compresses.
• Do not put ice on the burn; it can cause more tissue damage.
• Do not put butter, ointments of any kind, petroleum jelly, vanilla, or powder on the burn. These can deepen the skin damage.
• Cover the burn area loosely with a sterile gauze pad.
• Call a doctor if redness and pain continue for more than three hours, pain is severe, or blistering occurs.

**Assessing sunburn** There are degrees of sunburn severity:
• *First degree.* Redness and slight irritation of the topmost layer of the skin. A first-degree sunburn may be treated at home, without the necessity of professional medical help (see below).
• *Second degree.* Redness and irritation that penetrate the top and second layers of the skin and cause blistering. A second-degree burn requires medical intervention for treatment. Children who have suffered second-degree sunburns need to be monitored throughout their lives for skin cancer.
• *Third degree.* This type of sunburn occurs rarely and affects the top, second, and third layers of the skin. Third-degree sunburns can cause permanent scarring and blistering. Because the sun's rays penetrate the skin's pain fibers, a third-degree burn may be painless. If your child has a severe sunburn that's accompanied by fever or chills, severe blistering, dizziness, delirium, dehydration, or shock, seek medical help immediately. Also regularly monitor your child for skin cancer.

**Treating minor sunburn**
• Place a cool, clean compress on the area, or let your child play in a tub of cool water. Add a half cup of baking soda or colloidal oatmeal to the water to help ease pain.

**PARENTS ALERT**

## Sunburn Ointment Warning

Ointments made to soothe adult sunburn pain are not appropriate for children, unless specifically prescribed by your child's doctor. Note that dibucaine, an anesthetic in some ointments, is extremely toxic to children if swallowed.

• Avoid covering the burn. Clothing rubbing against the burn can cause discomfort.

• Apply a light, unscented moisturizing lotion to the skin. During the first 24 hours, don't apply petroleum jelly because it can retain heat. Also, avoid medicated creams—such as hydrocortisone or benzocaine—which may irritate burned skin.

• Avoid sunlight until the burn heals. It takes a week to 10 days for a sunburn to heal completely.

• Offer pain relivers. If the child complains about stinging skin, give him acetaminophen, appropriate for his age and weight.

• Offer plenty of water to replenish lost fluids. Sunburn hampers the skin's ability to retain water.

**Treating severe sunburn** Take your child to the doctor immediately. Do not put any ointment, butter, antiseptic spray, or anything else on the burn. Do apply cool compresses.

**Treating blisters caused by minor burns** Wrap the injury in a cool compress. Do not put any ointment on the injury. Do not break the blister.

## Convulsions and seizures

*For more information about the causes of convulsions and seizures, see **page 598**.*

Convulsions and seizures can have a number of causes and can vary in their intensity.

### Treating convulsions and seizures

• Call 911 for any convulsion or seizure of unknown origin and for any convulsion or seizure that appears more severe than usual in a child who has a convulsive disorder. While awaiting help:

• Roll your child on his side so that he doesn't choke on vomit or saliva.

• Do not place anything in his mouth. Don't worry that he could swallow his tongue; he can't.

• Make sure he doesn't roll off a bed or sofa or bang into something and injure himself.

• Have your child seen by his health-care provider, who will determine the cause of the seizure.

# Drowning (near drowning)

As soon as your child has been removed from the water, see if she is breathing. If she is able to breathe, turn her on her side to allow her to vomit, if necessary. Then take her to an ER immediately for assessment.

If she is not breathing, begin the following emergency treatment immediately.

### Treating near-drowning victims
- Begin CPR.
- Even if your child seems lifeless, or doesn't respond after a few minutes, continue performing CPR.
- Do not leave your child alone in order to search for a phone or help. If someone is with you, have that person go for help or call your local emergency service.
- Perform CPR until your child is able to breathe and has a pulse of 80 to 100 beats per minute. At that point, you can run for help.
- Take her to an ER immediately, or if help has been summoned, wait for the paramedics to arrive. After a near-drowning experience, your child will probably need to be hospitalized for observation if she has inhaled water, lost consciousness, or stopped breathing.

See **page 675** for information on CPR.

# Ear injuries

Seek medical attention if:
- Blunt-force or sharp-object injury is severe.
- Ear lobe is torn.
- You cannot dislodge an object from your child's ear.

**Blunt-force or sharp-object injury** If your child receives a blunt-force injury to the ear or has accidentally poked her inner ear with a sharp object, seek medical help immediately. Note if there's bleeding from the ear canal, if your child doesn't seem to hear as well as usual, if she complains of pain, or if her earlobe begins to swell.

## PEDIATRICK
### *Removing a Bug from the Ear*

If a bug crawls into your child's ear don't try to retrieve it with a swab or tweezers. Instead, fill the ear canal with mineral oil, using an ear dropper. The bug will drown, which will alleviate your child's discomfort. If the bug doesn't float to the surface where you can remove it, seek medical help.

**Torn earlobe** If your child has torn an earlobe, take her to the doctor, but first wash the injury and apply an antibacterial ointment and cover the wound with a sterile gauze pad.

**Object in ear** If your child has stuck something in his ear, you can see the item, and it's easy to grasp, use tweezers to gently remove it. Don't, however, put tweezers into the ear canal. If the item is made of metal, try using a magnet to draw it out, holding the magnet outside the ear canal. Take your child to the doctor or the emergency room if you cannot safely remove the object yourself. Also seek medical help if your child complains of pain for more than a few minutes after the object is removed.

# Electrical shock

It is important to be extremely vigilant not only in child-proofing your home, but in taking care to keep small appliances away from your small child.

## Treating electrical shock
In the event your child does get her hands into an outlet or onto an appliance that emits an electrical shock:
• Disconnect the appliance immediately, or turn off the power to the outlet. If this is impossible, use a nonmetallic object, such as a broom handle, chair cushion, or a chair leg, to push the child away from the electrical current. If your child is in or is touching water—if, for example, she has grabbed a hair dryer that has fallen into a sink—do not touch the water yourself.
• Begin CPR.
• Even if your child seems lifeless, or doesn't respond after a few minutes, continue performing CPR.
• Do not leave your child alone in order to search for a phone or help. If someone is with you, have that person go for help or call your local emergency service.
• Perform CPR until your child is able to breathe and has a pulse of 80 to 100 beats per minute. At that point, you can run for help.
• Take her to an ER immediately, or if help has been summoned, wait for the paramedics to arrive. Your child will probably need to be hospitalized for observation after being shocked, if she has lost consciousness or stopped breathing.

# Eye injuries

If your child sustains a blow to an eye or has had an irritant enter his eye, prompt action can ease the discomfort and, in the case of serious injury, preserve his eyesight. Seek medical help if:

- He has suffered a severe blow or puncture wound to his eye.
- He has gotten a caustic chemical in his eyes.
- You cannot remove a small particle from his eye or if the particle has scratched the cornea of his eye.

**Blow to the eye**  Cover the eye with a cool compress, if possible. If the eye appears damaged, go the ER. If possible, call ahead and ask that a pediatric ophthalmologist be ready for your arrival. Otherwise, request to see a specialist once you've arrived at the ER.

**Chemicals in the eye**  If any caustic substance enters your child's eye:

- Read the caution label on the packaging and follow the instructions given.

If the caution label is unavailable:

- Call your local poison-control center for instructions.
- Dust away any dry chemicals.
- Flood the eye with water, ideally for 15 minutes.
- Take your child to the ER or have him examined by a pediatric ophthalmologist immediately.

**Foreign object in the eye**

If sand, an eyelash, sawdust, or other minute irritant enters your child's eyes:

- Flush eye with lukewarm water up to 15 minutes, or until object washes out.
- Don't use a tissue, cloth, or cotton swab to remove the object; you could damage the cornea.
- Don't allow eye rubbing. Give your child a toy to handle to discourage her from rubbing her eye.
- If redness persists for more than 10 minutes, your child complains of pain, or you can't get the object out, take her to an ophthalmologist or her pediatrician.

**Minor irritants**  If shampoo, soap, cosmetics, or non-machine dishwashing detergent irritates your child's eyes:

- Tilt your child's head back. (If she's too young to follow instructions, hold her eye open with your index finger and thumb.)

• Run a steady, gentle stream of lukewarm water from the faucet or from a glass into a the eye for about 15 minutes.
• Instruct your child to blink frequently as the water runs over her face.

## Fainting

Any number of things can cause your child to feel faint, including extreme heat, going for a long time without eating, and shock. Children who hold their breath when they're angry may also faint.

Treating fainting incidents:
• If your child faints, immediately check to see if she is breathing. If she isn't, start CPR.
• If she is breathing, loosen any tight clothing around her neck and waist.
• Turn her head to the side and use your fingers to clear her mouth of any food to prevent choking.
• Don't offer any food or drink.
• Call her doctor immediately.

*See **page 675** for information on CPR.*

## Frostbite

Exposure to temperatures below 28°F (−2°C) can trigger mild frostbite in a young child. Frostbite first appears in the extremities such as the fingers and toes, nose, and ears. Symptoms include numbness, a whitening of the skin, or, in more severe cases, blistering.

If you suspect that your child has developed frostbite, seek medical care.

**Treating frostbite**  All possible cases of frostbite need to be evaluated by a medical professional. All rewarming should be medically supervised.

If you cannot get to a treatment facility immediately:
• Cover the affected areas with extra clothing; a warm, wet washcloth; or blankets. Or, submerge the frostbitten hand or foot in a bowl of warm (not hot) water, or place the frostbitten area next to normal-termperature skin to warm it gradually. As rewarming

occurs, your child should feel a tingling and burning sensation and her skin should turn red.
• Don't attempt to warm the affected area too quickly by using hot water or placing your child's hands over a radiator or other heat source.

## Hand and finger injuries

Seek medical help if:
• There's a possibility that bones are broken, for example, if there is swelling or observable deformity. If your child can't straighten his finger, it may be broken.
• There's profuse bleeding.

*For information on broken bones, see **page 671**.*

**Treating smashed fingers** A smashed fingertip will typically turn red and become swollen. To curb pain and reduce mild swelling, give your child an ice pack or cold cloth to wrap around his finger for 10 to 15 minutes. Never apply ice directly. If he suffers increased pain or swelling or develops a fever during the next few days after the injury, call the doctor.

If the fingertip bleeds:
• Wash it gently in cold water with an antibacterial soap.
• Elevate your child's hand above his heart and apply pressure by holding the fingers snugly with a soft, clean cloth—a washcloth is ideal. Unwrap the cloth every 5 minutes to see if the bleeding has stopped.
• Once the bleeding stops, have your child hold an ice pack against the injured finger for about 20 minutes to reduce swelling. Then, apply an antibacterial ointment and an adhesive bandage.
• Call your doctor if a cut is deep, bleeds persistently, or there is blood under the fingernail and/or a shattered nail. Your child may need stitches.

## Head and neck injuries

Seek medical help for any head or neck injury that results in loss of consciousnes, vomiting, lethargy, amnesia, or if your child simply doesn't "look right" after an injury.

**Assessing the injury**  Three factors determine the seriousness of a head injury: the speed at which the child was traveling when the bump occurred, the type of surface he hit or that hit him, and the height he fell from. If the height of the fall is equal to or less than the height of the child, serious injury is less likely. But every head injury must be taken seriously to rule out concussion.

**Treating head injuries**  Seek immediate medical attention if your child received a severe blow or fell a long distance. If your child shows any of the following symptoms after a blow to the head, have him seen by a doctor immediately, take him to the ER or call 911:

- Loss of consciousness
- Confusion, lethargy, lack of coordination, difficulty speaking clearly
- Inability to focus eyes. Unequally dilated pupils. The child's eyes cross, or vision seems impaired.
- Convulsion
- Headache that doesn't go away. Extreme irritability in a baby could signal a headache after a head injury.
- A large wound, or a smaller one that doesn't stop bleeding
- Repeated vomiting for 15 to 20 minutes
- Breathing that is unusually slow, rapid, or irregular
- Inability to stop crying
- Leakage of clear liquid from the nose or ear
- Appearance of dark purple circles around eyes or behind ears within 24 hours of injury
- A depression in the skull
- Unusually pale or grayish skin color

*For information on convulsions, see page 682.*

**Treating a minor head injury**  Large, discolored bumps—or "goose eggs"—commonly pop up after a blow to the head. They are generally unrelated to the seriousness of the injury, and you can reduce swelling by applying a cold compress. Don't offer food or milk right after a bump on the head. Instead, give your child water. If the water stays down, continue with her regular diet.

You don't need to force your child to stay awake following a minor head bump, but you should observe her carefully. Check on her every few minutes for two hours after the injury. If her breathing is regular and she isn't unusually restless, you can relax. If it's nighttime, check on her every couple of hours and awaken her once or twice during the first night after the injury; if you can't rouse her, call for medical help.

# Heat exhaustion and heat cramps

**Assessing heat exhaustion** Signs that your child has been hot for too long and may be becoming dehydrated include:

- Fainting
- Headache
- Dizziness
- Fatigue
- Nausea
- Restlessness
- Decreased urine production
- Pale, clammy skin
- Rapid, weak pulse
- Fast, shallow breathing
- Vomiting

**Treating heat exhaustion**
- Take your child immediately to a cool room or the shade.
- Give her water, continually offering one to one and a half ounces per pound of body weight, over the course of one hour. Once she's no longer thirsty, she should continue to drink, but not as frequently.
- Bathe her in room-temperature water.
- Call the doctor if symptoms don't subside within 10 to 15 minutes after treatment or if the child cannot keep fluids down. If she's severely dehydrated, she may need to receive fluids intravenously.

**Treating heat cramps**  Heat cramps result in pain in the arms, legs, back, or abdomen. To relieve the pain:
- Give the child water, as described above.
- Gently massage or stretch the affected muscle.
- Apply an ice pack wrapped in a towel to the cramp. Don't place ice directly on the skin.
- Call the doctor if your child can't walk or the pain isn't relieved by fluids within 10 to 15 minutes.

# Heat rash

This condition, also called prickly heat, is a rash brought on by too-warm clothing or by heavy lotions that plug sweat glands, trapping perspiration beneath the surface. Heat rash is signalled by the sudden eruption of small, red, itchy dots, especially on the back, chest, and other unexposed parts of the body. These often disappear when the child cools down.

### Treating heat rash
- Remove clothing from affected area.
- Lightly sponge your child with tepid water. Or, apply a cool (not icy-cold) compress.
- Sprinkle corn starch that has been chilled in refrigerator onto the rash. Be careful not to let your child inhale the powder.
- Apply calamine lotion to soothe itch, keeping the lotion away from areas near mouth and eyes, though.
- Call the doctor if scratching causes the rash to bleed, making it susceptible to infection; if your child has a fever, loses his appetite or seems ill; or if the rash lasts more than a few days, worsens, or scabs.

## Heat stroke and sunstroke

**Assessing heatstroke and sunstroke**  These conditions occur when the body's heat-control system, overwhelmed by high heat, shuts down. Both are medical emergencies. Heat stroke and sunstroke can affect the heart, central nervous system, kidneys, or liver, and may prove fatal. Symptoms include:
- Headache and general fatigue
- In later stages, fever of 105°F or higher, confusion, seizures, coma.

**Treating heatstroke and sunstroke**
- Immediately remove child from heat and call for medical help.
- Give him water to drink and pour tepid water over him to lower his body temperature.

## Mouth injuries

Seek medical attention if:
- Severe bleeding occurs.
- The tongue is severely cut or severed.
- A permanent tooth is knocked out or chipped.

**Treating injuries to the inner mouth**  If your child gets a scrape or cut inside her mouth, you can relieve her pain and control bleeding by having her suck on a Popsicle. If bleeding doesn't stop after 10 minutes or a cut appears deep or long, call her dentist or doctor. Also call the doctor if your child receives a puncture wound, from a pencil, stick, or another sharp object. Puncture wounds can become infected and the doctor may decide to prescribe antibiotics.

### Treating a split lip
- If possible, rinse the area with cool water.
- Then hold an ice pack or ice cubes wrapped in a clean wash cloth on the injury to curb bleeding and relieve pain. Don't apply ice directly to the skin.
- If the bleeding persists for more than 10 minutes or the cut is deep, call your child's doctor.

### Treating a knocked-out tooth
If a permanent tooth is knocked out and you are able to retrieve it:
- Hold the tooth by the crown (not the root) and rinse it under gently running water.
- Place it in tap water or milk and take it with your child to his dentist. The dentist may be able to reimplant the tooth if less than 45 minutes has elapsed. An older child—age 5 or up—may hold the tooth in his mouth between his molars and cheek, or under the front part of his tongue en route to the dentist, providing that he can remain calm.

  If the tooth cannot be retrieved, take your child to the dentist once the wound has healed. Your dentist may recommend implanting a false tooth to guide the growth of the surrounding teeth and to restore your child's smile and ability to chew properly.

### Treating a broken tooth
- Carefully clean dirt from the mouth, using sterile gauze soaked in warm water.
- Remove any parts of a broken tooth from your child's mouth to prevent him from swallowing them.
- Place the chip in tap water or milk and take it with your child to his dentist. The dentist may be able to bond the chip to the tooth.
- Take your child to the dentist right away for treatment.

### Treating tongue injuries
- Stop the bleeding by pressing on the cut with a piece of sterile gauze or a clean washcloth.
- If the cut doesn't stop bleeding or appears deep or long, call your child's dentist or doctor.

# Nose injuries

Seek medical help if:
- There is profuse bleeding after first-aid treatment.
- The cartilage may be broken.
- An obstruction cannot be removed.

## Assessing the injury
- If your child's nostrils appear asymmetrical, this could indicate that cartilage is damaged.
- If clear or bloody fluid leaks from the nose, this could be a sign that the delicate barrier at the back of the nose may have been broken, allowing spinal fluid to leak out.

**Treating a broken nose** Take your child to the ER. Do not press against the injury, though loosly holding an ice-filled bag over the injury can reduce pain and swelling.

## Treating a nosebleed
- Have her sit in an upright position, leaning slightly forward so she doesn't swallow or choke on blood.
- Using your index finger and thumb, gently pinch the lower part of the nose for about 5 minutes.

**Treating nasal obstructions** If your child has stuck something up her nose, you may have a very visible clue—such as a portion of the object dangling from her nostril. But she may have pushed the object so far up that it becomes lodged there for a day or longer. In that case, your first warning may be a foul odor emanating from her nose. Objects that linger in a nostril can also cause a bloody discharge. To treat an obstruction:
- If you can see the item your child has stuck up his nose and it's soft, such as a piece of bread, try to grab it with a pair of tweezers.
- If the item is too far up the nostril to grasp or it is hard—like a bean—ask your child to blow her nose; she may blow the object out.
- If this fails, take her to her doctor for a "professional" removal.

---

**PEDIATRICK**

## *Cold Packs for Nosebleeds*

Cold packs can stop nosebleeds by constricting blood vessels. Try placing an ice bag, a bag of frozen peas, or a cold can of soda on the back of your child's neck, forehead, or against her upper lip for several minutes.

---

## *When to Call the Doctor*

If the bleeding continues for more than 10 minutes, call your child's doctor. Also if your child has frequent nosebleeds that aren't caused by colds, allergies, or by picking, his doctor should examine him to find the cause.

# Poisoning

Dozens of common household and lawn-care products, medicines, as well as certain plants and seeds, can be poisonous to your child if she ingests or inhales them. If you suspect that your child has swallowed a substance, has chewed on or consumed a poisonous plant or mushroom, has had skin or eye contact with a toxin, or has inhaled a poisonous gas, chemical, or smoke, immediately call 911 or your area poison control center. The number should be posted by your phone or programmed into an automatic-dial phone. Keep a bottle of syrup of ipecac handy to induce vomiting if the poison control center advises you to do so. If syrup of Ipecac is not available, you can induce vomiting with sour milk (made by adding lemon juice to fresh milk).

Seek medical help if:
• Your child has swallowed or inhaled any poisonous substance.
• Your child has been poisoned by tainted food.
• Your child's skin or eyes have been exposed to toxic substances.
• Your child is unconscious, has difficulty breathing, develops a severe rash, or vomits profusely.

**Assessing the situation**  Whenever possible, know what kind of poison your child has been exposed to. Read the packaging of any chemicals for specific first-aid treatments. Bring remnants of any ingested food, plants, seeds, or other poison to the ER for identification. Knowing the substance will also guide the poison-control experts and medical professionals in treatment choices.

**Treating poisoning by ingesting (swallowing) harmful chemicals**  Call 911 or poison control as soon as possible. Do not induce vomiting unless directed to do so.

**Treating inhalation (breathed-in) poisoning by toxic fumes, gases (including carbon monoxide), or smoke**
• Take her outdoors and away from the toxins immediately so she can breathe fresh air.
• Loosen her clothing.
• If she isn't breathing, start CPR.
• Call 911 or poison control as soon as possible.

*See **page 675** for information on CPR.*

### Treating chemical skin-contact poisoning

- Remove contaminated clothing. Discard it or wash separately from the rest of your laundry in hot water.
- Drench the skin with water for at least 15 minutes.
- Wash your child's skin and hair thoroughly with soap and water. Dry him and wrap him in a blanket.
- Call poison control for advice.

### Treating chemical injuries to the eyes

Eye membranes absorb pesticides and other chemicals faster than any other external part of the body and damage can occur in just a few minutes.

- Hold the lid open and gently wash eye with cool running water from the tap or hose for 15 minutes or longer.
- Rush the child to a hospital emergency room or ophthalmologist.

## Poison ivy, oak, sumac, etc.

A number of common garden plants and trees can trigger skin irritations, and because kids have tender skin they are more prone than adults to adverse reactions. The oils (resins) from poison ivy, poison oak, and poison sumac are particularly noxious and affect most people. Contact with these plants causes an itchy red rash. Kids pick up the oil by brushing against the plant or its leaves or by touching anything that has come in contact with the plant, including pets, clothing, gardening tools, sports equipment, or camping gear. Typically, the rash, complete with blisters, appears within 24 hours of exposure and can last for one to three weeks.

If you suspect your child's skin has been exposed to a plant toxin:

- Remove contaminated clothing. Use gloves or take other appropriate measures to ensure that you do not become infected. Also take measures to prevent the spread of the toxin from clothing onto additional skin areas as you remove your child's clothing.
- Immediately flush the affected area with lots of water for 5 to 10 minutes.
- Call your child's doctor for a recommedation for an OTC or prescription topical medication that will quell itching, usually a hydrocortisone product. The physician may also recommend that you give your child an an oral OTC antihistamine, such as Benadryl, to relieve itching.

- Wash your child's contaminated clothing separately from the rest of the family laundry.
- Clean non-machine-washable shoes with equal parts rubbing alcohol and water.
- If poisonous plants grown in your yard, have them removed by a professional lawn service. Be sure that the service itself does not treat the problem with toxic chemicals. Never burn poisonous plants because the fumes are toxic.

**To curb itching after exposure:**
- Apply a cool compress to itchy areas. Dip a clean washcloth into cool water or a mixture that is equal parts milk and water. Wring it out and place it on the rash until itching is eased.
- Let your child soak for 20 to 30 minutes in a tub filled with tepid or cool water and a handful of colloidal oatmeal (available at most drugstores). Gently pat her dry when she gets out of the tub.
- Keep your child out of the sun until her rash subsides. Sunlight will aggravate a rash.
- Call your child's doctor if the rash develops pus, which is a sign of infection; if your child's face, eyelids, or hands swell; or if itching is severe.

**Treating ingestion of a poisonous plant**
- Look for tell-tale signs of sap or bits of leaves, seeds, or bulbs on your child's face, fingers, and inside her mouth.
- Remove any visible particles and try to identify them.
- Call poison control for directions. Be ready to supply identifying information about the ingested plant. Be sure to have a bottle of syrup of ipecac on hand at all times for emergencies.

# Shock

Shock may occur when your child has lost a large amount of blood or fluid in the wake of a severe injury. It may also occur as a result of severe infection or an allergic reactio (for example, to a bee sting).

Symptoms include:
- Disorientation or confusion
- Cold, clammy, sweaty skin and/or chills
- Rapid pulse or rapid or shallow breathing
- Pale skin

- Faintness
- Nausea and/or vomiting

**Treating shock** Call 911 immediately if your child shows symptoms of shock. Until emergency medical help arrives:
- Place your child on his back and loosen any tight clothing, such as belts or collars.
- Elevate his legs by placing them on a pillow or folded blanket or a tote, beach, or diaper bag.
- If possible, cover him with a sheet or light blanket.
- If your child's breathing is shallow—that is, he's having difficulty breathing—raise his head and shoulders slightly. (Don't raise or move his head or neck if you suspect he's suffered a neck injury, however.)
- Don't offer food or drink.

## Splinters

To remove a splinter:
- Gently wash the area with soap and water.
- Numb the area by holding an ice cube wrapped in a washcloth against the skin for a minute or so before attempting to remove the splinter.
- Using a pair of tweezers that have been sterilized in alcohol or washed in hot soap and water, grasp the end of the splinter and gently pull. If you can't get the splinter out, soak the area in warm, soapy water for 10 to 20 minutes several times a day for two or three days; the splinter may work its way out.

Your child needs medical intention if:
- The splinter is very large or deeply embedded, or is glass or metal.
- The area around the splinter swells or turns red, indicating an infection.
- Your child's tetanus vaccination isn't up-to-date; he should get a booster.

**PEDIATRICK**

### Splinter Strategies

- **Before removing a splinter,** cover the area with teething gel. This will numb the site enough to make splinter removal painless.

- **If you have trouble finding a splinter in your child's finger,** take her into a dark room and shine a flashlight on her finger. You should be able to see the splinter's shadow. Mark the spot with a pen so you'll know where to apply the tweezers.

- **If the wound isn't too deep,** try removing the splinter with Scotch tape. Just press the sticky side against the splinter and gently lift it out.

## *Your Family's First-Aid Kit*

In addition to medicine cabinet musts, every family needs first-aid supplies. Optimally, you should have one kit at home and one in the car or otherwise available when traveling. In all cases, the medical kit needs to be safely out of reach of children.

### Tools and Equipment

- Clean cloth (such as a washcloth, for cleaning wounds)
- Adhesive and non-stick bandages in assorted sizes
- Individually wrapped sterile gauze pads
- Roll of sterile gauze
- Roll of adhesive tape
- Triangular bandage and large safety pins (for a sling)
- Stretchable bandage (such as an Ace bandage, for treating sprains)
- Sterile cotton balls and cotton swabs
- Heating pad or hot water bottle
- Ice pack (A frozen bag of peas or other food will work for your home kit; for travel, buy "crushable" ice packs, available at most drugstores.)
- Small, blunt-tip scissors
- Angle-tip tweezers
- Thermometers
- This book or other first-aid manual

### Medications

- Antibiotic ointment and spray for cuts and scrapes
- Hydrogen peroxide
- Antihistamine (such as Benadryl) for allergic reactions
- Anti-itch cream (1% OTC hydrocortisone cream) plus calamine lotion for bug bites
- Children'-strength acetaminophen and/or ibuprofen
- Adult-strength acetaminophen and/or ibuprofen and/or aspirin
- Syrup of ipecac (to induce vomiting if poison is ingested; call your poison control center before administering)
- Rubbing alcohol (to sterilize tweezers, scissors, etc.)

# Your Special-Needs Child

Your child may require special care, due to accident, birth injury, genetics, contagion, the environment, or other factor, and for that reason you, too, need support and guidance. In this chapter, you'll learn how to serve your child's physical and emotional needs best, helping him achieve his potential, deal with the frustrations that his physical or mental limitations or treatment regimen may cause, and find the resources that will help you deal with the additional challenges of parenthood.

## *Living with and loving your special-needs child*

If your child has suffered an injury or has been diagnosed with a serious illness, you're likely caught up in something of a time warp—looking back on the good times before the crisis and looking forward to that time in the future when everything may be as it should be again. If your child was born with a genetic condition or has suffered a birth injury that alters the future you imagined for him, you probably feel cheated, as well as angry and, perhaps, guilty. And even if you've become accustomed to the condition that affects your child, you may be frustrated and fatigued, wondering not just about today but about what the future holds for your child and for you.

There's no simple route to finding the right care, the right balance between your child's needs and the rest of your family's needs, and no guarantees that everything will work out exactly as you want it to. No family has guarantees of a perfect future, of course, but you are more aware than most of what can go wrong.

## Your feelings

As the parent of a special-needs child, especially if your child has a severe disability, it's only natural that you may feel angry at your child because she isn't the perfect little person you envisioned; you may resent her because of the extraordinary amount of time you spend caring for her. You may also be angry at your partner if he doesn't share the burden equally. You will probably experience guilt as well— about your anger, especially when it's directed toward your child—and about your child's condition. You might feel that you did something wrong during your pregnancy that led to her disability, or that you failed to do something that could have prevented the condition. If your child was injured in an accident, you may constantly blame yourself—or your partner—for not doing everything you could to prevent the accident.

Because all of these feelings—anger, resentment, blame, and guilt—are normal, you need to channel them into something that will work for you and your family. To make your feelings work for you:

- **Acknowledge them.** State once how you feel. If you place blame on someone close to you, including yourself, say it just one time. If you're angry at your child, don't be afraid to admit that to yourself, and to a trusted, nonjudgmental ally, if you choose.

**PARENTS RESOURCES**

### Educating Your Child

All states are legally mandated by Public Law 101-476 to provide "free and appropriate public education" to disabled children ages 3 to 21. Each state also has programs for children from birth to age 3, but not all are free. Contact the early-childhood-intervention program in your area for more information.

**Parent Training and Information Centers (PTI's).** PTI's are federally funded advocacy centers that provide training and information to parents to help them participate more effectively with professionals in meeting the educational needs of children with disabilities, including referrals to early intervention programs. Each state has at least one PTI. To locate the PTI in your state, call the **National Information Center for Children and Youth with Disabilities** at (800) 695-0285 or visit www.nichcy.org.

### Books for Parents

**The Child with Special Needs: Encouraging Intellectual and Emotional Growth** by Stanley I. Greenspan, M.D., et al. (Perseus Press).

**In the Shadow of Illness: Parents and Siblings of the Chronically Ill Child** by Myra Bluebond-Langer (Princeton University Press).

**Creating Schools for All** (Council for Exceptional Children). To order, call (888) 232-7733 or write:
Department K80827
1920 Association Drive
Reston, VA 20191-1589

• **Put negative feelings aside.** Even though it may be very difficult, move on from feelings that aren't serving anyone. The truth is that no matter who is to blame, dwelling on those feelings doesn't change the present situation. On the other hand, seething with anger, resentment, or guilt toward those who also care about your child does change the present in a way that serves no one.

• **Allow positive feelings.** When things go terribly wrong, there's often a refusal to acknowledge anything good, as if such an acknowledgment trivializes the seriousness of the current situation. It doesn't. Finding something to laugh about and something to enjoy affirms both the present and the future. It's not a betrayal of your child to embrace life. The opposite is true.

• **Know that your feelings will change.** Whatever you're feeling, it will change over time. One day, you may despair. Another day, you may enjoy great hopefulness and joy. And then back again, and again. Sometimes you'll experience the gamut of feelings in a single day—or even a single hour. Allow yourself to look back and ahead at the range of emotion, and try not to get stuck in any one place.

**Taking care of yourself**  It's important to think of yourself and your needs as you go about meeting your child's needs. Given the level of dependency your child has on you, your well-being is the best gift you can give your child. If between medical crises, doctors' appointments, and other pressing matters, you see no relief for yourself, it's time to develop a plan to carve out some time for attending to your own needs. Only when your own batteries are recharged can you give your child your best. Some ways to give yourself some care are:

• **Join a support group.** Other parents who are experiencing or who have experienced many of your same joys and sorrows are in the best position to share their wisdom and their strength.

• **Share your feelings.** Talking about your feelings with others who care about you, such as friends and family, a counselor or therapist, your or your child's doctor, or a clergy person, can help you deal with them and resolve your emotional conflicts. If you find, however, that some people are unable to help you, try not to be too disappointed in them, which will just drain your energy. Instead, work to find someone else to whom you can talk.

- **Set aside a regular breaktime.** As much as you are focused on your child's needs, you need time away. Arrange for sitters, friends, and family members, to give you a half-hour or other set time when you can relax.
- **Find an additional focus.** Give your mind another place to go, even when you're involved in your child's care. For instance, while you're waiting in a doctor's office, spend time knitting, doing a crossword puzzle, or reading a novel. Meditate. Work on project that requires concentration.
- **Find a peaceful place.** Whether it be your backyard garden, a place of worship, or a calm part of your own brain, go there whenever you feel the need for solace.

## Your marriage

Parents of a special-needs child—especially one with a severe disability or a life-threatening condition—face new stresses on their marriage. Caring for your child may take up the major part of your day. How should you divide the responsibilities? If you and your partner both worked outside the home before your child was born, will one of you have to quit your job in order to assume care? The cost of medical care may be exorbitant: What can you do to avoid fights about money matters, as well as find the resources to provide the best care for your child? If you have other children, they, too, will need attention, love, and good care. Will you and your partner have the time and energy to fully meet their

**PARENTS RESOURCES**

### Financial Resources

If your private health insurance does not cover all of your child's medical needs, state-aid programs or private organizations may be able to help. Most hospitals and public health clinics have social workers or patient advocates on staff who can direct parents to government or private organizations that may be able to provide financial support. Your child may also be eligible for these federal programs:

***Supplemental Security Income (SSI)*** is available from the federal Social Security Administration to children or adults who are disabled or blind if they have limited income and resources. Payments are made on a monthly basis. In most states, children who receive SSI are also eligible for Medicaid. Also, a disabled child younger than 22 may receive Social Security Disability Insurance (SSDI) benefits if his parent is disabled, retired, or deceased. After a child receives SSDI benefits for 24 months, he becomes eligible for Medicare. For SSI and SSDI, contact the **Social Security Administration** at (800) 772-1213 or visit www.ssa.gov.

***Medicaid.*** If your income is too high for SSI, you may still qualify for Medicaid, especially if your income is significantly reduced because of medical expenses. In some states, the child's "assets" are considered separate from his parents'; this way, the child may qualify for Medicaid.

***Federal Title V Program.*** Under this program, states receive funds to provide rehabilitation and other services for disabled children under 16 who qualify. Contact your state social services department for information.

needs? And you and your spouse need time alone together in order to continue your loving relationship. If you are faced with overwhelming responsibilities, how can you maintain your marriage?

Start by setting aside time to talk openly and honestly with each other on a regular basis. Share all your concerns and fears with each other. It may help for you to write down your problems or concerns on a sheet of paper, leaving space for possible solutions you can arrive at together. As you start to work together to solve each problem—how to pay your child's medical bills, how to divide your workload, etc.—you will begin to feel more in control, united in your efforts, and supportive of one another. If you find, though, that you simply can't communicate effectively with each other, or that each discussion ends up in a fight, consider having a third, impartial party join your discussions. Look for a counselor who has experience working with the parents of special-needs children. Your child's doctor or an organization that deals with your child's particular disability may be able to refer you to such a person.

If one of you works outside the home, make sure that that person spends a good amount of time with your child during the evening and on weekends to allow the parent who cares for the child during the day to have some time off.

## Your other children

Making sure that your other children's needs are met can be a struggle when one child's needs necessarily take more time. It's easy to get so caught up in caring for a disabled child that you may not be aware that your other children are feeling confused, resentful, or—in some cases—unloved.

Siblings of special-needs children behave in various ways. Some try to get their parents' attention by acting out at home or school. Other children strive to be perfect to protect their parents from any additional concerns, a situation that is unhealthy for them. Some become overly protective of their special-needs sibling, giving up their own social life so they can spend all their waking hours with him. Finally, some kids simply accept the fact that their sibling comes first and always will. These

---

**PARENTS RESOURCE**

### *Help for Siblings*

**A.J. Pappanikou Center**
249 Glenbrook Rd., U-64
Storrs, CT 06269-2064
(860) 486-5035

kids are quiet. They don't seem resentful, but underneath, they may be very sad and may even become clinically depressed.

If you are the parent of a special-needs child, your other kids feel loved, well cared for, and important.

## Support for Siblings

### Do...

allow your other children to help take care of their special-needs sibling or do chores around the house to help you out, but be sure to remind them that they have a right to do things they enjoy as well.

give your healthy children the opportunity to discuss their concerns about their disabled sibling as well as aspects of their life that are not related to their sibling.

express gratitude for any help, but remind your child that it's the parents' responsibility to raise children, including his disabled sibling.

be sure to celebrate the special occasions in your nondisabled child's life. His birthday parties should center around him and his needs. If he's in a school play, try your best to attend or send a loved friend or relative in your place.

plan times for pleasurable, one-on-one activity with each child. Concentrate fully on that child and take the opportunity to catch up on what she's doing and how she's feeling.

plan fun family times—such as picnics—when all of you can enjoy time together.

have regular family meetings, at which everyone can discuss their concerns. Be sure all your children get a turn to share their feelings and ideas.

give your nondisabled child lots of hugs and kisses. Tell her you love her, rather than assuming she knows.

explain your disabled child's condition to your nondisabled child according to his level of understanding.

give each of your children the opportunity to join support groups to discuss their feelings among their peers.

### Don't...

use your healthy child as a baby-sitter, confidant, or defender of your disabled child. When you feel overwhelmed, it's tempting to rely on your healthy child, but he shouldn't have to act more mature than he is.

become angry with kids who act out in order to get attention. Instead, set aside time to discuss their feelings with them.

assume that your nondisabled child is absolutely fine just because she isn't complaining or acting out. She may be covering up her feelings.

allow your child to feel guilty because he is "normal."

overindulge your nondisabled child in order to make up for time you aren't able to spend with him.

expect that in every sibling argument your healthy child should give in.

# Helping your child cope

You cannot make your child's disability or illness go away, but you can help her develop the attitude and skills that will serve her.

**Building a positive self-image** All children, of course, need to have a good feeling about who they are, what they can do, and how they look. Some children with an illness or a disability require special sensitivity to achieve a good self-image. To help your special-needs child have a positive sense of herself:

- **Practice responses to others' comments.** If your child is old enough and is able to formulate her own responses to any comments that people may make regarding her condition, let her choose the kind of response she wants to make, whether it be explaining (again) about her condition, leaving it to you to respond, or simply ignoring those comments.
- **Give her plenty of reinforcement.** While handling an illness certainly takes up a lot of time and energy, it's important not to let your child define herself by her illness. If she's a terrific artist, has an interest in baseball, loves fashion, or is a whiz at mathematics, make sure that these aspects of her identity get full play. Keep up, as much as possible, her social world and support her interests.
- **Discipline consistently.** It's comforting to every child to know your expectations for her behavior and to accept consequences for misbehavior. A child who's undergoing difficult treatments or who has to confront physical or emotional limitations especially needs the safety of boundaries. This is not to say that you can't indulge your child, particularly during a stressful event, but it's better for your child to know that some things—like your willingness to correct her—have not changed.
- **Let her do all that she can.** Try not to be overly protective. Don't do for you child what she can do for herself, including chores around the house and as much of her self-care—dressing, playing—as she can. Let her engage in any activities that are age-appropriate if she's even minimally able to do so.

**PARENTS RESOURCES**

## Help for Children with Disabilities

**The U.S. National Library of Medicine** provides referrals to a network of 3000-plus medical libraries nationwide. It also operates online computer databases of health-related information.
(888) 346-3656, www.nlm.nih.gov

**National Rehabilitation Information Center** provides referrals and information about rehabilitation to disabled people.
(800) 346-2742, www.naric.com

**National Organization for Rare Disorders** provides information on symptoms and treatments.
(800) 999-6673, www.rarediseases.org

**Rural Information Center Health Service** provides information and referrals on health-delivery programs in rural areas.
(800) 633-770l, www.nal.usda.gov/ric/richs

**National Health Information Center** provides health information and referrals to general public, medical professionals, and educators.
(800) 336-4797, www.nhic-nt.health.org

**Medic Alert Foundation** is a service for people who, because of illness or disability, may not be able to speak for themselves. Provides members with Medic Alert bracelets or necklaces.
(800) 432-5378, www.medicalert.org

**American Board of Medical Specialties** verifies board certification of physicians.
(800) 776-2378, www.certifieddoctor.org

**National Bone Marrow Donor Program** provides information to patients.
(800) 627-7692, www.marrow.org

**Children's Hospice International** provides information and support for families who have a terminally ill child.
(800) 242-4453, www.chionline.org

**National Information Center for Children and Youth with Disabilities**
(800) 695-0285, www.nichcy.org

**Federation for Children with Special Needs**
**Technical Assistance for Parents Program (TAPP)**
(617) 236-7210, www.fcsn.org

**National Easter Seal Society**
(800) 221-6827, www.easter-seals.org

**Note:** Additional specific-condition resource listings are contained throughout this chapter.

# Accident-related disabilities

Spinal cord injuries (SCIs) and brain injuries are the leading causes of accident-related disabilities among children. The organizations listed in the resource sections can provide information on the most up-to-date research on treatment options and support services.

## Brain injury and spinal cord injury (SCI)

Every year, more than one million children in the United States sustain brain injuries, ranging from mild to severe trauma, according to the Brain Injury Association.

Pediatric spinal cord injury (SCI) is defined as an acute traumatic lesion of the spinal cord and roots. After the initial trauma is treated at a medical facility, your child's care will best be provided by a rehabilitation facility.

### Finding the right pediatric rehabilitation program

Rehabilitation hospitals and programs that are designed for adults usually don't maintain a separate facility exclusively for children. As an alternative to a general rehab center, you may want to look for facilities and/or programs that place kids with SCI or brain injury in rehabilitation units with other children who have chronic disabilities. This often provides families and children with opportunities to share common experiences and information with each other, and may lead to the development of support networks within the community.

Kids with SCI or brain injury are generally better off if they undergo rehab with other children who are actively involved in the rehabilitation process. In some cases, kids are placed in units with peers who are too ill for rehabilitation, and this can limit the healthier child's progress.

**PARENTS RESOURCES**

### Spinal Cord Injuries

**The National Spinal Cord Injury Association (NSCIA) and In Touch with Kids Network**
8701 Georgia Ave., Suite 500
Silver Springs, MD 20910
(800) 962-9629
(301) 588-6959
www.spinalcord.org

### Brain Injuries

**Brain Injury Association**
105 North Alfred St.
Alexandria, VA 22314
(703) 236-6000
www.biausa.org

Check to see if the program is accredited by the Commission on the Accreditation of Rehabilitation Facilities (CARF) or the Joint Commission on Accreditation of Healthcare Organizations (JCAHO). In the case of SCI, has the facility been designated as a Model Spinal Cord Injury Center by the National Institute of Disability Research and Rehabilitation (NIDRR)? Is the SCI program part of an SCI rehabilitation system operated by the state?

# Acquired/chronic illnesses

A child may be perfectly healthy at birth, only to develop a serious, chronic condition, such as asthma or diabetes, or a life-threatening disease like cancer, later on. While the majority of kids don't develop chronic or potentially fatal illnesses, knowing the warning signs of certain conditions will help you get early treatment for your child if she does develop an illness.

## Asthma

Approximately 13 million Americans—nearly 5 million of whom are under the age of 18—have asthma, a chronic inflammatory disease of the airways, which causes recurrent episodes of wheezing, as well as other coldlike symptoms.

A rise in childhood asthma is a particular cause for concern. Between 1982 and 1993, the incidence of asthma in children under 18 rose by 80 percent. The National Heart, Lung, and Blood Institute (NHLBI) of the National Institutes of Health estimates that more than 7 percent of U.S. children have the disease.

Hospitalizations due to severe asthma attacks are also on the rise, primarily in kids age 4 and under, according to the Centers for Disease Control and Prevention (CDC). In 1980, the rate of asthma hospitalizations for children under age 1 was approximately 33 per 10,000; by 1992, the rate had more than doubled, to 67 per 10,000. For children between the ages of 1 and 4, the rate jumped from 39 per 10,000 to nearly 60 per 10,000.

Asthma-related crises are preventable, however. The first step is an accurate diagnosis. Often, early symptoms are inaccurately diagnosed as less severe allergies or colds. It's only after repeated attacks that asthma is considered. According to the American Medical Association, more than half of asthmatic children outgrow their asthma by age 21. For many others, attacks become decreasingly severe as they grow older. Kids who've experienced asthma, however, need to be aware that the condition could return later.

**Types of asthma** In 1997, The National Heart, Lung, and Blood Institute (NHLBI) issued new asthma diagnosis, treatment, and prevention guidelines and recommended that asthma be reclassified into four stages: mild intermittent, mild persistent, moderate persistent, and severe persistent.

The mildest form involves symptoms appearing less than twice a week and only brief exacerbations or "breathing crises." The severest form includes continual symptoms, prolonged crises, limited physical activity, and a lung function of less than 60 percent of the normal level. The type of asthma your child has should determine the treatment, including the use and dosage of various medications.

**Diagnosis and treatment** If your child shows any symptoms of asthma, and his doctor can't find another cause for his coughing or wheezing, your child should be refered to a pediatric allergist who specializes in the treatment of asthma.

Allergists diagnose asthma by taking a personal and family medical history. A child is more likely to develop the condition if a family member or close relative has had either asthma or an allergic condition such as hay fever or eczema.

The allergist will also give older children a "peak flow test." During the procedure, the youngster blows hard and fast into a tube that is attached to a device that measures his airflow. If his ability to blow—his "peak flow"—is less than it should be for his age and size, that's a clear sign that his bronchial tubes have clamped down. The doctor will then give him some asthma medicine and if his peak flow is normal after he takes it, it's pretty certain that he has asthma.

Diagnosing asthma in an infant is more difficult, but the allergist may have the baby inhale asthma medications to see if she responds. Tests may also be done to rule out other conditions.

When the condition is managed carefully, most episodes of asthma clear up on their own or can be controlled by use of a bronchodilator, medication that opens the airways. But occasionally, an asthma attack is so severe that your child requires hospitalization.

Emergency treatment at home or in the hospital may include oxygen administration, corticosteroid drugs, and a bronchodilator administered through a nebulizer (a machine that turns liquid medications into a mist that the child can inhale), or an intravenous injection of aminophylline. If these measures don't work, the child will be put on a ventilator, a machine that forces pressurized air or oxygen into the lungs.

To prevent emergencies, the NHLBI strongly recommends that doctors treat the underlying inflammation of the airways rather than just treating symptoms as they occur. Preventive treatments include using inhaled corticosteriods and/or cromolyn sodium. Children as young as 2 may benefit from a once-a-day dose of Singulair, a cherry-flavored pill that has been shown to prevent attacks. It's vital to work out a treatment plan with your child's physician that takes your child's particular allergy into account.

**Managing your child's asthma** In addition to removing the allergens that may trigger an attack, it's imperative to treat the underlying inflammation of the airways rather than simply treating the symptoms when symptoms do appear. As well as making sure your child's asthma is controlled by the proper medications, follow these recommendations:
- Evaluate allergies. Determine what specific allergens trigger your child's attacks. Your doctor may do allergy skin tests to pinpoint offending substances.

**PARENTS ALERT**

## Cockroaches Trigger Asthma in Kids

Cockroaches may cause 25 percent of all asthma in inner city areas, according to a major 1997 study financed by the National Institute of Allergy and Infectious Diseases. Proteins found in the insects' saliva, droppings, and remains seem to be the triggers.

To cut your child's risk of developing asthma—or of having an asthma attack caused by exposure to cockroach protein—caulk cracks and seal holes that allow the bugs to gain access to your apartment or house; cover all food, including pet foods; seal garbage; wash dishes as soon as you have used them; and put out roach traps. If you use insecticides to kill roaches, be sure to place them in areas where children and pets cannot get to them.

• Elimate triggers. The NHLBI strongly recommends that you minimize or eliminate environmental allergies and that you not expose your child to second-hand cigarette smoke; that your child forgo some foods to which she might be allergic; and that you find new homes for your furry or feathered pets. Step up housekeeping to keep dust and mildew under control, and avoid using products with fragrences.

• Filter the air. Consider installing an air conditioner in your child's room, rather than leaving her window open for ventilation. Use a dehumidifier in damp areas like basements; dust mites thrive in humidity. Clean the dehumidifier at least once a month. Buy an air purifier, ideally a mechanical one with a HEPA filter. An electrostatic air purifier requires very careful, frequent cleaning, and isn't as efficient.

• Design your child's bedroom for health. Remove curtains, upholstered furniture, and carpeting, especially if it's on concrete flooring. Encase her mattress and pillows in an airtight cover. Wash bed linens weekly in hot (130°F.) water. (After doing the laundry, turn the heater back to 120° to help prevent scalding.) Make sure plush toys are washable and made of synthetics. Encase pillows and mattresses in mite-reducing covers.

• Follow the prescribed medication schedule. It's essential that, even in the absence of symptoms, your child adheres to the medication schedule that his allergist has determined is best for him.

• Monitor the condition carefully. Get yourself and your child in the habit of using a peak-flow meter, once he's old enough to do so, so that you're able to see precisely, on a day-to-day basis, what his air flow is and, on the advice of your child's physician, to adjust his medications. Learn to use a stethscope so that you can listen for wheezing upon exhaling, a good way to determine if your child's symptoms are actually an asthma episode or a common cold.

• Call the doctor immediately if symptoms are severe.
Other symptoms that require a call to the doctor include:

• A fever with persistant cough, or wheezing that doesn't respond to the prescribed medications.

• Vomiting that precludes taking oral medication.

• Difficulty speaking or sleeping because of coughing, wheezing, or an inability to breathe properly.

• Side effects such as nausea, vomiting, loss of appetite,

headaches, hyperactivity, or shakiness, brought on by the drug theophylline, which is sometimes prescribed for asthmatics.

To treat crisis symptoms, inhaled beta-2-agonists (bronchodilators such as Albuterol, Proventil, and Ventolin) can be used—but they should be used with great caution, since overuse or overdose can lead to life-threatening episodes. Beta-2-agonists work by relaxing and widening the airways, allowing for normal breathing. The NHLBI does not recommend daily use of beta-2 drugs, and urges that parents not use over-the-counter broncholdilators, such as Primatene. Instead, they should get a prescription beta-2-agonist from their child's doctor, and use it only as needed.

### Keeping kids with asthma active

- Help your child choose exercises that have rest periods, such as softball or tennis.
- Consider swimming. Some asthmatic kids find that swimming is an ideal exercise, since the warm temperature and moist air make breathing easier. But beware of pools that are highly chlorinated; chlorine may trigger an asthma attack in susceptible children.
- Because attacks are more likely to occur in the morning, your child may want to schedule exercise during the afternoon.
- Your child should warm up properly, doing some stretching exercises as well as mild aerobic activities, such as walking.
- Help older kids learn how to do deep-breathing exercises; these will help increase the amount of air she's able to inhale and exhale.
- Suggest that your child do deep-breathing for 5 to 10 minutes after exercising.
- Make sure your child keeps a bronchodilator with her for use if an attack should occur.
- If possible, your child should avoid outdoor exercise during very dry cold weather, or when the pollen count is high or nearby grass has just been cut.

**PARENTS ALERT**

## When Asthma Requires Medical Help

Call your child's doctor immediately (or take her to a hospital emergency room or call 911) if she:
- Has severe trouble breathing, especially if the breathing is rapid and you notice that the chest wall seems to be "pulled in" when she inhales, or if there is forceful grunting when she exhales.
- Acts agitated, very lethargic, or confused, or her eyes or fingertips look blue or her skin appears darker than usual.
- Experiences chest, throat, or neck pain.

## Children with Asthma and Other Allergies

**National Heart, Lung, and Blood Institute**
(301) 592-8573
www.nhlbi.nih.gov

**The Asthma and Allergy Network/Mothers of Asthmatics**
(800) 878-4403
www.aanma.org

**The American Lung Association**
(800) LUNG-USA
www.lungusa.org

**Asthma and Allergy Foundation of America Information Helpline**
(800) 727-8462
www.aafa.org

**Lung Line**
(800) 222-5864

**The National Allergy Bureau and American Academy of Allergy, Asthma, and Immunology** For weekly pollen and mold-spore counts for many parts of the country, call (800) 9-POLLEN or (877) 9-ACHOO, or visit www.aaaai.org/nab.

The following companies offer products that can help reduce your child's risk of developing asthma or of having an allergy attack:

**Allergy Control Products, Inc.**
(800) 422-DUST
www.allergyproducts.com

**National Allergy Supply, Inc.**
(800) 522-1448
www.natlallergy.com

**Allergy Clean Environments**
(800) 882-4110
www.allergyclean.com

**Allergy Free**
(800) ALLERGY
www.allergy-free.com

## Cancer

Approximately 8,800 children were diagnosed with cancer in 1997, according to the American Cancer Society (ACS). Though cancer is the leading cause of death in children under age 15, mortality rates have declined dramatically in the last few decades. Thanks to advances in treatments, 70 percent of children who are diagnosed with cancer survive five years or more. The orgnaizations listed in the resource sections can provide the most up-to-date research on treatment options and support services.

**Warning signs and symptoms** It can be difficult for parents to recognize the warning signs of cancer in kids; that's why it's important that your child have regular medical and ophthalmological (eye) checkups. The following persistent symptoms may signal cancer: an unusual mass or swelling anywhere in or on the body or face; a sudden tendency to bruise easily; paleness or fatigue that can't be linked to a specific condition; persistent pain in an arm or leg or somewhere else in the body; limping; a prolonged, unexplained fever, even a low-grade one; frequent headaches, especially those accompanied by vomiting, and sudden vision changes; or unexplained, rapid weight loss.

## Acute lymphocytic (lymphoblastic) leukemia

Leukemia is not a single disease; rather it is several diseases that affect the blood-forming tissues of the body—including the lymph system, the spleen, and the bone marrow. About 1 in 23,000 kids develops some type of leukemia. The disease usually occurs between the ages of 2 and 6.

**Symptoms** include unusual fatigue or drowsiness, loss of appetite, abdominal pain, headache, and a general feeling of being unwell.

About half of kids also have fever as well as bleeding from the nose and gums, or under the skin, resulting in bruising. Children may have enlarged lymph glands, spleen, liver, or testicles. In some forms of leukemia, bone or joint pain is a chief symptom.

**Diagnosis and treatment** If your child's doctor suspects that she has a type of leukemia, your child will undergo a series of blood tests, as well as other tests.

Treatment for leukemia usually involves chemotherapy, which kills cancer cells. Other treatments include bone marrow transplants and central nervous system therapies that help prevent leukemia cells from growing in the brain.

## Children with Cancer

*Note: Many of these organizations offer a variety of pamphlets and books on managing cancer and cancer treatment.*

**The American Cancer Society (ACS)**
(800) ACS-2345
www.cancer.org

**The National Cancer Institute/Cancer Information Service**
(800) 4-CANCER
cis.nci.nih.gov

**The National Children's Cancer Society, Inc.**
(800) 5-FAMILY
www.children-cancer.com

**Association for Research of Childhood Cancer, Inc.**
P.O. Box 251
Buffalo, NY 14225-0251
(716) 681-4433

**Children's Leukemia Research Association, Inc.**
585 Stewart Ave., Suite 536
Garden City, NY 11530-0478
(516) 222-1944
www.childrensleukemia.org

**Candlelighters Childhood Cancer Foundation**
(800) 366-2223
(301) 657-8401
www.candlelighters.org

**Children's Organ Transplant Association, Inc.**
(800) 366-2682
www.cota.org

If your child has leukemia, he should be treated in a specialized center that is equipped to deal with the demands of the disease—from both a physical and emotional point of view. The National Cancer Institute (NCI) can help you locate such a facility.

## Diabetes (type 1)

Juvenile diabetes, once commonly known as insulin-dependent diabetes mellitus (IDDM), and referred to today as type 1 diabetes, occurs in children and young adults. It is believed to be inherited.

In kids with type 1 diabetes, the pancreas doesn't produce

enough insulin—a hormone the body needs to burn glucose. Glucose is a type of sugar that the body produces for energy, when starches and sugars are digested. When insulin levels are too low, unused glucose can build up in the blood and flow over into the urine. As a result, the body's cells don't get enough glucose and start to burn fat instead.

**Symptoms**  The most common symptoms of diabetes include frequent urination (this can be hard to spot in a child who wears diapers, but a sudden increase in the number of wet diapers is sometimes a clue), increased thirst, excessive appetite, unexplained weight loss, and extreme fatigue.

**Diagnosis and treatment**  If your child's doctor suspects he has diabetes, your child will undergo blood and urine tests for a positive diagnosis.

Type 1 diabetes should be treated by a medical team experienced in the care of children with diabetes. The team should include a primary physician or pediatrician, a nurse-educator, a dietitian who can help you create an eating plan that meets your child's unique needs, and, if possible, a social worker who can help you and your child deal with emotional concerns. To monitor vision, your child should also see an ophthalmologist each year. For recommendations and for listings of diabetes specialists, contact your local Juvenile Diabetes Foundation International (JDF).

**Managing your child's condition**  You'll need to keep your child's blood sugar levels as close to normal as possible. This involves achieving the right balance between insulin levels, food intake, and physical activity.

You can monitor your child's blood glucose level yourself with a commercially available blood glucose monitoring system. A member of your child's medical team can also show you how to take a drop of blood and place it on a chemically treated strip, which is then placed in a meter for reading. You'll also be instructed to be alert for any signs of shock. You will also learn to monitor your child's urine for ketones, which are a warning sign of ketoacidosis,

---

**PARENTS ALERT**

## When Diabetes Requires Medical Help

If your child shows signs of low blood sugar (confusion, inattention, drowsiness, paleness, heavy perspiration, trembling, lack of coordination, sudden hunger, and/or dizziness) give her sugar or sugary foods immediately. If low-blood sugar leads to unconsciousness, rub the inside of her mouth with sugar. If she doesn't respond within 15 minutes, give her an injection of glucajon and take her to the ER.

## *For Children with Diabetes*

*Juvenile Diabetes Foundation International* **(JDF)** offers numerous publications about managing IDDM.
 120 Wall Street
 New York, NY 10005-4001
 (800) JDF-CURE
 (212) 785-9500
 www.jdf.org

*National Diabetes Information Clearinghouse,* a service of the National Institute of Diabetes and Digestive and Kidney Diseases/National Institutes of Health, answers questions and distributes publications about diabetes.
 1 Information Way
 Bethesda, MD 20892-3560
 (301) 654-3327
 www.niddk.nih.gov/health/diabetes/ndic.htm

**Pamphlets on Diabetes**

The following pamphlets are available from JDF
 *Your Child Has Diabetes*
 *Monitoring Your Blood Sugar*
 *A Child with Diabetes Is in Your Care*
 (for teachers and caregivers)

a dangerous complication. Show baby-sitters, caregivers, and your child's teacher how to monitor glucose; write out detailed instructions for them as well.

Your child's doctor or nurse-educator will also teach you how to administer insulin injections. Your child's doctor will determine the number of daily insulin injections he needs. Try to stick to a schedule so you don't forget one. Vary the site of insulin injection so you give each area a rest between injections. Your local JDF chapter can supply you with charts that show various places on the body where insulin can be injected. Keep insulin at room temperature so injections will feel more comfortable. You and your partner and your child's other caregivers should all learn to give injections. When traveling, carry food and insulin in your hand luggage. Also carry a letter from your doctor, explaining why you have syringes in your suitcase or carry-on luggage. Bring spare bottles of insulin in case a bottle breaks. Keep in mind that changes in climate may affect your child's insulin needs. Discuss this with your doctor before traveling. Make sure your child gets the right amount of exercise, plus nutritious foods.

**Feeding your insulin-dependent child** After your child has had an insulin shot, she must eat. If a baby with type 1 diabetes isn't hungry, you'll need to use a dropper to feed her some formula. Check labels on commercial baby foods and packaged products to see if they have added sugars; avoid those that do. Your child shouldn't binge on concentrated sweets, such as sodas, candy, and frosting, but she can eat the same foods you and your family enjoy. The only difference is that the amount of food she eats and when she eats it should be as consistent as possible. She may require a mid-morning and mid-afternoon snack to help keep her blood sugar on an even keel.  If your baby is ill and vomits after an insulin injection, he needs to eat something that has enough carbohydrates to ward off an insulin reaction, but won't upset his stomach, such as ice-pops. Feed your child before she exercises.

## Epilepsy

Epilepsy is a disorder caused by abnormal electrical activity in the brain, which leads to recurrent seizures or convulsions. It's important to distinguish between epilepsy and "febrile seizures," which many infants experience due to a sudden rise in temperature. Epilepsy, on the other hand, causes recurrent seizures—sometimes as many as 100 an hour or as few as one or two a year. Both illness and brain injuries can lead to epilepsy. Children with cerebral palsy or autism are more prone to the disorder than are other children. Certain stimuli, such as flashing lights, can sometimes trigger a seizure in susceptible people. But most epileptic seizures occur spontaneously. Most people with epilepsy develop the condition during childhood or adolescence. There's no way to tell whether a child's epilepsy will disappear as he gets older, but some children—especially those with absence seizures—do eventually outgrow their condition. In others, seizure frequency seems to decrease with age.

**Types of seizures** An epileptic seizure can range from mild to severe and may last for only a few seconds to more than five minutes. While many children with epilepsy experience only one type of seizure, some experience two or more types.
- *Generalized tonic-clonic seizures*, also called *grand mal seizures* or convulsions, affect all the muscles and motor functions of the child's

---

### Type 2 Diabetes

Non-insulin-dependen diabetes (NIDDM)—also called type 2 diabetes—which usually strikes adults, seems to be on the rise in children, according to a 1997 study reported in the journal *Pediatrics*.

Kids with NIDDM do produce insulin, but not enough to meet the body's needs, especially if the child is overweight. In some cases, the child's body is resistant to the effects of insulin. Most cases of NIDDM do not require insulin injections. Instead, diet, weight reduction, and oral hypoglycemic medications are used to keep the condition under control.

The researchers found that kids with NIDDM were overweight, and about 92 percent had a body mass index higher than the 90th percentile for their height, age, and sex.

If your child is overweight, has a family history of NIDDM, and has hypertension (high blood pressure), he should be checked fort Type 2 diabetes—even if he shows none of the typical symptoms, such as increased thirst and frequent urination. Early-stage NIDDM may present no symptoms.

*For more information about febrile seizures, see* ***page 598***.

**PARENTS ALERT**

## When Epilepsy Requires Medical Help

If either of the following events occur, call your child's doctor. If you can't reach her, call an ambulance or take your child to a hospital ER:
• A generalized tonic-clonic seizure lasts more than five minutes.
• Your child has two of these seizures in a row without regaining consciousness.

body. The child loses consciousness and may fall, stiffen, and begin to jerk or twitch as his muscles tense and relax. He may stop breathing briefly and his skin may have a bluish tinge. After a minute or two, the jerking gradually stops and the child starts to breathe normally and regains consciousness. Following the episode, his muscles relax and he may lose control of his bowels or bladder. He'll probably be drowsy and confused or disoriented and won't remember what has happened. Post-seizure effects usually clear up within a few hours.

• *Absence seizures*, also called *petit mal seizures*, cause the child to lose consciousness momentarily. The child may sit perfectly still, or he might blink rapidly or move his mouth or arms. This "blank" period can last from a few seconds up to a minute or so. In some children, these momentary seizures occur hundreds of times a day, or even as much as 75 to 100 times an hour, and can significantly impair their ability to learn and function.

• *Atonic seizures* trigger a sudden loss of muscle tone. In some kids, the head falls forward or back. Other children fall to the ground. Because atonic seizures can lead to severe head injuries, children who have them must wear protective helmets until their condition is controlled.

• *Myoclonic seizures* cause brief muscle jerks that can involve the entire body or just the face or arms. A child may have a single myoclonic seizure, or a series of them—which can lead to a tonic-clonic seizure.

• *Infantile spasms* usually affect babies under 6 months of age and occur in clusters. A baby who has an infantile spasm may look startled or as though he is in pain. He may suddenly pull his knees and arms up to his stomach. If he's in a sitting position, his head and arms may fall forward. Often, the baby cries out.

• *Partial seizures* may cause jerking movements of one part of the body and affect the way things look, sound, smell, and taste to the child having the seizure. In a "simple" partial seizure, the child remains conscious. The seizure often starts with an abnormal twitching movement, as well as tingling in the extremities. Some children experience hallucinations of smell, vision, or taste. Afterward, the child can usually remember what has happened. A "complex" partial seizure alters the child's consciousness so he's unaware of what is happening. He may look dazed and won't respond when spoken to. He may also experience involuntary actions, such as smacking his lips, picking at his clothing, or moving his arms and legs. He may also stand up and walk around or run or scream, or he might mumble. When the seizure has ended, the child will remember little or nothing about what has happened. If your child has a partial seizure, avoid trying to keep him from walking or running, unless he is clearly in danger.

**Diagnosis and treatment**  If your child has several seizures, her doctor will want to test for epilepsy as well as rule out other problems, such as a metabolic disorder. Your child will undergo a physical and neurological exam. The doctor will also take personal and family medical histories, noting if any other members of your family—parents, grandparents, aunts, uncles, cousins—had epilepsy. The doctor will also probably order an EEG (electroencephalograph), a test that measures brain wave activity. Other diagnostic tests may include MRI (magnetic resonance imaging) scans, which take pictures of the inside of the brain, PET (positron emission tomography) scans, which picture brain function, and CT (computerized tomography) scans, which take pictures of the inside of the head.

Anticonvulsant medications can be used to effectively control epileptic seizures in most children. These may cause side effects, such as drowsiness, lethargy, hyperactivity, loss of muscular coordination, stomach aches, or sleep problems, but for most children the side effects are mild. In the rare incidence that medications don't work, doctors may consider brain surgery to repair possible damage in an area of the brain. A strict diet, known as the ketogenic diet, may also be prescribed. For more information about this diet, contact the Epilepsy Foundation of America.

**Managing your child's condition**  After your child has had a seizure, comfort her, especially if she's lost control of her bowels or bladder. Reassure her that this is just part of the seizure and that it's okay. If your child has frequent seizures, keep an extra change of clothes handy—in her cubby at school, at a friend's house, etc. Avoid appearing anxious or upset. Make sure your child wears all appropriate protective athletic gear—like a helmet, knee and elbow pads, and wrist protectors—while participating in sports. Although you should always supervise kids when they are near water, it's especially critical in the case of a child who has epilepsy. Your child should swim only in pools that are continuously supervised by

See **page 682** for information on handling a seizure.

## For Children with Epilepsy

**The Epilepsy Foundation of America (EFA)** offers information about epilepsy diagnosis and treatment and refers families to community resources. The EFA has affiliates across the country which offer a wide variety of services, including counseling, support groups, contact with other families, medical referrals, and legal assistance.
(800) EFA-1000
(301) 459-3700
www.efa.org

### Books for Parents

*Seizures and Epilepsy in Childhood: A Guide for Parents* by John M. Freeman, M.D., Eileen P.G. Vining, M.D., and Diana J. Pillas (The Johns Hopkins University Press)

*A Guide to Understanding and Living with Epilepsy* by Orrin Devinsky, M.D. (F.A. Davis Company)

*The Epilepsy Diet Treatment: An Introduction to The Ketogenic Diet* (second edition) by John M. Freeman, M.D., Millicent T. Kelly, R.D., L.D., and Jennifer B. Freeman (Demos Medical Publishing). *Caution:* Parents should not attempt to start their child on this diet without the advice and supervision of a physician who is very familiar with it.

*The Americans with Disabilities Act: A Guide to Provisions Affecting Persons with Seizure Disorders*

*Your Child and Epilepsy: A Guide to Living Well* by Robert J. Gumnit, M.D. (Demos Medical Publishing)

### Books for Children

*Lee, the Rabbit with Epilepsy* by Deborah M. Moss (Woodbine House); All ages.

*Dotty the Dalmatian has Epilepsy* (from the Dr. Wellbook Collection, Tim Peters & Company); Ages 2 to 6.

qualified lifeguards, if you can't be with her. Tell lifeguards at pools and camps that your child has epilepsy. Tell your child's baby-sitter, teachers, and other caregivers about her condition. Give them written instructions that explain what to do—and what not to do—if she has a seizure. Alert your child's doctor to any medication side effects your child experiences. If your child is taking medication and becomes listless or weak for no apparent reason, call her doctor immediately.

# HIV and AIDS

HIV is the human immunodeficiency virus that causes AIDS, or acquired immune deficiency syndrome. When HIV enters the body, it invades many cells and eventually destroys them. Some white blood cells—an important part of the body's immune system—are also destroyed, and the infected person can't fight off infections and illness. HIV-infected moms can transmit the virus in the womb to the fetus or through their breast milk to their nursing infants.

**Symptoms** include failure to thrive, unusual fatigue, night sweats, swollen glands, diarrhea, fever, developmental delays, and neurologic symptoms.

Children with HIV often develop life-threatening opportunistic infections, including pneumocystis carinii pneumonia (PCP), cytomegalovirus (CMV) disease, a lung infection called lymphocytic interstitial pneumonitis (LIP), and candidiasis, a yeast infection that can cause unrelenting diaper rash and infections in the mouth and throat that make eating difficult. Children with HIV also suffer the usual childhood bacterial infections—but more frequently and more severely than uninfected kids.

About 20 percent develop serious disease in the first year of life. In the remaining 80 percent, the disease progresses more slowly, and many don't develop the most serious symptoms until the grade-school years or even adolescence.

**Diagnosis and treatment** A blood test called polymerase chain reaction (PCR) is highly accurate in diagnosing HIV infection in children 6 months and younger. Doctors can also culture samples of an infant's blood and test it for the presence of HIV. Currently, PCR assays or HIV culture techniques can identify about one-third of newborns who are HIV-infected. The tests can also identify approximately 90 percent of HIV-infected infants by 2 months of age, and 95 percent by 3 months of age.

Two anti-AIDS drugs, AZT and didanosine (ddI), which slow the growth of the virus, are widely used to treat infected children. Zalcitabine (ddC) and stavudine (d4T) are also available for use in children.

In 1997, the U.S. Food and Drug Administration approved the use of protease inhibitors (Norvir and Viracept) in children. Although protease inhibitors are not a cure, when used in combination with AZT and other antiviral drugs, they have significantly suppressed the AIDS virus to undetectable levels in adults. Other drugs, such as antibiotics and anti-fungals, are used to treat the opportunistic infections that occur in HIV-infected kids.

**PARENTS RESOURCES**

### For Children with HIV and AIDS

**AIDS Clinical Trials Information Service**
(800) TRIALS-A
www.actis.org

**AIDS Hotline**
(800) 342-AIDS
www.ashastd.org/nah/nah.html

**CDC National Prevention Information Network**
(800) 458-5231

**HIV/AIDS Treatment Information Service**
(800) HIV-0440
www.hivatis.org

**The Pediatric AIDS Foundation**
(415) 883-1796
(310) 395-9051

**The Pediatric Oncology Branch of the National Cancer Institute**
(301) 496-4256
www.dcs.nci.nih.gov/pedonc

**Managing your child's condition** The following precautions can help protect your child from opportunistic infections:
- Be alert for any changes in your child's health or behavior. If you notice anything unusual, call her doctor. For a child with AIDS, little problems can quickly turn into big problems.
- Talk to your child's doctor before she receives any immunizations or booster shots. Some vaccines could make her sick. No child with HIV—or anyone in the household or anyone caring for the child—should take the live polio vaccine.
- Try to keep your child away from adults or children with infectious diseases, especially chicken pox. If your child comes into contact with anyone who has chicken pox—or who has been near somebody with the disease—call her doctor immediately.
- If your child gets a cut or scrape, wash it immediately with soap and warm water and put a bandage over the entire lesion, taking precautions to protect yourself as well.
- Make sure that you, your other children, and your child's regular caregivers get a yearly flu vaccination. This will prevent you and them from getting the flu and passing the illness to your child.
- Follow stringent household and personal hygiene routines.
- Be especially careful not to feed your child unpasteurized milk, raw eggs, or undercooked beef, pork, chicken, fish, or other meats. Avoid shellfish and "organic" foods since they may harbor bacteria, fungi, and/or molds.
- Keep your child away from litter boxes and sandboxes that a pet or other animal has used. Infected children should avoid lizards (including iguanas) and pet-store turtles, which can carry salmonella.

# Juvenile rheumatoid arthritis (JRA)

About 200,000 children in the U.S. have some type of arthritis. The most common form affecting children is juvenile rheumatoid arthritis, which affects approximately 71,000 American children. JRA is an autoimmune disease, in which the body's immune system attacks the body itself. There's some evidence that in kids with JRA, white blood cells called lymphocytes lose the ability to distinguish parts of the body—such as the cartilage in the joints—from harmful agents like germs or bacteria. This leads to the release of chemicals that may attack and damage the body's own tissues.

**Types of JRA** Signs and symptoms of JRA can surface—then disappear—from day to day. Or, they may occur in the morning, but not in the afternoon, or in the evening—only to subside by bedtime. Joint pain and stiffness may be hardly noticeable one day and so severe the next that the child has great difficulty moving. There are three forms of JRA: polyarticular, pauciarticular, and systemic.

*Polyarticular JRA* Polyarticular JRA affects five or more joints. This form of JRA causes stiffness in the small joints of the fingers and hands, though the knees, hips, ankles, feet, neck, and jaw can also be affected. It often affects the same joint on both sides of the body. Some kids have a low fever, a positive blood test for rheumatoid factor, and nodules or lumps on the elbow or other parts of the body that receive repeated pressure from chairs, shoes, or other objects. More girls are affected than boys.

*Pauciarticular JRA* This form of JRA affects four or fewer joints. The most common symptoms are inflammation, pain, and stiffness of the large joints, such as the knees, elbows, and ankles, often affecting a joint on only one side of the body. It can also cause an eye inflammation called iridocyclitis.

*Systemic JRA* This form affects both the joints and the internal organs. The most common symptoms are fevers, usually beginning in the late afternoon or evening. The fever may be intermittent, but can last for weeks or months. Children with systemic JRA also suffer from chills and shaking. Pale red spots on the chest and thighs, and sometimes on other parts of the body also appear. Joint inflammation may begin with the fever, or it may start weeks or months later. Some children have inflammation of the outer lining of the heart, the heart itself, or the lungs; anemia; a high white blood cell count; and enlarged lymph nodes, liver, and spleen. Boys and girls are equally affected by systemic JRA.

Although JRA is a chronic disease which may last for many years, some kids eventually get well and experience no significant or permanent disability. Occasionally symptoms disappear for months or years; this is called a "remission." No one can predict which children will experience long-term remissions or be "cured." But most kids with JRA are able to lead active lives, keeping up with

**PARENTS RESOURCES**

### For Children with JRA

**Arthritis Foundation** and **The American Juvenile Arthritis Organization (AJAO)**
(800) 283-7800
www.arthritis.org

**Lung Line**
(800) 222-5864

school and social activities. When flare-ups do occur, changes in the child's schedule may have to be made.

If your child has JRA, he will probably suffer intermittent joint inflammation, which causes heat, pain, swelling, and stiffness in the joints. The skin over the affected joints may become red as well. Because it hurts to move an inflamed joint, your child may hold his arm, wrist, or leg in a bent position. If he holds the joint in one position for a long time, the muscles around it may become stiff and weak. The tendons may then tighten and shorten, causing a deformity called "joint contracture." Proper exercise, prescribed by your child's doctor, can help prevent this.

Children with severe JRA have long-lasting inflammation that can damage the joint surfaces. This joint erosion can cause pain and limit the range of motion in the limb or digit. Occasionally, joint inflammation speeds up or slows down the growth centers in bones, which can make bones longer, shorter, or bigger than they should be.

**Diagnosis and treatment** If your child has symptoms of JRA, his doctor will conduct a thorough physical exam, which will rule out other illnesses that include arthritis symptoms. If JRA is suspected, the doctor may suggest that an ophthalmologist check your child's eyes for signs of iridocyclitis. She may also refer your child to a pediatric rheumatologist, a physician who specializes in the diagnosis and treatment of childhood arthritis. There are a number of laboratory tests, including blood work, that can help doctors diagnose JRA, but no one test provides positive proof. Your child's doctors may also order X rays of certain joints to rule out other conditions, such as a bone infection or fracture. They may also take a sample of fluid from one or more joints to see if an infection is present.

Treatment programs usually include medications, exercise, eye care, dental care, and a healthy diet. Some children find that their pain and stiffness can be eased by combining traditional medical treatments with progressive muscle relaxation, deep breathing, and guided imagery. A number of medications can control inflammation and pain. Your child's doctor will probably start with nonsteroidal anti-inflammatory drugs (NSAIDSs, such as ibuprofen, naproxen, and tolmetin), or aspirin. While aspirin is generally not recommended for children because of the risk of Reye syndrome, doctors do use it to treat JRA. But they carefully monitor the child for any adverse reactions. If those treatments don't work effectively, the doctor may add more potent anti-rheumatic drugs or cortico-steroids. All of these drugs have side effects, but by experimenting with various medications, your child's doctor should be able to find one that provides relief with a minimum of side effects. Your child's doctor will also frequently test your child's kidney and liver function to make sure the drugs aren't causing serious harm.

Occasionally, surgery is used to relive pain, ease joint contrac-tures, or to replace a damaged joint, but surgery is usually neces-sary in severe cases only.

**Managing your child's JRA** In addition to medications, your child's doctor will probably recommend some or all of the following:
• Exercise is an essential part of treatment for JRA. Exercise keeps the joints mobile, helps keep muscles strong, aids in regaining lost motion or strength, and makes everyday activities, such as walking, easier. Your child's doctor may recommend therapeutic exercise, such as range-of-motion exercises, sports, and various recreational activities. A physical or occupational therapist can work with your child to outline an exercise program. During exercise, make sure your child wears protective equipment, such as elbow pads and knee pads, to prevent further injury to her joints.
• A healthy diet is important since some kids with JRA have nutri-tional problems associated with their illness, such as loss of ap-petite, which can lead to weight loss and poor growth.
• Good dental care is a must, since some kids with JRA have difficulty flossing or brushing their teeth. Your child's dentist can suggest various toothbrush handles, electric toothbrushes, floss holders, and rinses that will help your child keep his teeth and gums healthy. Tell your child's dentist about your child's JRA, especially if your child has had a joint replacement. He may need to take an-tibiotics before any dental treatment.
• Regular eye exams are critical. Your child should see an oph-thalmologist as soon as he is diagnosed and should have regular checkups.

# *Birth defects and injuries*

Birth defects occur in one of every 28 births, according to the March of Dimes. The term "birth defects" covers a range of about 3,000 abnormal conditions, ranging from heart defects to skeletal deformities to body chemistry abnormalities. The good news is that many children born with a birth defect go on to lead full, active lives.

**Types of birth defects** There are five major types of birth defects:
• Malformations present at birth. These include spina bifida, cleft palate, and heart malformations.
• Metabolic defects. These are diseases of body chemistry, and include cystic fibrosis, PKU, and muscular dystrophy.
• Blood disorders, such as sickle cell disease and haemophilia.
• Chromosomal abnormalities that result in conditions such as Down syndrome.
• Perinatal damage. Injuries to the fetus before or during birth, such as cerebral palsy.

## Malformations present at birth

Birth defects such as club foot and cleft palate, heart abnormalities, and spina bifida (open spine) can occur in some children. In many cases, doctors are able either to surgically repair the malformation or to lessen the severity of the problem.

### *Cleft lip and/or palate*

A cleft is an opening or split that occurs in parts of the lip, the roof of the mouth (the hard palate), or the soft tissue in the back of the mouth (soft palate). Normally, such openings are present in early fetal development, but close by the tenth or twelfth week of gestation. In about 1 out of every 700 babies, the openings fail to close.

Clefts may be very mild or very severe. A baby may have just a single notch in the upper lip—or a complete opening in the lip, extending into the floor of the nostril and upper gum. Clefts of the lip may occur on one or both sides. Cleft palate can occur alone or along with a cleft lip. One or both sides of the palate may be involved. Children with clefts may also have ear and dental problems. Untreated, clefts can lead to problems with feeding and speech development.

**Treating clefts** If your child was born with a cleft, her doctor will probably recommend specialists who will work together in her treatment. Most cleft teams include a primary pediatrician, a plastic surgeon, dental specialists, an otolaryngologist (an ear, nose, and throat specialist), a speech-language pathologist, an audiologist (hearing specialist), a psychologist, and a social worker.

A cleft lip and/or palate is corrected surgically. Most surgeons feel that a cleft lip should be repaired when the baby is about 3 months old, while cleft palate repair is usually done between 12 and 18 months. Kids may need additional surgical procedures as they grow.

Because some primary and permanent teeth may be missing, or may grow abnormally around a cleft, an orthodontist may need to use braces to reposition your child's teeth. Oral surgeons can reposition segments of the upper jaw, when needed, to improve its function and appearance.

**Managing your child's condition** Babies with a cleft lip usually don't have much trouble feeding, but those with cleft palate may have difficulty sucking forcefully. Though babies with small cleft palates have more success breast-feeding, those with larger clefts have great difficulty. If you want to make sure your baby drinks breast milk, express it into a bottle and feed it to your baby.

If your baby has a cleft palate, you can make sure he gets enough to eat by:
• Holding him in a sitting position to help keep breast milk or formula from leaking into his nose through the cleft.
• Using a preemie nipple on a squeeze bottle, and gently squeezing the bottle to help your child get enough milk or formula.
• Using a soft nipple with a cross-cut opening, which will allow the milk or formula to flow more freely.

Babies with cleft palate are especially prone to middle ear disease since the cleft allows fluid to build up in the middle ear. This can lead to mild or moderate hearing loss, as well as middle ear infections. Treated properly during infancy and early childhood, hearing loss needn't be permanent.

All babies with cleft palate should be examined by an audiologist

**PARENTS RESOURCES**

## *Birth Defects*

*March of Dimes Resource Center*
1275 Mamaroneck Avenue
White Plains, NY 10605
(888) MODIMES
www.modimes.org

(hearing specialist) during the first three to six months of life. Hearing should be tested regularly in babies and children who have cleft palate.

Your child may need some psychological counseling in order to deal with the difference in appearance a cleft causes. (Even though clefts can be repaired, multiple surgeries may be necessary to reduce lip deformities and scars, a process that could take years.) Also, your child may feel self-conscious about any speech problems that occur because of a cleft palate.

## *Clubfoot*

Clubfoot is a term that describes several types of ankle and foot abnormalities which are usually present at birth. The defect can be mild or severe, and one or both feet can be affected. Clubfoot is one of the most common of all birth defects; about 1 in 400 American infants is born with the condition each year. Boys are affected twice as often as girls.

**Types of clubfoot** There are three major types of clubfoot: In the most severe type, the foot is twisted inward and downward. This type is referred to as *equinovarus*. When both feet are "clubbed," the toes of each point toward each other. The cord in the heel may be tight as well, which makes it impossible for the baby to draw his foot up to a normal position. A more common and less severe type of clubfoot, *calcaneal valgus*, causes the foot to be sharply angled upward and outward at the heel. In the mildest type of clubfoot, *metatarsus varus*, the front part of the foot is turned inward. The condition is present at birth, but may not be diagnosed until the child is a month to several months old.

**Diagnosis and treatment** The condition may not be readily apparent. A child may have difficulty standing and walking. Toddlers with clubfoot look like they are walking on a stiffened leg or "peg" since the foot doesn't move up and down like it should.

When both feet are affected, the child may walk on the balls of his feet. If they are badly twisted, he may walk on the sides or the top part of his feet. These areas may become hardened or lumpy or infected.

If the condition is mild, a physical therapist may teach parents how to exercise the baby's foot to move it into proper position. Also, the baby may sleep in shoes connected to a bar that hold the feet in the correct position. In moderate to severe cases, plaster casts or surgery help realign the foot.

With early treatment, most kids with clubfoot go on to wear regular shoes and lead a full, active life, walking normally and taking part in sports.

## Congenital heart defects

Each year about 32,000 American babies are born with a congenital heart defect. These defects are the most frequent congenital malformations in newborns, and can range from from mild to severe. A congenital defect occurs when the heart or blood vessels near the heart don't develop normally prior to birth. The most common are septal defects. Kids with septal defects have an opening between the wall (septum) that separates the right and left sides of the heart. Such a defect is often called "hole in the heart."

For information about murmurs, see **page 613**.

For information about arrhythmias, see **page 614**.

**Types of septal heart defects** There are two kinds of septal defects:

• *Atrial septal defect* (ASD) In this condition, there's an opening between the two upper chambers of the heart, which allows some blood from the left atrium (blood that's already traveled to the lungs) to return via the hole to the right atrium, instead of flowing through the left ventricle, out the aorta and to the rest of the body. Many kids with ASD have few—or no—symptoms. But they can encounter serious problems later in life if the defect isn't detected and repaired. ASD occurs in about 64 to 104 per 100,000 births. ASD is sometimes detected when a child's parents notice that she tires or seems pale while nursing. But often, the condition isn't detected until later in childhood, sometimes during the preschool years, when the child's doctor hears a heart murmur through a stethoscope.

• *Ventricular septal defect* (VSD) In this condition, there's an opening between the two lower chambers of the heart. Some blood that has returned from the lungs and has been pumped into the left ventricle flows into the right ventricle through the hole, rather than being pumped into the aorta. The heart, which has to pump extra blood, is overworked and can become enlarged. VSD ocurs in about 160 to 200 per 100,000 births.

**Symptoms** may be apparent at birth or not show up until later in childhood, adolescence, or adulthood. A major clue in infants and young children is "cyanosis" or a blue tinge of the skin, especially on the fingers, toes, and lips. Babies and toddlers may be easily fatigued. Some are so tired that they have trouble nursing. Children with congenital heart defects may have weakness and poor weight gain.

**Diagnosis and treatment** If symptoms of heart problems, a family history of heart defects, or other indications are present, your child's doctor will conduct tests to diagnose or rule out heart problems. The doctor may order X rays, which will reveal important information about your child's lungs and the size and shape of his heart. Your child will also have an electrocardiogram (EKG), in which a machine receives tiny electrical impulses from the beating heart and records them in a zig-zag pattern on a moving strip of paper; or an echocardiogram (ECG), a procedure that uses high-frequency sound waves to get a picture of the heart and its valves while they are in motion. Blood tests may also be performed.

In some cases, these preliminary tests won't provide enough information for a diagnosis and the cardiologist will recommend more tests. These complex tests should be done at a hospital that has a diagnostic staff specially trained to care for babies and children with heart disease.

Drugs may be used to control symptoms of some defects, and surgery may be performed to repair defects (especially ASD and VSD). Surgery may be performed as early as the first few months of life. When a heart defect is diagnosed before birth, medications may be used to correct the condition before the baby is born.

Because kids with a ventricular septal defect are at higher risk for infection of the heart's walls or valves (a condition called endocarditis), they need to take high doses of antibiotics before and after certain dental and surgical procedures.

**Managing your child's condition** Most kids with congenital heart defects can lead a fully active life. In fact, doctors usually encourage children to engage in regular physical activity, which strengthens their hearts and cardiovascular systems. If your doctor gives the thumbs up, let your child take part in a variety of activity that is typical for a child his age, whether it be helping a toddler learn to climb steps or a preschooler learning to bike. Occasionally, doctors do advise that children avoid certain strenuous activities.

## Hirschsprung's disease

Hirschsprung's disease is a congenital disorder in which a segment of the intestine, usually near the anus, lacks the nerve cells that control the rhythmic movement of the bowel—making it difficult for stool to pass through the colon and out the rectum.

**Symptoms** include chronic constipation, bloating, poor appetite, and a failure to thrive.

**Diagnosis and treatment** A barium enema may show the narrowed rectal segment of the intestine, but absolute diagnosis must be made through a surgical biopsy of the colon to confirm the absence of nerve cells.

Treatment involves surgically removing the narrowed intestinal segment and rejoining the normal colon to the normal colonic or rectal segments.

## Spina bifida

Spina bifida—often referred to as "open spine"—is a defect of the child's backbone and, sometimes, the spinal cord. It's one of a group of birth defects known as neural tube defects. The neural tube is a structure in the embryo that develops into the fetal brain and spine. Every fetus's spine is open when it first forms, but it usually closes within 29 days after conception. In children with spina bifida, however, the spine doesn't close completely. About 1 in 2,000 infants is born with some form of spina bifida.

**Types of spina bifida** Spina bifida ranges from mild to severe. In the mildest form, there is a small defect or gap in a few of the small bones that make up the spine. The spinal cord and nerves are usually normal, and the child will probably experience no problems from the defect and won't require any special treatment.

In another form, which is the rarest, a cyst consisting of membranes that surround the spinal cord pushes through the open part of the spine. The spinal cord and nerves are usually normal. The cyst, which can be small or grow to the size of a grapefruit, can be removed by surgery, which allows the baby to develop normally.

The most severe form of spina bifida often involves a cyst that encompasses the nerve roots of the spinal cord—and sometimes the cord itself. Or, there may be no cyst, but part of the spine and nerve are exposed. Babies with severe spina bifida are at risk of infections, such as meningitis, until their spine is closed surgically, usually within 48 hours after birth.

**Treatment** If your baby is born with the mildest form of the condition, no treatment is usually needed. Surgery is required in moderate to severe cases. Babies with the most severe form are usually operated on within 48 hours after birth.

Surgery involves releasing the spinal cord from the cyst and replacing it in the spinal canal. The cord is then covered with muscle and skin. After surgery, a physical therapist can instruct you how to exercise your baby's legs. Later on, toddlers are fitted with leg braces and special crutches which help them walk. Some children need to use a wheelchair. Since many kids will have problems with leg paralysis and bowel and bladder control throughout life, orthopedists and urologists will be a part of their health-care team.

About 70 to 90 percent of kids with severe spina bifida also have a condition called hydrocephalus—or "water on the brain." This occurs when the cerebrospinal fluid, which cushions the brain and spinal cord, doesn't drain normally due to the spinal defect. As fluid collects in and around the brain, the head enlarges. Untreated, the condition can cause mental retardation. Treatment for hydrocephalus involves drainng the fluid from the brain through a surgically inplanted "shunt."

# Metabolic defects

Metabolic defects occur when cells aren't able to produce proteins or enzymes needed to convert certain chemicals into others—or when cells fail to carry particular substances from one area of the body to another. Symptoms of metabolic disorders may not surface until weeks or months after a child's birth.

## Celiac disease

Celiac disease is a digestive disorder that occurs when foods containing the protein gluten, such as wheat, barley, oats, or rye, are introduced into a susceptible baby's diet. The gluten triggers an immune reaction in the lining of the small intestine, rendering it incapable of absorbing essential nutrients, and the child fails to thrive.

**Symptoms** include abdominal cramps, foul-smelling diarrhea, weight loss and poor growth, and irritability.

**Diagnosis and treatment** The child's doctor will start by ruling out other problems, such as lactose intolerance. She may then surgically remove a small piece of the child's intestine for a laboratory analysis. The procedure, which does not require a general anesthetic, is done by passing a small tube through the baby's mouth to the small intestine. If the doctor finds that the lining of the intestine is damaged, she will recommend a gluten-free diet. Rice and rice cereals are often recommended in place of grains. If your child is diagnosed with celiac disease, it's important to check all food labels to make sure they do not include any gluten-containing foods.

Doctors usually do a second biopsy once the child's condition has improved, to confirm their original diagnosis. If your child does have celiac disease, he'll have to steer clear of gluten foods for the rest of his life. He may also need vitamin supplements to replace vitamins contained in grains.

*For information on lactose intolerance, see **page 517**.*

## Cystic fibrosis (CF)

Cystic fibrosis is an inherited disease that causes the exocrine glands in the body to function abnormally, leading to respiratory and digestive complications. The exocrine glands produce thin secretions, such as sweat, mucus, tears, saliva, and digestive juices. These secretions are carried through small tubes—or ducts—to the skin or internal organs. But in a child with CF, these glands often produce thick, sticky secretions that clog ducts. Plugs of mucus occur most often in the lungs and the intestines and make breathing and proper digestion difficult.

About 2,000 American children are born with CF each year, according to the Cystic Fibrosis Foundation.

While there is no cure for CF, researchers are progressing in their attempt to develop a gene therapy drug that could wipe out the disease. Continued therapy, including, in some cases of advanced lung disease, lung transplants, has changed the prognosis considerably from a generation ago, when the disease was fatal to most youngsters with symptoms. For children born now with CF, the prognosis is good.

**Symptoms** include wheezing; persistent cough with excessive mucus; recurrent bouts of pneumonia; failure to thrive or gain weight—even if the child has a good appetite; abnormal bowel movements, including chronic diarrhea and/or frequent, bulky, greasy, and foul-smelling stools; salty-tasting skin; nasal polyps; and enlargement, or clubbing, of the fingertips and toes.

**Diagnosis and treatment** About 10 to 15 percent of babies with CF are diagnosed at birth. In most of these children, a blockage in their bowels—caused by thickened mucus—is the first symptom. But in the majority of cases, the diagnosis is made during the first three years of life, when children develop other symptoms of the disease. A handful of those with the disease don't develop symptoms until later in childhood, adolescence, or even in adulthood.

If CF is suspected, the disease is diagnosed by measuring the salt content in the child's sweat (CF causes large amounts of salt to be excreted in sweat). Since babies under 1 month of age usually don't produce enough sweat for accurate testing, a DNA test can be used to identify CF gene mutations, and a blood test done two to three days after the baby's birth can also identify and measure a chemical involved in the disorder.

For most CF kids, proper therapy, which clears mucus from the airways, can slow damage to the lungs. Your child's doctor will prescribe physical chest therapy, exercise, antibiotics, and medications that can be inhaled to help make breathing easier. A physical therapist can teach you how to perform chest therapy for your child. Additional therapies include a nutritional plan; enzyme supplements to keep the pancreas working and to aid in weight gain and decrease bouts of diarrhea; and vitamin therapy with water-soluable vitamins. Your child's doctor will perform periodic lung function tests to see how well she is breathing, as well as phlegm cultures to check for evidence of an active infection in the lungs. If your child experiences an intestinal obstruction, his doctor will probably treat it with an appropriate diet and enzyme replacement; special agents that help break up the thick mucus and stool in the intestine; and enemas.

**Managing your child's CF** Your child's medical team will work with you to alleviate each of the problems associated with CF. These include:
• Providing respiratory therapy. You or another therapist will "thump" your child's chest and back to unclog mucus daily. Eventually, everyone with CF develops lung disease, but how severe it will be and how soon it will occur varies from person to person.
• Preventing salt loss. Hot weather, strenuous exercise, and fever can cause your child to sweat profusely and lose excessive amounts of salt. If she loses too much salt, she may experience fatigue, weakness, fever, muscle cramps, abdominal pain, vomiting, heat prostration or heat stroke, and/or dehydration. You can treat salt depletion by having your older child carry her own salt shaker with her so she can take in extra salt. In most cases, though,

## PARENTS RESOURCES

### For Children with CF

**Cystic Fibrosis Foundation** offers information on managing CF, plus various publications. CFF can refer you to 113 CF care centers nationwide, which provide high-quality, specialized care for people with CF.
  6931 Arlington Rd.
  Bethesda, MD 20814
  (800) FIGHT-CF
  www.cff.org

The Cystic Fibrosis Foundation offers the publication **Consumer Fact Sheet: An Introduction to Chest Physical Therapy**, which describes this form of therapy in detail. To order, call the foundation.

**Cystic Fibrosis Services, Inc.** This home-infusion and pharmacy service is a subsidiary of the Cystic Fibrosis Foundation and offers lower-cost drugs; negotiation with insurance and managed-care agencies for coverage; and home infusion therapy at a lower cost.
  (800) 541-4959
  www.cff.org/cfservices.htm

**Books**

**Cystic Fibrosis: A Guide for Patient and Family** (second edition) by David M. Orenstein (Lippincott-Raven).

allowing your child to eat salty foods and add salt to other foods will help her avoid salt depletion. When your child sweats a lot—during exercise, or hot weather, or a fever—encourage her to drink more fluids and to increase salt intake. A few kids with CF must avoid taking in too much salt because of other medical conditions. You don't need to restrict your child's activities to prevent salt loss, but she may need to avoid situations that promote excessive sweating.

• Encouraging physical exercise. Exercise stimulates coughing, which helps clear the lungs, and helps loosen mucus in the lungs so that it can be easily coughed up. Exercise also helps strengthen your child's breathing muscles.

• Monitor the diet. Your child may not absorb the needed nutrients from his foods. Also, the mucus that is supposed to lubricate his intestines may become so sticky and thick it can block them, causing failure to gain weight; diarrhea; bulky foul-smelling stools; abdominal pain or discomfort; and excessive gas. In addition to enzyme and vitamin supplements, your child's doctor may prescribe a high-calorie diet. While kids with CF need to consume the same healthy foods other kids eat, some need more calories for proper growth and development. If your child has a problem gaining weight, also ask his doctor about giving him a nutritional supplement.

## Muscular dystrophy (MD)

Muscular dystrophy is an inherited muscle disorder that causes a slow but progressive degeneration of muscle fibers.

**Types of MD** There are several forms of muscular dystrophy, which are classified according to the age at which symptoms appear, the rate at which the disease progresses, and the way in which it is inherited. *Duchenne muscular dystrophy* (DMD), which is the most common form, is rarely diagnosed before age 3. *Becker's muscular dystrophy* (BMD) is less common and occurs later in childhood, but produces many of the same symptoms as the Duchenne form. About 1 in 3,500 newborn males is affected by DMD or BMD.

With currently available treatment, most children with DMD lose their ability to walk by about age 12, and few survive their teen years. However, continued research offers hope to children recently diagnosed. Boys with DMD often, but not always, have a below-average intelligence. People with BMD often live to age 50.

**Symptoms** A child with Duchenne muscular dystrophy may be slow in learning to sit up and walk. Once symptoms appear, the condition progresses rapidly, and affected kids tend to walk with a waddle and have difficulty climbing stairs. When they try to get up from the floor, they may use their hands to push against their ankles, knees, and thighs—something known as "climbing up the legs." Some children with DMD have curvature of the spine, which makes them look swaybacked and barrel-chested. Despite their weakness, the muscles—especially calf muscles— look bulky; this occurs because degenerated muscle is replaced by fat. A child with BMD shows symptoms later than age 3 and the condition progresses more slowly than DMD.

> **PARENTS RESOURCE**
>
> ## *Musculary Dystrophy*
>
> *Muscular Dystrophy Association* provides information about all types of muscular dystrophy and can refer you to 230 clinics and 200 support groups in the U.S. Also has an "Ask the Experts" forum staffed by 100 top clinicians and scientists who can answer your questions about MD.
> (800) 572-1717
> www.mdausa.org

**Diagnosis and treatment** A blood test can be performed on the child to look for high levels of certain enzymes released from the damaged muscle cells. A test of electrical activity in the muscles and a muscle biopsy may also be done. Doctors look for a protein called dystorphin, that is missing, deficient, or abnormally formed in children with MD.

There is no cure for either form of muscular dystrophy, nor are there any truly effective treatments at present. However, gene therapy research for both BMD and DMD is promising. Corticosteroid drugs have been found to slow muscle destruction in DMD. These drugs do have serious side effects, though, including bone loss, high blood pressure, increased susceptibility to infections, and psychological difficulties—so use must be carefully monitored by your child's doctor.

**Managing your child's MD** If your child has DMD or BMD, help him remain as active as possible for as long as possible. Physical therapists can teach your child various exercises that will help keep his muscles in good condition. In some cases, surgery can be done on the heel cords to help your child walk more easily.

## PKU

**Children's PKU Network (CPN)** provides information to parents whose children have recently been diagnosed with PKU. CPN also assists parents in acquiring medical formula, specially formulated low-phenylalnine food items, scales, and bread bakers to families who are faced with financial crisis situations and/or insurance denial. CPN has regional councils with volunteers who act as national liaisons between clinics, families, health professionals, and the CPN national office, and offers articles, research studies, and videos about PKU, as well as a semiannual newsletter, UPDATE.
(619) 233-3202
(858) 509-0767

**National PKU News** newsletter, published three times annually, includes information on the latest clinical and genetic research; news about PKU formulas and diet; tips for diet management; news of PKU-related parental and professional meetings; and a section for young children with PKU.
6869 Woodlawn Avenue NE, #116
Seattle, WA 98115
www.pkunews.org

You and your child's physical therapist can also teach your child how to do deep breathing and how to cough effectively in order to improve respiratory functioning.

## PKU (phenylketonuria)

Phenylketonuria—better known as PKU—is an inherited disorder of the body's chemistry. Left untreated, PKU can cause mental retardation. However, most newborns with the disorder are diagnosed and treated early, which prevents retardation. About one baby in 12,000 is born with PKU in the United States.

Kids with PKU cannot process part of a food protein called phenylalanine. As a result, it builds up in the bloodstream—and this buildup can lead to brain damage.

**Symptoms** At first, children with PKU seem fine. But when they are about 3 to 5 months old, they start losing interest in their environment. By the time they reach 12 months of age, they have become mentally retarded—unless their condition has been diagnosed and their diet adjusted. Kids with PKU are often irritable, restless, and destructive. Many have dry skin or suffer repeated rashes; some have a "musty" odor. They are physically well developed and, among Caucasians, tend to have blonder hair than their relatives.

**Diagnosis and treatment** In most developed countries, babies are tested for PKU before they leave the hospital. (Tests are accurate when done after the baby is 24 hours old.) Testing involves analyzing a few drops of blood taken from the baby's heel. If the blood has more than a normal amount of phenylalanine, more tests are done to make a correct diagnosis.

Treatment involves extensive dietary monitoring. Your doctor can prescribe a special formula that has had the phenylalanine removed. Later, your child's diet can expand to include certain vegetables, fruits, some grains, and other low-phenylalanine foods. Because your child needs an adequate amount of protein for proper growth and development, she will need to continue drinking a special formula that's high in protein—but has little or no phenylalanine.

If your child has PKU, make sure she receives her medical care from a pediatrician who specializes in caring for kids with PKU, and a nutritionist who can develop a customized diet to suit your child's needs.

**Managing your child's condition** Your child must avoid breast milk, regular formula, cow's milk, cheese, meat, fish, and eggs, all of which contain fairly high amounts of phenylalanine. Throughout her life, she should also avoid any beverages or foods containing the artificial sweetener aspartame (Nutrasweet or Equal).

# Blood disorders

A number of blood disorders, such as hemophilia and sickle cell disease, can occur during childhood. Blood disorders are often diagnosed at birth, even though the affected babies look healthy.

## Hemophilia

Children with hemophilia have blood that doesn't clot properly—due to the absence of a particular blood protein, *factor VIII*. As a result, they suffer recurrent bleeding, most often into the joints. Most kids with hemophilia are male, and about 1 in 10,000 babies is born with the disorder.

Hemophilia tends to be hereditary, with affected males passing a defective gene on to none of their sons but to all of their daughters, who become carriers of the condition. Some of the sons of carrier females may develop the disease, and some of the daughters of carriers may become carriers themselves. (Carriers can be identified by a blood test.)

**Symptoms** Hemorrhaging into the joints and muscles often begins during toddlerhood, when the child puts pressure on his joints and muscles as he starts to walk. The bleeding episodes are painful and, unless treated promptly, can lead to crippling deformities of the knees, ankles, and other joints. Injuries such as scrapes or cuts and even minor surgery, such as a tooth extraction, can cause profuse, life-threatening bleeding. Kids may also suffer frequent bruising or blood in the urine, which can signal internal bleeding.

**Diagnosis and treatment** The disorder is diagnosed by blood-clotting tests. Bleeding episodes are controlled by injections (infusions) of concentrated factor VIII (the concentrate is made from donated blood). Infusions must be given as soon as possible after bleeding has started, and some children receive regular doses of the factor as a preventive treatment.

The National Haemophilia Foundation (NHF) operates local treatment centers throughout the U.S. that provide medical and additional services for children and adults with bleeding disorders. Treatment at these specialized centers is highly recommended.

**Managing your child's condition** Your local NHF treatment center will provide the support services you need, including physical therapy to cope with the effects of joint bleeds and social work services to advocate for your child. If your child has hemophilia, he can safely take part in activities appropriate for his age, perhaps taking additional precautions such as wearing knee or elbow pads when riding a trike.

## Von Willebrand's disease

Caused by a defective gene, von Willebrand's disease is a clotting disorder that affects males and females equally.

Children with von Willebrand's have a reduced concentration of a certain factor in their blood that helps platelets plug injured blood vessel walls. This factor also forms part of factor VIII, which is crucial for clotting. When von Willebrand factor is missing, neither blood coagulation nor platelet plug formation can occur normally—and the child tends to bleed excessively.

**Symptoms** include profuse or excessive bleeding from the gums, nose, or cuts. In severe forms of the disease, the child develops bleeding deep into the joints and muscles.

**Diagnosis and treatment** Blood-clotting tests and measurements that reveal reduced levels of von Willebrand factor in the blood are used for diagnosis.

Various treatments are available. Cryoprecipitate (a preparation obtained from normal blood plasma) injections can help prevent episodes of bleeding. Also, injections of the drug desmopressin can raise the body's natural production of von Willebrand factor.

## Sickle cell disease

Sickle cell disease is an inherited blood disorder that causes episodes of painful swelling in joints, as well as damage to vital organs, such as the kidneys, liver, and gallbladder. In some cases, the condition can lead to death, usually in childhood or early adulthood. The disease affects a red blood cell protein called hemoglobin. Hemoglobin is responsible for carrying oxygen from the lungs to every part of the body. Normally, red blood cells are round and flexible and move easily through blood vessels. But in people who have sickle cell disease, the cells become deformed—changing into a sickle- or banana-like shape. These distorted cells clump together and clog blood vessels. Sickle cells may also become trapped in the liver and spleen, where they are destroyed. This leads to a shortage of red blood cells, a condition referred to as "anemia."

Kids with sickle cell disease may grow more slowly than other children, may develop a curved spine, and enter puberty later than normal. They also have an increased risk of infection, particularly pneumococcal pneumonia and meningitis. When blood vessels are blocked for a long time, tissue can be destroyed, leading to organ damage. About 10 percent of children with sickle-cell disease suffer strokes.

---

**PARENTS RESOURCES**

### For Children with Sickle Cell Disease

**Sickle Cell Disease Association of America, Inc.**
3345 Wilshire Blvd., Suite 1106
Los Angeles, CA 90010-1880
(800) 421-8453
www.sicklecelldisease.org

**National Heart, Lung, and Blood Institute**
P.O. Box 30105
Bethesda, MD 20824-0105
(301) 592-8573
www.nhlbi.nih.gov

## When Sickle Cell Disease Requires Medical Help

Symptoms that should be reported to your doctor immediately include faintness or dizziness, unusual drowsiness, or a temperature over 103°F.

**Symptoms** include chronic fatigue, shortness of breath, and difficulty breathing. Painful swelling can occur in the joints, especially in the fingers and toes, because not enough oxygen-carrying blood is able to reach these areas. This blockage of blood vessels is called a sickle cell pain "crisis." Some crises are mild and last for only a few minutes; others are severe, lasting a week or two, and some children must be treated at a hospital.

**Diagnosis and treatment** A blood test (hemoglobin electrophoresis) can identify people who carry the sickle cell trait or who have the disease. A prenatal test can determine whether the fetus will have the disease or will be a carrier. Many medical centers and sickle cell treatment facilities offer carrier testing and genetic counseling.

There's no cure for sickle cell disease, but researchers are exploring ways to reduce the severity and frequency of pain crises. Good, regular medical care also helps limit damage to organs.

If your child has sickle cell disease, her doctor can recommend medications that will help ease her pain during a crisis. The doctor may also prescribe folic acid and other supplements to curb anemia. Other treatments include the use of steroids to shorten a crisis; ongoing antibiotic therapy to help prevent pneumonia in young children; and blood transfusions during a severe crisis.

A 1997 international study, sponsored by the National Heart, Lung, and Blood Institute, has found that regular blood transfusions (transfusion therapy) are 90 percent effective in preventing strokes in children with sickle-cell disease. To identify patients at high risk of stroke, doctors use a modified brain-scannning method called transcranial Doppler screening. This ultrasound technique measures the velocity of the blood flow in the brain, indicating major arteries that have narrowed due to sickle cell disease.

## Managing your child's condition

*For information on vaccinations, see **pages 543–547**.*

• Keep vaccinations up to date. Make sure your child gets his immunizations on schedule, especially the Hib vaccine. Your child should also receive the pneumococcal vaccine, which prevents pneumonia and meningitis, and the hepatitis B vaccine. Flu vaccinations are also recommended.

• Limit anxiety. As with all chronic illnesses, it's important that your child focus on childhood, not on the condition. Try not to worry about when the next "crisis" is going to occur. If you aren't constantly worried, it's likely your child won't worry as much about possible crises. Also consider substituting the words "pain attack" for "crisis" when talking with your older children. The word "crisis" may make your child feel dangerously ill.

• Keep up communication with your child's doctor. Ask your doctor which symptoms require a call.

• Share information with caregivers. Because kids with sickle cell need to urinate frequently, alert your child's teacher and others so that your child is readily allowed to use the toilet when he must.

• Watch the diet. Even though a child with sickle cell disease has a form of anemia, she doesn't have low stores of iron, so there's no need to ask her to eat loads of iron-rich foods. Don't give her iron supplements, unless her doctor tells you to do so. Try to avoid prodding your child to eat when she isn't hungry. Kids with sickle cell often have poor appetites. Instead, keep nutritious snacks on hand and let her have them when she feels like it.

## Chromosomal abnormalities

If there are too few or too many chromosomes on each of the body's cells, or if a part of a chromosome is missing or has been broken off and reattached to another chromosome, a chromosomal disorder such as Down syndrome or fragile X syndrome may occur.

### Down syndrome

Down syndrome, also known as trisomy 21, is a combination of defects including some degree of mental retardation and certain characteristic facial features. About 30 to 50 percent of babies with Down syndrome also have congenital heart defects, and many have visual and hearing impairment or other health problems. The severity of Down syndrome—and its complications—varies greatly from child to child. About 1 in 800 to 1,000 babies is born with the disorder.

Many children with Down syndrome learn to read, write, and solve math problems and are able to take part in school activities. Special education programs help children develop their skills and abilities as fully as possible. Certain high-achieving kids are "mainstreamed" into regular schools at some point, taking both special education classes as well as courses with nondisabled students.

*For information on congenital heart defects, see **page 729**.*

*For information on hearing impairment, see **page 754**.*

*For information on eye problems, see **page 757**.*

### Children with Down Syndrome

**National Down Syndrome Society**
(800) 221-4602
(212) 460-9330
www.ndss.org

**National Down Syndrome Congress**
(800) 232-NDSC
(770) 604-9500
www.ndscenter.org

**CMR Down Syndrome Center**
CWRU-School of Medicine
1621 Euclid Ave.
Cleveland, OH 44115-0210
(216) 621-5858

**Books**

**Babies with Down Syndrome: A New Parents' Guide** by Karen Stray-Gundersen (Woodbine House)

**Symptoms** Kids with the disorder usually have delayed development—sitting up and walking and talking later than other children. They also have distinctive features. Down syndrome children are usually shorter than normal and have poor muscle tone.

**Diagnosis and treatment** If your doctor suspects your newborn has Down syndrome, your child will undergo a blood test to determine whether a chromosomal abnormality is present. Prenatal testing can also determine whether a child has the disorder.

Complications common to children with Down syndrome are specifically treated. About 10 to 20 percent of children with Down syndrome have intestinal malformations that require surgery. Heart disorders and digestive problems are also more common in Down syndrome kids, and surgery is often required to correct them.

Children with the condition are at higher risk of thyroid problems and leukemia. They also tend to have numerous colds, as well as frequent bouts of pneumonia and bronchitis.

Early intervention programs are essential for helping to maximize your child's physical and emotional development.

**Managing your child's condition** Most kids with the disorder are able to do many things other kids can do.

• Encourage independence. Your child will walk, talk, dress himself, and learn to use the toilet with your help, but he may master these things a little later than usual. Early intervention programs, started in infancy, can help kids achieve these developmental milestones earlier. Encourage your child to play with other children who share the disorder as well as with her siblings and nondisabled friends. Children with Down syndrome tend to be affectionate and friendly and enjoy socializing with other kids and adults.

• Keep vaccinations up to date. Because your child may be at higher risk for infections, you need to make sure she receives all her childhood immunizations on schedule.

• Maintain communication with your child's health-care team. Be sure that she receives regular medical checkups, and sees an ophthalmologist at least once a year. If early tests detect a hearing problem, she'll need regular hearing checks, and may need to be fitted with a hearing aid. All babies born with Down syndrome should be examined by a pediatric cardiologist, and should have an echocardiogram—a procedure that shows images of the heart, its valves, and its ability to function—during the first two months of life.

• Encourage physical activity. Allow your child to take part in any physical activities she feels comfortable doing. Because kids with Down syndrome are prone to gaining excess weight, good physical fitness is important. However, it's essential that some children avoid extending their necks backward during exercise. Because certain Down syndrome kids have an abnormality in the ligaments of their neck, they risk severe spinal injury if the neck is extended too far. Your child's doctor may want to X ray her neck before she takes part in any vigorous activities, such as tumbling or doing somersaults.

## Fragile X syndrome

Fragile X syndrome is an inherited chromosomal abnormality that affects about 1 in 2,000 boys in the general population and about 1 in 4,000 girls.

Fragile X syndrome is the second most common cause of mental retardation in males, following Down syndrome. Most children with fragile X syndrome are mild to moderately retarded, but about 25 percent are severely retarded. Some children with

---

**PARENTS RESOURCES**

### Children with Fragile X Syndrome

**FRAXA Research Foundation**
45 Pleasant St.
Newburyport, MA 01950
(978) 462-1866
www.fraxa.org

**The National Fragile X Foundation**
P.O. Box 190488
San Francisco, CA 94119
(800) 688-8765
(510) 763-6030
www.nfxf.org

The following books are offered by the National Fragile X Foundation:

**Boys with Fragile X Syndrome** by Rebecca O'Connor, M.A.

**Transitioning "Special" Children Into Elementary School** by Jayne Dixon Weber

**Fragile X Syndrome: A Handbook for Families and Professionals** by Brenda Finucane, et al.

**Issues and Strategies for Educating Children with Fragile X Syndrome: A Monograph** by Phil Wilson, et al.

*Some children with fragile X also have autism, see* **page 750**.

fragile X have very mild symptoms—or no symptoms at all. Girls are often symptom-free, though about 30 percent are developmentally delayed or are mentally retarded.

**Symptoms**  Symptoms of fragile X syndrome may be apparent at birth, or may not show up until early childhood—or even later. Some extremely mild cases are never diagnosed. Symptoms include slightly enlarged ears, a high palate in which the roof of the mouth is narrow and deep, and flat feet. Boys with the disorder have large testicles. Infants with fragile X also tend to have a single crease in the palm instead of the double crease that others have.

*For information on mental retardation, see* **page 752**.

**Diagnosis and treatment**  Often, a delay in speech is a doctor's first clue that a child might have fragile X syndrome. Also, an unexplained family history of mental retardation may alert the child's doctor to the presence of the condition.

Increasingly, researchers are hopeful that a cure will be discovered. Current research suggests that the condition can be prevented and, possibly, reversed. In the meantime, early treatment and intervention can help your child. Treatment usually includes special education, speech and language therapy, and occupational therapy.

Medications such as methylphenidate (Ritalin) are sometimes useful in controlling hyperactivity and poor attention span in school-aged kids. It's important that a special education expert who has worked with fragile X children assess your child's overall development, including behavioral problems and learning strengths and weaknesses. A doctor who has experience working with such children will need to assess your child's special medical needs and set up a treatment program that includes regular checkups.

# Perinatal damage

Any number of things can lead to damage to the fetus before or during birth.

## *Cerebral palsy (CP)*

Cerebral palsy is a neuromuscular disorder. Kids with CP have an abnormality in an area of the brain that controls movement and muscle tone. About 1 to 2 children per 1,000 are born with cerebral palsy. Extremely low-birthweight babies (those under 3½ pounds) and premature infants are more prone to CP than larger, full-term babies. More boys than girls have the disorder; multiple-birth children are at higher risk than singletons.

**Symptoms** Because some children with CP have such mild symptoms, it's possible that a diagnosis may not be made until a baby is 6 or 7 months old, and some kids aren't diagnosed until their second year. A child between 2 and 6 months may have the following symptoms:
• His head "sags" when you pick him up. His neck will seem even limper than other babies' heads.
• His body feels limp and floppy.
• He feels stiff, and when you hold him in your arms, he arches his back and neck as though he is trying to push you away.

A child between 6 and 10 months may have the following symptoms:
• She will continue to have tonic neck reflex, which is normal for younger babies, but not for 6-month-olds. You'll notice that when your baby's head turns to one side, the arm on that side will straighten; the opposite arm will bend as though she's involved in a sword fight.
• She may reach out with only one hand and will make a tight fist with the other hand.

A baby over 10 months may have the following symptoms:
• He avoids crawling; instead, he moves around on his bottom (older children may move along on their knees).
• If he does crawl, his movements will appear lopsided. He may use one hand and leg to push himself along, dragging his opposite hand and leg.
   Other symptoms include spasticity, poor neck control, failure to sit or stand at the normal ages, speech delay, floppy or stiff muscle tone, and seizures.

**Diagnosis and treatment** Diagnosis is made primarily by observation. If your child's doctor diagnoses CP, he'll refer her to an early-intervention program, staffed by physical, occupational, and speech and language therapists, as well as nurses, social workers, medical consultants, and early childhood educators who are trained in special education.

*For information on strabismus. see **page 597**.*

The physical and occupational therapists can teach you specific physical exercises that will help prevent joint contracture as well as strengthen weak muscles. Early childhood educators can assess your child's intellectual and cognitive abilities. Speech and language therapists will help your child communicate more effectively, if her speech or hearing is impaired. (Some kids with CP learn to communicate via special computers.) Some kids have vision difficulties, caused by weak coordination of the eye muscles. About 3 out of 4 kids with CP have strabismus (crossed eyes) that needs early correction.

Other treatments involve the use of braces or splints and orthotics to correct shortened limbs or prevent scoliosis. Surgery is sometimes used to relieve spasticity. Medications can help control seizures.

Early-intervention programs also provide or recommend special utensils and toys that your child can use more easily, as well as furniture that can be adapted to your child's needs.

# *Emotional disorders and mental illness*

## Depression

Depression can occur at any age—even in toddlers. About 5 percent of children and adolescents suffer from severe depression at some time in their lives. Loss of a parent, sibling, or beloved pet can trigger depression in a susceptible child. So can stressful situations at school or at home, such as being continuously snubbed by schoolmates, or experiencing tension in the home because a parent has lost her job. Children with learning disorders or behavioral problems are at higher risk for depression.

**Symptoms** of depression in kids are often different from those in depressed adults—and a parent may be unaware that their child is depressed. Warning signs of depression include sad appearance, talk of sadness, frequent nightmares, changed behavior and behavior problems, frequent headaches or stomach aches that seem to have no cause and don't improve with treatment, changes in eating or sleeping patterns, poor social interaction, and persistent anxiety.

**Diagnosis and treatment** If you suspect that your child may be depressed, even mildly, ask her pediatrician to refer you to a mental-health expert who specializes in the diagnosis and treatment of depression in children. Counseling can help some children feel more in control of their lives and aid them in learning to view situations—and themselves—more positively. Other children require antidepressant medications and/or antianxiety drugs in addition to counseling or psychotherapy. When a child's depression is diagnosed and treated early on, he has a lower risk of suffering major depressions in adolescence or adulthood.

# Obsessive-compulsive disorder (OCD)

Between 2 to 3 percent of the general population suffers from obsessive-compulsive disorder, and experts estimate that 1 out of every 100 kids under age 20 is affected to some extent. The condition is marked by low levels of serotonin, a neurotransmitter in brain cells. Children with OCD rely on rituals or compulsions to reduce anxiety.

**Symptoms** include excessive worrying, taking an unusually long time to complete routine tasks, repeatedly asking for reassurance about trivial matters, checking and rechecking to make sure that something has been done—like locking a door or putting away all toys, repeating words or numbers. For instance, the child believes he must do this to keep "bad" things from happening. Some children also have verbal or physical tics.

---

**PARENTS RESOURCES**

### *Children with Depression*

***American Academy of Child & Adolescent Psychiatry***
3615 Wisconsin Ave., NW
Washington, DC 20016-3007
(800) 333-7636
(202) 966-7300
www.aacap.org

***National Mental Health Association***
1021 Prince Street
Alexandria, VA 22314
(800) 969-6642
(703) 684-7722
www.nmha.org

***National Mental Health Services/ Knowledge Exchange Network***
P.O. Box 42490
Washington, DC 20015
(800) 789-2647
www.mentalhealth.org

***National Institute of Mental Health***
(301) 443-4513
www.nimh.nih.gov

**Diagnosis and treatment** In addition to making a diagnosis based solely on symptoms, the doctor may test for signs of strep infection, which has been linked to sudden-onset OCD.

Obsessive-compulsive disorder is a very treatable condition. In about 90 percent of cases, doctors are able to significantly reduce symptoms by combining cognitive or behavioral therapy with serotonin reuptake inhibitors (SRIs), such as the antidepressant drug Paxil. These drugs allow a more "normal" amount of serotonin to remain in the brain, and this seems to reduce OCD symptoms. It can take as long as 12 weeks for the medications to work, though. A child psychiatrist should monitor the effectiveness of the medication, as well as check your child frequently for any side effects, such as sleep disruption or impulsivity.

A child psychiatrist or psychologist who specializes in the treatment of children with OCD can help your child learn to break his repetitive patterns, as well as providing ways for him to constructively alleviate his fears and concerns.

## Pervasive developmental delay (PDD)/autism

Pervasive developmental delay (PDD), also known as autism, is not a disease or "condition," but rather a disorder or abnormality that involves many aspects of a child's life, including his relationship with his parents, siblings, and friends; his language and social abilities; and his ability to learn. Because affected children tend to be very withdrawn, parents often say their child "lives in his own little world." About 4 in every 10,000 children are affected and almost three times as many boys as girls have PDD.

**Symptoms** usually develop within the first 30 months of life—and often during the first year. Infants and toddlers who have PDD don't cuddle or make eye contact. They may not respond to affection or touch. A baby with the condition may push away from a parent who tries to cuddle or nurse him. Additional symptoms vary from child to child, but some of the more common ones include being overly quiet, passive, or focusing intensely on the same toy for hours at a time; hyperactivity or aggression, including inexplicable tantrums, or sudden screaming fits; inappropriate behavior, including harming himself or others; incessant rocking back and forth or from side to side, continual head banging, twitching, and walking on tip-toe; unusual fears; difficulty learning manual tasks; infrequent laughter or smiles; rare hugs or kisses for parents; playing alone, with little interest in making friends; delay in speaking, or not speaking at all, or speaking in a robot-like manner; and unusual sensitivity to noise or light, but underresponsive to pain. Some kids have an outstanding skill, such as rote memory (memorizing and then reciting hundreds of phone numbers from the telephone book for example), or extreme musical ability.

**Diagnosing and treating PDD** Your child will be given a number of medical tests to rule out a metabolic problem, as well as to determine whether he has additional problems, such as seizures or mental retardation. Once the medical team learns more about your child's symptoms and abilities, they can devise an individualized treatment program that focus on behavior, communication, and social skills.

Though there's no cure for PDD, a variety of therapies can help reduce or eliminate some of the behavioral problems associated with the disorder. Treatment must be tailored to meet the child's specific needs, since one child's symptoms may be mild to moderate, while another's are severe. No one treatment or treatment program works for every child. If your child's doctor suspects that he has PDD, he should be diagnosed by a team of people who are experienced in diagnosing and treating the conditions: a neurologist, a child psychiatrist or psychologist, a developmental pediatrician, a learning disabilities diagnostician, a speech-language pathologist, and an audiologist.

In addition, his diet may be adjusted. Some children with autism have allergies or sensitivities to certain foods, especially those containing yeast or gluten. No thorough scientific studies prove that dietary changes help reduce symptoms of PDD, but some parents and professionals have reported that dietary adjustments have brought about positive changes in a child's behavior.

There is no specific drug to treat autism, but a number of medications are used to treat specific problems, such as seizures, hyperactivity, aggression, obsessive/compulsive behavior, and anxiety. Order the information package "Medications" from the ASA.

**Finding the right program** Effective programs include a range of services from at-home care to residential treatment programs. When choosing a program:
• Beware of any program or technique that promises to be effective for every child with autism.
• Beware of any program that doesn't stress individual "tailoring" of treatment.
• Realize that each treatment represents only one of several options for autistic children and that children usually need a number of therapies.
• Be aware that some new treatments haven't been scientifically validated. Approach a new therapy with skeptical optimism, and make sure they won't harm your child in any way.

# Mental retardation

A child or adult is considered to have mental retardation based on three criteria: his intellectual functioning level (standard IQ) is below 70 to 75; he has significant limitations in two or more adaptive skill areas, such as communication and social skills; and his condition has been present from childhood. About 2.5 to 3 million people in the United States have mental retardation.

About 87 percent of mentally retarded people are only mildly affected and are just slightly slower than average in learning new information and skills. As children, their condition may not be apparent and often, kids aren't diagnosed until they enter school. These individuals most likely will be able to live independent lives in their community, care for themselves, and hold jobs. The remaining 13 percent—those with IQs under 50—have serious problems with learning and independent functioning. But early intervention, specialized education, and support during adulthood can lead to satisfying lives in the community for these children, too.

**Symptoms** Mental retardation is more commonly diagnosed early on in children with an IQ of 50 or lower. Doctors and parents suspect that something is wrong when a baby doesn't develop certain motor skills—such as holding his head up by himself or sitting up unsupported—on the same timetable as other children.

Some kids with mild to moderate mental retardation seem fine physically during their first few years of life, developing motor skills just like other children, and a delay in speaking is the first clue that they aren't developing normally. Toddlers and preschoolers may have trouble counting, putting together puzzles, or recognizing colors. Grade-schoolers may not be able to learn to read, write, or do math problems.

**Diagnosis and treatment** If your child's doctor suspects that your child might have mental retardation, she will refer her to a pediatric developmental specialist or a pediatric neurologist. These professionals can administer a variety of tests in order to make an accurate diagnosis.

---

**PARENTS RESOURCES**

## Children Who Are Mentally Retarded

**The Arc of the United States**
1010 Wayne Ave., Suite 650
Silver Spring, MD 20910
(301) 565-3842
www.thearc.org

**American Association on Mental Retardation (AAMR)**
(800) 424-3688
(202) 387-1968
www.aamr.org

**Special Olympics**
(202) 628-3630
www.specialolympics.org

## Publications

The following are available from The Arc. To order, call (888) 368-8009:

**The Arc's Family Book,** by the Arc

**Toilet Training Children with Mental Retardation** by Molly C. Gorelick, Ed.D.

Early-intervention programs have had remarkable results in reducing the predicted incidence of subnormal intellectual functioning in high-risk infants and children. Most kids with mild retardation can learn to read and write, do some types of math problems, and, eventually, hold jobs and live on their own or in a supervised group home in the community. Those with moderate retardation may learn to read and write and eventually hold a job, but they often need a great deal of supervision and will need to live at home or in a group home setting. Children with severe retardation may not be able to learn to read or write, but very often they can learn to dress and feed themselves and use the toilet properly. As adults, many are able to live in small supervised group homes.

**Managing your child's condition**   In addition to providing your child with appropriate educational opportunities, it's vital that you give him as much independence as possible, and the social skills, and self-esteem that will help him develop to his potential. At home:
• Encourage your child to do as much as he is physically and intellectually able to do, but don't make him feel inadequate if he's unable to accomplish all that you would like. Your patience will serve him well.
• Provide your child with toys that will challenge—but not unduly frustrate—him.
• Read frequently to your child, and encourage his participation in the process. For instance, you can ask him to tell you what he liked about a particular story.
• Let him test his abilities. If necessary, assist him in tying his shoes or buttoning his shirt—but wait to see if he's able to manage on his own. Each time your child masters a skill or performs a task, he will feel proud and competent.
• Praise your child when he masters a task.
• Work with your child to choose certain jobs she can do around the house. By giving your child responsibilities, you'll help him see that he is an important, contributing member of the family.

# *Sensory disorders*

Sensory disorders involve the partial or complete loss of one of the body's sensory organs. The most common sensory disorders are hearing and vision loss.

## Hearing loss and impairment

Approximately 1 out of every 1,000 children is born deaf, according to the National Institutes of Health (NIH), and many more are born with less severe degrees of hearing impairment—or develop a hearing problem during childhood.

Children who can't hear properly during infancy and early childhood are at risk of delays in speech and verbal language skills. There's also evidence that hearing impairment can impact negatively on social, emotional, cognitive, and academic development.

The first three years of life are generally regarded as the most important period for language and speech development. But, in the United States, the typical hearing-impaired child isn't diagnosed until he's almost 3 years old, and some degrees of less severe impairment may go undetected for many more years.

**Types of hearing loss** Three types of hearing loss can occur in children. With *Conductive hearing loss*, the child has a structural abnormality in the outer ear canal or middle ear—or excessive fluid in the middle ear that interferes with proper conduction of sound. With *Sensorineural hearing loss*, there's an abnormality of the inner ear or the nerves that carry sound messages from the inner ear to the brain. In *Central hearing loss*, changes occur in the auditory centers of the brain, due to heredity, injury, disease, or, rarely, a tumor.

**Symptoms** There are varying degrees of hearing loss, and not all hearing-impaired children are deaf. In some, the loudness of sound is decreased. In others, the child can hear sounds but cannot understand words.

**Diagnosis and treatment** In infants, the lack of startling at loud sounds is often the first clue. In toddlers, delayed speech can signal hearing impairment. If hearing loss is suspected, your child's doctor will refer your child to a specialist for a diagnosis. Children

*For a list of behaviors that can signify hearing loss, see page 611.*

with temporary hearing loss caused by repeated bouts of otitis media can be treated with antibiotics as well as ear tubes, which help drain excess fluid from the middle ear. Once the fluid is removed, hearing should return to normal.

Kids with conductive hearing loss caused by a malformation of the outer or middle ear often require a hearing aid. When the child is older, reconstructive surgery may be done to repair the malformation and restore normal or near-normal hearing.

Children with sensorineural hearing loss may also benefit from a hearing aid, but the device won't completely restore their hearing. Children 2 years and older who haven't benefited from a hearing aid and have bilateral hearing impairment may be candidates for cochlear implants, tiny electronic devices placed in the inner ear.

---

**PARENTS RESOURCES**

## *Hearing-Impaired Children*

**National Institute on Deafness and Other Communication Disorders (NIDCD) Information Clearing House**
(800) 241-1044
(800) 241-1055 (TTY)
www.nih.gov/nidcd

**The National Institutes of Health (NIH) Office of Medical Applications of Research**
Building 31, Room 1B03
31 Center Dr., MSC 2082
Bethesda, MD 20892-2082
(301) 496-5641
www.odp.od.nih.gov/omar

**American Academy of Audiology (AAA)**
(800) AAA-2336
(703) 790-8466
www.audiology.org

**American Association of the Deaf-Blind (AADB)**
(800) 735-2258
(301) 588-6545 (TTY)

**American Society for Deaf Children**
P.O. Box 3355
Gettysburg, PA 17325
(800) 942-ASDC
(717) 334-7922 (voice/TTY)
www.deafchildren.org

**American Speech-Language Hearing Association**
(800) 498-2071
(888) 321-ASHA
(301) 571-0457 (TTY)
www.asha.org

**Auditory-Verbal International**
(703) 739-1049
(703) 739-0874 (TTY)
www.auditory-verbal.org

**Better Hearing Institute**
(800) EAR-WELL
www.betterhearing.org

**Cochlear Implant Association**
(202) 895-2781

The implants sometimes restore limited hearing so that the child is able to distinguish words. Children with sensorineural hearing loss usually must learn to lip-read, and/or to use a combination of spoken and sign language.

**Managing your child's condition** Begin early. If your child has a hearing impairment, intervention should be started as soon as possible. Education programs include teaching kids how to use devices that help them to hear or speak; sign language; lip reading; and listening skills. A speech/language pathologist and other specially trained hearing disorder experts can work with your child. Educate yourself about education options. When your child is ready for a toddler program or preschool, discuss her educational options with her doctor. The type of school your child attends will depend on the severity of her impairment. She may be mainstreamed into a regular school and attend classes with hearing children. Or, she may attend a regular school that has a special program for hearing-impaired kids. There are also private schools for children who have severe hearing disabilities. Take extra safety precautions. Because your child may not hear warning sounds, like honking horns, bike bells, or fire alarms, you must be extra vigilant. Check with your local transportation department to have "Deaf Child Area" signs posted in your neighborhood.

# Visual impairment

About 1 out of every 1,000 children in the United States has a serious visual impairment. Of these kids, 80 to 85 percent have some vision. Very few visually impaired children are totally blind—unable to see anything, including lights or shapes, and only 2,560 children nationwide under age 5 are "legally blind," which means their vision is severely limited though they may have some vision in one or both eyes.

The term "visual impairment" refers to any condition in which the eyesight cannot be corrected through surgery, with medication, or by corrective lenses, to what is considered "normal." Some children have a significantly reduced "field of vision." That is, they don't see things that aren't directly in front of them or close to being in front of them.

**Diagnosis and treatment** Doctors use tools like penlights and illustrated or colorful cards to measure an infant's visual acuity. In toddlers and older children, they also use picture cards, and visual field tests, which measure field of vision. It's very difficult to determine exactly how much a visually impaired infant or toddler can see, and often doctors and parents don't know the degree of impairment until the child can talk and tell them what he does and doesn't see. An eye exam is part of neonatal care and should be a continuing part of your child's pediatrician visits. If you notice any cloudiness or other oddity in your child's eyes or any behavior that indicates difficulty seeing, have her examined by a pediatric opthamologist. Treatment often includes corrective lenses, and depending on the cause of the sight loss, additional measures. Specific causes and treatments include:

*Retinopathy of prematurity* (ROP), a condition that can cause partial or complete loss of vision in premature babies. In full-term babies, the vessels that supply blood to the retina, the inner layer of the eye, which serves as a light receptor, are completely matured. But in premature infants, the vessels continue to grow after the baby is born, and abnormal vessels and scar tissue can form inside the child's eyes.

Babies with ROP may have mild to moderate impairment in visual acuity—or total loss of vision. The more premature the baby, the higher her risk of developing ROP or having a severe form of the condition.

Doctors use several types of treatments to prevent ROP from reaching a severe stage. Laser and cryotherapy (freezing) can curb abnormal growth of the blood vessels in newborns. In some cases, a child's retina may have become partially or totally detached (separated from the back of the eye), and a doctor will have to surgically reattach the retina.

If your child has ROP, he should be monitored by a pediatric ophthalmologist throughout childhood and into adulthood. Although some kids with mild ROP see clearly, they may have other problems, such as farsightedness, nearsightedness, astigmatism, strabismus, and/or glaucoma and will need corrective lenses or treatment for those conditions.

*Retinitis pigmentosa* (RP), a hereditary degeneration of the retina. It begins with night blindness, in which the child has difficulty seeing in dark or dim rooms or outdoors at night. Gradually peripheral vision is reduced. Some children with the condition retain some central ("tunnel") vision, while others lose all vision. Children with central vision don't require large-print materials, since they can see fairly clearly through the central part of the eye. They usually have difficulty moving through crowds of people or participating in playground activities, since their peripheral vision is decreased. There is no effective treatment for RP, though children with the condition can learn to adapt to the condition, and research continues for a treatment.

**Managing your child's condition** Taking these steps can help your child feel safe and reach her potential:
- Avoid startling. Blind or visually impaired infants are often startled or frightened when someone suddenly picks them up because they can't see that person coming. When you enter your child's room or walk over to her play yard, softly say her name, or coo, or talk gently to let her know you're approaching. Lightly touch, then stroke her arm before picking her up.
- Before handing a rattle or some other object to your baby, gently touch her hand so she knows that you will give her something.
- Guide your baby's hand to help her feel and enjoy different textures, like skin, soft cloth, plush toys, and foods with interesting textures. By doing this, you'll encourage her to reach out and grasp objects.
- Touch your baby as much as possible, so she'll be more aware of person-to-person contact.
- When your baby is ready to start walking, hold her in a standing position and walk her. After a while, she'll catch on to the idea that this strange new movement is fun. You can also help her hold onto safe, rounded couch or table corners to support herself, as well as teach her how to use them to pull herself up.
- Say your child's name often, even if you're just passing through the living room on your way to the kitchen. This will help her be aware of your constant presence and she won't feel as though she's been left all alone.
- Explain to your toddler what certain things are. For example, when he is learning to use the toilet, let him feel toilet paper and explain and show what it's used for.
- Help your child piece together parts of a whole. For example, guide her hand over a dog's face, ears, back, legs, etc. This way, she will learn to mentally "see" or perceive an entire object, animal, or person.

• When choosing toys for your child, look for ones that talk or make sounds, have bright colors, high contrast, or give off light, feature a variety of textures and surfaces, stimulate thinking and creativity, and encourage movement and exploration, including climbing and riding toys.

• Take extra precautions to keep your child safe while trying not to undermine her sense of independence.

---

**PARENTS RESOURCES**

## Visually Impaired Children

**National Association for Parents of the Visually Impaired, Inc. (NAPVI)**
(800) 562-6265
(617) 972-7441
www.spedex.com/napvi

**American Foundation for the Blind (AFB)**
(800) 232-5463
(212) 502-7600
www.afb.org

**American Council of the Blind**
1155 15th Street NW., Suite 1004
Washington, DC 20005
(800) 424-8666
(202) 467-5081
www.acb.org

**The Library of Congress National Library Service for the Blind and Physically Handicapped**
1291 Taylor Street NW
Washington, DC 20542
(202) 707-5100
www.lcweb.loc.gov/nls

**National Association for Visually Handicapped**
22 West 21st Street
New York, NY 10010
(212) 889-3141
www.navh.org

**National Organization of Parents of Blind Children, A Division of the National Federation of the Blind**
1800 Johnson Street
Baltimore, MD 21230
(410) 659-9314

# Part 4

# Safe and Sound

Making sure your child is safe is one of the major worries—and responsibilities—of parenthood.

While you cannot protect your child from all the dangers he will encounter along his journey to adulthood, and no amount of childproofing can substitute for adult supervision, you can take measures right now to provide safeguards at home, on the road, and out in the world. And doing so will help put your mind at ease, allowing you to strike a balance between worrying about your child's every move, having constantly to tell her "no" or "don't touch," and letting her explore safely. Perhaps most important, by providing your child with a healthy, safe environment you will enable her gradually to gain the skills and experience she needs as she grows up.

You have a lot more information than your parents did about how to prevent accidents, and there are many new child-safe devices widely available from retail outlets and direct-mail catalogs that make childproofing and safety much easier.

# CHAPTER 1

......................................................................

# Childproofing Your Home

You can begin to ensure a safer world for your child by childproofing your home.

It's easy to underestimate and overlook many potential household hazards. Unlike an adult, your child does not know, for example, not to touch a hot burner, not to grip the sharp blade of a knife, not to swallow laundry detergent, or not to stick a fork into an electrical outlet. He has not yet developed the skills and abilities necessary to understand what actions can be dangerous and what products or objects could harm him. Curiosity drives him forward and he learns by exploring with all of his senses, through trial and error, by steady and relentless investigation.

That's why, when you examine your own house, you need to look at it from child's-eye view. It sounds like a lot of work, and it is. Sometimes, it's hard not to feel like you're going overboard, especially since someone will inevitably remark, "Our parents didn't do all this, and we turned out okay." The fact is that accidental injuries are the number one cause of death in children under the age of 5. Each year, a million children in this country receive medical care because of accidental injury. As many as 50,000 children suffer permanent damage, and 4,000 die. You don't want your child to become one of those statistics.

Get down on your hands and knees and look, touch, reach up, and take note of what could threaten the safety of your child. Go from room to room in every part of the house, then remove or correct any potential hazards. Information in this chapter will help you become aware of dangers you might not have known about and tell you what you can do about them.

# Your child's room

In addition to the careful choices you made when you got ready for your baby's arrival, you'll need to continue to examine your child's bedroom as she grows, making the necessary changes in response to increasing mobility. In addition to choosing a safe crib, you'll need to examine every nook and cranny of the room.

As in the rest of the house, electrical outlets in your child's room should be securely plugged, appliances safely placed and cords kept out of reach, radiators covered, windows and window treatments made safe, and safety gates put in place where necessary. Keep in mind, too, that your child's needs—and her abilities to maneuver and move about, crawl, reach, and climb—change as she grows, so it's necessary periodically to reevaluate and make appropriate changes in your youngster's room and throughout the house. Following are points to consider when choosing items for your child's room and safety tips on using them.

*See **pages 7–17** for information on safe equipment for your newborn.*

## Bedding

Elaborate bedding, beautifully displayed at furniture stores and in catalogs, is lovely to look at, but, in truth, simpler bedding is the safest choice for kids. In general:
- **Avoid too much cushioning, decorative pillows, and quilts, which can cause suffocation.**
- **If your child is prone to allergies, select synthetic fabrics.** (For severely allergic kids, encase the mattress and pillows in covers that reduce or elmininate allergens.)
- **Steer clear, too, of headboards and footboards** that contain openings large enough to trap a child's head.

### Adjusting the crib as your child grows
Once your child is beyond the newborn stage, you'll need to make adjustments in her bedding:
- **Always lock the side rail in its raised position** whenever you place your child in the

**PARENTS ALERT**

### No Pillows

Infants should not have any pillows—or comforters, sheepskins, or other soft bedding in their cribs because these all pose a potential suffocation hazard. Once a baby can pull herself to a standing position, at around 8 months of age, or is able to climb, at about age 1, pillows can be used as stepping stones, resulting in falls from cribs.

When your child graduates to a bed, at around age 2 or so, you can give her a small, firm child's pillow. At around age 4, she can start to use an adult pillow if she finds it more comfortable.

crib. Test the dropside latches to make sure your baby cannot open them. When fully lowered, the top of the side rail should be at least four inches above the mattress, even when the mattress is at its highest position.

- **Do not place a crib** near radiators, heating vents, lamps, or other plugged-in appliances, window blind or window-shade cords, climbable furniture, or windows.
- **Never hang any object,** such as a toy on a string or a laundry bag, on the corner post or nearby where a child could become caught in it and strangle.
- **As soon as your child can stand up,** adjust the mattress to the lowest position and remove the bumper pads.
- **When your child reaches about 35 inches in height or has shown interest in climbing,** she has outgrown the crib and it's time to move her to a bed. It's a good idea to place cushioning on the floor around the crib as your baby reaches the toddler stage for added protection until you make the transition to a bed.

## Toddler beds

The transition from crib to bed can be made easier by choosing the right bed for your toddler. Additionally, if you use the same mattress and bedding that your child is used to from his crib, the transition to a toddler bed will be easier for him. Following are a few pointers:

- **Make sure the bed is sturdy** and not in danger of collapsing. Periodically check the joints, especially if your child jumps on his bed or if you're using a metal-framed bed, in which screws are more likely to jostle loose.
- **Choose a toddler bed that is low to the ground.** It's easier for your toddler to get into, and, should she fall out, the distance to the floor is not great and chances of injury are slim. Place a rug or other padding along the side and open end of the bed for added protection in cushioning falls. Some parents choose to place a futon or mattress directly on the floor at this stage rather than using a toddler bed.
- **Choose a bed to which guardrails can be easily attached.**
- **Choose a simple design.** The best bed frames have simple, nonornamental, head- and footboards without cutouts or protrusions.
- **Place the bed safely in the room.** Be sure to place your toddler's bed safely away from windows, heating units, wall lamps, and drapery and blind cords. To avoid the risk that your toddler could

become trapped between the side of the bed and the wall, place the bed with the headboard, rather than the side, along the wall.

## Adult-size beds

It's important to remember that infants should not be put to sleep in adult-size beds, since they can easily roll off onto the floor. No baby or young child should sleep on a bed that's against a wall where he could get trapped between the mattress and the wall and suffocate. Toddlers, too, may roll off and injure themselves or manage to move the bed away from a wall and get themselves wedged between the bed and the wall. Water beds are considered dangerous for infants, as well, because they, too, can pose a risk of suffocation.

While smaller child-size beds are fine as long as your youngster is small enough fit comfortably, sooner or later, a larger bed becomes appropriate. An adult-size bed can seem scary to a young child who is used to a smaller, cozier space. Some children, however, find moving to an adult-size bed an exciting adventure.

When your child is old enough to sleep in her toddler bed without falling out, she is probably ready for a big bed. Of course, guardrails are still an option, if needed. Low beds are a little safer than high ones, though, since they minimize the risk of injury should the child fall out. A bit of padding in the form of a carpet or folded quilt next to the bed can add to your child's safety. Make sure any bed you choose is sturdy, and place it safely away from heating units, windows, appliances, and cords.

## Bunk beds

Bunk beds can be risky business for little ones and are not recommended for children under age 6. Kids love them, but they can be dangerous for two reasons: it's a long fall from the top bunk to the floor, and, if the beds collapses, the child in the lower bunk can be seriously injured. If you do choose a bunk bed, place it in a corner for added structural support and to block two potential sides for falling out. In addition, observe the following safety precautions:

- **Be sure the top mattress fits snugly** and cannot slip over the edge of the frame.
- **Install guardrails on the top bunk.** The gap between the side rail and guardrail should be no greater than 3½ inches. Be sure your

child can't roll under the guardrail when the mattress is compressed by his body weight. Make certain the guardrails are at least five inches above the top of the mattress. Secure guardrails firmly to the frame with nails or screws, since a loose rail can trap a child or allow him to fall. It's best to install a guardrail on each long side of the upper bunk, even if one side is against the wall, since children can get trapped between the bed and wall if no rail is in place.

• **Inspect the supports under the upper mattress.** Wires or slats should run directly under the mattress and be securely fastened at both ends. There should be two or more supports made of heavy wire, wood, or metal below the top mattress. If the upper mattress is supported only by the frame or by too few supports, it could come crashing down onto the lower bunk.

• **Use the correct size mattress for the bed.** Bunk bed mattresses and frames come in two sizes. Placing a regular-size mattress on an extra-long frame creates gaps that a child could fall through.

• **Check the joints between top and bottom bunks.** Make sure that the top and bottom bedposts fasten together, or must be lifted at least 1¼ inches in order to separate them.

• **Watch for gaps.** Spaces between the footboard, headboard, and guardrails should be no more than 3½ inches. If the spaces are larger, nail or screw a board in place to cover dangerous gaps.

• **Make sure the ladder is anchored to the bed frame.** If it isn't, secure it to the frame of the bunk with nails or screws. Repair or replace loose or missing rungs immediately.

• **Make sure all welds on metal-frame beds are sound and not cracked.**

**Bunk bed rules** In addition to the above structural considerations, establish a few rules of the bed for your children to follow:

• **Forbid horseplay.** A bunk bed isn't a jungle gym. In addition to the risk of a child falling, bouncing and jumping could weaken the structure and cause it to collapse.

• **Make sure children use the ladder** to get in and out of the top bunk; they should not jump from the top bunk or step on furniture to reach it.

• **Don't allow children under age 6 to go on the top bunk.**

• **Don't let more than one person on the top bunk at a time.**

• **Use a night-light to help children see the ladder in the dark.**

# Playpens and play yards

You can turn any room in the house into a mini-playroom for a baby with a playpen. Playpens or play yards, as some prefer to call them, become useful when children begin to crawl. While some children take to them quite well, others hate being confined and resist their playpens with a vengeance. Playpens are not substitutes for supervision or company, however, and they should be placed so that you can keep an eye on your child while letting your child keep an eye on you. When choosing a playpen, follow these safety guidelines:

• **Look for mesh netting with a very small weave**—less than ¼ inch by ¼ inch to prevent fingers from becoming entwined. The space between slats on wooden playpens should be no more than 2⅜ inches to prevent a baby from getting caught.

• **Always keep the drop side up and make sure the locking device** is secure. A baby can roll into the pocket created between the mesh and playpen pad and suffocate. A child who can stand may climb over the lowered side and/or injure her fingers on the unlocked hinge.

• **Make sure vinyl- or fabric-covered rails and padding don't have holes or rips.** Loose material can tear off and choke a child.

• **Check the staples that attach the mesh to the floor of the playpen** and make sure they're secure. A child can choke on a loose staple.

• **Never use a playpen that has a torn mesh weave.** Even a small tear can enlarge suddenly and trap a child's head.

• **Don't string toys across the top of the playpen.** Any danglimg string or cord puts children at risk for strangulation.

• **Avoid putting large toys, bumper pads, or boxes in the playpen.** A child may use them to try to climb out.

• **Never use an enclosure made from an accordion-style fence.** A child can get her head caught in the openings and the V-shaped spaces.

# Shelves, cabinets, dressers, etc.

Young children are inherently curious and often have surprisingly long reaches and can grab things in an instant. Therefore, items which could pose safety hazards must be stored securely out of reach. And the storage spaces themselves must be secure.

• **Make sure all shelves, cabinets, and dressers are stable** to eliminate the danger of their falling down or toppling over. Sometimes this may require bolting units to the wall.

• **Place cushioning corner guards** on any furniture with sharp edges.

• **Do not place enticing toys on high shelves.** A child may try to climb up to reach them.

• **Never leave a dresser drawer open,** since children can easily pull a dresser down onto themselves or climb into the bottom drawer, with the same result.

• **Store only safe items in drawers that can be reached and opened by little hands.**

• **Install safety latches on dresser drawers and cabinets** that you don't want children to open.

• **For closets and cabinets to which children have access,** install devices that prevent them from closing all the way and pinching little fingers.

• **Make sure drawers cannot be pulled easily** all the way out of their frames.

• **Make sure knobs and handles are tightly screwed onto the drawers.** Loose doorknobs and handles pose a choking hazard.

*safety gates on all windows*

*closet doors secured*

*corners padded*

*bureaus anchored to the wall*

*no sharp corners on the bed*

*no lid on toy chests*

*A safe child's room*

*safety covers on all outlets*

# Bathroom

Standing water, scalding hot water, hard and slippery surfaces, pretty poisons in the guise of toiletries and medications, razor blades, and electrical appliances—ordinary components of practically any bathroom—are hazards that warrant childproofing attention. *Never* leave a child alone and unsupervised during bath time.

## Water hazards

- **Never let even a small amount of water stand in the tub.** Children have been known to drown in as little as two inches of water. Toilet bowls and diaper pails pose similar drowning hazards to curious, top-heavy toddlers. Choose diaper pails with locking lids, and always close the toilet lid after use. Invest in a special child-safe toilet lock that is easy for adults to maneuver, but difficult for your child to figure out.

- **Water temperature in your water-heating system should not exceed 120°F.** Set the water heater to a maximum of 120°F to prevent the possibility of scalds. For added protection install an antiscald device. Double-check water temperature with a bath thermometer. If your house was built in the mid-1980s or later, antiscald valves may be built into your plumbing. If not, several different types of do-it-yourself retrofit devices that stop the flow of water when the temperature reaches 115°F are available. Whole-valve replacements maintain a maximum temperature of 115 to 120°F and compensate for any changes in water pressure and temperature that may occur; they are best installed by a plumber.

- **Install childproof tub and sink knobs,** so a child cannot turn the water on. Also use a faucet cover that pads the faucet and prevents burns caused by brushing up against it when it's hot. They are available in countless fun shapes, colors, and characters.

**Hard, slippery surfaces** A wet tub or wet tile floor can be extremely slippery. Injuries can easily occur if a young child slips as she sits, stands in, or climbs in or out of the tub. Place a nonslip mat or appliqués at the bottom of the tub and a nonskid rug or bathmat on the floor next to the tub. Always wipe up water that has splashed onto the floor quickly, so it will not add to the risk of slipping. Commercial padding is available that fits snugly over the top edge of

*For information on safe bath time routines, see **page 832**.*

the tub, cushioning the hard surface and preventing serious injury should a child fall against it. Or drape a thick damp towel over the tub side during your child's bath.

**Avoiding shock** Cap all electrical outlets not in use with safety covers. Make sure outlets are protected by ground fault circuit interrupters (GFCI) to safeguard against electrocution. Always unplug small appliances such as hair dryers and curling irons when not in use, and put them safely out of the reach of children. Remember, too, that some items can retain enough electricity to cause shock after they have been turned off. Do not use appliances near a bathtub or sink full of water and keep the toilet lid closed when small appliances are in use. As an added precaution against electrocution, do not use space heaters or extension cords in the bathroom.

**Whirlpool baths** Children age 5 and up generally can use whirlpool baths safely, but only under careful supervision. Children under 5 years of age should stay out of hot tubs and whirlpool baths, since water jets can easily overpower a young child. Another potential hazard is the force of the suction from the water intakes, which may be powerful enough to trap a person—even an adult—beneath the surface, especially if their hair gets ensnared. For that reason, it's important to caution family members against putting their heads under water. Never use a tub or bath with a faulty or missing suction intake drain cover.

In addition, make sure water temperature is no greater than 104°F, if children are going to be using the bath, since high temperatures can scald a child's sensitive skin or damage internal organs. Limit the time your child spends in the bath to 15 minutes. Get her out sooner if she becomes drowsy or flushed.

## Bathroom supplies

Lock away all bathroom cleaning products and supplies. Most are toxic when ingested and harmful if they come into contact with skin or eyes, and some are so potent that just inhaling the fumes can cause serious damage. Medications—over-the-counter preparations from aspirin to vitamins and those prescribed by a doctor—are best safely locked away in a special chest, drawer, closet, or medicine cabinet.

Easy-to-install medicine chest locks are available that are simple for an adult, but not a child, to operate. (Note that many medications are best stored in a room other than the bathroom, since the heat and humidity may cause them to deteriorate.)

For added protection, make sure medication comes in child-proof containers. Toiletries—from shampoo and deodorants to perfume and cosmetics—should not be accessible to very young children. Place them high and well out of sight and reach or lock them up. Be sure to check the area around your tub and shower, removing shampoos, conditioners, and razors.

Also secure hampers or laundry shoots so a child cannot become trapped or fall in, and put safety locks on any windows. Lock away the garbage can inside a cabinet or under the sink so that it, too, is out of a toddler's reach. If you keep a cat litter box in the bathroom, choose an enclosed model with small opening or place it behind a childproof gate. (Cats easily learn to jump over.)

blind cord shortened

safety covers on faucets and handles

toilet locked

all medications and cosmetics safely out of reach

safety outlet installed

thermometer

nonskid mat

accessible cupboard latched

hamper latched

*A safe bathroom*

# *Around the house*

As your little one moves throughout the house she will be exploring every nook and cranny. Much of her exploration will take place as she creeps, crawls, or toddles across the floor—which makes the floor one of the primary places you'll need to check for potential hazards. She'll also encounter other interesting passageways—doors, windows, and stairways—that provide access to other areas of potential exploration both inside the house and leading to the outdoors. These, too, need to be carefully safeguarded to prevent accidents and injury.

## Doors, floors, windows, and stairways

**Doors**  Doors both provide and prevent access—functions that may be double-edged swords when it comes to childproofing. Children can be conveniently confined, of course, in a secure, comfortable, and visible environment by using a safety gate spanning a door frame while keeping the door itself open. Closed doors with locks and latches serve as handy barriers to areas that are hazardous and off-limits to young children. Door alarms, which sound a loud buzzer for a few seconds after a door has been opened, can provide a good back-up measure.

Dangers, however, can occur when doors prevent you from getting access to your child or cause entrapment, such as when a youngster accidentally locks herself (or you) inside a room or closet. Take preventive measures by using hook-and-eye latches or bolts placed high on the door, instead of the self-locking doorknob variety. Make sure that walk-in closets can be opened from the inside as well as outside. Hanging a towel over the top of a door will prevent it from closing completely and can provide an effective temporary solution. Doorknob covers can also be effective for some types of locks on doorknobs.

Doors—on anything from cabinets and cars to rooms—can also pinch little fingers. Be careful when opening and closing them, making sure that your child's hands or fingers aren't caught on either the open or the hinged side, and teach your child to take precautions around doors. Lessen the tension of house doors that close automatically so they will shut with less force. Or try attaching door stoppers to the tops of doors or their top hinges to prevent them from locking children in and pinching fingers.

**Glass doors**   Make sure that glass on all doors—from those on shower stalls to ones leading onto a deck or patio—is specially glazed for added safety. Look for the permanent mark in the lower corner showing the manufacturer's name, type of safety glass, and thickness. It's also a good idea to apply decals or stickers to the glass panels at your child's eye level, especially on large, sliding doors, to make them more obvious and immediately noticeable. You'll need to take precautions so your child can neither open nor close sliding doors on his own. To keep these doors locked, install a lock guard, available at most hardware stores. Or you can insert a heavy-duty, spring-loaded curtain rod between the outside frame and edge of the sliding door to prevent young children from opening it. To keep the door from sliding shut on your child when you need to keep it open, insert a small, rigid object, at least six inches long, into the groove at the base of the door.

**Floors**   In addition to keeping the floor free of debris (especially important if you're involved in 2 a.m. feedings), you want to make sure that the floor is splinter-free and nonslippery.

Secure all area rugs with rubber backing. Throw rugs or scatter rugs can be particularly dangerous if they do not have nonskid backing. If you use them, be sure to use a skid-proof pad underneath. Never use a scatter rug at the top of the stairs.

Avoid thick carpeting and rugs with long pile, such as shag carpets, which may obscure small or sharp objects such as buttons and pins that can be potentially hazardous. On any floor surface, if you have dropped pins or needles, use a magnet to find any stray metal hazards. Check carpets for loose threads or loops that could catch feet or little toes. Clean and dry or remove water-damaged carpets.

If your child has asthma, refrain from covering the floors with

---

**"IT HAPPENED TO US"**

## Glass Door Hazard

One summer's day last year, I decided to take a break and visit a friend in the neighborhood. I brought my 3½-year-old along with me. We were all sitting on the patio when my son said he was thirsty. My friend got up and went inside to pour him a glass of juice. He wanted to stay inside for a few minutes to finish it, and my friend came back outside with me. We didn't think much of leaving him alone in the house for a couple of minutes, since I could clearly see what he was doing through the sliding glass doors. After finishing his cookies, my son decided he wanted to come back outside—in a hurry. Not realizing that there was a closed glass door between him and the sunny outdoors, he ran full speed into it, smashing against it face first. Fortunately, the door was sturdy enough to withstand the blow and did not shatter. Although my son did not get cut, he had a severe nosebleed and a sizable bump on his forehead. If there had only been a decal or sticker at his eye level, he would have noticed the glass and not hurt himself running into it.

wall-to-wall carpet, which is a magnet for dust mites. Also damp mop regularly to reduce dust—and dust-mite—accumulation. To prevent the danger of inhaling toxins, keep children out of a room where a rug is being shampooed and for several hours afterward.

**Windows** Make sure you have window guards firmly installed in all rooms where windows are accessible to children. Be sure however, not to block a fire exit. You can also use locks on double-hung windows that allow windows to be opened only a few inches for ventilation. Or, open windows from the top only. Never rely on a window screen or storm window to prevent your child from falling out. Make sure you do not place furniture that a toddler can climb up on next to a window. Also put decals or stickers at your child's eye level to alert him to the fact that there is glass in large picture windows or floor-to-ceiling windows.

---

**PRODUCT POINTERS**

## Choosing and Using Child-Safety Gates

Installing a safety gate can help protect your child by confining him inside a room or keeping him out. Never assume, however, that the gate alone will keep your child safe. Gates are no substitute for your watchful eyes. The gates themselves can be a hazard if they are installed incorrectly, are not in good repair, or are unsafe by design. In 1994, nearly 1,200 children age 4 and under were injured as a result of safety gates. To make sure you choose a gate that is safe and use it effectively, follow these tips:

• **Select tall gate**—at least 32 inches high—to keep a toddler from climbing over it.

• **Make sure that if the gate has diamond-slat openings,** they are no more than 2⅜-inches wide. Vertical slats should be spaced no more than 2⅜-inches apart.

• **Choose a gate that stands securely in place.** A hardware-mounted gate anchors to the walls. An expanding-pressure gate is set to the width of a doorway with a bar or handle and is held in place by a spring mechanism. If you have a pressure gate, make sure the expanding bar is on the side opposite the child. Otherwise, she could use it as a foothold for climbing or pinch her fingers in it. Check rubber end caps which hold pressure gates against walls after each use. Dirty caps don't grip well.

• **Use a hardware-mounted gate at the top of stairs.** A pressure gate may not be secure enough to withstand the weight of a toddler, causing her to tumble down the stairs.

**Window treatments**  Window treatments can also pose risks. To minimize the hazards follow these guidelines:

- **Make sure that curtains are far enough away from heat sources** so they cannot be blown into them and possibly catch fire.

- **Make sure that there are no dangling cords** from blinds or curtains within your child's reach. Tie cords up high or use cord shorteners available through child-safety product sources.

- **Avoid cords that form a continuous loop.** They are particularly dangerous. Cords should be cut and reconfigured to form two separate cords, eliminating the nooselike loop. To eliminate the loops, cut the cord above the end of the tassel, remove the equalizer buckle, then slip the new tassels onto the two new cords that you have created. Breakaway tassels that separate if a child becomes entangled in the cord loop are also available.

- **Be sure any plastic or decorative pulls on blinds or cords are safely attached** and will not come off and become a potential choking hazard.

- **Make sure all shades, blinds, etc., are securely installed** and will not come crashing down.

*Safety gates are a must once your child becomes mobile.*

**Stairways**  Stairways are enticing to toddlers and can pose a danger to older children and adults, as well. To childproof your stairways:

- **Install safety gates** at the top of the stairs, and bottom if necessary, to prevent climbing up or falling down as soon as your child starts to crawl.

- **Make sure stairs are not slippery.** Nonskid padding especially made for stairways is available and handy for basement or garage steps.

- **If you carpet your stairway,** be sure carpeting is firmly secured to each stair and that there is no loose hardware.

- **Stair railings should be secure and free of splinters.**

- **Make sure slats are spaced no more than 3½ inches apart.** If they are, invest in a banister guard.

- **Use caution around open-backed stairs** that toddlers could slip through.
- **Never place objects on stairway;** they are a tripping hazard.
- **Use a night-light near stairways** and have light switches placed within easy reach of both top and bottom stairs.

## Furnishings

It's hard to imagine that ordinary room furnishings could pose potential threats to your child's safety. Look closely, though, and you'll see there are plenty of risks. Most of them are quite easily minimized, however.

**Bookshelves and other furniture** Toddlers might be tempted to crawl up onto bookshelves, TV stands, or use dresser drawers as stairs, so take measures to secure unsteady pieces, bolting them to walls or floors. Remove pieces that cannot be secured. Make sure, too, that all tabletops are securely anchored to their bases. Unsteady floor lamps may need to be removed, secured, or placed in a spot where they are unlikely to cause problems.

Remove dangerous items from shelves that little hands can reach. Hazards for children include not only breakable items such as glass, but also dishes of nuts or hard candy that might pose a choking hazard. Remember, as your child grows so does her ability to reach higher places.

**Sharp-cornered and glass furniture** Check coffee tables, end tables, and other furniture for sharp edges. Use protective cushioning to soften the blow should your youngster fall against the piece. If possible, temporarily remove pieces that have sharp edges or corners that could be hazardous to a young child who runs into them. Glass can be especially dangerous, since glass can cause serious injury if broken. Glass shelving can be particularly dangerous and is best relocated until children are older. If any piece of furniture contains posts on which your child's clothing could become entangled, remove the post or put the furniture item away until later.

**Cushioned furniture** Soft cushions and upholstery are a suffocation risk for infants, especially those under 6 months of age. Be particularly careful of bean-bag type seating or cushions filled with plastic foam (polystyrene) beads. Never place infants on water beds, sheepskins, or other plush surfaces.

**Rockers and recliners** Even though rocking chairs are a soothing addition to the nursery, be aware that they can be risky business around young children, since the chair's very function makes it unstable. It's wise to place a rocker off-limits for a while and, certainly, remove it from a toddler's room. Children may end up banging their heads on the chair as it tilts forward when they're trying to climb into it. Or they can tumble over backward or forward, especially if the chair is in the middle of the room. Little fingers and toes are in danger of being crushed by rockers in use by others, so be aware of little ones who might be crawling around the floor if you are using a rocker.

Recliners pose an even more serious potential for harm. Children can quite easily become wedged in them, pinching arms and legs between seat and sides or between the foot stool portion and main part of the chair. Some children have had their heads trapped between the chair seat and leg rests. Their own body weight forces the leg rest to fold down. *Never* let young children play on reclining chairs. If you have a recliner, make it off-limits to children under age 6 and/or tie the mechanism in the closed position.

**PARENTS ALERT**

*Exercise equipment*

Keep all exercise equipment out of reach. Exercise bikes, rowers, stair steppers, and other mechanical devices contain a number of gears that could entrap your child. Even two-pound weights could cause harm if a child drops one on himself.

# Kitchen

Did you ever notice how people tend to congregate in the kitchen at parties? It's often where the action is—where people like to be. Young children are no exception. There's practically no end to the fascinating things for little ones to explore in the kitchen. Adults engaged in preparing meals are bustling around, pulling colorful, interesting items from refrigerators and cupboards left, right, and center. Things are going on out of a toddler's sight on counters and stoves, and he yearns to see what and participate. That's why he's always reaching up at you while you're trying to cook.

The combination of all this activity, the child's innate curiosity, and your sometimes divided attention means that it's especially important to childproof the kitchen. Of course, you should never leave your young child unattended in the kitchen. The greatest concentration of household appliances, including plenty of sharp, heavy, and hot items, is found in the kitchen. The following outlines where many hazards can occur and how to minimize the risks.

*A safe kitchen*

refrigerator latched

drawers secured

burners covered

stove latched

no slippery rugs on the floor

all accessible cupboards latched

dishwasher latched

# General safety in the kitchen

To keep your child safe in the kitchen, you'll need to take note of the following:
- **Check for sharp edges and corners** where children could bang heads or injure their eyes. Install protective guards or cushioning.
- **Secure all knobs and handles.**
- **Seal off all electrical outlets with safety plugs.**
- **Keep floor skid-proof.** Use nonskid rugs. Wipe up spills immediately.
- **Install safety latches** on all cabinets and cupboards with contents that could pose risks to children.
- **Keep spices out of children's reach.** Many are toxic.
- **Use a child-resistant garbage can** or keep your trash behind closed doors in a locked cabinet.
- **Dispose of plastic bags safely** by tying each in a knot before throwing it in the trash.
- **Keep aluminum foil, waxed paper, and plastic wrap dispensers away from children.** The serrated edges on the boxes can cut little fingers.
- **Don't leave small objects that could pose choking hazards within striking range of little fingers.** That includes toothpicks, rubber bands, and paper clips, as well as food.
- **All alcohol should be securely stored out of a child's sight and reach.** After a party, make sure to empty all glasses.

*For information on toxic spices, see **page 509**.*

# Stove
- **Make sure stoves, ovens, and burners are in good working order.** If fueled by gas, regularly check that there are no leaks and that pilot lights function properly.
- **Use back burners whenever possible.** Some of the most common accidents occur when a child reaches up and grabs a pot or pan, spilling the hot contents over himself. When it's necessary to use the front burners, turn all pot handles toward the back so they are not as easy to reach.
- **Keep flammable objects such as curtains, towels, oven mitts, and debris away from the stove.**
- **Make sure handles on pots and pans are secure, not loose.** Tighten them if they are wobbly, or if they can't be fixed, throw the pots and pans out.

## *Microwaving Safety*

Microwave ovens are useful and efficient if they are used properly. However, it's not so easy to use them safely. It's best not to let children under 12 years old use them.

Microwave cooking and heating pose special hazards. Since microwaves heat from the inside out, both the container in which the food was heated and the food itself may feel cool to the touch, but there could be hot spots inside. Using a microwave oven to heat baby food or formula in bottles is not recommended because of the uneven heat and potential for scalding.

Steam escaping from such items as microwave popcorn bags or unvented containers may be dangerously hot, too. In addition, steam pressure buildup can cause some sealed containers (including plastic baby bottle liners) to explode and some materials (i.e., plastic containers used to package such items as cottage cheese) to melt or leach into foods. Even the outer membrane of an egg yolk, if left intact when microwaved, can allow so much pressure to build up inside the yolk that it will explode when pierced, potentially causing severe burns. Make sure to pierce the yolk or scramble the egg before microwaving. Always use containers that are safe for microwave ovens, heat food for the recommended period of time, and operate the appliance according to the manufacturer's guidelines.

- **Place childproof covers on stove and oven knobs or remove knobs** entirely from the stove so that burners and oven cannot be turned on easily by a child. Knobs can be stored conveniently in a drawer or on a shelf, out of your child's reach.
- **For extra safety, use a stove guard** that helps prevent little hands from touching hot surfaces.
- **Check for hot surfaces.** Some units are poorly insulated and the outside may get hot enough to cause burns. Check the outside of your oven when it's at roasting temperature to make sure it's only warm, not hot, to the touch. If it does become too hot, install a safety gate at the kitchen door and keep children out of the kitchen during cooking times.
- **Always turn the oven off when not in use,** and never use it to heat a room.
- **Be careful opening the door of a hot oven** when a child is standing by. He may try to touch the inside of the door, or may get a face full of very hot air.
- **Bolt the stove to the wall** if you have a low oven or broiler door so that the stove will not tip over should a child open the door and stand on it.

# Refrigerators and freezers

- **Use a childproof door latch,** Velcro or buckle type, to secure the door shut.
- **Remove refrigerator magnets.** Children can choke on small items, and colorful refrigerator magnets are particularly enticing.
- **Warn children not to touch ice-cold surfaces with their tongues.** Your child's tongue will stick to the surface.

- **For added precaution keep glass bottles and jars off easily accessible shelves** and never store batteries or film or other interesting inedible objects in the refrigerator.
- **Remove doors from old appliances** you are replacing as soon as the new ones arrive. Refrigerators as well as coolers, freezers, and other larger airtight appliances can entrap a child who may crawl inside and be unable to get out. Also, as soon as your child is old enough to understand, instruct her never to hide in any appliance.

## Dishwasher

- **Never leave sharp implements, including knives, inside the dishwasher.** No doubt, your child will see you placing dishware into and out of the dishwasher and will want to do the same. If you do place sharp utensils in the dishwasher, make sure they are pointed downwards during the cycle, and remove them as soon as they are washed. Also remove breakable items immediately.
- **Use a childproof appliance latch for added protection.**

## Garbage disposal

- **Use a disposal cap** to prevent objects from shooting back out after you've put them down into the disposal.
- **Teach children never to reach down into a place they can't see, such as a sink drain with a disposal unit.**

**PARENTS ALERT**

### Dangers in Detergents

The powerful substances that get laundry and dishes clean can pose serious risks to children. Dishwasher detergent, in both powder and liquid form, is particularly hazardous. Because of its high alkalinity, it can be as corrosive as drain cleaner. Trouble can happen even if detergents are generally safely locked away. Even the residue left in the dishwasher after dishes have been washed can be harmful. To protect your child, follow these tips:

• **Buy detergent that has a child-proof cap** or store in a child-proof container. Keep out of children's reach.

• **Don't add detergent to the dishwasher until you are ready to turn on the machine.**

• **Remove detergent residue from the machine after each wash.**

• **If your child gets detergent on her skin, wipe it off with a dry towel and rinse the area with cool water.** Get medical attention if the area looks inflamed.

• **Do not induce vomiting** if your child swallows detergent. Wipe any detergent from her mouth with a dry towel and call your poison control center, physician, or 911 immediately.

• **If detergent gets into your child's eyes, rinse them under lukewarm water** for several minutes, then head for the emergency room.

### Hair Caught in Mixer

My 3-year-old daughter is fascinated by everything in the kitchen. One day last winter I decided to make a chocolate cake from scratch. My ever-curious daughter wanted to help, of course, so I let her add some of the ingredients that I had measured out. I left the electric mixer running in the bowl to beat in some of the ingredients. While I was searching for the vanilla, I suddenly heard my daughter scream. She had leaned over the mixing bowl and accidentally got her hair caught in the beater. Fortunately, my old mixer was not very powerful and I was able to pull the plug out quickly. My daughter escaped severe injury, fortunately, but she was terrified. It taught me how quickly accidents happen and how dangerous ordinary household appliances can be.

# Small kitchen appliances

• **Unplug toasters, blenders, coffee makers, food processors, and other small appliances** when not in use and store them out of the reach of children.

• **Use cord shorteners** to take up the slack in appliance cords so that the cords are less likely to dangle.

• **Never use a knife or other metal object to unclog a toaster.** This could cause electrocution. If something becomes lodged in a toaster, unplug it and wait a few moments before trying to extract it. Shake it loose, or use a wooden spoon to dislodge it.

# Dining area

Whether you have an eat-in kitchen or a separate dining room, observe the following:

• **Repair or dispose of rickety chairs.**

• **Shove chairs back in place flush against the table** when not in use. Don't let them stand out from the table where they may be treated as steps for a toddler to climb.

• **Secure tables with center pedestals.** Tables that have center pedestals rather than corner legs are more likely to topple over if a child's weight bears down on the sides. Teach your child never to lean on the table's edge.

• **Make sure tabletops are securely anchored to bases.**

• **Be wary of folding or collapsible tables and chairs.** Brace them so they are secure around children or remove folding tables and chairs when not in use.

• **Check for protruding nails, splintered wood, staples, sharp bolts, and jagged edges.** Get down on all fours and take a look at the undersides of your tables and chairs.

• **Place fine china, glassware, and other breakable items safely behind closed doors.**

• **Do not keep a cloth on the dining table.** Toddlers are likely to pull it—and everything on it—down off the table and on top of themselves.

# High chairs

High chairs place young children at a convenient level for feeding, while allowing them to share in the dining experience with the rest of the family. They also have the added benefit of restraint. High chairs, however, can be dangerous. Keep the following safety pointers in mind when choosing and using a high chair. Be careful, too, when using high chairs or booster seats in a restaurant.

- **Choose a chair in which the back of the seat is a simple, rounded style,** not one with corner posts, which could potentially catch on a bib tie and pose risk of strangulation.
- **Look for a high chair with a tray that locks firmly into place.** When locking the tray, check that the baby's fingers are out of the way.
- **Make sure the chair has both waist and crotch straps.** Always fasten them when using the chair. A child who isn't secured can stand up and fall or slide beneath the tray and strangle.
- **Make sure the safety straps function and are firmly attached,** especially if you use a secondhand chair. If they aren't, contact the manufacturer to order new ones.
- **Choose a chair with a wide base for stability.**
- **Check the legs to see that caps, plugs, or coverings are firmly attached.** If loose they can cause the chair to wobble or pose a choking hazard if they fall off.
- **Check the folding mechanism,** making sure the locking device is securely latched.
- **Don't place a high chair close to tables, counters, or walls**. By pushing against these surfaces, a child can cause the high chair to fall over.
- **Don't let your child stand in a high chair or climb into it on his own.**

**Booster seats and table-attached models**  There are two general types of booster seats—those that attach to the chair and

---

### "IT HAPPENED TO US"

## *Our Child Was Scalded*

I couldn't image how quickly accidents could happen until one did. My husband and I were sitting at the dinner table with our 18-month-old daughter in her hook-on high chair. The telephone rang and I got up to answer it, setting my just-poured cup of steaming-hot coffee down next to my plate. The next thing I heard was my daughter's shriek of pain. No sooner had I set my cup down, then she reached over to grab it, spilling it over her arms and hands before my husband had a chance to intervene. We immediately ran her hands and arms under cold water, but it was clear that the injury was worse than we had first thought. We rushed her to the emergency room where she was treated for second-degree burns. Now I know to keep hazardous implements and hot liquids well out of her reach.

**PARENTS ALERT**

## *Setting the Table for Safety*

Young children have a knack for grabbing onto things that parents might assume are safely beyond their reach—a point to keep in mind when setting the table.

When setting a table with young children around, do not put sharp implements such as steak knives and sharp-tined forks out in advance. Wait until guests are seated to complete the table setting. Be careful, too, when serving hot foods and beverages. Place serving dishes and coffee- or teapots away from a young child.

Keep small food items such as olives away, too, since they pose a choking risk, and make sure other diners do not leave pits, toothpicks, and the like within a child's reach.

Be careful with glass and china items. which may shatter when knocked over or dropped. Use sturdy plastic cups for young children to drink from.

those that attach to the table or countertop. A chair-based booster seat meant for automobile use can double as a booster seat in a restaurant or at home. A household booster seat, however, is not meant for use in the car.

Your child should be able to sit up straight with good balance on his own before he can safely use a booster seat. Generally, booster seats are not recommended for children younger than 18 months of age. If you use the chair-attached model, choose a chair that is sturdy, and has a flat seat and straight back. Make sure the seat is securely attached to the chair before placing your child on the seat. Then strap him in safely.

If you choose a seat that hooks onto a counter or table top, make sure that your child's feet cannot reach any surface. It's a common misconception that placing an attachable seat over a chair provides added protection, but the opposite is true. If your child's feet can touch the chair beneath the suspended seat, he can push himself up, toppling the chair and dislodging the booster seat. Be sure, too, that the counter or table to which the hook-on chair is attached is stable enough to support it. Never attach a seat to a pedestal-based table. Follow the manufacturer's recommended weight limits—typically 40 pounds. The chair you choose should have strong clamps so it attaches firmly to the table, and strong, safe straps like those recommended for high chairs, above.

# Laundry room

Children often find the laundry or utility room or area attractive. The large, warm, humming washing and drying machines, piles of clothing, and colorful bottles and boxes of cleaning supplies are fascinating to explore. If you have a separate laundry or utility room, it's a good idea to place it off-limits to small children by shutting, and safely latching, the door, since so many products used in cleaning and laundering are toxic. If possible, tend to laundry duties, including ironing, when children are napping or supervised by other adults.

Never leave laundry and cleaning supplies out on top of the appliances or on the floor. They are best locked away in a childproof cabinet, even if the room itself is locked. Whenever possible, choose cleaning products that have child-resistant caps and lids.

Be careful, too, with piles of laundry. Drawstrings on sweat pants, for instance, can pose strangulation risks, and loose buttons can come off easily, creating a choking hazard. Properly dispose of empty containers by throwing them away in a sealed receptacle. Dispose of plastic garment bags by tying them in knots before tossing them to prevent accidental suffocation. Use trash cans with childproof lids and tie plastic bags in tight knots to reduce risk of strangulation.

## Washer and dryer

To a child, large laundry appliances like washers and dryers can look like great places to hide or intriguing spaces to explore. Once they are inside, they may not be able to get out. Take the following precautions with these appliances:

- **Always keep doors of large appliances closed.**
- **Lock doors with childproof latches.**
- **Make sure the appliances will not tip over** and that they are close enough to the wall so that youngsters cannot squeeze behind them.
- **Turn the power off to washer and dryer** if possible, when they are not in use.

## Iron

- **Do not allow iron cord to hang down** within reach of a child's grasp. One tug and the iron could come tumbling down.

- **Never leave a hot iron unattended.** Turning your back for a few seconds could spell disaster if the iron falls on top of a child or he reaches up and touches the hot surface.
- **Remember, irons stay hot long after they are shut off.** Remove the iron to a safe spot to cool, then put it away. Always unplug it when not in use.
- **To reduce the risk of fire, consider investing in a self-turn-off model.**
- **Keep ironing supplies, such as spray starch, out of children's reach.**

# Indoor play spaces

Your child's playroom should be kid friendly—a place where she can relax and have fun in a safe and secure space. Ideally, it should be located so that you can keep a pretty close watch on what's going on. Childproof the room as you would any other room in the house, installing window guards, making sure that electrical outlets have safety plugs; electrical cords, lamps, etc., are out of the way; fixtures and furniture are sturdy and in good repair; and there are no sharp corners and edges for a child to fall against and hurt herself. Be sure, too, that your child will not be able to lock herself inside the room.

Keep all unsafe furniture—rocking chairs, for instance—out of the playroom. Likewise for hazardous substances.

Make sure there are cozy spots where your child can curl up and settle down with a book or a quiet game. Child-size furniture is good for her to use, too, since it reduces the risk of falling from adult-height seats. Have plenty of age-appropriate toys on hand that are both safe and easy to reach.

If you have more than one child using a playroom, you are going to have to keep your older child's toys out of the younger one's reach. Teach your older children that babies and toddlers can choke on small items including small parts that might break off toys, and enlist their help in watching out for dangers. Also teach older children to securely close or latch bins, cabinets, and closets that hold potentially hazardous items and to put their toys safely away after use. Childproof latches are handy to use in this case, since older children can be taught how to open and close them, but they are still difficult for toddlers to manipulate. Don't, however, put young children in charge of their younger siblings, since they simply aren't capable and it would be unfair to expect this degree of maturity from them.

## Choosing safe toys

*Also see **page 846** for information on using toys and sports equipment safely.*

Choose toys that are appropriate for your child's age and abilities. Read toy labels to note recommendations for age. These recommendations are based on the physical ability of the child to play with the toy; the mental ability of a child to know how to use a toy; the play needs and interests present at various levels of a child's development; and the safety aspects of the particular toy. To help keep playtime safe and fun, follow these pointers when choosing toys for your children:

**Toy safety checklist**    When choosing toys for your child, review these safety standards:

- **Is the toy well made and sturdy?** If not, it could break apart, potentially injuring a child.
- **Does the toy have a safe finish?** Paint should be nontoxic and durable so the finish doesn't peel.
- **Are art supplies such as crayons, paints, and modeling dough nontoxic?** Look for the ACMI (Art and Creative Materials Institute, Inc.) seal certifying the products' safety.
- **Are toys, including stuffed animals, washable?** If not, they can become breeding grounds for germs.
- **Does the toy have heating elements or electrical connections?** Battery-powered toys are acceptable as long as the batteries and wires are safely enclosed and inaccessible or the toy is used only under close supervision.
- **Are rideable toys stable, sturdy, and in good repair?**
- **Are there any sharp points, edges, or brittle, breakable parts** that could cause injury or entrap small hands, feet, or fingers?
- **Does the toy make loud noises?** Noise levels greater than 100 decibels can damage your child's hearing. "Caps" used in cap guns are dangerous if used indoors or closer than 12 inches from your child's ear.

## Keeping Older Kids' Toys Out of Reach

To help my 5-year-old son remember to store his toys out of his 18-month-old sister's reach, I took an old bread box—the kind that has a door that swings open from top to bottom—and painted it like a treasure chest. I placed it on a shelf he could reach, but that is too high for his little sister. For added protection, I put a safety strap with a child-safe buckle around the box, encircling it top to bottom. Now when my son wants to play with his toys, he goes to his private treasure chest and removes what he wants. When he's finished, he locks his toys up safely inside again.

• **Does the toy involve throwing or shooting projectiles?** Many such toys are best avoided because of potential injury, especially to eyes. Make sure if your older child plays with bow and arrow sets, safety darts, etc., that they are used safely, away from younger children, and with constant adult supervision. Also make sure that any parts such as rubber suction cups do not fall off and become a choking hazard to younger children.

• **Avoid latex balloons.** Be aware that one of the greatest choking hazards for children is uninflated balloons and the pieces of burst balloons. Opt for mylar balloons.

**Choosing toddler toys** Observe these additional safety checks when choosing toys for children under the age of 3:

• **Is the toy—or any part of the toy—small enough to swallow?** To test the safety of a toy, invest in a truncated cylinder. This clear plastic tube, available in many retail outlets, allows objects to pass through it that are too small to be given to a child under 3 years of age. This includes marbles, small interlocking blocks, small balls, and many toy accessories and game pieces.

• **Can parts be bitten off?** Balls and other toys made of foamlike materials may be hazardous if the child bites off pieces and attempts to swallow them.

• **Does the toy have internal springs, gears, or hinges?** Toddlers could put them in their mouths and choke.

• **Does the toy have a string?** Strings, ribbons, or cords longer than six inches place your child at risk for strangulation. Avoid such toys or remove or trim the strings.

## Toy storage equipment

Let your child herself choose toys she would like to play with by storing them in areas that are easily accessible to her. (It's up to you, of course, to limit the selection by providing only those toys that are safe.) Sturdy, low open shelving works well, as do colorful storage cubes. Avoid tall dressers with deep drawers that are both hard to reach and difficult to keep neat. If you use a toy chest or toy box, follow these guidelines:

- **Use a toy box that does not have a top, or select one that has a lightweight, removable lid or sliding doors or panels.** Be sure, however, that any sliding features are child-safe and cannot pinch hands or entrap heads.
- **If the toy box has a hinged lid, make sure that it has a spring-loaded support** that holds the lid open at all angles, so it can't come crashing down on your child's head or hands, and she cannot become trapped inside. If the lid doesn't stay open to any angle, either remove the lid or install a support.
- **Choose a toy box with rounded or padded edges and corners.**
- **Make sure the toy chest you choose has ventilation holes to allow for air circulation, since children may crawl inside.** Do not block ventilation holes by shoving the box firmly against a wall.
- **Make sure the lid does not latch.** A child might become trapped inside.

# Electrical systems

A faulty electrical system can be hazardous for two reasons: risk of shock or electrocution, and fire. Be sure that your home has been wired professionally by a licensed electrician and periodically inspect wiring and electrical equipment for signs of wear and tear. And remember that misuse of even a properly functioning system can also result in accidents.

## General precautions regarding electricity

Following are precautions to take when dealing with electrical systems and appliances.

- **Install safety plugs in outlets not in use.**

## Basement Safety

Use basements as living areas only if they are leak-proof and have adequate ventilation. Use dehumidifiers, if necessary, to maintain humidity between 30 and 50 percent. Check for radon. If basements are used primarily for storage, or if they house such heavy-duty household equipment as furnaces, hot-water heaters, and oil storage tanks, as well as laundry machines and supplies, or additional freezers and refrigerators keep them off, limits to kids.

If, however, you use your basement as actual living space and kids are going to be playing there, childproof the area as you would any other part of your home.

- **Have ground fault circuit interrupters installed** in outlets in the kitchen and bathroom and have regular outlets grounded to reduce the risk of shock.
- **Check all cords and plugs for wear and tear** and repair and replace them if they are frayed or damaged in any way.
- **Repair or replace any outlet or switch** that feels hot to the touch, sparks, or makes hissing noises.
- **Do not overload sockets** by plugging more appliances into them than they can hold.
- **Avoid using an extension cord with a high-energy appliance.** If you must, use a special heavy-duty cord. Do not run extension cords under rugs or over doorjambs, where they could get pinched, damaging their safety insulation.
- **Never bypass a three-pronged plug.** Never replace a three-pronged plug with a two-pronged plug or try to adapt it to fit into a two-pronged plug outlet by using an extension cord or adapter. Many household appliances and other equipment that use a lot of electricity are designed with three-pronged plugs which are grounded for safety purposes.
- **Always remove plugs from sockets by grasping the plug,** never by tugging on the cord.
- **Do not let electrical cords dangle or pose a tripping hazard.** Run them as close to the wall as possible and take up the slack. Use special devices available in hardware and many houseware stores to guide or consolidate cords, or use electrical tape to adhere them to wall or floors. Run them out of sight and behind furniture to keep them away from children, especially toddlers, who might be tempted to chew on them and could suffer serious injury. Do not, however, run electrical cords under rugs or carpeting.
- **Always replace a burned-out fuse with one that is rated for that circuit.** Replacing it with a larger one could cause the circuit to overload and catch fire.
- **Never use electrical appliances near water,** such as hairdryers near the bathtub, or even a non-battery-powered radio by the kitchen sink. Dry your hands before you touch anything that is plugged in, including the cord.

- **Always use the proper-wattage bulb.** Check the fixture for the maximum wattage it can support and never exceed the limit.
- **Be careful about placement of lighting fixtures.** Bulbs get very hot and can cause severe burns if touched. In addition, lamps can cause fires if they fall or otherwise come into contact with flammable materials.
- **If you attempt any electrical repairs or installations yourself,** remove the fuse or trip the circuit breaker—rather than simply turning off the power by the switch.

## Household appliances

The countless appliances in your home are wonderful conveniences, but they can become household hazards if they are not properly maintained, if they malfunction, or if they are not used in accordance with manufacturers' instructions. Young children, especially, are at risk because they do not understand the potential for injury.

As you childproof your home room by room, examine all appliances, both large and small, from several perspectives. Think about their placement and function and view them from your child's-eye level. Consider whether the appliance is in danger of toppling over when pulled on or pushed against. Make sure electrical cords are in good condition, not frayed, and that they do not dangle enticingly within your child's reach. Also be sure to keep electrical units away from sinks and tubs and other water sources, since an electrical appliance, even if turned off, can cause electrocution if it falls into the water. Often, it's best to unplug any small appliances and to place them out of children's reach altogether when they are not in use.

Pay close attention to units that generate heat, from toasters and stoves to space heaters and lights, since burns and scalds are among the most common household injuries. In addition to the cautions listed above regarding kitchen and laundry-room appliances, take special note of precautions regarding these appliances:

**PARENTS ALERT**

### *Halogen Lamp Hazards*

Halogen floor lamps, especially torchère-style models, have been implicated in numerous house fires. Because of the risk, they have been banned from many public places, such as college dormitories. They are not recommended for any home.

Although halogen bulbs use less energy than incandescent bulbs, they burn hotter. Items accidentally tossed into the bowl-shaped lamp—a paper airplane, T-shirt, or stuffed toy, for example—could easily catch fire. Fires can result as well if the lamp is knocked over onto a rug or bedding, or if curtains or drapes are blown across the lamp.

**Beauty appliances**  Don't leave curling irons, electric hair curlers, and hair dryers unattended while they are plugged in or still warm. They stay hot after they are turned off and may cause burns.

**TVs, stereos, and VCRs**  Firmly anchor TVs and stereos to prevent their toppling. VCRs are best placed out of reach, since your curious child may injure his fingers if he places them in the tape slot. Lock shields are also available for protection.

**Electric blankets**  Never place an infant on an electric blanket. Doing so can cause her to become dangerously overheated. In fact, do not use electric blankets on beds for children under 12. Do not fold or tuck in an electric blanket on your own bed. Folded or crimped heating coils pose a fire risk.

## Heating, cooling, and air-filtration systems

Always keep safety in mind when you are choosing and maintaining systems that heat and cool your family's living space. Appliances that heat or cool—from furnaces and space heaters to air conditioners, both central and window varieties—tend to be heavy power users and place high demands on electrical systems, so it's important to make sure wiring and circuitry is in good repair and capable of safely tolerating the electrical load. Never plug more than one high-energy-use appliance into the same outlet to guard against system overload, which can be a fire hazard.

Heating and air-conditioning systems can be a source of microbial or carbon monoxide contamination if they are not properly cleaned and maintained. Clean devices regularly according to manufacturers' guidelines and change all filters on humidifiers, dehumidifiers, furnaces, and air-conditioning units regularly.

**Air conditioners**  Using an air conditioner in warm weather rather than opening the windows can decrease the amount of airborne pollens inside the home as well as make the room temperature more comfortable. But it is important to use an air conditioner properly. Make sure that all room air conditioners are correctly installed and securely anchored, and be sure they are plugged into the right kind of outlet. They should not be placed inside the window in such a way that they can be used as a step for a child to stand on. If the unit protrudes out the window at a height at which a child or adult could be harmed by running into its sharp corners, enclose it in a metal cage with rounded corners. Be sure to clean the unit regularly, replacing or washing filters and cleaning all ducts. If a unit has been exposed to the outdoors or stored for the winter, be sure to wash it thoroughly. For many units, this involves using a high-powered hose to wash away pollutants such as bird dropping and grease-trapped dust that have accumulated on and within the metal housing. Remove dust from the indoor vents, too. Check the manufacturer's guidelines for cleaning your units.

**Air purifiers** Room air purifiers can remove allergens from the air and are particularly useful in homes in which any resident suffers from asthma or other allergies. Placing filters over forced-air vents and installing central air cleaners, which are more effective than single-room devices, can help, too, by cutting down on the amount of dust and dust mites circulating in the air. Check that your unit is HEPA (high-efficiency particulate air filtration) certified. A HEPA filter on vacuum cleaners or air filters must, by law, capture 99.97 percent of all particles down to 0.3 micron—about 200 times smaller than the width of a human hair. The filter screens out pet dander, pollen, dust, mold, and bacteria, all of which cause allergy sufferers discomfort.

**Dehumidifiers** Keeping air humidity low by using a dehumidifier can also help curtail dust mites, which do not thrive as well in dry surroundings. Dehumidifiers also inhibit the growth of mold, to which many people are allergic. Treat dehumidifiers with mold-inhibiting sprays for extra protection, and clean them according to the manufacturer's guidelines.

**Humidifiers and vaporizers** Warm-mist or steam humidifiers and vaporizers use boiling water to produce steam. A child may be

---

**"IT HAPPENED TO US"**

## Steam Vaporizer Hazard

Our family learned first-hand that steam vaporizers should not be used around children. Our 13-month-old daughter had a cold. To ease her congestion while she napped, I placed a vaporizer on the bookshelf in her room. Before putting her in her crib, though, I left the room briefly. Just a few seconds later, I heard a scream. My daughter had reached into the steam and burned herself. We rushed her to the nearest hospital, where she was treated for serious burns of her right hand. The burn subsequently healed, but two of my daughter's fingers are permanently disfigured because of scar tissue. Before this happened I never realized how dangerous a vaporizer could be or how quickly accidents can happen.

burned by reaching into hot steam or knocking an appliance over, spilling boiling water on himself. It's better, therefore, to use a cool-mist or ultrasonic humidifier, which releases cool moisture into the air. Nonetheless, always make sure the device and its cord are out of your child's reach, and clean the unit as recommended by the manufacturer.

**Space heaters** There are several different types of space heaters, all of which can be hazardous. A child can be burned by touching the heater, kerosene heaters can emit toxic vapors, and fires can start if the heater is knocked over or is placed close to flammable materials. If you must use a space heater, take the following precautions:

* **Choose an electric model and place a spark-arresting screen around it.**
* **Choose a model that automatically shuts off when toppled over.**
* **Instruct children to stay away from it.**
* **Make sure the heater is at least three feet away from furniture, curtains, and other flammable materials.**
* **Make sure the cord is not a tripping hazard.**
* **Don't leave the appliance plugged in and in an empty room.**
* **Never use a space heater to dry clothing or towels.**
* **If you use a kerosene heater use only clear, grade A-1 kerosene, never gasoline, camp stove fuel, or yellow kerosene.**
* **Never use the kitchen stove as a space heater**—a child may touch the door or reach inside, resulting in serious burns. Leaving a gas stove on with the door open can also cause dangerous levels of carbon monoxide to accumulate very quickly.

## Furnace and air-duct safety

Have a professional install your home heating system and have it checked regularly—at the beginning of each winter season is a good time. Maintenance checks should include making sure that furnaces are not cracked or missing panels or flue caps to be sure exhaust gases can escape from the home properly. Carbon-monoxide levels should be monitored as well by installing carbon-monoxide detectors throughout your home. Make sure air ducts are well maintained, not cracked, and that they are properly secured in place. Also monitor them to make sure they do not become hot enough to cause a fire. Do not store combustible objects on or near them.

Grills that cover ducts need to be installed properly and must remain sturdy and secure. Grill guards and deflectors that help prevent little fingers from exploring them are available for hot-air ducts. If you have a grate over a floor furnace duct, make sure it is secure enough to bear the weight of an adult. Since some floor grates can get hot enough to cause burns when the heat is on, place a screen around it for additional protection. Never dry clothing or towels on a register or grate, which may cause a fire.

## Fireplace safety

The warm glow of a fire is comforting. Be careful, though, when using a fireplace. Be sure to have the fireplace, flue, and chimney professionally serviced to check for problems, and have it cleaned at least once a year to remove any buildup of soot or creosote. Have a spark guard installed on top of the chimney to keep sparks from igniting the roof.

Burn only firewood in your fireplace—not plastics, chemically treated wood, or newspapers, especially those with colored inks, which may give off noxious fumes and/or cause dangerous substances to build up in the chimney. Do not use barbecue lighter fluid or gasoline to start a fire in the fireplace.

Place a spark-arresting screen in front of the fireplace and make sure it is always in place when you have a fire burning. Although a glass screen is most effective in preventing sparks from entering a room, it does get hot. If you have a glass screen, it's advisable to place another mesh screen in front of it to prevent little hands from getting burned. If you have a child under the age of 4, remove the screen's handles so she cannot easily grab the screen and pull it over on herself. Also keep fire tongs, pokers, and other tools out of reach. They retain heat long after being used and may be sharp as well.

Remove the gas key to a gas-fueled fireplace and place it safely out of reach to make sure that a child cannot accidentally turn on the gas, allowing it to spew into a room, or start a fire. Learn the proper way to operate a fireplace, keeping fires small, and making sure there is sufficient ventilation while the fire is burning. Be aware that smoke from the fireplace may cause symptoms in children with allergies, and refrain from using fireplaces when they are present.

*Also see **pages 858–61** for information on home fire safety.*

# *Indoor pollutants*

S ome safety precautions involved in childproofing a home—barring access to stairways, for instance—seem fairly obvious. But what about the dangers you don't see? Tasteless and odorless substances in the air, on surfaces, and in the drinking water can threaten the health of your family. Young children are particularly vulnerable since they breathe more quickly than adults, their skin is more permeable, their metabolisms faster, and their immune systems are not as well developed.

Pollutants in the home can be particularly potent, too, because they tend to be more concentrated in an enclosed environment. The Environmental Protection Agency (EPA), for instance, reports that concentrations of air pollutants are often two to five time higher indoors than out, even in cities. On a positive note, however, you can substantially cut your family's risks by taking a few simple steps. Following are facts you need to know and preventive measures you can take to safeguard your family against common contaminants and toxins:

## Asbestos

Asbestos is a naturally occurring mineral fiber. It is used in the home because of its excellent fire retarding and insulating properties and may be found in a variety of places, including heating equipment, pipe housing, fireplaces, exterior siding and roofing, and ceiling and flooring materials. Asbestos poses little risk when it is not disturbed. Trouble occurs when it starts to deteriorate and crumbles, releasing fibers into the air and onto surfaces. Inhaling the fibers, which may be invisible to the naked eye, may cause cancer of the lungs and chest lining as well as scarring of lung tissue anywhere from 15 to 45 years after exposure. Be particularly vigilant when planning any renovation.

**PARENTS RESOURCE**

To learn about asbestos removal contact your State Department of Health for regulations and advice, or call the **EPA Toxic Substance Control Act Hotline** at (202) 554-1404. You can also visit the EPA website at www.epa.gov.

**Safety precautions to reduce asbestos risks**
- If you suspect that a material contains asbestos, do not disturb it or try to remove it yourself.
- Seal off intact asbestos that is exposed. The American Lung Association recommends creating an air-tight seal around it with plastic sheeting and duct tape. Or hire a contractor who can build an enclosure around the material or spray it with an encapsulating compound.
- If asbestos is deteriorating and crumbling or if you are remodeling, removal is essential. Get professional advice and assistance by looking in the Yellow Pages under "Asbestos" for contractors who can analyze and possibly remove deteriorating asbestos.

## *Common Household Toxins*

Following are the most common toxic household chemicals:

alcoholic beverages

ammonia and cleaning products containing ammonia

antifreeze

boric acid

cosmetic items, especially hair
straighteners and nail-
polish removers

drain cleaners

fertilizers

furniture polish

gasoline and kerosene

laundry and automatic
dishwashing detergents

lighter fluid

lye

medicines of all kinds,
including vitamin and
mineral supplements
(especially iron)

oven cleaners

paints and paint thinners

pesticides and insecticides

rust removers

toilet bowl cleaners

weed killers

window washer fluid

Many other seemingly benign substances found around the house can be harmful if ingested, such as bubble bath, shampoo and shaving cream, ordinary dishwashing liquid, lipstick, toothpaste, and pet food.

## Carbon monoxide (CO)

Colorless, odorless, tasteless, this gas can kill—most often while kids and parents are sleeping. While higher amounts of the gas are responsible for poisoning deaths, exposure to low levels of carbon monoxide over a period of weeks can cause flu-like symptoms, including fatigue, headache, and muscle ache, and may also trigger lung ailments and cause neurological problems. There are many potential sources of carbon monoxide in your home, including fuel-burning heaters, space heaters, fireplaces, and vehicles.

**PARENTS ALERT**

### *Carbon Monoxide Dangers*

Any household appliances that are fueled with gas, oil, kerosene, or even wood may produce carbon monoxide. Carbon monoxide is a serious risk for children, because they have higher oxygen requirements than adults and carbon monoxide directly interferes with oxygen delivery to vital organs. The use of home heating equipment is often the source of many of these unfortunate incidents. It is highly recommended, therefore, that carbon monoxide detectors, which sound an alarm before carbon monoxide accumulates to dangerous levels, be installed in every home. Choose one of the two types of detectors approved by the Underwriters Laboratories Standard UL 2034 and recognized by reputable health and safety organizations: a basic plug-in model or a battery-operated detector. The battery-operated model is designed to detect lower levels of carbon monoxide and is therefore somewhat more sensitive than the plug-in type.

Although both kinds of detectors provide protection against carbon monoxide poisoning, professional metering equipment provides the most accurate readings of CO levels. The detectors should be placed in bedrooms and on the wall or ceiling at least 15 feet from the fuel-burning appliances. Additional detectors on every level provide added protection. Additional precautions include the following:

• **Never operate gasoline-powered engines in a confined space**.

• **Never use charcoal grills inside the home, directly outside an open window,** or in an attached garage, even if the door is open.

• **Have all your household fuel-burning appliances checked.** Look at the color of the gas burner flames and pilot lights. A blue-colored flame indicates that fuel is burning efficiently. The flame should not be yellow.

• **Never use your kitchen stove to heat a room.**

# Formaldehyde

Formaldehyde is contained in quite a few products, from particleboard to adhesives in carpeting. It is released over time, but the fumes are strongest when a product is new. Not everyone is sensitive to formaldehyde, but it has been linked to itchy eyes and throats, headaches, and nausea in some people. Its connection to cancer is not clear at this time. To minimize potential hazards, choose products that are well sealed or formaldehyde free. Choose only furniture and other items that are formaldehyde free for your child's room, to minimize exposure. If you have formaldehyde-containing products in your home, try placing household plants (choose nontoxic varieties) around the house to absorb some of the fumes.

**PARENTS RESOURCE**

If you are concerned about formaldehyde in your home or suspect high levels are present in a particular product, call the **EPA Toxic Substance Control Act Hotline** at (202) 554-1404, or visit their website, www.epa.gov.

# Household chemicals

Many ordinary household products are dangerously toxic if ingested. Some are extremely caustic, causing skin irritation or burns, and serious injury to eyes. Some are dangerous even if inhaled, especially in a poorly ventilated area. Always read labels before using products and follow all recommended precautions and directions. Always store cleaning products, toiletries, medicines, lawn-care products, gasoline, and beverage and medicinal alcohol out of children's reach in childproof places.

### Safety precautions for storing household chemicals
- **Choose items with childproof caps** whenever they are available.
- **Always cap the item when it's not in use.**
- **Lock up hazardous substances in childproof places.**
- **Do not spread powdered chemical pesticides—even boric acid—or spray liquid pesticides on food-preparation surfaces** or where children can come into contact with them. If you must spray, do so when children are not in the house.
- **Do not put nonfood items in food containers,** such as storing bleach in a juice jar.
- **Be careful of fumes.** Fumes from some household products such as bathroom tile cleaners and even deodorant are toxic and should be used only in well-ventilated areas. Read instructions and

*For some safe cleaning routines, see **page 831**.*

## Nontoxic Substitute Cleaning Products

Because children's taste buds are not well developed, an unpleasant flavor or odor may not deter them from ingesting a poisonous substance. Your child may find a bottle of detergent as appealing to drink as a glass of juice. You may want to consider substituting nontoxic cleaning products for the commercial varieties. Following are a few suggestions:

• **Carpet Cleaner.** Cut a potato and use the cut side to rub out stains on your carpet. Rub until the stain is no longer visible.

• **Shower Curtain Cleaner.** To get mold and soap scum stains out of a shower curtain, saturate a sponge with vinegar and wipe the curtain clean.

• **Wallpaper Cleaner.** To remove smudges from wallpaper take a slice of ordinary white bread and rub until the dirt disappears.

• **Microwave or Standard Cleaner.** Take ¼ cup of baking soda and add enough water to make a thick paste. Use a sponge to apply the paste to the inside of your oven and door, then rinse clean.

• **Window Cleaner.** Mix 3 tablespoons of cornstarch with ½ cup water. Use a cotton cloth to dab into the mixture and rub onto the window. Rub until the film disappears.

• **Floor Cleaner.** Pour 2 tablespoons of vegetable-oil-based liquid soap into a bucket. Add ½ cup vinegar, then 2 gallons of water. Mix and mop.

• **Stainless Steel Cleaner.** Pour some baking soda into a small bowl and dip into it with a damp sponge. Rub onto stainless steel until it's clean. Rinse with warm water and polish dry.

use accordingly. Choose a pump spray over an aerosol, if available, in personal-care and household cleaning products. Be aware, too, that toxic fumes may emit from volatile organic compounds, the most common of which is formaldehyde.

• **Keep children out of a room where a rug is being shampooed** and for several hours afterward. Some research has suggested a possible link between young children exposed to freshly shampooed rugs and Kawasaki syndrome, a rare illness that can lead to heart disease.

• **Follow environmentally safe guidelines for the disposal of toxic substances.** Do not leave them around the house or yard where children could get into them. Do not toss them into an open (or easily accessible) garbage can. When disposing of toxic or potentially toxic substances, call your local sanitation department or the EPA for guidelines. (In addition to being dangerous, improper disposal is also illegal in most areas.)

• **Choose nontoxic and environmentally friendly products whenever possible.**

## Lead

Exposure to lead can cause serious health problems. Babies are particularly vulnerable because their bodies absorb lead much more quickly than an older child's or adult's. Because their central nervous systems are still developing, a baby's health can be adversely affected by lead exposure. A blood level of 10 micrograms of lead per deciliter of blood is considered "elevated" in children, and some experts feel that every 10-microgram increase may cause an irreversible drop of one to three points in a child's IQ.

Often, children with elevated blood lead levels show no signs of lead poisoning, or the signs may be mistaken for another condition such as colic in infants or attention deficit syndrome in older children. Higher lead levels may result in digestive problems, changes in sleep patterns, and increased or decreased activity levels. Very high lead levels can trigger seizures, nerve paralysis, deafness, and, in rare cases, death.

Lead paint in homes poses the highest risk to children, and about 75 percent of all private homes and apartments built before 1980 contain some lead-based paint. Often the lead paint is hidden under newer layers of paint, and when the new paint starts to crumble, old chips or lead dust are released. House renovations may also expose lead-based paint and stir up lead dust. Babies and toddlers—who are apt to crawl around and chew or suck on paint chips, which are sweet-tasting, or who may put pacifiers, teething rings, and toys carrying lead dust into their mouths—are most at risk.

Exterior house renovations can result in lead deposits in the surrounding soil, as can leakage from parked cars that may have used lead-based gasoline in past years. Another source of lead poisoning is drinking water. Pipes lined with lead or pipes with lead soldering around the joints, as well as faucets made with brass or bronze may contain lead, which leaches into the drinking water. Experts estimate that approximately 30 million Americans have water with lead levels that exceed the acceptable level of 14 ppb (parts per billion).

### Safety precautions to reduce the risk of lead contamination

Experts recommend that children be tested for lead exposure between the ages of 9 and 12 months. If you know your home contains lead, everyone living there should be tested. Over-the-counter home testing kits are available to check lead in paint and water, but professional testing is likely to be more accurate. Local health and water departments may be able to provide you with information on how to get paint and water samples tested for a small fee.

---

**PARENTS RESOURCE**

You can contact the **National Lead Information Center Clearinghouse** for a list of laboratories in your area that can analyze paint and dust samples, (800) 424-LEAD or www.epa.gov/lead/nlic.htm.

## Lead Poisoning

Last year we journeyed north to visit my parents, who live in a 30-year-old house in Massachusetts. Our 19-month-old son was fascinated by the large windows in the old house and spent a lot of time holding on to the sill, looking out. One day I discovered that he had a mouth full of paint chips. Apparently he had been gnawing on the windowsill all along! We took him to a doctor who tested his blood for lead. The test showed that his blood contained an "elevated" amount of lead

The doctor advised me to feed him foods rich in calcium and iron, which reduce the amount of lead absorbed by the body, and have him retested a few weeks later.

Of all the measures I had taken to childproof my parents' home, I hadn't given the windowsills a second thought.

### If lead is present in your home

• **Use a wet cloth to remove any paint chips or paint dust** you find on the floor.

• **Wet-mop floors and wet-wipe surfaces often,** especially windowsills and where walls meet the floor. Wear rubber gloves and use powdered dishwasher detergent with a 5 to 8 percent phosphate content. Do not sweep or vacuum floors that may have lead dust or paint chips on them.

• **Wipe sills with a wet cloth before and after opening window,** and keep opening and closing to a minimum, especially in your baby's room.

• **Run cold tap water for 60 seconds or longer** before using it to mix formula or to drink. Always use cold, not hot, tap water for consumption, including water for cooking.

• **Choose stainless steel over brass or bronze faucets** when replacing old fixtures.

• **Wash your child's hands often,** especially before he eats. Also wash pacifiers, toys, and teething rings frequently.

• **Include adequate amounts of iron and calcium in your baby's diet.**

• **If you plan to renovate a lead-contaminated area of your home, hire a qualified licensed lead-abatement company.** Vacate the premises during the renovation. This is vital in the case of young children and pregnant women, since lead can travel through the placenta and affect the fetus.

## Radon

Radon is a colorless, odorless, radioactive gas that is formed by the breakdown of natural uranium in rocks and soil. Outside, the gas disperses into the air and concentrations are so low that they do not pose a health hazard. Inside, however, concentrations can build to dangerous levels, especially in homes that are closed up and very well insulated. Radon can enter your home through pipes, drains, sumps, and cracks in the foundation.

Exposure to radiation in radon is linked to between 7,000 and 30,000 deaths a year, according to the Environmental Protection Agency. An estimated one out of every 15 homes in the United States—including city apartments below the third floor—has radon levels the Environmental Protection Agency considers unsafe.

**Safety precautions to reduce the risk of radon contamination** To determine radon levels, the EPA advises testing in the lowest living area of your home. (Avoid testing in kitchens and bathrooms, which may have good ventilating systems, and concentrate on other living areas.) Most hardware and building-supply stores sell home-testing kits. Short-term tests take air samples for 2 to 90 days. (For greater accuracy the EPA recommends averaging the results of two readings.) Long-term tests monitor air for longer periods. The air samples are then sent to a lab to be analyzed. For quicker results, hire a private contractor to do the testing. (Look in the Yellow Pages under "Radon.")

**What to do if radon levels in your home are high**
- **Cover and seal basement drains, pipes, and sumps, and plug cracks in the foundation with sealing compound.**
- **Immediately retest,** since some entry points may have been missed, and continued high levels point to a need to search further for additional sites that need sealing.
- **Vent radon outside if necessary.** A contractor can install a venting pipe that will draw radon from beneath the house and disperse it into the outside air.
- **Retest for radon every few years,** since entry points may open up again or new ones form.

# Treated and pressurized wood

It's not advisable to use wood treated with chemical preservatives or pesticides in areas where it is likely to come into frequent contact with skin. Children's skin is more permeable than adults', so they are at greater risk for absorbing more of the toxic chemicals. Instead of treated pine or other non-weather-resistant wood, use a type of wood that is naturally weather resistant outdoors, such as redwood, cedar, and cypress. Be especially careful not to choose treated wood in your child's backyard play equipment.

*See **page 815** for more on outdoor play equipment safety.*

Some treated wood can be painted over, which enables you to seal the chemicals in. Often, treated wood cannot take paint, however, so it's best to check with a building supplier who knows before you try it. If children will be coming into contact with flooring made of treated wood, use outdoor carpeting to cover it, seal it with polyurethane, or replace it with wood that isn't chemically treated. Dispose of any scraps or sawdust from treated lumber promptly, but do not burn it, especially in a wood-stove or fireplace. Burning will release toxic substances into the air.

## Water supply

The statistics are frightening. The U.S Environmental Protection Agency estimates that roughly 30 million Americans—about one in eight—are exposed to potentially harmful microbes, pesticides, lead, or radioactive radon whenever they drink a glass of tap water or take a shower in their own homes. The three leading contaminants of tap water in this country are microbes, agricultural chemicals, and lead, with high levels of bacteria and fecal residue being the most common violations of safe-water standards. What can you do to ensure the water you drink and bathe in is safe?

**PARENTS RESOURCES**

For laboratories that test lead in water, contact the **Environmental Protection Agency's Safe Drinking Water Hotline** at (800) 426-4791 or the **Water Quality Association** at www.wqa.org.

**Safety precautions to reduce the risk of tap water contamination**

• **Find out where your water comes from.** A quick call to the customer-service number listed on your water bill should give you the answer. Or ask your landlord for the name of your water supplier if you live in an apartment or rental house. Where your water comes from will tell you a great deal about what might go wrong and the contaminants it contains. Surface sources of water—lakes, rivers, and reservoirs—put you at greater risk for microbial contaminants, such as *E. coli*, *Giardia lamblia*, and *cryptosporidium*, all of which can cause severe gastrointestinal distress, including nausea, cramps, and diarrhea with the accompanying risks of dehydration. Ask your water supplier if there have been any recent problems with microbial contamination and how efficient the filtration system is. (Water from deep wells is less likely to contain microbes, but have it tested to be sure.) Once you know what the risks are, you can take measures to reduce those risks by installing the appropriate filters, switching to bottled drinking water, and changing the way you cook to keep your family safe.

• **If you have a well, test it once a year for contaminants.** A simple and inexpensive coliform test will alert you to the presence of harmful bacteria in your water supply. You should also test for nitrates and radon.

• **Keep bottled water on hand.** Especially if you live in an agricultural area, drink bottled water during peak run-off months. It is far less likely to contain contaminants. The high-risk periods for nitrates in your water are spring and summer.

• **Buy a water-filtration unit.** Simple carafe types filter out chlorine, and some also filter out lead. More expensive under-the-sink or counter types are also good for eliminating or reducing microbes and pesticides.

• **Boil water for newborns** and any people with depressed immune systems. Bring cold tap water to a rolling boil, then immediately remove from heat, and allow to cool. Do not boil for a longer period of time, since doing so may concentrate lead levels. Boil even bottled water unless it is certified as pure, since about a quarter of bottled water sold is simply municipal water that has been filtered — in other words, tap water. Even waters labeled "purified" are not sterile enough for newborns.

## Tobacco smoke

Don't smoke or allow others to smoke in your child's presence. Passive, or second-hand, smoke contributes to millions of illnesses in children each year, according to a study conducted at the University of Massachusetts Medical Center, in Worcester. According to the researchers, the harm caused to kids by passive smoking includes an increase in respiratory disorders and ear infections.

## Other contaminants

Indoors, levels of pollen and fungi are generally lower than outdoor levels, but these substances can blow indoors when windows are left open on high-pollen days. In addition, molds and funguses can

"IT HAPPENED TO US"

## Contaminated Water

Our 1-year-old daughter came down with a bad case of diarrhea. I took her to the doctor for an exam, and found that she was suffering from a severe gastrointestinal infection caused by *E. coli* bacteria. The doctor thought that her infection was probably caused by contaminated tap water. I was shocked. I had read in the newspaper that *E. coli* had been found in the water, but I'd also read that the problem had been cleared up. He advised me not to let my family drink the tap water yet. My daughter recovered quickly, but the incident really shook me up. After that we installed our own under-the-sink water filtration system. We now use only filtered water for drinking and cooking.

grow indoors in damp areas and where water is allowed to stand. To reduce exposure to airborne biological contaminants take the following steps in your own home:

• **Install and use fans vented to outdoors.**

• **Clean cool-mist and ultrasonic humidifiers** in accordance with manufacturer's instructions and refill with clean water daily.

• **Empty water trays in air conditioners, dehumidifiers, and refrigerators frequently.**

• **Mop up water in leaky basements and cellars** as quickly as possible and keep damp areas dry.

• **Clean up immediately any mold or fungus that develops.**

**Ventilation** Be sure to provide adequate ventilation to the outside for steam and moist air from laundry and kitchen units and in bathrooms, installing exhaust fans if necessary. When the weather permits, open the windows regularly to replace household air, making sure that the open windows are child-safe.

# Remodeling safety

Remodeling a home can be a trying situation at best. Construction always seems to take longer than expected and can be more disruptive than you've ever imagined. In addition to inconvenience, however, remodeling can present hazards. Ideally, remodeling is best done while you and your family are temporarily living elsewhere or on vacation. Since it isn't always practical or possible to vacate your home during remodeling, however, the following precautions are advisable:

• **Hire qualified professionals** to do the work and make sure it will follow current building codes for safety and sound structure.

• **Keep the part of the home under construction off-limits to youngsters.** Temporary dividers or walls can be installed to make the area inaccessible. A worksite is not a safe place for little ones, since tools may be left around, electrical wires exposed, nails within easy reach, etc. It's impossible to childproof the area effectively.

• **Vacate if any hazardous substances such as lead-based paint or asbestos are going to be exposed and disturbed or removed,** until it's safe to return. Always have such materials dealt with by practiced professionals who are familiar with environmentally sound removal methods. Also ask in advance when toxic substances such as paint strippers or floor varnishes are going to be used and determine what types of products are being used. Check manufacturer's instructions on application and ventilation requirements. Some fumes are more dangerous and take longer to dissipate than others. You and your family will be safer and more comfortable if you are not home when certain materials are applied.

• **Have your contractor take measures to minimize dust.** Cloths can be hung to curtail the spread of plaster or sawdust, and sanders can be equipped with dust bags that catch some of the debris. Nonetheless, it's practically impossible to prevent some dust from entering living areas. Try to keep a few rooms in the house clean by closing doors and wiping off feet before entering the room and frequent vacuuming.

• **When the job is finished, inspect the area for potential hazards,** looking for any debris, empty or half-empty containers, sharp nails, and other harmful objects that may have been left behind, and childproof the area as you would other rooms in your house.

# Outdoor areas

The great outdoors—even a small backyard—seems like a vast expanse to a child eager to explore every fence, tree, rock, flower, mound of dirt, and blade of grass—or sprig of poison ivy. While you can't childproof the whole world, you can attend to potential hazards in your own yard, and you can take precautionary measures to keep your child constrained within home-turf boundaries, at least while they're young. You might try fencing in a small area stocked with toys and free of hazards including poisonous plants. Fenced in areas, however, are not substitutes for supervision. A toddler should not be left to play on her own outdoors.

You and your family share the outdoors with many creatures, great and small. In some areas, wild animals may be a hazard. Be wary of those that are acting odd or appear to be ill. For example, raccoons that approach during the day or that appear to be disoriented may be affected with rabies. Do not try to control or catch such animals yourself. Instead, call the appropriate authorities in your area. Even relatively innocuous animals may bite or scratch if cornered, so teach your child to respect them and keep a safe distance.

Insects are another matter. Teach your child that certain insects like wasps or bees may harm them and that they should not be disturbed. As much as possible, avoid bites by mosquitoes, ticks, and other insects by wearing protective clothing.

Following are potentially hazardous areas around your home and tips on how to make them safer.

## Barbecue areas

Cooking outdoors can be lots of fun and barbecued food seems to taste extra special. Whenever there's cooking going on, though, there are potential hazards of fire and burns and inhalation from fumes. Young children should be kept a safe distance away from grilling areas at all times—there are too many dangerous items around, from the toxic and flammable fuels used to start charcoal fires to the long and sharp utensils used to turn food. Remember, too, that grills retain heat for a long time and coals may be red-hot inside, even though their outer surfaces appear ashen and cool.

**Safety precautions when using outdoor cooking equipment**
When you prepare and cook food outdoors, there are as many precautions to observe as indoors, and, in some respects, even more.
• **Choose equipment wisely.** Look for models that are sturdy and well made. It's easier if they are readily transportable so they can be brought out when needed and safely stored away when not in use.
• **Use grills only in well-ventilated, open spaces.** Never use charcoal grills inside the home, directly outside an open window, or

in a garage, even if the door is open, because of the risk of carbon monoxide poisoning. Don't allow children to be downwind of barbecue smoke for long periods of time. An occasional whiff from a distance won't hurt, but prolonged exposure is ill advised. Never place a grill near any combustible materials, such as shrubbery or trees or along the side of the house.

• **Use fuels safely**. Flammable fuels present dangers, both because of their combustible nature and because they are toxic if ingested. Always use them according to suggested guidelines, applying the fire starter before the fire is lit, not afterward to boost the flame, for example. Immediately put away after use. Store containers out of children's reach. Never store gas grills fueled with propane in a place accessible to children. As an added precaution, use a safety lock to prevent the lever on the propane tank from being accidentally switched to the open position.

• **Watch for heat.** Because they are generally not insulated, outdoor grills tend to get hot all over, and they retain heat for a long time. Coals, too, remain hot for many hours. Let all grills cool thoroughly after using them. Douse charcoal with water to make sure coals are "dead."

• **Exercise caution with barbecue tools.** You might be more likely to leave knives or other sharp implements lying around outside, for example, or be more easily distracted in a less-confined outdoor area. Remember that implements such as long-handled forks and prongs are not only sharp, but they also get hot enough to inflict burns. When not in use, store barbecuing tools out of children's reach.

• **Supervise.** Never allow young children to remain unattended in the barbecue area, from the time the grill is ignited until the equipment is thoroughly cool and sharp implements are safely out of reach. It's best to have one adult tend the barbecue and another keep an eye on the kids a safe distance away.

## Balconies and decks

Balconies can be enticing to children, who enjoy peering down from them to spy on the world below. Exterior balconies and decks can provide a place to get a little fresh air, well within the confines and comfort of your own home. Accidents can happen, however, if children tumble over the top or get stuck or fall through the slats.

To make balconies and decks safe, follow these guidelines:

- **Banister posts should be sturdy, secure, and no more than 3½ inches apart.**
- **Posts should be vertical,** since horizontal rails can be used as climbing steps.
- **If vertical slats are built onto a horizontal bar above floor-level, check the distance between the bottom bar and the floor**—children should not be able to squeeze underneath the railing.
- **Railing should be high enough to prevent children from easily tumbling over.** The railing should also be at least 36 inches high. Even a low deck a step or two above the ground can be hazardous, since it's all too easy to step backwards or slide a chair back and fall off the side. Higher decks and balconies of course involve potentially greater risks.
- **Check railings and posts for protruding nails or splintering wood.**
- **Use banister guards or balcony/deck netting** for added protection to prevent children from falling over or through the slats or putting their heads or limbs between them, especially if the distance between slats is greater than the recommended distance.
- **Never place furniture near the balcony rail** or allow children to play or climb up on the banister or railing.
- **Be sure deck furniture is stable or keep children off of it.** Youngsters can easily get caught between the interwoven plastic straps of some outdoor furniture. See also about lawn furniture below.
- **Choose nonbreakable drinking and eating utensils.** It's safer to use plastic than glassware outdoors.
- **Be aware of sliding-glass-door hazards.**
- **Teach children never to toss anything over the railing.**
- **Supervise children whenever they're playing on a balcony or deck.**

*See **page 773** for information on sliding-glass doors.*

## Hot tubs

Hot tubs, like whirlpool baths, are not safe for children under age 5 to use, since strong water suction and water jets can overpower a small child and cause him to loose his balance and slip beneath the surface. Older children may use hot tubs safely if the following guidelines are followed and if they are closely supervised.

- **Make sure that the water temperature is no greater than**

104°F. High temperatures can scald a child's sensitive skin or damage internal organs.

- **Limit soaking time to 15 minutes.** If your child becomes drowsy or flushed, get her out of the water sooner.
- **Enclose an outdoor hot tub with a fence** that is at least four feet high and has a self-closing, self-latching gate that a young child cannot open.
- **Cover the tub with a locking cover made of rigid plastic or wood** when it is not in use. Completely remove the cover whenever you use the tub, so a child cannot get trapped underneath it. Drain any water from the cover's surface so a child cannot drown in it.
- **Never use a hot tub with a missing or broken grate.** A drain without a grate can exert a pull strong enough to hold an adult under water. In addition, teach your child never to put her head beneath the water's surface. Hair can get sucked into the intakes and trap her under water.

### PARENTS ALERT

## *Choking Hazards*

Be aware that barbecue fare can present choking hazards to young children. Hot dogs are one of the major offenders for youngsters under age 5.

# Driveways and garages

Driveways and garages are hazardous places for children to play for several reasons. One, of course, is that cars enter and exit and drivers may have difficulty seeing a child in the vehicle's path, especially when backing up. A driveway, however, is sometimes one of the few smooth surfaces for children to use for wheeled toys, skates, etc., so it is often a place they like to play.

Garages are often repositories for a host of hazardous equipment and toxic substances and are best placed off-limits to young children unless the children are closely supervised by adults.

**Driveways**   Each year about 100 children ages 1 to 4 are killed when they are hit by an automobile. A great number of these accidents happen when the child is struck by a car being backed out of a driveway by a friend or relative. The risk of injury increases when driveways are shared and when a play area is not fenced off from a driveway. Most accidents occur when a child follows a driver outside; when a driver is aware that a child is nearby but fails to check for him; or when a child suddenly darts into the path of a car that is backing up.

## *Automatic Garage Door Openers*

Automatic garage-door openers can be deadly. Particularly dangerous are those devices installed before 1993, prior to federal standards requiring that doors reverse automatically when they come into contact with an object.

If you have an automatic garage door opener, make sure it has a reverse safety feature and that it is in good working order. Have the door installed by a professional. Mount controls high on the garage wall beyond the reach of children and keep the remote control out of your child's hands. Also take these precautions:

• **Remove any door handle or hook** that could catch on a child's clothing.

• **Teach your child to wait until the door has stopped moving** before entering or exiting the garage.

• **Never open or close the door if you can't see it clearly.**

• **Check the reverse feature once a month.** If the door doesn't reverse, disconnect the automatic opener and open and close the door manually until the automatic device is repaired or replaced.

A toddler or preschooler is simply too young to understand that a driveway can be a dangerous place and does not know enough to watch out for himself. Therefore, the following precautions are advisable:

• **Have an adult watch your child** to keep him from following you to the car.

• **Walk around the car** to make sure a child is not behind or underneath it. Nearby toys could be a tip-off.

• **Check your rearview and sideview mirrors** frequently for children.

• **Refocus, and recheck the area around you**—after you've put the keys in the ignition and fastened your seat belt.

• **Be extra alert when driving a van or pickup truck,** since it's more difficult to see child from these vehicles.

• **Honk and/or call out** to any child you suspect may be in the immediate area.

**Garages, workshops, and outdoor storage sheds** Think about what's in your garage, workshop, or storage shed for a moment and it quickly becomes clear that it's a potentially hazardous environment for children. These spaces house not only a car, but often sharp tools and implements, toxic and flammable substances from insecticides and fertilizers to pest poisons and gasoline, perhaps empty bottles and cans, plus countless items that could fall over onto a child and cause injury. Even the garage door can be dangerous. (See opposite.) The garage generally is not a safe place for an unsupervised young child to be, and it's best to keep it off-limits to her. That doesn't preclude taking the following precautionary measures to prevent accidents, however.

• **Use cabinet and drawer latches and electrical outlet covers** as you would in other parts of the house, and keep hazardous implements and substances safely locked away.

• **Don't leave lengths of rope lying around** or hanging down from hooks.

• **Store ladders in a horizontal position,** so a child cannot climb up them.

• **Disconnect power tools when not in use.** Plug locks are available that attach to cords and prevent their insertion into electrical outlets.

• **Properly dispose of any incendiary materials** such as piles of old newspapers and magazines, old clothing, and soiled, oily rags. Do not store gasoline or other flammable liquids near gas and hot-water heaters.

• **Never store a discarded appliance in a garage without first removing the door.**

• **Lock the car doors.** Little fingers are easily crushed by a car door and there are plenty of potential hazards inside the car should a young child enter it unsupervised.

• **Use special precautions with garage doors.** Garage doors are heavy and can cause serious injuries. Both automatic and manual doors can crush fingers and cause severe head injuries, even death. The safest kind of manually operated garage door has a counterbalance system rather than a long coil spring. Make sure automatic garage doors have a device that automatically stops the door or reverses it when it comes into contact with an object.

## Yards and gardens

Making sure your yard, lawn, and surrounding areas are safe for children is also important. Nature, although wonderful, is not always friendly, even cultivated nature. That's where supervision and education come into play. For example, you and your family may enjoy plants and flowers, inside the house and out, or harvesting crops from a garden, but it's important for children to learn that not all plants are edible—some are extremely poisonous. Teach your young child never to eat anything without asking you first and keep a close watch to make sure that he doesn't put things into his mouth that do not belong there. Always lock away small bulbs (which may be toxic) and plant seeds, since, even if they aren't poison, they pose a choking hazard for small children. Some flowers and vegetables can be hazardous

**PARENTS ALERT**

### *Tool Safety*

Never allow a child age 9 or under to use anything with a sharp edge. Power tools are particularly hazardous. Put tools and implements away as soon as you are finished using them. Never place garden tools on the lawn or soil with tines pointing upward, and never lean them against a wall with tines or blades pointed outward.

**PARENTS ALERT**

### *Poisonous Mushrooms*

Some wild mushrooms can cause serious illness— and even death if eaten. Teach your child to stay away from any mushrooms she sees outdoors. If she does eat a wild mushroom, call your poison control center immediately.

if ingested or even if their sap merely comes in contact with skin. Your first line of defense is to teach children that some plants are not good for them—they can cause tummy aches, skin irritations, or worse.

**Poisonous plants**   There are literally hundreds of poisonous plants, and many of them are very common. Learn to identify poisonous plants and eliminate them from your gardens and yard. Your state cooperative extension agency will help you identify plants if you provide them with samples.

If your child has ingested a poisonous plant or has a severe reaction to contact with one, contact your local poison control center.

*For a list of common hazardous plants, see **page 818**.*

**Lawn equipment hazards**   Exercise extreme caution while operating any motor-driven lawn equipment. Lawn mower accidents kill 15 kids annually. Another 8,000 under age 14 are treated every year for mower-related accidents. Children have been run over by ride-on mowers or have fallen from them. Others have suffered cuts or amputations when they have slipped under push-type or rider mowers or stuck their hands or feet into the moving blades. Small children should not be allowed to play with or around gas- or electric-driven lawn maintenance equipment.

**Pesticides**   Each year, approximately 80,000 children are exposed to or poisoned by a pesticide product that has been stored improperly, according to the Environmental Protection Agency. A nationwide EPA study revealed that almost half of surveyed households with children under age 5 had at least one pesticide stored within their reach. Pesticides applied to plants and flowers usually dissipate within a few hours or days; the real danger lies in exposure to the concentrated products if the child ingests or inhales a pesticide.

**Lawn furniture**   Make sure outdoor furniture is free of splinters, protruding nails or screws, peeling paint, and sharp edges or corners. Also be wary of folding chairs or stools that might pinch and injure little fingers (or heads) and furniture that is unstable and easily tipped over. Chairs with interwoven straps may pose hazards too, since a child's head could become entrapped in the weave.

Also take care not to place furniture near railings on an outdoor deck. Children can climb onto the furniture and topple over the railings.

**Other yard safety points** Make your yard as safe as you can by following these precautions:

- **Keep hazardous substances out of your child's reach.** This includes fertilizer and leftover paint, as well as items like garden tools and automotive supplies.
- **Don't leave garden hoses lying around,** especially in the sun, which can heat water trapped within them to a dangerously high temperature.
- **String clotheslines out of your child's reach.**
- **Install ground fault circuit interrupters** in outdoor electrical sockets to prevent shock.
- **Choose a safe fencing material** if you fence in your yard, or fence off a smaller play area. Wood should be smooth and devoid of splinters and untreated. A chain-link fence should be free of any barbs. Make sure gate latches are childproof and stand three or more feet from the ground.
- **Fence off trash cans and other hazards** so your child can't go exploring inside them.

## Outdoor play equipment

Keep safety in mind when your child uses outdoor play equipment, at home, at playgrounds, and on the road.

- **Choose sturdy, age-appropriate equipment.** Do not install outdoor gyms that your toddler will "grow into," since these are likely to include equipment that is not suitable for a child his age.
- **Position equipment correctly.** Be sure to place equipment such as swings far enough away from walls, fences, and trees, so that children will not bump into them while they are using the equipment.

**PARENTS ALERT**

### *Keep Sandboxes Safe*

Even the sandbox can pose hazards if you don't take precautions. Pets or rodents may leave disease-carrying droppings; spilled food and drink can attract insects; and rocks, small toys, or glass can cut or choke a child. To safeguard your sandbox, follow these tips:

- **Buy a fresh supply of natural sand each year.** This light tan, sterilized sand is sold at hardware and gardening stores. Don't buy white, powdery, artificial sand made of crushed rock; it may contain asbestos.

- **Keep the sandbox in a sunny, rather than shady area.** Ultraviolet rays kill microorganisms.

- **Place the sandbox at least 10 feet from your home if the house was built before 1970, or if you suspect it may have been painted with lead paint.**

- **Use a sifter to check sand weekly for unwanted contents, especially if the sandbox is left uncovered.**

## Lawn- and Garden-Care Product Cautions

What's good for the garden may be lethal to your child. A child who touches, drinks, or inhales pesticides or other lawn-care products is at high risk for poisoning. To reduce this risk:

• **Minimize your use of these substances.** Minimal spot treatments with a less toxic product rather than subjecting a large area to toxic treatments may suffice.

• **Buy only EPA-registered products.** Check the label for an EPA registration number.

• **Make sure any service you hire is licensed** by your state and belongs to a standards-setting group.

• **Keep children and pets inside** when you apply a pesticide. Close windows if you spray. Don't let kids or pets on or near a treated area until the product has dried—check the label.

• **Remove children's and pets' toys** from the yard before pesticide is applied. Cover items like a sandbox with a leak-proof disposable plastic tarp.

• **Never leave an open container of fertilizer or pesticide lying around.**

• **Never transfer lawn-care products to another container.**

• **Store lawn and garden products in a locked cupboard or shed.**

• **Follow label instructions** when disposing of expired products and empty containers.

• **Be aware if neighbors plan to use these products.** If so, find out how long your child should stay away from the area.

Also be careful that equipment does not interfere with high-traffic areas. For instance, don't place a slide to exit onto a bicycle-riding area or place the swings too near the sandbox, where the extended legs of the swinger could hit another child.

• **Follow proper maintenance and use procedures.** When installing play equipment yourself, follow instructions carefully. Conduct regular safety checks of all equipment, looking for jagged edges, protruding bolts, splintering wood, cracks, and other damage. Baby swings should have securely latching safety belts with a crotch strap.

• **Ensure a soft landing.** Many outdoor injuries are caused by falls. Make sure there is a soft surface—about 12 inches of loose sand, loose mulch, or special foamlike tiles or rubber mats—around all equipment.

• **Teach children how to use equipment correctly.** Stress the importance of using equipment safely—not twisting swings, for instance—and not walking in front or in back of a swing in motion.

### What to know when choosing home play gym equipment

• **Wood structures:** Wood that's treated and/or pressurized should be avoided, unless the chemicals within the wood can be sealed in with a few coats of nontoxic paint. Keep in mind that sealing with lacquer paint will make the equipment more slippery.

• **Metal structures:** Metal gets hot in the sun, so check it before each use. Rustproofing is a good idea since this will maintain the integrity of the metal unit longer. Be sure to use a nontoxic material when rustproofing. Avoid metal swing seats, which are far more likely to cause injuries than soft, rubberized materials. Encase metal chains on swings with plastic to avoid pinching fingers.

• **Plastic structures:** Plastic is a good choice, provided that the self-contained units are properly anchored.

# Away from home

Families with young children usually childproof their homes, but you can't assume that every home is safe for your child. Keeping your child safe is always your responsibility, so you need to supervise your child closely. Survey the scene for obvious hazards such as a busy road, swimming pool, deck with rails, ill-kept swingset, discarded boards with sharp nails, and other dangers and make sure your child stays clear of them.

You may want to do some quick, temporary childproofing if the situation allows for it. It's easy, for instance, to secure dangling cords, turn pot handles to the rear, and open windows from the top instead of the bottom when you're away from home. The amount of childproofing you do will usually depend on how long you are going to be staying and how well you'll be able to keep an eye on your child.

Always check the furniture, including the crib, in a room where your child sleeps. Map out fire-escape routes in advance and explain them to your children if they are old enough.

When staying with close friends or relatives, you may want to request some advance safeguarding tactics like having them lock toxic substances in a cabinet, closet, or cupboard with a safety latch, installing a safety gate at the top and bottom of stairs, putting in window guards or locks, installing smoke detectors if they are not already in place, and posting emergency numbers for the fire department, police,

## Traveling Tips

Whenever my family (which includes an 18-month- and a 3-year-old) are staying overnight away from home, I bring along a few easy-to-carry supplies for quick childproofing. I take a couple of bungee cords to secure cabinets and drawers, ten or more electrical outlet covers, a bottle of ipecac syrup, a couple of doorknob covers to keep the kids out of off-limit rooms, and some good old multipurpose duct tape for taping cords and dangling objects out of the way or even covering up more electrical outlets if need be. I also carry a strap to use on shopping carts or booster seats and high chairs in restaurants. In addition I carry a couple of small night-lights and an intercom so I can listen to what's happening in the room the children are sleeping. It helps me sleep better, too, knowing I'm in touch with what's going on.

and poison control center by the telephone. Be sure to take safe equipment such as high chairs, a portable crib, and car seats with you and leave them there if people are going to be caring for your child while you are not there. Always travel with your own first-aid kit.

Always follow your routine safety procedures even if you are in other people's homes or cars. Never allow yourself to forget the seatbelts or infant car seat "just this once"—it's not worth the risk.

*Look out for these and other poisonous plants in your own and others' homes.*

## Common Hazardous Plants

Here are some of the common plants that may pose risks for your child. Your local poison control center can provide a complete list.

| PLANT | POISONOUS | SYMPTOMS OF INGESTION |
|---|---|---|
| Amaryllis | Bulb and sap | Nausea, vomiting, and diarrhea |
| Autumn crocus | Seeds and tubers | Abdominal pain and fever; ingestion can be fatal |
| Daffodil | Bulb | Digestive upset |
| Dumb cane (dieffenbachia) | Sap | Can cause swelling of tongue, excess salivation, vomiting; painful to skin, lips, mouth |
| Hyacinth | Bulb | Stomach cramps, vomiting, diarrhea |
| Iris | Entire plant | Nausea, vomiting, diarrhea |
| Lily of the valley | Entire plant | Heart irregularities |
| Morning glory | Seeds | Hallucinations |
| Mushrooms | All of certain varieties | Diarrhea, vomiting, hallucinations, seizures, liver failure |
| Potatoes | Sprouts and vines | Nausea, vomiting |
| Rhubarb | Sap | Skin irritation |
| Tomatoes | Leaves and vines | Nausea, vomiting, diarrhea |
| Tulip | Sap | Skin irritation |
| Yew berry | Seeds | Extremely deadly; seek medical attention immediately if ingested |

# Outdoor Water Safety

W hether on vacation or enjoying your own backyard pool, keep a constant eye on your child while near water.

## General water safety guidelines

To guard your child against water-related accidents, the National SAFE KIDS Campaign recommends you do the following:

- **Supervise your child closely at all times** when she's near a swimming pool, a lake, a river, at the beach, and even in a wading pool. Never leave her alone for a second—even to answer the phone. Kids can drown in a matter of seconds or minutes in just a few inches of water. Never let your child swim alone.
- **Empty or cover kiddie pools when not in use.** Fence in an in-ground pool, and make above-ground pools inaccessible to children without adult supervision.
- **Have your child wear an approved personal flotation device (PFD)** when she is near water or in a boat, even if she knows how to swim.
- **Never rely on inflatable toys as safety devices.**
- **Have your child wear a brightly colored suit** so you can spot him more easily when he is swimming in a pool or lake or is at the beach.
- **Keep a flotation ring and a long-handled pole on boat docks.** If your child falls into the water, throw the ring to her and extend the pole so she can grab onto it.
- **Caution kids not to jump from docks or boats.** There could be big rocks under the dock or boat, and even though an outboard motor has been turned off, the blades may still be in motion.

**Special precautions for keeping infants safe in and near the water**  For children up to age 1, observe the following precautions when playing in and around water:
- **Don't take a baby into a pool or other body of water before she has good head control;** she should be able to lift her head consistently to a 90-degree angle to prevent the possibility of her head accidentally bobbing under water. This ability generally comes at around 4 or 5 months of age.
- **Never submerge your baby's face in water.**
- **Water temperature for infants under 6 months** should be comfortably warm—between 84 and 87°F. Air temperature should be at least 3° warmer.
- **Don't keep your baby in the water for longer than half an hour,** or she may become dangerously chilled.
- **Hold onto your baby at all times** when playing in the water.
- **Observe your baby's reactions carefully** and discontinue water activity if she becomes unhappy.
- **Never leave your infant unsupervised in a flotation device, or in or near water**—including a wading pool.
- **Never leave the supervision of a baby to an older child.**
- **Never leave your infant in a stroller near a pool.**

**Special precautions for toddlers and preschoolers**  Toddlers and preschoolers are more apt than babies to be harmed in and around outdoor sources of water because they can get near it themselves and because they often think they are more capable than they are. Parents, too, often let down their guard, especially if their child has had any form of swimming lessons. To keep your mobile child safe:
- Teach your child to swim when he's ready.
- Be aware a child can be floating and still drown. Many recreational flotation devices will buoy a child's arms or body, but will actually push his face into the water. Water wings, bathing suits with flotation devices in them, air mattresses, and even life preservers are no substitute for proper supervision.
- Teach children that different bodies of water may require different cautions. Water in lakes may become suddenly deeper. Waves at the ocean shore may have dangerous undertow. Keep young children by your side in natural water sources. Be sure he understands the depth levels of pools, and stays where he can touch the bottom if he's not swimming.

• Make sure your child knows never to dive in water less than nine feet deep. Diving in shallow water can cause head and spinal cord injuries and even death when the diver strikes the bottom.

## Swimming lessons

While a dip in a warm pool with parents is a fun activity for a baby or toddler, the American Academy of Pediatrics recommends that serious swimming lessons not begin until a child is about age 5. Water-play activities can begin sooner, as long as parents make sure that their kids don't overdo it by letting a child swallow pool water or stay in the pool when she is chilled, or by prodding a particularly frightened child into the water.

To make sure that babies and toddlers feel good about their "lessons," look for programs that emphasize comfort, fun, and safety and that require that parents be in the water with their babies and toddlers at all times. This is to help the babies feel secure and to prevent them from going under and ingesting pool water. The water should be about 90°F, and the classes should be no more than 30 minutes for under-3-year-olds and 45 minutes for kids ages 3 to 6.

Children who are reluctant to take the plunge should never be forced. Parents should allow them to sit on the side of the pool just dangling their feet in the water. For your reluctant swimmer, look for a program in a pool that either has a very shallow low end or that provides a "water table," on which kids can stand during their lessons. To help keep kids from developing painful "swimmers' ear," which can cause them to equate discomfort with swimming, dry kids' ears thoroughly as soon as they leave the water. If a child begins to tremble or if her lips turn blue, remove the child from the pool immediately, even if the lesson has more time to go.

## Pool and pool-area safety

Approximately 300 children under age 5 drown each year in home pools, spas, and hot tubs, and nearly 2,000 more are injured in pool-related accidents. Because young children can drown in small amounts of water, even baby wading pools pose risks. Children under age 5 should be constantly supervised around all water sources. Empty all water out of your wading pool when it's no longer in use and either turn it upside down or deflate it.

## "IT HAPPENED TO US"

### *Bike Riding Near a Pool*

I know most pool accidents happen during warm weather, but my 4-year-old son almost drowned at the end of December. I had been outside with him, watching while he rode his new bicycle on the pool deck, but I took him inside with me so I could rest. I left him watching a video in the family room, which looks out onto the pool area, but I made a critical mistake: I didn't deadbolt the door leading out to the pool before I went into the bedroom to take my nap. Twenty minutes later I got up and walked into the family room. My son was not there. Looking toward the pool I saw his bicycle, hung by a pedal upside down in the water. I rushed out and saw him clearly face-down at the bottom of the pool. I jumped in and pulled his limp body onto the deck. Fortunately, my previous lifeguard experience had taught me how to give mouth-to-mouth resuscitation. He came around and started to cry softly. I brought him inside and laid him on the sofa, then I dialed 911. The ambulance came and the medics rushed him to the hospital. His temperature had dropped to 88° and doctors were worried that he had aspirated vomit into his lungs. The prognosis was not clear. It wasn't until the next afternoon that doctors told us my son was going to be OK.

For built-in and aboveground pools:

- **Prohibit running and jumping** in a pool area or along a dock.
- **Install nonslip material** around the pool perimeter.
- **Put up a fence or gate** around the pool area to ensure that your child (or other children) can't get access without an adult. The fence should be at least five feet high (or meet building code standards in your area). Slats should be no more than 3½ inches apart. The fence should have a self-closing, self-latching gate, and the lock should be high enough that a child can't reach it. Do not leave lawn furniture or other objects onto which children could climb near the fence.
- **Never leave children alone** near a built-in pool, regardless of whether there is water in it.
- **Keep all electric appliances out of the pool area.** If you have electric outlets in the outdoor pool area, hire an electrician to put in ground-fault circuit interrupters.
- **Never bring breakable glass or plates into the pool area.**
- **Keep the pool area well lit at night.**
- **Keep all pool-cleaning substances and electric pool appliances locked away.**
- **Make sure the pool drain is securely covered by a grate and check it regularly.**
- **Instruct children never to play or sit on the grate and to keep their fingers and feet away from it.**
- **Keep the pool water clean, bacteria-free, and at the recommended pH level.**
- **Keep rescue equipment (a long pole, at least one life preserver, and a long rope with life ring) by the pool.**
- **Mark where the water gets deep with a rope with buoys.**
- **Use a safety pool cover that can support at least 30**

**pounds of weight per square foot.** Secure the cover over the pool during the months it's not in use, and make sure there are no spaces through which a child could slip. Be sure no large pockets of water collect on top of the pool cover—children have drowned on top of pool covers in these puddles.

- **Invest in a motion-sensing device** that will sound if anything goes near or falls into the pool.
- **Keep a phone by the pool and post emergency numbers.** You should not have to leave the pool area to answer the phone or to call for help.
- **Get CPR certification and refresh your training each year.** Also make sure that anyone supervising your child near water knows how to swim and how to perform CPR.

## Boating and dock safety

Always make sure children wear suitable life jackets or life preservers (called PFDs—personal flotation devices) whenever they are on board a boat. There are several types of life jackets available; the safest models are designed to keep an unconscious person in a vertical position or leaning toward his back in the water for a long period of time. Choose one that is approved by the U.S. Coast Guard and make sure it fits properly. Any PFD should keep your child's head and mouth out of the water. Try it out in the water. If it doesn't work, return it and get a different one. Life jackets should be available for every person on a boat. Also have on board at least one life ring on a rope that can be thrown out to a person in the water. Never let children sit on top of seats, on gunwales, or on the bow of the boat.

Don't allow children to run around on docks. For added safety, have your child wear a PFD while he's dockside, even if he's a good swimmer, since a child who falls into the water may panic and forget how to swim. Keep a life ring handy to toss into the water in case someone needs it. Make sure there are no protruding nails or sharp edges splintering wood on the dock to cause injury.

# CHAPTER 2

# Safe Routines

Following safe routines throughout the day, at home and away from home, is just as important as providing a child-safe environment. The more habitual your safe routines become, the easier they will be to follow. Make it a habit to try to foresee as many potential hazards as possible. This doesn't mean that you and your family can't have fun or that you have to live in a constant state of fear. It simply means that you need to take precautionary measures wherever you can—from eating food that's safe to choosing safe sports or play equipment. And, of course, you need to set good examples, for instance, by buckling up for safety whenever you get into any vehicle and by wearing a protective helmet when you're riding a bicycle.

Much of safety consciousness is about developing a habit of awareness and being alert. During a summer outing, for instance, survey the picnic grounds or beach for broken glass, know if the water is safe for swimming and where lifeguards are stationed, investigate the restrooms or locker facilities, and determine a meeting place for your family to gather should anyone become lost. At public places from motel rooms to theaters, be aware of exits and emergency evacuation routes and point them out to your children. Before long they will become automatic, and, by your good example, your children will develop a safety-conscious attitude, too.

## At-home activities

It's easy to learn about safety procedures and initiate safe routines at home, but sometimes mundane activities can become so routine and so numerous that it's easy to overlook safe practices and tempting to take a few short cuts in the name of saving or energy. Remember, though, that accidents happen quickly. They're not planned. Leave a hot iron or an open bottle of cleaning solvent within a toddler's reach for a moment while you run to answer the door and it could spell disaster. Take the time to make sure safeguards are in place at all times. It will pay off in the long run.

# Knowing your home

Perhaps the most important element in safeguarding house and family is knowing the electrical, water, heating, and other systems in your own home. You don't need to become an expert mechanic, plumber, or licensed electrician, but it pays to know a few basic household procedures. Find out, for instance, where the main water supply is and how to shut it off in case of a burst pipe or major water leak. Know where the circuit breakers are and how to shut off the electricity. Have flashlights (in good working order) strategically placed around the house where you can have easy access to them. Review the above periodically to make sure the information is fresh in your mind should you need it. (Older children can learn this, too.)

Knowing your home includes an awareness of the function and location of emergency items. Fire extinguishers, for instance, will be of no use if they don't work or you don't know where they are or how to operate them. A fire exit is useless if it's blocked or locked and you can't find the key or forgot the combination. Emergency numbers should be up to date and posted near every phone.

*See **pages 762–823** for information on childproofing your home.*

# Cooking and food-handling routines

Food safety is an important concern for everyone, but it is particularly crucial for youngsters because they are more vulnerable to chemicals such as pesticides and food-borne organisms that cause illness. Children are at higher risk because their intestinal tracts absorb substances more easily than those of adults, their immune systems aren't as strong, and their developing brains are more susceptible to long-term damage. Cooking and handling food in safe ways, therefore, is essential to your family's well-being.

*For information on childproofing your kitchen, see **pages 777–84**.*

**Handling meat, poultry, and fish** Each year bacteria—primarily *E. coli*, salmonella, and staphylococcus—are responsible for over 30 million food-borne illnesses and up to 500 deaths. Often the contaminated foods turn out to be meat, poultry, fish, and eggs. Fortunately, many food-borne illnesses can be eliminated by thorough cooking. Key guidelines to think about when cooking and handling these products are:

- **Use caution when handling raw or rare meat, poultry, fish, and shellfish.** Using an antibacterial soap, thoroughly wash hands after handling uncooked or undercooked food before you touch anything else—other foods, a pot handle, your apron, etc. Use the same procedure for any containers, utensils, or surfaces that have come into contact with uncooked or undercooked food. Use paper towels when drying hands, surfaces, and utensils, since using a cloth involves the risk of spreading contaminants. Carefully discard wrappings.

• **Never allow children to handle rare or raw meats or fish or wrappings.** Find some other way for him to help out in the kitchen other than making hamburger patties or meatballs. (If you take a child fishing, make sure that she either wears protective gloves or thoroughly washes her hands after handling her catch.)

• **Always thaw meat, fish, and poultry in the refrigerator or microwave,** not on the counter. Once thawed, cook immediately.

• **Cook meat, poultry, and fish thoroughly.** Red meat should be cooked until uniformly brown. Poultry should be cooked until no pink remains and juices run clear. To be especially safe, use temperature as your guide: the USDA recommends that ground beef be cooked to 160°F, poultry to 165°F, and steaks and roasts to 140°F. Well-cooked fish will "flake" or fall apart when you gently cut into it. It's very important that children never eat raw or rare meats or sushi.

• **Roast poultry unstuffed.** It's safer to roast poultry unstuffed, since stuffing inside a bird takes a long time to reach a safe temperature. Cook stuffing separately.

*See the Food Storage Guide on pages 829–30.*

• **Eat or freeze meat, poultry, and fish within two days of buying, and beef, veal, pork, and lamb within three days.**

• **Store all food—cooked or uncooked—at cold temperatures that inhibit the growth of bacteria.**

• **Store meat, fish, and poultry packages on a plate** in the refrigerator to keep juices from dripping onto other foods. If juices come into contact with other foods, wash them thoroughly.

### Raw hot dogs

*"Is it safe for my child to eat raw hot dogs?"*

Raw meat is not safe to consume. However, what people generally refer to as "hot dogs" are generally fully cooked, smoked meat products. (Check the label on the package for the words "fully cooked.") They may be eaten unheated like many cold cuts, or served heated up by boiling, grilling, etc.

Like any perishable meat product, however, hot dogs need to be kept in the refrigerator or freezer. They can be used up to a week after the sell-by date if kept in cold storage. For best quality retention, use frozen hot dogs within two months of freezing. As with all meat products, defrost in the refrigerator or microwave. Never leave hot dogs at room temperature for more than two hours—one hour if the temperature is 90°F or above, to avoid food poisoning.

The real danger from hot dogs is choking, so if you serve them to your child, make sure they are cut both lengthwise and sliced into small pieces.

**Handling eggs** Eggs may be dangerous if not handled, stored, or cooked properly, primarily because of the risk of salmonella poisoning. To minimize your risk of food poisoning follow these guidelines:

- **Use only Grade A eggs that do not have any cracks.** Also, wash your hands after touching cracked raw eggs, and throw eggshells in the garbage.
- **Store eggs in their carton** in the main section of the refrigerator, not in the door where the temperature is not as cold.
- **Wash eggshells before you crack them.** There may be bacteria on the shells as well as in the egg itself.
- **Always cook eggs until they are firm and not at all runny.** Soft-boiled and poached eggs (unless poached until the yolk is hard), however, are not recommended for children.
- **Avoid consuming raw or undercooked eggs in other products.** That includes not licking the spoon, bowl, or beaters if raw eggs are used in cookie dough or cake batter and not eating traditional Caesar salad dressing. (Most commercial Caesar salad dressings do not contain raw eggs and are, therefore, safe.) In making batters, use dehydrated egg mixtures or liquid pasteurized eggs if you want to let the kids lick the bowl or spatula.
- **Wash your hands and all cooking utensils with hot, soapy water before and after contact with raw eggs or foods that contain them.** Also wash hands after handling egg shells. Don't

**PARENTS ALERT**

## E. coli in Cider

Although *E. coli* outbreaks are most often associated with meat products, other foods may be contaminated. One potential hazard is unpasturized apple cider, the kind often sold at roadside stands and farmers' markets. (Apples are exposed to bacteria when they come in contact with contaminated manure.) To avoid possible infection, buy only pasteurized cider.

## Symptoms of Food Poisoning

Symptoms of food poisoning may come on immediately or even days after exposure. Symptoms include vomiting, diarrhea, cramps, and bloody stools. If you suspect food poisoning, consult a health-care professional.

allow children to handle raw egg shells. (They may, however, safely take the egg shell off a hard-boiled egg.)

• **Never leave raw eggs or foods containing eggs at room temperature** for more than two hours. (That includes Easter eggs. If you color eggs or have an egg hunt, do not eat the eggs if they have been at room temperature for over two hours. You can always use them for decorative purposes, then discard them, substituting freshly cooked eggs for consumption.)

**Pesticides in produce** You are right to be concerned. Fruits and vegetables are some of the best foods to feed your family, since they contain so many vitamins and minerals plus fiber. Nonetheless, major studies conducted by the National Academy of Sciences and other groups have shown that a substantial number of foods contain pesticide residues. There is ongoing debate, however, over the risks they pose. There are measures, though, that you can take to reduce your family's risk of pesticide exposure.

• **Wash or peel fruits and vegetables.** Wash with plain water and use a stiff brush to remove surface grit and some of the chemicals that have been sprayed on produce. Any fruit or vegetable that has been waxed should be peeled since washing alone won't remove the contaminants. It is impossible to remove pesticides that are absorbed into produce from the roots, so your best bet is to choose safe produce that you know has been grown without pesticides.

• **Buy locally and in season.** Outdoor stands and farmers' markets are usually supplied by nearby growers. The less distance produce has to travel, the fewer post-harvest chemicals are needed to retard spoilage and aging.

• **Consider buying organically grown products.** Supermarkets and farmers' markets often stock foods grown without pesticides. Be aware, however, that these tend to be more costly. Additionally, organically grown produce may harbor pests and microorganisms that are not present in treated foods.

• **Don't use dangerous pesticides at home.** If you grow some of your own produce, use environmentally friendly ways to control pests. Information is available from many sources, including your state cooperative extension agency.

## Food Storage Guide

The U.S. Department of Agriculture suggests following these general food safety tips on food storage:

• Purchase packaged products before the marked expiration date.

• If product has a "Use-by date," follow that date.

• Follow any additional handling recommendations printed on the product.

• Set your refrigerator so that the main compartment temperature is a constant 40°F. Freezer temperature should be 0°F.

• Once a perishable product is properly frozen, it may be considered safe indefinitely.

• Discard any foods that have developed a bad odor, flavor, or appearance.

### REFRIGERATOR STORAGE (40°F or below)

**Fresh or uncooked perishables**  If perishable, take the food home immediately after purchase and refrigerate it promptly. Freeze it if you can't use it within the time frames recommended on the chart below.

| Product | Storage times after purchase |
| --- | --- |
| Poultry | 1 or 2 days |
| Beef, veal, pork, and lamb | 3 to 4 days |
| Ground meat and ground poultry | 1 or 2 days |
| Fresh variety (organ) meats | 1 or 2 days |
| Cured ham, "cook before eating" | 5 to 7 days |
| Uncooked sausage (pork, beef, or turkey) | 1 or 2 days |
| Eggs | 3 to 5 weeks |

**Storing packaged meats that have been sealed at the plant**  Packaged products, such as cold cuts and vacuum-sealed corned beef, are safely stored in your refrigerator. Follow the "Purchase by" and "Use by" guides printed on the package. If product has no date, cook or freeze the product by the times shown on the following chart. If the package cannot be resealed after opening it, transfer the remainder to a sealable sandwich bag or an air-tight container.

| Processed Product | Unopened | After Opening |
|---|---|---|
| Cooked poultry | 4 to 7 days | 3 to 4 days |
| Cooked sausage | 3 to 7 days | 3 to 4 days |
| Sausage (hard/dry, shelf-stable) | 6 weeks (pantry) | 3 weeks (refrigerator) |
| Corned beef (uncooked, in pouch with pickling juices) | 5 to 7 days | 3 to 4 days |
| Vacuum-packed dinners (commercial brand with USDA seal) | 2 weeks | 3 to 4 days |
| Bacon | 2 weeks | 7 days |
| Hot dogs | 2 weeks (but no more than 1 week after "sell-by" date) | 7 days |
| Lunch meats | 2 weeks (but no more than 1 week after "sell-by" date) | 3 to 5 days |
| Ham, fully cooked | 7 days, sliced; 3 days, whole | 7 days |
| Ham, canned (labeled "keep refrigerated") | 9 months | 3 to 4 days |
| Ham, canned (shelf stable) | 2 years (pantry) | 3 to 5 days (refrigerator) |
| Canned meat and poultry (shelf stable) | 2 to 5 years (pantry) | 3 to 4 days (refrigerator) |

### FREEZER STORAGE (0°F.)*

| Item | Months | Item | Months |
|---|---|---|---|
| Bacon and sausage | 1 to 2 | Meat, cooked | 2 to 3 |
| Casseroles | 1 to 2 | Poultry, uncooked whole | 12 |
| Egg whites or egg substitutes | 12 | Poultry, uncooked parts | 9 |
| Gravy, meat or poultry | 2 to 3 | Poultry, uncooked giblets | 3 to 4 |
| Cooked ham, hot dogs, and lunch meats | 1 to 2 | Poultry, cooked | 3 to 4 |
| Meat, uncooked roasts | 9 | Soups and stews | 2 to 3 |
| Meat, uncooked steaks or chops | 4 to 6 | Wild game, uncooked | 8 to 12 |

*Time guides are for quality and taste only. Frozen foods remain safe indefinitely.

**Canned goods** Canned goods sometimes display noncoded "open" or calendar dates that indicate that the product is of peak quality or best if used by that date. For those canned goods that do not have such a date, the USDA recommends the following guidelines:

• **High-acid canned foods** such as tomatoes, grapefruit, and pineapple, can in general be stored for 12 to 18 months.

• **Low-acid canned foods** such as meat, poultry, fish, and most vegetables will keep 2 to 5 years if the can remains in good condition and has been stored in a relatively cool, dry place.

## Household cleaning

Keeping a tidy home with children around can be a tall order. There is a difference, though, between "messy" and "dirty." Children crawl around the floors, touch every surface they can reach, and put many objects, including their hands, into their mouths, so maintaining a reasonable level of cleanliness makes sense. It's impossible to create a sterile environment in your house, but a sanitary one is desirable and healthful.

### Safe cleaning routines

• **Make germ-breeding areas a top priority.** Keeping food preparation and eating surfaces, diaper-changing, and bathroom areas as clean is particularly important.

• **Pay special attention to floors.** Regular floor mopping and carpet vacuuming to keep floors free of items that might cause harm if stepped on or swallowed is a good idea. Time your floor mopping so that the floor is dry during periods that family members will walk on it, since a wet floor can be extremely slippery.

• **Empty buckets immediately.** Keep kids away from buckets when you are mopping floors or washing the car. Children have drowned in buckets. The chemicals in cleaning buckets are also harmful when they get onto your child's skin or into his eyes. Empty all buckets as soon as you are done with them.

• **Beware of allergens.** Eliminating dust, mold, pet hair and saliva, and other allergens will add to the comfort levels of those prone to allergies.

**PARENTS ALERT**

### Commom Non-Food Choking Hazards

According to theAmerican Red Cross, the top non-food culprits include:

• Deflated balloons and balloon pieces
• Coins, pins, buttons, and other small items
• Small toys and toy parts
• Medications
• Other items include baby powder, beverage can pop tops, cigarettes, and cigarette butts

*For information on treating allergies, including preventive measures, see page 553–59.*

## PARENTS ALERT

### *No Sponges*

Keep sponges out of your baby's reach. The soft texture invites your baby to chew and could present a choking hazard if a piece is bitten off. Also, if a child sucks on soap-laden sponges, she can ingest too much soap. Additionally, sponges that have been in use for a while can harbor a multitude of bacteria.

• **Exercise extreme caution with household cleaning products.** Be aware that cleaning products, especially tough ones designed to cut through all sorts of grime, can be harmful. Use them and store them safely. It's also best, if possible, to use stronger solvents when children are not in the area.

• **Keep kids in view or out of the area when doing dangerous jobs.** Whenever you're using chemicals or equipment that could hurt your child, have him in full view or, better yet, away from home during these activities. Window cleaning can be dangerous if windows are open when young children are in the area. Make sure your child is in close view or being supervised by an appropriate adult elsewhere when you are vacuuming, since it's difficult to hear over the sound of the machine.

### Carpet-cleaning concerns

*"I've heard that the chemicals used in carpet cleaners can make kids sick. Is this true?"*

Some research has suggested a possible link between young children exposed to freshly shampooed rugs and a set of symptoms described as Kawasaki syndrome, although the risk has not been clearly established. No single brand of shampoo or method of cleaning was associated with the illness. Other studies have not been able to show any link at all between carpet cleaning and Kawasaki syndrome. Researchers continue to study Kawasaki syndrome and the effects of rug cleaning solutions on children, but in the meantime, it's a good idea for you to be on the safe side and keep any young children out of the room when the carpet is being cleaned and for several hours afterward.

*For information on choosing and using household chemicals, see **page 799**.*

## Safe bath time routines

Bath time can be great fun, especially as your baby gets to the toddler stage and learns to enjoy splashing around a bit and playing with tub toys. Nevertheless, bath time requires an extra dose of vigilance.

**Bath time safety**  Bath time can be dangerous if precautions are not taken to guard against two of the most common childhood accidents: drowning and burns from scalding.

By the time they're toddlers, most children will make some attempts to wash themselves, and by age 4 or 5, most will be fairly adept at managing much of the washing routine, provided bathroom safety precautions are in place. Following is the recommended procedure for safely bathing your child:

• **Make sure the room is childproofed**—padded, nonslip surfaces in place; faucet covers in place; scald-proof fixtures installed; and toxic substances and electrical appliances out of reach.

• **Never leave your child alone in the bath.** Approximately 80 American children—most of them 4 years of age and under—drown each year in bathtubs. Drowning can occur in as little as one inch of water and can happen in a few seconds.

• **Ignore distractions.** If you have an answering machine, let it take messages during bath time. Or bring a cordless phone into the bathroom to allow you to take brief calls without leaving your child's side. If you must leave the bathroom, take your child with you. Don't leave another child in charge of a sibling who's in the bath, even if they're sharing the bath.

• **Use warm, not hot water.** Young children have tender skin and exposure to water at 140°F can cause a third-degree burn in as little as three seconds. When filling your child's tub, it's good practice to start with cold water, then to add hot, and to turn off the hot water before turning off the cold. Mix the water around to eliminate any hot spots. Always test the water with either your elbow or a bath thermometer before you place your child in the tub. Bath water should feel pleasantly warm, but cooler than the water you would bathe in. The bath temperature should register between 85 and 90°F on a thermometer. Never turn the hot water back on while your child is in the tub. If your child tells you that the water is too hot, take his word for it and add cooler water. To prevent burns from touching the hot-water spigot, install a protective faucet cover.

• **Prevent entrapment.** It's a rare child who doesn't wonder what

## PARENTS ALERT

## Bath Seats and Rings

Babies between the ages of 6 and 9 months statistically are at highest risk of drowning while using bath seats or rings. These devices, which are intended for babies 6 months and older, help support the infant during bath time. Most of the seats have three or four legs with suction cups that attach to the bottom of the tub. Accidents occur when the suction cups release unexpectedly, allowing the device and the baby to tip over into the water. Infants may also become trapped if they slip between the legs of the device. Older babies, usually over 8 months, may try climbing out of the seat and subsequently drown.

To prevent such accidents, do not rely on bath rings or seats to keep a baby safe—never leave a baby alone in the tub. Fill the tub with just enough water to cover the infants' legs—it's sufficient for bathing, and, although it won't prevent it entirely, decreases the risk of drowning. Finally, attach suction cups only to a smooth surface. They will not stick to textured, repainted, ridged, or nonskid tub surfaces.

*For more on childproofing the bathroom, see **pages 769–71**.*

would happen if she stuck her big toe into the faucet. To prevent mishaps, turn the tub-spout cover to block the faucet opening and use a drain stopper to keep fingers and toes from getting caught in the drain.

• **Prevent slips.** Keep splashing that causes water to get onto the floor to a minimum and dry up puddles as they occur. It's also a good idea to install antislip decals or a rubber mat inside the tub and place a nonskid rug next to the tub to reduce the risk of slipping. (But see Parents Alert regarding nonskid surfaces and toilet seats and rings.) Remember that wet babies and children are slippery, so you will need to use both hands to grasp your child securely under the arms as you lift or guide him into and out of the water. Wrapping a towel around your child before lifting him out can give you the traction you need.

• **Keep all needed supplies within easy reach,** including towels to prevent chills upon getting out of the bath.

• **Remove any potential tubside dangers,** such as shavers and open shampoo bottles.

• **Drain the tub as soon as the bath is finished.**

### Showers for kids

*"Are showers safe for kids? Is a preschooler too young?"*

Most preschoolers are too young to bathe by themselves and therefore showers, which are difficult for you to monitor, are not recommended. Since you need to be nearby to catch a child before she falls, you'd need to keep the shower door or curtain open, which increases the possibility of a wet and slippery floor. However, if your child does want to shower, stay close. Put towels on the floor to sop up the water that is likely to land there. And be sure that no one uses the toilet that's on the same pipeline. Flushing will cause a drop in cold water to your child's shower and could result in scalding.

# Pets and other animals

While you don't want to make your child fearful of animals, he does need to know safe routines when handling or approaching animals.

- **Teach kids never to approach an animal they do not know.** Kids need to know that not every animal is approachable, even if it's on a leash held by a trusted neighbor. They should always ask the pet owner's permission to pet an animal. Caution children, particularly, never to approach a wild animal or any animal that looks sick or that is not behaving normally. For instance, raccoons are nocturnal creatures and any raccoon that meanders into your yard in the daylight can rightly be suspected of being ill. Likewise, kids shouldn't handle injured animals that they find. Sick and injured animals can carry a number of diseases, including rabies, which can be fatal.
- **Remind kids never to pick up a cat.** Cats and kittens are particularly skittish when it comes to being handled and may scratch in an attempt to get away. When children have permission to hold a cat, make sure that their legs and arms are covered.
- **Don't allow kids to handle reptiles or amphibians.** Many carry salmonella and for that reason, the sale of turtles, salamanders, and others as pets has been banned in a number of localities. If your child does touch a reptile or amphibian or its cage or dishes, have him wash his hands with an antibacterial soap.
- **Show kind pet practices.** Never allow your child to harm an animal or play too roughly with it. An animal that's treated roughly will respond in kind.

# *Travel and outings*

From the point that you bring your child home from the hospital, he will accompany you on outings around the neighborhood, to the grocery store, to doctors' appointments, on visits to friends and family, to parks and playgrounds, on vacations, perhaps to daycare, preschool, and on to school. Eventually, he will have to get from one place to another on his own, which is why it is important to instill safe habits and routines as early as possible and practice them repeatedly. Also, since children are keen observers of their surroundings and will study you constantly, set a good example by practicing the safety procedures that you preach.

*For information on your baby's first outings, see **page 50**.*

# Stroller and pram travel

Strollers and prams or carriages can be great conveniences for transporting babies and even some of their paraphernalia. Once infants can sit, often as early as 6 months of age, use a stroller, not a carriage. Carriages aren't safe for older babies since they can easily fall out. Look for equipment that has certification from the Juvenile Products Manufacturers Association (JPMA). The U.S. Consumer Product Safety Commission advises looking for the following when choosing a stroller or carriage:

• **Choose a stroller in which the leg openings can be closed when used in the carriage position.**

• **Choose a stroller and carriage which has a base wide enough to prevent tipping,** even when the baby leans over the side. If the seat can be adjusted to a reclining position, make sure the stroller does not tip backward when the baby lies down.

• **Make sure there are no exposed coil springs or sharp edges.**

• **Make sure the stroller has a restraint system** that includes a combination seat belt and crotch strap.

• **Check the restraint system** to make sure it is strong and durable, fits snugly around your child, and can be easily fastened and unfastened. Use it each time you place the baby in the stroller.

• **Make sure that the brake is easy and convenient to operate and actually locks the wheels.** Brakes on two wheels provide an extra measure of safety.

• **If a stroller has a shopping basket for carrying packages it should be low on the back of the stroller and in front of or directly over the rear wheels.**

When using a stroller or carriage follow these safety tips:

• **Always use the restraint system whenever you place your baby in the stroller.** Otherwise your infant might slip feet first through a leg opening, entrapping his head between the seat and the handrest bar.

• **Never allow standing in a carriage or stroller.**

• **Never leave your child unattended** in either a carriage or a stroller.

• **Keep your child away from the stroller when folding or unfolding it.** Children's fingers have been crushed and even amputated in parts of the folding mechanism.

• **Never hang shopping bags over the handles.**

# Pedestrian routines

Start teaching your child basic street rules as early as possible. Keep in mind, however, that just because she can repeat the rules to you doesn't mean she is ready to apply them effectively and consistently. Pedestrian injuries are the leading cause of preventable death in children ages 4 to 8; about 1,000 children age 14 and under die from them each year. It's particularly dangerous for children under 10 to cross the street alone—they can't accurately judge distances well enough to be safe.

Always set a good example when you are with your child. Don't jay walk or dart across the street to make the light. Help your child learn pedestrian rules:

• **Practice safe routines out loud.** Tell a young child exactly what you are doing when you stop, look, and listen. Make it a habit to stop at crosswalks and to stop and wait before stepping into the street, no matter how little traffic there is.

• **Stop at driveways as well as before crossing streets.** Point out that lights on the back of cars light up when they are in reverse, and listen together for the high-pitched beeping sound that trucks make when they back up.

• **Stay out of the street when playing.** Young children must learn that roadways are dangerous and off-limits.

• **Watch out for cars.** Children need to understand that just because they can see a car doesn't mean the driver can see them.

• **Cross only at a corner,** preferably one with a crosswalk, stop sign, or traffic signal.

• **Stop, look, and listen.** Whenever you and your child cross the street, teach him to pause and check for traffic in all directions before stepping onto the roadway—and continue to look both ways until across. But keep in mind that even though he may repeat your instructions, he's too young to actually remember to use them.

• **Walk, don't run, across the street.** A running child is more likely to stumble and fall, or fail to check and stop for cars.

• **Never dart out into a street, driveway, or parking lot.** Fifty

## *Teaching Children Street Smarts*

To help teach my kids about street safety, I played a little game with them whenever we were out walking on the street. It turned out to be a good exercise. I asked each of my two boys when they were about 4 years old to identify cars by telling me if they were coming toward us, moving away from us, or backing up. It's difficult for very young children to do, but it made them look hard at cars moving on the street and helped them develop a sense of how they were moving. I think for a while that whenever they saw a car that question came into their mind and it helped them become safer pedestrians.

to 70 percent of injuries to school-age children occur when kids rush into the street from between parked cars or from behind bushes and other shrubbery.

- **Seek out escorts.** For children under 10 who are walking alone, teach them to get help from a crossing guard or trusted adult.
- **Watch out for police cars and other emergency vehicles.** They may move fast and run red lights. Instruct your child to wait until such vehicles pass.
- **Walk on the left side of the street, facing oncoming traffic.**
- **At night, think bright.** If your child must walk along the street when it's dark have him wear bright clothing with reflective patches or tape.

**Rainy weather safety**  While a little rain certainly won't hurt your child, there are some safety rules he should learn to follow:
- **Never jump into a puddle through which you can't see the bottom.** Some puddles are quite deep. After a heavy rain, soil and pavement erosion can turn a crack in the ground into a knee-deep or bigger hole.
- **Avoid storm drains.** These can become torrents during and after a rainstorm.
- **Be careful with umbrellas.** Children should only use ones with rounded spoke and top tip and with nonpinching folding mechanisms. Also teach your child never to use his umbrella as a weapon.

## Car travel

Motor vehicle crashes are the leading cause of unintentional injury-related death among children ages 14 and under. Riding without adequate restraints is the number one risk factor for death and injury, which is why it is so important to use child safety seats and safety belts and harnesses correctly whenever your family travels by car—either yours or someone else's.

Be very aware of your own driving habits, since you are in the best possible position to keep your child safe. Practice defensive driving at all times. Don't speed or tailgate or engage in any other unsafe practices. Keep your temper, even when another driver cuts you off or tailgates you. Always remember that getting to your destination five or ten minutes later is preferable to not getting there at all.

When traveling with your family by car follow these safety guidelines:

- **Always use the proper restraints.** Make sure kids are in their car seats or, if they're big enough, in seat belts. Use your own seat belt on every ride. Make it a rule that you do not leave until everybody is safely situated in appropriate car seats and has fastened seat-belt restraints.
- **Keep kids in the back seat.** The safest place for children to ride is in the back seat. Never place an infant in the front seat of a vehicle that has a passenger-side air bag. If a child must ride in the front seat equipped with an air bag, set the seat as far back as possible from the dashboard, but do not recline it, and buckle up the child snugly with a shoulder/lap belt or in a car seat with its own shoulder harness, depending on the age and size of the child.
- **Don't overcrowd the vehicle.** When several people are traveling in the back seat, it's imperative that there be one belt for each person. Sharing the same belt is dangerous. Only seat as many people as the car was designed to hold.
- **Watch out for car doors.** Always look to make sure feet, hands, and fingers are safely out of the way before closing them. Be particularly careful with sliding van doors.
- **Insist that children behave in the car.** There should be no roughhousing, throwing objects, grabbing the steering wheel, or playing with door locks and buttons. If children are screaming and acting, up pull over to the side of the road and don't resume travel until the uproar subsides.
- **Always turn off the motor and remove your keys** when you park the car.
- **Do not store heavy or sharp objects on the back window shelf of a car.** They could come flying off and cause injury in the event of a sudden stop.
- **Park so that your child can exit the car on the sidewalk side,** not on the side facing a busy street.
- **Never leave a child unattended in the car,** locked or otherwise.
- **Do not allow passengers to ride in the flat bed of a truck,** or anywhere but inside the passenger compartment, securely buckled up.

**Choosing and using safety seats and restraints** There are several kinds of child safety seats. Some seats are made only for infants; convertibles may be adjusted to fit children from birth to age 4.

"IT WORKED FOR ME"

## A "Beary" Good Idea

I had a hard time getting my 4-year-old to wear her seatbelt without making a fuss until I got a little belt for her favorite teddy bear. Now whenever we are in the car she takes teddy along and faithfully straps him in, then buckles up herself.

*Always place your toddler in a forward-facing safety seat in the back seat.*

Safety boosters are for children who have outgrown regular safety seats but are not yet tall enough for regular shoulder straps. When choosing and using seats, follow these guidelines:

• **For infants:** Infants under 26 inches tall and weighing less than 20 pounds should ride facing the rear in a semireclined infant or convertible safety seat. Never place a rear-facing infant seat in the forward position.

• **For children over 20 pounds:** Once your child reaches 20 pounds or 26 inches and can sit up by herself, you can move her to a forward-facing safety seat. If you put a toddler in a safety belt alone, the belts will probably not fit correctly.

• **For children over 40 pounds:** When your child reaches 40 inches tall or approximately 40 pounds, you can move her into a booster seat. Booster seats help elevate a child so that the seat belt falls across his chest. There are three kinds of booster seats: seats with shields, those without shields, and seats with removable shields. Follow manufacturer's instruction for use of each type. Boosters with shields are for use with lap belts alone. Boosters without shields are for use only with the vehicle lap/shoulder belt. Boosters with removable shields are for use without the shield to make combination lap/shoulder belts fit right. Add the shield when only a lap belt is available. Do not use shield boosters for children under 40 pounds. A child should stay in a booster seat until the back of her head is higher than the vehicle's seat back. Then she can start using regular seat belts alone.

Many kids, however, outgrow boosters when they are still too small for the lap and shoulder belts to fit properly and comfortably. Fortunately, products are available that help solve the problem. One is a padded nylon sleeve through which you thread the shoulder belt and reposition it. Another device is a two-foot-long slotted plastic bar that also repositions and secures the lap and shoulder belt. Both are widely available. Some car manufacturers are also addressing the issue and offer seat belts with clips that reposition the shoulder belt away from a child's face and neck. In addition to choosing the right restraint, you must use it properly and make sure it is in good condition.

• **Make sure the seat itself is safe.** Designs have been modified and improved, but products continue to be recalled. Every safety seat made for sale in the U.S. today must be crash-tested and labeled with the name of the manufacturer, the date made, and a statement that the seat complies with federal safety standards. Used or borrowed safety seats may or may not be safe. If you have a used car seat make sure it was never in a crash, it is in good repair with no cracks, it is less than ten years old, preferably less than five, and it has all of its parts, including instruction booklet.

• **Always place your child in the back seat.** Front passenger air bags can kill a child; even if the air bags are disabled or your car does not have air bags, the back seat is the safest place for your child to ride.

• **Install the car seat according to the manufacturer's recommendations.** Keep the manufacturer's instructions with the car seat, perhaps in the glove compartment. Make sure the seat is compatible with your automobile or make the necessary adjustments suggested by the manufacturer. This is essential; some researchers estimate that as many as 95 percent of car seats are installed improperly.

• **Make sure that the seat belt will hold the seat firmly in place.** Some harness belts, particularly those designed to allow nonabrupt movement, require installation of a locking clip. Otherwise, a sudden swerve could cause the child seat to tip over. Install the clip if necessary.

**PARENTS RESOURCE**

For any questions about safety seats, including recent product recalls, call the **DOT Auto-Safety Hotline** at (800) 424-9393 or (888) 327-4236, or visit www.nhtsa.dot.gov.

# Public place safety

Whenever you take your child to a public place—a store, theater, or restaurant, for example—you need to be aware of potential dangers and to steer your child away from them.

 • **Look for open windows or chutes, slippery floors, automatic doors,** and other structural hazards.

 • **Be aware of exits and emergency evacuation exits** wherever you are and point them out to your children.

 • **Avoid deserted places.**

 • **Avoid overcrowded places.**

 • **Point out the helpers that your child could turn to if separated from you.** Point out what uniformed police officers, museum guards, park attendants, or other officials look like and explain to your child that those are the people she should turn to for help in an emergency.

 • **Teach kids to stay put if they are lost.** If a child can't directly see the person to whom he could turn for help if he's lost, teach him to stay put and not run around trying to look for you once you've been separated. You will find him more easily if he stays in one place.

**Public restrooms** Unfortunately, safety in public restrooms today has become an issue. Try to use only restrooms you regard as safe and always accompany a young child to the restroom. It's safer for young boys to use the ladies room with female caretakers than to go into a suspicious-looking facility alone. With young girls, try to enlist the help of a reliable female such as a store clerk, to accompany a child into the ladies room if you are a male caretaker. If a child is old enough to use the restroom alone, make sure you can keep an eye on the door while he or she is using the facility. Instruct the child to do what he or she needs to do and get out promptly.

*See **page 817** for quick childproofing tips.*

**Hotel and motel safety** If your family is going to be staying in a hotel or motel overnight, inspect the property in advance if you can. Check the room for potential hazards and eliminate them as best you can. Make sure it is in a safe location, structurally and hygienically sound. If a site inspection is not possible, choose a reputable company name you trust. If you are going to be using facilities other than your room, check them out first before you allow your older children to venture off on their own.

Discuss with your child what to do should he become lost or

confused. Some hotels offer baby-sitting arrangements and programs for children. Make sure you are comfortable with the people, the environment, and the proposed activities before entrusting your child to a stranger's care.

Young children should not be left unattended in a hotel or motel room. Always keep the door locked and teach children not to open the door if someone knocks. Ask them to call you if, for instance, you are in the shower when someone knocks. Also teach them the safety-wise telephone behavior of not divulging much information to a stranger on the phone. Tell your child to get you immediately if the phone rings and he answers it. If you are temporarily unable to talk on the telephone, instruct your youngster to tell the caller to ring back later and hang up. If he is old enough, instruct him to take a name and number and say that you will call back later.

## Plane travel

Even though you don't need to purchase a ticket for children under 2 years old, get one anyway, if you can afford it, so that you'll have a seat on which to put his infant seat. Otherwise, try to book an off-peak flight that is likely to have a spare seat. This way you can strap him in when the "fasten seatbelt" light is on. Request a bulkhead seat so that you'll have extra room in which to maneuver.

Make sure your infant seat will fit properly on an airplane seat, and that the label states that it's certified for use on an airplane. During takeoff and landing, give an older child something to suck on or gum to chew so that his ears won't hurt from the change in pressure. Don't drink hot coffee or tea when flying with your child; if the ride suddenly gets bumpy, you could spill it and burn him.

**Flying with an infant**  There's no magical age at which an infant can travel on an airplane. However, you can help your baby feel more comfortable during the flight, by observing the following tips:
• **Give your baby a pacifier or bottle during takeoff and landing.** Sucking and swallowing will help to clear her ears and ease any discomfort she may feel.
• **Carry on plenty of essential supplies,** including bottles, diapers, and wipes; a two-hour flight can turn into a six-hour delay. Bring a blanket and variety of clothing in case the temperature on the plane is too cold or too hot.

- **Dress your baby comfortably.** If you want to show her off in the fancy outfit from Grandma, put it on her when you arrive.
- **Make sure your baby is restrained.** Airlines permit children under 2 to ride in parents' laps. However, the Federal Aviation Administration advises that children who weigh less than 20 pounds sit in a rear-facing safety seat approved for use on aircraft.
- **Consult your pediatrician if your baby has an ear infection or cold.** Depending on the severity of the baby's illness, your doctor may advise you to postpone the trip.

## Shopping routines

Be safety minded even when you are performing everyday routines like going shopping. A key point to keep in mind is to be alert. It's easy to become preoccupied looking for particular items, comparing prices, and trying not to forget anything on your list. Often, too, shopping is done betwixt and between in a rush to get home or to another appointment. It's really easier in the long run to plan shopping excursions so you have the necessary equipment, including strollers or baby carriers, with you in the store.

Be especially careful in shopping malls or supermarket parking lots where many other shoppers are hurrying in and out from all directions on foot and in cars. Never allow children to run around or play with shopping carts in parking lots or store aisles.

**Not getting separated**  Once you are inside a store, one of the biggest dangers is that you and your child will become separated. If you are not using a baby carrier or stroller, teach your child to stay close to you at all times. Some parents find hand holders—telephone-cord-like devices that attach to you and your toddler's wrist—a big convenience. It's a more appealing way of keeping track of a child than putting him on a leash or harness, and it saves you from having to stoop over constantly, trying to hold on to your toddler's hand. Stress the importance of not ever going off with strangers.

---

**"IT HAPPENED TO US"**

### Toddler Takes Off in the Store

I decided one day to make a quick, unplanned stop at a large hardware store to pick something up and brought my son along minus his stroller. The store didn't have shopping carts, so I couldn't put my son in the cart seat. I looked up at the aisle signs to try to figure out where the item that I needed was and my son just took off. Several cashiers saw him go by, but none thought to stop him. Finally, I was able to locate him, but after that experience, I'm reluctant to take him into any store without a stroller. I told him that if he ever gets separated from me again, not to keep running—just stand still. I explained that if he stays in one spot I will find him.

**Safe escalator use**  Each year 2,500 children age 14 and under are injured in escalator accidents. Three out of four accidents are the result of falls; most of the rest happen when a child's hand, foot, shoe, or clothing becomes trapped in a moving step. Following these tips when using escalators with your child:

- **Always carry a baby or very young child.**
- **For toddlers and older children, make sure that shoelaces are tied and that pants or skirts don't drag.** (Drawstrings should already be removed or cut short to prevent strangulation.)
- **Teach your child to face forward and stand in the center of the step, so his feet aren't near the edges.**
- **A child should always grasp the handrail;** if he can't reach it, hold his hand.
- **Show your child how to lift his feet and step off at the end of the ride.**
- **Don't let your youngster play or sit on an escalator or ride the handrails.**
- **Don't take your child in a stroller or cart on an escalator;** it can easily tip or get caught in the steps. Instead, look for an elevator or ramp. Or hold your child and ask a passerby for help carrying the folded stroller.
- **Use the shutoff button,** usually located at the top and bottom of the stairs near the handrail, if you need to stop the escalator in an emergency. If you can't reach it, ask someone to press it for you.

**Shopping cart safety**  About 25,000 children are injured each year when they fall or jump from shopping carts, or when the carts they are riding in tip over. More than 600 youngsters are injured seriously enough to require hospitalization. The Consumer Product Safety Commission has recommended that stores equip carts with safety belts for children. Strapping children in will keep them from standing up or jumping from carts, but it will not prevent the cart from tipping over. The top-heavy design of most grocery-store shopping carts makes them inherently dangerous. It's safer to transport a baby in a front or back carrier rather than a cart, or have a companion push a toddler in a stroller. If you do place your child in a shopping cart, use the safety strap. (You can buy one in a juvenile products store to bring with you in case there is none on the cart.) Never attach a car or infant seat to a cart, use the seat provided. Never allow a child to sit or stand in the cart's basket, and don't let

an older child push the cart or ride on the outside when a youngster is in the seat. Keep a close eye on children when they are riding
in your shopping cart—don't leave them alone, even for a second.
Accidents happen fast.

## Bike, trike, and roller skate safety

Wheels are wonderful things for a child. They bring a sense of freedom and provide fun forms of exercise. Between 18 months and 3
years of age, children love wheeled toys that they can ride on or
push and pull around. These can be great fun to use outdoors, but
make sure ride-on toys have a broad base for stability. Do not allow
children to ride these toys in the driveway, especially when cars are
entering and exiting. Since they're so low to the ground, it's virtually
impossible for a driver to see them.

From ages 3 to 5 children start to enjoy more complicated
rolling equipment, such as beginner roller skates and tricycles.
These have a down side, though. When children get wheels, the potential for accidents increases. Nearly 400,000 children ages 14 and
under are treated in hospital emergency rooms for bicycle-related
injuries each year. To keep your young rider or skater safe:

• **Restrict riding and skating to safe areas.** Where your child
bikes or skates is a major concern—streets and roadways with automobile traffic are dangerous places for young children to be, with
or without their own wheels. Nearly 90 percent of all bicycle-related
deaths are a result of collisions with automobiles. Even driveways
can be hazardous when cars are pulling in or out. Restrict children
to sidewalks and paths until they are old enough to ride well and observe basic traffic rules. Generally, children under the age of 10
should not ride on the street unless accompanied by an adult.
Younger children are especially vulnerable to accidents because
they lack the coordination, peripheral vision, and judgment needed
to ride safely in the street. Once on the road, cyclists must ride with
traffic and obey all signs and signals.

• **Teach safety rules.** In addition to keeping them out of the flow
of automobile traffic, teach kids to avoid dangerous stunts, such as
a roller skater holding on to the back of a moving bike.

- **Make sure your children wear protective gear.** Children must wear helmets whenever they are skating or cycling. When roller-skating, they should also wear wrist and elbow guards. Knee guards, too, are a good idea. Young children riding with an adult in a bicycle seat also must wear helmets.
- **Make sure clothing fits snugly,** so that no loose cords or clothing can become entangled either in a bike itself or in bushes and other things in the environment.
- **Start on a soft surface,** such as grass, just to allow your child to feel what it's like to stand or ride on wheels.
- **Teach your child how to stop.** A very important skill to learn as early as possible is how to stop—without crashing into something. Learning how to control moving and stopping on bikes and skates is an integral factor in keeping safe as well as having fun.

**Choosing and using trikes and bikes**  Most children are ready for a tricycle around age 3; some, a bit earlier. When choosing a trike, look for one that has a sturdy frame and big wheels, and is built low to the ground, which will make it less likely to tip over. Check that your child can easily grasp the handlebars and his feet can touch the pedals. If he has to struggle to reach either, he could lose his balance. Ideally, you should be able to adjust the seat and handlebars by a range of three to four inches, so your child can comfortably ride the trike until he graduates to a two-wheeler.

A safe age for children to start to use a bicycle is usually from 6 to 8 years, though some younger children have the strength and balance needed. Many may be able to ride one sooner with training wheels.

A beginner does best on a sturdy single-speed model with coaster, or foot, brakes. Tires should be 1 to 1½ inches wide for stability. In choosing a bike, look for one that is appropriate for your child's size. Don't buy a larger bike and expect him to grow into it. Check that he can place the balls of his feet on the ground while seated on the bike and can easily reach the handlebars with his elbows slightly bent. If the bike has a center bar,

**"IT WORKED FOR ME"**

### *Encouraging Helmet Use*

My daughter was very reluctant to wear a helmet whenever she rode her bike, despite the fact that I had explained to her repeatedly how important it was for her safety. One day when we were shopping she pointed out a helmet on the shelf that had caught her attention. We found her size and tried one on to make sure it fit well. She was able to fasten and unfasten the strap all by herself, too, which made her very happy. We bought it for her and now she wears it without fail whenever she rides her bike. Letting her choose her own helmet made all the difference.

have him straddle it. His feet should be flat on the ground, and there should be at least one inch of clearance between his crotch and the bar. Adjust the handlebars and seat as your child grows. Check equipment regularly for steering and brake control. If the bike doesn't come with a bell or horn and front, side, and rear reflectors, buy and install these additions.

**Choosing and using skates**  A safe age to start children skating is around 4, although some kids can manage earlier than that. The old-fashioned (out-line) type of roller skate with two parallel rows of wheels on each skate is more stable and easier for a youngster to learn to use than in-line skates, with wheels placed in a single straight line down the center of the skate. Some skates are convertible from out-line to in-line. Skates should fit snugly enough on the feet not to wobble. They can be a size or so too large (use heavy socks or foam pads to take up some room), but they should fit firmly around the ankle for support.

*Your child should wear her helmet whenever she rides her bike.*

**Choosing and using helmets**  In choosing a helmet, follow these guidelines:

• **Make sure the helmet is well made.** For all-around protection, choose a helmet with a seal of approval from the American Society for Testing and Materials (ASTM), the American National Standards Institute (ANSI), or the Snell Memorial Foundation.

• **Make sure it fits well.** The front should be less than an inch above the eyebrows; the sides should cover the ears; and the back should cover the little bump at the base of the skull. The helmet should be snug enough not to slip off when you tug on it, but it should allow enough movement for comfort, so your child does not feel pinched or choked.

- **Opt for a hard-shell helmet for children older than 2,** for the greatest protection. Choose a foam helmet for kids 2 and under—hard-shell helmets are too heavy for young children's neck muscles to support. Make sure the helmet has a fabric covering, though. Should a child fall, foam can stick to the road's surface, causing neck injuries; fabric allows the helmet to slide.

- **Look for an easy-to-use clasp.** Most children under 8 will need help manipulating the clasp. Older kids should be able to work it on their own. If it's too difficult for them they won't wear the helmet.

- **Look for reflective material** so that if your child cannot make it home before dusk, he will be visible.

- **Check the helmet regularly** to make sure that it still fits your child and that it has not been damaged. If you spot defects such as cracks, dents, missing foam, or torn fabric, buy a new helmet.

# CHAPTER 3

# Community Concerns

Ideally, the community in which you live is a safe, nurturing environment for your family. But, of course, the world is not a perfect place. Human-made problems and natural disasters affect the lives of everyone. Environmental pollution threatens the vital natural resources. Public places may not be designed or maintained with health and safety in mind.

While it is impossible to childproof the world or to confine your children to the safety of your home, you can curb environmental pollution and other hazards. These actions are not foolproof, but they do offer some measure of protection by lowering the risks.

## *Environmental pollution*

Many organizations, including the U.S. Environmental Protection Agency (EPA), recognize that children face an array of complex environmental threats to their health—from asthma-inducing air pollution to toxic chemicals. Because children are in the process of physically developing, they are more susceptible than healthy adults to the effects of environmental toxins—from lead in paint to illness-causing microbes in drinking water. While currently some action is being taken at the federal government level to enforce laws relating to safe pesticide use, higher standards for drinking water, and stricter air-pollution control, parents need to take steps to minimize the risks for themselves and their families.

Part of the process involves implementing and teaching environmentally sound practices in your own home. For instance, teach your children the four R's: reduce, reuse, recycle, and respond. Children love to get involved in good causes, and the environment can become one of your family's concerns. You and your children can dispose of trash in environmentally safe ways. It's easy, for example, to have children help sort and recycle bottles, cans, and plastics, or contribute to your own compost pile. Think "green" and choose environmentally safe products, from laundry detergents to lawn and garden supplies.

There are additional steps you need to take, however, to safeguard your family from dangers of pollution and environmental contamination. Following are precautions you can take right now.

# Air pollution

Air pollution causes a wide variety of adverse health effects that range from eye irritation to heart and lung damage, and even to premature death. Asthma-related deaths, for example, are on the rise in children and young people, increasing as much as 118 percent between 1980 and 1993, according to the Centers for Disease Control. Many of the most common air pollutants can contribute to respiratory illnesses, including asthma, and the EPA estimates that more than a quarter of the nation's children live in areas that fail to meet national air-quality standards.

Air pollution has other adverse effects, too. It can impair visibility, reduce crop production, and damage ecosystems, national parks, wilderness areas, and natural bodies of water.

Air pollution comes from many different sources:
- **Stationary sources,** such as factories, power plants, and smelters.
- **Mobile sources,** including cars, buses, planes, trucks, and trains; also wildfires, windblown dust, and volcanic eruptions.

It can also occur indoors—inside your home, as well as in hospitals, hotels, offices, schools, and factories. To limit the damaging effects of air pollution, be aware of air quality both indoors and out and correct any problems that are within your direct control.

**Indoor pollution**  If your child frequently complains of being tired or not feeling well when she comes home from school, the air in the building could be making her sick. About 19 percent of the

## Checking Indoor Air

For a health hazard evaluation of your office, call the **National Institute for Occupational Safety and Health Information Service at the Centers for Disease Control and Prevention** at (800) 35NIOSH, www.cdc.gov/niosh, or contact the **Occupational Safety and Health Administration**, (202) 693-1999, www.osha.gov.

The **EPA**, at (202) 554-1404, www.epa.gov, may also be helpful.

A free "Indoor Air Quality Tools for Schools Action Kit" is available from the **Indoor Air Quality Information Clearinghouse**, www.epa.gov/iaq. Fax requests to (703) 356-5386 or call them at (800) 438-4318.

nation's public schools have unhealthy air, according to the General Accounting Office. The culprits? Poor ventilation, mold growth in leaky roofs or ventilation systems, fumes from chemicals used in cleaning and in art, science ,and photography classes and even cigarette smoke that drifts into rooms from the teachers' lounge.

Poor air quality can lead to headaches, coughing, congestion, sore throats, itchy eyes, or nausea—all of which affect a child's ability to concentrate in school. Typically, children begin to feel better an hour or so after they get home.

If your child consistently complains that she doesn't feel well when she comes home from school, ask other parents if their kids have similar symptoms. Also, ask your doctor if she suspects indoor pollution may be triggering your child's after-school symptoms. If it appears that the school has a pollution problem, meet with the principal; ask how the school monitors air quality; how rooms are ventilated; and whether there's a no-smoking policy for teachers and other staff in the building. Then work with the school administration and other parents to increase the school building's health.

**Outdoor air quality** Outdoor air quality, or course, is more difficult for individuals to control. It pays to be an environmental advocate and to be aware of what sort of pollutants might be present in your own community. Local community organizations and local and national environmental and public health organizations such as the Clean Air Network of the Natural Resources Defense Council and the American Lung Association can help you. You can also contact the EPA and your state, regional, or local air pollution control agencies to receive information directly on Clean Air Act activities. Monitoring of pollutants is carried out by EPA, state, and regional air pollution control agencies, and by the owners of individual sources of pollution, such as factories. Air pollution monitoring stations are set up all over the country, collecting information on at least six primary pollutants. Contact the EPA, or your state, regional, or local air pollution control agency, for information on monitoring programs and monitoring reports of your area.

In the meantime, if you live in an area where air pollution is a problem, listen to the radio or television for air-quality reports. Keep babies and young children inside, if possible, when air quality is poor. If you are driving in congested areas, try to choose times when traffic is lighter so you don't get stuck in a traffic jam with your baby. If you do get caught in heavy traffic, close the car windows and turn on the AC. Avoid long walks along city streets on hot muggy days, especially if you or your child has lung problems such as asthma. Also avoid strenuous activity and exercise outdoors in heavily polluted areas.

If you or your family suffers from allergies, check the newspaper or listen to the radio or TV for pollen counts and stay inside in air-conditioned rooms if possible to minimize exposure to allergy-triggering substances during peak times. Finally, because environmental pollution has taken a heavy toll on the earth's ozone layer, people are more vulnerable to the damaging effects of the sun's rays. Be sure that your family is protected from ultraviolet rays year round by wearing protective clothing and sunscreen (for children over 6 months of age).

## Water contamination

Each year, hundreds of beaches are closed because of pollution, particularly the presence of raw sewage. Throughout the country signs are posted warning people not to swim in or eat fish taken from countless lakes and rivers. Water pollution affects not only where we swim and what we eat but, of course, what we drink. Contaminated drinking water poses serious risks to children, especially infants, who drink more fluids per pound of body weight than adults. Children also tend to be more vulnerable to the effects of microbial contamination. The EPA estimates that in 1995 alone, a total of 30 million Americans drank water from systems that violated one or more public health standards, and approximately 13 million people are served by systems that do not filter their water and hence do not adequately protect against contaminants.

Before your family swims in lakes, rivers, streams, or ponds, or eats fish caught in those waters, find out if the water is safe to swim in and if fish taken from those sources is safe to eat. Obey all

*For information on testing drinking water, see **page 804**.*

warnings to the contrary. Caution your children against drinking water from natural sources such as streams or lakes. While it may look clean, the water may contain dangerous microbes or toxins.

Be especially careful with drinking water. In areas where water is suspect, drink only bottled water and avoid using ice cubes made from the local water. At home, ensure a safe supply of drinking water.

# Public spaces and places

While you can't modify all the public buildings and gathering places in your community, you can make it a point to become involved in the civic life of your community by monitoring and reporting public health and safety hazards to your local authorities. You also need to recognize hazards and to avoid them whenever possible.

## Structural hazards in the community

In the course of your week, as you go about your usual routine, make it a point to be aware of safety issues in your community. Here are areas where you should report problems before they cause harm to your family or someone else's:

- **Traffic and road conditions:** malfunctioning or missing street and traffic signs and lights, potholes, broken curbs, and obstructions, such as an overgrown tree.
- **Storm damage:** downed power lines, toppled or damaged trees, localized floods.
- **Construction and/or repair work** that poses hazards, such as removal of lead or asbestos without proper safeguards, blocked public spaces, insufficient barriers to protect citizens from falling debris.
- **Insufficient lighting** in public and private places, such as supermarket parking lots.
- **Overcrowding** in public transportation or at community events, which could cause injuries if there's a crowd surge.
- **Missing, blocked, or inadequate fire escapes and fire exit signs.**

# Playground safety

Playgrounds are great places for having fun. They can, however, be the scene of a high number of accidents. In 1994, for example, more than 146,000 children ages 2 to 14 were treated for injuries, mostly from falls at playgrounds. Always supervise and watch your children. More than 40 percent of injuries are related to lack of adult supervision. Check grounds and equipment each time your child uses the playground, since the passage of time and heavy use erode equipment. There are no federally mandated playground safety standards, so it is up to parents and community leaders to evaluate the play equipment children use. Be on the lookout for equipment hazards, surface dangers such as broken glass, as well as other children or bullies who might engage in rough play and ominous-looking strangers who could possibly abduct your child. Also make sure your child uses the equipment safety—no standing on swings or jumping off slides, for example.

If you are bringing a toddler to a playground, she will be watching older children and want to imitate them. It's important to encourage her play, but at the same time you need to recognize her limits and teach her safe ways to work within them, making sure, for instance, that she grabs onto swings with both hands and that she takes turns on the slide, one child at a time.

**Playground equipment** Items that get a lot of use need to be frequently inspected. Following are tips to help you safeguard your child:

• **Check the surface under the equipment.** Sixty percent of all playground-related injuries result from falls onto hard surfaces, such as concrete, asphalt, grass, and dirt. The best surface consists of 9 to 12 inches of wood chips, pea gravel, loose mulch, or sand. Synthetic foamlike tiles or rubber mats designed for playground use are also acceptable.

• **Check the safety and integrity of the equipment.** Do not let your child use any equipment that is not anchored properly or has missing, cracked, or otherwise damaged parts. Check the

---

**"IT WORKED FOR ME"**

## Teaching Playground Safety

I had a lot of trouble getting my daughter to remember to wait her turn when using the slide. She would start up the ladder before the child in front of her could get in position to slide down. I turned the "one at a time" rule into a game among her and her friends by creating a new version of "tag." Now the children don't start up the ladder until the child who has just used the slide comes back around, taps her on the arm, and says, "You're it."

equipment for deteriorating wood that could cause splinters, as well as any rusted bolts. Make sure that spaces between ladder rungs and other openings are less than three inches wide or more than nine inches wide. Platforms, ramps, and bridges should have guardrails to prevent falls. Guardrails and slats should be less than 3½ inches apart, so a child's head can't get caught. Slides and climbing equipment intended for 2- to 5-year-olds should be no higher than six feet above the ground. Slides and monkey bars should not be higher than six feet off the ground for preschoolers and seven feet for school-age kids.

- **Make sure equipment is age appropriate.** Toddler swings should have leg dividers to prevent kids from slipping out. Children's heads can get stuck in narrow openings. Don't allow toddlers to play on seesaws. They can too easily be propelled off, or pinch fingers and catch legs under the board when it touches the ground. Toddlers are not coordinated enough to mount and dismount safely.

- **Don't let your child play on a heavy metal or hard molded plastic animal or gliding swings.** These pose a serious threat of pinching as well as possible other injuries if your child uses them too vigorously.

- **Swings should be far enough apart**—at least two feet from side to side—so that one swing doesn't crash into another.

- **Swings, seesaws, and other pieces of moving equipment should be at least 12 feet apart** to create a safe "fall zone." This also reduces the risk of a child getting hit by a swing or another youngster.

- **All equipment should be at least six feet from any walls or fences.**

- **Check for hot metal surfaces** on equipment such as a slide, which may get hot enough in the sun to cause burns.

- **Avoid using equipment with "S" hooks** or five- to ten-inch rings. "S" hooks can dislodge and children can get their heads caught in large rings.

Swings, seesaws, and other pieces of moving equipment should be at least 12 feet apart.

Openings between ladder rungs should be greater than 9 inches.

The area below equipment should be covered with mats or 12 inches of sand.

Soft ground covering should extend at least 6 feet around the perimeter of equipment.

The ground should be clear of objects than can injure your child or cause her to trip.

# Home Fire Safety

Home fires can be quick and deadly. They tend to occur when least expected, often in the middle of the night. Fires and burns are the third leading cause of unintentional injury-related death among children in the United States. Protecting your family from fire-related dangers is a two-step process. First, take precautions to keep your home as fire-safe as possible. Second, teach your family, even young children, what to do in case of fire.

## Fire prevention

The National Fire Protection Association (NFPA) recommends these fire safety tips:
- **Install smoke detectors** on each level of your home. Consider installing automatic fire sprinklers.
- **Never smoke when drowsy or in bed or permit anyone in your family to do so.**
- **Use sturdy, stable, tabletop ashtrays** and check for smoldering butts in furniture—especially after parties. Douse all butts with water before disposing.
- **Never leave cooking food unattended.** Keep cooking areas clean and clear of combustibles.
- **Use portable space heaters with care.** Keep them away from combustibles.
- **Have your chimney and central-heating system inspected** at least once a year and cleaned if necessary.
- **Plug only one heat-producing appliance into an electrical outlet.** Never override or bypass fuses or circuit breakers. Avoid running extension cords across doorways or under carpets.
- **Replace frayed or worn electrical plugs and cords, including extension cords.**

- **Store matches and lighters out of the reach of children.** Use only child-resistant lighters.
- **Never store gasoline inside your home.** If necessary, keep a small quantity in an approved, locked safety container in the garage or outdoor shed.
- **Store paints, thinners, and other flammable liquids in their original containers, well away from heat, sparks, or flame.**
- **Keep your attic free of combustibles** such as newspapers and magazines.
- **Never leave small children alone in the home.**
- **To prevent electrical fires** plug up electrical outlets with outlet safety covers. Do not use cracked or old extension cords.

**PARENTS ALERT**

## *Help Firefighters Find Your Home*

Identify your house with large address numbers that the fire department can see easily from the street. Put stickers on windows of your children's rooms so that firefighters can locate them quickly.

## Fire escape planning

Every family member needs to know where safety exits are and have escape routes planned in advance. Ideally, your home should have at least two ground-level exit doors, preferably at opposite ends of the building.

How your family responds in a fire emergency will most likely depend on how well you have prepared. The NFPA recommends these basic fire-safety practices:

- **Plan escape routes in advance.** Make sure there are two clear exits from each room, such as the door and a window, and that everyone knows these escape routes and has practiced using them. Keep escape routes unobstructed. Escape ladders can be installed from upper windows. (You'll need to keep one window free from child-safety guards to allow for escape. Open this window from the top only or install a safety lock that allows only limited opening at other times.)
- **Make sure everyone in your home is familiar with the sound of your smoke detector's alarm.**
- **Decide on a safe location outside your home** and instruct all members of your household to meet there in the event of fire, so you'll be sure everyone is out of the building.
- **Post the fire department's emergency number** by every phone so you can report a fire in another location. Never call the

fire department from your home phone during a fire in your home if doing so will slow your escape.

• **In the event of fire, leave your home immediately,** go directly to your meeting place, and account for all members of your household. Do not go back inside.

• **Have one person call the fire department from a neighbor's phone.** Tell the dispatcher your name, address, the exact location of the fire, and whether anyone is still inside. Stay on the phone until the dispatcher tells you to hang up.

• **Practice your escape plan** at least twice a year with all members of your household.

**High-rise precautions** If you live in an apartment building there are additional fire-safety guidelines to follow. Many of these tactics also apply to other multiple dwellings, such as hotels:

• **Mark the location of the nearest manual fire-alarm box on your escape plan,** so you can alert other tenants to the fire as you are making your escape. If your building has no such alarm, shout and pound on doors as you leave the building, but leave the full evacuation of the building to the fire department.

• **Never use an elevator during a fire.** Heat and smoke could kill you if the elevator stops at a floor where the fire has spread, and a power failure caused by the fire could trap you in the elevator.

• **Close the door and cover all cracks where smoke could enter,** if smoke or fire is blocking the exit from your apartment. Use damp towels, if possible, to seal cracks.

• **Don't jump.** If your apartment is two stories or more above the ground, do not jump from your window. Telephone the fire department, even if the fire trucks have arrived, and tell the dispatcher where you are trapped. Signal firefighters from your window by waving a white cloth.

• **If possible, open your windows at the top and bottom** so fresh air can enter through the lower opening and smoke can leave through the upper opening. Do not break the window. If opening the window draws smoke into the room from any source, close the window immediately.

# Fire extinguishers

Every home should have a fire extinguisher installed in plain view, above the reach of children, near an escape route, and away from stoves and heating appliances. Ask your local fire department for advice on the best locations in your home. Used properly, a portable fire extinguisher can save lives and property by putting out a small fire or containing it until the fire department arrives. Portable extinguishers for home use, however, are not designed to fight large or spreading fires. Even against small fires, the NFPA deems them useful only under certain conditions:

- The operator must know how to use the extinguisher. There is no time to read directions during an emergency.
- The extinguisher must be within easy reach and in working order, fully charged.
- The operator must have a clear escape route that will not be blocked by fire.
- The extinguisher must match they type of fire being fought. Extinguishers that contain water are unsuitable for use on grease or electrical fires. (See below for ratings.)
- The extinguisher must be large enough to put out the fire. Many portable extinguishers discharge completely in as few as 8 to 10 seconds.

Fire extinguishers are available in three classes to match the three basic types of fires. All fire extinguishers are labeled using standard symbols for the classes of fires they can put out. A red slash through any of the symbols tells you the extinguisher cannot be used on that class of fire.

- **Class A:** Ordinary combustibles such as wood, cloth, paper, rubber, and many plastics.
- **Class B:** Flammable liquids such as gasoline, oil, grease, tar, oil-based paint, lacquer, and flammable gas.
- **Class C:** Energized electrical equipment including wiring, fuse boxes, circuit breakers, machinery, and appliances.
- **ABC Multipurpose:** May be used on any type of fire.

Extinguishers are also rated for size: for example, 2A:10B:C. The rating is expressed as a number from 1 to 40; the larger the number the larger the fire the extinguisher can handle. Higher-rated models are usually heavier, though. Make sure you can hold and operate the extinguisher before you buy it.

## PARENTS ALERT

## Using Extinguishers

If you are ever faced with a Class A fire and don't have an extinguisher with an "A" symbol, don't hesitate to use one with a "B:C" symbol. However, it is very dangerous to use water or an extinguisher labeled only for Class A fires on a Class B or Class C fire.

# Index

## A

Acetaminophen, 539, 542, 579, 652
Acne, 72
Acquired immune deficiency syndrome. See AIDS
Activity boards, 155
Acupuncture, 528
Adenoiditis, 550–3, 588
Adoption, 362–7
　discussing, 365
　health considerations, 363–4
　infant, 362–3
　interracial, 364–5
　and self-esteem, 364
Aggression, 241–2, 393–4, 396, 750
AIDS, 720–2
　precautions, 722
Alerts
　alcohol, 121
　allergy, 555, 556, 558, 624
　appliances, 781
　aspirin, 643
　asthma, 710, 711
　baby-proofing, 116
　baby walkers, 151
　bath seats/rings, 833
　bedtime bottles, 29
　bouncing, 18
　bubble bath, 482
　carbon monoxide, 798
　car safety, 52
　choking, 515, 811, 831
　clothing hazards, 49, 489
　colds, 574
　detergents, 781
　diabetes, 715
　diapering after polio vaccine, 35
　diet in pregnancy/nursing, 516
　ear washing, 45
　epilepsy, 718
　exercise equipment, 777
　fevers, 600
　fifth disease, 602
　fleas, 481
　food, 509
　food avoidance in nursing, 24
　food storage, 119
　footlockers, 776
　garage door openers, 812
　halogen lamps, 791
　heat illness, 497
　hepatitis, 620
　hidden allergens, 518
　hives, 624
　honey danger, 55
　iron supplements, 561
　lawn/garden products, 816
　lice shampoo, 610
　medications, 536, 542, 558
　mumps, 636
　overheated bottles, 30
　pain relievers, 587, 710
　pertussis, 638
　poisonous plants, 814
　potty seats, 266
　rehydration liquids, 581
　rubella during pregnancy, 607
　sandboxes, 815
　shrimp safety, 604
　sickle cell disease, 742
　skin irritation, 582
　sleep apnea, 638
　sleep positions, 41
　sound levels, 612
　sponges, 832
　strollers, 17
　sunscreen, 495
　table safety, 784
　talc use, 34
　teething, 121
　ticks, 499
　tool safety, 813
　whooping cough, 638
Allergies, 29, 57, 72, 73, 553–9, 576
　to animals, 555–6
　antibiotic, 540–1
　in autism, 752
　and breast-feeding, 24
　causes, 553
　diagnosing, 554
　eggs, 507
　emergency treatment, 666
　environmental, 556–9
　food, 55, 118, 515–20
　hereditary, 515, 553
　and hives, 624
　injections for, 558
　medications, 558
　reducing risk of, 55
　seasonal, 559
　severe, 554
　sudden-onset, 554
Amblyopia, 535, 592, 596
Anemia, 559–61, 629.
　　See also Sickle cell disease
　causes, 560
　sickle-cell, 602
　symptoms, 560
　treatments, 560–1
Anesthesia, 532–3
　in circumcision, 4–5
"Angel kisses," 58
Anger, 311–12, 401–2
Antibiotics, 539–41, 583, 585, 587, 627, 657
Anticipation, 127, 140
Antihistamines, 542, 558, 571, 576, 582, 637
Ants, red, 668
Anxiety, 108, 186
　separation, 207, 235–6, 378, 409, 427
　sources of, 246
　stranger, 152, 153, 244
Apgar test, 53
Apnea, sleep, 57, 561–2, 638
　causes, 561
　symptoms, 561–2
　treatment, 562
Appendicitis, 562–3
　causes, 562
　symptoms, 563
　treatment, 563
Appetite
　decrease, 60, 180
　regulating, 181
Appliances, childproofing, 781, 791–2
Arrhythmia, 614–15
Art, 323–4
Arthritis, 528
　juvenile rheumatoid, 722–5
Asbestos, 796–7
Aspirin, 536, 710
　baby, 539
Asthma, 57, 534, 576, 707–12
　activity with, 711
　diagnosis, 708–11
　reducing risks of, 54
　triggers, 710
　types, 708
Astigmatism, 592–3, 596, 758
Atherosclerosis, 509
Atrial septal defect, 729
Attention deficit disorder, 426, 563–8
　causes, 564–5
　diagnosing, 565
　diet in, 567–8

symptoms, 564
treatment, 566–7
Attention span, 174, 301
for reading, 253
Au pairs, 373–4
Authority, questioning, 304
Autism, 717, 751–2
Autonomy, 189, 206

## B

Babysitters. *See* Childcare
Back injuries, 667
Balancing, 224
Balconies, childproofing, 809–10
Bandages, 48
Barbecue areas, childproofing,
808–9
*Bartonella henselae*, 572
Bassinets, 8
Bathing
during colds, 61
cross-gender, 230
encouraging, 481–2
frequency, 45, 481
immersion baths, 44
infants, 13–14, 42–6
newborns, 13–14
with parents, 44–5, 230
safety, 769–71, 832–4
siblings, 448–9
sponge baths, 42, 43, 44, 601
supplies, 13–14
thermometers, 14
toys for, 482
warm towels, 45
water temperature, 43
whirlpool baths, 770
Beds and bedding, 8–10
adult-size, 765
bunk, 765–6
cribs, 763–4
safety, 117, 763–8
toddler, 189–91, 764–5
Bedtime
night-lights, 492
power struggles, 225–6
rituals, 40
routines, 384–5, 491
schedules, 163–5
snacks, 164
Bed wetting, 266, 269–71
Bees, 498, 668, 669

Behavior
aggressive, 393–4, 396
anticipating consequences
of, 211
antisocial, 409
attention-getting, 171, 242,
394–5
change in, 548, 574, 644, 652
destructive, 398
inappropriate, 751
modeling, 314, 392, 452
negative, 168
overreacting to, 395–6
positive, 383–8
reckless, 301, 302
in school, 425–6
social, 406
stereotypical, 290
and timing, 382
unacceptable, 388–403
understanding, 381–3
Benadryl, 571, 573
Bilirubin, 70
Biofeedback, 528
Birth defects and injuries
celiac disease, 733
cerebral palsy, 746–8
chromosomal abnormalities,
743–6
cleft palate, 726–8
clubfoot, 728–9
congenital heart defects, 729–31
cystic fibrosis, 734–6
hemophilia, 739–40
Hirschsprung's disease, 731
hydrocephalus, 732
malformations present at birth,
726–33
metabolic defects, 733–43
muscular dystrophy, 736–8
perinatal damage, 746–8
phenylketonuria, 738
sickle cell disease, 741–3
spina bifida, 731–3
von Willebrand's disease, 740–1
Birthmarks, 58–9
Birth order, 213, 440–2
Bites
animal, 667–9
emergency treatment, 667–9
human, 667, 669
insect, 498, 499, 668, 669
Biting, 394–5

Bleeding, emergency treatment,
669–71
Blepharitis, 593
Blisters, 579, 671
Blood disorders
hemophilia, 739–40
sickle cell disease, 741–3
von Willebrand's disease, 740–1
Blood pressure, 625–6
Bonding, 87–8, 97
with fathers, 110, 168, 208–9
siblings, 434
Bones
emergency treatment, 671–3
fractures, 530
injuries to, 671–3
Boredom, 124
*Borrelia burgdorferi*, 631
Bottle-feeding, 2–3, 28–31
bottle temperature, 30
microwave use for, 30–1
nighttime, 31
positions, 29
schedules, 28
supplies, 11
Botulism, 604
Boundaries
exceeding, 305
setting, 171, 184, 229
sexual, 229
testing, 207
Bowel habits, 549
Bowel movements
newborn, 34
Bowlegs, 161, 568
Bragging, 307
Brain
connections, 112–13
damage, 599
development, 157
and epilepsy, 717
growth, 112–13
inflammation, 589–90
injury, 706–7
neural connections in, 157
power, 157–9
Breast-feeding, 2–3, 21–7, 116
and allergies, 24
colostrum, 22
discomfort in, 3, 27
feeding positions, 25
"first milk," 22
food avoidance in, 24

Breast-feeding, *cont.*
  and immunity to disease, 54, 55
  and jaundice, 69
  latching-on, 22, 27
  milk production in, 24, 25, 26
  premature babies, 96–7
  schedules, 23–4
  supplies, 11
Breath-holding, 399
Breathing
  difficulty, 60, 549, 551, 574,
    674–8
  emergency treatment, 674–8
  labored, 574
  mouth, 551, 552
  rescue, 674–8
Bronchiolitis, 568–9, 575
Bronchitis, 569–70
Bronchodilators, 711
Bruising, 570
Bumper pads, 10
Burns, 678–82
  chemical, 678, 680
  contact, 680
  electrical, 678
  emergency treatment, 678–82
  fire-caused, 680
  friction, 680
  infected, 679
Burping, 30–1

**C**

Caffeine, 519
Calcium, 514
Calories, 503–6
Cancer, 712–14
  leukemia, 570, 599, 713
Candida, 38
Candidiasis, 721
Canker sores, 570–1
Carbohydrates, refined, 520
Carbon monoxide, 798
Cardiopulmonary resuscitation,
  675–6, 684, 686
Carriers
  front, 15, 51, 87
  infant, 15
  sling, 87
Cars, leaving children in, 52
Car seats, 15, 838–41
  convertible models, 15
Cataracts, 66, 535, 596

Cat-scratch disease, 571–2
Cause and effect, 140, 156, 196,
  205, 423
Celiac disease, 733
Cerebral palsy, 717, 746–8
Chairs
  booster, 783–4, 840
  highchairs, 10, 783
  safety, 782
Checkups
  neonatal, 53
  routine, 526–7
  well-baby, 82–4, 161
Chemotherapy, 713
Chicken pox, 546–7, 572–3, 590
Chiggers, 668
Childcare, 368–78
  changing, 375–6
  childcare centers, 370–1
  feelings about, 377
  finding, 368–76
  group, 369–70
  in-home, 372–5
  safety factors, 371
  selection factors, 368–9
  staffing ratios, 370
Childproofing, 131, 166
  bathrooms, 769–71
  bedrooms, 763–8
  homes, 762–95
  indoor play space, 786–9
  kitchens, 777–84
  outdoor areas, 807–17
  playpens, 767
Chiropractors, 528
Chlorpheniramine, 576
Choking, 118, 676–8
Cholesterol, 509
  high, 623–4
Chromosomal abnormalities
  Down syndrome, 742–5
  fragile X syndrome, 745–6
Circumcision, 4–5
  anesthetics for, 4–5
  and diapering, 35
  and toilet training, 265
Cleft palate, 68, 352, 726–8
Climbing, 147, 162, 183, 224
Clinging, 153, 169, 207
*Clostridium botulinum*, 55, 604
*Clostridium perfringens*, 604
*Clostridium tetani*, 655
Clothing

  chewing on, 313
  choosing, 278
  comfortable, 48–9
  differing opinions, 347
  infants, 47–50
  selecting, 48–9, 489
  shoes, 150
  sleepwear, 49
  storage, 50
  washing, 50
Clubfoot, 728–9
Cognitive development
  stimulation for, 94–5
  1 to 2 months, 93–5
  2 to 3 months, 111–14
  4 to 5 months, 127–30
  6 to 7 months, 139–45
  8 to 9 months, 155–9
  10 to 12 months, 172–6
  13 to 18 months, 195–202
  19 to 24 months, 211–18
  in 2 year olds, 249–60
  in 3 year olds, 290–9
  in 4 year olds, 319–26
  in 5 year olds, 351–60
Colds, 573–5
  in infants, 59–61
  symptoms, 59–60
  treatment, 60
  and vitamin C, 575
Cold sores. *See* Herpes virus
Colic, 61–2, 629
  "carry," 61
Color blindness, 594
Colostrum, 22
Communication, 87
  and aggression, 241
  body movement, 206
  conversational, 112, 113, 128,
    144–5, 157, 175, 176
  in divorce, 462–4
  gestural, 172, 173
  increasing, 172
  by signing, 176
  songs, 111
  in stepfamilies, 470–2
  through emotion, 106
  with toddlers, 176
  verbal, 252
Congestion, nasal, 59, 574, 645
Conjunctivitis, 594–5
Conscience, 317–18
Constipation, 62–4, 577–8, 731

Constipation, *cont.*
  chronic, 578, 731
  heredity in, 62
  idiopathic, 577
  recognizing, 63
Convulsions, 57, 549, 688
  emergency treatment, 682
Cooperation, 282
  encouraging, 387–8
  learning, 321
Coordination, 166–7, 224
  eye-hand, 148, 179, 205, 224,
    328, 329, 360, 597
  hand, 302
  large muscle, 224
  motor, 331
  in toddlers, 220, 273
Cortisone, 558
Coughs, 64, 575–6
  nonproductive, 575–6
  productive, 576
  suppressants, 576
  and teething, 121
Counting, 319
Coxsackie virus, 578–9
Cradle cap, 72
Cradles, 8
Craniosynostosis, 103
Crawling, 116, 133, 150–1, 177, 178
  sit-down, 151
Creativity, 213, 277, 302, 323–4,
  354, 406
  encouraging, 254–7
Cribs, 8–9
  mobiles, 18
  portable, 10
Croup, 579
Crying, 95, 168
  allowing, 120
  and colic, 60
  newborns, 91
*Cryptosporidium*, 804
Curiosity, 211, 226, 291
  anatomical, 228–9
  sexual, 228, 229
Cursing, 395–6
Cuts and scrapes, 670
Cyanosis, 730
Cystic fibrosis, 57, 633, 734–6
Cystitis, 657, 658
Cysts, mouth, 71
Cytomegalovirus, 721

**D**
Dairy products, 507, 518
Dancing, 205–6
Dawdling, 389–90
Death, 464–5
  books on, 350
  discussing, 349–50
  and spirituality, 349–50
Decision-making, 192
Decks, childproofing, 809–10
Decongestants, 576
Defiance, 231, 232, 335, 396–8, 409
Dehydration, 21, 52, 67, 579–81
  in infants, 64–5
Dental care, 486–9, 533–4.
  *See also* Teeth and teething
  with arthritis, 725
  infant, 46
Depression, 90, 748–9
Dermatitis, 581–3
  atopic, 72, 581–2
  contact, 581, 582
  seborrheic, 38, 72
Development
  brain, 157
  cognitive, 93–5, 111–14, 127–30,
    139–45, 155–9, 172–6,
    195–202, 211–18, 249–60,
    290–9, 319–26, 351–60
  comparisons, 135
  conscience, 317–18
  coordination, 166–7
  delays in, 103
  and discipline, 383
  emotional, 85–93, 106–10,
    123–7, 136–9, 152–4, 167–71,
    185–95, 230–49, 276–90,
    304–18, 335–51, 422
  friendships, 170–1
  individual rates, 134, 135
  language, 104–5, 139, 144–5,
    197–9, 211, 214, 251, 325–6,
    419
  milestones, 134, 136, 178, 211
  motor, 101, 163
  muscle, 132
  neuromuscular, 160
  physical, 77–80, 101–6, 115–30,
    131–45, 147–51, 160–7,
    177–85, 204–6, 220–30, 301–3,
    328–35
  relationships, 106–7, 123, 136–7,
    153, 168–9, 186–7, 207, 231–2,
    277, 305

social, 107, 113
speech, 104–5
Diabetes
  hereditary, 714
  juvenile, 57, 714–17
  type 1, 714–17
  type 2, 717
Diapers, 32–8
  and circumcision, 35
  cleaning, 35
  cloth, 7, 12, 34–5
  disposable, 7, 11–12, 34
  gender differences, 35–6
  normal contents, 34
  for older babies, 167
Diarrhea, 583–4
  causes, 65
  and diaper rash, 38
  in infants, 65–6
  and milk, 584
  newborn, 34
Diet and nutrition, 500–20
  in arthritis, 725
  and attention deficit disorder,
    567–8
  and cystic fibrosis, 736
  for epileptic children, 719
  food groups, 506–7
  in phenylketonuria, 737–8
  preschoolers, 505–6
  toddlers, 503–4
  vegetarian, 508
  vitamins and minerals, 508–9,
    512–14
Diphtheria, 543–4, 584–5
Directions, following, 250
Disabilities, accident-related,
  706–7
Discipline, 379–403
  and child's temperament, 382
  and developmental stage, 383
  and parenting styles, 379–80
  sharing, 380–1
  and single parenting, 456
  with special-needs children, 704
  in stepfamilies, 474
  strategies, 400–1
  time-outs, 400–1
  toddlers, 171
  understanding, 379–83
  verbal correction, 400
Dislocations, 585, 672
Divorce, 459–64

Down syndrome, 68, 569, 742–5
Drawing, 211
Dressing
  independently, 275–6
  infants, 47–50
  routines, 489–90
  seasonal, 494–6
  self, 220–1, 273, 302
  for summer, 52
  for winter, 52
Drooling, 116
  and teething, 121, 122
Drowning (near drowning), 682–3
Dust mites, 556, 557, 774

E

E. coli, 604, 658, 659, 804, 806, 827
Ear(s), 484–5
  cleaning, 484
  drops, 538
  infections, 2, 54, 65, 66, 574,
    583, 585–9
  injuries to, 683–4
  piercing, 484–5
  tubes, 588
  washing, 45
  wax, 484
Eating. See also Feeding
  dilemmas, 502
  family meals, 502
  good habits, 180–3
  healthy, 500
  lack of interest in, 180
  patterns, 160
  picky, 501
Eczema, 72, 73, 581–3
  and circumcision, 4
Education
  early, 404–29
  for hearing impaired, 757
  kindergarten, 417–29
  readiness for, 407–9
  special, 754
  Title V programs, 701
  waiting to begin, 408–9
Egocentrism, 206
Electrical shock, 684
Electrolyte replacement solution,
  65, 542
Emergencies
  blue coloration, 56
  epiglottitis, 590–1

first aid in, 664–97
food poisoning, 605
meningitis, 634–5
preparedness for, 664–5
pyloric stenosis, 57, 74
Emergency room, 528–9
Emotional development
  1 to 2 months, 85–93
  2 to 3 months, 106–10
  4 to 5 months, 123–7
  6 to 7 months, 136–9
  8 to 9 months, 152–4
  10 to 12 months, 167–71
  13 to 18 months, 185–95
  19 to 24 months, 206–10
  in 2 year olds, 230–49
  in 3 year olds, 276–90
  in 4 year olds, 304–18
  in 5 year olds, 335–51
Emotional disorders, 748–52
  autism, 750–2
  depression, 748–9
  obsessive-compulsive disorder,
    749–50
  pervasive developmental delay,
    751–2
Empathy, 201, 276, 305, 310, 318
  encouraging, 236
Encephalitis, 589–90
  primary, 590
  secondary, 590
  viral, 640–2
Endocarditis, 731
Epiglottitis, 590–1
Epilepsy, 717–20
  managing, 719–20
  seizures in, 717–19
Esophageal reflux, 55, 74
Exercise, 493
  for arthritis, 724, 725
  and cystic fibrosis, 736
  stress-relieving, 654
Expectorants, 576
Experimentation, 141, 321
Exploration, 142–3, 166
Extroversion, 337–8
Eye(s). See also Vision
  blow to, 685
  care of, 534–6
  chemicals in, 685
  color, 83, 116
  conditions, 66–7
  drops, 538, 539

focus, 66
foreign objects, 685
infections, 67
injuries, 684–5
"lazy." See Amblyopia
problems, 535, 591–8
wandering, 67. See Strabismus
yellowing, 57, 69–70, 549

F

Fainting, 598, 686
Fairness, 317
Family
  birth order of children, 213,
    440–2
  grandparents, 126–7, 336, 366
  impact of adoption on, 366
  only children in, 452
  planning, 436–40
  preparation for new siblings in,
    442–5
  relationships, 250, 336
  siblings, 336, 430–5, 436–52
  spacing children in, 436–40
  stepfamilies, 466–76
Fantasy, 214–15, 291
  play, 308
Farsightedness, 595
Fats, 509
Fear
  of the dark, 231, 280
  of death, 279, 350
  exploring, 193
  of falling, 19, 85
  of Halloween, 281
  in infancy, 19, 85, 124–5, 151
  introducing, 193
  lack of, 166, 184
  in preschoolers, 279–81
  respect for, 193
  of school, 426–7
  school bus, 429
  of separation, 225–6, 244,
    415–16, 419
  of storms, 231, 280
  of strangers, 244
  in toddlers, 191–4, 225–6, 244–5,
    279–81
  of unknown, 191, 192, 279
  of walking, 151
Feeding
  bottle, 2–3, 11, 28–31

breast, 2–3, 11, 21–7
 diabetic children, 716–17
 drinking from cups, 149–50
 and ear infections, 2, 29
 formula, 2, 3, 28, 29
 infant, 10–11
 newborns, 2–3
 nighttime, 31, 119–20
 positions, 25
 preschoolers, 505–6
 self, 132, 133, 148, 220–1, 302
 sleep during, 31
 solids, 102, 116, 118–21
 and sudden infant death syndrome, 2
 supplies, 10–11
 toddlers, 503–4
 with utensils, 302
 water, 30
Feet
 clubfoot, 728–9
 flat, 150, 603
 orthotics for, 603
Fever, 57, 67–8, 598–602
Fibbing. *See* Lying
Fifth disease, 602
Fire safety, 858–61
First aid, 664–97
 allergies, 666
 back injuries, 667
 bites and stings, 667–9
 bleeding, 669–71
 blisters, 671
 bone and joint injuries, 671–3
 breathing difficulties, 674–8
 burns, 678–82
 choking, 676–8
 convulsions, 682
 drowning/near drowning, 682–3
 ear injuries, 683–4
 electrical shock, 684
 eye injuries, 685
 fainting, 686
 finger injuries, 687
 frostbite, 686
 hand injuries, 687
 head injuries, 687–8
 heat exhaustion/cramps, 688–9
 heat rash, 689–90
 heat stroke, 690
 kits, 697
 knocked-out teeth, 691
 mouth injuries, 690–1

 neck injuries, 687–8
 nose injury, 692
 poisoning, 693–4
 seizures, 682
 shock, 695–6
 splinters, 696
 split lip, 691
 sprains, 671–3
 sunstroke, 690
 tongue injury, 691
Flatulence, 606
Fleas, 481, 637, 668
Flu. *See* Influenza
Flukes, freshwater, 668
Fluoride, 488
Folic acid, 513, 742
Fontanels, 20–1, 57, 101, 549
 fused, 103
Food. *See also* Diet and Nutrition
 allergies, 118, 515–20
 bedtime snacks, 164
 canned, 828, 831
 cereals, 118
 commercial baby, 119
 finger, 118
 groups, 506–7
 juices, 120
 lean substitutes, 511
 pesticides in, 828
 poisoning, 603–5, 661, 827
 portions, 180
 preferences, 160, 182–3
 safety, 825–31
 snacks, 180
 solid, 102, 116, 118–21
 storage and handling, 119,
  825–31
 trying new, 180
 vegetarian, 508
Formaldehyde, 799
Fragile X syndrome, 745–6
Freezers, childproofing, 780–1
Friendships and friends, 170–1,
  242–4, 336
 best, 346
 disagreements between, 345–6
 imaginary, 285, 291
 making, 305–6
 parental, 110
 preschoolers, 305–6, 344–5
 school parents, 428
 toddlers, 282–6, 305–6
Frostbite, 494, 496, 686

Fruits and vegetables, 506
Frustration, 124–5, 168, 186, 192,
  231, 232, 242, 281–2, 339, 341–2
Furniture, infant, 8–9

**G**

Games
 artistic, 258
 balance, 184
 ball, 224
 board, 353
 body, 143
 climbing, 183
 conversational, 127–8
 copying, 184
 counting, 174, 259
 cycling, 223
 dancing, 114
 dropping, 175
 fine-motor, 274–5
 group, 183
 hiding, 174, 184
 imitative, 174, 221
 interactive, 107, 114, 128, 143
 marching, 206
 mirror, 114
 musical chairs, 206
 outdoor, 183
 repetitive, 175, 200
 rhyming, 296
 singing, 114, 143
 sorting, 155
 stacking, 178
 thinking, 216
 throwing and catching, 183
 toddler, 175–6, 183–5, 257–8
 for 2 to 3 month olds, 107, 114
 for 6 to 7 months, 143
 water, 175, 201, 224
 word, 215–16
Garages, childproofing, 811–13
Gardens, childproofing, 813–15
Gassiness, 61, 606, 736
Gender
 identity, 228
 play, 309–10
 roles, 290
 skill differences, 273
 toddler's understanding of,
  194–5
 and toys, 201–2

Genitals
  inflammed, 660–1
  interest in, 133–4, 304–5
  play with, 304–5
  tenderness, 549
  touching, 227
Gestures, 107
*Giardia lamblia*, 804
Giardiasis, 607
Glasses, 535–6
Glaucoma, 66, 535, 596, 758
Gluten, 733
Grains, 506
Grandparents, 126–7, 336, 366
Grasping, 113, 140, 142, 179
  pincer, 142
Gratification, delaying, 386–7
Grief, 350
Grooming
  baby hair, 46
  infants, 14
  toddler, 221
Growing pains, 607–8
Growth
  bone, 151
  charts, 84, 617
  cognitive, 250
  differing rates of, 222
  emotional, 306
  intellectual, 293, 306
  measuring, 222–3
  steady, 178
Guaifenesin, 576
Guilt, 154
Gyms
  baby, 18
  play, 102

# H

Hair, 101
  birth, 132
  care, 482–4
  first cutting, 135
  grooming, 46
  infant care, 45–6
  lanugo, 77
  ornaments, 46
  tangles, 483
  twirling, 312, 313
  washing, 45–6
Haircuts, 135, 483–4
Hand

  injuries, 687
  preference, 172, 302–3, 328
  washing, 478–9
Hand-foot-and-mouth disease.
  *See* Coxsackie virus
Havrix, 620
Hay fever, 559
Head
  banging, 138, 313
  circumference, 82–4
  injuries, 687–8
  lice, 480, 609–10
  lifting, 101, 116
Headaches, 608–9
  migraine, 528, 608–9
Health
  bathing, 481–2
  dental care, 486–9
  ear care, 484–5
  exercise, 493
  habits, 478–99
  hair care, 482–4
  hand washing, 478–9
  nail care, 485–6
  seasonal concerns, 494–9
  sleep needs, 490–1
  supplies, 14
Hearing
  checks, 68–9, 301
  concerns, 68–9, 610–13
  in infants, 68–9, 79, 104
  loss, 105, 352, 610–11, 754–7
  problems, 57, 252, 754–7
  and pronunciation, 252
  vocabulary, 173, 177
Heart
  atrial septal defect, 729
  conditions, 613–15
  congenital defects, 729–31
  disease, 509–10
  murmurs, 613–14
  ventricular septal defect,
    729–30, 731
Heat
  cramps, 689
  exhaustion, 496, 598, 688–9
  prickly, 73
  rashes, 73, 689–90
  stroke, 67, 690
Height, 82–3, 135, 161, 182, 220,
  301, 615–17
  measuring, 222–3
  predicting, 222

Heimlich maneuver, 677–8
Hematuria, 618
Hemophilia, 739–40
*Hemophilus influenzae*, 591
Hepatitis, 545–6, 604, 618–20
Herbalism, 528
Heredity
  and allergies, 553
  and constipation, 62, 577
  and diabetes, 714
  in hemophilia, 739
  and sensitivity, 310
Hermangiomas, 58
Hernia, 57
  infant, 624–5
  inguinal, 620
Herpes virus, 572, 590, 621–2, 647
Hiccups, 69, 622
Highchairs, 783
Hirschsprung's disease, 62, 577,
  731
Hitting, 394–5
HIV. *See* AIDS
Hives, 624
Hormones, 89
Hornets, 668
Horsefly, 668
Hospital visits, 530–3
Humidifiers
  cool-mist, 14, 60, 569, 794, 806
  ultrasonic, 794, 806
  warm-mist, 793
Humor, 128, 143, 215, 352–3
Hydrocele, 624–5
Hydrocephalus, 732
Hydrophobia, 640–2
Hygiene
  bathing, 481–2
  dental care, 486–9
  ear care, 484–5
  hand washing, 478–9
  nail care, 485–6
  nose blowing, 479–80
  practices, 478–81
Hyperactivity, 565, 750. *See also*
    Attention deficit disorder
  and sugar, 520
Hyperopia, 595
Hypertension, 625–6
Hyperthyroidism, 599
Hypothyroidism, 62, 577, 578

# I

Ibuprofen, 539, 542, 652, 710
Identity
    gender, 228
    sense of, 170, 213
    sexual, 290
Illness, acquired, 707–25
Illness, chronic, 707–25
Imagination, 214–15, 277, 291, 294–6
Imitation, 196
Immune system, 53, 56, 515, 553, 722
Immunity
    in adopted infants, 363–4
    and breast-feeding, 2
    to illnesses, 480
Immunizations, 526, 527, 543–7
    chicken pox, 546–7
    DTaP, 543–4, 585, 655
    free, 544
    Haemophilus B, 546
    Hepatitis B, 545–6
    MMR, 545
    polio, 544–5
    questions on, 543–4
Impetigo, 626
Inattentiveness, 389–90
Independence, 185, 189, 191, 203, 206
    drive for, 207
    encouraging, 232, 277–8
    increasing, 407
    teaching, 214, 245
    testing, 304
Infalyte, 580
Infants
    abilities and knowledge, 78, 101–2, 111, 116–17, 132–3, 139–40, 147–8, 155–6, 161–2, 172–3
    adjustment to, 86–8
    adopted, 362–3
    bathing, 13–14, 42–6
    beds and bedding for, 8–10
    bed sharing, 41
    bedtime, 40
    birthmarks in, 58–9
    caring for, 19–52
    cognitive development, 93–5, 111–14, 127–30, 139–45, 155–9, 172–6
    colds in, 59–61

colic in, 61–2
constipation in, 62–4
diapering, 7, 11–13
emotional development, 85–93, 106–10, 123–7, 136–9, 152–4, 167–71
facial expressions, 77
fears in, 19, 85, 124–5, 151
feeding, 10–11
feelings in, 85, 106–7, 123–4, 136–9, 152, 168
fussy, 91–3
growth spurts, 24
health, 53–74
hearing in, 68–9, 79
holding, 19–21
jaundice in, 69–71
massage for, 81–2, 97
naps, 39, 40–1
newborn, 1–74
outings, 50–1
people preferences in, 154
physical development, 77–80, 101–6, 115–30, 131–45, 147–51, 160–7
preferences in, 21
premature, 96–9
shoes for, 49
skin conditions, 71–3
sleep needs, 41–2
sleep patterns, 38–42
smell sense in, 80
smiles, 78
social development, 107, 113
sun protection for, 52
supplies for, 7–19
talking to, 87
taste sense in, 80
vision in, 79–80
vitamins, 23
vomiting in, 74
Infections
    bacterial, 67, 584–5, 586, 599, 626, 627, 648–9, 653, 656–7, 721
    cytomegalovirus, 721
    ear, 2, 54, 66, 551, 574, 583, 585–9
    eye, 67
    gastrointestinal, 661
    intrauterine, 68
    mouth, 721
    opportunistic, 721

oral, 73–4
pneumocystis carinii pneumonia, 721
skin, 626
upper respiratory, 575
urinary tract, 65, 265, 618, 658–60
vaginal, 660–1
viral, 67, 586, 599, 618–20, 627, 643
yeast, 38, 721
Influenza, 575, 627–8
Inoculations, 527, 543–7
Insects, 808
    bites, 498, 499, 669
    in ears, 683
    repellents, 498, 499
Insecurity, 231
Insulin, 714
Intelligence, 354
    bodily-kinesthetic, 355
    and breast-feeding, 2
    interpersonal, 354
    intrapersonal, 355
    linguistic, 354
    logico-mathematical, 354–5
    and muscular dystrophy, 736
    musical, 354
    spatial, 355
    understanding, 292–4
Interaction
    in infants, 123
    observation of, 211
    for reinforcement of concepts, 141
    social, 211
    thought/muscle, 113
    verbal, 113
Interrupting, 392
Intoeing, 638
Introversion, 337–8
Iodine, 514
Ipecac, 542
Iridocyclitis, 724
Iron, 514


# J

Jaundice, 57, 549, 619, 628
    abnormal, 71
    benign, 69
    causes, 69
    in infants, 69–71
    physiologic, 69

Jealousy, 186
Joint Commission on Accreditation of Health-Care Organizations, 6
Juice, 181–2
Juvenile rheumatoid arthritis, 722–5

## K

Kawasaki syndrome, 832
Kindergarten, 417–29
    readiness for, 418–21
Kindness, 305
Knock-knees, 568

## L

Labial adhesions, 628–9
Labyrinthitis. *See* Ear; infections
Lactose intolerance, 65, 517–18, 583, 733
La Leche League, 23, 25–6
Language
    babbling, 127, 144–5, 173, 217–18
    baby signs, 176
    body, 156, 187
    concepts, 359
    delays, 296–7
    development, 104–5, 139, 197–9, 211, 214, 251–2, 325–6, 419
    exploration of, 198
    inappropriate, 395–6
    learning, 141, 215–16, 325–6, 407
    mimicry, 127, 157, 170
    oral, 422
    pronunciation, 319
    putting thoughts into, 250
    rhythm of, 216
    second, 158–9, 288
    sentences, 211, 319
    sign, 114, 176
    skills, 217–18, 406, 422
    social, 156
    socially appropriate, 229
    spoken, 157
    talking, 217–18
    understanding of, 144–5
    vocabulary, 177
    vocalizing, 116, 139
Lanugo, 77
Laundry room, childproofing, 785–6

Layettes, 7, 8
Lead, 800–2
    and constipation, 62, 577
    poisoning, 62, 479, 577, 629–31, 801–2
Learning
    about differences, 288–9
    academic, 422–3
    to anticipate, 127, 140
    cooperation, 321
    difficulties, 629
    disabilities, 328
    by doing, 212
    by experience, 211, 319–20
    by experimentation, 141, 156, 196
    by exploration, 142–3, 166, 211, 319–20
    free-form opportunities, 320
    good sportsmanship, 331, 333
    language, 141, 215–16, 325–6, 407
    and listening, 94, 111
    manners, 314–17
    math, 258–9, 321–3
    mental processes in, 250
    mouthing objects, 129, 140
    by object manipulation, 196–7
    by observation, 111, 128, 173
    practice, 127–8
    problem-solving, 196
    reinforcement, 174
    rote, 293
    science, 321–3
    sensual, 196, 199
    to share, 236–8, 283–4
    step-by-step, 187
    stimulation for, 94–5, 292
    styles, 250, 293, 354–6
    through conflict, 406
    through play, 320
    through questions, 407
    through senses, 94
    tolerance, 289, 348
    trial-and-error, 179, 212
Leukemia, 570, 599
    acute lymphocytic, 713
Lice, head, 480, 609–10
Limits
    desire for, 305
    setting, 379–403
Lisping, 352
Listening skills, 94, 111, 358–9, 407

Liver disease, 69–70
Lockjaw. *See* Tetanus
Loneliness, 285–6
Lying, 317, 318, 390–1
Lyme disease, 499, 631–2

## M

Magnesium, 514
Make-believe, 214–15
Malabsorption, 632–3
Manners, 314–17
    table, 315–17
Massage, 97
    infant, 81–2
Mastitis, 27
Maternity leave, 377
Mathematics, 258–9, 321–3, 359, 423
Measles, 545, 590, 633–4
    German. *See* Rubella
Meat, poultry, fish, and eggs, 507
Medicaid, 701
Medical care, 521–42
    alternative, 528
    emergency room, 528–9
    hospital visits, 530–3
    medical history, 521–4
    X-rays, 529–30
Medications, 536–42
    administration, 537–9, 540
    AIDS, 721
    allergy, 558
    antianxiety, 749
    antibiotics, 65, 539–41, 583, 585, 587
    anticonvulsant, 719
    antidepressant, 749
    antifungal, 74
    anti-inflammatory, 710, 724–5
    anti-seizure, 65, 583
    arthritis, 724–5
    in attention deficit disorder, 566
    children's, 537
    doses, 536
    elixirs, 537
    expectorant, 576
    first aid, 697
    for heart problems, 730
    herbal, 528
    interactions, 497
    liquid, 537–8
    overdose, 536

over-the-counter, 536, 576
for premature babies, 97–8
prescription, 536
safety, 770–1
sickle cell, 742
storage, 541–2
suspension, 537
syrups, 537
Memory, 140, 174
retention, 172
Meningitis, 634–5, 649
bacterial, 68, 634
viral, 634
Mental illness, 748–52
Mental retardation, 733, 738, 743, 745–6, 752–4
Messiness, 199
Metabolic defects, 733–43
celiac disease, 733
cystic fibrosis, 734–6
phenylketonuria, 738–9
Microcephaly, 103
Microwave ovens, childproofing, 780
Migraine headaches, 528
Milia, 72
Milk, 29
Mirrors, safety, 18
Misbehavior
limiting, 388–403
responding to, 388–93
understanding, 381–3
Mites, 668
Mobiles, crib, 18
Mobility
climbing, 147, 162, 183, 224
crawling, 133, 150–1, 177, 178
running, 204, 224
squirming, 133
stances, 161
standing, 133, 134, 161–2
walking, 149–51, 162, 177, 178
Modesty, 230, 352
Mold, 556, 557–8, 805–6
Moles, 59
Mongolian spots, 58
Mononucleosis, 635
Moods, 167, 168
Morality, 317, 347
Mosquitoes, 668
Motion sickness, 635–6
Mouth
blisters, 579

canker sores, 570–1
cysts, 71
infections, 73–4, 721
injuries, 690–1
patches, 73
Mouthing objects, 129, 140
Mucus
in eyes, 67
nasal, 60
Multiples, 430–5
bonds between, 434
differing personalities in, 432
equipment and supplies for, 430–1
individuality development, 432–3
Mumps, 545, 590, 636–7
Muscular dystrophy, 736–8
Becker's, 736
Duchenne, 736, 737
Music, 141, 174–5, 354
bedtime, 165
and movement, 205–6
Myopia, 595–6
Myringotomy, 588

N
Nails
biting, 312, 313
brushing, 485
care of, 485–6
clipping, 14, 46–7, 485
infant, 14, 46–7
products, 485–6
Narcissism, 186
Nasal
congestion, 59, 551, 574, 645
discharge, 574
drops and sprays, 60, 538, 542, 554
injury, 692
Naturalyte, 580
Navels, 32, 77, 103
Nearsightedness, 595–6
Neck injury, 687–8
Negativism, 186
Neural tube defects, 731–3
Neuromuscular disorders, 746–8
Newborns, 1–74
Niacin, 513
Night-lights, 492
Nightmares, 245–6

Night terrors, 246–7
Nosebleed, 692
Nose blowing, 479–80
Novocain, 534
Nursery rhymes, 216–17
Nursery school, 404–17
accomplishments in, 405–6
changed attitudes about, 416–17
evaluating, 411–13
goals in, 406–7
need for, 404–5
reluctance to attend, 416–17
selecting, 410–11
teaching methods in, 410–13
Nursing, 2, 3, 21–7.
See also Breast-feeding
biting while, 122
feeding positions, 25
food avoidance in, 24
schedules, 23–4
Nutrition. See Diet and nutrition

O
Object permanence, 139–40, 155, 195
Obsessive-compulsive disorder, 749–50
Olean, 519
Olestra, 519
Orthotics, 603
Otitis media. See Ear; infections

P
PABA, 495
Pacifiers, 5, 40, 91, 92, 137, 234–5
Pain relievers, 5, 122
Papular urticaria, 637
Parasites, 607, 639, 668
Parents
adjustment to new baby, 86–8
authoritative, 380
bathing with, 44–5
divorced, 459–64
fear of separation, 419
feelings about special-needs children, 699–700
getting sleep, 40
guilt in, 154
handling anger, 401–2
involving both, 90
keeping up old friendships, 110

Parents, *cont.*
  noncustodial, 471
  permissive, 380
  privacy for, 190
  resumption of sexual relations, 112
  single, 453–66
  styles, 213, 379–80
  as teachers, 111
  time for selves, 145, 186, 457, 700–1
  widowed, 464
Parents, single, 86, 453–66
  by choice, 464–6
  dating, 458–9
  and discipline, 456
  scheduling for, 453, 455–6
  support systems for, 457–8
Parents Without Partners, 458
Patience, 153, 386–7
Pedialyte, 65, 580
Penicillin, 584
Penis
  circumcision, 4–5
  erections, 228
  post-circumcision, 35
Perfectionism, 338–9
Perinatal damage, 746–8
Personality. *See also* Temperament
  inborn, 109, 239
  introspective, 213
  understanding, 109
Pertussis, 543–4, 637–8
Pervasive developmental delay, 751–2
Pesticides, 814
  in food, 828
Pets, 54, 88
  illness from, 481
  safe routines, 834–5
  ticks and fleas, 499
Phenylketonuria, 738–9
Phobias, 193
  school, 427–9
Physical development
  coordination, 166–7
  1 to 2 months, 77–80
  2 to 3 months, 101–6
  4 to 5 months, 115–30
  6 to 7 months, 131–45
  8 to 9 months, 147–51
  10 to 12 months, 160–7
  13 to 18 months, 178–85

19 to 24 months, 204–6
  in 2 year olds, 220–30
  in 3 year olds, 273–6
  in 4 year olds, 301–3
  in 5 year olds, 328–35
Physicians, 525
  choosing, 5–6
  well-baby checkups with, 82–4
  when to call, 56–7, 548–50, 576, 579, 599, 608, 650, 661, 692
Pigeon toes, 638
Pillows, 10, 763
Pinching, 394–5
Pink eye. *See* Conjunctivitis
Pinworms, 639
Plants
  common, hazardous, 818
Play. *See also* Games; Toys
  dates, 242–4
  equipment, 221
  exclusionary, 308–9
  fantasy, 214, 291, 308
  gender-neutral, 202
  gender-specific, 309–10
  grown-up, 258
  gyms, 205
  imaginary, 257–8
  imaginative, 215
  joining in, 205, 212, 221
  learning through, 320
  make-believe, 250
  outdoor equipment, 815–17
  parallel, 243
  physical, 221, 223–5
  pretend, 231, 259–60, 262, 308
  safe spaces, 786–9
  solo, 212–14, 393
  styles, 308–10
  superhero, 287
  violent, 286, 393
  water, 224
Playpens, 767
  portable, 10
Pneumocystis carinii
  pneumonia, 721
Pneumonia, 65, 575, 576, 583, 639–40
  bacterial, 640
  viral, 640
Pointing, 147, 173
Poisoning, 693–4
Poison ivy/sumac, 694–5
Polio, 544–5
  vaccine, 35

Pollutants
  air, 851–3
  asbestos, 796–7
  common household, 797, 799–800
  environmental, 850–4
  formaldehyde, 799
  lead, 800–2
  pressurized wood, 803–4
  radon, 802–3
  water, 804–5, 853–4
Port wine stains, 59
Postpartum blues, 88–90
Posture, 220
Potassium, 514
Praise, 169–70, 185, 189, 232, 307, 451
Prams, 16–17
  safety, 836
Prednisone, 588
Prematurity, 96–9
  developmental stages, 98–9
  and hearing, 68
  vision problems in, 758
Preschool, 404–17
  accomplishments in, 405–6
  changed attitudes about, 416–17
  evaluating, 411–13
  goals in, 406–7
  need for, 404–5
  reluctance to attend, 416–17
  selecting, 410–11
  teaching methods in, 410–13
Preschoolers
  abilities and knowledge, 273–4, 291–2, 301–2, 319–20, 329, 351–3
  cognitive development, 290–9, 319–26, 351–60
  diet and nutrition, 505–6
  emotional development, 276–90, 304–18, 335–51
  fears of, 279–81, 415–16
  feelings in, 276–7, 304–6, 335–7
  physical development, 273–6, 301–3, 328–35
  play styles, 308–10
  rejection among, 284–5
Prickly heat, 73
Problem-solving
  learning, 196
  with siblings, 449–51
  skills, 214, 291, 320–1, 423

Protein, 512
Ptosis, 596–7
Punishment, 379
Pyelonephritis, 658, 659
Pyloric stenosis, 57, 74, 640

# R

Rabies, 640–2, 808
Radon, 802–3
Rashes, 642
  diaper, 7, 12, 34, 36–8, 57
  heat, 73, 689–90
  in infants, 71–3
  seborrheic, 38
  yeast, 38, 721
Reading, 87, 142, 148, 174, 252–4,
    294–6, 298–9, 352, 359, 423–5
  early, 424–5
  pre-reading skills, 356–7
  preschooler, 324–5
  readiness, 325
  refusal, 326
  skills, 423
Reflexes, 78
  extrusion, 118
  grasping, 78
  Moro, 78, 93
Refrigerators, childproofing, 780–1
Regression, 247–9, 268–9, 445
Rehabilitation programs, 701
  spinal cord injury, 706–7
Rejection, 284–5
Religion. *See* Spirituality
Resources
  adoption, 367
  AIDS, 721
  alternative medicine, 528
  asbestos removal, 796
  asthma, 712
  attention deficit disorder, 564,
    565, 566
  autism, 751
  birth defects, 728
  bleeding disorders, 739
  brain injuries, 706
  breast-feeding, 23
  cancer, 714
  car seats, 841
  cerebral palsy, 747
  childcare, 376
  choosing a physician, 5
  cleft palate, 727

  congenital heart defects, 730
  cystic fibrosis, 735
  on death, 350, 466
  depression, 749
  diabetes, 716
  Down syndrome, 744
  early education, 421
  emergency treatment, 666
  epilepsy, 720
  fragile X syndrome, 745
  head lice, 609
  hearing impairment, 756
  home-adaptation for special-
    needs children, 707
  hospital visits, 530
  juvenile rheumatoid arthritis,
    723
  lead, 801
  left-handed goods, 303
  Lyme disease, 632
  mental retardation, 753–4
  multiples, 435
  muscular dystrophy, 737
  obsessive-compulsive disorder,
    750
  phenylketonuria, 738
  prematurity, 99
  Ronald McDonald Houses, 700
  sickle cell disease, 741
  single parents, 465
  special education, 699
  special-needs children, 699, 701,
    705
  spina bifida, 732
  spinal cord injuries, 706
  stepfamily, 476
  urinary tract infection, 658
  vision problems, 760
Respiratory syncytial virus, 54,
    642–3
Retinitis pigmentosa, 758
Retinopathy of prematurity, 758
Reye syndrome, 539, 643–4, 652
Rheumatic fever, 644
Rhinitis, 559, 644–5
Riboflavin, 513
*Rickettsia rickettsii*, 646–7
Ring stackers, 155
Ringworm, 645–6
Rocking, 313
Rocky Mountain spotted fever,
    499, 646–7
Rolling over, 148

Rooting, 78
Roseola, 647
Routines
  bedtime, 40, 163–5, 384–5, 491
  consistency in, 164
  daily, 232–6
  dressing, 489–90
  establishing, 105–6, 232–6,
    383–5
  mealtime, 180–3, 383–4
  memorization of, 172
  for multiples, 432
  pedestrian, 837–8
  reversed, 104
  safe, 824–34
  sense of security from, 232–6
  shopping, 844–6
  sleep, 42, 163
  toileting, 261–71
  toy cleanup, 384
Rubella, 68, 545, 590, 606–7
Rubeola, 633–4
Rudeness, 304, 305
Rugs, nonskid, 14
Running, 204, 224

# S

Safety, 761–856
  airplane, 843–4
  appliance, 791–2
  automobile, 52, 838–41
  away from home, 817–18
  with bandages, 48
  barbecue areas, 808–9
  basement, 790
  bathing, 14, 42, 832–4
  bathroom, 769–71
  bedroom, 763–8
  beds and bedding, 8–9, 117
  bike/roller skate, 846–9
  boating, 823
  cleaning routines, 831–2
  with clothing, 49
  cooking/food-handling, 825–31
  deck and balcony, 809–10
  during diapering, 32–3
  doors, 772–3
  ear washing, 45
  electrical, 789–91
  fire, 858–61
  fireplace, 795
  floors, 773–4

Safety, *cont.*
  furnace, 794–5
  with furnishings, 776–7
  garden, 813–15
  gates, 178, 774
  helmets, 848–9
  hot tub, 810–11
  household, 162
  indoor play spaces, 786–9
  kitchen, 777–84
  laundry room, 785–6
  nursery school, 413
  outdoor, 807–17
  pedestrian, 837–8
  pet, 834–5
  play equipment, 815–17
  playground, 855–7
  playpen, 767
  from pollutants, 796–806
  pool, 821–3
  pram, 836
  preschool, 413
  public places, 842–3, 854
  remodeling, 806–7
  sandbox, 815
  school bus, 429
  sense of, 190
  shopping routines, 844–6
  in sports, 332–3
  stairway, 775–6
  stroller, 836
  toddler, 225
  tool, 813
  travel, 819, 835–49
  water, 769–70, 810–11, 819–23
  window, 774–5
  yard, 813–15
Salmonella, 605, 647–8
Scabies, 648
Scalds, 680–1, 783
Scarlatina, 648–9
Scarlet fever, 648–9
Schedules. *See* Routines
School
  achievement, 425
  fears, 426–7
  getting started, 421–5
  kindergarten, 417–29
  problems, 425–6
  readiness for, 418–21
  resistance to, 427
  transitional, 422
School buses, 429
Science, 321–3

Scoliosis, 748
Scrotum, 77
Seats
  car, 15
  portable, 18
Security
  objects, 138–9, 210
  sense of, 85
Sedatives, 532
Seizures, 57, 549
  absence, 718
  atonic, 718
  emergency treatment, 682
  febrile, 598
  grand mal, 717–18
  myoclonic, 718
  partial, 718–19
  petit mal, 718
  tonic-clonic, 717–18
Self
  awareness, 125–6, 136, 177, 185
  concepts, 290
  confidence, 186, 339–41
  consciousness, 275, 428
  discipline, 331, 380
  dressing, 220–1, 273, 302
  esteem, 240, 275, 306–7, 331
  feeding, 148, 220–1, 302
  image, 306, 704
  reliance, 187, 190, 213
  sense of, 154, 250, 278
  stimulation, 229
  sufficiency, 340
  touching, 227
Sensitivity, 168, 310–11
Sensory disorders, 754–60
  hearing impairment, 754–7
  visual impairment, 757–60
Separation, 108, 137
  anxiety, 207, 235–6, 378, 409,
    427
  emotional, 177
  fear of, 225–6, 235–6, 244,
    415–16, 419
  role of, 125–6
Sexuality
  answering questions about, 229
  family nudity, 228
  interest in, 304
  playing doctor, 229
  questions on, 304
  teaching about, 229–30
  toddler, 227–30

Shape sorters, 155
Sharing, 283–4, 406
  among siblings, 448
  battles, 238
  chores, 278, 279
  concept of, 209
  meaning of, 236–8
  practice in, 279
  readiness for, 231, 236
  resistance to, 237
  understanding, 209
Shock, 695–6
  electrical, 684, 770
Shoes, 150
  for infants, 49
  selecting, 490
  tying, 302, 329
Showing off, 334–5
Shyness, 136, 153, 239–41
  inherited, 239
  and school, 409–10
Siblings, 336, 430–5, 436–52
  bathing together, 448–9
  disagreements among, 449–52
  introduction of new, 443–5
  preparation for additional,
    442–5
  relationships, 445–6
  sharing among, 448
  spacing, 436–40
  and special-needs children,
    702–3
  in stepfamilies, 475–6
Sink liners, 14
Sinusitis, 649–50
Skills
  academic, 407, 408, 420
  classification, 423
  climbing, 179
  cognitive, 93–5, 111–14, 127–30,
    139–45, 155–9, 172–6, 203,
    249, 290–9, 319–26, 351–60
  communication, 319
  comparison, 423
  conversation, 296
  dexterity, 179, 225
  eye-hand, 148, 179, 205, 224
  fine motor, 118, 131, 162, 179,
    204–5, 220–1, 273, 274–5,
    301, 328
  grasping, 113, 140, 142, 179
  gross motor, 131, 134, 178, 204,
    206, 220, 328

language, 144–5, 217–18, 250, 406, 407
large-muscle coordination, 224
listening, 358–9, 407
math, 423
motor, 160, 419
negotiating, 278–9
oral language, 422
perceptual, 419, 422
physical, 187
pre-reading, 356–7
problem-solving, 214, 291, 320–1, 423, 452
reading, 423
sequencing, 423
showing off, 334–5
social, 172, 236, 331, 354, 406, 419, 420, 422
thinking, 216
verbal, 172, 241, 409
writing, 423
Skin
blemishes, 77
care in infants, 45
conditions, 57, 71–3. *See also* Rashes
facial, 77
infections, 626
lotion, 45
paleness, 549
peeling, 73
sunscreen for, 52
winter protection, 52
yellowing, 57, 69–71
Sleeping
naps, 39, 40–1
need for, 490–1
newborn patterns, 38–42
nightmares, 245–6
resistance to, 163
in stroller, 165
through night, 39–40, 119–20
toddler naps, 185
Sleepovers, 340–1
Sleepwear, 49, 490
flame-retardant, 50, 490
Smoking
and asthma, 54
and ear infection, 54
and sudden infant death, 55–6
Snoring, 650
Socialization, 123–4, 240
Social Security Disability

Insurance, 701
"Soft spot." *See* Fontanel
Sore throat, 551, 650–1
Spatial concepts, 142, 360
Special-needs children, 698–760
coping skills development, 704
disciplining, 704
reinforcement for, 704
and siblings, 702–3
Speech
babbling, 127, 173, 217–18
comprehension, 172
development, 104–5, 197–9
evaluation, 296
infant, 104
lisping, 352
mimicry, 127, 157, 170
nasal, 551
pronunciation, 319
razzing, 128
sentences, 211, 319
stuttering, 297–8
talking, 217–18
vocalizing, 116, 139
Spina bifida, 731–3
types, 732
Spinal cord injury, 706–7
Spirituality
beginning, 347–51
and tolerance, 348
Splinters, 696
Sports, 301, 354
and coordination, 331
good sportsmanship, 331, 333
gymnastics, 332
organized, 332
safety, 332–3
for 5 year olds, 331–4
Sprains, 671–3
SSDI. *See* Social Security Disability Insurance
SSI. *See* Supplemental Security Income
Stairs, 162
*Staphylococcus aureus,* 605
Stepfamilies, 466–76
blending lifestyles in, 472–3
discipline in, 474
forming relationships in, 466–8
new babies in, 475–6
siblings in, 475–6
Stomach ache, 651–3
"Stork bites," 58

Stoves, childproofing, 779–80
Strabismus, 535, 597, 748, 758
Strangers
anxiety over, 152, 153
fear of, 244
Strawberry marks, 58
Strep throat, 653
*Streptococcus mutans,* 486
Stress, 528, 598, 654
physical symptoms, 342
relieving, 312–14, 342–4
Strollers, 16–17
fold-up, 17
safety, 836
umbrella, 17
Stuttering, 297–8
Styes, 597–8
Sudden Infant Death syndrome, 55–6
and bed sharing, 41
and breast-feeding, 2
causes, 55
sleeping positions, 41, 55
and smoking, 55–6
Sugar, 520
hidden, 520
Sunburn, 496, 497–8, 681–2
Sunglasses, 498
Sunscreen, 52, 333, 495, 542
Sunstroke, 496, 690
Supplemental Security Income, 701
Supplies
bathing, 13–14
feeding, 10–11
grooming, 14
health, 14
infant, 7–19
travel, 14–17
Suppositories, rectal, 539
Swaddling, 93
Sweeteners, artificial, 519
Swimmer's ear, 589
Swings, infant, 17–18
Swollen glands, 654–5
Symbols, 250
Symptoms
adenoiditis, 551
AIDS, 720–1
allergy, 516, 518, 554
amblyopia, 592
anemia, 560
appendicitis, 563

Symptoms, *cont.*
arrhythmia, 615
astigmatism, 593
attention deficit disorder, 564
autism, 750–1
blepharitis, 593
blocked tear duct, 593
botulism, 605
bronchiolitis, 568–9
bronchitis, 570
cancer, 713
canker sores, 571
cat-scratch disease, 572
celiac disease, 733
cerebral palsy, 747
chicken pox, 573
colds, 59–60
colic, 61
color blindness, 594
congenital heart defect, 730
conjunctivitis, 594
constipation, 577
Coxsackie virus, 578–9
croup, 579
cystic fibrosis, 734
cystitis, 659
dehydration, 64–5, 580
depression, 748
dermatitis, 581, 582
diabetes, 715
diarrhea, 583
diphtheria, 585
dislocations, 585, 672
Down syndrome, 744
ear infections, 66, 587
encephalitis, 590
epiglottitis, 591
febrile seizures, 598
fifth disease, 602
flat feet, 603
flatulence, 606
food poisoning, 605, 827
fragile X syndrome, 746
gassiness, 606
giardiasis, 607
growing pains, 608
head lice, 609
hearing impairment, 755
hematuria, 618
in hemophilia, 739–40
hepatitis, 605, 619
hernia, 620
herpes, 621

impétigo, 626
influenza, 628
jaundice, 69–70
labial adhesions, 629
lead poisoning, 630
leukemia, 713
Lyme disease, 631
malabsorption, 632–3
measles, 633
meningitis, 634
mental retardation, 753
mononucleosis, 635
mumps, 636–7
muscular dystrophy, 737
obsessive-compulsive disorder, 749
papular urticaria, 637
pertussis, 638
pervasive developmental delay, 750–1
phenylketonuria, 738
pinworms, 639
pneumonia, 640
ptosis, 596
pyelonephritis, 659
rabies, 641
respiratory synctial virus, 643
rheumatic fever, 644
rhinitis, 645
ringworm, 645
Rocky Mountain spotted fever, 646
roseola, 647
rubella, 606–7
rubeola, 633
salmonella, 648
scabies, 648
scarlet fever, 649
sickle cell disease, 741–2
sinusitis, 649
sleep apnea, 561–2
stomach ache, 651, 652–3
strabismus, 597
strep throat, 653
stress, 342
styes, 597–8
swimmer's ear, 589
swollen glands, 654
teething, 121
tetanus, 655
thrush, 73–4
tonsilitis, 551
tuberculosis, 657

urethritis, 659
urinary tract infections, 659
vaginal infections, 660
von Willebrand's disease, 740
whooping cough, 638
Syringe
bulb, 14
nasal, 60

T
Tables
changing, 11, 12–13, 32, 116
safety, 784
Talking, 217–18
Talking back, 396–8
Tantrums, 171, 191, 205, 207, 231, 398–9, 409
Tear ducts, 66
blocked, 593
Teeth and teething
baby, 328, 329–30, 486
braces, 534
brushing, 221, 486–7
care of, 486–9
"congestion," 121
dental visits, 533–4
drooling with, 121
emergency treatment, 691
first, 116, 121–2
first molars, 328
flossing, 487–8
fluoride, 488
loosening, 328
permanent, 330
plaque, 486, 488
problems, 330–1
swallowing, 330
in toddlers, 220, 223
tooth fairy, 330
wisdom, 330
Television, 216
age-appropriate, 299
and diet, 510
and fear, 280
limiting, 299, 354
monitoring, 216
Temperament, 285–6
basic, 125
and discipline, 382
inborn, 125
individual, 85
in infancy, 21

and physical development, 134
Temperature
    nighttime, 492–3
    rapid rise, 598
    taking, 67–8
    and teething, 121
    underarm, 601–2
Testicles, 624–5
    undescended, 57, 657–8
Tests
    AIDS, 721
    Apgar, 53
    asthma, 708
    blood, 70, 721
    for cancer, 713
    computerized tomography, 719
    cystic fibrosis, 734
    echocardiogram, 730, 745
    electrocardiogram, 730
    electroencephalograph, 719
    eye, 535, 757
    flat feet, 603
    genetic, 742
    hearing, 68–9
    for heart problems, 730
    for jaundice, 70
    lead poisoning, 630
    magnetic resonance imaging,
        719
    PKU, 737
    prenatal, 744
    speech and hearing, 296
    speech development, 252
    transcranial Doppler screening,
        742
Tetanus, 543–4, 655
Therapy
    alternative, 528
    behavioral, 750
    central nervous system, 713
    cognitive, 750
    occupational, 747
    physical, 732, 737, 740, 747
    rehydration, 65, 580, 635, 638
    respiratory, 735
    speech, 252, 298, 757
Thermometers
    bath, 14
    digital ear, 601
    forehead strip, 601
    oral, 601
    rectal, 14, 63, 601
    selecting, 600–1

Thiamin, 513
Thinking
    abstract, 158
    games, 216
    mathematical, 158, 322
Throwing, 177, 178, 183
Thrush, 73–4
Thumb sucking, 138, 313
Ticks, 498, 499, 646, 667
Tics, 655–6
Time
    kid, 357
    learning, 357–8
    quiet, 343
    sense of, 211, 249, 319
Time-outs, 382, 400–1
Tips
    bathing, 47, 482, 483
    bedtime, 226, 491
    bed wetting, 270
    clothes storage, 50
    colic, 62
    constipation, 63
    contaminated water, 806
    on dawdling, 389
    dental visits, 533
    diapering, 36, 37
    exercise, 493
    experimentation, 279
    feeding schedule, 42
    hair, 484
    hair twirling, 312
    head lice, 609
    hiccups, 622
    lead poisoning, 802
    morning routines, 416
    nail care, 47, 485
    nightime fears, 246, 247
    one-on-one time with baby, 87
    oral rehydration, 580
    playground safety, 855
    postpartum blues, 89
    on schedules, 416
    self-image, 306
    sibling squabbles, 448
    special-needs children, 704
    stepfamily, 470, 471
    storytime, 217
    street safety, 837
    toys storage, 788
    travel, 819
    water safety, 822
    on whining, 393

Title V programs, 701
Toddlers
    abilities and knowledge, 178,
        195–6, 211–12, 220–1, 249–51,
        273–4, 291–2, 301–2, 319–20
    aggression in, 241–2
    bed sharing, 189–91
    cognitive development,
        195–202, 211–18, 249–60,
        290–9, 319–26
    decision-making with, 192
    defiance in, 231, 232
    diet and nutrition, 503–4
    disrobing, 228
    emotional development, 185–95,
        230–49, 276–90, 304–18
    exercising control, 199
    fears in, 191–4, 225–6, 231,
        244–5, 279–81
    feelings in, 185–6, 206–7, 230–1,
        276–7, 304–6
    friendships of, 242–4
    gender understanding, 194–5
    insecurity in, 231
    love of repetition, 200
    need for order in, 233
    physical development, 177–85,
        204–6, 220–30, 273–6, 301–3
    play styles, 308–10
    regression in, 247–9
    rejection among, 284–5
    sense of ownership in, 209
    shyness in, 239–41
    social styles, 239–44
    strong opinions in, 189
    willfulness in, 231
Toe-walking, 656
Toileting
    accidents, 265–6
    beginning, 263–6
    for boys, 265
    daytime, 263–6
    difficulties, 268–9
    nighttime, 267
    readiness for, 261–3
    refusal, 269
    teaching, 261–71
Tolerance, 348
Tonsilitis, 550–3
Toys
    activity centers, 156
    age-appropriate, 18, 200–2
    bath, 482

Toys, *cont.*
  categorization, 201
  dexterity, 179
  fine-motor, 274–5
  and gender, 201–2, 290
  imitative, 201
  infant, 17–19
  interactive, 212
  for make-believe play, 250
  manipulative, 200–1
  mechanical, 250
  musical, 18, 258
  nesting, 156
  ownership of, 173, 210, 237
  play-alone, 213
  preferences, 168
  puzzles, 250, 258, 274, 353
  safe, 787–8
  skill-building, 221
  soft, 18
  sorting, 156, 179
  stacking, 156
  storage, 788–9
  toddler, 200–2, 788
  water, 201
  weapons, 287–8
Transitional objects, 210
Treatment, emergency
  allergies, 666
  bites, 667–9
  bleeding, 669–71
  bone and joint injuries, 671–3
  burns, 678–82
  convulsions, 682
  drowning (near drowning),
    682–3
  ear injury, 683–4
  electrical shock, 684
  eye injuries, 684–5
  fainting, 686
  finger injury, 687
  frostbite, 686
  hand injury, 687
  head injury, 687–8
  heat exhaustion/cramps, 688–9
  heat stroke, 690
  mouth injuries, 690–1
  neck injury, 687–8
  nose injuries, 692
  poisoning, 693–4
  seizures, 682
  shock, 695–6
  sunburn, 681–2

sunstroke, 690
Treatments
  adenoditis, 552
  AIDS, 721–2
  allergies, 554, 555
  amblyopia, 592
  anemia, 560–1
  appendicitis, 563
  arrhythmia, 615
  arthritis, 724
  asthma, 708–11
  attention deficit disorder, 566–7
  autism, 751–2
  blepharitis, 593
  blocked tear duct, 593
  bronchiolitis, 568–9
  bronchitis, 570
  cancer, 713
  canker sores, 571
  cat-scratch disease, 572
  celiac disease, 733
  cerebral palsy, 747–8
  chicken pox, 573
  cleft palate, 727
  clubfoot, 728–9
  colds, 60, 574–5
  colic, 61–2
  congenital heart defects, 730–1
  conjunctivitis, 594–5
  constipation, 63–4, 577–8
  Coxsackie virus, 579
  croup, 579
  cystic fibrosis, 734–6
  dehydration, 65, 580–1
  depression, 749
  dermatitis, 581–2
  diabetes, 715
  diarrhea, 66, 583–4
  diphtheria, 585
  dislocations, 585, 672
  Down syndrome, 744–5
  ear infection, 66
  ear infections, 587
  emergency, 664–97
  encephalitis, 590
  epiglottitis, 591
  epilepsy, 719
  febrile seizures, 598
  fever, 68, 599, 600
  fifth disease, 602
  flat feet, 603
  flatulence, 606
  food poisoning, 605

fragile X syndrome, 746
frostbite, 686
gassiness, 606
giardiasis, 607
growing pains, 608
headache, 608–9
head lice, 610
hearing impairment, 755–6
heart murmer, 614
heat exhaustion/cramps, 688–9
heat rash, 689–90
hematuria, 618
hemophilia, 740
hepatitis, 619–20
hernia, 620
herpes, 621–2
hiccups, 69, 622
Hirschspung's disease, 731
hives, 624
hydrocele, 625
hypertension, 626
impetigo, 626
influenza, 628
jaundice, 70–1, 628
labial adhesions, 629
lead poisoning, 630–1
leukemia, 713
Lyme disease, 632
malabsorption, 633
measles, 633–4
meningitis, 634–5
mental retardation, 753–4
mononucleosis, 635
motion sickness, 636
mouth injuries, 690–1
mumps, 637
muscular dystrophy, 737–8
obsessive-compulsive disorder,
  749–50
papular urticaria, 637
pertussis, 638
pervasive developmental delay,
  751–2
phenylketonuria, 738–9
pinworms, 639
pneumonia, 640
ptosis, 596–7
pyloric stenosis, 640
rabies, 642
respiratory synctial virus, 643
rheumatic fever, 644
rhinitis, 645
ringworm, 646

Rocky Mountain spotted fever, 646–7
roseola, 647
rubella, 607
rubeola, 633–4
salmonella, 648
scabies, 648
scarlet fever, 649
sickle cell disease, 742
sinusitis, 650
sleep apnea, 562
sore throat, 650–1
spina bifida, 732–3, 733
steroid, 588
stomach ache, 652–3
strabismus, 597
strep throat, 653
styes, 598
sunburn, 682
swimmer's ear, 589
swollen glands, 655
thrush, 74
tics, 656
tonsilitis, 552
tuberculosis, 657
undescended testicles, 658
urinary tract infections, 660
vaginal infections, 661
vision problems, 757–9
vomiting, 661–2
von Willebrand's disease, 741
whooping cough, 638
Triglycerides, 623
Trisomy 21. See Down syndrome
Tuberculosis, 656–7
Tubs, 14
Turn-taking, 406
Twins. See Multiples
Tympanostomy tube, 588

U

Urethritis, 657, 658
Urinary tract infection, 658–60
Vaginitis, 660–1

V

Vaccinations, 527, 543–7
Varicella. See Chicken pox
Vegetarianism, 508
Ventricular septal defect, 729–30, 731

Violence, make-believe, 286–8
Viruses, 67
cold, 573
Coxsackie, 578–9
croup, 579
hepatitis, 618–20
herpes, 572, 590, 621–2, 647
human immunodeficiency. See AIDS
human papilloma, 662
influenza, 575
respiratory syncytial virus, 54, 569, 643
rubella, 606–7
varicella-zoster, 572
Vision
cataracts, 66
changes in, 328, 713
checks, 301
color sense in, 80
concerns, 66–7
glaucoma, 66
in infants, 79–80
and prematurity, 66
tunnel, 758
Vision problems, 57, 591–8, 757–60
retinitis pigmentosa, 758
retinopathy of prematurity, 758
Vitamins and minerals, 519
infant, 23
necessary, 508–9, 512–13
Vocabulary
building, 217, 296–8
expansion, 291, 296
hearing, 173, 177
increasing, 203
preschooler, 319
speaking, 250
toddler, 319
Vocalizing, 116, 139
Voice recognition, 94
Vomiting, 57, 74, 549, 651, 652, 661–2
projectile, 57, 74, 549, 640
during rescue breathing, 675
and spitting up, 74
von Willebrand's disease, 740–1
Vulvovaginitis, 660–1

W

Walking, 149–51, 162, 177, 178
Warnings. See Alerts
Warts, 662
Wasps, 668
Water
contamination, 806, 853–4
pollution, 804–5
safety, 819–23
supply, 804–5
Weaning, 120–1
Weight, 82–3, 161, 182, 220, 615–17
and baby fat, 135
gain, 101
loss, 713
management, 510–11
Whining, 392–3
Whooping cough, 543–4, 637–8
Willfulness, 231
Windburn, 496
Writing, 423–5

X

X-rays, 529–30

Y

Yards, childproofing, 813–15
Yeast
diaper rash, 38
rashes, 721

Z

Zinc, 514

## Acknowledgments

*We would like to thank the following individuals and organizations, all of whom contributed their time and expertise to this book:*

American Academy of Child and Adolescent Psychiatry • American Foundation for the Blind, Inc. • American Heart Association • Gail Blatt, National Institute on Deafness and Other Communication Disorders • Brain Injury Association, Inc. • Children's PKU Network • Cystic Fibrosis Foundation • Epilepsy Foundation of America • Cindy Hyatt, M.S.W., C.S.W. • Juvenile Diabetes Foundation International • Susan La Venture, National Association for Parents of the Visually Impaired, Inc. • Nancy Merberg • Muscular Dystrophy Association • National Fragile X Foundation • National Heart, Lung and Blood Institute • National Mental Health Association • National Spinal Cord Injury Association • The Pediatric AIDS Foundation • Susan Rafkin, The National Children's Cancer Society, Inc. • The Ryan White Foundation • Joann Schellenbach, American Cancer Society • Sickle Cell Disease Association of America • Rose Ann Soloway, American Association of Poison Control Centers • Janet Weinstein, National Center for Learning Disabilities • Michael Woltz, V.M.D.

*Thanks to Gena Merberg for taking photographs and to the following moms, dads and kids who modeled for our illustrator:* Henry, Nicholas and Tory Burch • Alex, Shelby, Debbie and Evan Merberg • Jane Smyth Reese • James Tobin • Morgan Elizabeth Wilcock

Many thanks to our enthusiastic editor at Golden Books, Laura Yorke, and to her fabulous assistant, Lara Asher.

We are extremely grateful to our friends at Gruner + Jahr: Lisa Cooperstein first made this series possible and Tammy Palazzo stepped in to see it through.